Rice
Global Networks and

Rice today is food to half the world's population. Its history is inextricably entangled with the emergence of colonialism, the global networks of industrial capitalism, and the modern world economy. The history of rice is currently a vital and innovative field of research attracting serious attention, but no attempt has yet been made to write a history of rice and its place in the rise of capitalism from a global and comparative perspective. *Rice* is a first step toward such a history. The 15 chapters, written by specialists on Africa, the Americas, and several regions of Asia, are premised on the utility of a truly international approach to history. Each one brings a new approach that unsettles prevailing narratives and suggests new connections. Together they cast new light on the significant roles of rice as crop, food, and commodity, tracing how it shaped historical trajectories and interregional linkages in Africa, the Americas, Europe, and Asia.

Francesca Bray is Professor of Social Anthropology at the University of Edinburgh. She is the author of *The Rice Economies: Technology and Development in Asian Societies* (1994); *Technology and Gender: Fabrics of Power in Late Imperial China* (1997); *Technology and Society in Ming China, 1368–1644* (2000); and *Technology, Gender and History in Imperial China: Great Transformations Reconsidered* (2013).

Peter A. Coclanis is Albert R. Newsome Distinguished Professor of History and Director of the Global Research Institute at the University of North Carolina at Chapel Hill. He is the author of *The Shadow of a Dream: Economic Life and Death in the South Carolina Low Country, 1670–1920* (1989) and *Time's Arrow, Time's Cycle: Globalization in Southeast Asia Over La Longue Durée* (2006) and the coeditor of *Environmental Change and Agricultural Sustainability in the Mekong Delta* (2011).

Edda L. Fields-Black is Associate Professor of History at Carnegie Mellon University. She is the author of *Deep Roots: Rice Farmers in West Africa and the African Diaspora* (2008).

Dagmar Schäfer is Director of Department 3, Artefacts, Knowledge, and Action at the Max Planck Institute for the History of Science, Berlin, and Professor of Chinese Studies at the University of Manchester. She is the author of *The Emperor's Silk Clothes: State-Run Silk Manufacturing in the Ming Period, 1368–1644* (1998) and *The Crafting of the 10,000 Things: Knowledge and Technology in 17th-Century China* (2011) and coauthor of *Weaving an Economic Pattern in Ming Times, 1368–1644* (2002).

Rice

Global Networks and New Histories

Edited by

FRANCESCA BRAY
University of Edinburgh

PETER A. COCLANIS
University of North Carolina, Chapel Hill

EDDA L. FIELDS-BLACK
Carnegie Mellon University

DAGMAR SCHÄFER
Max Planck Institute for the History of Science

CAMBRIDGE UNIVERSITY PRESS

CAMBRIDGE
UNIVERSITY PRESS

University Printing House, Cambridge CB2 8BS, United Kingdom

One Liberty Plaza, 20th Floor, New York, NY 10006, USA

477 Williamstown Road, Port Melbourne, VIC 3207, Australia

4843/24, 2nd Floor, Ansari Road, Daryaganj, Delhi - 110002, India

79 Anson Road, #06-04/06, Singapore 079906

Cambridge University Press is part of the University of Cambridge.

It furthers the University's mission by disseminating knowledge in the pursuit of education, learning and research at the highest international levels of excellence.

www.cambridge.org
Information on this title: www.cambridge.org/9781107622371

© Cambridge University Press 2015

This publication is in copyright. Subject to statutory exception and to the provisions of relevant collective licensing agreements, no reproduction of any part may take place without the written permission of Cambridge University Press.

First published 2015
First paperback edition 2017

A catalogue record for this publication is available from the British Library

Library of Congress Cataloging in Publication data
Rice (Cambridge University Press)
Rice : global networks and new histories / [edited by] Francesca Bray, University of Edinburgh, Peter A.
Coclanis, University of North Carolina, Chapel Hill, Edda L. Fields-Black, Carnegie Mellon University,
Dagmar Schäfer, Max Planck Institute for the History of Science
pages cm
ISBN 978-1-107-04439-5 (hardback)
1. Rice – History. I. Bray, Francesca, editor.
II. Coclanis, Peter A., editor. III. Fields-Black, Edda L., editor.
IV. Schäfer, Dagmar, editor. V. Title.
SB191.R5R4434 2015
633.1'8–dc23   2014023784

ISBN 978-1-107-04439-5 Hardback
ISBN 978-1-107-62237-1 Paperback

Cambridge University Press has no responsibility for the persistence or accuracy of URLs for external or third-party internet websites referred to in this publication, and does not guarantee that any content on such websites is, or will remain, accurate or appropriate.

Contents

List of Figures	*page* vii
List of Tables	ix
List of Contributors	xi
Foreword by Giorgio Riello	xiii
Acknowledgments	xix
Introduction: Global Networks and New Histories of Rice *Francesca Bray*	1

PART I: PURITY AND PROMISCUITY

Introduction *Francesca Bray*	37
1. Global Visions vs. Local Complexity: Experts Wrestle with the Problem of Development *Jonathan Harwood*	41
2. Rice, Sugar, and Livestock in Java, 1820–1940: Geertz's *Agricultural Involution* 50 Years On *Peter Boomgaard and Pieter M. Kroonenberg*	56
3. A Desire to Eat Well: Rice and the Market in Eighteenth-Century China *Sui-Wai Cheung*	84
4. Rice and Maritime Modernity: The Modern Chinese State and the South China Sea Rice Trade *Seung-Joon Lee*	99
5. Promiscuous Transmission and Encapsulated Knowledge: A Material-Semiotic Approach to Modern Rice in the Mekong Delta *David Biggs*	118

6. Red and White Rice in the Vicinity of Sierra Leone: Linked Histories of Slavery, Emancipation, and Seed Selection 138
   Bruce L. Mouser, Edwin Nuijten, Florent Okry, and Paul Richards

PART II: ENVIRONMENTAL MATTERS

Introduction 163
Edda L. Fields-Black

7. Rice and Rice Farmers in the Upper Guinea Coast and Environmental History 167
   Edda L. Fields-Black

8. Reserving Water: Environmental and Technological Relationships with Colonial South Carolina Inland Rice Plantations 189
   Hayden R. Smith

9. Asian Rice in Africa: Plant Genetics and Crop History 212
   Erik Gilbert

10. When Jola Granaries Were Full 229
    Olga F. Linares

11. Of Health and Harvests: Seasonal Mortality and Commercial Rice Cultivation in the Punjab and Bengal Regions of South Asia 245
    Lauren Minsky

PART III: POWER AND CONTROL

Introduction 275
Peter A. Coclanis

12. The Cultural Meaning of Work: The "Black Rice Debate" Reconsidered 279
    Walter Hawthorne

13. White Rice: The Midwestern Origins of the Modern Rice Industry in the United States 291
    Peter A. Coclanis

14. Rice and the Path of Economic Development in Japan 318
    Penelope Francks

15. Commodities and Anti-Commodities: Rice on Sumatra 1915–1925 335
    Harro Maat

Bibliography 355
Index 399

Figures

P.1	Overview maps: (a) Asia, (b) Europe and Africa, and (c) Africa and Americas	*page* xxii
2.1	Distributions of percentage sawahs under sugar cane for the years 1880 and 1920	73
2.2	Relations between percentage sawahs under cane and population density for 1880 and 1920	75
2.3	Relations between percentage sawahs under sugar cane and sawah area per capita for 1880 and 1920	76
2.4	Relations between percentage sawahs under cane and rice yield per unit sawah for 1880 and 1920	77
2.5	Relations between percentage sawahs under cane and wet rice production per capita, 1880 and 1920	78
2.6	Relations between percentage sawahs under cane and arable land per capita for 1880 and 1920	79
2.7	Distribution of percentages of sugar cane sawahs per district for each Residency in 1920	80
2.8	Livestock per unit of arable land in 1880 and 1920	82
2.9	Relation between numbers of livestock in 1880 and 1920 at Residency level	82
3.1	Rice regions in China, ca. 1920–1950s	87
5.1	Hydro-ecological zones of the Mekong Delta	120
6.1	Phylogenetic relationships among 315 West African rice samples using UPGMA	154
6.2	Close-up of the phylogenetic relationships of the Japonica cluster and its subclusters	156
8.1	Scarps and terraces of the Lower Coastal Plain, central South Carolina	194
8.2	Charleywood Plantation with new rice fields	195
8.3	Windsor Plantation, with rice fields in division "A" and flanking canal wrapping around division "B"	205

9.1	Population clusters identified by PCA in JMP Genomics software	221
10.1	Graph of 5-year running averages for four Lower Casamance stations	231
10.2	Location of our Jola study communities and the regions where they are found	233
11.1	Death rates during the 1908 Malaria epidemic in Punjab	253
11.2	Malaria distribution in Bengal	258
11.3	Seasonal mortality in the Punjab	272
13.1a	Geographic distribution of pounds of rice produced in Southwestern states 1880–1900	294
13.1b	Geographic distribution of pounds of rice produced in Southwestern states 1910–30	295
15.1	Map of a tobacco estate on Northeast Sumatra	341

Tables

2.1	The land, population, and rice-production characteristics of the sugar regions of Java in 1920	page 58
2.2	Production of kilocalories per capita per day for selected years, Java	67
2.3	Rice production per hectare (in kgs unhusked rice) for selected years	68
2.4	Correlations of percentage sawahs under cane with other variables	74
2.5	Correlations of the agricultural variables for districts	81
2.6	Correlations of livestock per unit of arable land with other variables at Residency level	83
6.1	Japonica rices at Mogbuama (Sierra Leone) in 1983 and 2007	158
13.1	Rice production in the United States, 1839–1919 (millions of pounds of clean rice)	299
13.2	Southwest Louisiana's share of total rice production in Louisiana, 1879–1929	309
13.3	Mean yield of clean rice per acre, southwest Louisiana, 1879–1929	311
15.1	Origins of rice imports of the Netherlands Indies, in the mid-1910s	346
15.2	Rice imports of four major districts of Sumatra, in the mid-1990s	346

Contributors

David Biggs Associate Professor, History, University of California–Riverside, USA

Peter Boomgaard Professor, Environmental and Economic History, KITLV/Royal Netherlands Academy of Arts and Sciences, Leiden, Netherlands

Francesca Bray Professor, Social Anthropology, University of Edinburgh, UK

Sui-Wai Cheung Associate Professor, History/Research Centre for Ming-Qing Studies, Chinese University of Hong Kong

Peter A. Coclanis Albert Ray Newsome Distinguished Professor, History, University of North Carolina–Chapel Hill, USA

Edda L. Fields-Black Associate Professor, History, Carnegie Mellon University, Pittsburgh, USA

Penelope Francks Research Associate, School of Oriental and African Studies, London, UK

Erik Gilbert Professor, History, Arkansas State University, Jonesboro, USA

Jonathan Harwood Professor Emeritus, History of Science, University of Manchester, UK

Walter Hawthorne Professor, History, Michigan State University, East Lansing, USA

Pieter M. Kroonenberg Professor, Social Science, Leiden University, Netherlands

Seung-Joon Lee Assistant Professor, History, National University of Singapore

Olga F. Linares Senior Staff Scientist, Smithsonian Tropical Research Institute, Panama City, Panama

List of Contributors

Harro Maat Universitair Docent, Knowledge, Technology and Innovation, Wageningen University, Netherlands

Lauren Minsky Assistant Professor, History, New York University–Abu Dhabi, UAE

Bruce L. Mouser Professor Emeritus, History, University of Wisconsin–La Crosse, USA

Edwin Nuijten Senior Researcher, Plant Breeding and Sustainable Production Chains, Louis Bolk Institute, Driebergen, Netherlands

Florent Okry Researcher, National University of Benin, Cotonou, Benin

Paul Richards Professor Emeritus, Technology and Agrarian Development, Wageningen University, Netherlands

Dagmar Schäfer Director, Department III, Max Planck Institute for the History of Science, Berlin, Germany

Hayden R. Smith Adjunct Professor, History, College of Charleston, USA

Foreword

Giorgio Riello

"We can't stop buying rice just because it is expensive. Maybe, we will increase our roti consumption." The words are those of Damini Gupta, an Indian housewife interviewed by *The Times of India* at one of the many malls in Bangalore while buying provisions in January 2013. Comments left on the "readers' opinion" provided further opinions on the matter. While some prompted other readers to change their consuming habits – "switch to wheat" said one of them as it is good for diabetes – most of the 17 comments hinted at wider issues: "how many quintals of rice is rotting due poor infrastructure in another comic situation," one of them said. Another was vociferous that "we should stop giving loans to Farmers." Others thought it a government conspiracy and a "mismanagement by terrorist Kangress [*sic*]" or simply a failure on the part of the state. Praveen from Mangalore argued for a wider political economy perspective: "the govt lifted ban on export of nonbasmati rice 6 months back. It's time to impose it back, we export and our people suffer. Now onion prices also increased." Jaideep Shenoy, also from Mangalore, put jokingly: "If the people can not have rice, they can have cake instead. :).".[1]

Anyone who thought that "rice is easy" might change one's mind by reading the pages of *The Times of India*. Today, as five centuries ago, rice is a complex topic. It is not just a staple in the diet of billions of people but also one of the most important crops in the world. Yet, unlike cod, salt, or chocolate among the foods and beverages, and indeed silk, cotton, silver, or even copper among the globally traded commodities, rice has so far evaded both popular and scholarly analyses on a world scale. Until the recent increase of the price of rice – and indeed many other staple foodstuffs such as coffee and sugar – few popular accounts had ever given a thought to rice

---

[1] "Should we stop eating rice?" by R. Sunitha Rao, *The Times of India*, 23 January 2013: http://timesofindia.indiatimes.com/business/india-business/Should-we-stop-eating-rice/articleshow/18141554.cms

beyond the idea that it is the food of Asia par excellence. This stereotypical view of rice contrasts with a rather complex history as conveyed in this book in at least two major ways. First, rice is not a crop or a commodity of just one area of the world. Throughout its history, the cultivation, trade, and consumption of rice has affected vast parts of Asia, Africa, and the Americas. In China rice started to be cultivated more than 10,000 years ago; it was also domesticated very early in South and Southeast Asia, where its cultivation spread widely through antiquity. It was grown in Europe by the tenth century CE and was introduced to the Americas in the early sixteenth century as part of the so-called Columbian exchange. By the precolonial period, rice cultivation was widespread in West Africa.

Italians like their risotto and the Japanese their rice *nuka*; Caribbean cuisine is famous for its coconut rice with beans; and any Indian meal is incomplete without rice. Therefore, one could think of a global history of rice as something that is cultivated and consumed in different parts of the world. Yet, this might be a simplistic or simplified view. A second feature of the complex story of rice is that – as for many other commodities – it does not come in only one standard variety. There are at least three distinct species of rice, and within each species there are hundreds of types depending on cultivation and suitability to different purposes. Indeed, as the introduction to this book reveals, variety is just one of the reasons that makes "rice resist any easy reification." Rice is a "varied commodity" that relies on a diverse range of systems of cultivations, organizations of labor, gender relations, and so on. Indeed as *The Times of India*'s article shows, rice is at the core of people's consumption habits, it is a concern of the state, a commodity whose production requires heavy infrastructural investment, and a product that competes with other foods worldwide.

The challenge faced by the editors and contributors to this volume is at once that of recovering the complex history of rice in its long and geographically diverse history; and to convey it in a clear and concise way. This is no easy task. As the field is vast, they collectively decided to follow William McNeill's suggestion that scholarship of a global nature needs to know what "to leave out." This book, therefore, focuses on the last five centuries. This is no random choice as the "discovery" of the Americas at the end of the fifteenth century reshaped the contours and redesigned the relational logic between different world areas. In the past two decades world and global historians have produced a vast array of studies addressing how the past half a millennium generated many of the structures, challenges, and achievements that dominate the debate over our present-day globalized world. Globalization has become an everyday expression signifying the increasing interconnectedness of the world. The awareness that globalization is not just a recent phenomenon but has slowly emerged over the centuries has been one of the key themes embraced by global history. Economic historians, in particular, have been interested in understanding not just how the economic connectedness of the world affected people's lives, but also the disparities of wealth across different world areas. A second concern has, therefore, been what is called "divergence": the different paths of economic development that saw the West industrialize while most of Asia and Africa lagged behind.

The language and concerns of economic history that dominate debates over globalization and divergence have been influential in the shaping of narratives of a global type. However, the past decade has seen the emergence of a global history that is more multidisciplinary and addresses topics that are not limited to economic development. At least three of these new areas are relevant for this book. First, the history of science and technology now engages with the importance of embedded knowledge, of different "epistemic cultures" and of the transmission of useful and reliable knowledge across world areas. Second, commodities have become a way to reflect on commercial but also material and cultural contact across time and space. Moving beyond the traditional remit of the history of trade, commodities are today a way of considering complex global processes that link together resources, technologies, manufacturing, exchange, power, and the agency of states and consumers. Finally, there is an emerging body of scholarship on global consuming practices. From the work of Brewer and Porter and de Vries for Europe, several world areas are crafting sophisticated studies on consumer behavior, the importance of exotic and foreign goods, and on consumers' tastes and preferences that will hopefully result in a global reconsideration of the very meaning of consumption.

The analysis of these new trends in global history could continue. My point here is that this book challenges easy pigeon-holing. Francesca Bray in the introduction to Part I asks "What happens when we reframe the well-worn production-focused debates that have structured standard readings of economic history to incorporate evidence about consumer tastes, peasant agency, the ideological dimensions of technical choice, or the resistance of pollen to human control?" Indeed, what happens when well-known approaches are scrutinized with fresh eyes? It turns out that a more eclectic approach might be needed. The choice made here is not to reduce the story of rice to simply one of economic development; or one of agrarian knowledge and associated technologies; or one of a commodity called "rice"; or indeed one of a foodstuff consumed across the world. Embracing only one of these perspectives would not "do justice" to rice, but would also limit the potential of this study and its contribution to global history. *Global Rice* rather than being "exclusive," engages with different bodies of literature, and by doing so it connects debates and problems that have so far been seen as separate.

So far so good, but how are good intentions translated into action and even more importantly, good results? First, one of the ambitions of this book is to bring together distinct discourses without denying their specificity, their logic and their heuristic importance. The point here is not, as for many popular accounts, to narrate a unified history of rice across time and space, but to consider histories of rice through their connections, their entanglements and at points through comparative methodologies of analysis. The Green Revolution of the 1960s and 1970s, for instance, was a drive to purify farming landscapes across the world. Yet, knowledge and ideology stemming from Western labs came to create different vectors of change in places such as China, Southeast Asia, and India. While their histories are connected and in dialogue with each other they also show profound contrasts. The same could be said of the nature and power of institutions, of gender, race, and class relations in riziculture, of the relationship between endogenous and exogenous forces in each world area, of the role of the state, of labor relations, and the like.

A second important factor underpinning this project is more of a practical nature. The premise of the intellectual endeavor that supports this work has been rather different from traditional ways of organizing scholarship. Rather than gathering a group of scholars, each of whom attempts to construct a separate argument that is exclusive of any other alternative interpretations, in this book contributors admit the limitations of their interpretations and "compare notes" with each other. Some might object that scientific labs have long worked on the principle of collaboration – teamwork as it is called. Yet, historians are less acquainted with such ways of drafting scholarship. It is only in recent years that large collaborative research projects have made an entrance in the historical arena, frequently at great expense of public money. More well-known is the format of the edited book, often the result of a conference or series of workshops gathering together like-minded people to discuss a topic or problem. The result is in-depth analysis: a collective work of excavation that drills deep across the vast surface of history often limiting the field to narrow temporal and geographical coordinates. In this sense, *Global Rice* is very different from an edited volume. As observed earlier, it covers broad geographical and temporal coordinates, spanning at least four continents and several centuries. And more importantly, its aim is to connect different themes, methodologies, and even disciplines.

The ways in which this book has been conceived is not its only point of distinction. The field of global history has addressed vast temporal and spatial expanses mostly by privileging macro approaches. In the attempt to paint grand canvases of history, the brushstrokes of global historians have been rather large, sometimes using economic and sociological theories as generalization devices. In practical terms, this has meant an over-reliance on secondary sources rather than the engagement with primary research. It has also meant that the quirky detail, the colorful anecdote, and indeed the personal and subjective have not fared well in recent global historical narrative. It is always difficult to single out examples of bad practice, but let me say that such difficulties have plagued my own work on cotton. A field dominated by a vast secondary literature, my approach to writing a global history of cotton textiles has been rather macro, therefore glossing over the specificity of individual areas and focusing instead on topics relevant to a preconceived set of questions. Such an approach would however not work for rice. This is not just because of the large number of topics that rice raises and the empirical ground that scholars need to cover. Another important reason is that the history of rice throws at us a series of different questions and is characterized by the co-existence of different scholarly traditions and debates.

As the general introduction and chapters in this book observe, at least two large-scale debates have been at the core of histories of rice: the "black rice thesis" of the Atlantic region and the "agricultural involution" or "growth without development" of early modern China. Both of them deal with issues surrounding the cultivation of rice. The black rice thesis emphasizes the transplantation from West Africa to the Americas of a set of agricultural skills and a system of gendered knowledge. By contrast, agricultural involution underlines instead how rice encouraged small-scale improvements, rather than a search for radical transformation, thus running into the trap of decreasing returns. One is positive, the other rather negative; one is connective, the other fosters comparisons; one is set in the Atlantic, the other in East Asia. There might seem to be little common ground and yet as contributors make it clear, power, gender, the agency of state and individuals, and decision-making processes are common themes that cut across these two broad debates. Similar linkages, contrasts, and mutual comparisons help also at the level of individual factors and micro histories: Is the social cohesion brought about by rice unique to Asian societies? Is the role of labor in the Atlantic so different from Asia in the conveying of knowledge? Is multi-activity associated with rice cultivation everywhere? Are water resources always key to rice cultivation? And so on.

This book thus engages with local experiences and with a micro-set of issues, often conveyed through the expertise of individual contributors. Yet, this is not a simple gathering of precious information that simply adds to our knowledge of rice. Each fact, interpretation, and explanation comes to form a dot in a large canvas. Rather than large strokes, here the big *tableau vivant* of rice is formed by the mercurial nature of different voices that are in dialogue and sometimes in contrast with each other. The editors made the conscious decision of emphasizing the different logics shown by historical evidence, the malleable lines of evolution and the many differences and dissonances of a history of rice on a global scale. This is a point of radical departure for the simple reason that the vast majority of global history has embraced instead the opposite view in the belief that models or meta-narratives should be the end-point of large-scale historical analysis. Here instead we see a different strategy of presentation and explanation at play. A series of recurrent themes such as economic development, modernization, the role of the state, knowledge and agrarian practices, standardization and homogenization of commodities, and so on are considered through a variety of lenses and are often contextualized within specific historical and historiographical settings. Yet at the same time authors enter into a dialogue with each other and cluster into at least three major "constellations" on "Purity and Promiscuity," "Environmental Matters," and on "Power and Control."

I would like to conclude my brief analysis by reflecting on the peculiarity of using rice to write global history. By now, it should be clear that rice defies established ways of writing the global as it does not present a linear or unified narrative. There is also a certain non-permeability of area studies (the geographic clustering of historical scholarship) that does not help. The story of rice is also one of moments of profound change accompanied by stasis and of acute opposition between different forces, most evidently local cultivators vs. state administrations or capitalist interests. One might say that especially when we focus on riziculture there is however a great deal of potential for comparative analysis to allow for a deeper understanding of commonalities, differences, and peculiarities. The transfer of agronomical knowledge, of tools, and technologies and the adaptation of rice varieties and systems of cultivations are further global themes of a connective nature. Yet, in a reverse of common expectations, rice turns out to be a "disappointing" global commodity. Today, possibly at the peak of its globalization, only 5–7 percent of the total world rice production is traded internationally. One might ask how much rice is actually a good example of a failed global commodity or even a so-called anti-commodity in which global forces lead to the creation of specific "indigenous" forms of production and in which the global is not about worldwide processes but concerns co-existence of a multitude of different experiences on a global scale. In many ways, this is a global story that brings us back to the local, to the preoccupations of the Indian housewife Damini Gupta or a similar head of household in Bangladesh, Brazil, Cambodia, Laos, Madagascar, Myanmar, Nigeria, or Vietnam, all countries in which rice provides a substantial part of the daily caloric intake. Here we see the potential to see local consuming patterns in the light of global processes and forces. The five centuries of history considered in this book thus provide an insight into the daily lives of cultivators, administrators, businessmen, and consumers who rarely thought of themselves as part of any global history and yet each of them came to be a tile in the mosaic of a large-scale history.

Acknowledgments

Support from the Max Planck Institute for the History of Science, Berlin, Research Group Concepts and Modalities: Practical Knowledge Transmission, Dagmar Schäfer and from the Centre for Chinese Studies, of the University of Manchester, enabled the production of this working group book. In March 24–26, 2011, the authors who eventually joined this book project were able to meet for a workshop on "New Histories of Rice," in Berlin. Our thanks go to all the contributors for their serious engagement with the volume's topic. In an unusual spirit of good fellowship, they never failed to react promptly and patiently to the smaller and greater demands of the editing team as the theme, focus, and arrangement of the book as a whole took shape. Our joint work was exciting and stimulating.

Figures P.1 a–c assemble data from various contributions in the book to illustrate the diversity of topics and issues of regional approaches to rice that inform the global view (and conversely also how the global view informs regional debates). Lee, for instance, tackles the regional diversity of rice production in early twentieth century China, while Maat, interlinking with such data, highlights contrasts between import and export regions in Dutch East India around the the 1910s. (The size of the colored circles reflects import–export balance (adjusted from Smits 1919).) Debates around the African continent in this book underline circulation/flows/exchanges. Gilbert, for instance, discusses the flow of various genotypes into and out of Africa and thus also provides selective data on rice characteristic of various other macro-regions of the world. But Gilbert's samples do not adequately reflect the importance of indigenous West African rices (*glaberrima*), discussed in the chapters by Mouser and Fields-Black and rendered on Figure P.1b by the ellipses. Regions tackled in the book are highlighted in grey.

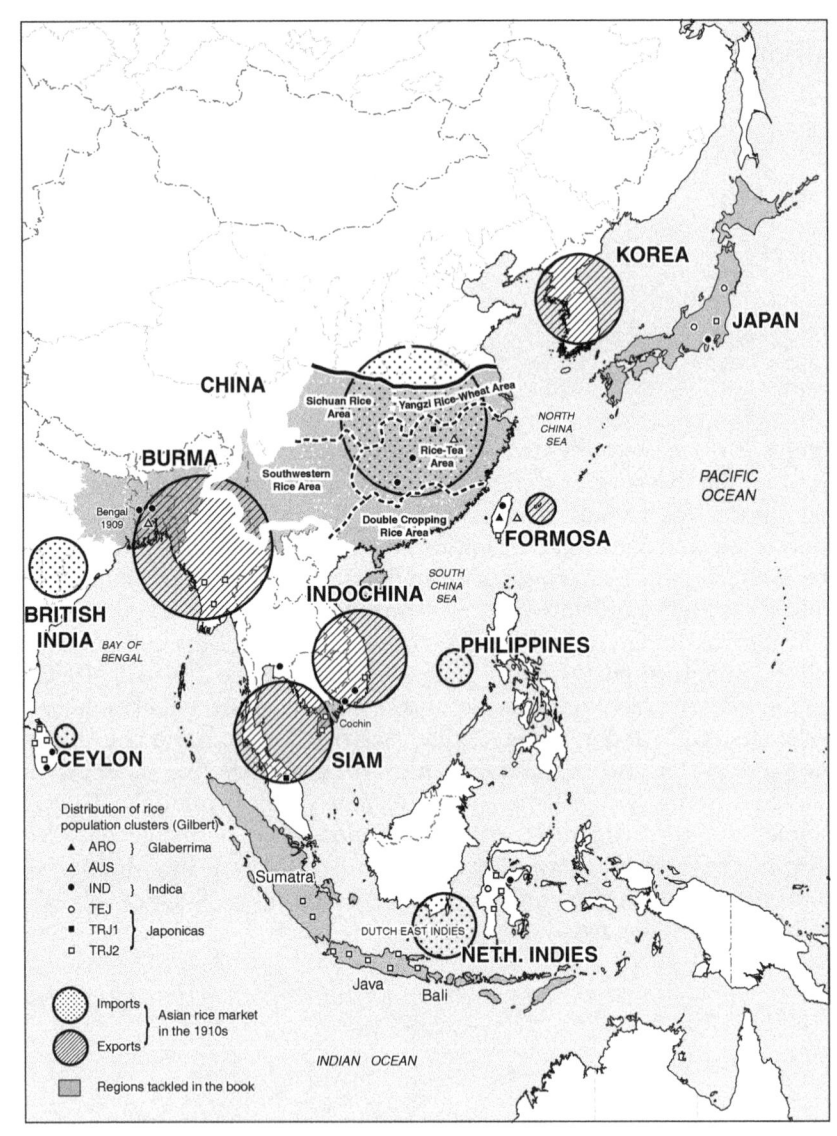

FIGURE P.1a. Overview map Asia

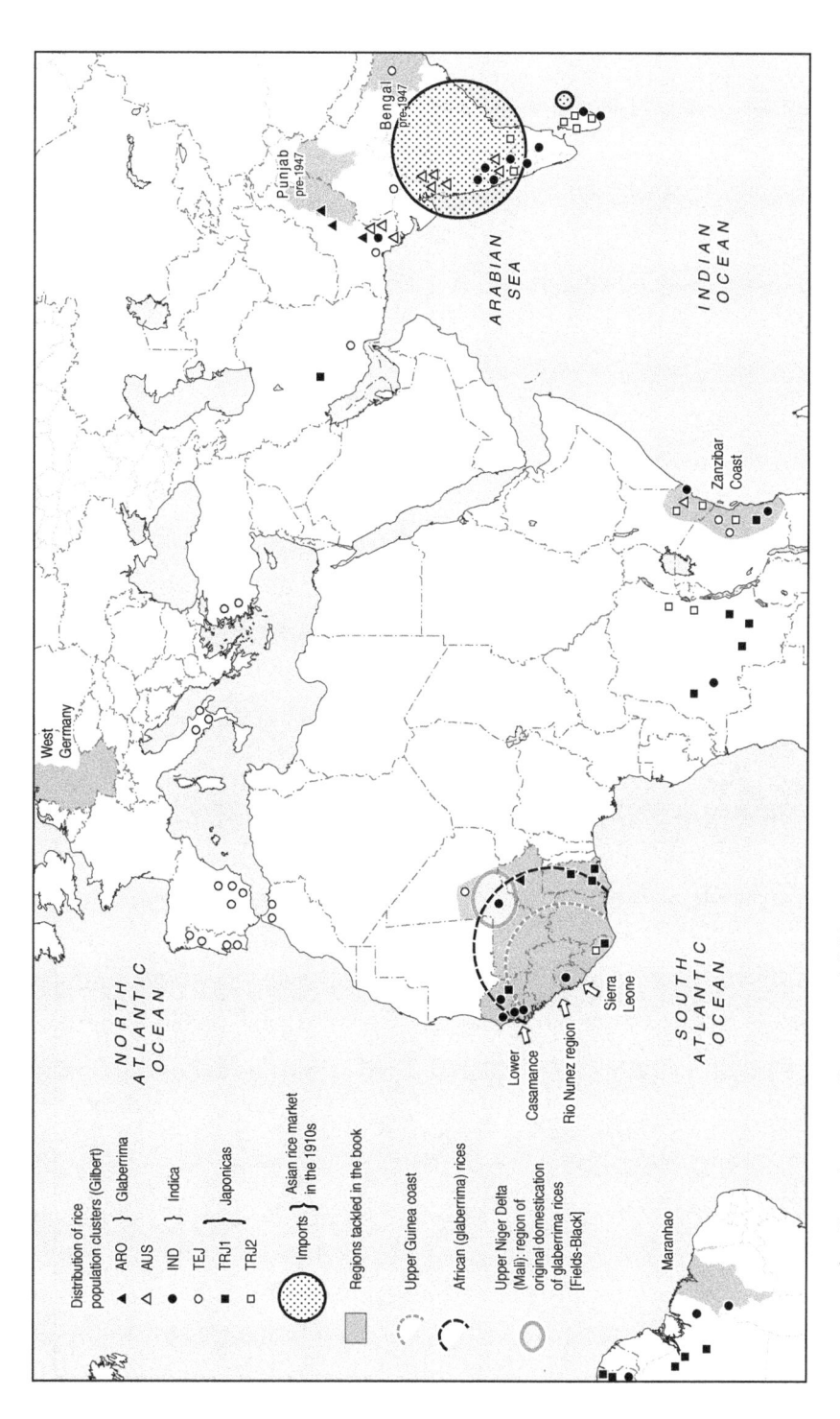

FIGURE P.1b. Overview map Europe and Africa

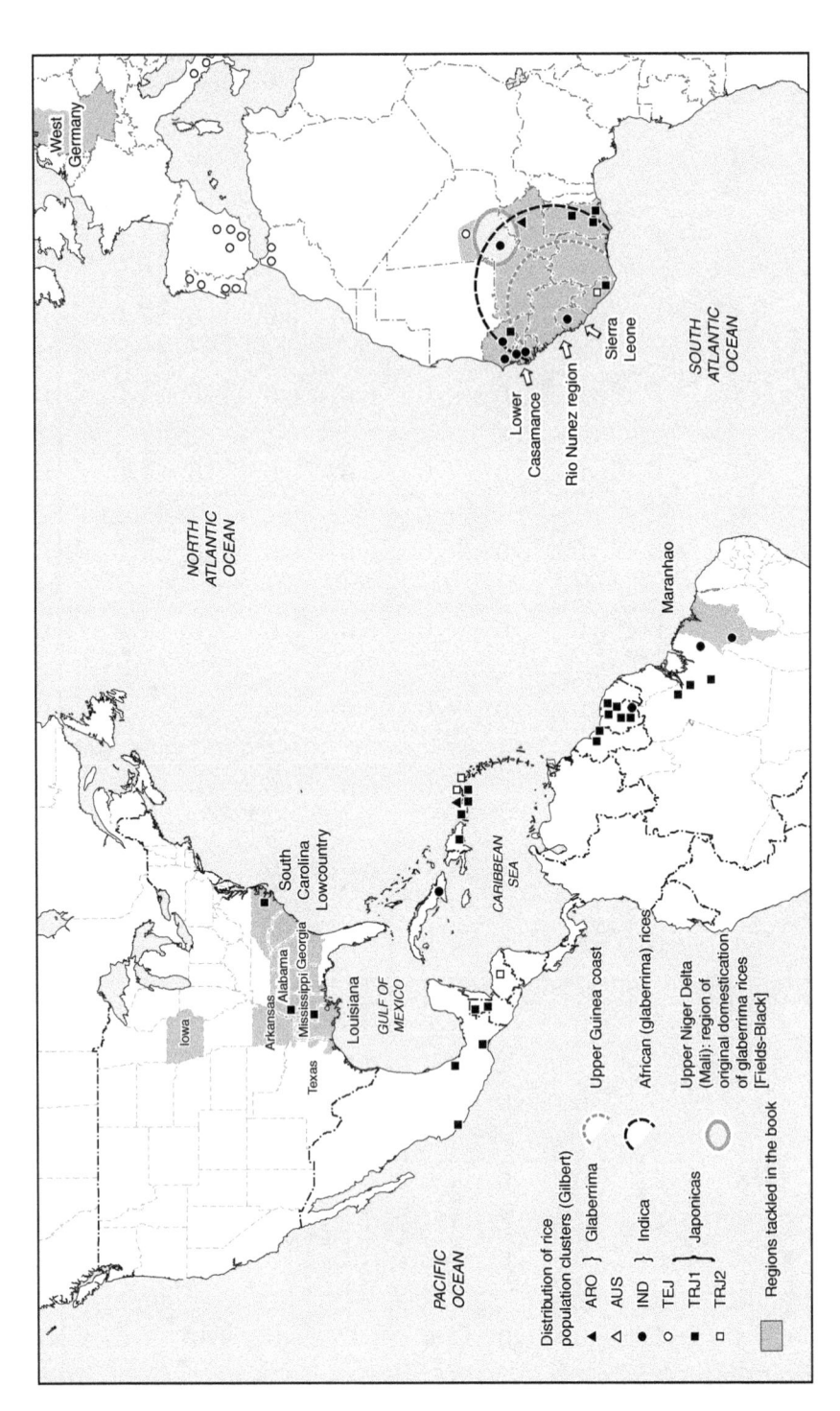

FIGURE P.1C. Overview map Africa and Americas

Introduction

Global Networks and New Histories of Rice

Francesca Bray

The history of rice is intricately entwined with the emergence of the early-modern world economy and the global networks of industrial capitalism. As a crop, food, and commodity, rice has played a critical role in shaping and linking the histories of Africa and the Americas, Europe, and almost every region of Asia. An essential staple of colonial growth and postindependence development programs, today rice is food to over half the world. How did this come about? How much can we recuperate of the history of the flows and interchanges, the introductions and *métissages*, and the shifts in patterns of production, consumption, and trade that made rice into a global commodity? And what might a focus on rice and its multiple facets, dietary and symbolic, genetic, economic, and political, contribute to the flourishing field of global history?

THE CHALLENGE

Our global rice project began early in 2010, with a panel on "New histories of rice" organized by Edda Fields-Black at the invitation of the American Historical Association (AHA). It is not often that a mere crop captures the attention of the historical profession, but the liveliness, not to say ferocity, of the debate around the "Black Rice thesis" clearly made it a newsworthy theme.[1] The AHA panel comprised papers by three Atlantic historians[2]: I was the commentator. As an Asianist I was astonished by the strangeness, the striking unfamiliarity of the questions and assumptions of historians discussing rice in Africa and the Americas; they were equally astonished by mine. And yet we were all talking about different parts of the same elephant:

---

[1] E.g., Carney 2001; Eltis et al. 2010.
[2] Max Edelson joined Edda Fields-Black and Peter Coclanis on the panel. He was unfortunately unable to join us in our subsequent workshop and book project.

rice in the early-modern world economy. We decided to pursue the comparison, and this book is the result.

With its challenging propositions about what the plantation economy of the United States might owe to West African knowledge systems, the Black Rice controversy addresses big issues about knowledge, inequality, power, and the sources of wealth, with implications that would seem to reach well beyond national or even hemispheric borders. Yet we realized that the exciting challenges and contrasts raised by the Black Rice debate had apparently bypassed China historians. Conversely, the questions that preoccupied historians working on rice in East or Southeast Asia barely featured in the Black Rice debates – for instance the impact of rice-farming systems on long-term environmental history,[3] national imperatives of food self-sufficiency,[4] merchant cultures,[5] the impact on state or farmer choice of evolving consumer markets,[6] the ideology of rice-breeding and other agricultural improvement programs,[7] the negotiation of irrigation strategies between state and locality,[8] or rice and national identity.[9] Meanwhile, the Black Rice scholars took it for granted that rice farming was integral to the growth of a modern capitalist economy, while in the East Asian context rice farming was more often taken as an obstacle to economic development.

The balkanization of regional historiographies of rice is striking and at the same time surprising. Granted, rice systems initially developed independently in different parts of the world, in diverse environmental niches and within different social matrices. Yet for the last four centuries the regional histories of rice as crop, as food, and as commodity have been inextricably entangled with the emergence of the early-modern world economy and with the global networks and commodity flows of industrial capitalism. But although rice was grown, traded, and consumed across intersecting circuits of exchange that stretched from Brazil to Japan, the historiography of rice has remained regionally segmented, articulated to distinct problematics. It is remarkable how widely the historical questions asked about rice differ between regions, or even between countries within a region, and how little dialogue there has been across these geographical divides. It is as if the local fields of enquiry occupied watertight compartments, forming a fragmented patchwork of intellectual communities unaware of each others' agendas.

Paradoxically, one obstacle to dialogue, comparison, and synthesis may be precisely that regional historians are so keenly aware of the links between rice

---

[3] Elvin 2004; Boomgaard 2007b; Bray 2007a; Harrell 2007.
[4] Francks 1983; Will and Wong 1991.
[5] Hamilton and Chang 2003.
[6] Francks 2009; Montesano 2009.
[7] Maat 2001; Moon 2007.
[8] Bray 1986; Lansing 2006; Li 2010.
[9] Ohnuki-Tierney 1993; Cwiertka 2006.

and modernity in their own bailiwicks. One cannot complain that rice has been neglected as a historical agent or a shaper of paradigms, ranging from the Black Rice thesis of the Atlantic region to models of "agricultural involution" or "growth without development" for early-modern China, and the concept of "industrious revolution" as proposed by analysts of Japan's particular path to modernity. Clearly, such debates are nested in very specific, regional problematics of historical change, and framed by quite distinctive questions about the material basis of society, about nature and human agency, knowledge and control, progress or the morality of power. Therefore, few historians have thought to ask what the similarities or distinctions between regional histories and historiographies of rice might signify, how they might connect, or which new factors demand our attention if we compare China with the southern United States or Java with Senegal.

Rice: Global Networks and New Histories suggests how much we have to gain from breaking down the barriers and taking each other's preoccupations seriously. Rice history is currently a vital and innovative field of research attracting serious attention within the broader discipline. An impressive number of challenging and illuminating regional studies have appeared in the last few years.[10] But although regional historians are well aware that their local studies are part of a broader picture, as yet no attempt has yet been made to write a history of rice and its place in the rise of capitalism from a global and comparative perspective.[11] *Rice: Global Networks and New Histories* is a first step toward such a history.

Global history sets out to show how different regions of the world became linked, how they co-evolved toward a modern ecumene, what traveled along global networks and what did not, where the flows quickened and where backwaters or pockets of resistance lay, and how local matrices of environment and endowment, of social, political and material practice fed into global patterns or values. At the same time the global perspective is inherently comparative, pressing us to think critically about our locally generated questions or models: If we ask Black Rice questions about late imperial China, will it disrupt our current interpretations, prompt new questions, or inspire us to adopt new methods? And if a new research tool challenges prevailing narratives about rice in British India or Georgia, could it usefully be taken up by historians of Japan or Brazil?

---

[10] Among the recent regional histories are works by several of our contributors, including Cheung 2008, Fields-Black 2008, Hawthorne 2003, Lee 2011, and Stewart and Coclanis 2011.

[11] Sharma 2010 offers coverage of several regions, but it is a very different enterprise from global history, consisting of unrelated country histories and spanning over ten thousand years. Such histories were written for sugar (Mintz *Sweetness and power* [1985]) and for maize (Warman *Corn and Capitalism* [2003, first published in Spanish 1988]) almost 30 years ago. They became instant classics, setting the stage for vibrant new fields of comparative scholarship that are still going strong today.

Our collective brief in *Rice: Global Networks and New Histories* was to think both globally and comparatively about local cases, seeking to highlight and test the deep-rooted assumptions naturalized within regional research and debates, and to identify cross-cutting themes that would illuminate standard questions in new ways. In particular, we wanted to highlight and explore the nature of the local-global articulations that shaped local histories of rice as crop, food, and raw material, and the international networks of trade, labor, expertise, taste, and genetic materials in which localities participated or from which they were excluded. One valuable lesson to be drawn from recent work both in global history and in science and technology studies is that, rather than drawing categoric distinctions between production and consumption, or scientific research and farmer practice, or nutrition and ritual, we can often learn more from our historical sources by recognizing that making, doing, and using are in practice inextricably entwined, as are economic, social, and symbolic value, or dietary and cultural sustenance. So rather than attempting comprehensive coverage of the rice-growing and rice-eating world, or organizing the chapters by geography or date, or by unhelpful categories like production or consumption, we decided to focus on a small number of powerful, richly suggestive cross-cutting themes.

The 15 chapters of *Rice: Global Networks and New Histories* are written by specialists on Africa, the Americas, and several regions of Asia. Most of the contributions are richly empirical, locally embedded case-studies, some are synthetic reflections, others are speculative and explore the potential and implications of new research tools such as genetic mapping.[12] Each one brings a new approach that at some level unsettles prevailing narratives and suggests new cross-disciplinary linkages. The book is organized in three sections: *Purity and Promiscuity*, *Environmental Matters*, and *Power and Control*. We envisage these themes (explained more fully in the introductions to the sections) as conceptual bridges to disciplines currently setting trends in global history, respectively: the history of science, environmental history, and studies of governmentality.

The authors of *Rice: Global Networks* approach the comparative and global history of rice at several levels. The novel methods they deploy, and the big questions they ask, are premised on "the utility of a truly international approach to history. Regional or national approaches to the subject, self-contained and self-absorbed as they often are, will not do in this case."[13]

The authors thus seek new ways to connect micro- and macro-level histories (e.g., Biggs, Fields-Black, Smith). They propose a number of new approaches to

---

[12] Mouser et al. and Gilbert pioneer the use of genetic mapping to trace historical patterns of crop diffusion and breeding. Fields-Black suggests new ways to incorporate historical linguistics into regional history. Biggs and White both use topographical and hydrological mapping as tools.

[13] Coclanis 1993b, 1051.

regional histories, notably through reconceptualizing the significance of rice in specific contexts (e.g., Cheung, Linares, Hawthorne, Maat). They identify some promising angles from which to develop better comparative analysis, and explore new ways to integrate histories of rice into the complex interwoven flows of goods, people, capital, knowledge, and power that converge to form the history of capitalism (e.g., Lee, Boomgaard and Kroonenberg, Coclanis). The contributions borrow stimulating ideas from cultural history (Hawthorne), science and technology studies (Biggs) or the history of medicine (Minsky): What happens when we pay serious heed to the suffering bodies of workers in the rice-fields, or introduce the Latourian concept of the assemblage into an analysis of landscapes in the Mekong Delta? Individually or collectively, the chapters also highlight inconsistencies and contradictions between interpretations, places where the dots refuse to join, where data are absent, where analytical frameworks won't travel, or where a new method of investigation raises awkward and apparently intractable questions. They also highlight and explore various irreducible tensions: tensions, for instance, between local and global values attributed to rice; between rice as subsistence crop, commodity, or foodstuff; or between the profuse variety of rices and of rice farming systems, and the pressures toward homogeneity that come with taxation, international trade, scientific breeding, and modern ideals of agricultural development. The work, in other words, is still in progress: we are at the exciting stage where new questions are coming thick and fast, but we are not sure where they will lead us.

In the rest of this introduction I will first set the scene in very general terms, sketching out some features of rice as a global crop and commodity in the early-modern and modern era. Then I consider what is at stake in two contrasting debates about rice history, the Black Rice debate in Atlantic history, and the involution debate in East Asian history. I go on to discuss some of the contrasting approaches to rice and society that characterize different regional histories, question the rice-ness of rice in different contexts, and conclude with some reflections upon making connections, across space and across time.

GLOBAL RICE

What might we mean when we talk of rice as a global crop or commodity? Cotton and porcelain have each recently been claimed as the first global commodity,[14] and the arguments made in support of these claims are instructive. The long-term trends and outcomes that they identify constitute a common matrix within which the history of rice also unfolded, and the cases of both porcelain and cotton highlight similar – though by no means identical – opportunities for fusing material and cultural analysis.

---

[14] Riello and Parthasarathi 2011; Finlay 2010.

Porcelain and fine cottons both began their global careers in around 1400 or 1500. In both cases local Asian industries were feeding high-quality goods into expanding export markets that eventually spanned the globe. Early-modern European monarchs, states, and entrepreneurs sought doggedly to discover or recreate the techniques for making fine Indian prints and Chinese porcelains. One goal was import-substitution, to staunch the drain on the national coffers. But as both new technologies were mastered not long before the first stirrings of industrialization, it was not long before European textile and ceramic manufacturers began to aim for mass production and mass markets, at home and abroad, ushering in the age of mass consumption.

The preindustrial long-distance trade in porcelain and fine ceramics had significant cultural as well as technical impact, creating an ecumene of aesthetic values, visual motifs, and new manners (including introducing Europeans to the dinner plate as a replacement for the trencher). Inter-regional flows of cotton goods and expertise had likewise promoted new tastes and patterns of consumption, but it is cotton's key role in triggering the English industrial revolution and its consequences that commands most attention from global historians. Developments in the intercontinental organization of cotton cultivation and production between the late-eighteenth and mid-twentieth century were integral to the rise of industrial capitalism, colonialism, and modern markets, and to the consolidation of new hierarchies of class, race, and expertise, of new international divisions of labor and resources whose legacy still endures.

As a crop, food, and commodity, rice likewise acquired global significance over the last four or five centuries. Although it was not a high-value commodity like fine cottons and porcelain, it also appeared initially to Europeans as a typically Asian product and source of wealth. In 1506, just a few years after Columbus claimed Hispaniola for the Spanish crown, the Dutchman John Huyghen van Linschoten recorded his impressions of Bengal. It was a land, he wrote, "most plentiful of necessary victuals, specially *rice*, for that there is more of it [in that country] than in all the East, for they do yearly lade divers shippes [therewith], which come thither from all places, and there is never any want thereof."[15]

The thriving trade of the Asian oceans was a source of wealth and of desirable commodities that Europeans longed to break into and control, indeed Columbus had been seeking a shorter westward route to the Indies when he set off across the Atlantic. Spices, rare woods, and costly dyestuffs, exquisite printed cottons, lustrous silks, and porcelain were among the luxury goods that traveled the Asian routes, and it was these high-value goods that the Europeans initially coveted. But traffic in mundane necessities like raw

---

[15] Quoted by Minsky (this volume), emphasis added.

cotton and silk, iron nails and pots, copper cash, timber, and rice was equally vital to the expanding manufactures and markets of the Asia trade. Entrepots and industries, like armies, march on their stomachs: rice cultivation spread and intensified through tropical and temperate Asia in step with flourishing states, demographic expansion, rising prosperity, and a steady growth of commercial cropping, manufactures, and cities. With the conquest of the Americas, Europeans soon saw good reasons and opportunities for launching into rice-production themselves.

By 1700 rice was the chief provision of the slave trade between West Africa and the Americas; it subsequently became the main staple of colonial labor forces throughout the tropical zone. The eighteenth-century rice plantations of Brazil and Carolina harnessed African skills and labor to produce rice for export to Europe and to European colonies in the Caribbean. Through the nineteenth century, as they expanded their colonies through Asia, the British, French, and Dutch colonial powers carved out new export rice-zones in Burma, Indochina, and Indonesia to meet the expanding needs of empire, in the process pricing the rice industries of the Americas out of the market. Independent kingdoms in Southeast Asia, notably Siam but also smaller states like Kedah, also entered the fray and opened up new rice frontiers to feed miners, plantation workers, and growing urban populations through the Western colonies.

Rice farming as a source of accumulation and growth was by no means confined to colonial contexts, however. Until the late eighteenth century the Chinese economy was probably the largest in the world. The immense wealth and power of late imperial China was rooted in a system of intensive, small-scale rice farming that supported commercial cropping, rural manufactures, and a huge volume of trade. While the state invested heavily in developing rice production to feed its population and sustain the army and government, shifts in markets were equally important in shaping the balance between rice farming and other economic activities in any given locality. In Mughal India, which rivaled China in early-modern times as an exporter of manufactures, the state promoted rice farming to support the expansion of commercial cropping. In Japan advances in rice-based farming powered first the dynamic urban and commercial growth of the Tokugawa shogunate, and then the ambitious modernization, industrialization, and militarization programs of the Meiji state.

In their encounters with colonial-industrial capitalism the rice economies of India, China, and Japan each followed a different path. Under British rule the rice systems of Punjab and Bengal were further diversified and intensified to support the production of colonial export crops like indigo, cotton, and sugarcane. China had no formal colonies of its own, but by the late nineteenth century Chinese millers and merchants controlled most of the rice trade not only in China itself but also throughout Southeast Asia, including the

European colonies. Meiji Japan met its remorselessly expanding resource needs by seizing colonies for itself, annexing Taiwan and Korea and taking control of their rice production.

From around 1600 or 1700 the rice industries and consumption practices of the New World and the Old were gradually linked up through overlapping and often competing circuits of exchange, of rice itself, and also of labor, skills, technology, and agronomic knowledge and models. As demand increased, rice steadily conquered new territories. Paddy-fields crept down from river-valleys to flood-plains and coastal mangrove swamps, and up from valley floors to dizzying tiers of mountain terraces. By the mid-nineteenth century new technologies for draining, pumping, and levelling meant that swampy deltas and flood-plains could be turned into paddy fields for the first time. In Cochinchina, Burma, and Siam export rice-industries were set up, partly to feed migrant workers on the mines and plantations of European colonies through South and Southeast Asia, and partly to undercut imports of rice to Europe itself from America or Bengal.

The new Asian rice-bowls, though they operated on a much larger scale than traditional farms, still relied on intensive use of labor. But a revolutionary change took place in Louisiana beginning in the 1880s. There, as Peter Coclanis explains, immigrant Bonanza farmers and agronomists from the mid-West succeeded in "turning rice into wheat," transforming virgin land into vast tracts of paddy that could be irrigated, tilled, and harvested with machines. Instead of requiring the minute and continual toil of many workers, now one or two men could run a huge farm whose labor requirements amounted not to man-days but to man-hours. A new, productivist model for industrial rice farming was born. It proved its worth in Louisiana and later in California, and in the terms of modern economics it appeared supremely efficient and advanced compared to the micro-farms of old Asia. This model has since been exported around the world, first by colonial governments, later by modernizing independent states, frequently as part of a broader Green Revolution package. But its record has been checkered.

Even today we can still map an exuberant profusion of local varieties and types of rice, of ecological niches, and farming practices that elude the Green Revolution model of monoculture "miracle rices" grown with tractors, chemical fertilizers, and herbicides in large, rectangular fields. There are still good reasons for some farmers to choose dry rices, floating rices or rattoon rices; to select from a host of continually evolving landraces, some hybridized with "miracle rice" breeds; to till pocket-handkerchief terraces or patches of swidden cleared in the forest. Modern, large-scale rice farming quite often succeeded on lands where no rice had previously been grown; it often failed where improvers tried to transform existing small-scale farming. Success or failure hinged not only on the natural, but also on the social and political environment in which such radical transformations of the landscape were attempted.

One reason for the enduring appeal, despite its proven limitations, of the mid-Western model of rice farming is that it embodies key aspects of industrial or even corporatist rationality: it is capital-intensive, brings economies of scale, and prioritizes labor productivity. As Jonathan Harwood explains, this is by no means the only rationality that has been applied to scientific seed-breeding, but within the broader matrix of capitalist and commercial interpretations of efficiency and progress, it has come to prevail. A capitalist mode of production is "encapsulated," as Biggs puts it, in the high-yielding varieties developed by US-trained crop-scientists over the last century. A recurring theme in the following chapters is how modern rice gradually took shape – in constant tension with the specific requirements of local environments and social formations – as a global crop, a scientifically tailored instrument of development that governments and corporations, policy-makers, economists, and scientists strive to deploy in the form of "universal varieties" that they hope will thrive – and prove acceptable as food – anywhere in the world.

Faith in transferable seeds or technologies, what Latour calls "immutable mobiles," is by no means confined to the modern era: in about 1100 Chinese state bureaus for agricultural development were distributing imported seed of quick-ripening rices to farmers. But the pace quickened and confidence in universals grew in the colonial era, as science was applied to crop selection. Scientific rice-breeding was part and parcel of the colonial enterprise in French Indochina, of nation-building in Republican China and postindependence Senegal, and of succeeding visions or ideologies of international development from the Green Revolution of the 1960s to the International Rice Research Institute's current project for Golden Rice. Today centralized scientific rice-breeding is widely accepted as a global solution to global problems of hunger and poverty. The contributors to this book offer various explanations of how and why the idea of universal rice has come to be so persuasive and so powerful, despite the resilience of alternatives. Some focus on recent processes, others trace its roots back to a more distant past.

Whether we stand in China or Louisiana, Sierra Leone or Bengal, it is clear that the local history of rice is closely entwined with worldwide trends in colonial and capitalist expansion, and with the emergence of modern science and institutions. The question is how we might weave the different strands together to produce something more than a patchwork of local stories. Here let me briefly compare two local debates about rice, history, and capitalism. The incommensurability between them, I suggest, reveals deeper agendas within the historical enterprise. Exposing these underlying goals and values suggests some promising new points of reflection at the level of global history.

WHAT WE TALK ABOUT WHEN WE TALK ABOUT RICE: DEBATES AND AGENDAS

The terms of the Black Rice debate, in a nutshell, are as follows.[16] The Black Rice thesis is that African workers in the rice-fields of South Carolina or Brazil were not simply carrying out tasks defined by white farm-owners but effectively transplanting or recreating a West African set of agricultural skills and knowledge system. In her book entitled *Black Rice*, Judith Carney drew upon ethnographic evidence from West Africa to propose that women were the chief custodians of rizi-cultural skills and knowledge, and therefore the chief agents of technological transfer across the Atlantic. The evidence on which the Black Rice arguments are based has been fiercely contested by other historians. Some argue that there is no convincing evidence that the majority of rice-plantation workers in the Americas came from the African regions (mainly the Guinea Coast) where rice was grown; others contest the role of women as purveyors of technical skills. Still others believe that the rice-systems of the colonial New World are better understood not in terms of simple binaries of power and knowledge between black and white, but as much more complex hybrids.[17]

With its challenging propositions about what the plantation economy of the United States might owe to West African knowledge systems, the Black Rice controversy addresses big issues about knowledge, inequality, power, and the sources of wealth, with implications reaching well beyond national or even hemispheric borders. It also raises tricky methodological questions about sources and interpretation.

As a historian of China the familiar debate with which I grapple is quite different: it is about agricultural involution and the historical trajectory of rice-based agrarian economies like imperial China. For anybody not familiar with the term, it was coined by the anthropologist Clifford Geertz. Geertz' *Agricultural Involution*, published in 1963, is a study of the social and ecological impact of the colonial "Cultivation System" (*Cultuur Stelsel*) in Java. Geertz argued that there is something technically special about wet rice as a staple. In Java the capitalist dynamism of the colonial sugar-plantation sector offered a dramatic contrast with the peasant rice farming which fed its laborers. Geertz argued that the technical characteristics of irrigated rice farming in Java permitted infinite small-scale increments in output, but these were achieved largely through the intensification of labor inputs, achieved not through development of the means of production, but through the reinforcement of the traditional, non-capitalist social institutions within which rice farming was embedded. Involution occurred in Java, Geertz argues, because there was no industrial or urban sector to absorb surplus population;

---

[16] For more critical detail see the chapters by Fields-Black, Smith, and, especially, Hawthorne.
[17] For example, Smith (this volume); Hawthorne 2003.

in Meiji Japan, by contrast, there was no involution partly because a growing industrial sector was attracting peasants off the land, and partly because new labor-saving technologies were becoming available to Japanese farmers.

The influence of *Agricultural Involution* on historians of Asian and other non-Western civilizations has been tremendous. Less overtly political than Karl Wittfogel's claims, published just six years earlier, that large-scale irrigation works like those typical of imperial China both require and support the totalitarian institutions of "Oriental despotism," Geertz' concept of agricultural involution continues to frame some key debates in comparative history, in particular explanations of China's historical "backwardness"[18] or contestations of the Geertzian model.[19] I come back later to recent challenges to the concept of agricultural involution from historians of Indonesia. For now, I explain why it was so enthusiastically accepted as the key to explaining China's history.

The Chinese puzzle was how to explain a story of apparent failure. Joseph Needham set the terms most clearly, arguing that until about 1400 China was the world leader in scientific and technological creativity – but then this creativity ground to a halt. China was rapidly overtaken by Europe, in science, in economic growth, and in military and political power. The scientific and industrial revolutions took place in Europe, not China. Why? Needham's culprits included the stifling effects of bureaucracy and a supposed indifference on the part of the Confucian elite to Nature and practical knowledge. Drawing on Geertz as well as on Japanese scholarship on China, in *The Pattern of the Chinese Past* Mark Elvin incorporated the mode of agrarian production into this explanatory model.[20]

According to both Needham and Elvin, the heyday of Chinese scientific and technological achievement was the Song dynasty (960–1279). Underpinning the surge in experimentation and intellectual brilliance was what Elvin dubbed the "Song-dynasty Green Revolution." In order to raise tax revenues to protect its borders and feed its population, the Song state financed irrigation works and land reclamation projects, promoted the use of new rice varieties, farm equipment, and cultivation techniques such as multiple-cropping, disseminating information through local magistrates' courts and the circulation of agronomic

---

[18] Wittfogel's arguments about technology and the totalitarian state, published at the height of the Cold War (Wittfogel 1957), were enthusiastically welcomed in the West both within and beyond the academy. Geertz' concept of involution implied that real development could only come from *outside* Java – and thus meshed very well with the principles of development theory.

[19] For the 2010 AHA panel, the economic-environmental historian Li Bozhong proposed a paper (which unfortunately he was not able to present) which used meteorological records and data on rice yields and labor to show that a century-long decline of both land and labor productivity in rice farming in the Lower Yangzi region after 1823 "was due primarily to climatic cooling *and not, as is frequently argued, to agricultural involution*" (emphasis added).

[20] Needham 1969, 16, 190; Elvin 1973.

treatises, and encouraging uptake through tax breaks and loans. This "package" resulted in a short-term surge in agricultural output and in household-based production of textiles and other commodities. Its long-term impact, however, was to trap the rural population, and by extension the Chinese state and Chinese society, into an involutionary dynamic such as Geertz had described for Java. In Elvin's account the roots of China's decay thus grew inexorably from the dynamics of its growth patterns.

Elvin's paradigm-setting study became one of the most influential works on China ever written. Various adaptations were made by economic historians of China to explain what they saw as China's inherent failure to develop toward modernity, leading to a decline in dynamism post-1400 that was nevertheless combined with a well-documented long-term growth in farm and commodity output. Elvin proposed the idea of a "high-level equilibrium trap" to explain this model of arrested development, Philip Huang and others used terms like "stagnation" or "growth without development."[21] Historians of the "California School" argue on the contrary that China continued to develop in the post-Song period, although along ideological, institutional, and technical paths different from those experienced in Europe or North America. They argue that the Chinese agrarian state's economy matched Europe in crucial indicators at least until 1750 or 1800, and that China was a key player in the emergence of modern forms of organization of capital, and in shaping "modernity." It was not the tendencies of native rice farming systems that channeled China's nineteenth-century degeneration into "the sick man of Asia," but a constellation of factors including climatic change and the predatory incursions of the Western powers.[22]

In an early contribution to what became the Californian model, I proposed that what I termed the "skill-oriented," small-scale, low-capital path of rice farming intensification typical of East Asia had a quite distinct dynamic from the typical model of agricultural development in Britain or its temperate-zone colonies. The rice-based dynamic, I argued, was by no means inherently involutionary. More typically, it effectively sustained patterns of rural economic diversification and income generation that often increased labor productivity and household output – albeit without the spectacular returns of large-scale mechanization.[23]

I conceived of my skill-oriented model as a response to what I had learned about the relations between rice farming and national development in

---

[21] Huang 1990.
[22] Landmark studies of the California School include Wong 1997, Pomeranz 2000, Marks 1998, Frank 1998, Li 1998, and Arrighi et al. 2003.
[23] Bray 1986; Li 1998; and see below for further detail on the forms of economic diversification that rice economies supported. Gender complementarity and the fundamental economic contributions of female work were recognized by Chinese policy makers as a key factor to be incorporated into economic policy and official interventions (Bray 1997; Pomeranz 2003).

Japan.[24] Francks' chapter confirms that it remains consistent with more recent scholarship on Japanese economic development. Curiously, the case of Japan appears flatly to contradict what are still prevalent arguments about Chinese stagnation. The intensification of rice-based farming in Tokugawa Japan, starting in about 1600, mirrored (and indeed in many ways was explicitly modeled on) earlier Chinese precedents like the Song Green Revolution. As in China, increased output of rice and other crops supported urbanization, the expansion of manufacturing, and increased consumption levels. The Meiji government (1868–1912) imposed rigorous policies for further intensification of rice farming as part of its modernization drive, in order to support very successful policies of industrialization and military expansion.

In Japan's case the deliberate promotion of small-scale skill-oriented rice farming – a commitment that as Francks explains continues to influence Japan's ecological, economic, and political landscape today – is viewed by economic historians of Japan as unproblematic, albeit distinctive, when it comes to capital accumulation, industrial-level economies of scale, or a spirit of innovation. It cannot just be, as Geertz proposed, that Japan's rice-economy was qualitatively transformed after the Meiji state adopted Western policies of scientific and industrial development starting in the 1870s. Indeed the Japanese economic historian Akira Hayami proposed a contrast between an "industrial revolution" in England ca. 1800 and an "industrious revolution" in Tokugawa Japan. The English revolution depended on high capital inputs to achieve economies of scale, whereas the Japanese revolution put to work mental habits and physical skills moulded by the traditions of small-scale rice farming and rural craft production. This idea of an industrious revolution was then reworked in a European context by Jan de Vries, who proposed a revisionist account of the European Industrial Revolution's roots and dynamics based on the intensification of small-scale household production. De Vries argued that between roughly 1550 and 1800 households in northwestern Europe worked more hours and allocated more of their labor to specialized production for the market. They made the time for this work by purchasing some goods that they had previously made for themselves. The profits they made by their sales allowed them to purchase more consumer goods, thus raising their living standards, albeit sacrificing some leisure in return. De Vries in turn provided a new analytical framework for the revisionist arguments of the California School, who have documented similar patterns in early modern and modernizing China.[25]

There are two important stakes in the East Asian involution debates, both of them highly political. One is the question of *modernization and progress*: Were the demands and institutions of rice-based societies inimical to the rise

---

[24] Especially Smith 1959, Hayami 1967, Ishikawa 1981, and Francks 1983.
[25] Hayami 1967, 1992; de Vries 1994; Pomeranz 2003.

of capitalism, industrialization, and liberalization – in other words, to the emergence of modernity (that is, modernity as viewed from Europe or North America)? Closely connected to the question about modernity is another question, this time about *creativity*. If rice-economies do tend historically toward involution, is this because they typically increase output through tiny anonymous improvements, rather than encouraging the search for radical transformations, noble inventions, or discoveries of the kind associated with the rise of a scientific mind-set and an inventive engineering culture in the modern West?

The debates about rice and history in East Asia have generated challenges to Eurocentrism and intellectual racism at various levels. They invite us to rethink the qualities and values of non-Western civilizations, their specific historical dynamisms, their impact on world history, their contributions to modernity, and their right to recognition on the world stage. They also invite us to rethink our teleologies, and in particular to question how much of "the modern" is really Western – they thus require us to relativize many of our certainties.

The same is true of the debates around rice and history along the shores of the Atlantic. Yet the register, the terms in which these challenges are expressed, the underlying inequalities which they address, are instructively different. The East Asian debates challenge ideologies of Western supremacy. They operate generally at the level of national or regional history. Whether in China or Japan the nature, ideology, and reach of *the state* are key considerations; regimes of exploitation and control are seen as located within the society, rather than imposed by alien forces.[26]

The debates around Atlantic rice systems, on the other hand, are shaped by the critical discourses developed to address the historical experience of the United States and its relations with Africa, in particular slavery and its modern legacies. Three intertwining regimes of subordination, *race*, *class*, and *gender*, structure the research agendas. In its strongest formulations, the Black Rice thesis has two complementary goals of restoring agency and worth to subordinated social groups. First: to show us that the knowledge and skills of supposedly powerless and ignorant black slaves shaped the development of the Southern plantation economy, American engagements in world trade, and the American path to industrial capitalism. Second: along Black Athena lines, to demonstrate the creativity of African societies, especially African women, and the world-historical impact of their inventions. An interesting point that strikes the East Asianist is that there is never any suggestion here that rice-growing is somehow incompatible with radical social change, or with the growth of industrial capitalism. On the contrary, in the Atlantic-American context it seems that the dynamics of rice farming are assumed to be the very opposite of involutionary.

---

[26] Francks 1984 and this volume; Wong 1997; Mazumdar 1998; Buoye 2000.

Introduction

In contrasting the Atlanticist with the East Asian debates about rice and history, we are clearly far from exhausting the comparative possibilities. Among the alternatives that might have been explored, we could for instance have included the arguments about rice and colonial/postcolonial development in Burma, Indonesia, or Vietnam, or about rice and nation-building in nineteenth-century Siam. Or we might have chosen to compare the history and historiography of rice with other important crops like wheat, corn, or cotton in a single geopolitical context, for instance in North America or India. One particular interest of the East Asia–Atlantic comparison is that it contrasts two distinctive modes of production. In China and Japan small-scale peasant production of rice was integral to a mixed rural economy, embedded within an interventionist agrarian state for which the rural sector was the primary source of income and accumulation. The rice-system that grew up in the American South was an export industry; the plantations were commercial enterprises competing for foreign markets within a largely laissez-faire national economy.

RICE AND SOCIETY

This brings me to my next theme: the articulations of rice farming to the social order. Within the framework of the Atlantic field of rice history, observed contrasts, continuities, or ruptures in the social embedding of rice farming and its regimes of exploitation have served to highlight interpretive issues in the social mechanisms of technology transfer and innovation. As Eltis et al. put it:

Broadly speaking, two contrasting models dominate interpretations of Atlantic history. One draws on Old World influences to explain the nature of societies and cultures in the Americas, while the other assigns primacy to the New World environment. One stresses continuities, the other change. The polar extremes are persistence and transience, inheritance and experience. An emphasis on inheritance prioritizes the cultural baggage that migrants brought with them, whereas a focus on experience highlights the physical and social environments, such as climate, natural resources, and settlement processes, that they encountered. In modern parlance, one approach focuses on folkways, the other on factor endowments.[27]

Where technical knowledge is concerned, in its strongest form the Black Rice thesis proposes that a complete "knowledge system," comprising seed, tools, and water-management devices, and gender-specific divisions of labor, knowledge, and material skills, was in effect transplanted from the West African coast to the natural swamplands of the Carolina Lowcountry or Brazil.[28] Other interpretations, for example by Edelson, portray a complex

---

[27] Eltis et al. 2010, 1329.
[28] Carney 2001.

process of adaptation and fusion, noting for instance that British planters in the Carolinas were already interested in rice. Although we do not know whether their knowledge came from descriptions of rice farming in East Asia, Italy, or India, we do know that English writers on agronomy like Samuel Hartlib (ca. 1600–1662) advocated introducing wet-rice to suitable extensions of British territory in order to reduce national expenditure on imports. Edelson argues that British planters recreated home-grown techniques for draining and channeling water in the Lowcountry, providing a material matrix within which a new technical system of rice-cultivation emerged through experiments and negotiations combining British, African, and Amerindian skills, knowledge, and goals.[29]

Hayden Smith proposes that one key to a more rooted understanding of the creolization of knowledge and skills that went into building the hybrid rice-systems of the Americas lies in environmental micro-history. Smith's fine-grained study of successive modes of inland rice farming in the South Carolina Lowcountry focuses on topography, asking how it affected choices not only about the location and technical organization of rice-fields, but also about which land people identified as suitable for settlements. Smith suggests that one could build outward from rice-fields and houses to follow the inhabitants, enslaved and free, through the landscape, focusing in particular on access to the wider world. This ambitious project would, Smith suggests, illuminate the role of topography in shaping a region's culture and society.

Terrain, topography, and hydrology also feature prominently in Biggs' historical mapping of the political geography of the Mekong Delta. Rice's natural promiscuity means that humans must work hard to maintain the varieties that suit their needs. Biggs takes rice-seeds as encapsulations of changes in labor, technology, science, and the politics of settlement. Focusing on four different sub-groups of rice (long-stem and short-stem landraces, high-value cultivars and high-yield cultivars) suited to different ecological niches and modes of production, and locating them in actor-networks of resources and expertise, Biggs unfolds a history of successive waves of settlement, of distinctive forms of government, and of wars and resistance, culminating in the recent transformation of the Delta into a showpiece of Green Revolution technology. While this might seem a logical and thus stable outcome, Biggs successfully demonstrates both its contingency and its precarity.

Olga Linares' longitudinal study of responses to drought in three rice-growing Jola villages in the Casamance region of Senegal similarly illustrates the pertinence of Smith's suggestion. Of course an anthropologist is at an advantage here, since she is free to follow people and resources as they move. Linares' ethnography has unusual historical depth, tracing detailed

---

[29] Edelson 2006, 2010.

fluctuations and shifts in the productivity, acreage, and practices of rice farming over more than three decades, since the onset of a prolonged drought period in 1968. She compares the resilience of rice-production and the sustainability of village-based livelihood in three distinctive eco-zones. Like Lauren Minsky in her analysis of the complex associations between disease, environment, and economy in India, however, Linares rejects simplistic ecological determinisms, arguing that gender and generational roles and relations, and the insertion of villagers into broader networks of employment and commerce, are just as important as ecology in explaining the differences between the villages.

As in the Javanese regencies analyzed by Boomgaard and Kroonenberg, in each of the three communities studied by Linares the demands of rice production shape but do not determine broader patterns of economic activity, including communal infrastructural work and gender divisions of labor. Before the drought Jola households typically combined subsistence rice farming with cash-cropping of groundnuts, and often produced small surpluses of rice too. Since the drought commodity markets have changed, the government now imports cheap rice from Asia, and increasing numbers of villagers migrate to the cities for work. The context is of course contemporary, yet many of the factors to which Linares draws our attention are also pertinent for understanding historical micro-shifts elsewhere, for example in pre-modern China or Japan. They do not translate easily, however, across the Atlantic to large-scale slave-labor plantations.

History and anthropology are closely linked in African studies generally, hence studies of rice-growing in seventeenth- and eighteenth-century African settings, like their modern counterparts, specifically address the connections between the requirements of rice cultivation and local forms of government, access to land, gender regimes, age sets, and the rights of locals versus "outsiders." The chapters by Mouser, Fields-Black, Linares, and Hawthorne all take up these themes. But once we cross the Atlantic this form of sociological analysis usually cedes to parsing the emergent properties of a society where planters and settlers, slaves and laborers, Africans, indigenes, and whites mingle, offering an infinity of forms of collaboration or exploitation that eventually consolidate into a "plantation economy."[30]

What seems to feature much less dramatically in the American than in the African analyses – understandably given the looming shadow of slavery – is the question of whether rice farming in itself shapes institutions of social cohesion. This is, however, an important problematic in East Asian and in Southeast Asian rice histories, most marked perhaps in Japanese scholarship. A strong streak of Marxist materialism can be discerned in the Japanese

---

[30] Smith, this volume; Edelson 2010.

models of "tightly" and "loosely organized rural societies," which nevertheless reflect important realities of village organization on the ground.[31]

There are two main considerations here. First, in the patchwork of tiny fields belonging to different farmers that makes up any gravity-fed or poldered irrigation unit, it is in the collective interest to ensure that water is distributed fairly. If local rulers or state officers want full coffers rather than starving peasants on their hands, they need to ensure that upstream villages leave a fair share of water for villages downstream. Second, Asian irrigated rice farming is marked by two very high peaks of labor demand (transplanting and harvesting). Families or communities pool their labor on a rota basis to help each other with these key tasks, and these labor-exchange groups play an important role in structuring other economic or social activities. After land reform in China, the Communist government organized peasant labor into "work brigades" that were essentially the old labor-exchange groups; in Malaysia, agricultural development officers in the 1970s used *gotong-royong* labor-exchange groups as convenient conduits to disseminate new technology.[32]

The tensions between private and collective interest, exploitation and mutual dependence, are a recurrent theme in studies of East and Southeast Asian rice systems. The Balinese *subak* (local irrigation management organizations) are famous as probably the most intricate and perfect example of a society and landscape organized around rice farming: the dazzling tiers of rice-terraces that cascade down the mountainous slopes are kept perpetually green thanks to regular meetings of all the *subak* farmers in the local water temple. Yet even within a single *subak*, competition for water between descent-groups threatens agreement. How, then, is equilibrium sustained within and between the numerous *subak* that adjoin along a watershed? In his most recent work on the *subak* the anthropologist Steven Lansing argues provocatively that the complex interweaving over space and time of ritual, social, and technical interventions is a historically "self-organizing process" that channels contending interests to generate a common commitment to order and shared prosperity.[33]

While the mystique of the *subak* has attracted a succession of Western historians, folklorists, and anthropologists, Japan has its own tradition of mystical-materialist explorations of the imperatives of rice farming, referring back for example to medieval village regulations that sentenced any farmer breaking irrigation rules to expulsion from the village.[34] In imperial China's gigantic river-systems, like the Yangzi basin, the imperatives of flood prevention had to be measured against those of crop irrigation and transport. There

---

[31] Ishii 1978.
[32] Bray 1986; 2009.
[33] Lansing 2006.
[34] Tamaki 1977.

historians have examined how the cross-cutting or contradictory interests of state, region, and community, and of bureaucrats, landlords, or small farmers were negotiated and translated into material practice or political agendas, and how the tensions between private and collective goals and resources have sculpted modern landscapes and economic decision making.[35]

Japan is perhaps the most conspicuous example of a successful modern "rice economy." Francks' chapter describes the policies and institutions through which the state mobilized multifunctional rural households to build a modern, competitive industrial economy that even today is still, to a visible extent, shaped by and organized around the needs and affordances of small-scale rice farming. As Francks remarks, if rice today is still the symbol of an authentic Japanese life, this reflects how tightly rice farming has been integrated into Japan's industrial formation and consumer practices.

East or Southeast Asianists, then, agree with Black Rice scholars like Carney in assuming that a "commitment to rice-production"[36] profoundly shapes the social as well as the physical contours of rural landscapes, in ways that – while not imposing uniformity at the level of micro-environment[37] – often overarch political or geographical boundaries. The Asianists also take for granted that rice is a crop grown by small farmers – an understanding widely reflected in ideologies and practices of government across the region, whether in precolonial, colonial, or postcolonial times.[38]

In East or Southeast Asian contexts, economies of scale simply did not work in rice farming: skills were more effective than expensive equipment in raising yields.[39] While there was much landlordism in East Asian rice regions, farms were small and plantations unknown, even for the cultivation of valuable cash-crops like tea or sugar. In the technically sophisticated Yangzi Delta in the 1660s about half an acre of rice-fields was considered enough to feed a family, while the rest of the holding was used for cash-crops like cotton or vegetables, or planted with mulberries to feed silkworms. Some families preferred to buy rice on the market so they could devote all their land and labor to cash-crops. Rice farming served as a sheet-anchor for economic diversification in China. We see a historical ripple-effect over the centuries: productive rice-regions like the Lower Yangzi or the Pearl River Delta shift to higher-value commodities like textiles or sugar, while former backwaters

---

[35] Li 2010.
[36] Carney 2001; Eltis et al. 2007; Fields-Black, this volume.
[37] See the chapters by Fields-Black and Linares.
[38] See Maat, this volume, on Smits. Suzanne Moon's study of technological development in the Netherlands East Indies also documents cases where the interaction of colonial idealism and scientific practice led the Dutch to commit to small-scale change in their "development of the native peoples' (Moon 2007).
[39] Bray 1986, 115, 148–155. Only in the 1970s, when the Japanese started designing miniature machines specifically for tilling, transplanting, and harvesting wet-rice, did the situation begin to change.

become new centres of the internal rice trade. Some formerly poor mountainous regions establish thriving industries in bamboo paper or tea and begin to import rice. Then around 1800 the Lower Yangzi turns back to rice farming, and once again pioneers advanced techniques.[40]

In colonial Java too, despite Geertz' portrayal of agricultural involution, the heterogeneity, resilience, and flexibility of the small-scale rice system is well documented. Boomgaard and Kroonenberg note that Geertz' interpretation of the Javanese rural economy "has been praised and imitated by many scholars who worked on areas other than Java, and vilified by most Java scholars." Their critical re-evaluation of what Geertz characterized as a "mutualistic" relationship between sugar and rice on Java highlights the importance of activities that Geertz simply omitted from his analysis: raising livestock, growing a wide range of crops, or working as laborers in neighboring non-sugar regencies, for example. Boomgaard and Kroonenberg's reconstruction of peasant agency, demographic and economic, neatly complements arguments about peasant economic agency spelled out by Maat for Sumatra.

Geertz was hardly alone among social theorists in suggesting that the "native" sector of colonial or modern economies consisted of low-tech, largely subsistence activities that were reactive, determined by the penetration of a more highly developed capitalist sector. The same attitude frequently informed colonial policy as well as postcolonial development policy around the world. In exploring different rice farming strategies among smallholders in colonial Sumatra, Maat's concept of "anti-commodity" draws attention to the ambiguity of rice and other peasant crops or products. Now used for subsistence, now sold as commodities, such goods are produced by peasant households in a flexible response to the formal capitalist sector of commodity production. Peasant choices are certainly contained within colonial or postcolonial systems of economic segmentation, but can also be seen as resisting or mobilizing them.

In the case of Sumatra, the colonial government attempted to install a system of irrigated, intensive wet-rice farming in the lowlands; success was at best mixed, even though the government manned the schemes with properly "industrious" rice-farmers brought in from Java. Most of the rice on Sumatra continued to be grown by smallholders who combined upland, dry rice with commercially competitive production of cash crops like rubber. Yet this crucial component of the rural economy, linked though it was into international commodity markets, remained largely invisible at policy level. As Maat reminds us, colonial and postindependence agronomists, economists, and modernizing governments almost invariably equated efficient commodity-production with large-scale, plantation-level production, and productive rice farming with irrigated lowland rice.

---

[40] Bray 2007a; Li 1998; Marks 1998.

Introduction 21

Mouser and his co-authors provide a West African angle on anti-commodities, tracing "the reworking of rice as a commodity in international trade into an item more suited to local needs" in postindependence Sierra Leone. What is particularly interesting here is their application of a newly emerging research tool, namely the genetic mapping of rice varieties, to postulate a history of small-farmer seed-selection and breeding pursued over decades following emancipation in the 1920s. Farmers shaped and reshaped local rice genetic resources in counterpoint to colonial and post-independence official strategies for modernizing the rice sector. In Sierra Leone as often elsewhere, Green-Revolution policies and universal varieties proved unsustainable, but farmers have successfully developed a range of varieties from crosses not only within but across species. Some do well only in local niches, others fulfill the goal of universal varieties, thriving in a wide range of conditions. Linares' account of Jola farming complements Mouser's molecular analysis, elaborating the ecological, economic, and social factors that guide farmers' choices between the types of rice on offer.

COMMITTED TO RICE: GROWING, EATING, TAXING, TRADING

What does it mean to depend upon rice as a key resource, whether as a crop, a food, a raw material, or a trading commodity? One challenge to the historian is that wherever rice is grown it has a tendency to hog the picture. One thing that is very striking about rice is that most people think that "Rice is Nice," even if it's a new food to them. Rice is tasty, rice is elegant, rice looks good as well as tasting good. Almost everywhere it is available rice is high-status food, the preferred dish for rituals, feasts, and ancestral offerings as well as for rental payments and taxes.[41] If we ask whether a society, or region, is "uniformly committed to rice,"[42] or even what part rice might play in its rural economy, its trading circuits or its dietary practices, we need to take into account that rice seems (at least in local eyes) to have an exceptionally high degree of symbolic magnetism.

In late imperial Chinese records, for example, since taxation was in rice or its equivalents, a prefecture would be categorized by its rice output even if all the rice the peasants harvested went to the landlord and the tax-man, while they themselves ate sweet potatoes.[43] Japan offers an even more dramatic case. A key element in the ubiquitous modern "theory of Japaneseness" (*nihonjin ron*) is the belief that rice is the staple food upon which Japanese civilization has been built from its inception, and that various typically Japanese social and psychological traits come from eating and growing rice

---
[41] Hamilton 2004.
[42] See Fields-Black, this volume; Eltis et al. 2007.
[43] Cheung, this volume; Huang 1990; Mazumdar 1998.

the Japanese way. Schoolbooks teach children that rice cultivation has sustained and molded Japanese society for over 2,000 years. Each spring TV programs show the emperor ceremonially turning a furrow in a rice-field. Athletes' trainers insist that they must have Japanese, not imported, rice if they are to reach their full physical and mental potential. Politicians support wasteful systems of rice farming as an unassailable national legacy. Francks' chapter analyzes rice as the basis for modern Japanese patterns of both production and consumption. Meanwhile Katarzyna Cwiertka demonstrates the key role that militarization and colonization played in establishing rice as the expected everyday staple for lower-class Japanese, and the complex symbolic place of rice in contemporary Japanese culture is vividly portrayed in a study by the anthropologist Emiko Ohnuki-Tierney entitled *Rice as Self*. Historians like Charlotte von Verschuer show that the myth of Japan as a rice-centred civilization dates back a thousand years, although it was only at the turn of the twentieth century that rice first became a staple food for many Japanese, including rice-farmers.[44] So how did the myth of rice emerge?

First, as von Verschuer notes, rice held a special political role in Japan from early times. Unlike shifting cultivation or even dry fields, wet-rice fields could be easily located, measured, and recorded. Rice was the only cereal whose production was routinely taxed; the state and local rulers alike tried to encourage or impose rice cultivation wherever possible, while farmers for their part preferred to grow other cereals which were not only tax-free but required much less work. Not surprisingly, the powerful prevailed and the area under wet-rice increased inexorably over the centuries.[45]

How did rice acquire its special symbolic status in Japanese culture? In the twelfth century, scholars writing commentaries on Japan's earliest texts, compilations of history, myth, and poetry produced in the seventh century, began to gloss generic references to cereal crops or to foods generally as references to rice.[46] This trend of equating all food or grain with rice was consolidated in Edo scholarship, between 1600 and 1850. Between 1870 and 1920 the modernizing Meiji government translated the cult of rice beyond classical scholarship, generating a popular discourse of origin myths and national essence that fed into educational texts as well as political speeches. In other words, over time the special political role of rice and its place in

---

[44] Cwiertka 2006; Ohnuki-Tierney 1993; Verschuer 2005.

[45] James C. Scott's latest book (2009), initially entitled "Why civilizations can't climb hills," offers a refusenik model of this dynamic of encroaching state control in mainland Southeast Asia. Maat and Biggs (this volume) discuss respectively how shifting cultivation of rice in Sumatra (known to the colonial authorities as *roofbouw* or "robbery cultivation"), and upland fields or floating rice-crops in the Mekong Delta, similarly eluded the control of the central state.

[46] A similar trend can be observed in China, where the word *fan*, a generic term for the boiled or steamed form of whatever is the local staple grain, has increasingly come to be equated with rice.

the elite diet was manipulated to create an image of Japan as a nation of rice-eaters.[47] As the history of the myth has been researched, we historians of agriculture have had to go back to our sources to look more carefully at what they might tell us about rice in Japanese food culture.

Acknowledgement of the myth of rice in Japan also requires us to rethink critically the significance of medieval and early-modern Japanese agricultural treatises, all of which treat rice-production as the cornerstone of farming practice. The ideological status of rice farming in Japanese political philosophy coincides with that of China in key respects. In evaluating good husbandry Japanese elites, like the Chinese political class, focused on industriousness: with the back-breaking work of transplanting and weeding, rice farming involved spectacularly hard work compared to most other crops and hence represented the moral and political quintessence of good farming.[48] In Chinese political ideology rice farming was one element in a cosmo-political dyad: men ploughed while women wove textiles, thus between them feeding and clothing both their own families and the state. The painful drudgery involved was not a moral good in itself, but rather the sacrifice required to maintain social harmony and thus ensure the continued beneficence of Heaven. Farming handbooks gave detailed instructions for growing the beans or sweet potatoes that village families routinely ate, but only rice warranted a woodcut illustration, and that illustration generally emphasized the ritual and symbolic importance of rice farming.[49]

How rice-growing skills feed into personhood differs greatly around the world. In China the labor and skills of rice-growing were mostly (if not exclusively) performed by men and coded male, but there were no specific male virtues or powers associated with the occupation. In each of the three Jola villages that Linares discusses the gender division of labor was different. Yet one kind of work was exclusively male: whenever dykes had to be built, canals dredged, or rice-fields reclaimed from mangrove swamps, it was the young, strong men who set to, working together in age-mate teams. Taking the Balanta of Guinea-Bissau as his ethnographic case-study, Hawthorne looks more closely at the masculine qualities associated with the heroic tasks of mangrove rice farming in West Africa, this time in the context of the Black Rice debate.

The Black Rice thesis not only celebrates the achievements of Guinea Coast rice-farmers in bringing ricicultural skills to the Americas, but infers that these skills were empowering. One of Carney's key arguments – hotly

---

[47] Verschuer 2005; Ohnuki-Tierney 1993.
[48] Verschuer 2005. In later historical theory this translated, as we have seen, into the human qualities underpinning an "industrious revolution."
[49] Bray 2007b. Until about AD 1000 Setaria millet, the most important cereal crop of northern China, was the iconic cereal. By around 1000 the economic centre of China had definitively shifted south, and with the loss of the northern provinces to the Tartars in 1126 the focus of political, technical and symbolic attention shifted to rice.

disputed by Eltis – is that Guineans (and in particular Guinean women) were in demand among Carolina planters, who were ready to pay higher prices for their rice-growing skills. These skills, according to Carney, then served the Guinean slaves on the plantations as a trading good or bargaining chip that allowed them to negotiate a degree of control over their own labor. Eltis disputes this interpretation on the basis of the records for the origins and purchase prices of slaves.[50] Hawthorne's chapter takes a very different tack, focusing on the meaning of work. He points out that although the *means of production* were the same on both sides of the Atlantic, the *mode of production* was entirely different. In Guinea rice farmers worked within a lineage or domestic mode of production. Working on rice made men of boys and women of girls. A skilled rice-worker was a desirable marriage partner, and the Balanta characterized themselves as hard workers, different from their "lazy" neighbors who grew less-demanding crops or raised livestock. On the slave plantations of Brazil work in the rice-fields became a "deculturing experience": "In their homelands, Upper Guineans never performed hard work for hard work's sake. They labored long hours over rice because society rewarded those who did so and punished those who did not. The American plantation system stripped away social rewards, making rice labor for white masters little more than drudgery ... African conceptions of personhood, ritual obligations, and collective cultural identity were broken."

The brutal hardships faced by slave workers on the Brazilian rice-farms were extreme. Owners favored newly opened land instead of permanent fields, so much of the labor involved felling and clearing. Workers succumbed to untreated wounds, burns, and diseases, undernourishment, lack of sleep, and absence of solace. Conditions on the plantations of Carolina were somewhat less extreme, given that the slaves there worked under a "task" system that notionally left them some time for themselves. In each case, of course, as slaves the workers had no choice about how long or how hard they worked. How, then, did peasant rice-farmers fare under conditions of what Chayanov called "self-exploitation?" Naturally, the pleasures or pain associated with growing rice differed considerably, as did the degree of risk: shifting cultivation required fewer hours of drudgery than permanent fields, tenants had to work hard enough to pay their rent and the tax-man as well as feeding their family, farms that grew mostly rice were vulnerable to flood or drought, families embedded in markets were at the mercy of price fluctuations .... Although these generalities are well known and can often be glimpsed in filigree through other sources, historical studies that specifically address the bodily health of farmers are rare.

---

[50] Carney 2001; Eltis et al. 2007.

While Hayden Smith's chapter acknowledges the health considerations that shaped settlement patterns in Carolina, it is Lauren Minsky's contribution that puts the health of farmers centre-stage, reminding us of "a central paradox of the modern world: hunger, malnutrition, and disease severely haunt the people who produce the staple food-grains that nourish and sustain the world's population."

In Bengal and Punjab rice production intensified through the nineteenth and early twentieth century, as part of a wider development of commercial cropping that included export crops like jute, indigo, and sugar. During this time, Minsky shows, both morbidity and mortality increased significantly among farmers. But Minsky challenges deterministic formulations that link rice with malaria, cholera, or other tropical diseases "simply by virtue of its being a 'wet' crop." Rather, she shows, deteriorating health levels resulted from the intensification of mixed commercial cropping systems, which entailed a steady increase in inputs of water, fertilizers (including human waste), and labor, and relentless pressure on land previously devoted to non-irrigated crops or pasture.

Rural populations in both Bengal and Punjab suffered from chronic infections as well as increasingly lethal seasonal epidemics. Minsky takes the case of malaria to show that patterns of infection, immunity, and resistance differed significantly between the two regions, in part because different mosquitoes thrived in each zone, in part because the seasonal presence of mosquitoes differed with distinctive regional rain patterns. But in each case those most vulnerable to disease were the poor, already weakened by hunger, malnourishment, and exhaustion. Punjab and especially Bengal have good claims to be described as rice economies, but although the quantity of rice produced in the region increased, the majority of Punjabis and Bengalis ate less rice as time went by. Poor or landless families bought food rather than growing their own, and even the coarser varieties of rice were often beyond their means. As Minsky concludes, historians and policy makers alike need "to apprehend how commercialization shaped social inequality as manifested in differential food entitlements, metabolic demands, and risk of exposure among classes." Contrary to the mantras of development policy, intensifying food production does not necessarily mean that poor people will eat better or become healthier.

In focusing on the fate of the poor Minsky traces a history of diet, but not a history of consumption. In current social theories of consumption what is at issue is consumer choice: what influences it and what impact does it have, whether on markets or on identities. Consumers are by definition choosers, agents, seeking to fulfill needs packaged as desires and desires packaged as needs. A destitute farm-laborer in Bengal is not a consumer, since hers is, as Bourdieu puts it, the choice of no-choice. In Minsky's account the consumers who drive and benefit from economic growth are largely hidden: her spotlight is turned elsewhere. But similar processes of commercialization and market penetration marked the economy of South China in the eighteenth century, and Sui-Wai Cheung's contribution traces a complementary history of consumption, focusing on taste and dietary improvement.

Cheung argues that in focusing too narrowly on production methods and demographic growth, historians have hitherto neglected the importance of taste and consumer choice in interpreting the (much-studied) history of the Chinese rice industry. Cheung draws our attention to a popular distinction between *zhuliang*, "main food," and *zaliang*, "coarse food." Urban and rural families alike aspired to eat *zhuliang*, which in south and central China referred to rice, as often as possible. "Coarse foods" like sweet-potato were not only considered less palatable and nutritious, but they bore the stigma of poverty. Those who could afford rice had strong preferences for different types, varieties or seasons, and as Cheung shows, these preferences profoundly shaped rice markets, import levels, and farmers' crop-choices. As in the case of India, the farmers who grew rice often lived off coarse foods like sweet potatoes themselves. Yet increasing numbers of Chinese people could afford to indulge their "desire to eat well" some if not all of the time.[51]

Cheung discusses a period when most rice consumed in China was produced within the country, with rice traders (and the state) controlling flows between provinces. But as Seung-Joon Lee points out in his chapter, rice imports from abroad, particularly from Nanyang (Southeast Asia), were growing in importance and already emigrant Chinese millers and merchants were taking control of rice-production and trade through the region. By the Republican era (1911–1937) the "rice masters" of Hong Kong controlled the rice supplies of China's great cities like Shanghai and Canton. They made higher profits on Nanyang imports than on Chinese-grown rice, and their influence on prices and preferences was decisive in shaping markets. The rice masters' expertise was legendary: they could assess the quality and flavor of a shipment at a glance, fulfilling the finicky expectations of urban consumers.

Unfortunately rice imports in the early Republic were so high that they tipped the trade balance into the red, while Chinese rice production was languishing in the absence of markets. Kuomintang (KMT) leaders were alarmed: How could China withstand the inevitable onslaught of Japan unless it could feed itself? They chose a properly modern solution: science would save China. In collaboration with Cornell the KMT set up a precursor of the Green Revolution program, where national and provincial experimental stations developed high-yielding varieties of rice and wheat, and extension programs were established to encourage farmers to adopt the new seeds along

---

[51] See also Latham 1999, 112, discussed below. Rice-farmers in Guangdong Province today still aspire to provide their families with three meals of rice daily (Santos 2011). Meanwhile, after decades pursuing the productivist goal of simply producing greater quantities of rice, the Chinese government is now encouraging research to develop new varieties that will meet consumer expectations of quality (Zader 2011).

with chemical fertilizers. The new rices yielded up to 30 percent more, but they did not keep well or taste good. They proved a resounding failure on urban markets.

Things might have turned out differently, Lee argues, if the KMT had taken the expertise of the rice masters seriously and addressed palatability as well as yield in their breeding programs. But, as Harwood notes, top-down, productivist, Green Revolution-type policies are obsessed with quantity. Palatability is a distraction; the needs, preferences, and vulnerabilities of the smallholder farmers whose lives are targeted for improvement are neglected; consumer tastes and preferences are ignored in favor of calorie counts and breakdowns of vitamin or protein content. This is not a purely modern problem: Cheung records eighteenth-century Chinese officials noting dismally that southerners, however hungry, refused food aid in the form of northern millet or beans: "The people in southern Jiangsu are used to eating rice, they do not eat coarse food."

As the foregoing discussion indicates, those who grow rice may not eat it, those who trade it may not consume it, those who willingly eat one kind of rice may be reluctant to eat another sort. What, then, would a "commitment to rice," uniform or not, look like historically? This is the question that frames Edda Fields-Blacks' interdisciplinary enquiry. Fields-Black seeks to trace and explain the complex relationships that captives from different regions of the Upper Guinea Coast may have had to rice and rice production: Were they experienced rice-farmers, and if so was rice the primary crop or just one of many? Was rice their preferred food or a trading good? What opportunities for rice farming existed and what were its attractions in a region where food-production was constantly vulnerable to drought? Fields-Black critically assesses what information can be drawn from travellers' accounts, archaeology, environmental history, and relative chronology linguistics, to piece together a preliminary history of rice-production and its relations both to the Atlantic slave trade and to inland trading networks. She draws a picture of great diversity: some micro-regions of Upper Guinea were growing rice for subsistence; others relied more upon drought-resistant fonio (millet); rainfall determined the season's choice. Although rice was growing in importance, the region was by no means committed to rice in the seventeenth and eighteenth centuries, Fields-Black concludes.

Mouser et al.'s chapter overlaps chronologically with Fields-Black's, but takes the story of West African rice from the high period of the Atlantic slave trade and through to the present, emphasizing the relations of production within which different types or varieties of rice were introduced, bred, or disseminated. Mouser's study supplements historical documents with the morphological and genetic analysis of 315 farmer varieties collected in the West African coastal zone in 2008, throwing new light on the processes and motivations of farmer breeding, and on the capacity of rice to interbreed not only between varieties but also between the two species of African and Asian rice, *Oryza glaberrima* and *Oryza sativa*, that had long been thought to produce only sterile hybrids outside the laboratory. Mouser and his co-authors are particularly interested in charting the ingenuity that African farmers have devoted to adapting introduced "Carolina" japonica rices to their needs since they were first introduced from America in the late eighteenth century.

Erik Gilbert, in contrast, applies similar genetic evidence, now using samples from East Africa as well as the Atlantic coast, to explore the origins and dispersal of Asian *sativa* rices through the whole continent. Gilbert's overarching question is how and why Asian rices came to be so important. "In areas where African *glaberrima* rice was once predominant, Asian rice is now the preferred crop. In many other parts of the continent where native rice was never domesticated and riziculture is relatively new, Asian rice is the only rice cultivated." From the preliminary genetic evidence, Gilbert infers that there were three, or possibly four, separate introductions of Asian rice to Africa, resulting in the existence of distinct populations. He notes that "none of the three main African populations of *sativa* rice is limited to the continent, rather they are intercontinental and embrace the Americas, southern Europe, and Southeast Asia, leaving a botanical trace of human contacts between continents." Gilbert considers the chains of ecological niches along which *sativa* rices might have traveled from the east coast to the west, but concludes that unlike other Asian crops such as bananas or sorghum, rice did not in fact cross the continent in premodern times. While this genetic evidence is still tentative it throws up some interesting challenges. Why, for instance, are no connections between India and East Africa traceable, as one would have expected given the strong trading links?

A CURIOUS COMMODITY

After this long discussion of how the diversity of rice affects historical interpretation, one might well ask whether rice is special *as rice*, and if so, how? In a few regions of the world rice is now grown, like wheat or corn or soy, on a huge scale, on highly mechanized farms. In most places, however, even though farmers now use machinery and industrial inputs, rice is distinguished from other major cereal crops by the much smaller scale of fields, machinery, and farms, and by the large amounts of skilled labor still needed to grow the crop and to maintain irrigation systems. As Peter Coclanis remarks in his introduction to the section on *Power and control*, "whether we are speaking of cultivation practices, water management, labor protocols, market forces, or political imperatives, rice, especially under irrigation, has long been perceived as a crop predisposed to, if not demanding, high levels of power and control, manipulation, and machination." There have been many arguments made and challenged over the decades, particularly by historians of East and Southeast Asia, about the ways in which the specific demands of rice cultivation shape societies. In this introductory survey I try to avoid the pleasures and pitfalls of production-centered technological determinism to see what might emerge if we begin from different viewpoints. What happens, for example, if we begin with rice not as a crop but as a commodity?

From the perspective of the world's central futures markets, rice is rice just as wheat is wheat, sugar is sugar or steel is steel. The provenance may affect the quality, but not the intrinsic nature, of the commodity. And yet if we look more closely, whether at the processes of production or those of consumption, rice resists such easy reification. From the perspective of production, for the farmer, the rice breeder, the agronomist or the miller, the requirements, constraints, and affordances of rice as a plant or as a crop are infinitely variable. Of course this does not apply only to rice. But for various reasons – including the characteristic scale and skilled inputs already mentioned, and the fact that rice is usually eaten as a whole grain rather than in flour-products or porridges – rice has proved more resistant than most major staples to the types of standardization and homogenization, social, environmental, and agronomic, associated with industrial-type production and marketing of foods.

When we shift our focus to marketing and consumption, it becomes clear that, at least in those regions where rice was the preferred staple, rice was at best imperfectly fungible as a commodity. Consumers who could afford to exercise choice had marked preferences as to the variety, species, region, and season of rice. As Cheung notes, color, taste, aroma, shape and size of grain, consistency, translucence, and medical properties were all factors that shaped markets, not to mention whether the grains were whole or broken, fresh, mature, or stale. Rice merchants had to be experts in far more than a simple scale of good to bad quality. Trading circuits might overlap at certain points, but even today there is no single, homogeneous world market in rice.

A few years ago the economic historian A. J. H. Latham was asked to contribute a volume on rice to the series "Routledge Studies in the Modern World Economy." Pondering what to call his study, Latham settled upon *Rice: The Primary Commodity*. Rice, he noted, has outstanding claims to be considered not just *a* but *the* primary commodity, since about half the world's population depends on rice for a large part of their diet today, more than on any other staple crop. And yet, as Latham remarked, there is a paradox here, for despite its importance and ubiquity rice "does not figure in the world's great marketplaces. The Chicago wheat market has no parallel in rice [...] Rice is traded by dealers and governments across the world in what appears a bewildering network of contacts."[52]

In these respects, rice as a commodity is perhaps closer to tea (or to modern coffee) than to wheat: it combined mass markets and niche markets well

---

[52] Latham 1998, 1.

before the late twentieth-century revolution in the means of consumption. Several contributions to this volume, including the chapters by Biggs, Cheung, Lee, Linares, and Minsky, consider intersections or overlaps between mass and niche markets, but the issue certainly deserves further attention. Even as rice came to be treated as a cheap bulk starch, exported and shipped around the world to feed colonial workforces and the urban poor, markets for different types and qualities of rice remained segmented. Yet pressures to treat rice as "just rice" mounted steadily. Imperial Chinese or colonial Indian famine relief programs were premised on the equivalence of different types of rice. This attitude was further entrenched in modern seed-breeding practice, and in the national or international programs for food security and poverty relief to which much scientific breeding is geared. Food aid post–World War II has been another vehicle for the homogenization of rice, and for consolidating its rank as the world's most common staple. This in turn provides leverage for universalist projects to breed new rices as "global" solutions to hunger and malnutrition.

THE VIEW FROM HERE: CASTING OUR NETS WIDER

An honored strategy in global history is to compare how the world looks from different places. As an example, once again I take the Atlantic viewpoint as my foil, to suggest how it could be linked to a China-centered history through a more ambitious articulation of micro- and macro-regions.

The Black Rice debate required historians of rice to redraw territorial boundaries as well as interpretative frames. Claiming that African workers in the rice-fields of South Carolina or Brazil were not simply carrying out tasks defined by white farm-owners but effectively transplanting or recreating a West African agricultural knowledge system, scholars like Littlefield, Carney, and Hawthorne argued for a radical remapping of the cultural geography of the Atlantic slave trade and its flows of people, knowledge, and power (including conventional accounts of gender).[53] In arguing that rice cultivation in the Carolinas was rooted in practices from the Guinea Coast, they also challenged the geographical boundaries of what had formerly been thought of as independent technical systems of rice production (one of world-historical importance, one negligible) to treat them as components of a single zone within which knowledge flowed West across the Atlantic – but from Africa, not from Europe. Moreover, in order to substantiate and develop their arguments, supporters of the Black Rice thesis have become increasingly interdisciplinary, working in and across a range that includes not only economic history, social history, and history of technology but also the history of food, ethno-linguistics, or ecology. The Black Rice thesis has been

[53] Littlefield 1981; Carney 2001; Hawthorne 2003.

hotly or more mildly contested on numerous grounds,[54] but one unchallenged achievement of the Black Rice scholars has been to put rice cultivation in West Africa clearly on the map of economic history.

The terms "Atlantic history" and "the Atlantic world" have been common historiographical currency for quite a few years now, which certainly helped smooth the path for the kind of re-zoning of rice history that the Black Rice scholars proposed. They were not proposing a new region. Instead they argued that a new trading good, namely rice-growing knowledge and skills, should be added to the many and various goods that traveled along the well-worn pathways criss-crossing a landscape (or rather seascape) that was self-evidently a region, namely the Atlantic. What was novel was not the connection between West Africa and South Carolina. The novel element in the Black Rice thesis was the argument that one of the acknowledged goods transported along this route, in this direction, was technical expertise – along with the reversal of conventional intellectual and power hierarchies inherent in such a transfer. Rice went Atlantic, but the Atlantic as a region was by now a comfortably familiar zone.

Yet broad as the Atlantic Ocean may be, it is not the world. It is all too easy, as Peter Coclanis has argued in a series of publications, to treat it as The Pond (my word, not his), that is to say, a self-contained system of circuits and exchanges removed from the influence of broader flows or other Ponds.[55]

Looking from the Americas outward, the chief market for rice was Northern Europe. By the eighteenth century European demand had forged what Coclanis terms a "world market" in rice. This market catered to a spectrum of uses, with wide variations in elasticity of demand. When other cereals were scarce and expensive, rice might be used as cheap food for the poor, for troops, or for animals; for the well-to-do, rice was a desirable addition to a varied diet; as an industrial material, rice and its by-products served for brewing, paper-making, or the manufacture of starch. This variety means it is difficult to explain precisely why rice-prices or levels of demand varied. When rice farming was established in the early eighteenth century in what was then the British colony of Carolina, producers were competing for the rice markets of the metropolis with Brazil and Italy. But once Britain had established colonial control over Bengal in the 1780s, Bengal rice began to nudge US competitors out of North European markets. By the 1830s the Dutch East Indies had entered the fray; then Burma from the 1850s, and Siam and Cochinchina a few years later. Various explanations can be offered for South and Southeast Asian success in out-competing America on this Europe-centered "world market" in rice, including the versatility of collaboration between Asian and European capital, favorable climate and terrain, or low

---

[54] Eltis et al. 2007; Edelson 2010.
[55] Coclanis 1993b, 1995, 2006.

labor and capital costs. What is clear, however, is that the long-term history of the American rice industry was closely articulated with the history of rice in Asia and cannot be understood in "Atlantic" terms alone.[56]

But is it not necessary to extend these links still further? Before being drawn into the European and colonial rice-trading circuits of the nineteenth century, Vietnam, Siam, the Philippines, Indonesia, and the Eastern fringes of the Indian Ocean were closely knit into trading links with China in a zone that the Chinese referred to as Nanyang, the Southern Ocean. Although it never surpassed internal Chinese markets in either volume or worth, the Nanyang trade was enormous; by the late eighteenth century, however, Chinese trade with Europe was drawing level. Whether to Nanyang or Europe, China exported chiefly manufactured goods, ranging from iron nails, cooking pots, and copper coinage to silk brocades and porcelain; its imports were chiefly raw materials, silver bullion or coin, and rice. Robert Marks documents the complexity and flexibility of internal and external trading patterns in the Canton region from 1685 to 1850. Imports included dyestuffs from Nanyang and raw cotton from northern China, Nanyang, and British India. The region exported cotton cloth, silk fabrics, and sugar to other parts of China and to Nanyang. Europeans purchased silk, cotton goods, and tea, and brought raw cotton, silver, and opium in return. Local farmers had turned their paddies over to mulberries or sugar; like the urban workers they now ate rice from the upstream provinces and Nanyang. Often they were quite fussy about the kind of rice they would eat, thus determining the choices of the farmers who supplied them.[57]

Writing of the end of the same period but from a different perspective, Latham notes what initially seems a puzzling fact. By the mid-nineteenth century an international market for rice had emerged in which Burma, Siam, and French Indochina exported rice while Ceylon, Malaya, the Dutch East Indies, the Philippines, and China imported rice. No mystery, says Latham, why plantation and mining economies powered by immigrant labor would import rice, but why would China need to do so? Was it a production problem that indicated that China was suffering from adversity and incapable of feeding itself? On the contrary, says Latham: the data on rice prices and markets show that regions like Canton or the Lower Yangzi had chosen to give up rice production to specialize in other crops and products, making them sufficiently prosperous to purchase their preferred food: rice. "Incomes were increasing in an economy which was expanding under favourable market conditions. The source of the dynamism was increased productivity in agriculture and rising incomes due to advancing

---

[56] Coclanis 1993b, 1052, 1995, 148, 154–5; Montesano 2009.
[57] Marks 1998, 1999; Cheung, this volume.

specialization. [...] Rice is a luxury not a necessity and China was on the move."[58]

Despite the importance of imports through the early modern period, however, the bulk of the rice eaten in China was produced inside the country. There is no space here to do justice to the many studies by Chinese, Japanese, and Western scholars of the internal rice market in China.[59] Suffice it to say that it was enormous. Granted not all farmers could afford to eat rice; moreover in most of North China wheat, sorghum, or millet were more common both as crops and as food. Yet by the early Ming dynasty (1368–1644) as many as 12,000 government barges, each carrying 25 tonnes, shipped tax rice north each year to supply Beijing and the troops along the northern frontiers; by mid-dynasty the capacity of the barges had been increased to 45 tonnes. These figures do not include the tax rice used directly at the local or provincial level, and the volume of tax rice paled in comparison with the amounts of rice circulated around the country on the open market by rice-merchants.[60] The ebb and flow of interlinked regional economies at different levels of development, shifts in comparative advantage, changing demands for different crops or manufactures, the impact of climatic fluctuations, natural disasters or war, as well as changes in government policy on pricing or levels of food self-sufficiency, all affected the production and flows of rice within China and the demand for rice imports. Meanwhile foreign sources of rice shifted in response to internal factors and to external competition between producers. Thus Siam had traditionally exported large quantities of what was politely known as "tribute rice" to Canton and Amoy, but by the eighteenth century the Siam traders could not get high enough prices for their rice in China and moved instead to markets in Japan and the Ryukyu Islands.[61]

We thus see a chain of connections emerging whereby the fortunes of rice production in the Atlantic region were ultimately linked not simply to the Indian Ocean region, but to the China-centered trading zone of Nanyang, to the internal rice-markets of China, which in the eighteenth and early nineteenth century influenced rice markets around Asia, and even to the remote Ryukyu Islands, midway between Japan and Taiwan. And yet it is not obvious how these different nodes and regions were articulated.

At what period, if ever, and across which regions, did an integrated world rice market operate, for example?[62] What kinds of barriers might separate geographical units, what shared interests connect them, and how far might a given sack of rice travel along the network, whether as a commodity, an

---

[58] Latham 1998, 1999, 110, 122. See also Cheung, this volume.
[59] See Cheung, this volume and Cheung 2008 for surveys of the literature.
[60] Brook 1998, 46, 118; Wang 2003; Cheung 2008.
[61] Zurndorfer 2004, 7.
[62] Coclanis 1993b, 1072–5 argues for its emergence by the end of the nineteenth century; Latham, as we have seen, denies its existence (Latham 1998).

object of consumption, or a symbolic good? For some consumers rice was a luxury, for others the everyday staple, and for others it was just one among several sources of cheap industrial starch. Farmers might happily grow certain kinds of rice, which they themselves found quite unpalatable, for the market, and factors of this kind must have influenced how species or varieties traveled, along with husbandry skills.[63] Some rice-producing regions exported the bulk of their produce, in others most rice was consumed locally and only small surpluses entered international markets.[64] For Siam the dramatic expansion of the rice industry in the nineteenth century was part of a strategy of nation-building, while its neighbors (Burma, French Indochina) were developed as colonial rice-baskets to enrich the metropolis.

Other countries that produced rice were governed according to an official commitment to food self-sufficiency. This was true of late imperial China, where most officials continued to mistrust markets long after they were irrevocably implanted.[65] An official "knowledge system" operated to complement or where necessary override the workings of the open market or the influence of local oligarchies. This system included the management of irrigation networks, of long-distance transport facilities by river, canal, and sea, and of a network of public granaries, as well as minute attention to rice output and prices.[66] Lee's chapter describes the new technologies that were incorporated into the official arsenal for promoting rice self-sufficiency during the Republican period (1911–1937), including protective tariffs, railways, and modern scientific rice-breeding programs. Like later Green-Revolution packages the Republican project emphasized quantity rather than quality, and ultimately failed to reduce the consumption of imported rice.[67] The project did, however, have a very significant afterlife beyond China's borders:

---

[63] This would be equally true of exchanges between farmers and of official efforts to disseminate new farming methods or crops, whether in Song China or in modern states (Bray 2008).

[64] Speaking of the period after World War II, Latham writes, "The rice that enters the world rice market is residual or 'left over' rice, surplus to the needs of the exporting countries. They take what they need for their own consumption, and export the remainder. [The market] is *'thin'* because the amounts of rice traded are very small in proportion to the amount of world rice production, as most producers and exporters are also major consumers of rice themselves. Less than 5 per cent of annual world production enters the world market. This would be no problem if the sellers and buyers in the market were the same year by year. But the market is in fact extremely *volatile*, with sellers and buyers changing all the time, according to the state of their own crops" (1998, 27, emphases added).

[65] Brook 1998; Wong 1997.

[66] Will and Wong 1991; Marks 1998, 1999.

[67] The goal of food self-sufficiency has determined policy in many Asian states in more recent years (Malaysia and South Korea come to mind). Postindependence reluctance to depend on food imports from capricious neighbors or world powers played a decisive role in shaping agrarian policy and the promotion of Green-Revolution technologies in many developing nations.

After its defeat in China's civil war, the Nationalist government fled to Taiwan in 1948, taking with it the national research facilities, and rice research continued in Taiwan. The successfully bred semi-dwarf rice, Taichung Native 1, was the major outcome from Taiwan's Taichung Research Station, and this was subsequently used by the International Rice Research Institute (IRRI) to crossbreed with other strains to develop various improved semi-dwarf varieties [disseminated throughout Asia as part of the Green-Revolution package].[68]

Our goal in *Rice: Global Networks and New Histories* is to harness the concerns of global history to establish a creative dialogue between regional schools, to explore the potential for sharing innovative methods or interpretive frameworks across local boundaries, and to propose tactics for counterposing micro- and macro-history that contribute to a richer understanding of both local and global processes.

Rice played a critical role in shaping and linking the histories of Africa and the Americas, Europe, and almost every region of Asia. It made crucial contributions, at local, regional, and international level, to the emergence of colonialism, industrial capitalism, and the modern world order. As in the case of porcelain or cotton, the spread of rice cultivation and consumption across the early modern and modern ecumene raises challenging questions about the lineages and the effective reach of today's prevailing models of economic rationality and techno-scientific efficiency. The contributors to *Rice: Global Networks and New Histories* explore the catalysts or obstacles to the circulation of grain, genetic materials, technical knowledge, people, and capital that shape the formation and lifespan of a trading circuit or a system of production. In emphasizing consumption equally with production, global history also brings a salutary corrective to a tendency within economic and technical history to treat all types of rice as essentially indistinguishable packages of calories. As our contributors demonstrate, neither global nor local approaches can afford to neglect the essential qualities of a commodity in appraising the relations between supply and demand, production and consumption, hunger and desire, aesthetics and fashion. As historians, we cannot afford to ignore the power politics encapsulated in a seed or a sack of rice.

---

[68] Shen 2010, 1035.

PART I

PURITY AND PROMISCUITY

Francesca Bray

INTRODUCTION

Rice is largely self-pollinating and rather less promiscuous than most cereals. Normal rates of cross-fertilization are around 1 percent, although depending on climate and on variety, cross-pollination rates of up to 30 percent have been observed. In some circumstances hybrids are unusual and thus likely to attract a farmer's attention; in others, farmers will have to struggle against their crop's promiscuous tendencies to cross with other rice-varieties nearby, or with the wild relatives that infest rice-fields as weeds. Mobilizing the variability of rice has allowed farmers over the millennia to select and develop thousands of landraces to fill a mosaic of micro-variations in terrain and climate, and a spectrum of needs. But agriculture is also an exercise in purification and the control of variation, in the simplification and tidying of farming landscapes, the breeding and maintenance of pure strains, the production of grain that meets recognized standards.

Regimes of purification seek greater control, more predictability and increased efficiency – and yet they also contain the threat of sterility and vulnerability. Contagion and disorder, wildness, promiscuous cross-breeding, and unpredictable variation threaten the reliable order yet also guarantee its future, constituting the actual or figurative biodiversity that is an essential source of novelty, fertility, and new energy. Laboratory-bred varieties like IR-8, the "miracle rice" of the 1960s, were designed to carpet paddy-fields across tropical Asia smoothly with a single, ideal variety, yet such "universal" rices are hybrids whose very existence depends upon access to the infinite variety of genetic material contained in land-races, weedy relatives and wild rices, collected from across the world and carefully preserved in germ-plasm banks adjoining the great breeding laboratories.

Maintaining purity against the threat of taint, pollution, or contagion is, as the anthropologist Mary Douglas pointed out in *Purity and Danger*, a universal if infinitely varied human endeavor. Purifying procedures, intellectual, symbolic, technical, and managerial, have profoundly marked the history of farming and food production. Selecting similar ears for seed-grain, weeding a plot, planting only one crop in a field, breeding white cattle with white and black with black: these are all simple and obvious techniques of purification that date back to the origins of farming. More complex measures often took place at the level of government, like setting standards for the quality of grain paid in taxes or sold in markets, or offering farmers instruction in "improved" methods; alternatively, merchants or networks of savants or progressively minded farmers might contribute to the circulation and standardization of knowledge and technology.

With the rise of industrialization, commercial and scientific crop-breeding, and agronomic science, trends toward the standardization and homogenization of farming methods and products became still more marked. The Green Revolution of the 1960s and 1970s was, in essence, a drive to purify farming landscapes across the world, weeding out local particularities and variety to propagate what was envisaged as a universally valid model of efficient grain production. As noted by Harwood, the Green Revolution encountered many challenges, both technical and social, and was at best a partial success; nevertheless, its homogenizing goals and strategies still appeal so strongly in certain powerful quarters that we are currently being promised a New Green Revolution.

Although unprecedented in its scope and scale, and in its degree of entanglement with the rationalities of laboratory science and of corporate capitalism, the Green Revolution descends from a long historical line of projects to control and improve farm production by imposing greater uniformity. Sometimes the initiative came from the state: in twelfth-century China, for example, all farmers throughout the Southern provinces had to pay part of their taxes in rice, and the acceptable varieties and qualities of rice were clearly stipulated. Other forms of regulation might operate at local level, for instance within an irrigation unit the constraints of water-control meant that farmers would all need to plant varieties that could be transplanted and harvested at much the same time. In other cases it was the demands of urban consumers, channeled through rice-merchants, that contributed to standardizing rice production, much as supermarkets today regulate the production choices of the farmers who supply them.

But what kind of order or uniformity were at stake in any specific case? Were types of rice classified and valued according to shape, color, genetic make-up, the type of terrain in which they would grow, or the ease with which they fitted into a complex mixed economy? What degree of wildness, disorder, variation, and contingency went into maintaining the health and vigor of any particular rice-based system of production, consumption, taxation, or trade? When states devised policies for improving rice-farming, how were concerns for peasant incomes, national food security, or export earnings weighed against each other?

Scientists are nowadays most likely to define the purity of a rice variety in genetic terms; they may compute its value in terms of output, hardiness, resource use, nutrition, or even, sometimes, that elusive quality "palatability." Biggs suggests that we might think of highly valued rice-grains or rice-seeds in any specific historical context – whether it be IR-8, the Champa rices distributed by the Chinese government in the twelfth century to encourage double-cropping, or the floating rices sown by NLF soldiers and other populations on the run in the Mekong Delta – as Latourian assemblages, the momentarily stable products of a continuous struggle by human actors to channel and control natural promiscuity and environmental uncertainty. The genetic information contained in a rice-grain "encapsulates" a history of various kinds of knowledge, skill, and desire converging to produce not just a particular variety of rice, but also a material, social, and political landscape.

Modern rice-breeding programs and agricultural development programs take uniformity as a virtue and prioritize high yields and economies of scale. During the heyday of the Green Revolution irrigation schemes, subsidized prices for approved seed and fertilizers and farm-gate purchase systems combined to flatten out and homogenize rural landscapes, blanketing them in smooth carpets of just one or two varieties of modern rice. Historically, farmers developed rice-varieties adapted to local ecology; now local environments were rebuilt to meet the needs of "universal" rice-breeds.

Looking at the dramatic remodeling of Asian landscapes to accommodate "miracle" rice-varieties in the style to which they were accustomed, one might assume that its special requirements for water and for level fields make rice (or at any rate wet-rice) a rather inflexible crop, most efficiently grown in standardized monocultures. In fact, as every chapter in this section demonstrates, rices are remarkably flexible in the range of terrain they can occupy, and in the combinations of cropping systems and economic activities that they support. Modern crop breeders and agronomists could have taken the path of enhancing local systems and supporting diversity and small-scale farming (in the words of an early twentieth-century German plant scientist, "The best agricultural rule I know is 'specialise, don't generalise'").[1] Harwood explains how instead a "cosmopolitan" breeding strategy and ideology of progress came to prevail, becoming common sense for the majority of the international community of scientific breeders and development experts.

The chapters in this Part address the tensions and interplay between purity and promiscuity, and between uniformity and diversity, that shaped the historical evolution of rice-farming systems through a period marked by the penetration of commodity markets, the disruptions of colonialism and imperialism, shifting nationalist imperatives, the rise of modern agricultural science and development models with global claims. They also challenge

---

[1] Kiessling 1906: 330–331; quoted in Harwood, this volume, fn. 4.

some prevailing models of historical analysis that over-simplify or stereotype rice-based rural economies, like Geertz' concept of "agricultural involution," or explanations that treat all kinds of rice as equivalent. All draw our attention to the tensions and heterogeneity beneath the surface of rice histories that have often been construed in over-simplified terms. Harwood traces the institutional and political history of "universal varieties." Boomgaard, an environmental and economic historian, and Kroonenberg, a statistician, have joined forces to re-evaluate Geertz's alluringly simple model of rice-based economies. Cheung reminds us that "modern" challenges like national food security, export earnings, and the tyranny of urban tastes over rural livelihoods, were already burning issues in eighteenth-century China. Lee and Biggs' papers trace the intellectual, political, and personal networks through which the rationality of scale economies and uniformity came to be consolidated as the commonsense solution to rural problems in Asia, whereas Mouser et al. show us the very different fortunes of the cosmopolitan breeding strategy in Sierra Leone, where farmers took breeding back into their own hands.

New forms of evidence, new cross-disciplinary collaborations, and new types of historical question go hand in hand. What challenges do research techniques like genetic mapping bring to the botanical-social history of rice? What happens when we reframe the well-worn production-focused debates that have structured standard readings of economic history to incorporate evidence about consumer tastes, peasant agency, the ideological dimensions of technical choice, or the resistance of pollen to human control? The chapters in Part I look attentively at past categorizations, meanings, and uses of rice. They map in sensitive detail the environmental, economic, symbolic, social, and political territories within which specific local systems of rice-farming emerged and evolved. In emphasizing the interweaving and increasingly convergent circuits of genetic, commodity, and knowledge transmission from which modern, globally embedded practices of rice production emerged, they propose challenging new approaches to the history of rice as seed, as commodity, as food, and as symbol of national strength and modernity.

I

Global Visions vs. Local Complexity: Experts Wrestle with the Problem of Development

Jonathan Harwood

This chapter is the odd one out in Part I. Unlike the other authors gathered here, I know very little about rice cultivation and its social, political, and economic relations. My work has focused instead upon large-scale agricultural transformations – in Europe ca. 1900 and in the developing world since 1945 – with particular attention to the role of plant breeders.[1] While attending the workshop from which this volume emerges, however, I was struck by several themes common to both rice cultivation in the global South and to the contexts with which I am familiar. I discuss one of those themes here.

A striking feature of agricultural history in many countries since at least the nineteenth century (and perhaps much longer), has been a recurring attempt to revolutionize it through imposing uniformity. A new set of techniques thought to be uniquely powerful is introduced throughout a region in the belief that it will boost production everywhere. Usually, however, these fail[2] and often for the same reason. Namely, they neglect to take account of diversity: of the enormous variation in growing conditions as well as in economic circumstances across the region in question.

Those familiar with James C. Scott's *Seeing Like a State* (1998) will recognize how much this chapter owes to that wonderfully provocative book, though my concern here is less with states as agents of grand transformative schemes than with the experts who devise and implement such schemes. Where my analysis departs more substantially from Scott's, however, is in our portrayals of the expert community. While he tends to treat the expert community as a largely unified group that carries out such schemes without dissent, I argue that the grand dreams of agricultural transformation have often been contested. A substantial minority of experts has challenged them, arguing that such schemes can never do justice to the actual diversity of

---

[1] Harwood 2012.
[2] Mouser et al. in this volume; Maat 2001; Bonneuil 2001.

farming conditions.³ This issue has not been resolved, and the tension between universalizing and particularizing approaches to development persists right into the present.⁴ There is evidently more than one way to organize a revolution. In this chapter I outline three contexts, drawn from different times and places, in which the expert community has been divided on this question.

1. THE LOCAL VERSUS THE COSMOPOLITAN

I begin in early nineteenth century Europe. At that time farmers nearly everywhere planted what are usually called "local" varieties (sometimes termed "traditional" or "farmers" varieties). These were varieties that had been grown in a region for generations and were thus necessarily well-adapted to local soil and climate conditions through the process of natural selection. They were also adapted to local cultivation practices since for generations they had survived farmers' annual decisions as to which plants should provide the seed for the next season. And that meant that they were also "unfussy": they could produce a decent yield even in regions where growing conditions were relatively poor.

From about mid-century, however, as the effects of mineral fertilizer upon plant growth became more widely known, farmers keen on higher yields began to experiment. What they found was that their local varieties could not tolerate large amounts of such fertilizer. Typically the plants grew so tall and their stems became so thin that they toppled over in wind or rain ("lodging"). In an attempt to get round this problem, some experimentally inclined farmers sought to isolate unusual plants from their fields (or occasionally to construct them via crossing) which were better able to use fertilizer. The popularity of such improved varieties with their neighbors led some of these farmers to rely upon breeding as their principal occupation. Commercial breeding of this kind emerged first in Britain and France but spread in the latter half of the century to several continental countries.

The commercial breeder's strategy was what I have called a "cosmopolitan" one.⁵ The basic aim of this strategy, as its name implies, was to develop one outstanding variety that would produce good results everywhere. The starting point for breeding was generally a high-yielding variety. This plant was then selected further to ensure that it gave high yield under "intensive" cultivation conditions, that is, those thought to maximize yield: careful soil preparation, liberal use of mineral fertilizer, and thorough weeding and pest-control. Such outstanding varieties were then known in the German-speaking

---

³ cf. Scott 1998, 288–306. Recent work on colonial agricultural science has also taken exception to Scott's portrayal of expert consensus (Beinart et al. 2009; Barton 2011; Tilley 2011).
⁴ van der Ploeg 1992.
⁵ Harwood 2012, 45ff.

world as "universal varieties" (*Universalsorten*). Just when and where the earliest claims for them were made I don't know. What is clear is that in the German-speaking world, at least, such claims were common around 1900.[6] Indeed, some empirical evidence pointed toward the existence of such varieties. For example, the wheat variety "Squarehead," imported from Britain to the continent in the 1870s, proved successful in a wide variety of countries across western and eastern Europe.[7] And from the 1890s a German commercial variety named "Petkuser rye" was enormously successful in locations all over Germany as well as in Sweden.[8] Similarly, the "Hana barley," an improved local variety from the Hana region in Hungary, was adopted in many European countries.[9]

Despite their remarkable yields, however, by the 1880s it was becoming apparent that commercial varieties were not faring well in regions where growing conditions differed from those in which they had been bred. In Württemberg, for example, the Petkuser rye was widely planted except at high altitudes where a local variety fared better.[10] Similarly, although versions of Squarehead wheat produced the highest yields where climate and soils were favorable, in poorer growing conditions they were generally inferior to local varieties. Part of the problem with commercial varieties was ecological. Since they had been bred by firms in central and north Germany, they were ill-adapted to south Germany where soil types and climatic conditions were not only very different but also enormously diverse.[11] Moreover, the cultivation methods used on such smallholdings were also very diverse, thus ruling out any generic solutions.[12] But there were also economic obstacles. One was that since commercial varieties were bred to do well under intensive cultivation, they were too "fussy" for most small south German farms where intensive cultivation was much less common.[13] And even where commercial varieties were actually suitable

---

[6] To be sure, most of the evidence is indirect. There are few published claims for the existence of such varieties (Kühle 1926; Stadelmann 1924), but the large number of refutations of such claims (eg, Kulisch 1913, Scharnagel 1936) suggests that the notion must have been quite common in breeders' circles at that time.

[7] Schindler 1928.

[8] Nilsson-Ehle 1913.

[9] Schindler 1907.

[10] Fruwirth 1907.

[11] The problem was not confined to Germany; British growers had noticed the problem already by the 1840s. The results when growing the same wheat variety on different soils were so different, one farmers club remarked, that it was "impossible to decide on the merits of any one kind for universal adoption" (quoted in Walton 1999, 47).

[12] Scharnagel 1953. In the global South today the ecological diversity that poses a stumbling block to any purportedly universal variety also exists even within a single farm. Peasant farmers often prefer to plant several varieties of a given crop in order to make allowance for slightly different soils and conditions on different patches of their land.

[13] For example, Kryzymowski 1913.

for particular localities, they were substantially more expensive than good quality local varieties and thus unaffordable for most farmers.[14] Lastly, brewers and millers, in Germany at least, often regarded local varieties of barley and wheat as of higher quality than commercial ones. As a result, the "universal variety" had plenty of critics, who drew attention to local failures. Indeed, many critics went further, ruling them out in principle. The director of Baden's plant-breeding station, for example, insisted that "no one will ever be able to breed a universal variety."[15] Another breeder declared that varieties that thrive throughout Germany just do not exist. The director of Bavaria's plant-breeding station put it more gently: "As desireable as universal varieties would be, I have little hope that we will ever achieve them." And a division head at one of Saxony's experiment stations was less charitable: claims for universal varieties were either based on a mistake or were downright deceitful.[16]

But the critics did not merely carp; they also pursued a different breeding strategy, best described as a "local" one. This approach was based on quite different premises. Its aim was not to develop a single outstanding variety but instead a multitude of improved ones, each well-adapted to a particular growing condition.[17] The starting-point for breeding, therefore, was not one outstanding high-yielding variety but rather many local varieties, each chosen because it offered high quality and was well-adapted to a particular locale. The breeder's task was to increase the yield of these plants. And the fact that a local variety generally consisted of many genetically distinct lines, often varying greatly in yield, meant that this could be achieved by selection quite quickly. If the vision underlying the cosmopolitan strategy was a physiological one – in the sense that the breeder sought to develop a single plant-design that was maximally efficient at using fertilizer and sunlight – the local strategy was rooted in an ecological perspective. Starting with an awareness of the enormous variability of growing conditions – in both ecological and economic respects – the breeder judged that it would be easier to increase the yield of a well-adapted plant than the adaptedness of a high-yielding one.[18]

---

[14] Dix 1911. Spanish rice planters in the 1940s were in a similar situation. Faced with possible shortages of water and mineral fertilizer, they often thought it not worth spending money on high-yielding varieties (Camprubi 2010).

[15] Lang 1909, 614.

[16] Respectively, Böhmer 1914; Kiessling 1924, 15; and Steglich 1893.

[17] As one proponent of the local strategy remarked, "The best agricultural rule I know is "specialize, don't generalize'" (Kiessling 1906: 330–331).

[18] Although Stephen Biggs' discussion of different models of agricultural innovation (Biggs, S. 1990) has little to say about plant breeding as such, it provides a wider framework in which my analysis might be placed. What I have called the cosmopolitan breeding strategy offers a specific instance of what he has called the "central source" model, in which new technology is generated in central research institutions and transferred "down" to national and regional

The local strategy was pursued in a new kind of research institution that emerged in various parts of Central Europe around the turn of the century, the state-supported plant breeding station: in Switzerland (1898, 1907), Austria (1902), Alsace (1905), and in the German states of Bavaria (1902), Hessen (1904), Württemberg (1905), Baden (1908), and Saxony (1908).[19] These stations conducted a wide range of activities. All of them devoted considerable effort to testing available plant varieties in order to advise the small farmers in their region which of these were suitable for the prevailing growing conditions. Many of the stations also undertook the development of new varieties, seeking to breed crop plants that were better-adapted to local conditions. In addition, stations took responsibility for improving those crops of local importance which had been neglected by commercial breeders. Several stations also offered courses in plant breeding so that interested local farmers could learn how to carry out basic selection procedures. And at least one station devoted a great deal of effort to helping small farmers organize themselves into local crop improvement associations so that they could more effectively market their produce. The aim of the stations in general was to improve the productivity of small farms but more particularly to free the smallholder from dependence upon the allegedly "universal" varieties produced by commercial breeding. By the 1920s they had begun to do just that. The largest of them was bringing a substantial number of improved varieties to market, and commercial breeders, feeling the pinch, complained of "unfair competition." By then local and cosmopolitan strategies were competing for public approval and state support.

2. FRAILTIES OF THE GREEN REVOLUTION

Given the achievements and limitations of these early-twentieth-century approaches to breeding, one might have expected that subsequent attempts to revolutionize agriculture would proceed somewhat more cautiously (or at least eclectically). In fact some breeders do appear to have abandoned the search for universal varieties but by no means all.[20] If we shift, for example, to the Green Revolution (GR) in the global South after 1945, it looks in many respects like a reprise of what had gone before.

Like their counterparts in mid-nineteenth century Europe, peasant farmers in the developing world – who make up the vast majority of farmers

---

institutions for modification before eventually reaching farmers. Conversely, the local breeding strategy is an example of what Biggs calls the "multiple source" model in which technology is generated by many institutions and groups, including farmers, and diffuses in several directions.

[19] For a similar approach among French maize-breeders in the 1940s and 1950s, see Bonneuil and Thomas 2009, 182.
[20] Engledow 1925; Bundesverband Deutscher Pflanzenzüchter 1987, 42.

there – have long relied upon local varieties. It has been estimated, for example, that around 40,000 varieties of rice were being grown in India ca. 1980.[21] At that time the Bangladeshi Rice Research Institute identified 4,500 different varieties in their country but reckoned that the total number might be twice as high.[22] As in Europe ca. 1900, many experts regarded such local varieties as inferior since they did not produce as high yields as did western commercial varieties nor did they respond well to mineral fertilizer. And as before, GR breeders saw their task as replacing these numerous varieties with a small number of powerful new ones that would have a major impact everywhere.

Since the aim of the postwar GR programmes was to boost agricultural productivity, their breeders once again adopted a cosmopolitan strategy. As the Rockefeller Foundation's agricultural officials declared in 1954:

> The basic problems concerning rice are universal problems which can be properly attacked in one central laboratory which would then make the results available to all. Many of the really fundamental physiological, biochemical and genetic problems are essentially independent of geography [...].[23]

The authors' confidence in this strategy was probably based on the success of the Foundation's Mexican Agricultural Program. By selecting for wheat varieties that fared well in various regions of that country despite differing day-length, Norman Borlaug managed to produce not merely high-yielding varieties but also "widely adapted" ones that also did well in parts of Pakistan, India, Egypt, and elsewhere.[24]

In the 1960s, for example, the International Rice Research Institute's (IRRI) new high-yielding rice variety was billed as a "miracle variety" that would thrive throughout southeast Asia.[25] The conceptual framework underlying this work was that of the "crop ideotype." As its earliest proponent put it, in a "crude attempt at perfection,"[26] the breeder draws upon plant morphology and physiology in order to design a model plant whose characteristics – for example, length and strength of stem, size and orientation of leaves, ratio of grain weight to total plant mass, and so on – should in principle enable it to produce the maximum yield when planted in a field at high density. Such "near-universal" varieties, as the Ford Foundation called them in 1969, would thrive wherever cultivation practices were adjusted to

---

[21] Farmer 1979, 307.
[22] Biggs, S. 2008, 491.
[23] cited in Chandler 1982, 2.
[24] Myren 1970.
[25] Cullather 2004. As one former IRRI scientist later commented, at the Institute there was an implicit belief in the existence of a "universal peasant society" and a single type of traditional agriculture which meant that "IRRI doesn't care about variation"(Anderson et al 1991: 91).
[26] Donald 1968, 387; see also Jennings 1964.

accommodate them.[27] The result was a "technological package" consisting of high-yielding varieties of wheat or rice, mineral fertilizer, and pesticide. Introduced in regions that enjoyed abundant rainfall or irrigation, the package duly succeeded in doubling or tripling cereal yields.[28]

Among politicians as among scientists, however, the decision to adopt this technological package was controversial. In India, for example, there was a good deal of struggle between different factions within the government, and some experts who advocated an alternative development strategy based on local varieties were marginalized.[29] Rice-breeders in some southeast Asian countries expressed doubt over IRRI's claims for wide-adaptation. In Bangladesh, for example, rice scientists were divided over whether a centralized or localized breeding strategy was more effective. On the release of the miracle variety IR-8 in 1966, Philippino breeders doubted its quality and taste while some – even at IRRI – knew that it was vulnerable to pests.[30] Disagreement among IRRI's staff continued throughout the 1970s. At the end of the decade the head of the Institute's Cropping Systems Division bluntly rejected the strategy that had been dominant at the Institute since its establishment, saying "The illusion that agricultural production can be served by massive centrally planned research does a disservice to the farmer [...]."[31]

The sceptics' reservations appear to have been justified. By the late 1960s the GR had become the subject of intense controversy that continued for the next decade. Some critics focused upon the new technology's damaging environmental impact.[32] But what attracted most critics' attention was the fact that despite large increases in cereal yield and production, in many areas

---

[27] Anderson et al. 1991, 70. This issue of a variety's suitability for a range of growing conditions was regarded as a secondary matter. One advocate of the crop-ideotype approach (Hamblin 1993) has insisted that the first systematic presentation of the approach was widely misunderstood. Its author had not in fact claimed that such ideotypes would thrive in all growing conditions; his view was instead that different ideotypes would need to be designed for each environment. From my point of view, however, the fact that the ideotype concept was misunderstood in this particular way is a nice indication that the idea of "universal" varieties was still very much in the minds of breeders during the 1970s and 1980s and that it remained controversial.

[28] Although GR programmes into the 1960s were dominated by U.S. agricultural scientists, the cosmopolitan breeding strategy was more widespread. It was, for example, also the dominant approach taken after 1945 at France's Institut national de recherches agronomiques (Bonneuil and Thomas 2009).

[29] Rudra 1987. One high-profile rice-breeder at the Central Rice Research Institute – who oversaw a valuable collection of local varieties, which included both high-yielding and pest-resistant varieties – was unceremoniously retired. When he responded by moving with the collection to a provincial rice research institute, the authorities closed the institute (Juma 1989, 92–3).

[30] Anderson et al. 1991.
[31] cited in Anderson et al. 1991, 90.
[32] Dahlberg 1979.

the GR seemed to make relatively little impact upon rural poverty and malnutrition, and in some regions poverty had actually increased.[33] The explanation given for this apparent paradox was that throughout the developing world the GR's package was taken up earlier and more often either by large landowners – who gained the most from the technology – or by those smallholders who enjoyed access to good land and irrigation. Smallholders on poor or rainfed land gained much less, and the landless poor were often worse off.[34] The overall effect of introducing the technology was thus to widen the gap between rich and poor in the countryside.

The reason for this differential uptake was that GR varieties were unsuited to most farmers' needs in tropical regions. For one thing (as in Central Europe fifty years earlier), they were expensive. High-yielding seed was about twice as expensive as local varieties; mineral fertilizer had to be purchased; and since the new varieties were often vulnerable to disease, pesticide also had to be applied. Second, in their preoccupation with increasing yield, GR breeders had neglected other traits that were just as important for smallholders, if not more so. Thus, the new varieties were much more sensitive to weather conditions, pests, and disease than were local varieties.[35] And lastly, as might have been expected from the cosmopolitan strategy that informed their development, because GR varieties were designed to flourish where there was an abundant and well-controlled water-supply, the large majority of farmers had no benefit from them.[36] Having been designed to grow in irrigated paddies, for example, the dwarf variety IR-8 could not cope with the periodic flooding in rainfed areas.[37] As a result, in some regions local rice varieties were preferred to IRRI's; although yielding less, they required no fertilizer, were pest-resistant, and needed no irrigation. If some breeders were surprised by this preference, Central European peasants would have understood it very well.

Tucked away in the experiment station, breeders of cosmopolitan persuasion were evidently out of touch with the ecological and economic diversity of growing conditions. But that was not all; splendid isolation also meant that breeders were out of touch with the *cultural* diversity of the regions they were supposed to be serving. One of the points that emerges clearly from several of the chapters in Part 1 of this volume is that "taste" is rather more important than many green revolutionaries recognized. Sui-Wai Cheung, for example, reminds us that people care intensely about the quality of what they eat, not just its effect on the palate and upon health but also its cultural meaning

---

[33] For example, Griffin 1974.
[34] Ruttan 1977.
[35] Chambers 1977; Pinstrup-Andersen and Hazell 1985.
[36] On average about a quarter of the agricultural acreage in the developing world is irrigated, and the proportion in Latin America and Africa is much smaller (FAO 2004: table A5).
[37] Farmer 1986.

(e.g., its associations with social status). Even in times of famine, he shows, the people in some regions could not be persuaded to eat "coarse foods." Nevertheless, somehow this message seems to have eluded Chinese agricultural scientists two centuries later. For as Seung-Joon Lee shows, in their boundless enthusiasm for boosting yields, Chinese breeders of the 1920s and 1930s were less concerned with quality than were rice merchants, such that their new high-yielding domestic varieties were unable to compete with those that the merchants imported. Similarly, as David Biggs demonstrates, at about the same time in Indochina French colonial scientists' and businessmen's attempts to strengthen exports – by introducing new varieties of rice, which they believed would be more popular in European markets – floundered in the face of the preferences of Chinese and Japanese consumers. A generation later the GR's breeders were still oblivious to the cultural importance of quality. Soon after his arrival in India in the mid-1960s, bearing the high-yielding dwarf wheat varieties that he had bred in Mexico, Norman Borlaug was told that his varieties lacked the taste and quality of the local varieties used for chapattis. The new technology, some Indian commentators feared, was endangering culinary tradition. Objections of this kind, Borlaug retorted, were "minutia" and could be sorted out later.[38] The same story was repeated with rice. Despite its very high yields, consumers in several regions found IR-8 to be inferior to local varieties in its taste and cooking properties.[39]

Like their cosmopolitan counterparts in Central Europe ca. 1900, therefore, the GR's breeders greatly underestimated the extent of local diversity – be it ecological, economic, or cultural – and the obstacles that would pose.

3. AND SINCE THE REVOLUTION?

In one sense the GR was obviously a gigantic experiment. It bears asking, therefore, what has been learned from it. Above all, has it moderated the universalizing ambition of green revolutionaries? The answer, I think, is "initially yes but ultimately no."

Had one posed this question during the 1970s, 1980s, and 1990s, the answer would almost certainly have been "yes." In response to criticism of the GR, experts' attention began to shift during the 1970s toward the needs and circumstances of small farmers. Initially, for example, experts had been frustrated by the fact that their technologies were being adopted only partially by small farmers (or not at all) and had attributed this to ignorance or conservatism. By the 1970s, however, evidence was accumulating that demonstrated that smallholders were not irrational or incompetent in their choice

---

[38] Cullather 2010.
[39] Anderson et al. 1991.

of technology; their farms were actually quite efficient, once one took into account the constraints under which they had to operate.[40]

What was also becoming clearer was that smallholders did not passively adopt technology but rather experimented in order to improve it.[41] As several of the chapters in this volume indicate, this recognition has been a long time coming. Since the early nineteenth century most agricultural experts have consistently underestimated the innovative capacity of small farmers (Mouser et al.; Maat). Nevertheless, peasant farmers' ability to breed successful new rice varieties has been known for some time. A classic case is the farmer-bred variety "Shinriki," which was later recognized and promoted by Japanese experiment stations from the late nineteenth century.[42] The point is underlined by other authors in this volume. Both Biggs and Minsky, for example, show how historical migrations into different ecological regions have obliged farmers to develop new varieties and cultivation practices. I presume a similar improvisatory skill was required of those West African rice farmers who were brought as slaves to North America.

If peasants were actually rational and innovative, however, that suggested that the GR's breeders were out of touch with farmers' needs. From the 1970s, therefore, a variety of new approaches to agricultural research were developed. These sought to narrow the gap between experiment station and farm. One approach was to allocate a larger role to social scientists. Previously their function in research teams – where they were involved at all – had been merely to assess the social consequences of introducing new technology; henceforth they were to play a role from the outset in the design of the technology.[43] Another approach ("farming systems research") paid more attention than heretofore to the ways in which small farms actually operated. More particularly, the idea was to focus not upon single crops (as was the overriding tendency among breeders) but upon the entire *system* of production on such farms. And by "system" they meant not just the biophysical factors in production but also the socioeconomic context of the farm. Once researchers took a view of the farm as a whole, it would be easier to identify at which point in the system an intervention could be made that would improve productivity most effectively. A third approach ("agroecology") was based on the premise that since GR methods were both expensive and damaging to the environment, the researcher's task was to develop cultivation methods that could increase yields sustainably, replacing commercial agrochemicals as far as possible with locally available manuring methods or alternative forms of pest-control.

---

[40] Schultz 1983 (first ed. 1964).
[41] Biggs 1980; Richards 1985.
[42] Ishikawa and Ohkawa 1972.
[43] Cernea and Kassam 2006.

Breeders responded to criticism of the GR in several ways. One response was to broaden the scope of breeding work so as to include crops and traits that were of particular importance to smallholders but had so far been neglected. From the mid-1970s, for example, various international agricultural research centers began to do more work on crops such as sorghum, millet, pulses, cassava, and yams. Moreover, they began to spend less time trying to increase yields and more on improving traits important to smallholders such as yield-stability, taste, and cooking properties. And centers like IRRI devoted more attention to developing varieties that were pest-resistant (so as to reduce the need for pesticide) and better adapted to unfavorable (e.g., non-irrigated) growing conditions.[44]

In 1975 a first step in decentralizing rice breeding took place when IRRI stopped developing its own "finished" varieties and instead began handing over promising breeding material to national research institutes in the global South which would finish off the breeding process as they saw fit.[45] Nevertheless, for the most part these attempts to make breeding more "peasant-friendly" still left control in the hands of breeders at the experiment station. A more radical approach was to reject the cosmopolitan breeding strategy altogether. Apparently unaware of their Central European predecessors, proponents of "participatory plant breeding" (PPB) argued that the best way to obtain well-adapted varieties was to breed locally in the relevant marginal conditions.[46] If one took already adapted local varieties as the starting material and established through consultation with farmers the kinds of varieties they valued, there was much less risk of developing varieties whose traits were of no use to the locals. The extent of farmer-participation in PPB varies widely. Often the breeding is conducted by experts with farmers merely providing breeding material or being consulted on choice of variety. But where varieties for a wide range of growing conditions are required, this arrangement is seen as prohibitively expensive. In this case it makes both ecological and economic sense for breeding to be carried out by the farmers themselves who work in those environments. The justification given for proceeding in this way is that farmers are thoughtful experimenters who typically possess more extensive knowledge of their local growing conditions, crops, and farming systems than do experts (though it has often taken the latter a while to realize this[47]).

By now "sustainability" and "participation" are to be found in virtually all reports and strategy documents issued by development agencies. But the actual impact of the new post-1970s approaches upon agricultural research has been rather more modest. By the late 1980s, for example, international

---

[44] Lipton 1978.
[45] Chandler 1982, x.
[46] Ceccarelli 1989; Simmonds 1991.
[47] Ashby 1990; Marglin 1996.

donors were beginning to withdraw funding for farming systems research. In the case of agroecology, despite evidence of sustainable cultivation practices that can increase yields in unfavorable growing conditions, only a very small proportion of the budgets of international agricultural research centers has actually been devoted to developing technology that does not require commercial agrochemicals.[48] As far as PPB is concerned, debate on the subject has been sharply polarized over the past decade. PPB has been strongly resisted in various places, by conventional breeders as well as by some ministries of agriculture.[49] While some breeders are receptive, most are said to consider PPB an unnecessary alternative to conventional breeding. Though breeders are now agreed on the necessity of developing varieties suited to the needs of smallholders, therefore, they are still as divided as ever over the most effective strategy for doing so.

Despite longstanding arguments for the ecological and economic diversity of farming (as well as for the cultural diversity of consumption preferences), the cosmopolitan breeding strategy today is alive and well. Commercial breeding in sub-Saharan Africa, for example, is largely centralized (on grounds of cost), resulting in varieties that are not well-adapted to the regions where they are grown.[50] Nevertheless, confidence persists that (near-) universal varieties are possible. As a breeder from the private-sector declared, "As a general rule, the more consistently a variety excels in any one locale, the more widely adapted it will be to many locales."[51] At the moment the proponents of new "biofortified" rice varieties (e.g., rich in iron or vitamins) are claiming – despite evidence to the contrary – that these varieties will preserve their desireable properties in all growing conditions.[52] And at IRRI breeders are attempting to construct a "new plant type" that will maximize yield in tropical regions. (When one looks more closely, however, it is evident that this new rice is expected to thrive in the irrigated and otherwise favorable growing conditions for which the type is designed; no mention is made of its suitability for rainfed or upland regions.[53]) While undoubtedly influential, however, this quasi-deductive approach to breeding has failed to win over all breeders or even crop physiologists.[54] After more than a century of argument,

---

[48] Tripp et al. 2006.
[49] Biggs 2008.
[50] DeVries and Toenniessen 2001; Lynam 2011.
[51] Duvick 1990, 41.
[52] Brooks 2011.
[53] Virk et al. 2004. Several years ago the International Centre for Maize & Wheat Improvement succeeded in developing a very similar wheat variety. Based on a new "architecture," it was extraordinarily high-yielding. On the other hand, it required large amounts of fertilizer, and at the time of its announcement, breeders did not yet know in which regions it would be able to grow (anon. 1998).
[54] Marshall 1991; Duvick 2002.

therefore, breeders still do not agree whether or not the quest to design miracle varieties is sensible.

CONCLUSION

Just why opinion on this issue has been – and continues to be – so sharply divided is a large and important question but one whose definitive answer must be deferred. At the moment I can offer only a tentative explanation for the controversy in early-twentieth-century Germany. There the contrasting breeding strategies can be attributed to the differing institutional affiliations of the two factions. For the most part, the proponents of universal varieties were commercial breeders (supported by a few prominent academics) who, for understandable reasons, sought to develop varieties that would flourish virtually anywhere. When those varieties did well in tests that had been conducted in a relatively small number of regions, therefore, they were quick to generalize, proclaiming such varieties' universal suitability.[55] Proponents of the local strategy, on the other hand, tended to be concentrated in public-sector breeding stations whose mission was to serve the small farmer. By virtue of these institutional affiliations, however, the two groups of breeders also became familiar with very different kinds of farming. As we have seen, commercial breeding was concentrated in regions with good soil and moderate climate, whose large and well-capitalized farms provided a market for varieties that would flourish under those conditions, while "peasant-friendly" breeding stations were located in the South where growing conditions were so variable that no single variety could be expected to flourish outside a narrow locality.

If we turn, on the other hand, to the conflict between cosmopolitan and local breeders that has been ongoing since 1945, institutional affiliation would once again appear to offer at least a partial explanation. The power of a small number of multinational seed companies, for example, is almost certainly one reason for the continued vigor of the cosmopolitan strategy though the institutional basis for local breeding is not so clear. By the postwar era, however, the two sides' differential familiarity with peasant agriculture no longer looks plausible. To be sure, it has occasionally been suggested that those American breeders who dominated the first generation of the GR knew little about growing conditions in the developing world. But by the 1970s at the latest, scarcely any breeders working in the global South can have been *unaware* of the diverse conditions under which peasants there had to farm. The evidence suggests instead that they simply *ignored* such diversity in order to concentrate upon that minority of (wealthier) farmers who worked in favorable conditions (as though their motto was "Focus on the best and

[55] Remy 1908.

forget the rest").[56] In any event, a full account of the continuing debate after 1945 remains to be written.

Having surveyed three different contexts, however, I want to conclude by assessing what can be gained by comparative analysis of large-scale agricultural transformations. The analytical payoff seems clear. Although the GR is conventionally placed in the global South from the 1940s, historians of development and of colonialism have been arguing in recent years that what we now call "development" did not begin in 1945.[57] A well-known case in point is the remarkable agricultural development of Meiji Japan.[58] But the chapters in this volume take us further, broadening the basis for comparative analysis. What emerges are numerous recurring features among attempts at agricultural revolution: for example, the central role of rulers or states in initiating such schemes (Minsky, this volume), the political aims behind such schemes (Biggs and Lee, both this volume), and the kinds of technology deployed. In addition, as I have argued here, comparison reveals something fundamental about the nature of expertise: that its universalizing ambition is the source not only of its power but also of its fallibility.

But comparison offers more: analysis of this kind also makes history a potentially useful resource for policy. Over the past 20 years various academics and practitioners within the development industry have urged their colleagues to look more closely at the history of development in order to avoid unnecessary mistakes. And the literature in this field is littered with concern to "learn the lessons of the past."[59] But the "history" invoked is rarely systematic reflection. More often one finds a hastily cobbled-together and highly selective version of the past which can be used to justify a particular course of action,[60] and attention is usually focused only on the period since 1945. But what can history actually offer? Obviously it cannot provide a straightforward recipe for action since the future never simply recapitulates the past. It can, however, provide policy-makers with critical feedback ("What happened the last time this kind of approach was tried?"). And more generally, it can provide a list of issues to watch out for, a wider range of options from which to choose, a set of tools for thinking.

---

[56] Most breeders at an international conference on "breeding for lousy conditions," for example, resisted the idea of developing varieties suited to such conditions, reckoning that it made more sense to try to improve (thereby standardizing) the cultivation methods used on poor farms (terHorst and Watts 1983, 53, 74–75). One feature of the national agricultural research systems established in Latin America during the 1960s was that despite widely differing social, economic, and agricultural conditions from one country to another, their research systems were much alike. All had embraced technologies that worked well under a limited set of conditions (Pineiro and Trigo 1983).

[57] For example, Bray 1979; Cowan and Shenton 1996; Rist 2008; Cooper 2010.

[58] Francks 1984.

[59] For example, World Bank 2007, 226.

[60] Woolcock et al. 2011.

From the chapters in this volume, policy-makers should be able to learn a good deal about which approaches to agricultural development – in various places over many centuries – have been effective and which not.[61] The message that emerges from my own contribution, however, is: "Beware of experts bearing gifts," especially where the gift is a simple scheme built around a "miracle" technology. These invariably promise too much. Paradoxically, the professional rewards for producing solutions of universal scope, combined with the narrow and specialized training characteristic of modern expertise, mean that the agricultural scientist is often blind to the local complexity of production (and consumption).[62] In consequence, unless counter-measures are taken, the introduction of fancy new technology may well benefit some users but will almost certainly prove inappropriate for the many.

In Germany as well as Britain in recent years, those in the humanities and social sciences have had to suffer the fact that educational ministries have become enamored with remarkably narrow utilitarian criteria of "relevance" and "impact," which clearly favor funding of the natural sciences. The chapters in this volume, however, illustrate just how myopic such policy is. For history provides a reservoir of experience. And any fool knows that one can – or at least ought to – learn from experience.

---

[61] Or at least that minority of policy-makers who are genuinely concerned to alleviate rural poverty. The evidence suggests that policy for development has often been driven by quite different considerations (Harwood 2012, 173ff).

[62] Often blind but not always; for a counter-example see Riley 1983. As I have argued elsewhere (Harwood 2005), institutions of higher agricultural education have varied in important ways. Staff at some of them have been far more attentive to the needs of farmers – and correspondingly less concerned to abide by scholarly norms – than have those elsewhere.

2

Rice, Sugar, and Livestock in Java, 1820–1940: Geertz's *Agricultural Involution* 50 Years On

Peter Boomgaard and Pieter M. Kroonenberg

GEERTZ AND INVOLUTION

Do we love him or do we loath him? Do we love Clifford Geertz (1926–2006) because he put Java (and Bali) on the scholarly map with his well-written books that appealed to a large audience? Or do we hate him because his *Agricultural Involution* (1963) was such a travesty of Java's economic and social history of the nineteenth and early twentieth centuries? Geertz has been praised and imitated by many scholars who worked on areas other than Java but vilified by most Java scholars.

Personally, we, the authors, are inclined to applaud him for drawing our attention to Java as a nice case study of the possible linkages between population growth and the high rates of labor absorption in wet-rice cultivation. Although there is much to be criticized in his famous book, there is also much to be admired and to be learned. It is regrettable that as a cultural anthropologist he was ill-equipped for the nitty-gritties of archival research that should have been carried out but were not. The upside of this was that some 35 years ago, the first author found himself a fascinating topic for a PhD dissertation.[1]

In this chapter, we deal only with one particular aspect of the involution theory – Geertz's ideas about the allegedly unlimited capacity of Java's wet-rice fields (*sawah* in Javanese) for almost constant intensification during the colonial period (ca. 1820–ca. 1940) (see Figure P.1a). As Ben White pointed out, Geertz did not "provide [a] clear, operational and testable definition of 'agricultural involution' – a failure partly due to Geertz' preference for evocative similes and metaphors rather than direct concrete statements, which makes the book so delightful to read the first time and so infuriating thereafter."[2] Nevertheless, the main thrust of his arguments is clear.

---

[1] Boomgaard 1989.
[2] White 1983, 21.

Geertz's main point is that

> the output of most [rice] terraces can be almost indefinitely increased by more careful, fine-comb cultivation techniques; it seems almost always possible somehow to squeeze just a little bit more out of even a mediocre sawah by working it just a little bit harder .... The capacity of most terraces to respond to loving care is amazing.[3]

This is the ecological basis of (agricultural) involution. Secondly, Geertz argued that rice and sugar (cane) were ecologically "mutualistic":

> Sugar demands irrigation [and drainage] and a general environment almost identical to that for wet rice.... In the mutualistic relationship, the expansion of one side, sugar cultivation, brings with it the expansion of the other, wet-rice growing. The more numerous and the better irrigated the terraces are, the more sugar can be grown; and the more people – a seasonal, readily available, resident labor force [a sort of part-time proletariat] – supported by these terraces during the nonsugar portion of the cycle, can grow sugar.[4]

The historical implications of these factors were, according to Geertz, far-reaching. They created a society characterized by "shared poverty, social elasticity [in Geertz's terminology the opposite of social conflict], and cultural vagueness" ["an indeterminateness which did not so much transform traditional patterns as elasticize them"]. Agricultural involution led to growth without development, as no structural economic and social changes, no specialization, diversification, and industrialization, – sugar factories apart – occurred, and surplus labor was absorbed by wet-rice and sugar cultivation. It was basically just more of the same thing. While wet-rice cultivation formed the backdrop to high rates of population growth, these growth rates and the sugar industry siphoned off all potential for change, including an embryonic true proletariat. Such, in a nutshell, was the Geertzian view of agricultural involution's consequences.[5]

GEERTZ'S QUANTITATIVE DATA

Geertz presented the main evidence for this mutualistic argument in two tables. Here (Table 2.1) we reproduce the main part of one of them.

A short note is in order here regarding the "symbiosis" of rice and sugar in Java after 1830. When the literature about post-1830 Java mentions "sugar estates" or "sugar plantations," these estates are, as a rule, not real plantations, in the sense that one person, family, or firm owns a large tract of land planted to sugar. Certainly in the areas where the so-called

---

[3] Geertz 1963, 35.
[4] Geertz 1963, 55–7.
[5] Geertz 1963, particularly 103, 123.

TABLE 2.1 *The land, population, and rice-production characteristics of the sugar regions of Java in 1920.**

	% of land	% of wet-rice land	% of population	% of wet-rice production
37 main sugar regencies (47% of all regencies)**	34	46	50	49
98 main sugar districts (22% of all districts)	15	22	24	24
19 leading sugar districts (4% of all districts)	2.6	4.6	5.3	5.2

* Taken from Geertz 1963, 71; the title of the table was copied from Geertz.
** "Regencies" were administrative units governed by a Javanese civil servant called *regent* (he who rules) by the Dutch, and *bupati* by present-day Indonesians. A number of regencies constituted a "Residency," governed by a Dutch colonial official, the *Resident*.

Cultivation System had been introduced, that is in most Residencies of Central and Eastern Java, except the so-called Principalities (regions still governed by Javanese princes), sugar producers had to hire land from villages, inhabited by smallholders. This land was leased for a certain period of time, often two decades, during which always one-third of the arable land was planted with sugar – one harvest of which occupied the land for more or less 18 months – while on the other two-thirds, the original owners planted rice.

Much criticism regarding the agricultural involution thesis has been elicited by the "mutualistic" sugar–rice argument. Scholars have argued that rice and sugar did not have the same water requirements; that a field where wet rice was grown had to be resurfaced entirely; and the other way around, that sugar occupied the fields so long that only fast-growing rice varieties could be grown there after and before the sugar harvest, and that, therefore, average rice harvests dropped in the sugar areas such as Pasuruan.[6]

On the basis of Geertz's arguments one would expect that in the areas where sugar cane was grown on sawahs, rice production per unit land would be higher and more people would be living there.

Strangely enough, few people have looked carefully at the statistics Geertz published. If they had done so, they might have concluded that he did not exactly present a strong case. If we look at the first row of figures in Table 2.1, where data are given for the 37 main sugar regencies, we find that in 47 percent of the territorial units where the main sugar producing areas were to

---

[6] White 1983, 22–4.

be found in 1920, also 46 percent of all wet-rice fields could be encountered, as well as 50 percent of the population and 49 percent of the wet-rice production.[7] We fail to see how these figures can point at a mutualistic relationship between rice and sugar.

These findings are entirely unremarkable; in fact they are remarkable for their unremarkability. Expressed in words, it means that the main sugar areas, representing in total slightly under half of the number of regencies of Java, also contained slightly under half of the area occupied by wet-rice fields. Half the population of Java was living here, producing half of all wet rice. It also means that the areas where little or no sugar was grown represented about half of Java's territory, consisting of about half the area occupied by wet-rice fields and home to the other half of Java's population, who produced the other half of the wet-rice harvest. Therefore, there was virtually no difference between the sugar and the non-sugar half of the island, as the very small differences recorded fall squarely within the error margins!

The 98 main sugar districts in the second row are not doing any better, as all the variables score very close to one-quarter of the total number of districts, wet-rice acreage, population, and wet-rice production, respectively. They are, therefore, not doing better than the remaining three-quarters of the total number of districts.

Only in the last row do we see signs of the link Geertz thought to have discovered between wet-rice production and sugar. The 19 leading sugar districts, consisting of 4 percent of all the districts of Java, contained 4.6 percent of the wet-rice land and 5.3 percent of the island's population, and contributed 5.2 percent of the total wet-rice production. These districts, therefore, had a higher-than-average share in the wet-rice lands, the wet-rice production, and the population. However, the wet-rice production per capita was the same as the mean for the whole island, which means that the higher-than-average wet-rice production of these 19 leading sugar districts was caused by a combination of relatively high population density (30 percent higher than the mean), a 13 percent higher-than-average production per unit of wet-rice land, and a 15 percent higher-than-average availability of wet-rice land. So there was more rice land than average, even more people, and therefore a lower-than-average availability of sawah per capita, which then had to yield more rice per unit of land in order to keep the production per capita on the average level of the island. This is the more-or-less universal logic of

---

[7] We do not include the column "% of land" in our analysis. It is irrelevant what proportion of the total surface area of Java, which includes volcanoes and other mountains, lakes, rivers, swamps, and cities, was taken up by the regencies or districts in question. Geertz erroneously and misleadingly used precisely these surface area data as index base in the second part of the table we have partly reproduced in Table 2.1.

increasing production (yield) per unit of land when the average size of the landholdings becomes smaller.[8]

But what had been caused by what? Did, as Geertz argued (see earlier quote), the expansion of sugar bring with it the expansion of rice growing? As we have seen, outside the 19 leading sugar districts, it certainly did not.

A STATISTICAL INTERMEZZO

Geertz's data as represented in Table 2.1 only report percentages for groups of areas and they shed little light on the relative positions of areas on one variable, say sugar production on sawahs, with respect to their positions on another variable, say rice production per sawah or on the areas' population density. For more insight into such relations we need more information from other sources and we need other measures than simple percentages.

In 1920 the Dutch colonial government produced the *Landbouwatlas van Java en Madoera* (Agricultural Atlas of Java and Madura) containing detailed information on a large number of variables, primarily agricultural ones, both at the Residency and at the district levels. These figures are the basis for our further analyses and, incidentally, were the source of Geertz's data as well.

Correlations between two variables (say, sugar production on sawahs and rice production on sawahs) reflect primarily information on the relative rank orders of the districts on the two production variables. If a higher production of sugar generally goes together with a higher production of rice, and vice versa, the correlation will be high – say around .40. Correlations can in principle be as high as +1, indicating a perfect positive relation, and as low as −1, indicating a perfect inverse relation. In practical situations, correlations of +.70 and higher occur mainly if one measures the same variable twice in succession with similar measuring instruments. In fact in most applied sciences substantively interesting correlations are usually between .30 and .40. Squared correlations can be interpreted as the amount of variability of one variable explained by the other one. The fact that a correlation of .70 is rare implies that one may seldom if ever expect 50 percent explained variability or more and that between 10 percent and 16 percent is much more common. Thus, it is rarely the case that a single variable can explain on its own most of the variability of another one.

A word of caution about the interpretation of the correlations presented in this chapter is in order. Correlations based on a small number of

---

[8] It is clear that whatever relationship obtained in these leading sugar districts between sugar, rice, and population, it was only valid for a very small percentage of all districts.

observational units are rather sensitive to individual units that have vastly different values compared to the other units. This plays a role when we look at correlations for the 15– 20 Residencies but not for correlations for the 160 districts. We will signal such instable correlations for Residencies when appropriate.

Our discussion of the situation in Java in 1920, and sometimes in 1880 as well, will be primarily couched in terms of correlations.

MORE DETAILED ANALYSES

In this section, we present correlations we have calculated for all Java Residencies and districts in 1920, based upon the *Landbouwatlas* mentioned earlier. Occasionally, we have similar data for 1880 but only on the Residency level.[9]

Sawah under Cane and Population Density

The first question is whether increasing percentages of sugar cane on sawahs go together with increasing population density for Residencies and districts, respectively, something one might expect based on Geertz's reasoning, and based on the sample of 19 leading sugar districts. The correlations[10] are as follows:

1880, Residency level	.02
1920, Residency level	.48
1920, district level	.45

Apparently, there was no correlation in 1880, but in 1920 there was a positive medium-sized correlation, corresponding at the district level to a 20 percent explained variability of one variable by the other. As demonstrated in the Appendix, it should be noted that in 1880 there was not much sugar planted on sawahs as only two Residencies (Probolinggo and Pasuruan) had more than 5 percent.

The fact that there was no correlation at all in 1880, however, suggests that the direction of the causal arrow is not from sugar to population density but the other way around. In 1880, sugar was planted in districts with population densities varying from high to low, because at that moment the labor surplus in the high-density areas was hardly any higher than in the low-density ones. But when densities became much higher and cheap labor became increasingly available in the more densely settled areas, planting sugar in those districts became more attractive. As almost

---

[9] The 1880 data are taken from the *Koloniaal Verslag* (Colonial Report) of that year.
[10] All correlations reported in this chapter are the standard Pearson correlations applicable to continuous variables.

all activities regarding the cultivation of sugar cane were done by seasonal labor, it is unlikely that people had been migrating on a permanent basis to the sugar districts in large numbers between 1880 and 1920.

CAPITALIST ENTERPRISE AND SUBSISTENCE-ORIENTED SMALLHOLDERS

Sawah under Cane and Sawah per Capita

We should now find out whether there is a statistical link in our data between a high proportion of sawah under cane and low availability of sawah per capita, as suggested in the 19-district sample, which could be seen as a corollary of high population-density figures. The correlations are the following:

1880, Residency level	-.34
1920, Residency level	-.60
1920, district level	-.20

The correlations are varied: medium sized in 1880, rather high in 1920 at the Residency level, and, strangely enough, at the 1920 district level very low indeed, explaining only 4 percent of the variation in the dependent variable.

Maybe if sawahs became too small, which certainly might have been the case in high population-density areas, near-landless or entirely landless laborers were no longer available for seasonal labor in the sugar plantations, as they needed more permanent jobs. It is one of the problems in Geertz's study that he does not talk about nonagricultural labor at all, while we know from other, more recent, studies that around 1900 a fair proportion of Java's economically active population was landless (31 percent), and an almost equally large percentage should be regarded as nonagriculturists (29 percent), working in towns and cities and/or in nonagricultural jobs.[11] It has often been argued, for example in the more theoretical (Marxist) literature, that it was in the interest of capitalist enterprise to preserve a subsistence household sector where the reproduction of labor power could take place cheaply.[12] Too high a proportion of totally landless people was not attractive to the sugar entrepreneurs. Our findings appear to illustrate this case.

Sawah under Cane and Rice Production per Unit Sawah

In the sample of 19 leading sugar districts, a higher-than-average rice production per unit of wet-rice land was found, and we should try to find out whether these two variables were statistically related to each other:

---

[11] Boomgaard 1991, 34.
[12] See, e.g., Meillassoux 1981; Geertz agreed with this notion (e.g., 1963, 89).

1880, Residency level	.09
1920, Residency level	.34
1920, district level	.39

As with population density, we find no correlation at all in 1880, and positive but medium-sized ones in 1920. Thus, rice production per unit sawah alone only explains 15 percent of the variation in sawahs under cane at the district level, a modest explanatory value.

Sawah under Cane and Wet-Rice Production per Capita

Wet-rice production per capita in the 19-district sample was about average; in our data the relations between the two variables are as follows:

1880, Residency level	−.18
1920, Residency level	−.52
1920, district level	−.04

Our 1920 district-level data lead to the same conclusion as the Geertzian sample: no correlation between percentage wet-rice lands under sugar and wet-rice production per capita. The correlation in 1880 is also low. It is a bit of a riddle, therefore, why the Residency-level correlation for 1920 is so high (but negative). It explains 27 percent in the variation of the dependent variable, which is almost one-third. It suggests that if in a Residency the wet-rice production per capita was below average, there was a fair chance that the proportion of sawah under sugar cane was above average (and vice versa). However, such a causal link did not exist on the district level in the same year! Part of the explanation of this phenomenon is the "outlier" position of the Yogyakarta Residency: it had a very high proportion of sawah under cane in 1920, but scored very low with respect to wet-rice production per capita (see Appendix, Figure 2.5). If Yogya was excluded from the analysis, the correlation at the Residency level for 1920 would be much lower: −.22.

DWARFHOLDINGS ATTRACT SUGAR?

Sawah under Cane and Arable Land per Capita

But perhaps we should not look at sawahs per capita alone; what about all arable lands per capita? This is the data:

1880, Residency level	−.11
1920, Residency level	−.66
1920, district level	−.36

Again, the very high (but negative) correlation at the Residency level for 1920 is remarkable, implying that if in a Residency the quantity of arable land per capita was below average, it is rather likely that there would be a high percentage of wet-rice land under sugar, explaining 44 percent of the variation. At the district level the correlation was much lower, and only 13 percent of the variation is explained, a very modest predictor. Part of the explanation of the difference between Residency and districts levels in 1920 is, again, the outlier position of Yogya (see Appendix, Figure 2.6). If Yogya were excluded, the 1920 correlation at the Residency level would be -.45.

Both sets of figures – correlation coefficients between percentage sawah under sugar and sawah per capita, and between the first variable and all arable lands per capita – suggest that Residencies where peasants in 1920 were smallholders with really small properties ("dwarfholdings"), both wet and dry lands (*tegal(an)*), were likely to attract sugar cultivation (possibly because part-time labor would be easily available). The other way around – very small holdings due to cane growing – makes no sense, if only because sugar cane does not grow on dry lands. The high but negative correlation in 1920 at the Residency level between proportion under sugar and rice production per capita supports these findings: if average income in terms of rice was low, people would be looking for part-time jobs, which the sugar industry could offer.

At the 1920 district level, the variable "percentage of the sawahs planted to sugar cane" produces correlations of more than .3 (or less than -.3) for three variables only – population density (.45), arable lands per capita (-.36), and wet-rice production per unit of rice-land (.39). Therefore, there is a fair chance that sugar cane would be grown on a high proportion of the sawahs if population density was high, the rice production per unit sawah was high, and the quantity of arable lands per capita was low (while the chance of the proportion of sugar being above average would increase perceptibly if in the surrounding Residency the average landholding per capita would be low as well!).

SMALLHOLDER INTENSIFICATION AND THE INDUSTRIOUS REVOLUTION?

Summing up, we expect an above-average percentage of sawah under sugar in districts with a high population density. Such a district will often have lower-than-average sawah and arable lands per capita – especially in the latter case, when there are few dry lands in addition to sawah, chances are higher that more sugar is grown. This is another argument that sugar growing is not the cause but the result of the variable just measured, because growing more sugar could hardly lead to a low availability of tegal lands. Such a district would often have above-average rice yields per unit of sawah as well, which also made for a relatively big chance that an above-average percentage of sawah under sugar can be expected.

Smaller-than-average landholdings with higher-than-average yields per unit of land in areas with high population densities are par for the course – one neither needs wet rice nor sugar as explanatory factors. It is called (traditional, preindustrial) agricultural intensification by smallholders, and almost invariably leads to higher yields per unit of land, while stagnating or dropping output per worker.[13]

Sometimes, however, working harder, that is spending more working hours than before, could lead to higher production per worker as well, in which case some scholars have used the term "*Industrious* Revolution" (as opposed to *Industrial* Revolution). As will be shown presently, it could be argued that such a revolution took place in Java during this period.[14]

Returning for the time being to our case study, we argue that our findings that rice production *per capita* in such districts was about average are also in keeping with this "traditional" model. It is logical that such districts would attract the sugar industry, certainly if the alternatives were restricted (most lands being arable lands). However, as a rule, the quantity of wet-rice land per capita in the district should not be too low, or there would not be enough room for sugar. In contrast, lower-than-average per capita sawah lands in the surrounding Residency was a good thing for the sugar growers, because it would provide the temporary migrant laborers they needed during the busy seasons (preparing the land, planting, and harvesting).

LIVESTOCK REARS ITS HEAD

Finally, looking at the 1920 Residency-level correlations, there is a very high one that so far has not been discussed – it is a correlation of .59 between percentage sawahs under sugar cane on the one hand and the numbers of water buffaloes and cattle per unit of arable land on the other. Geertz does not talk about the presence of livestock, and the information is, alas, not available at the district level, so we cannot find out how the 19 sugar districts were doing in this respect. It also appears to have been a recent correlation, because in 1880 it was actually zero (.00)!

In 1920, this variable alone explains 35 percent of the variation in the other one. But which variable is the one that is explained by the other? Do we get large areas under sugar when livestock is abundantly available? Or is the presence of sugar conducive to livestock keeping?

As both buffaloes and cattle were used as plow-animals on sawahs in preparation for rice cultivation, one would expect a high and positive correlation between some measure for quantities of sawah or rice harvest and

---

[13] See, e.g., Booth 1988, 236; Netting 1993, 124–9.
[14] Hayami 1989, 3–5; see also De Vries 2008.

numbers of livestock per unit of land. However, the only really large correlation (the ones for percentage sawah of total arable, sawah per capita, and rice-production per unit of land are all low to modest) is between livestock per unit of arable and rice-production per capita, and that one is negative (-.70)! If there is a causal link between these two variables (and not only a statistical one), we must either suppose that the presence of above-average livestock numbers leads to lower-than-average availability of rice per capita, or that below-average availability of rice per head of the population is somehow conducive to more than average numbers of livestock per unit of arable land.

However unlikely it may seem prima facie, the latter link is the most plausible, albeit in an indirect way. The livestock density correlates rather highly (.61) with the proportion of arable lands sown with maize (corn) and a bit lower (.44) with the percentage of lands planted with cassava. It is well known that parts of the maize and cassava plants – stalks and leaves – were used as livestock feed, and the presence of cassava correlates strongly but negatively (-.75) with the availability of rice per capita. The correlation between availability of rice per capita and maize is also substantial and negative (-.45). The presence of both maize and cassava correlates negatively and fairly strongly with percentage sawah of arable land (-.54 and -.47 respectively) and quantity of sawah per capita (-.46 and -.49 respectively).

One may assume, therefore, that maize and cassava, grown in regions where percentage sawah of all arable land and sawah per capita were below average, as was the availability of rice per capita, attracted livestock keeping. As both maize and cassava were cultivated on dry lands, which needed manuring – in contrast to irrigated sawahs, which were (largely) fertilized by nutritious elements in irrigation water – the manure of cattle and buffaloes attracted maize and cassava growing.

The maize- and cassava-growing areas must have been particularly attractive to stockbreeders when there was a large sugar presence in the region, as the sugar industry needed livestock for many of its activities. The growing presence of livestock would then have constituted an extra attraction for more sugar cane growing enterprise, and so on and so forth. It is certainly possible that livestock, in turn, made the cultivation of maize and cassava even more attractive. It is, therefore, better to say that sugar attracted livestock and livestock sugar, as it was doubtlessly the case.

GROWTH?

But we have strayed rather far from the writings of Clifford Geertz. An important element in Geertz's Agricultural Involution theory is the notion that there was growth in numbers of people in Java, an increase in the harvested area (partly through double cropping), rises in per hectare productivity, but no growth in output per capita. On this issue he quoted the Dutch

TABLE 2.2 *Production of kilocalories per capita per day for selected years, Java.**

	1815	1880	1940
From arable	1,654	1,926	2,111
Total	1,917	2,288	2,408

* Taken from Boomgaard and Van Zanden 1990, 51. Included in the total are the produce of gardens, coconuts, and fish and meat.

economist J. H. Boeke, who described the same phenomenon, calling it "static expansion."[15]

But has the notion of static expansion been borne out by recent research? Table 2.2 presents data on this topic.

If we take the production of kilocalories per capita per day for a number of benchmark years as a reasonable proxy of agricultural production in the subsistence sector, it would appear that Geertz underestimated the growth in income per capita, although it has to be said that particularly during the second period the rate of growth was rather low. Much of this growth – and in this respect Geertz was right – was almost certainly generated by increased labor input per capita: people just worked harder; industrious revolution, indeed!

On the other hand, Geertz overstated his case with the following sentence; "Wet-rice cultivation, with its extraordinary ability to maintain levels of marginal labor productivity by always managing to work one more man in without a serious fall in per-capita income ([...])." Around 1940 agricultural economist G. J. Vink had already demonstrated that in many areas the input of labor was so high that its marginal productivity was zero.[16]

Capital investment hardly played a role in all this, apart from improvement in irrigation, undertaken by the colonial state, and the construction of better roads, another colonial project. However, between 1880 and 1940 the amount of sawah as percentage of all arable lands, dropped from 55 to 40 percent, which means that the construction of irrigation works had been outstripped by the growth of arable lands, which, in turn, had been driven by high rates of population growth, a topic to which we will return presently.

But there was no mechanization to speak of, while other forms of technological improvement appear to have played a very small role indeed, although it has to be admitted that we know next to nothing about, for instance, improved plows. We do know that some research had taken place on the

---

[15] Geertz 1963, 78–80. Geertz did leave the possibility open that after 1900 the Javanese standard of living might have improved gradually (p. 80)).

[16] Vink 1941, 91–106; Geertz 1963, 80; Boomgaard and Van Zanden 1990, 42; Boomgaard 1999, 182–3.

improvement of rice varieties, but not until the 1930s, and they were then planted on such a small scale that it is unlikely to have had much effect. Artificial fertilizer was introduced by many sugar plantations, but it is doubtful whether it played any role in the subsistence sector, where few people would have been able to buy it.[17]

STAGNATION

It is, therefore, not a total surprise, that the rise in yields per hectare, which was part of Geertz's agricultural involution package, did not take place between 1880 and 1920, but may have occurred during part of the nineteenth century. This is demonstrated in Table 2.3.

The figures for the early nineteenth century are very interesting, but also less reliable than later ones. However, even with an error margin of 10 percent or so, the trend appears to be clear.

Between 1815 and 1836 there is a drop in the yields, almost certainly because of the introduction of the Cultivation System from 1830. This system, introduced by the colonial government, required the peasantry to produce crops for the European market (sugar, indigo, tobacco) on part of their arable lands. They received a wage (*plantloon*) for doing so, which was subtracted from the tax (*Landrente*) they had to pay. If lucky, they were supposed to receive a small amount of money when the value of their crops was higher than the amount of tax due, but it is doubtful whether this money reached them (it may not have got further than the level of the regent, the district chief, or the village head at best). Usually, they may

TABLE 2.3 *Rice production per hectare (in kgs unhusked rice) for selected years.* *

	First crop	First and second crop
1815	1,650	
1836	1,360	
1860	1,660	
1880	2,265	2,100
1900		2,000
1921/1925		1,850
1931/1935		1,900
1936/1940		2,040

* Boomgaard and Van Zanden 1990, 41, 44. A small, but growing percentage of the sawahs was double cropped with rice – the second crop was planted during the dry season and the yields per ha. were therefore usually lower than those of the first crop.

[17] Boomgaard and Van Zanden 1990, 36–44; Boomgaard 1999, 176, 180–5.

have had to pay the balance between the two. Although some land clearing took place, the compulsory crops took up a notable proportion of the existing arable lands, and rice harvests suffered as a consequence, with famines in the 1840s in their wake.

Then, however, the most pernicious features of the Cultivation System were corrected and irrigation works carried out, resulting in a gradual improvement of yields. After 1870, the Cultivation System was gradually phased out. Around 1860, yields were back at their 1815 level, and by 1880 they had surpassed that. By how much is anyone's guess, because these years also saw concerted attempts at improving statistics of lands, harvests, and people, so that the higher figures in 1880 partly reflect improvement in recording.

After 1880, yields dropped, probably largely, as mentioned earlier, because irrigation did not keep up with population growth and land clearing. Only in the 1930s, when sugar more or less disappeared owing to the 1930s Depression (and, therefore, freed up good sawah land), and higher yielding rice varieties were introduced, yields were improving, although the level of 1880 was not reached again.[18]

It is, of course, ironical that it was the disappearance of sugar that was largely responsible for the higher rice yields, as this development is directly in conflict with Geertz's sugar–rice link. Here, yields were increasing because sugar was no longer cultivated on these rice-fields, not because there was a mutualistic link between the two crops!

POPULATION

Geertz was right about population growth. During most of the nineteenth and early twentieth century it was close to 1.5 percent per year on average, which was very high for Java (and higher than most countries around that time), where growth rates prior to 1800 had never been higher than 0.5 percent and usually closer to 0.1 or 0.25 percent annually on average.[19]

Geertz was not really interested in explaining these high population growth rates. Nevertheless, the few lines he dedicated to the topic contained a number of shrewd guesses. Basically, he presented the following features as (not) having influenced the rate of population growth:

- "Improved hygiene could hardly have played a major role until fairly late."
- "The Pax Nederlandica had perhaps more effect." Here he is referring to what others have called Pax Imperica, imperial peace, which stands for the suppression of indigenous warfare by the colonial powers.

---

[18] Boomgaard 1989, 82–3; Boomgaard and Van Zanden 1990, 36–47; Hugenholtz 2008.
[19] Boomgaard 1989.

– "Probably most important, and least discussed, was the expansion of the transport network which prevented local crop failures from turning into famines."[20]

Later, in a comparison between Java and Japan, he summarized his explanation as follows:

Rapid growth after 1830, evidently as a result of declining mortality due to improved communications and greater security and of increased fertility due to the labor-tax pressures of the Culture System; but not, save possibly for a brief initial period, as a result of generally rising Indonesian living standards.[21]

This is not the place for a detailed exposé regarding Java's high rates of population growth. Suffice it to say that his points are all relevant, that he probably underestimated the, however slightly, rising standards of living, and that he missed out on smallpox vaccination for the nineteenth century, and quinine and species sanitation, both against malaria, for the late nineteenth and early twentieth centuries.

However, most interesting of all, is what he says about rising fertility due to labor-tax pressure. This, among (historical) demographers is now better known as the demand-for-labor response. Recent research on Indonesian economic and demographic history suggests that an increased labor burden, with or without remuneration, has led historically (examples come from nineteenth and early twentieth-century Java and Sulawesi) to increased fertility, as much of the burden rested on women, who then wanted more children in order to share this burden, as children started assisting them at a very early age. The mechanism through which the increased labor burden was translated into higher fertility was the shorter breastfeeding period, and therefore the shorter period of lactational amenorrhea, and in the case of higher income possibly a drop in the age of marriage.[22]

Thus we return to the Industrious Revolution: people – and certainly women – started to work harder, either when they expected an increased income from the production of a certain crop or artisanal item, for instance because cheaper and safer transport led to a growing demand, or when labor burdens increased due to higher taxes in kind. In both cases women could wish to have more children, while their potential fertility increased because the heavier labor burden might shorten the period of breastfeeding, thus putting an earlier end to lactational amenorrhea (if they had not wanted these extra children, they could have use contraceptive methods or terminated their pregnancies or even committed infanticide, neither of which was frowned upon in many Indonesian and other Asian societies). Women might also desire to have more children to aid them, when they were in the

---

[20] Geertz 1963, 80 (note 58).
[21] Geertz 1963, 137.
[22] Boomgaard 1989, 192–5; Henley 2006, 315–19; Boomgaard 2007a, 212–13.

situation described by Geertz – more labor being needed to acquire a higher rice yield. There is no need to bring sugar into this story.

The first type of growth has also been called "Smithian growth," after Adam Smith, and is based on division of labor and regional specialization when good government, including law and order, or falling transport costs led to an increase in trade.[23] It is possible that this type of growth had been going on in Java during the nineteenth century, and probably to a lesser degree during the early twentieth century as well.

It could also be argued that some "Boserupian growth," after Ester Boserup, occurred, because in many areas more labor had been applied to the land, resulting in increased yields and reduced fallow.[24]

Much of the growth of the Javanese rural economy after ca. 1900, however, was a matter of expanding arable lands through land clearing. In areas where marginal productivity was (almost) zero, those who did not own land could often still clear new lands in the upland regions, if they did not want to (or could not) leave the agricultural sector entirely. Increased production of maize and cassava bears witness to this process.

A new growth spurt of the rural economy had to wait until the 1970s, with high rates of investment in the rural sector (Green Revolution, High Yielding Varieties, artificial fertilizer, rural credit, expansion of irrigation). Geertz, however, had been writing around 1960, when the agricultural sector was, indeed, stagnating.

CONCLUSION

Ironically, our statistical analysis points to a strong link between sugar and livestock, a factor missed by Geertz. It is through the production of maize and cassava – again, two factors neglected by Geertz – in the upland regions that this link appears to be established. It is likely that sugar attracted livestock, and livestock attracted sugar.

Our analysis has also shown that there was a fair chance that sugar would be grown on a high proportion of the sawahs if population density was high, wet-rice yields were high, and the quantity of arable lands per capita was low, while the chance of the proportion of sugar being above average would increase perceptibly if the average landholding per capita in the surrounding Residency would be low as well.

There is no evidence, however, that sugar cultivation led to high population densities and high rice yields. But it may have contributed to the local survival of fairly large proportions of smallholdings, by employing many smallholders, who constituted a class of part-time proletarians. However,

---

[23] See, e.g., Maddison 2005, 17.
[24] See, e.g., Boomgaard 1989, 203–4; Van Zanden 2000, 22.

sugar is not needed for this – in other parts of Java that role was played by (for instance) coffee.

In sum, it can be said that in areas of high population growth, average landholdings were small as a matter of course, and yields on the small- and dwarfholdings had to be high for lack of alternative sources of a similar income (combined with cultural preference, and possibly some compulsion from both the Javanese and the Dutch colonial state).

This state of affairs was the result of traditional agricultural intensification by smallholders (partly Smithian, partly Boserupian growth). After ca. 1880, rice yields stagnated (in contrast to what Geertz had argued), and most agricultural growth was generated by the clearing of new land, where more often than not non-rice crops were grown, such as maize and cassava. It was, therefore, possible that (again in contrast to what Geertz predicted) agricultural output and consumption per capita went on increasing, although not by much.

As demonstrated, Geertz got many of his facts regarding Javanese economic growth wrong, and for some of the links between sugar and rice he postulated there is little evidence. Therefore, the term Agricultural Involution could, in our view, be dropped. The usual terminology of economic historians suffices to describe what happened in Java during the nineteenth and early twentieth centuries.

ACKNOWLEDGEMENTS

The idea for this chapter was born when both authors spent their sabbatical at the Netherlands Institute for Advanced Study in the Humanities and Social Sciences (NIAS), Wassenaar, in 2003/4. This cooperation, by two authors formerly unacquainted, is an example of how NIAS can bring people together and stimulate research that otherwise might never have been carried out. We are grateful to the NIAS personnel for their unstinting support, and in particular thank Anneke Vrins-Aarts for converting the numerical data for 1920 published in the *Landbouwatlas* into a database.

APPENDIX

In the preceding pages correlations between percentage of sawahs under sugar cane and various other variables are presented. This appendix provides background data and statistics in order to explain some of the outcomes observed. Its character is necessarily more technical than the main text of the chapter.

Analysis at the Residency level

One of the problems in analyzing the data regarding cane on sawahs at the Residency level is that there are only 19 Residencies with valid data for this

Rice, Sugar, and Livestock in Java, 1820–1940

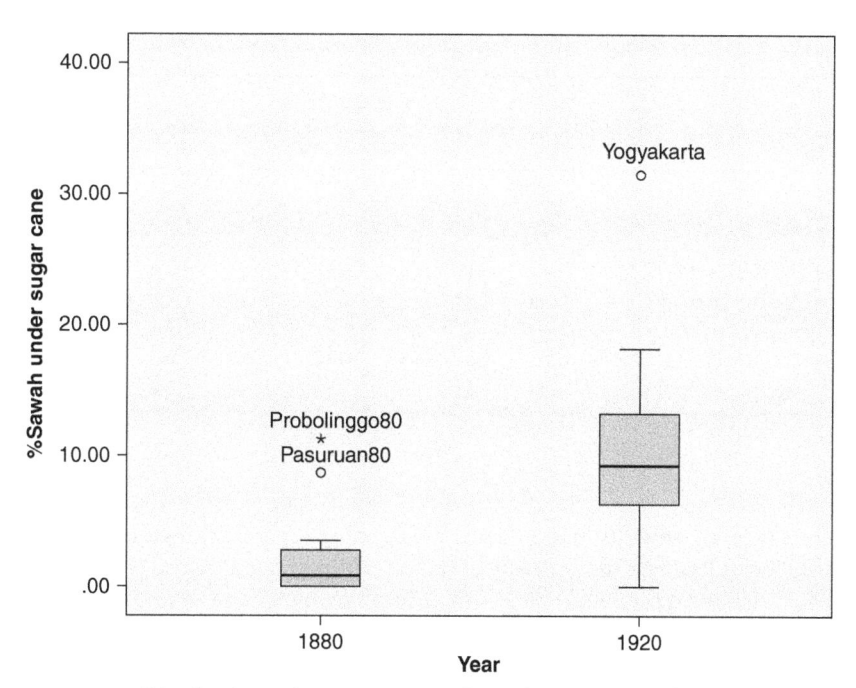

FIGURE 2.1 Distributions of percentage sawahs under sugar cane for the years 1880 and 1920.

variable in 1880 and 15 in 1920, so that statistics such as correlations are easily influenced by a single Residency with strongly deviating values. In this respect it is more insightful to look at the graphs of the relations in combination with the statistics than at summary measures such as means and correlations alone.

The interpretations in this chapter are primarily based on correlations with percentage sawahs under cane. Before looking at the correlations let us examine and compare the distributions of the variable "percentage sawahs under cane" at the Residency level for the two years under consideration

Each boxplot in Figure 2.1 shows the distribution of the variable in the year indicated. The size of the box is determined by the middle 50 percent of the observations and the bar indicates the median, the point that divides the distribution into its lower and upper half. Noteworthy is that the distribution in 1880 is characterized by very little variation. Apart from Probolinggo and Pasuruan no Residency had more than 5 percent sawahs under sugar cane. In 1920 not only the percentage of sawahs under cane had increased considerably but in addition sizeable differences emerged between the Residencies. Such variability is generally necessary to obtain high correlations with other variables. The Residency Yogyakarta was exceptional given its high

TABLE 2.4 *Correlations of percentage sawahs under cane with other variables.*

	Residencies						Districts	
	1880		1920 + Yogyakarta		1920 − Yogyakarta		1920	
Variable	R^2	R	R^2	R	R^2	R	R^2	R
Sawahs per capita	.12	−.34	.36	−.60	.25	−.49	.04	−.20
Arable land per capita	.01	−.11	.44	−.66	.21	−.45	.13	−.36
Wet rice per capita	.03	−.18	.27	−.52	.05	−.22	<.01	−.04
Population density	<.01	.02	.23	.48	.20	.44	.15	.39
Wet rice per unit of sawah	.01	.09	.12	.34	.22	.46	.11	.33

percentage of sawahs under cane in 1920 (32 percent), while all other Residencies had less than 20 percent.

Because the sample size is so small (only 23 Residencies in all and even smaller numbers with valid data for sugar cane on sawahs) it has been checked for each calculation for the year 1920 to what extent Yogya has a serious influence on the statistics calculated, in particular the correlations (see Table 2.4).

First we present an overview of the correlations of percentage sawahs under cane with a number of relevant variables. Note that although there are 444 districts, only 152 had valid data for sawahs under cane.

The correlations in Table 2.4 confirm that the variability in percentage sawahs under cane in 1880 is probably too small to find large systematic relations with other variables. Only the correlation with sawahs per capita (R = −.34) looks potentially interesting (see main text). On the other hand the correlations in 1920 are not only larger, but show also a fairly consistent pattern, in that the correlations with quantities per head are always negative, which is also true for the 1880 data. It would appear, therefore, that a relatively large availability of land and rice per capita, is not conducive to sugar cultivation. In contrast, high population density and high rice yields per unit of sawah (which are interrelated factors) go together with high percentages of sawah under cane. It is also evident that the data for Yogyakarta with its large percentage sugar cane sawahs is highly influential in determining some correlations. Overall it seems best to rely on the correlations without Yogya as the better representation of the statistical relationships in general.

Apart from the signs of the correlations, comparing the results for the Residencies with those of the districts seems difficult because their correlations are rather different. We present separate analyses for the districts later.

Rice, Sugar, and Livestock in Java, 1820–1940

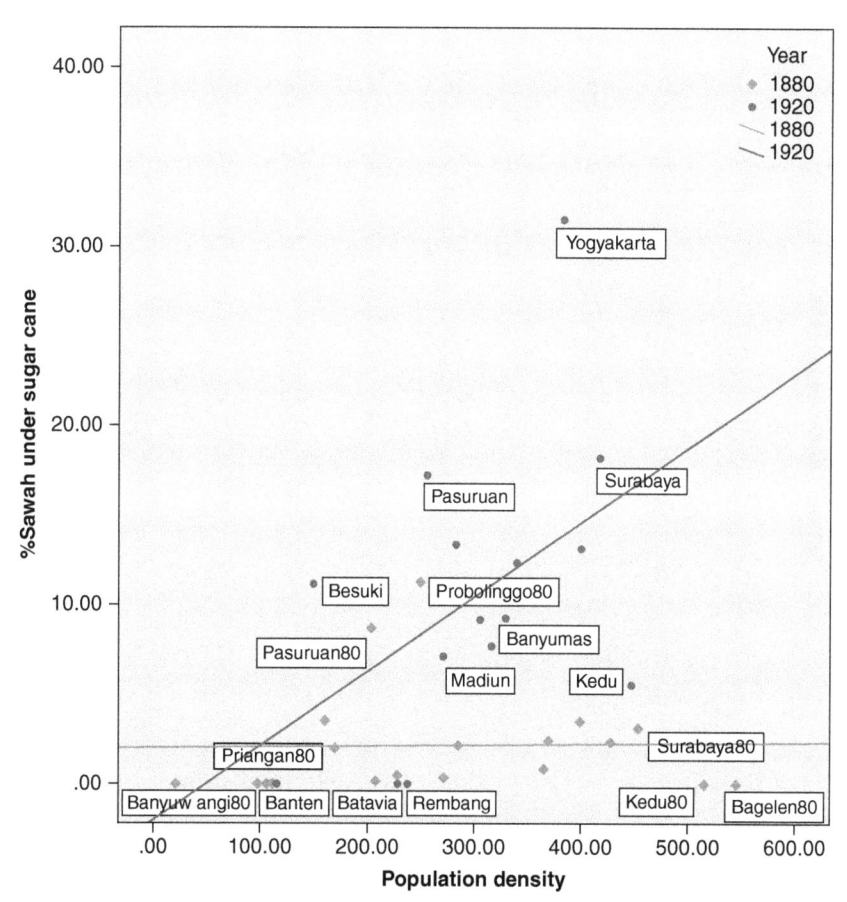

FIGURE 2.2 Relations between percentage sawahs under cane and population density for 1880 and 1920.
*1880 Residencies have the suffix 80; no suffix is used for 1920.

Figure 2.2 shows that the percentage of sawahs under cane was virtually independent of the population density in 1880 ($R = .02$), but there is a strong correlation in 1920 ($R = .44$; without Yogyakarta). The Residencies of Batavia, Rembang, and Banten had next to no sugar cane sawahs. In 1880 Probolinggo and Pasuruan were the only Residencies with sizeable amounts of sugar cane on their sawahs.

The $R^2 = .25$ ($R = .49$, without Yogyakarta) for 1920, $R^2 = .12$ ($R = .34$) for 1880, but note that the size of the correlation is primarily due to the values for Probolinggo and Pasuruan. For both years we observe a decreasing proportion of sugar sawahs as the sawah area per person increases (Figure 2.3).

From Figure 2.4 we deduce that there is no relation between these variables in 1880 ($R = .09$), but a sizable relation in 1920 ($R = .46$, without Yogyakarta).

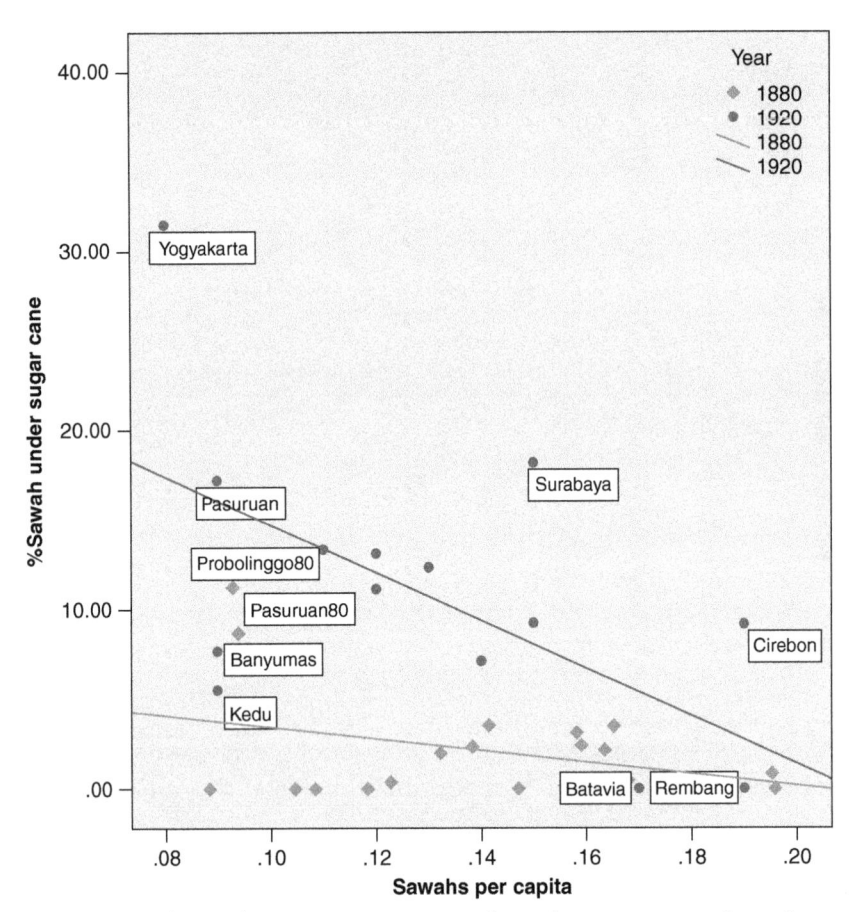

FIGURE 2.3 Relations between percentage sawahs under sugar cane and sawah area per capita for 1880 and 1920.

Thus, the higher the rice yield per unit sawah the larger the proportion of sawahs under cane.

Figure 2.5 shows that in 1880 there is a negligible relation between the two depicted variables, but a reasonable correlation in 1920, reinforced by the results from Yogyakarta ($R = -.22$, without Yogya, and $-.52$ including Yogya). This implies that as the availability of wet rice per capita increases, the proportion of sawahs planted to sugar drops.

The variables depicted in Figure 2.6 show, again, a negligible relation in 1880, but a fair correlation in 1920, reinforced by the results from Yogyakarta ($R = -.45$, without Yogya, and $-.66$ including Yogya). Thus, the more arable land per capita the lower the percentage of sawahs planted with cane.

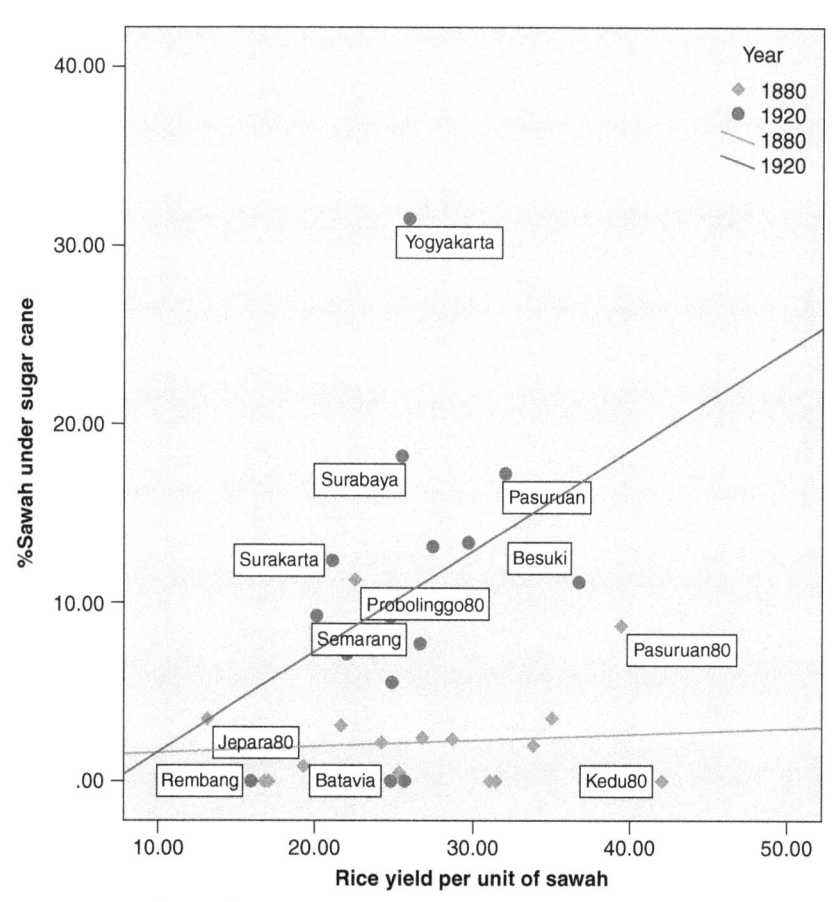

FIGURE 2.4 Relations between percentage sawahs under cane and rice yield per unit sawah for 1880 and 1920.

Analyses at the District Level

The number of districts is far larger than the number of Residencies, so that a more comprehensive analysis is possible. When comparing the results at the Residency and the district levels, it is important to realize that Residencies were not agriculturally homogeneous areas. As the districts were much smaller, they were usually more homogeneous, producing more contrasting data (for instance, almost no cane versus high proportions of cane). Because of this, one is more likely to really measure what one intends to measure. We cannot restrict ourselves to the district level as much information is only available at Residency level, particularly for 1880. Moreover, the influence of livestock can only be examined at the Residency level as no district-level livestock data survived.

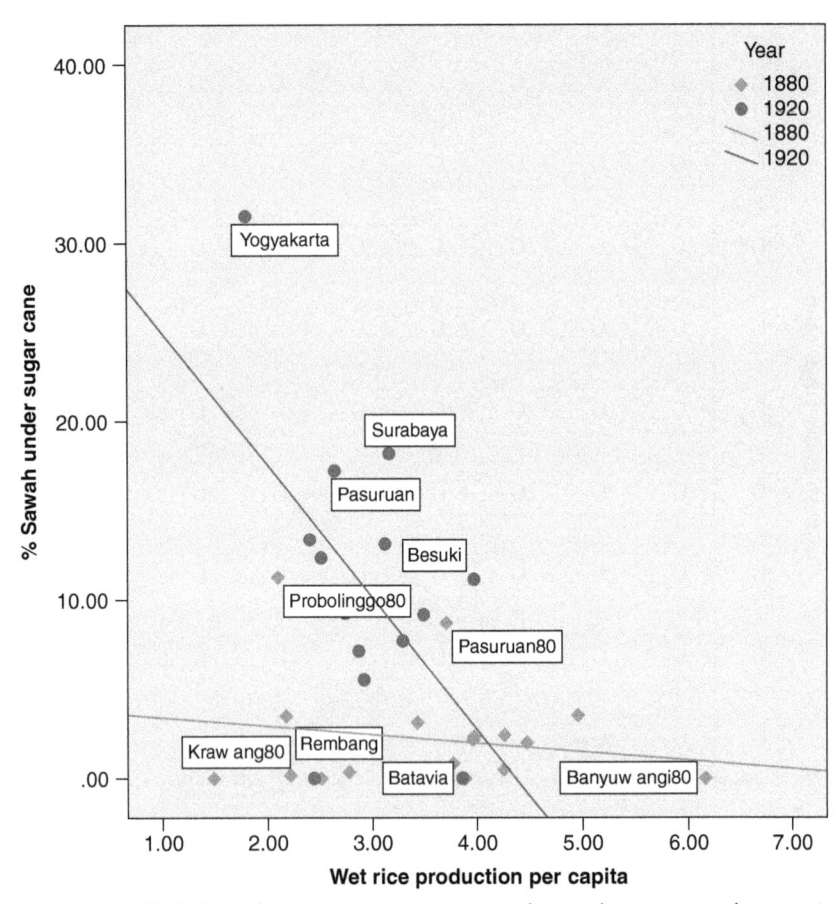

FIGURE 2.5 Relations between percentage sawahs under cane and wet rice production per capita, 1880 and 1920.

A quick impression of the heterogeneity of the Residencies with respect to percentage of sawahs under cane can be obtained by looking at Figure 2.7, which shows the distribution for each Residency. As before, the boxes in the plot show the values for the middle 50 percent of the districts in a Residency and each of the "whiskers" at the end of the box represents the lower or higher 25 percent of the districts. In Pekalongan the district numbered 131 is an outlier with an unusually high percentage of sawahs under cane for that Residency. The wide spread of the percentages within a Residency illustrates the agricultural differences within those areas.

One of the worrying aspects of the data is that the percentages of sawahs under cane are only available for 167 of the 444 districts. However, as none of the percentages are equal to zero, it is highly likely that the missing

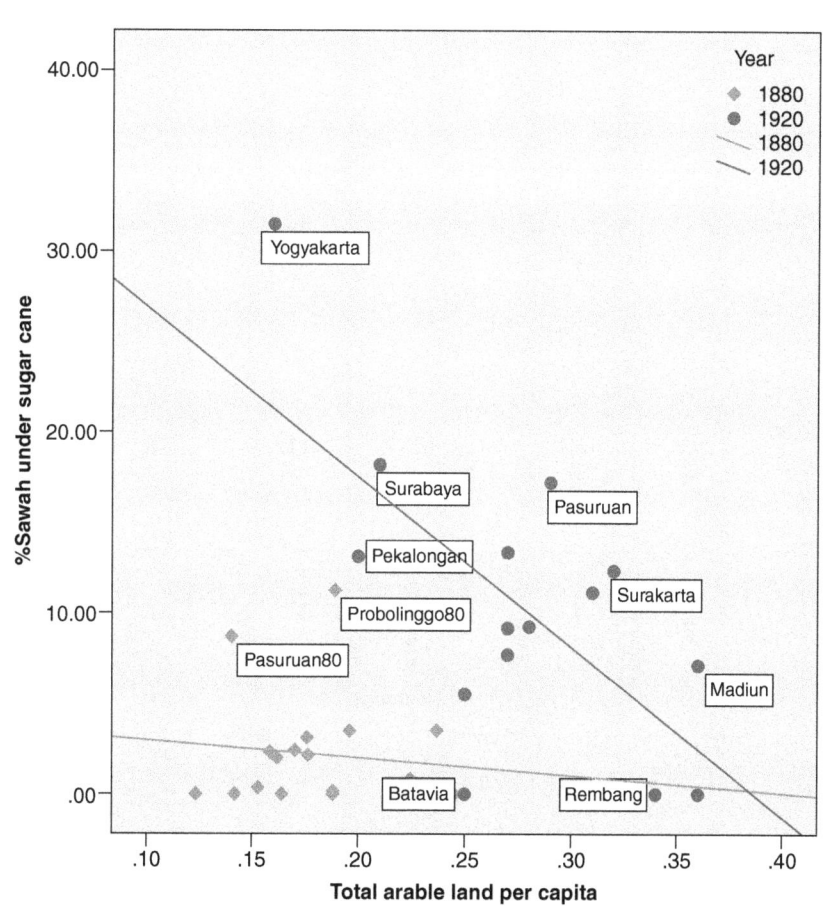

FIGURE 2.6 Relations between percentage sawahs under cane and arable land per capita for 1880 and 1920.

data indicate that there were no sugar cane sawahs in the relevant districts. However, the possibility that in a (small) number of cases "missing data" do, indeed, represent just that – the absence of data, cannot be excluded.

The analyses below are based on those districts with non-missing values for percentage of sawahs under cane, thereby excluding among others seven urban districts, and also all districts of the Residencies of Batavia, Banten, Priangan, Rembang, and Madura. After eliminating these areas we ended up with 160 districts. In total there were 152 districts that had valid observations for all six variables under consideration.

The most important question to be addressed here is which variables are the best predictors of the percentage sawahs under cane in the 152 districts.

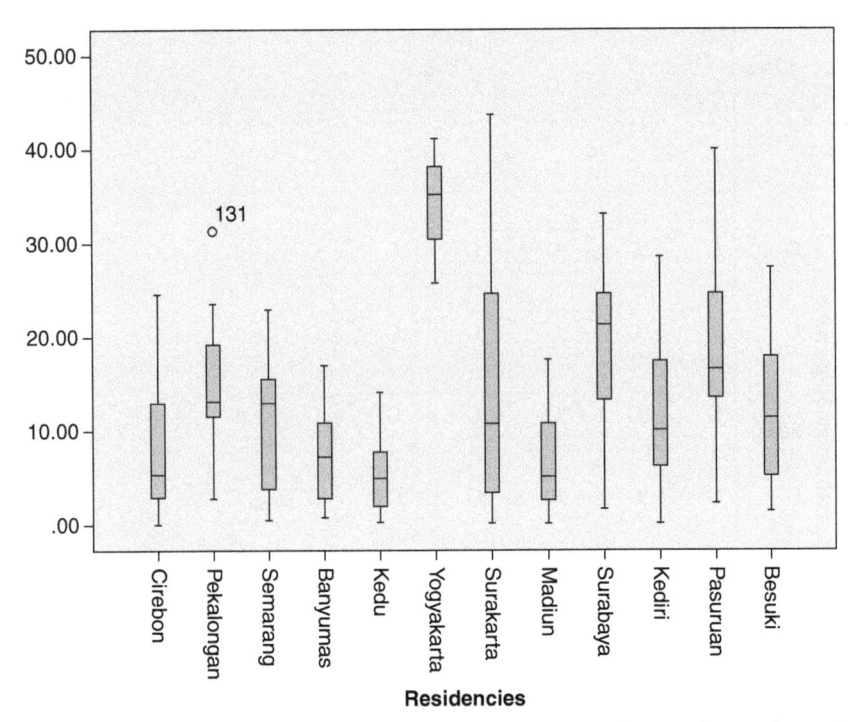

FIGURE 2.7 Distribution of percentages of sugar cane sawahs per district for each Residency in 1920.

To this end correlations were computed and regression analyses were carried out.

From Table 2.5 it is evident that population density ($R = .45$), wet rice per unit sawah ($R = .39$), and percentage arable land ($R = .28$) are the most important predictors for proportion sawahs under cane. However, two of the predictors are very highly correlated ($R = .65$): when the proportion arable land of the total area is high, population density is high as well. This means that for the analysis these variables carry the same predictive power and are more or less interchangeable. Our preliminary analyses showed that population density is a slightly better predictor so that we will restrict ourselves to this variable and rice per sawah to predict percentage sawahs under cane.

A regression analysis showed that for the 152 districts 32 percent of the differences in proportion sawahs under cane can be predicted by the population density of the district and the wet rice yield per unit sawah. The contribution to the prediction is 18 percent for population density and 10 percent for rice per sawah while their shared contribution is 4 percent ($R = .67$; $R^2 = .32$).

TABLE 2.5 *Correlations of the agricultural variables for districts.*

	% Sugar cane sawahs	Population density	Wet rice per unit sawah	% Arable land per total area	Sawahs per capita	Wet rice per capita
Percentage sugar cane sawahs	1.00	.45	.39	.28	−.14	.02
Population density	.45	1.00	.05	.65	−.23	−.06
Wet rice per unit sawah	.39	.05	1.00	−.11	−.28	.17
Percentage arable land per total area	.28	.65	−.11	1.00	.13	.15
Sawahs per capita	−.14	−.23	−.28	.13	1.00	.65
Wet rice per capita	.02	−.06	.17	.15	.65	1.00

The Role of Livestock (Residency Level)

The *Landbouwatlas* also presents information on livestock (buffalo and cattle) in the Residencies in 1920. There is also quantitative information on livestock for 1880, by Residency, but as they were not recorded in the same way in both years, it is difficult to assess for specific areas how the numbers of cattle and buffalo developed. But we can examine correlations as they are based on standardized units and are, therefore, independent of differences in scale.

Figure 2.8 shows that the numbers of livestock per unit of arable land in both years were distributed relatively regularly except that in 1880 Banyuwangi had a much larger quantity of livestock per unit of land than any other Residency. However, it should be noted that in Banyuwangi only 5 percent of the total surface area consisted of arable land while population density was extremely low. Unfortunately no information is available for this Residency in 1920 (as it had been merged with Besuki).

There is a very large correlation for the numbers of livestock per unit of land in 1880 and 1920 ($R = .76$), be it that for only 13 Residencies information is available for both years. As Figure 2.9 shows, the relative positions of the Residencies over time with respect to livestock have not changed much.

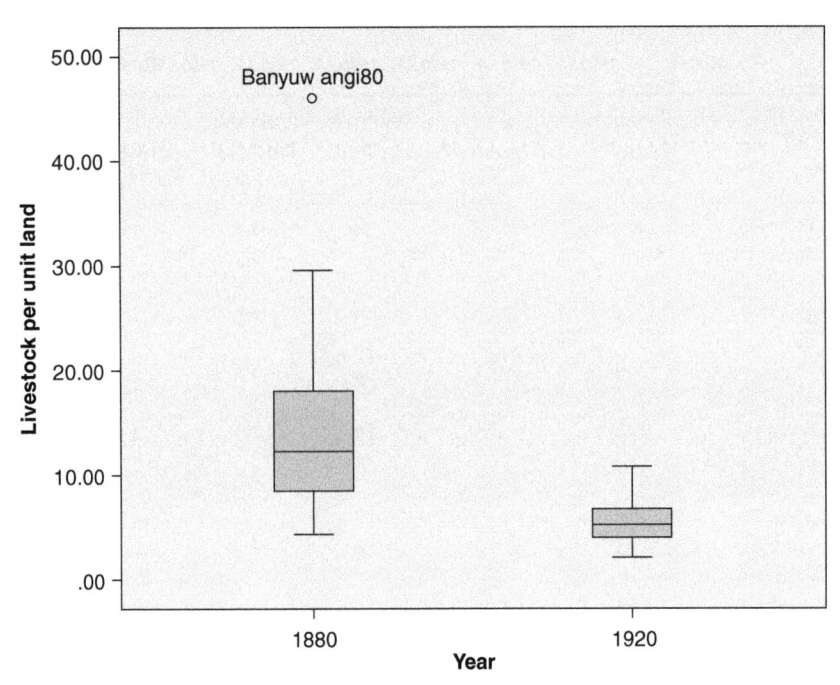

FIGURE 2.8 Livestock per unit of arable land in 1880 and 1920.

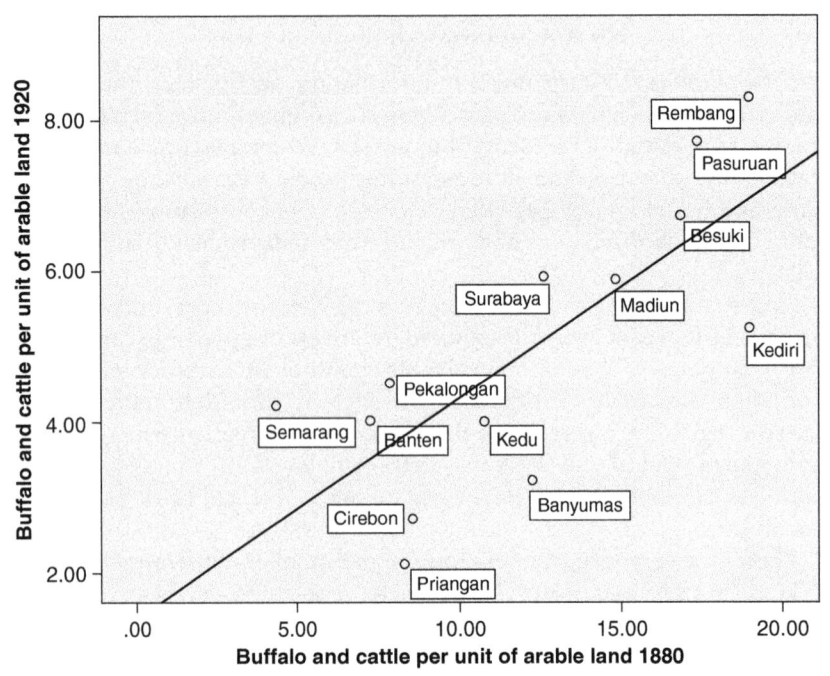

FIGURE 2.9 Relation between numbers of livestock in 1880 and 1920 at Residency level.

TABLE 2.6 *Correlations of livestock per unit of arable land with other variables at Residency level.* *

	Residencies		
Variable	1880 (N = 19) R	1880 (N = 18; without Banyuwangi) R	1920 (N = 17) R
Wet rice per capita	.24	-.34	-.70
Sawahs per capita	.02	-.55	-.38
Sawahs per unit of arable land	-.14	-.32	-.31
%Maize per unit of arable land	–	–	.61
%Cassava per unit of arable land	–	–	.44

*The data from 1880 and 1920 had 13 Residencies in common.

Banyuwangi was such an outlier in 1880 that it should be excluded from the correlations between livestock and the rice variables. If we do so, the data for 1880 and 1920 shows general consistency. Based on Table A4 we can say that numbers of livestock were inversely related to variables representing rice production and rice land, and in 1920 positively related to maize and cassava production.

The statistical relations between cassava and maize on the one hand and livestock on the other can only be studied for 1920. From Table 2.6 we discern that the correlations of livestock with percentage maize per unit of arable land ($R = .61$) and with percentage cassava per unit of arable land ($R = .44$) were considerable and positive, indicating that Residencies with much maize and cassava also had large numbers of livestock.

The situation for Yogyakarta in 1920 was somewhat different from the other Residencies in that it had a relatively large number of livestock, scored high in terms of cassava production, but medium to low in terms of maize. Yogya also produced much cane, to which a large presence of livestock might have contributed, and in turn stimulating stockbreeding.

3

A Desire to Eat Well: Rice and the Market in Eighteenth-Century China

Sui-Wai Cheung

In 1653 the 61-year-old Hangzhou scholar and historian Tan Qian completed his 108-chapter chronicle of the Ming dynasty, and realized his dream to visit Beijing. Built by the Yongle Emperor in the Ming in 1421, inherited by the Qing dynasty in 1644, the imperial capital was a repository of historical memories, as well as home to some famous rare book collectors, and Tan had imagined visiting the city for the 42 years it took him to write his history of the Ming. When his fellow villager Zhu Zhixi, an official in the court, invited Tan to work for him as a secretary, Tan accepted the invitation happily.[1]

The two-month journey from central to northern China did not dampen his enthusiasm; on arrival in Beijing, Tan Qian visited book collectors, conducted interviews with nobles, officials, and eunuchs of the previous Ming dynasty, and explored Beijing and outlying areas, often on foot in order to witness the place and its people from close up; whenever he discovered something interesting, even though it was only a ruined piece of wall, he took notes on it.[2] He walked until his feet became swollen and blistered; and he was often lost, but his passion for history as revealed in Beijing was not quenched by these problems.[3] He became homesick; and he missed eating rice.

Tan Qian did not like the dry, dusty weather of Beijing; in a letter to a friend, Tan grumbled that his nose and mouth were always filled with dirt.[4] But his worst problem was food. In Hangzhou, rice was the staple, but the major crops in northern China were wheat, millet, and sorghum. Tan saw rice fields scattered about in the metropolitan area of Beijing, but the price of rice

---

[1] Wu 1960, 2–4.
[2] Wu 1960, 5.
[3] Years later, he published a book called *Beiyou lu* (*Travels in Northern China*) with a preface written by Zhu Zhixi, who noted that Tan walked so much his feet blistered.
[4] Wu 1960, 6.

was still twice that in the south. For lunch and dinner northern people ate cakes made of broken wheat, millet, buckwheat, and beans. Unless they had guests, they did not cook rice. As the price was exorbitant, they purchased rice only in small amounts.[5] Tan did not get over his homesickness, and in 1656 obtained permission to return to Hangzhou.

The story of Tan Qian is evidence that rice was not always a staple in northern China. In fact, it only became so in recent decades, presumably due to widespread rice farming in northeastern provinces along with state-subsidized policies, especially in railway transportation. But even during the first half of the twentieth century rice was only a staple in southern China. Between 1928 and 1937, John Lossing Buck and his students in Jinning University studied agricultural land use in 168 districts in 22 provinces. Based on their data, Buck divided China into a northern wheat region and a southern rice region.[6]

In the rice region, cropping patterns varied due to differences in climate, soil, and other physical elements. In the northern district of Lower Yangzi River, for instance, farmers grew a crop of wheat and a crop of rice, while in its southern district the two crops were rice and tea (Figure P.1a). Farther south, farmers could produce two crops of rice a year.[7]

Many scholars tied population growth in China to rice cultivation. Ping-ti Ho, for instance, argued that the introduction of early-ripening Champa rice initiated an agricultural revolution that resulted in the population growth between 1000 and 1850. He noted that Champa rice (which matured in 60 to 100 days, unlike local varieties that took 150 days) made double-cropping possible, thereby increasing the food supply and ensuring population growth. According to Ho the dissemination of early-ripening rice and the spread of double-cropping was necessarily a slow process. Up to the end of the Southern Song (1127–1279) the early-ripening varieties were grown to a significant extent only in Zhejiang, southern Jiangsu, Fujian, and Jiangxi. During the Yuan (1279–1368) and Ming (1368–1644) the cultivation of early-ripening rice became widespread in the southwestern provinces and in Hubei and Hunan as well, the two provinces that have since become China's rice bowl. By the time of Matteo Ricci (1553–1610) double- and sometimes triple-rice cropping was common in Guangdong.[8]

But increasing rice farming does not necessarily instigate demographic growth. The weakness of Ho's population study was that he ignored the role of the market in food supply and demand. Even in the late imperial period, China was not a single economic unit. Some districts typically

---

[5] Tan 1960, 314.
[6] Buck 1956, 25, 39, 41. See his figure 1.3.1.
[7] Buck 1956, 27.
[8] Ho 1974, 169–95.

consumed more rice than they could produce, and the market became the institution that assured them of a grain supply from other districts. The successful development and dissemination of the new, early-ripening varieties of rice provided the context for China's self-sufficiency, but what drove that development was a market that balanced supply and demand.

When the market is examined, it becomes clear that rice consumption was based on people's food preferences and on what they could afford. The first question I want to address in this chapter is: "Why did people eat rice?" It is true that the climate in Buck's rice region in central and southern China was good for growing rice, but rice was not the only staple crop that grew well there. Why, then, did people choose to eat rice instead of another staple? My second question is: "What kinds of rice did they eat?" The answers to these two questions will enable us to understand the nature of the long-distance rice trade in late imperial China.

I shall examine the different strains of rice that were sold on the two major long-distance trade routes – the Yangzi River in central China (Area A on Figure 3.1) and the West River in southern China (Area B on Figure 3.1) – with an eye to how they fared in the market. Together, these two areas formed the most important rice consuming areas in traditional China.

TWO MACRO-REGIONAL RICE MARKETS

In eighteenth-century China, two large macro-regional, integrated markets took shape around the cities of Suzhou in the north and Guangzhou in the south. (Midway between Suzhou and Guangzhou, Quanzhou in Fujian made a third, but relatively small market; Quanzhou could import rice from both large markets, but mainly got its rice from Taiwan.)

In the first millennium the city of Suzhou was mostly low-lying plains and marshes. Then in 1127, when foreign conquest of north China forced the Song court to move south to Hangzhou, the Huai River became its foremost northern border in the east, and the Yangzi River a second northern frontier. Since the grain tax did not provide enough food for soldiers garrisoned on the Huai, the Song government had to buy rice from the market. Hangzhou, the capital, began to import rice from neighboring prefectures, especially from Suzhou.[9] Thus, Suzhou's agricultural development followed political events.

By the same token, the grain trade on the Yangzi began to decline in the latter half of the thirteenth century, when military skirmishes in the middle and lower Yangzi Valley disrupted the flow of traffic. In 1276 Hangzhou fell to Mongol invaders, and the resulting decline in Hangzhou's urban population reduced its need for long-distance grain. During the Yuan, the new

---

[9] Shiba 1968, 154–67.

FIGURE 3.1 Rice regions in China, ca. 1920–1950s, detail of overview map Figure P.1a.

capital was established at Beijing, far from the Yangzi; other than the grain tribute, the grain trade between the two regions was minimal.

In the late sixteenth century, the grain trade revived and flourished on the Yangzi. Due to commercial development, the Yangzi delta had a chronic shortage of local grain and needed to import it from upstream. This long-distance grain market expanded to include rice from Jiangxi, Hunan, and Hubei.[10] The central rice market now became Suzhou, which was a commercial emporium, a place to trade for silk and tea. Importing grain from upstream on the Yangzi, and raw cotton from North China via the canal,

---
[10] Kawakatsu 1992, 206–19.

Suzhou exported finished goods and luxury products in all directions, but particularly to Beijing and other cities. Merchants from its neighboring prefecture of Huizhou were well positioned to tap into this rising economy. They sojourned in large numbers in Suzhou, buying silk along the Yangzi River and the Grand Canal. They also were involved directly with overseas commerce.[11]

The West River region, as the other large integrated rice market, had the city of Guangzhou in Guangdong as its distribution centre. Guangdong imported rice from Fujian, Jiangxi, and Hunan, but most of all from Guangxi, via the West River. Like Suzhou, Guangzhou had been a fertile region in the twelfth century, and it exported rice via sea routes to neighboring provinces like Jiangsu, Zhejiang, and Fujian. But from the sixteenth century onward, the rice supply fell, and the city had to import rice from Guangxi.[12]

A DESIRE TO EAT WELL

Rice farming requires extensive capital and labor. Rice grows in water, and farmers had to inundate their fields to transplant the rice, and then drain the fields before harvesting it. Rainfall could provide only part of the water; most farmers had to work hard to get enough for their fields. The simplest way to get water, by hauling it from a stream in a bucket, was slow, hard work. The invention of the Chinese dragon wheel saved farmers from this kind of labor.[13] Irrigation was even more efficient: farmers built levees and canals to direct the water, sometimes making openings in the dikes or levees so water could flow from one paddy to another. But these tools and construction projects involved a large capital investment, and even when farmers could afford the cost, rice farming was labor-intensive. Transplanting the rice plants from the seedbed to the paddy field, in particular, was dirty, back-breaking work. It meant bending over all day to plant the rice, up to the knees (and the elbows) in mud and water, under the hot sun. Why, in the face of these difficulties, did traditional Chinese choose to plant rice?

During the eighteenth century rice was widely cultivated and eaten as a staple food in central and southern China, but so were wheat, millet, oats, buckwheat, yams, and sweet potatoes.[14] Contemporary Chinese categorized

---

[11] Marmé 2005, 38–9, 147, 197.
[12] Chen 1992, 18–9.
[13] Hammond 1961, 28, 41–3, 58. The dragon's tail was a long trough with a series of boards fitted crosswise along a revolving rope or chain. As they followed one another along the trough, they brought the water with them. The body of the dragon was a wheel that the boards went over to turn back in the other direction. The boards were moved by a man pumping with his feet on a wheel fastened to one side. See ibid., p. 43.
[14] According to a report from a high Guangdong official in 1729, apart from rice, wheat, and oats, Guangdong farmers planted millet, yams, and buckwheat. See *Yongzhengchao hanwen zhupi zouzhe huibian*, vol. 15, 119.

rice as "main food" (*zhuliang*), and the other staples as "coarse food" (*zaliang*). In central China, the most frequently eaten coarse foods were wheat, millet, oats, buckwheat, and yams; in southern China, sweet potatoes were the most prevalent.

Sweet potatoes, a crop from the New World, were the survival crop of the poor.[15] In 1749 acting Jiangsu Governor Yaerhashan wrote: "With regard to the sweet potatoes in Fujian province, 60 to 70 per cent of the poor people rely on them for food. Each catty costs only 2 to 3 *wen* [of copper cash]." Two years later, Fujian Governor Pan Siju stated that: "The poor families in Zhangzhou and Quanzhou eat many sweet potatoes as their daily staple. Therefore, 60 to 70 per cent of [their] hilly land [is used] to grow sweet potatoes." In 1752, Chen Hongmou, who had in that year taken over as governor of Fujian, said in his memorial: "Nowadays sweet potatoes and other coarse food are bountifully harvested everywhere. They are cheap and filling. Poor people are glad to buy them for their meal."[16] In Guangdong, the situation was similar. A 1752 memorial by the Guangdong Governor stressed the importance of promoting sweet potato cultivation in Guangdong: "Poor people [settling] in the mountains and [by] the seas (*shanhai pinmin*) generally rely on [the crop] as their subsistence food."[17]

At the same time, Qing Chinese considered the sweet potato an inferior food, and better-off families avoided eating it. Although food preference is a complex subject, Tsou and Villareal gave some reasons for the aversion. First, eating sweet potatoes regularly caused flatulence or "gas." Second, the sweet potato's high sugar content elevated blood sugar and reduced the appetite, a disadvantage for those who wanted to eat other foods at their meals as well. Third, sweet potatoes were associated with poverty. People who had been poor and were no longer seldom ate sweet potatoes, which reminded them of suffering and hardship.[18] Another reason for avoiding sweet potatoes was probably the matter of social standing. The correlation of poverty with sweet potatoes made them a low-status food, so even if people had never been poor they would not consider eating them, no matter how good they tasted. While

---

[15] Sweet potatoes were an American tropical crop originally, introduced to China in the sixteenth century. It is believed that a Fujian merchant discovered the sweet potato when he was buying American silver in Manila. He brought the vegetable back to Fujian and recommended it to his provincial governor, who saw the benefit of growing a tropical drought-resistant plant that was also a high-yield crop. A 1604 essay written by a Fujian official stated that every farmer in his province had planted sweet potatoes ten years earlier. See Chen, Qianlong edition, vol. 4, 741–3.

[16] *Zhupi zouzhe*, reel no. 56, pp. 1809–15; Guoli gugong bowuyuan *Gong zhong dang Qianlong chao zou zhe*, vol. 1, 743; vol. 4, 182. Wang 1986, 89 also observed the widespread consumption of the sweet potato in Fujian.

[17] *Gongzhong dang Qianlongchao zouzhe*, vol. 4, 252.

[18] Tsou and Villareal 1982, 37–42.

the idea of "eating well" implies eating food that is healthy and delicious, it also implies eating food that is high status.

During the Great Leap Forward in the late 1950s, the Guangdong government encouraged sweet potato cultivation since it had found that the same *mu* (Chinese acre) of land that produced 350 catties of husked rice could yield as many as 5,000 catties of sweet potatoes. The obstacle to the policy was the age-old prejudice against sweet potatoes. People in Leizhou Peninsula, the southern tip of Guangdong province, even had a saying that eating sweet potatoes made a person stupid. They used the term "big sweet potato" (*da fanshu*) to denote a useless person. This "wrong thought," according to the Guangdong vice governor, was more entrenched in cities than in villages, where sweet potatoes were a staple food.[19]

In the eighteenth century, rice fetched a higher price than sweet potatoes, and farmers grew it wherever the natural environment allowed. Sweet potato cultivation in southern China was successful mainly because its growing season fit the rhythms of rice cultivation: sweet potatoes grew well in the sub-tropical cool season of southern China and became a good winter crop there.[20] The root plant was less popular in temperate central China because the winter was too cold for it; during the warm seasons most farmers preferred to plant rice, while in the winter they grew other coarse food like wheat and barley instead of sweet potatoes.[21]

PRECIOUS RICE

Rice was the staple of choice in central and southern China. In 1738, when southern Jiangsu Province, the wealthiest district in central China, reaped a poor harvest, the Shandong governor offered to sell the Jiangsu government Shandong millet and beans for a reduced price. Nasutu, the governor-general of Jiangsu, Jiangxi, and Anhui, dismissed this suggestion, saying, "The people in southern Jiangsu are used to eating rice, they do not eat coarse food."[22] In a memorial to the imperial court a month later, Nasutu added that Shandong millet and beans could be sold only in northern Jiangsu Province, where eating habits were similar to those in Shandong.[23] While Nasutu's tone indicated a snobbish pride in the wealthier lifestyle of southern Jiangsu, where people could afford to eat rice daily, it also showed that he had no confidence in being able to sell the coarse food within the district, even during a famine.

---

[19] An 1958, 10, 13.
[20] For the temperature requirements of the sweet potato, see Cai and Yang 2004, 22, 24.
[21] Buck 1956, 69.
[22] *Zhupi zouzhe*, reel no. 54, 2351–4.
[23] *Zhupi zouzhe*, reel no. 54, 2423–30.

There were two main varieties of rice, *jing* (also called *geng*) and *xian*. They were differentiated by the stickiness, or starch content, of the cooked grain. *Jing* rice, which required an annual temperature lower than 16°C, was grown mainly in northern China, and modern Japanese rice (or Japonica rice), characterized by its unique stickiness and texture, was its offspring.[24] *Xian* rice required an annual temperature of over 17°C. It grew in the hotter climates of southern and central China, and as it contained little starch was less sticky.

The districts around Lake Tai in the lower Yangzi valley grew *jing*, the rice from northern China. It is still unclear why (or when) people in this area, called Jiangnan, began to grow and consume *jing*. Nanjing, for instance, though a city in the same latitude, could grow only *xian*. The scholar You Xiuling suspected that *jing* was not cultivated in Jiangnan on a large scale until the southern Song period (1127–1279), when northern nobles and wealthy families, fleeing the invading Jushen tribes, migrated to Jiangnan. Their desire for *jing* rice could be satisfied because the climate of central China had just entered a cooler phase, one that was suitable for *jing*.[25] Due to this cooler climate, farmers could produce only one crop each year.

Jing rice farming was rare, practiced only in the Yangzi Delta. During the eighteenth century central and southern China grew *xian* rice. *Xian* had an early-season (*zaoji*) strain and a late-season (*wanji*) strain.[26] In the Yangzi valley of central China, the growing season was short so farmers had to choose to plant either early- or late-season *xian*, plus a non-rice crop in the remaining months. But in Guangdong and Fujian in southern China, farmers mostly grew two crops of *xian* in well-watered paddies between March and November, plus a crop of sweet potatoes in the winter.[27]

The nature of rice consumption in southern and central China varied according to the production output. Rice was grown in two crops a year in southern China. Although those "poor people settling in the mountains and by the seas" still relied on sweet potatoes as their subsistence food, many families could afford to eat rice, or mix rice with their sweet potatoes. The amount of sweet potatoes in their cooked rice depended on a family's income, and on how much they were willing to spend on daily food. By contrast, in provinces like Hunan and Jiangxi along the Yangzi valley, where farmers produced only a single crop of rice per year, rice was more precious, and therefore, it is likely that the local population consumed more sweet potatoes or other coarse food.

The small output of *jing* rice, which was grown only in the areas around Lake Tai in central China, made this rice even more precious and led to a

---

[24] Ding 1983, 61; Ding 1957/1983, 29.
[25] You 1986, 80–2.
[26] Ding 1983, 78.
[27] Buck 1956, 69.

special storage method called "*dongchongmi*" (rice hulled in the winter) in Jiangnan. In the twelfth lunar month, Jiangnan people collected their harvested rice, removed the grain husk, polished the rice until it was white, and put it into ceramic urns. Then they added water, and sealed and stored the urns. After two months or more, when the water had softened the rice and the rice turned a yellowish color, it was ready to cook.[28] Although no one stores rice this way any longer, the practice was common in Jiangnan in late imperial China, and guaranteed that people would have their local rice all year round. It also kept mice and insects from eating the stored rice.

Eighteenth-century scholar Shen Chiran, although a native of Jiangnan, criticized his neighbors for their dependence on *jing*. According to him, despite the high price and limited supply of *jing*, people in Jiangnan prefectures like Suzhou, Jiaxing, and Huzhou considered *xian* to be "inedible" (*bukeshi*). During his 18-year stay in Xinshi town, Huzhou, he discovered that local people "alert each other not to eat *xian*" (*xiangjie bushi*). Although he exhorted them to change their rice-eating habits, it was like "beating a drum in front of deaf people."[29]

Jing rice went for high prices throughout Jiangnan. Akifumi Norimatsu attributed its price to the long growing season and heavy input of water, fertilizers, and labor.[30] In addition to production costs, the high price of *jing* was the result of its limited supply: farmers could normally grow only a single rice crop annually and could not even keep all of it for local consumption because of the rice tribute, which went to Beijing.[31] Local demand for rice was great, but the supply of *jing* was small.

The price of *jing* made its consumption an index of wealth in Jiangnan. In the seventh lunar month of 1725, the Jiangsu Governor noted in a memorial to the Yongzheng Emperor that:

In Suzhou Prefectural City, all better-off families (*youyu zhijia*) ate local late-season rice. For each *shi* [of local *jing* rice], the price was 1.7 to 1.8 taels of silver. Rice for "normal" (*xunchang*) [families] was all "guest rice" (*kemi*) from Jiangxi and Huguang (Hunan and Hubei provinces). Currently the market price for each *shi* was between 1.32 and 1.38 taels.[32]

---

[28] Shen 1808/1986, 3/15a. See also a recent interview about "rice" (*mifan*) in an oral history project titled *Jiaxing jiyi* (Jiaxing Memories) conducted and published in the Internet by the Jiaxing Library, Zhejiang. http://www.jxlib.com/jiaxingzl/jxjy/wen/mf.htm [accessed July 17, 2014].

[29] Shen 1808/1986, 3/5a-b.

[30] Norimatsu 1985, 159.

[31] The court in Beijing, in order to pay the wages of officials and soldiers in the metropolitan areas, levied a tax of about 2.4 million *shi* of *jing* rice from the provinces of Jiangsu and Zhejiang annually, and transported it via the Grand Canal to Beijing. See the quota of the grain tribute tax in Table 1.1 in Cheung 2008, 144.

[32] Zhongguo diyi lishi dang'an guan 1989, vol. 5, 496. See also Norimatsu 1985, 160.

Xian was the rice most often traded along the Yangzi Valley. Every autumn the *xian* from Jiangxi, Hunan, and Hubei was shipped downriver to the Yangzi Delta. From there the junks sailed southward via the Grand Canal. After paying duties at the Hushu Customs House, merchants unloaded much of their *xian* at Fengqiao, a town 4 kilometers west of Suzhou city. A 1743 memorial by Jiangsu Governor Chen Dashou depicted the scene on its riverbanks:

> Suzhou, as the centre of all directions, relies on sojourning merchants for more than half of the rice it consumes [...]. For this reason, along the riverbanks of Fengqiao town, [the tasks of] unloading rice from junks and putting it into warehouses (*zhan*) are conducted every day.[33]

As the redistribution center for *xian* in Jiangnan, Fengqiao town was extremely prosperous, and it was the demand for *xian* in Suzhou and other neighboring cities that made it so.

In summation, the cultivation and consumption of *xian* rice was behind the prosperous development of the long-distance rice trade along the Yangzi Valley in central China during the eighteenth century. Although *jing* was grown in the Yangzi Delta, or Jiangnan area, it was expensive. Those who could afford to eat rice, but not the local *jing*, ate the *xian* imported from the middle Yangzi provinces. In the next section, we turn to the rice trade on the West River in southern China, a region where *jing* was rarely grown.

XIAN RICE ON THE WEST RIVER

Guangdong Province was particularly suited to rice farming, with an elevation of 500 to 1,000 meters and a relatively flat topography. The most fertile area of the province was the Pearl River Delta, which covered 10 counties. The abundant water supply was a boon for rice farmers, as was the hot climate. The mean temperature was 14°C. in February, the coldest month, and 29°C. in July, the hottest. Humidity was high, and rainfall well-distributed at about 175 cm annually.[34]

Most of the land in Guangdong produced three crops a year, two of rice, and one of coarse food. Qu Dajun (1630–1696), a famous scholar in the Pearl River Delta, noted in his work *New Treatise on Guangdong* (*Guangdong xinyu*), that the harvest for the first crop (early-season strain) was between the fifth and sixth lunar months, and the second crop (late-season strain) between the ninth and tenth lunar months. After the autumn rice harvest, some farmers planted winter wheat in the same field. Wheat was never a daily food in Guangdong; people made wheat noodles and buns, but mostly as food for guests. Also, as Qu pointed out, the wheat grown in Guangdong was so

---

[33] *Lufu zouzhe*, reel no. 49, 2039.
[34] Buck 1956. 82–3.

inferior to that in central and northern China that some farmers simply let their land lie fallow in the winter, which saved them a lot of manure fertilizer for the spring rice crop.[35]

Both the early and late season rice strains were *xian*: early-season *xian* was higher in yield, but considered "hot" (*re*) in nature, while late-season *xian* was "cold" (*liang*) in nature and therefore more healthful; it deserved to be called an "excellent grain" (*jiagu*).[36] While the "hot" and "cold" designations of traditional Chinese medicine may sound strange to modern science, the point is that Guangdong people considered late-season *xian* healthier than, and therefore superior to, early-season *xian*. (Consumption preferences for seasonal rice varieties also occurred in other rice-farming societies. As shown in the study by Lauren Minsky in this book, in Punjab and Bengal autumn rice was more valued and expensive than spring rice.)

Even though Guangdong grew two crops of rice a year, it imported a great deal of rice, also *xian*, from its neighboring province Guangxi via the West River, first to Wuzhou Prefecture at the convergence of the Gui River and the Liu River, and then to the big cities of Zhaoqing, Foshan, and Guangzhou. Throughout the eighteenth century, the rice trade on the West River was prosperous in the second half of the year, which covered both harvests of early- and late-season rice in Guangxi.

But although they ate Guangxi rice, Guangdong people preferred the local *xian*. E'erda, the governor of Guangdong, made this point in his 1732 memorial:

> Whenever the [local] rice is dear in Guangdong, merchants from Guangxi can certainly make a profit. However, when the price [of local rice] is low, Guangdong merchants and civilians loathe the thin small grains of Guangxi rice, which are inferior to those big round grains of Guangdong rice, [and under such circumstances] they choose the Guangdong rice, making Guangxi rice un-marketable [...] Therefore, whenever the local rice is cheap in Guangdong, Guangxi merchants hesitate.[37]

In other words, Guangxi rice had a share in the grain market of Guangdong not because of its high quality, but because of its low price. When the price of local rice plummeted in Guangdong, as happened in 1732, the rice trade from Guangxi immediately came to a halt.

To sum up, the nature of the long-distance rice trade on the West River echoed that on the Yangzi River. Both the Yangzi Delta and the Pearl River Delta grew large amounts of rice, and their rice suited the tastes of local people. As local rice was usually more expensive, people who could not afford

---

[35] Qu 1985, 373–8.
[36] Qu 1985, 373. Qu stated that the yield of late-season rice was only two-thirds that of early-season rice in Guangdong. See ibid., 374.
[37] Guoli gugong bowuyuan 1977–79, vol. 19, 797.

it would eat rice imported from upriver. The result was a flourishing long-distance rice trade on both rivers.

CONCLUSION: PRODUCTION AND CONSUMPTION IN PRE-MODERN CHINA AND THE WORLD

In the early twentieth century, agriculture and economy were perceived as two separate and unrelated concepts. Agriculture was left outside the discussion on economic development, even while no one negated its primary importance. In China, as shown by Seung-Joon Lee in Chapter 3, politicians in the Republican government believed that the lack of food grown within the country, and the resulting lack of self-sufficiency, posed a threat to national security in a hostile international environment. China looked to agricultural reform to feed its huge population, inviting foreign specialists like John Lossing Buck to help them develop high-yield rice and wheat varieties (see Chapter 3, this book). Although the Republican government, as well as the Communist government that followed, were both aware of the importance of agriculture, they based economic development on industrial development, especially that of heavy industries. Farmers seemed to have nothing to do with modernization.

Theodore Schultz (1902–1998) did much to introduce economics into the discipline of agricultural study. Schultz questioned the charge that farmers were ignorant of market activities: "What does illiteracy imply? The fact that people are illiterate does not mean that they are therefore insensitive to the standards set by marginal costs and returns in allocating the factors they have at their disposal." He argued that in every country of the world, even those regarded by the West as backward, farmers grew crops in response to the market. In Panajachel, Guatemala, the community did not function as an isolated subsistence economy, but was closely integrated into a larger market economy. The people were obviously hard-working, thrifty, and astute about selling their crops, renting land, and buying things for consumption and production. In America, the Native Americans calculated the value of their labor in producing crops for sale or for home consumption against working for hire. They rented and pawned parcels of land and bought their few producer goods with an eye on the return. All of their business, many be characterized as money economies organized in their households as both consumption and production units, with strongly developed markets that tended to be perfectly competitive. Likewise, in Punjab in the 1920s and 1930s, cotton farmers took about the same amount of time to adjust their production to changes in the market as did their United States counterparts.[38]

---

[38] Schultz 1964, 34–5, 42–4, 49–50.

In 1932, Richard Henry Tawney added China to the discussion of agricultural economy, arguing that Chinese villages were not self-sufficient units either. In a district of Shandong Province, for instance, while the farmers ate the sorghum they grew, they usually exported 50 percent of their wheat, while in the city of Chengdu, Sichuan Province, economic stress compelled farmers to sell most of their crops immediately after harvest. Thus, Tawney concluded that Chinese farming was not for subsistence, but attuned to the market. Not only commercial crops like cotton, tea, tobacco, and silk, but also food crops, were raised largely for sale. Using Buck's data on 2,866 Chinese farms, Tawney further suggested that more than a third of the rice, about half of the wheat, beans, and peas, two-thirds of the barley, and three-quarters of the sesame and vegetables were produced for the market. The farmers in Buck's study disposed of 53 percent of their total output off the farm.[39]

Evelyn Rawski showed that market conditions even influenced farmers' decisions on what to grow a thousand years ago. The introduction of early ripening or Champa rice into China in the eleventh century changed the nature of rice cultivation, allowing double cropping in the southern provinces such as Fujian. Champa rice also had drought resistant qualities that enabled it to be grown in poorer soil. While Suzhou peasants continued to specialize in the older *jing* varieties, which were considered superior to Champa, to sell in nearby cities, they bought Champa rice in the market to pay their rice tax to the government. As a result, the Song court discriminated against Champa, too. It ordered that taxes and rent be paid in *jing* in the Yangzi Delta, imposing a 10 percent surcharge if Champa rice was used instead.[40]

Rice production increased in China from 1500 onward because of the growth of maritime trade. In the early sixteenth century, the discovery of silver mines in Japan attracted trade; junks laden with silk and porcelain from the coastal districts of central and southern China flocked to Nagasaki to trade for silver bullion. In the wake of this sudden prosperous trade in silver, which was accompanied by numerous raids on southeast coastal counties by both Japanese and Chinese pirates, the Ming government banned *all* private, foreign maritime trade as piracy. The imperial ban did nothing to terminate the silver trade, but attracted Portuguese merchants, who had colonized Malacca in 1511, to Macau to act as middlemen between China and Japan. In 1565 Spanish merchants occupied Manila; they immediately used the port as a commercial base for selling their silver from the New World. Maritime trade in silk and porcelain had declined by the eighteenth century, but the southeast coastal provinces trade remained profitable, exporting tea to the British East India Company in exchange

---

[39] Tawney 1966, 54–5.
[40] Rawski 1972, 40–1, 52.

for New World silver. The prosperity of maritime trade raised the living standard in southeast coastal provinces and allowed more people to change their diet from coarse food to rice, hence the increasing demand for rice in those areas.

The increased demand for rice in China paralleled developments in rice production elsewhere in the world, as other historians in this book will show. In the Mekong Delta, Vietnamese traveled from the north in the late 1600s, taking by force the land that Khmer communities had inhabited for centuries. Since the days of the Angkor Empire in 800 CE, the Khmers had grown rice in the delta. They built bunds to store water in alluvial plains, and practiced a flood-recession cultivation, producing a single crop of rice after the flood receded. The Vietnamese improved irrigation systems, introduced better rice seeds, opened new land, and built canals to connect the rice farms to the marketplace. Many Khmers did not adapt to these changes; they retreated to isolated mountain slopes where they continued to live a nomadic life, eating wild species of rice, catching fish, and collecting such forest products as honey and beeswax (see Chapter 5, this book).

In West Africa, as a result of maritime trade, rice became an important commodity for sale in new ports along the Upper Guinea Coast. By the end of the seventeenth century a double-cropping system of rice farming was well established there (see Chapter 7, this book). At about the same time, following the African slave trade, Carolina and other southeastern districts of North America developed rice cultivation; Edda Fields-Black and Peter A. Coclans will discuss this in depth, to examine the subject of knowledge transfer.

Where rice cultivation was highly commercialized, farmers diversified to meet customer tastes. For example, Bengal farmers grew the *aus* or the *boro* as their spring crop, and *aman* as their autumn crop. Unlike the late-season *aman* rice, which was valuable and marketable, both the *aus* and *boro* were low quality grains, bought by tenants and landless laboring classes who could not afford *aman* (see Chapter 11, this book). In China, as this chapter has demonstrated, consumers chose among various rice varieties. Markets in the Yangzi Delta sold local *jing* and imported *xian* from the Upper Yangzi Valley, with *jing* as the preferred, usually more expensive rice. Even when there was no *jing* for sale in southern China, markets provided at least four different types of *xian*: local late-season, local early-season, Guangxi late-season, and Guangxi early-season. Among these, the Guangdong late-season *xian* was the favorite grain of Guangdong natives, and the most expensive; the Guangxi early-season *xian*, an inferior grain, was the cheapest.

In the premodern world that this chapter refers to, rice was transported mostly by junks sailing along inland rivers or between neighboring coastal cities. Global rice trade was rare. In China, although the southeast coastal province of Fujian did import rice from other Southeast Asian countries (mostly from Siam and sometimes as much as 100,000 shi^{41} a year^{42}), this was not a regular practice.^{43}

The rice trade did not become truly global until the nineteenth century. The *xian* grown in Siam and Vietnam, for instance, dominated the Guangzhou market at the Pearl River Delta in the late nineteenth century, and then the Shanghai market at the Yangzi Delta in the early twentieth century. The advent of steamships, which reduced the cost of transporting grain between nations, was certainly a major cause of the rice trade becoming global, as were the differences in international market prices of rice from different countries.^{44}

---

[41] *Shi* was a measure of volume equal to 103.55 liters. Chuan and Kraus 1975, 79–98.

[42] Qing government documents record that rice imported into Fujian from Southeast Asian countries was approximately 90,000 *shi* in 1752, 80,000 *shi* in 1754, 123,000 *shi* in 1755, and 92,000 *shi* in 1756. Wang 1986, 92.

[43] An official 1756 report stated that the Southeast Asian rice import was particularly high between 1754 and 1758, ranging from 90,000 to 120,000 *shi* annually; but the amount sharply declined after 1758, and by 1765 the amount was insignificant. The report gave two reasons for the decline. First, poor rice harvests in Southeast Asia had led to higher prices. Second, Fujian merchants had been importing grain from abroad in order to get imperial degrees (and raise their status in society); once the degrees were awarded the merchants had little incentive to continue trade. Guoli gugong bowuyuan 1982–89, vol. 25, 812–14.

[44] Faure 1989, 117–32.

4

Rice and Maritime Modernity: The Modern Chinese State and the South China Sea Rice Trade

Seung-Joon Lee

Rice has a twofold significance in the history of China, being of both agricultural and commercial importance. Rice cultivation represented the foundation of Chinese agriculture from the beginning of the Chinese civilization, simply because rice was the staple grain for the majority of the Chinese population. Both the imperial state and individual farmers paid careful attention to technological improvements in rice cultivation, such as introducing high-yielding varieties, developing cultivation tools, and improving irrigation systems. The imperial state's constant efforts to compile and publish agricultural textbooks well illustrate how much the Chinese elite were keen on improving agricultural production.[1] At the same time, the commoditization of rice and other grain trade led to unprecedented prosperity in late imperial China. As early as the Ming-Qing transition (early 1600s), farmers were able to purchase rice and other grains in the markets rather than simply producing rice for self-consumption.[2]

In the early twentieth century, however, the Chinese elite believed that China's food problem was a menace to the country's progress toward modern nationhood because a failure to secure national food self-sufficiency would threaten national security under hostile international environments. The grain problem facing twentieth-century China did not simply mean rice shortages; rather, it stemmed from a bifurcated pattern of rice consumption. In southern coastal cities, large amounts of foreign rice imports (Southeast Asian rice varieties) were being popularly consumed because of their better quality and lower prices, whereas the countryside was suffering from a devaluation of domestic crops. Foreign-rice traders had all of the advantages in marketing, including spider-webbed commercial networks linking coastal port cities to Southeast Asian entrepots, well-advanced hardware facilities, and wide varieties of rice. More than anything else, these traders had their

[1] Bray 2008, 319–44.
[2] Chuan and Kraus 1975; Rawski 1972.

practical knowledge that allowed them to discern the qualities of various rice varieties, both local and foreign. This local technique was the basis of the foreign-rice traders' business success, simply because consumer satisfaction profoundly determined the market value of rice.

This chapter explores the political contest over two different forms of knowledge between the modern Chinese state and the Cantonese rice merchants who dominated the transnational rice trade throughout the South China Sea. Regarding food security as a core governmental task was not unique to China. To resolve the food problem, the modern Chinese state devised and executed a series of new economic policies that many countries commonly practiced in the early twentieth century, including the introduction of a protective tariff, building railways, the development of new rice breeding techniques, and devising new dietary suggestions. However, the Guomindang regime and its technocratic elite simply ignored the practical knowledge that the rice merchants garnered from their business experience, knowledge that was indispensable to satisfying consumer demands for certain degrees of rice quality. To the Guomindang elite, their mercantile practice meant nothing more than obsolescence that had to be eradicated under the scientifically proven guidance that the party's technocrats provided. The Central Agricultural Experimental Institute spearheaded rice-breeding experiments with the full support of the central authorities. The agricultural experts who learned new plant genetics in foreign universities and secured support from the Central Agricultural Experimentation Institute dealt with each rice species as a scientific object. They firmly believed that increasing agricultural productivity through agricultural science would be the best remedy for the Chinese food problem. In contrast, the rice merchants who treated each rice variety as a commodity developed their own understanding of rice through everyday commercial experience. In particular, Cantonese rice merchants who dominated the South China Sea rice trade had ample opportunities to acquaint themselves with different varieties of rice and their various market values. They sometimes accustomed themselves to popular rice varieties in a given local rice market. At other times, they took full advantage of multiple nationalities to maximize economic opportunity and minimize commercial risk throughout coastal China and Southeast Asia.[3]

Recent scholarship has cast a skeptical eye on the universal validity that Western science and technology has uncritically claimed. By illuminating the "indigenous" dimensions of the rice economy, Francesca Bray asserts that rice cultivation was a "skill-oriented" agricultural system distinguished from the "mechanical-oriented" counterpart in the West. Judith A. Carney reveals the significant contribution that the West African rice culture made on rice cultivation in the Americas.[4] However, few have gone beyond the production

---

[3] Lin 2001, 985–1009.
[4] Bray 1986); Carney 2001.

aspect of rice cultivation. A better understanding of the entire agricultural system should encompass the complete process of grain circulation from producers to consumers. The mercantile aspect is important in that it is the bridge linking agricultural producers in the countryside and food consumers in the cities. The rice merchants had nothing to do with the validity of modern agricultural science that Chinese agricultural experts enthusiastically imported from the West. Nevertheless, they were keen on the versatility of their own system of knowledge – practical knowledge that they made more sophisticated through business experience. By juxtaposing the mercantile aspect of "indigenous" techniques that the rice merchants appropriated and the Central Agricultural Experimental Institute, this chapter illustrates that there was an immeasurable distance in the ways of understanding rice varieties.

REPUBLICAN CHINA AND THE PERCEPTIONS OF RICE

It was well known that when the Guomindang lost the minds and spirits of peasants, it paved the way for the Chinese Communist Party's eventual victory in the decades-long political rivalry. However, this is not to say that the Guomindang members disregarded the agrarian question or only protected the landlords' interests. In fact, the Nationalists expended greater energy toward improving the rural problem than the communists could have done. The only distinction was that the Guomindang placed their emphasis less on the class relationships between the "haves" and the "have-nots" and more on the question of overall agricultural productivity. The Nationalists understood that their political victory over the communists would rely on whether they could improve Chinese agriculture as a whole. The concerns over the agrarian problem, particularly the emphasis on the scientific renovation of cultivation methods, can be traced back to the 1920s when Sun Yat-sen, the founding figure of the Party, drafted the Party's cardinal principle: "the Three Principles of People." Sun called for scientific rural improvement programs as the stepping stone to alleviate arduous peasant life in rural areas. Although Sun incorporated Marxian perspectives into his understanding of the poverty of rural China, as Marrie-Claire Bergère noted, Sun placed more hope in "increased production" through "technical modernization" rather than political "redistribution of land to the tillers."[5]

The Guomindang's new "Nationalist Government" in Nanjing and the comparatively peaceful years in the following decade (1927–1937) facilitated Sun's aspiration for scientific agricultural reconstruction. Having consolidated its power over key economic areas in Shanghai and the lower Yangzi area, the Guomindang came to expedite their forward-looking idea of

---

[5] Sun Yat-sen most directly addressed the rural problem with the "Principle of People's Livelihood," which was the most Left-leaning and, at the same time, the most equivocal part of his general argument. Bergère 1994, 388.

agricultural improvement. For example, the regime launched the National Economic Committee (*Quanguo jingji weiyuanhui*) to supervise "all publicly financed projects for economic development" in 1931. The Department of Agriculture (*Nongyechu*) was, together with the Irrigation, Transportation, and Hygiene Departments, one of the first four departments to deal with the urgent problems that required tremendous financial support.[6] Comparatively amicable international environments following the international recognition of the Chiang Kai-shek regime also helped to expedite the regime's ambitious agricultural reform projects. The League of Nations technical advisory groups led by Dr. Ludwig Rajchman, director of the Health Section of the League's Secretariats, spared no efforts in helping their Chinese counterparts in the Department of Agriculture. With the Cornell-Nanking program (Cornell's first international cooperation program), the College of Agriculture and Forestry at the University of Nanking took the lead in China's agricultural education and experimental programs.[7]

RICE AND NATIONAL SECURITY

To the Goumindang members whose cardinal purpose was fulfilling Sun Yat-sen's will at any cost, boosting Chinese agriculture meant more than improving poor peasants' livelihoods. To build a strong nation, or at least to survive as a nation under hostile international circumstances, nothing was more urgent than achieving self-sufficiency in the national food supply. The Japanese invasion of Manchuria (1931) and the construction of Manchukuo in the subsequent year, as well as the continuous military provocations in the northeastern area, enraged the Chinese public. Many party members came to realize that a clash with Japanese military forces was inevitable and would be on an unprecedented scale, although they obediently followed Chiang Kai-shek's appeasement policy. Having realized the significance of wartime provisions during World War I in Europe (1914–1918), the Guomindang asserted that China needed a new scientific program to improve agricultural productivity.

The Party's ruling elite's concern for national food security can be traced back to its inception. It was Sun Yat-sen himself, the founding figure of the Guomindang, who first drew attention to the issue of national food supplies by asserting that protecting food supplies was the quintessential task in the national revolution. In his third lecture on the "Principle of People's Livelihood," Sun asserted that the "question of national food supply

---

[6] The Department of Agriculture spearheaded a number of public programs for rural revival. In the early years, the Department concentrated its efforts on improving agricultural finance through village cooperation and technical improvements in sericulture and the cotton industry. Zhao 1970, 43; Kirby 2000, 143–4.
[7] Stross 1986, ch. 6.

(*qifan wenti*) was the life-and-death question of one nation." Before World War I, Sun, like politicians in many countries, had never seriously considered the question of the national food supply. Having tried to understand the outcome of the war, however, Sun realized the significance of food and national security. No question was more pressing than "why Germany had lost the War despite its superior military power." Once the Allies blockaded German seaports, concluded Sun, "Germans could no longer sufficiently feed their soldiers and civilians because Germany had not achieved self-sufficiency in food supply before the War."[8] Needless to say, Sun's warning resonated with Guomindang members in the 1930s. What if Japan blockaded Chinese seaports as the Allies had done to the Germans during World War I and cut off grain supply routes?

What alarmed the Chinese public even more was that, like Germany, significant portions of the food supply for the entire national population relied heavily on foreign trade.[9] Nearly all statistical research outcomes unequivocally indicated that, except for one or two years, China had imported huge amounts of foreign rice since the founding of the Republic in 1911. Foreign rice imports were more serious problems than wheat imports. Surprisingly, the amounts of foreign rice imports were so large that China's overall trade imbalance largely stemmed from the rice trade.[10] The vast majority of imported rice was consumed in southern coastal cities. In particular, Canton, the southernmost metropolis, was the largest foreign-rice importing city. Guangdong province was the most affected by rice shortages. According to the *Improvement of Chinese Agriculture* (*Zhongguo nongye zhi gaijin*), it is obvious that "Guangdong took more than two-thirds of the net imported rice." The Guomindang concluded that "once the problem of grain supply in Guangdong could be resolved, it would mean that more than half of the entire problem of the country would be resolved."[11] The question of the national rice supply not only concerned government officials, but also drew wide public attention throughout the country. For about four years from 1932 to 1936, more than 250 articles in both popular magazines and scholarly periodicals were published to discuss China's food problem.[12]

---

[8] This lecture was delivered on August 17, 1924. Sun Wen 1957, vol. 1, 216–17.
[9] In the late 1920s and early 1930s, quantification through statistical research supported by both statistics bureaus at different levels of local governments and non-governmental research institutes was an obvious scholarly trend. Numerical representation through quantification was widely believed to be the best and most objective way to understand social problems facing China. Lee 2011, 126–7.
[10] Xingzhengyuan nongcun fuxing weiyuan hui 1934, 53; Chang 1931, 27.
[11] In 1919, for example, Guangdong took 1.6 million piculs out of China's net rice import, 1.8 million piculs. In 1923, Guangdong alone took 1.7 million piculs, whereas the national net import was 2.2 million. Xingzhengyuan nongcun fuxing weiyuan hui 1934, 53.
[12] Zuijin simian jian shiliang wenti wenxian mulu 1936, 267–78.

THE CENTRAL AGRICULTURAL EXPERIMENT INSTITUTE

At the confluence of governmental concern and public attention lay the founding of the Central Agricultural Experiment Institute (*Zhongyang nongye shiyansuo*). In a national conference held by the Ministry of Agricultural and Mining in the inaugural year of the regime, all participating agricultural specialists, who were largely trained abroad, agreed unanimously that China needed a national research institution specialized in scientific research in the various fields of agriculture. Shortly thereafter, 14 agricultural experts, including John Lossing Buck and Harris H. Love, who were leading the Cornell-Nanking agricultural improvement program, were invited to organize the preparatory committee. If the Academia Sinica was the sole scholarly institution that was fully supported by the government in the fields of general humanities and pure sciences, the Central Agricultural Experiment Institute was the one that the state cared about most to meet the nation's urgent requirement: rural revival and self-sufficiency in national grain supplies. The rapid institutional development was remarkable. The Institute invited technical experts in fields such as veterinary studies, pedology, horticulture, sericulture, and agronomics.[13] Recruiting talents in the various fields of agricultural sciences was not difficult. Chinese students' studies abroad in the field of agriculture can be traced back to the last decade of the Qing dynasty. For example, Tang Youheng studied at the College of Agriculture and Forestry at Cornell between 1904 and 1908 before taking charge of the Guangdong Provincial Agriculture and Forestry Experiment Field.[14]

Despite political urgency, the Guomindang authorities assured professionalism in the Institute. Shortly after the inauguration, a new ambitious Minister of Commerce and Industry, Chen Gongbo, appointed himself as director of the Institute. He swore that the problem of national food self-sufficiency would be overcome before the end of his tenure.[15] However, substantial operational power was given to agricultural experts. For example, the new deputy director, Qian Tianhao, was the former director of the Natural History Museum at the Academia Sinica.[16] International support for the Institute and its experimental projects was also favorable. The new position of Engineer in-Chief (*zongjishi*), which would supervise all of the practical operations of the subdivisions, was given to Harris H. Love, who was a leading figure in the Cornell-Nanking agricultural science cooperation programs. John Lossing Buck (Pearl Buck's husband) was a standing advisory

---

[13] Before the official commencement of the institute's research activity in 1932, Dai Jitao, a prominent member of the Party, suggested changing the institution's name from "research" to "experiment" to fit better with the Party's orientation, which emphasized "practice" rather than "scholarly research." Shen 1984, part. 2, 40-1.
[14] Guangdong sheng zhongshan tushuguan 1992, 418.
[15] Chen 1936, 193.
[16] Shen 1984, part. 2, 41.

board member from the beginning. Under their direction, the Institute also reorganized departments specializing in horticulture, pedology, developing chemical fertilizer and pesticides, forestry, veterinary medicine, sericulture, and agricultural economics. The primary goal of the Institute was to develop high-yield rice and wheat varieties to supplement the insufficient national food supply. For the specific task of improving rice production, the authorities established the Center for Rice and Wheat Improvement as a subdivision of the Institute. The budgetary amounts assigned to the Center were the same as those assigned to the remaining tasks of the Institute.[17]

However, this does not mean that this new research center was only built to meet political demand. Many agricultural scientists agreed that the highest priority should be placed on plant breeding projects. From the viewpoint of agriculturalists, the Institute was the sole place offering a chance to practice scientifically the most audacious experimental projects in China. Chiang Kai-shek's Nationalist government was regarded as the *de facto* state that put Sun Yat-sen's unfulfilled goals into practice in the early 1930s. Many Chinese scientists believed that their scientific and technological projects would be aided by state support and, in turn, the outcomes would help China's painstaking transformation into a modern nation.[18] Thanks to this type of academic environment and the nearly unconditional support of the authorities, the Institute was able to hire prominent scholars in the field of agriculture.

RICE EXPERTS

No candidates were more suitable for the leading positions of the Center than Drs Zhao Lianfang and Shen Zonghan, who were two of the most prominent plant breeders. Whereas Zhao was known as the rice expert on account of his 1926 dissertation at the University of Wisconsin on the genetic engineering of rice, Cornell-trained Shen Zonghan specialized in wheat breeding.[19] Zhao and Shen drafted the "Plan for National Rice Self-Sufficiency (*quanguo daomi jigei jihua*)," and the "Plan for National Wheat Self-Sufficiency (*quanguo xiaomai jigei jihua*)," respectively in 1935.[20] Even before joining the Center, they were famous for their breeding techniques, particularly those producing high-yield crops. Zhao's first practical application of his knowledge after returning from the US took place in Guangxi province. When he was invited to the position of Engineer-in-Chief at the Guangxi Provincial Agricultural Bureau in 1928, he had to confront wild rice species that had

---

[17] Shen 1984, part. 2, 41–2; Li 2006, 113–14.
[18] For Chinese scientists' attitude toward the Republican Chinese state, see Wang 2002, 291–322.
[19] Zhao was appointed as head of the rice improving team and Shen was appointed as head of wheat improving team. Zhao 1970, 21–5. Shen 1984, part. 1, 81–3.
[20] Chen 1936, 193.

never been domesticated. What he was told by the local populace was that Guangxi wild rice had red dots on its surface (of each rice granule) even after husking and that this kept local consumers from eating these wild varieties. High-polishing with mechanical milling could remove the appearance of the spots, although this process tended to crush large portions of the granule. However, its ripening cycle was faster than that of normal white rice, so it could be used for double-cropping. Without hesitating, Zhao busied himself with crossbreeding these rice varieties several times. He finally created a new hybrid variety of rice that sustained higher yield yet completely lacked red dots.[21] Shortly thereafter, he had to leave the provincial position, as continuing political tension between provincial and central authorities did not provide a favorable research environment. However, he had no difficulty in finding a better academic position. He was invited to the College of Agriculture at the National Central University in Nanjing (*Guoli Zhongyang daxue*), where he served as a professor for six years until he was called again to the position of director of the Department of Agriculture at the National Economic Council in 1934.[22] Underlying Zhao's success was his rice breeding. For example, a new rice variety named No. 258, which Zhao and his research team bred at the University, was proven to increase yields to between 15 percent and 29 percent.[23]

Increasing productivity was equally important to Shen Zonghan, who was an expert in plant genetics, particularly wheat breeding. Shen was a professor of plant genetics at the University of Nanking (*Jinling daxue*), where several professors from Cornell taught and experimented with plant genetics under the two universities' cooperative research program. Shen was the leading figure in the "Cornell-Nanking Plant Improvement Project," which received the University's largest financial support because the project ensured an extramural funding source from the China International Famine Relief Commission. The Cornell influence was obvious on the campus at Nanking. For example, the College of Agriculture and Forestry was modeled after its counterpart at Cornell. From 1926 onward, Nanking's plant breeding methods followed what Cornell agronomist Harry Houser Love advocated.[24] Cornell-trained Shen was a reputable Chinese faculty member at the College. For example, his number of published articles was ranked among the top 20 percent of all authors in the history of the *Journal of the Chinese Agricultural Science Society*.[25] He was also a strong advocate of plant breeding. There was a famous episode involving Shen's fundamental

---

[21] Zhao 1970, 37.
[22] Zhao 1970, 41.
[23] This productivity was further confirmed after three-year experimental planting in six different districts in the middle and lower Yangzi River areas. Chen 1936, 216.
[24] Shen 1984, part. 2, 17, 27.
[25] Yang Jun 2008 23–29.

overhaul of Yenching University's new rural reform project in North China. In 1930, the Yenching University secured $250,000 (USD) of financial support from the China International Famine Relief Commission. When asked to review the original plan, Shen severely criticized it for lacking a detailed plan for plant breeding.[26] Shen strongly asserted that only scientific plant breeding could improve agricultural production and that this was the best way to remedy the Chinese agricultural problem. What provided him authority was his scientific achievement in wheat breading. For example, some wheat varieties that Shen had created at Nanking produced 32 percent more yields in 1933.[27]

Both Zhao and Shen believed that substantial financial support from the central authorities would enable the pursuit of an audacious crop breeding project. For example, accepting the position at the Central Agricultural Experimental Institute in the summer of 1934 was, recollected Shen, one of the hardest choices of his life, because it required him to leave the University of Nanking, where he could conduct his research with former colleagues and teachers from Cornell. Shen was afraid that there would be political intervention in his scholarly life in the government-sponsored institution. Moreover, he was the highest-earning faculty member at the College next to the Dean.[28] In the long run, however, he firmly believed that a public research institute supported by the central government would lead to the revival of Chinese agriculture as a whole.[29] Likewise, Zhao's passion for his rice improvement project was so strong that he often caused arguments at the director's office. In the inaugural year of the Institute, for example, Zhao's request for research funding was equivalent to one million *yuan* (Chinese currency) and was rejected by Director Xie Jiasheng and Deputy Director Qian Tianhao, who, Zhao lamented, had no experience in "agricultural improvement" and were too timid to understand the magnitude of his vision. Despite such minor troubles in the budget, the rice improvement program Zhao and his experimental team devised was hailed and adopted by many provincial authorities. In the Hunan province, for example, more than half of the Provincial Rice Improvement Committee members were filled with Zhao's formers students from the Central University.[30]

Shortly afterward, the Institute made great achievements in rice research. In order to achieve the nationwide "agricultural improvement," collecting and classifying local rice varieties was more important than anything else.

---

[26] The original plan suggested improving cattle-farming and subsequent milk production. It also called for fruit farming for higher-value business. Shen 1984, 25–26.

[27] The variety was named U. of Nanking No. 2905 (*Jinda 2905 hao*). Shen 1984, 14–15.

[28] According to his memoir, the usual salary increment in the College was 10 yuan per year, but Shen started his salary at 170 yuan in his first year (1927) and received 270 yuan in his fifth year (1931). Shen 1984, part. 2, 28.

[29] Shen 1984, part. 2, 43.

[30] Zhao 1970, 53.

For the three years between 1933 and 1936, the Institute collected 70,000 sample rice varieties from six provinces and officially recognized 2,031 varieties for further research. For this, as Zhao insisted, institutional cooperation with agricultural experts at the provincial level was quintessential. In particular, the Institute's supports concentrated on Hunan, Anhui, and Jiangxi provinces, three rice-sufficient provinces in which rice production was sufficient enough to support other provinces. The Institute trained rice experts and dispatched them to each province to help collect and classify local varieties. In return, their efforts at the provincial level provided good samples for the rice-variety standardization and breeding projects that the Institute pursued.[31] While encouraging the cooperation with provinces, the Institute led major rice-breeding projects. In 1936 alone, Zhao and his colleagues created six new high-yield rice varieties. In particular, new breeds such as *Zhongnong* No. 4 and *Zhongnong* No. 34 proved to have highest productivity.[32] In Zhao's recollection in the early 1950s, the Institute produced no less than 70 new high-yield rice varieties over a period of 20 years after its foundation, including a few years in Taiwan after 1949. Zhao also estimated that the rice fields that peasant household adopted and planted these new rice varieties reached about 5 percent of total arable land of China before the Guomindang fled to Taiwan in 1949.[33]

WAR AND AGRICULTURAL SCIENCE

As a matter of fact, it was the outbreak of the Sino-Japanese War (1937–1945) that accelerated the Institute's "Plan for National Rice Self-Sufficiency." Once the war broke out, the central authorities regarded food supply as the essence of national defense and increased the support to the Institute, because both supplying sufficient food to the frontline and sustaining minimum amounts to the home front would determine profoundly the outcome of modern warfare. In the early months of the war, the laboratories and experimental fields of the Institute were destroyed by Japanese aerial bombing. Following the Guomindang government that evacuated its capital in Nanjing and retreated to Sichuan province where the wartime capital was newly built at Chongqing, the Institute moved to Chengdu, the provincial capital of Sichuan in early 1938. However, the retreat to the hinterland turned into a turning point of the institutional development. The Institute could diversify its members, as it hired new staff with different educational and regional backgrounds. Most staff had graduated from, or experienced, agricultural colleges from 18 different provinces and cities. With the outbreak of the war, they flocked to Sichuan

---

[31] Zhao 1970, 55.
[32] *Zhongnong* was an acronym that indicates the Central Agricultural Experiment Institute. Zhao 1970, 410; Li 2006, 114.
[33] Zhao 1954, 136.

and rebuilt the Institute.[34] If the institutional emphasis was placed on rice-breeding experiments before the war, wartime priority was put on educating field instructors who would be dispatched to the countryside to teach peasant new cultivation techniques and basic knowledge of agronomy, veterinaries, sericulture, and so on. Through the one-year field-instructor training programs that the Institute operated, three to four hundred new field instructors were educated each year and dispatched to more than 50 counties that the Guomindang controlled to disseminate new agricultural knowledge. For this, the Institute hired more than 1,000 teaching and research staff by 1942. Financial supports that the Institute secured then amounted to 1,500 *yuan* (Chinese currency), including budget allocation from the central authorities and bank investments. This was almost double the amount that Zhao Lianfang requested from the government in the inaugural year of the wartime program in 1938.[35]

After the end of war, the task of agricultural experts in the Central Agricultural Experiment Institute changed dramatically. As the Guomindang lost China to the Chinese Communist Party in the ensuing Chinese Civil War (1945–1949), the Institute fled to Taiwan, following the line of the Guomindang regime's retreat. However, the changing international circumstances under the Cold War confrontation required a new role of the Chinese rice experts. In April 1943, key agricultural experts, including Zhao Lianfang and Shen Zonghan, were invited to Washington, DC to attend the Post-War World Food and Agriculture Conference as Chinese representatives. After the end of the war, this conference developed into the FAO (Food and Agriculture Organization) of the United Nation.[36] In 1955, Zhao Lianfang was appointed an "agricultural officer cum rice production expert" of FAO. When he flew to Rome, headquarter of the Organization, to collect the appointment letter, the Foreign Ministry of Taiwan issued a diplomat's passport to him. Yet Rome was not Zhao's final destination. Shortly afterward, he flew to Iraq to help to train about 30 Iraqi agricultural experts and their new rice breeding projects for three years. In 1963, he took the invitation of the Dominican Republic to take the position of agricultural advisor for one year.[37]

Shen Zonghan's career after 1949 was not different from Zhao's. While leading Taiwan's agricultural improvement program, Shen busied himself helping the new agricultural improvement programs in neighboring countries. Shen was the leading advisor for the College of Agriculture at the University of the Philippines throughout the 1950s and 1960s. He also

---

[34] Zhao 1970, 59–63.
[35] Zhao, 1970, 59.
[36] Shen 1984, 141.
[37] Zhao 1970, 418–22.

participated in the founding of the IRRI (International Rice Research Institute), an international non-profit organization specializing in rice research.[38] No place required Shen's knowledge and experience more than Vietnam where the war against communism became intensified. In 1959 Shen flew to South Vietnam to lead the team of Taiwanese agricultural experts to introduce new high-yield rice varieties to the Vietnamese peasants. Within 5 years, Shen's team of agricultural experts developed into the Agricultural Advisory Corps of Republic of China at Vietnam (*Zhonghua minguo zhu Yuenan nongye jishu tuan*) and the number of Taiwanese agricultural experts increased from 30 to 85.[39]

In short, the role of Chinese rice experts did not end with the defeat of the Guomindang regime in mainland China, but rather they continued to help the spread of new knowledge about rice.

THE SOUTH CHINA SEA RICE TRADE

Despite notable achievements in improving quantity, however, the agricultural improvement programs could not improve grain quality as quickly as was expected. As a matter of fact, the "inferior quality" of Chinese rice was the largest hindrance in correcting the food trade imbalance during the Republican period (1911–1949). Rice as a commodity required more sophisticated processes of quality control than industrial products because the former was more easily "perishable." Underdeveloped transportation infrastructure delayed the transportation of grain from the countryside to the city. At the same time, the mismanaged granary system led to grain being exposed to the open air for long periods of time and rotting or becoming damaged by insects even before it reached urban markets. To make matters worse, urban grain wholesalers did not trust their rural counterparts. Many middlemen between the countryside and the cities, in turn, tended to mix sand with the rice or water the rice (*chanshui chanza*) to achieve a heavier weight before it was measured at the grain markets in the cities.[40]

What the rice experts in the Central Agricultural Experiment Institute feared in the 1930s was the foreign-rice trade, particularly the Southeast Asian-rice trade, that blossomed in coastal China with cheaper prices and better quality. Because colonial authorities encouraged an export-oriented rice economy in Southeast Asia in the second half of the nineteenth century, rice became the most commercialized agricultural product on the world

---

[38] Ford Foundation and Rockefeller foundation provided $ 7million for the founding of the IRRI. Cullather 2010, 162. For more information about Shen's activity in the Philippines, See Shen 1980, 121, 271–74.
[39] Shen 1984, Part III. 84–85.
[40] Chen 1934, 23.

market.⁴¹ Southern coastal China became the major market for this transnational rice trade. Trading rice with Southeast Asia was nothing new to China. As early as the 1720s, the Kangxi emperor encouraged the importation of Siamese rice in order to relieve rice shortages in the Fujian Guaongdong provinces.⁴² Having begun as occasional efforts to relieve local rice shortages in the eighteenth century, the Chinese trade with Southeast Asian rice merchants grew to a burgeoning business that was two to three times more profitable by the mid-nineteenth century.⁴³

At the center of the blossom of the Southeast Asian rice trade was the overseas Chinese adaptation of the new business environment. The first steam-powered rice milling company in Bangkok, for example, was constructed by American businessmen in 1858. However, the business could not succeed, and ownership changed several times. Once Chinese merchants became familiar with such rice firms, however, the business flourished. By the turn of the century, Chinese merchants came to dominate the major rice industries throughout Southeast Asia. For example, 23 rice milling firms operated in Bangkok in 1893, and of these, Chinese owned 17 of the firms. Fifteen years later, the number of rice firms doubled, totaling 49. By then, Chinese dominance in the business became more obvious: only three firms were owned by Europeans, while Chinese merchants monopolized the rest.⁴⁴ The success story of the "Wanglee" rice firm was exemplary. Tan Tsu Huang (1841–1920), the founder of the firm, came to Siam in the 1860s as "a penniless Teochiu (Chaozhou, eastern part of the Guangdong province) lad of twenty." Tan initially operated junk trade and overseas shipping between China and Bangkok. As competition with European steamers became intensive, he had to develop his business specialty. In 1874, Tan opened his first rice firm, "Huang Huang Lee," in Bangkok. By the early 1900s, his family owned and operated two of the largest rice mills in Bangkok.⁴⁵ Rice business in French Indochina was not different from the business in Bangkok. In Cholon, four miles from downtown Saigon, where more than half of the

---

⁴¹ The opening of the Suez Canal (1859) and the introduction of the steam-powered milling machine accelerated the growth of the Southeast Asian rice trade. For about 50 years, the Southeast Asia rice trade conspicuously flourished. While Burmese and Siamese rice exports recorded more than 120 percent growth, Cochinchinese rice exports increased by 500 peercent in the second half of the nineteenth century. Adas 1974, 58; Ingram 1955, 38; Taiwan Sōtoku kanbō chōsaka 1925, 163.

⁴² Occasionally, the Qing imperial authorities encouraged the importation of Siamese rice to supplement rice shortages in subsequent decades. For example, Chinese merchants and gentries who imported 2,000 piculs of rice from Siam, were rewarded by the Qianlong emperor in the 1750s. Feng 1934, 225; Ingram 1955, 23.

⁴³ Sarasin 1977, 109–12.

⁴⁴ In another observation, the total number increased to 66 by 1919, out of which the Chinese owned 59. Stiven 1908, 144–6; Ingram 1955, 70–1.

⁴⁵ Suehiro 1989, 111; Wright and Breakspear 1908, 169.

rice firms in Cochinchina were located, the Chinese monopolized all of the large rice firms that produced over 300 tons of rice a day.[46] Aside from ownership, the Chinese were also dominant in the process of rice husking and trading, largely because, as it was said, "no one ha[d] better than their dexterity" in the business.[47]

HONG KONG AND THE CHINESE RICE MASTERS

To the rice firms in Southeast Asia, Hong Kong was the gateway to the Chinese market. In fact, Hong Kong's leading business was channeling Southeast Asian and Chinese trade, which was known as the "southern and northern trade (*Nanbei hang*)." The most prominent item in this trade was Southeast Asian rice.[48] West Bonham Street, where these rice trading firms gathered, was nicknamed the "Street of *Nanbei hang*." According to a survey conducted by Japanese observers in 1917, the "Street of *Nanbei hang*" was indeed the meeting place for northern and southern traders. Seven rice firms specialized in trading rice from Tonkin, six firms specialized in rice from Saigon, and eight firms specialized in Siamese rice. If these rice firms represented the sellers' interests, no fewer firms represented buyers from the "north." The same survey indicated that six firms worked for Guangzhou, four firms worked for Shanghai, and nine firms exported rice to Japan. There were even two specialized firms for trading with North and South America. By the 1930s, more rice firms were established to trade Southeast Asian rice to such northern cities as Tianjin, Qingdao, Weihai, and Dailian.[49] Actually, the *Nanbei hang* business took the lead in Hong Kong's commercial prosperity. Among the Chinese merchant community in Hong Kong, it was widely said that "all of Hong Kong money gathers on the Street of *Nanbei hang*."[50]

It was also said that the Street of *Nanbei hang* was not merely a "marketplace" (*shangchang*) but also a "battleground" (*zhanchang*) because "great numbers of well-experienced dealers" from all port cities across China "flocked like a thick forest (*gaoshou linli*)" to obtain high market-value rice varieties.[51]

---

[46] By the early 1930s, the Chinese-owned rice mills numbered 45, whereas there were 67 native-owned mills and 5 French mills. However, the Chinese dominated large firms. See Tsao 1932, 454–5.

[47] The middlemen who purchased rice from indigenous peasants and sold it to the rice firms were also ethnically Chinese. In 1937, one British Financial adviser to Thailand estimated that about 50 percent of the export price of rice was used to pay the miller, the exporter, and middlemen. Ingram 1955, 70–1.

[48] By 1917, the largest amount of rice handled in the Hong Kong rice market was Siamese rice; the second was French Indochinese rice before re-shipping to the Chinese market. *Shina no komeni kansuru chōsa* 1917, 258.

[49] *Shina no kome ni kansuru chōsa* 1917, 270–4; Huang 1998, 6.

[50] *Gongshang ribao* (Hong Kong Industry and Commerce Daily), 5 and 6 November 1935.

[51] Huang 1998, 4.

When rice shipments arrived, wholesale sellers put a notification (*paizi*) for all of the details such as vessel names, rice varieties, and opening times for wholesale bidding. Once the bidding started, it became intense as bidders attempted to reach mutually agreeable yet profitable prices. In the world of rice merchants, there was a special tool for their business, called the "secret abacus" (*midi suanpan*). Every bidder used this special abacus that was small enough to be held in one hand with a small panel to conceal one's bidding price from competitors.[52] Fierce competition did not overwhelm the rice traders' world; mutual trust was also established. As the largest buyers of Southeast Asian rice, Cantonese buyers were especially famous for wholesale price bidding, and some gained individual reputations on the *Nanbei hang*. These renowned and most experienced figures were influential when both sellers and buyers failed to make a deal. They acted as arbitrators and forced both parties to make a deal. Few challenged this arbitration. Of course, only a few prominent buyers were allowed to arbitrate, and the best of them was lauded as the master-hand (*gaoshou* or *nengshou*). This practice was accepted as an unwritten law in the Street of *Nanbei hang*.[53]

What qualified the master-hand was not only his bidding skill but also his technique of discerning rice quality, as the quality of rice was the most important factor in the rice business. In 1936, for example, one observer noted that, the "market value [of rice] depends largely on appearance, especially, shape, color, and opacity" because "rice was, in contrast to wheat, eaten as grain."[54] To check the quality of rice before wholesaling, Cantonese rice firms built liaison offices on the *Nanbei hang* and dispatched their buyers, called "Hong Kong residing buyers (*zhougang maishou*)." The basic yardstick for judging quality was measuring the amount of broken rice in a fixed amount of rice.[55] For better market value, however, buyers had to be conversant with other characters of rice varieties that were traded on the market, such as stickiness, aroma, and the hardness of a granule. One had to determine the quality of any given rice varieties and their market value at first glance. Indeed, discerning rice quality demanded a high level of professionalism, meaning it usually took many years to become a buyer. For this reason, the "Hong Kong residing buyer" was paid the second-highest salary in the rice firm, after the general manager.[56] This type of knowledge, perhaps called "practical expertise," was surely the reason that Hong Kong residing buyers were lauded as "masters" in the rice traders' world. One story of a successful Cantonese rice merchant reveals how much important practical knowledge flowed in the transnational rice trade.

---

[52] Huang 1998, 4.
[53] Guangdong sheng yinhang jingji yanjiushe (Guangzhou zhi miye) 1938, 38–39.
[54] Robertson 1936, 243.
[55] Faure 1990, 217.
[56] Guangzhou zhi miye 1938, 22.

A RICE MASTER AND HIS EXPERTISE

Chen Zupei, born in the Waihai village of Xinhui County in the Guangdong province in 1916, became one of the most famous rice dealers on *Nanbei hang* in the 1930s. Much like many Cantonese, Chen's family was well-exposed to the commercial world. As the Chen family was not well-off by any means, his father, Yunlu, had sailed to Tokyo. Having studied tanning techniques at a Japanese manufacturer, Yunlu returned home to open a shoe-making shop, but unfortunately, his business failed. Zupei, at the age of 14, had no choice but to finish his studies at the second year of junior school (equivalent to eighth grade) and migrated to *Nanbei hang*, Hong Kong. He managed to work as an errand boy for a Shandong manager, Zhong Shou, in his wholesale trader's firm. While helping the shopkeeper, Zupei learned about business. He acquainted himself with miscellaneous business techniques, from bookkeeping and the use of an abacus to delivering sample items to business acquaintances and gathering market information.

One day, Zupei learned that French Indochinese rice had arrived while his boss was gone meeting an important customer. From his experience at the shop, Zupei was aware that French Indochinese rice was popular among the northern customers with which his Shandong firms primarily dealt. Zupei also knew the market values of the different varieties of rice. Substituting for his manager, Zupei went to the marketplace to bargain with the seller. A short while later, the seller, probably a well-seasoned dealer, was stunned by this teenaged boy. Using his manager's "secret abacus" dexterously, Zupei made his tender accepted at last. The deal he made involved trading 300 bags of French Indochinese rice. Afterward, Zupei made successful deals again, which made him famous among the Shangdong traders working on *Nanbei hang*. It did not take long for Zupei to replace Zhong Xi and Chen Luquan, the two most famous managers in the entire Shangdong traders' guild in *Nanbei hang*.[57]

By 1936, at the age of 20, Zupei became the general manager, handling the entire rice trade for the Shandong merchants in Guangzhou. He was the representative buyer for Shangdong's four major rice firms: Weihai's *Rechengde*, Qingdao's *Fengtairen*, Dailian's *Taihexing*, and Tianjin's *Deheyong*. For this new enterprise, Zupei moved his headquarters to Guangzhou, only 83 miles north of Hong Kong. Because the Chinese authorities imposed the foreign-rice tax for the first time in 1933, after which tax rates continuously increased, operating the business at Guangzhou could save costs.[58] However, it was Zupei's early experience on *Nanbei hang* that boosted his business success; in particular, his knowledge of the qualities of many different varieties of rice and different consumer preferences. Zupei realized

---

[57] Huang 1998, 4.
[58] For more information about the foreign-rice tax, see Lee 2011, ch. 6.

that Guangzhou's local variety of "Gold Blizzard" (*Jinfengxue*) was regarded as second-tier rice by Cantonese customers because of its taste; those customers preferred the Silk Sprout (*Simiao*) variety. However, the production of Silk Sprout rice was limited, and it was expensive. Some Southeast Asian varieties were seen as alternatives: second-best in quality, but cheaper and readily available through the Hong Kong rice market. In particular, the variety of "Annam *geng* rice (*Annan gengmi*)" was a good substitute for Gold Blizzard. In contrast, Gold Blizzard rice was welcomed in the northern rice markets such as Beijing and Tianjin, as well as many port cities in Shandong. Many documents show Zupei's fair understanding of various market values of different rice varieties. Japanese observers noted that there was "little distinction between Cantonese and Siamese rice varieties," but "some higher quality local varieties were even much better than the best of Siamese rice."[59] According to a local gazetteer, the "shape of Annam *geng* rice was short and round. However, its taste was not fine."[60] Zupei also knew that Gold Blizzard was suitable for making congee that northerners liked, whereas Silk Sprout was suited for the southern palate favoring steamed rice. Zupei had no reason to hesitate to develop the business of the Gold Blizzard variety with Shandong customers. Though the market value of Gold Blizzard in the Canton rice market was not as high as that in Shandong, its production was quite extensive. Despite its "middle or lower grade of quality (*zhongxia*), therefore, according to the local gazetteer, many Cantonese peasant households tended to plant Gold Blizzard because it endured well in any weather condition."[61]

Discerning rice quality was indeed the centerpiece of Zupei's business success. Zupei valued any rice expert who could fairly judge the market value of certain varieties of rice. One day in 1937, Zupei strolled down the June Twenty-third Street of Guangzhou (*Liuersan lu*: a.k.a. the Shakee Rice street, where the city's wholesale rice merchants flocked) eastward. He found an old man standing in front of a rice shop, looking carefully at rice samples on his palm. Certainly, this was the way many rice masters practiced discerning the quality of rice before suggesting prices. The old man, whose last name was Yan, greeted Zupei. Shortly after exchanging polite greetings, Zupei jumped to bargaining as he recognized that the quality of the rice sample was extremely good. He could not know the price the old man suggested to sellers, but he estimated the best price would be 11 (Chinese) dollars and 50 cents per one hundred *jin*, which is equivalent to around 133 pounds. Later, both knew that they estimated the same price. Unexpectedly, the seller suggested a much cheaper price at 11 dollars and 20 cents. This deal would

---

[59] Silk sprout rice and such Southeast Asian varieties such as Rangoon rice, Tonkin rice, and Siamese rice commonly had thin and long granules. See *Shina no kome* 1917, 8–9, 284.
[60] *Panyu xian xuzhi* 1911, juan 12, 11b.
[61] Huang 1998, 6; *Panyu xian xuzhi*, juan 1911, juan 12, 14b.

produce a huge profit because the amount of rice that the seller wanted to sell totaled around 500 hundred. Instead of providing more competitive prices, the old man suggested that each would share each half. Zupei was impressed as much by the old man's rice discerning skill as by his attitude for fair trade. Afterward, Yan became one of the three men whom Zupei never forgot throughout his lifetime, as he recollected in his memoir, because such men taught him lessons about how business should be.[62] What Zupei's story tells us is that the practical knowledge that the rice merchants garnered from their business experience was indispensable in the success of the foreign-rice trade.

CONCLUSION

The twentieth century brought a profound change in the Chinese perceptions of rice. Before the outbreak of the war with Japan, nothing concerned the Chinese elite as much as the food problem. In the 1930s, many Guomindang members believed that China's food problem was caused not only by the unsecured and unpredictable rice supplies in the impoverished rural areas, but also by unhealthy eating habits that demanded more and more imports of foreign food stuffs, most conspicuously, highly polished white rice in coastal cities. To the Guomindang elite, the resolution of the Chinese food problem meant more than sustaining the basic level of people's livelihood that the late imperial Chinese state had long regarded as the cardinal purpose of the statecraft. Having realized the significance of food supply during World War I in Europe, the Guomindang came to treat rice as the quintessential agenda of national security; China had to reduce its trade deficit and ultimately achieve self-sufficiency before the imminent war with Japan. Under such circumstance, it was no surprise that modern agricultural sciences, particularly plant breeding, became the most-needed discipline. Agricultural experts, especially those who trained in foreign universities and, therefore, able to use the latest technology, were hired and promoted in both academic institutions and government positions. The building of the Central Agricultural Experiment Institute represented the Guomindang elite's aspiration for a scientific resolution of the food problem. Plant-breeding technology was certainly conducive to improving agricultural productivity.

However, agricultural experts' and the party's technocratic elite's rationale was entrapped in technological determinism. They paid little attention to the question of rice quality that was so important to rice consumers. In their understanding of the Chinese food problem, there was little room to consider the mercantile dimension of rice. From the viewpoint of rice-consuming public, however, rice was a unique staple grain, distinguishable from other

---

[62] Huang 1998, 9–10.

grains such as wheat and corn, because rice was directly cooked and consumed without any processing. Any given local dietary preference took shape in a local context. In Canton where foreign rice was most popularly consumed, few could understand Cantonese culinary preferences for rice varieties better than Cantonese rice merchants, who, next to the consumer public, judged and anticipated the particular consumer demands. As told above, there lay incommensurability between how the agricultural experts practiced scientific rice improvement programs in the Central Agricultural Experimentation Institute and the way in which the Cantonese rice merchants expedited the rice business.

5

Promiscuous Transmission and Encapsulated Knowledge: A Material-Semiotic Approach to Modern Rice in the Mekong Delta

David Biggs

Recent histories of rice in different places and eras have stimulated a lively debate about how the traffic in living things (*Oryza sativa* and, in some cases, even *Homo sapiens*) and accompanying transfers of knowledge and technology have reshaped regional histories. The debates, highlighted in this book's introduction, primarily concern questions about agency – where credit lies for the creation of a colonial-era cash crop in the case of the Carolina lowlands, distinctive agricultural landscapes in West Africa and Java, or in refined consumer tastes in China. Bringing these debates to the Mekong Delta in the long twentieth century (1880-present), I am repeatedly drawn to the observation that different types of rice existing simultaneously in this region signify different combinations of these material, economic, and knowledge-based relationships that have formed over time. The relative spread of one population of rice versus another tells us not only about ecology but also about shifts in world markets, access to technology, changes in labor, evolving state policies, even outbursts of war. So, rather than tell a history of rice as a sum total of rice produced in relation to changes in labor, technology, or science, this chapter aims to explore the modern histories of rice in the Mekong Delta as encapsulated in the grains of different varieties.

Rice is far more than a staple of commerce; in genetic, economic, and cultural terms it is a product of a remarkable web of interrelated processes. Proponents of actor-network theory might describe specific varieties of rice *assemblages* as they are really ongoing, evolving products of regulating, underlying, networked relationships. Sociologist John Law describes the actor-network approach as one that treats "everything in the social and natural worlds as a continuously generated effect of the webs of relations within which they are located. It assumes that nothing has reality or form outside the enactment of those relations."[1] Rice landraces and cultivars strike

---

[1] Law 2009, 141.

me as provocative examples of *assemblages* given their genetic propensity to hybridize or become "weedy" and thus useless without constant attention from humans involved in relevant scientific, trade, or agricultural networks. The survival of *Oryza* in certain highly cultivated forms depends upon these networks as well as key environmental factors remaining constant. Its proliferation as a world cereal, likewise, depends on larger networks of commodity traders, trans-oceanic modes of transportation, and newer inventions such as superphosphate or small, motorized pumps that permit sustained, higher yields. The genetic information contained in rice, its encapsulated knowledge, has also become more tied to global networks of scientists, international labs, multinational seed companies, and even the arcane world of patent law. Meanwhile, rice farmers, who possess knowledge about rice cultivation, have also become increasingly connected to agricultural extension offices sharing the latest methods to eradicate pests, increase yields, and use new technologies. So rice, especially rice varieties in the twentieth century, offers a lens for peering more deeply into the ways that innovation in science or technology, instances of war, and changes in policy have had major social and environmental impacts on society.

This chapter explores a twentieth-century history of rice in the Mekong Delta from the in-grain perspective of four different sub-groups of rice: long-stem and short-stem landraces, high-value cultivars and high-yield cultivars. (I use the term landraces to refer to traditional or heirloom varieties of rice developed by natural processes, usually over many years, and adapted to local environmental conditions. A landrace differs from a cultivar in the sense that a cultivar is selected via more labor-intense methods, often in experimental settings, and maintained by more rigorous methods of propagation and screening.) Within each of these groups – landraces, high-value cultivars and high-yield cultivars – are dozens to hundreds of varieties that, if examined more closely, could describe finer differences in rice breeding, rice trade, and ecosystems. This chapter keeps to a higher-level perspective, showing more general actor-networks associated with these four types of cultivated rice. The changing populations of these four types of rice reflect major differences in ecosystem (short- versus long-stem), policy (land races versus cultivars), and technology (landraces versus high-yield cultivars). As with most river deltas, the Mekong Delta is a patchwork of many different hydro-landscapes in one: alluvial banks, brackish water back swamps, and vast flood plains that are seasonally inundated under a meter or two of water. Each hydro-terrain presents different challenges to rice cultivators (Figure 5.1). As increasingly more humans have settled here, roughly one million in 1860 compared with over nineteen million today, rice species have followed them. Many hundreds of landraces have gone extinct while several dozen high-yield varieties now cover more than 90 percent of the delta's fields. However, this image of skyrocketing population growth and mass extinction for hundreds of landraces can be misleading. The reduced variety in plants makes key commercial

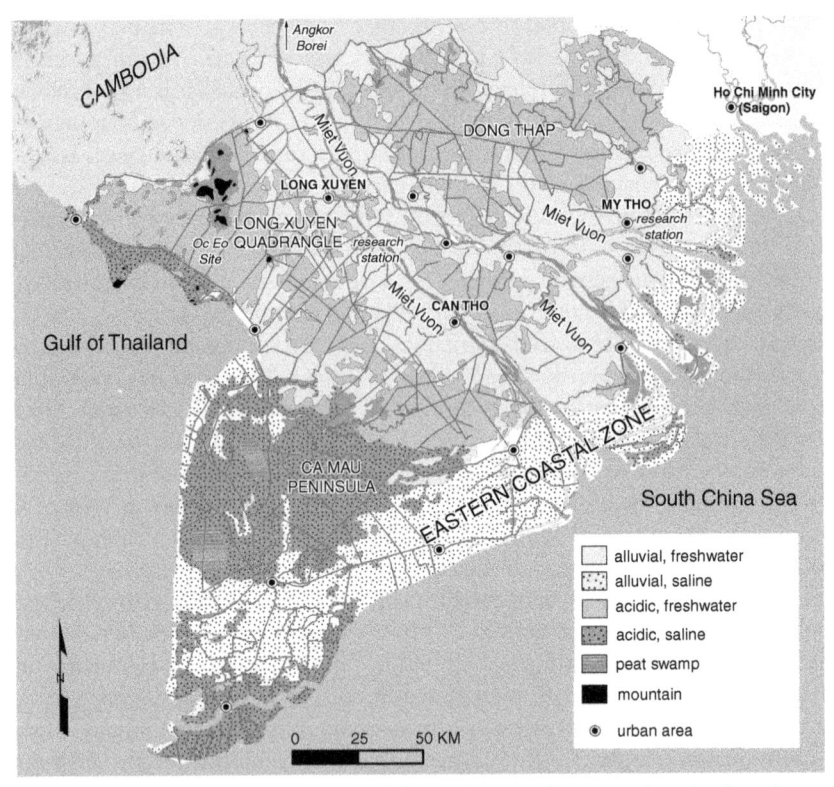

FIGURE 5.1 Hydro-ecological zones of the Mekong Delta. Map showing locations of research stations, major towns, and hydro-ecological zones of the Mekong Delta. Source: Author.

species more vulnerable than ever to evolving pests. Also, in the margins of many fields grow wild and weedy relatives that, without careful selection, can cross with commercial plants and produce less productive offspring. Thus, each grain of rice is not just a product of human labor but also a seed of encapsulated knowledge produced by human and natural events. Rice is also highly *promiscuous*, even capable of reproducing with other rice species, thus threatening in each successive generation to become less adapted, less useful without careful attention.

Managing sustained production in a rice field is a struggle! It requires steady applications (and updates) of traditional and scientific know-how. The color, taste, and nutritional properties of rice, its material properties, often ensure its survival in local and global commerce. Imagine farmers, scientists, and millers all locked in a struggle with rice's natural promiscuity. These different human activities – scientific research, weeding, grading – can in Latour's idea of actor-networks be construed as performances that ensure what he describes as the *durability* of a particular, social-natural *assemblage*, in this case a highly valued strain of rice.[2] There is a great monetary distance, for example, between highly coveted long grain rices such as Basmati or the Carolina golden varieties and the less fragrant, less colorful, broken varieties that end up in industrial starches and animal feeds.

Assuming this material semiotics perspective on rice in the Mekong Delta, the historical narrative that results is one best re-centered to particular rice types and the environments that supported them. The twentieth century was for rice as with other species one of accelerated movement, globe-spanning reach, rapid hybridization, and in many instances extinction. As with other species, rapid extinction of wild relatives such as *Oryza rufipogons* may mean the loss of potentially useful genes.[3] Most if not all aspects of rice production underwent major and rapid changes over the past century. Labor changed dramatically with the advent of new machinery and changing land use practices. The genetic makeup of rice also underwent rapid changes with the advent of high-yield rice seed in the 1960s and, more recently, with the mapping of rice genomes and the development of transgenic rice. Finally, the war that raged in the Mekong Delta in 1960s played a role in this history. Modern, high-yield rice became popular in government-controlled areas while landraces and wild species thrived in free-fire zones and "liberated" territory. With Vietnam's reunification after 1975 and especially its market-oriented reforms in 1986, just over 40 varieties of modern rice account for the majority of land planted in rice. Many of the hundreds of landraces have disappeared. At all points in this turbulent twentieth century, changes in rice reflect deep changes in political and agricultural economies.

CULTURES COLLIDING: LONG-STEM AND SHORT-STEM

Until as recently as 1980, large swaths of the Mekong Delta were annually flooded, turning into vast inland lakes dotted by a few stands of trees lining dikes and clumps of reeds, wild rice and deepwater rice greening the surface. Lands so bitterly contested in the Indochina Wars laid seasonally silent under a sheet of brownish, silt-laden water. During the war years, in flood season wild stocks of fish migrated downstream from Cambodia along with birds, mosquitoes, and snakes. This persistence of a seemingly wild, ancient landscape was of course an anomaly in the waning days of the Green Revolution. Vietnam's market-oriented "*doi moi*" reforms in 1986 and subsequent economic boom permitted a delayed boom for companies selling pesticides, fertilizers, and motorized equipment. The war-wilded floodplains and swamps have given way, rapidly, to a more familiar view in the late twentieth century of

---

[2] Latour 2005, 67.
[3] Vaughan et al. 2005, 113.

industrial agriculture. Vast Dutch-style polders now keep most of the seasonal floods out. They are filled with paddy, houses on stilts, and roadway billboards advertising the wares of chemical and agribusiness corporations.

This delayed wave of industrialization has finally blurred one of the most important dividing lines in any river delta: elevation. Elevation divides social groups, differentiates ecosystems, and plays an important role in the history of rice. For several millennia in the Mekong Delta, it played a central role in the spatial distribution of settlements and accompanying rice types. There are two main types of high-elevation land in the delta: island-like mountain outcroppings in the upper delta and alluvial banks in the lower delta. The mountain outcroppings straddle the present-day border between Vietnam and Cambodia and contain most of the ancient inhabited sites. This ancient history of settlement and rice (as early as 500 BCE) was generally unknown to the world before 1930. A French colonial administrator, Pierre Paris, using aerial photographs, detected an ancient canal system connecting these mountain outcroppings.[4] Louis Malleret, a librarian working for the Société des Études Indochinoises in Japanese-occupied Saigon, followed Paris' discoveries; and in 1943, he commenced an archeological dig at the most prominent canal nexus, Oc Eo. That work became the basis for his doctoral thesis in 1949 and resulted in a four-volume work, *l'Archéologie du Delta du Mékong* (published from 1959–63) that has, with more recent archaeological excavations, established these high-elevation sites as part of a regional, pre-Angkor or Oc Eo culture that lasted from approximately 500 BCE to 500 CE.[5] Even in the Vietnamese portion of the Mekong Delta today, most of the villages located near these ancient sites are still ethnically Khmer. Recent archaeological digs at such upstream sites as Angkor Borei suggest that farmers along these hills practiced bund irrigation at higher elevations and flood-recession irrigation at seasonally inundated slopes. Rice varieties in these areas tended toward shorter-stem landraces. Farmers broadcast long-stem, flood-tolerant varieties in the basins below; but most farm labor, scarce until recent times, was focused on cultivating rice in the flood recession zones.[6]

The other elevated region, alluvial banks or what Vietnamese locals call the *miet vuon* (garden strips), looks from the air like a web of silted banks hugging rivers, arroyos, and canals. It is in this elevated web that the majority of the delta's population expanded rapidly in the modern era (1700-present). All of the region's major towns and cities, some now approaching a million people, are located in the *miet vuon*, too (see Figure 5.1).

Modern settlement of the *miet vuon* from the 1600s was far from a peaceful process. A Vietnamese general, Nguyen Huu Canh, led a military

[4] Paris 1931, 223.
[5] Malleret 1959, 27–33.
[6] Fox and Ledgerwood 1999, 48.

campaign against Cham and Khmer forces in 1698. He finally seized Saigon for the Vietnamese crown and traveled along the Upper Branch (*Tien Giang*) of the Mekong close to the present-day Cambodian border. He later died from infection near present-day Long Xuyen.[7] His excursion was followed in the 1700s by successive waves of Vietnamese soldier-settlers. Vietnamese settlement was also augmented by several waves of Chinese Ming loyalists who fled the Qing Dynasty's anti-Ming campaigns of 1683. Chinese from coastal provinces such as Guangzhou and Fukien settled by the thousands along Southeast Asian rivers. They sought patronage from the royal courts at Hue (Dai Viet), Phnom Penh (Cambodia), and Ayutthaya (Siam); then over several decades, they capitalized on extensive mercantile experience in the South China Sea trade to establish new, thriving ports, some even as walled cities at such places as Saigon, My Tho, and Ha Tien. Even today, a quick tour along the roads or waterways of the Mekong Delta reveals how ethnic Khmer, Vietnamese, and Chinese communities became densely intermingled in the *miet vuon*. Towns such as Soc Trang have retained their original Khmer names, Theravada Buddhist temples, and Khmer scripts on signs, while Vietnamese and Chinese neighborhoods have grown around them.

While these elevated places are central to the history of settlement and rice cultivation, the vast depressions in the delta are also interesting as contrary spaces. The large, intersecting regions of back swamps, mangroves, tide marshes, and depressions cover more than two-thirds of the delta's surface area. These depressed regions were largely wilderness into the late nineteenth century. In the dry season, elephants roamed through grasslands along with herds of deer and large predators. Farmers routinely encountered cobras and other highly venomous snakes. Conversion of the depressions and marshes happened largely in response to events in the *miet vuon*. As Vietnamese officials and military units consolidated authority over the *miet vuon*, more and more Khmer families relocated into the floodplains, seeking refuge. The southernmost third of the delta, known as the Ca Mau Peninsula (Figure 5.1), was famous in the early 1800s as the kingdom's top producer of beeswax and honey. Khmer harvesters paddled canoes through dark mangroves, smoked out the hives and then collected the wax floating on the water surface.[8]

People who moved into the depressions did not have to abandon their rice, however. They switched varieties to long-stem landraces, either deepwater or floating varieties. Deepwater rice grows between 50–100 cm and possesses moderate elongation abilities during floods while floating rice grows longer than 100 cm and has very strong elongation abilities, able to grow well over a meter in just one week![9] Long-stem rice delivered less volume per hectare than

---

[7] Nguyên 1997, 12.
[8] Cooke 2004, 143.
[9] Catling et al. 1988, 11.

short-stem rice; yet for people living in far-flung, seasonal communities, sometimes on the run, floating rice was a vital staple.

In the Mekong Delta, when I asked (Vietnamese) farmers about who traditionally grew deepwater rice, the response was almost always "Khmer." On a trip to visit an agricultural research station near Can Tho in 2002, one farmer showed me a specially adapted "Khmer" tool with a longer curved sickle and explained that it was adapted to gather the longer rice stems. He also explained how, during the years of the National Liberation Front in the 1960s, he and his Vietnamese colleagues used the same tools to harvest rice in the base areas hidden deep in the mangrove swamps. He then showed me the shorter "Vietnamese" sickles and blades used to harvest short-stem rice. "Was floating rice a Khmer rice?" I asked. "Of course," he replied.[10] This story illustrates the sensitive issue of Viet-Khmer relations that, since Vietnam's occupation of Cambodia in the 1980s, taint any historical treatment of the delta's Khmer heritage. At the same time it also conveys how readily Vietnamese revolutionaries adapted the seed and tools when they were forced into depressed areas, thus suggesting that long-stem landraces and associated tools were easily transferred from one culture to another. Today, the few communities that still grow floating rice are for the most part Khmer; but affiliation with long-stem rice seems to have less to do with cultural preferences than class. Richer families live on higher ground and tend to grow short-stem rice.

There is strong evidence, however, to suggest that modern deepwater rice was a grain of choice in the delta's ancient past. Archaeological excavations at Oc Eo sites suggest that ancient towns (circa 300 CE) marketed floating rice. While upriver sites such as Angkor Borei (Figure 5.1) may have tended toward shorter-stem landraces in bunds and flood-recession areas, those living and working at the downstream port (the Oc Eo site) grew floating rice. The port city rested on wooden piers and the surrounding basin was likely flooded much of the year.[11] Exhaustion of timber supplies coupled with changes in the water table, the spread of malaria or piracy may have caused the demise of the port and its floating rice stands.[12]

Deepwater rice was the landrace of choice for those on the run; people who wanted to avoid greater integration into the state moved into the floodplains. Whether these were Khmer farmers seeking to avoid conscription or Vietnamese radicals building an insurgency in the 1930s, they typically opted for cultivation of floating or even wild rice (*Oryza rufipogons*). Floating rice was well adapted to growing not only in flooded fields but also in oxbow swamps and depressions that required limited attention when weeds were removed or seeds broadcasted. For people on the run, such rice formed an essential staple for foraging. A French lieutenant, leading a survey mission

[10] Biggs 2002a.
[11] Malleret 1962, 419.
[12] Nguyen 1994, 1–17.

across such a depression in 1871, described one journey through such a non-state space. Upon reaching the edge of an alluvial zone, his crew organized fifteen longboats in a Khmer village paddled by villagers who worked in the swampy areas. On their departure across the watery bowl (*vi thuy*) for which the village was named, he noted "the dugout becomes a species of broad shoe, slipping with speed on cut or curved grasses. Enough broad packages of rebel grasses form often, causing interruptions where it is necessary to carry the dugout by hand, through what can be called a *trâp* [pit]." The survey mission noted plantations of the tall grasses, indicating that they were likely actively cultivated. However, it also recorded the local name for the rice, "phantom rice," a name typically associated with the wild species *Oryza rufipogons*.[13] These blurred boundaries between cultivated and wild rice and fields and swamps contrasted sharply with the rectangular boundaries of fields in the *miet vuon*.

Thus, the cultures associated with short-stem and long-stem landraces were not so much defined by ethnicity as by their (vertical) position vis a vis the state. It should be no surprise that colonial engineers from the 1880s on targeted these vast, non-state areas for reclamation and offered concessions to French companies. The more densely populated *miet vuon* simply presented too much political resistance. Thus, much of the area in the depressions in the Mekong Delta became colonial-era plantations. By 1930, over nine thousand kilometers of canals opened up more than two million hectares in the old depressions to estates populated with several million migrants and tenants growing short-stem varieties. Older cultivators who lacked land title, including many Khmers, retreated further out from these encroaching estates to more remote swamps. It should be no surprise that the same estates, located in hydrologically vulnerable terrain, became prime battlegrounds for post-1945 revolutionary struggles. Vietnamese tenants, deeply in debt, joined the August Revolution en masse to fight against the return of French rule. This war escalated from the "French War" into the "American War." Many of the same areas became free-fire zones, and they remained seasonally flooded through most of the war years due to destruction or neglect on the canals and polders.

Because of the fighting, cultivation of floating rice (and short-stem landraces) persisted even as high yield rice and the Green Revolution had rapidly transformed other Southeast Asian deltas. In 1974, 500,000 hectares of land around Chau Doc and Long Xuyen were still planted in floating rice.[14] Land reform, both in 1970 and after 1975, largely eliminated deepwater and floating rice from the delta. The first reform, called Land to the Tiller, started in March 1970. It split up large landholdings, but it also placed limits on the maximum size of landholdings to three hectares. Farmers in the flood zone

[13] Brière 1879, 44.
[14] Vo 1975, 93.

typically farmed ten hectares since the single season crop generated only about one ton per hectare (compared to two or three tons/ha in a short-stem field or six for high yield varieties).[15] Both the pre-1975 Republic of Vietnam and the post-1975 Socialist Republic of Vietnam initiated policies that favored the further extension of small landholdings and high yield rice from the *miet vuon* into the flood plains. Reforms initiated in 1985 have, in the nearly 30 years since, resulted in over four billion USD invested in dikes and pumping stations to regulate much of the flood zones as short-stem polders. Meanwhile, rice production across the delta region has increased from roughly 1.5 tons per hectare in 1973 to over 7 tons per hectare today. This recent boom in rice production, however, has come at a price. An estimated 94 percent of all rice grown in the delta today is high-yield rice. This means that not only have land races of floating rice and long-stem varieties disappeared but so too have many short-stem varieties.[16]

THE RISE OF THE CULTIVAR

This global shift from land races to cultivars, plants that were selectively propagated for certain traits, has only recently given rise to concerns about biodiversity loss among rice varieties. Until the late 1990s, most researchers focused on the incredible proliferation of rice-growing operations. Starting from the perspective of a single cultivar such as "Carolina rice" (long grain *O. sativa*) imported from Java in the 1870s or the International Rice Research Institute's "IR8" imported from the Philippines in 1966–1967, one can trace outward the political forces and modernist overtones connected with their adoption. French rice researchers from the 1880s to the 1940s lamented the relatively low quality of export rice derived from the local landraces, and they sought repeatedly to acclimatize other, more desirable "races" in the delta soils. American agricultural advisors in the 1960s similarly sought to improve rice production to "win hearts and minds" and spark economic modernization in South Vietnam. A closer focus on modern cultivars also reveals a lot about politics and ideology, from the workings of colonial rice research stations to discourses on race, degeneration, and acclimatization, and more recently to the increasing influence of global research networks and multinational seed companies.

The first cultivar of interest, what French rice researchers called "Carolina rice" even though it was raised in Java, was by all accounts a flop. Repeated efforts to acclimatize the gold standard of commercial rice in the Mekong Delta failed. Failures, however, can be instructive. They point toward broader weaknesses in colonial society as it related to agriculture. Economic historian Peter Coclanis makes a compelling case for the role of Southeast

---

[15] Callison 1974, 89.
[16] Nguyen 2011, 48.

Asian rice in re-shaping the global rice trade by the 1860s; however, not all Southeast Asian rice was made equal.[17] In Cochinchina, professional organizations such as the Committee of Agriculture and Industry repeatedly published accounts of efforts to introduce varieties of Bengal or Carolina rice (from Java) to "improve" local varieties. There was a long-running discussion among French scientists and businessmen in the Committee about the problems with traditional rice. In one such meeting about the causes of inferiority of Cochinchina's rice in European markets, the Committee's businessmen pointed to a number of factors. For one, Vietnamese farmers cultivated many different varieties of rice. Among these varieties, one man noted, "there are some that must be worth as much as the most popular rice from other regions."[18] The problem, reiterated by Frenchmen for decades thereafter, stemmed from a lack of control in selecting grains in the fields and separating rice in processing.

Almost always, French discussions in such venues about problems in rice transshipment, selection, husking, and drying returned to the powerful roles played by Chinese companies and intermediaries. The role of Chinese families in the shipment and polishing of rice pre-dated the French in Saigon by more than a century. Frenchmen, from an early point in the colonial conquest, recognized that they could not outdo indigenous farmers and Chinese merchants in rice. As one famous colonial explorer, Auguste Pavie, noted about the French troops accompanying him on his forays up the Mekong, most Frenchmen simply could not give up their baguettes for rice. While the Vietnamese porters and Pavie himself enjoyed steaming hot bowls of rice at almost every meal, new arrivals from France "savored their bread" even as it grew moldy in the tropical heat.[19]

Even most French plantation owners were removed from working with rice. They relied on tenant farmers to cultivate the crop, Chinese businesses to ship it to mills and Chinese businesses in Cho Lon (present-day Ho Chi Minh City) to husk it and export most of the crop to Asian markets. This Asian minority's privileged position in the French colonial era continued an older arrangement begun in the 1600s across much of Southeast Asia. Chinese emigres fleeing the Qing Dynasty traveled in a fleet of merchant and military ships off the coast of central Vietnam. They asked the ruler of the southern half of Vietnam for asylum, and he quickly pointed them to the kingdom's far southern frontier with Cambodia. There they established mercantile posts at the present-day cities of Ho Chi Minh City (Sai Gon) and My Tho (Figure 5.1). These were not masses of impoverished Chinese peasants but well-organized groups of wealthy merchant families and military officers.[20]

---

[17] Coclanis 1993a, 251.
[18] Comité agricole et industriel de la Cochinchine 1872, 8.
[19] Pavie and Tips 1999, 69.
[20] Dai Nam Thuc Luc 1963, 91.

This ethnic division of rice shipment and polishing persisted throughout the colonial era and after. The autobiographical novel by Marguerite Duras, *L'Amant*, explores the problems of crossing social and racial divisions in colonial society as a French teenage girl living with her widowed mother in the Khmer town Sadec becomes a lover to a wealthy Chinese young man who gives her a ride from her mother's modest country home to his family's mansion in Cho Lon.[21] A 1992 film adaption by the same name shows in beautiful sweeps of cinematic landscape the transitions between ethnic lines that accompanied movement from fields and canals to urban mills and warehouses on the Saigon waterfront. Even after the creation of the Republic of Vietnam in 1955, ethnic Chinese families continued to pay large sums of money for monopoly rights to mill rice and sell it wholesale. With American commodity import programs in the 1960s came portable, diesel-powered rice mills from Japan and Taiwan. These portable machines presented the first significant threat to the old mills and the ethnic separation in the rice trade that had persisted for 300 years. For a time, older mill operators in government-controlled lands lobbied to prevent this technology from getting into the hands of farmers; so instead the small machines wound their way into insurgent-controlled lands. The National Liberation Front took up rice milling, and some NLF supporters even sold it in government-controlled markets to raise cash.[22]

Nature also conspired against French bids to control commerce. Rice traveled, from the 1860s to the 1960s, on longboats to larger waterways. From there it was transferred to flat-bottomed barges that navigated the delta's larger arroyos and canals to Cho Lon. French businesses, operating such fleets simply could not compete with local rice shippers. One surveyor in 1880 remarked:

From a purely economic point of view, in this country of river navigation par excellence, where each center [of the delta] would provide quite sufficient freight to feed a service of large riverboats ... to move rice freight distances of one hundred miles on assembled longboats with 10 to 15 oarsmen, moored against the bank when the current is opposing, obliged in each arroyo to wait until high tide to cross the sandbar, this is nonsense ... under this pretext our trade remains in the hands of the Chinese, thus we are conducting our commerce on their terms.[23]

Throughout the decades of colonial rule, from the 1860s to the 1930s, colonial businessmen and scientists lamented this perfect storm of factors that prevented them from getting higher prices for their rice, especially in Europe. Chinese businesses controlled the rice trade and Vietnamese rice farmers preferred to grow a wide variety of landraces in their fields. While

[21] Duras and Bray 2008.
[22] NARA-CP 1970.
[23] Rénaud 1880, 317.

other Southeast Asian colonies such as the Dutch Indies and British India sent much of their rice exports to European markets, three-quarters of Mekong Delta rice exports went for the most part to China. Japanese rice merchants even imported the "inferior" Mekong Delta rice to feed their own populations while exporting higher grade, Japanese rice to Europe.[24]

Also conspiring against the French was the promiscuous nature of rice and an inability to control the field conditions where rice grew. French boosters for improving rice exports repeatedly mentioned such ideal rice varieties as the famed "Goldseed" of Georgetown, South Carolina or the "Tanggerang" of Java. However, when entrepreneurs attempted to grow imported stocks of these varieties, within a few generations their offspring had outcrossed virtually all of their prized traits. They were simply outnumbered in field trials by ever-hybridizing, Vietnamese neighbors. French rice prospectors could not feasibly rid fields of these native landraces. Another problem, internal to the French colony, was a lack of political and financial support for building rice research stations. Where Dutch, British and American governments had funded active rice research stations by 1910, French support in Indochina was mostly lip service. This lack of funding in turn meant a lack of skilled technicians or a cadre of extension agents who might have been able to carry out efforts to introduce more profitable varieties. Wrote one such critic: "It is known that purebred progeny and pedigree comes from units through which the primary characters chosen were transmitted hereditarily keeping stability and homogeneity." The problem, then, was not a lack of knowledge but more a lack of will to maintain the hereditary *stability* of valuable seed.[25] In 1906, several wealthy French businesses even imported Javanese workers in an attempt to improve the quality of the plantation's output with imported Javanese know-how. As with the Javanese rice, however, migrant Vietnamese tenants quickly outnumbered the Javanese laborers. Dutch restrictions on the movement of Javanese labor after World War I finally put an end to the program.[26]

The general failures of the colonial state to "improve" rice varieties makes for an actor-network story of *indurability*, as told from the perspective of imported Javanese and Carolina wonder seeds that never took. Of course, if told by native Vietnamese or Khmers more interested in their own favored varieties, the flip side of this story, the *durability* of traditional cultivars might signify a kind of agri-cultural resistance. There was not a sufficient network of French rice technicians and Vietnamese extension agents to distribute seed and ensure proper controls to maintain traits. The commercial network was instead controlled by ethnic-Chinese businesses; and those businesses specialized in exporting varieties popular as basic foodstuffs to China and other

[24] Capus 1918, 30.
[25] Capus 1918, 36.
[26] Brocheux 1995, 27.

Asian countries rather than varieties preferred in European exchanges. So the role of taste, particularly Vietnamese, Chinese, and Asian tastes, for rice was another important factor in the lack of *durability* for "Carolina rice" or "Tanggerang." French failures to populate these special rice genomes, even in the floodplains where large plantations were established as factory towns, reflected at heart the deeper conflicts colonial authorities faced in gaining control over the millions of Vietnamese, Khmer, and Chinese who had been engaged in the rice trade long before the gunboats arrived.

Failures in "improving" rice cultivation during the early decades of the twentieth century, especially in the 1930s, turned some French agronomists into radicals who grew increasingly opposed to estate-run agriculture. René Dumont, a newly graduated agronomist assigned to a rice research station near Hanoi in 1931, published one of the first modern anthropological and geographical studies of Vietnamese rice in 1935. In it, he carefully studied traditional tools, rice types, water-lifting techniques, and planting techniques; he marveled at traditional environmental knowledge employed to maintain the Red River Delta's vast and ancient network of flood dikes.[27] The result of Dumont's study was one of the first in a series of encyclopedic works to come out on the intricacies of Vietnamese rice that have become models for rural anthropology. Given the circulation of such agronomists throughout the colonial empire, from Indochina to the South Pacific to West Africa, such works also contributed to an increasingly global field of tropical agriculture. It even launched some political careers. Dumont returned to France and advanced a more socialist view of agriculture in the 1950s; in the 1960s he regularly appeared on French television with harsh critiques of environmental damage brought by Green Revolution pesticides and fertilizers. In 1974, he ran as France's first environmentalist candidate for President (and lost). There were other famous and influential agronomists and geographers from this era, notably tropical geographer Pierre Gourou and Vietnamese anthropologist Nguyen Van Huyen (who after 1945 served as Ho Chi Minh's Minister of Education).

Among French colonial scientists involved with rice, one individual in particular, Yves Henry, played a pivotal role in fomenting these 1930s-era studies of rice agriculture. Henry, a former colonial servant in both West Africa and French Indochina published more than 30 works with the help of teams of indigenous researchers and French graduate students such as Dumont and Gourou. Henry rose to the position of Inspector General of Agriculture for the Colonies after the Paris Colonial Exposition in 1931. Before then he had studied the cultivation of cotton in the Senegal and Gambia Rivers and published extensively on rice in Indochina.[28] So, French

---

[27] Dumont and Nanta 1935.
[28] Henry 1906; de Vismes and Henry, 1928; Henry 1932.

networks of agronomists continued to expand, but they never again played a major role in the development of rice landscapes in Vietnam.

Flash forward to the mid-1960s and a very different modern rice story emerged. The recently formed International Rice Research Institute released "IR8" and farmers, at least in government-controlled areas, learned of the crop's incredibly productive results. With motorized pumps irrigating fields and access to chemical fertilizers and pesticides, farmers quickly became interested in claims that IR8 would double or triple crop yields. A series of other IRRI seeds followed in the 1970s. By 1994 some 42 IRRI varieties accounted for more than 60 percent of all rice areas in Vietnam. Since 1971, Vietnamese rice scientists such as the delta's most famous, Dr. Vo Tong Xuan, worked closely with IRRI and returned to fill top posts in rice research institutes and universities across Vietnam.[29] Since 1994, the percentage of land devoted to IRRI strains has now grown to over 94 percent! Thus, new networks of Vietnamese scientists, millions of farmers, seed merchants, and others have managed to re-populate the delta with a relatively small "family" of genotypes while many if not most of the hundreds of landraces once common in 1930 have disappeared, confined to 6 percent of rice-growing areas.[30]

If one considers the IRRI strains as a relatively homogenous group of modern cultivars, what is most amazing is just how *durable* in the actor-network sense this *assemblage* has been. IRRI varieties have simultaneously multiplied crop yields while leading to near-monoculture conditions for preferred varieties across large areas. Critiques of the Green Revolution, spurred largely by IRRI varieties, and negative impacts on biodiversity are well known. However, with respect to an actor-network approach, its impressive *how* IR8 and its cousins became so prolific so rapidly.

Contrary to the colonial example above, Americans did not play the leading role in popularizing IRRI rice *inside* Vietnam. American agencies, even the U.S. Army, introduced it to Vietnam beginning in 1967, but they only marginally succeeded in winning over cultivators. They did, however, play an important *supporting role* with respect to high-yield rice in the Mekong Delta. The Philippines-based research network that produced IR8 was supported by two American foundations and led by American scientists. The Rockefeller and Ford Foundations provided the International Rice Research Institute (IRRI) with initial funding in 1960; and the Philippines, a former American colony and an ally in the Cold War, provided logistical support via a former agricultural college founded by the former colonial government at Los Banos, Laguna. A history of IRRI's early years suggests an intensely American-focused operation, where senior American scientists and officials received compensation paid in dollars from the Rockefeller Foundation along the same lines as Americans working for U.S. government

---

[29] Brian Lee and the IRRI 1994, 49.
[30] IRRI 2012.

agencies and corporations in overseas posts. As in these other posts, there was a significant difference in salaries, too, between Americans and their Asian counterparts.[31]

The development of the first, commercially viable IRRI strain, IR8, reflects the role of this postcolonial institution: Americans running the breeding program and scientists from Japan, Taiwan, Thailand, and East Pakistan (Bangladesh) involved in the transmission of new varieties to their respective countries. IR8 was one of the first widely dispersed IRRI varieties. Rice breeder Peter Jennings, together with a handful of local research assistants, made 38 crosses in 1962 between short-stem Taiwanese varieties called *dee-geo-woo-gen* or Taichung Native 1 with long-stem, tropical *indica* varieties. The 8th cross (hence the name IR8), involved a cross between *dee-geo-woo-gen* and an indica variety popular in the Philippines called *peta*. From the cross, 130 seeds were generated. Seeds from the first generation (F1) yielded about 10,000 offspring. Taller, late-maturing plants in the second generation (F2) were separated, and seed from the shorter-stemmed plants were re-planted in a blast disease nursery. In the third generation plants (F3), those with strongest resistance to blast disease were separated. Seed from F3 was then planted into 298 rows to generate the fourth generation of plants. In this F4 field, on the 288th row, the 3rd plant was selected to be the progenitor for what was more technically labeled IR8–288–3. In late 1965, seed packets containing the offspring of IR8–288–3 traveled home with the Asian scientists to their domestic research stations. At stations in the Philippines, Hong Kong, Taiwan, and Malaysia, of all IRRI varieties tested, IR8–288–3 delivered repeatedly high yields, generally around 6,000 kg/ha.[32] Thus, in 1966, the Green Revolution was born.

While American scientists played a key role in directing the development of the high-yield rice genome in the Philippines, Americans in South Vietnam and the Mekong Delta played a more peripheral role in establishing high-yield rice due largely to the massive presence of American troops and violent fighting in rural areas. While the transfer of IR8 to rice research stations happened rather quietly in Thailand, in Vietnam transfers often involved more attention. For example, the U.S. Army flew several tons of seed into a flood-damaged valley north of Saigon by helicopter. Taiwanese agricultural advisors assisted farmers in caring for the IR8 seed, and reports from the harvest in January showed good results. However, just after the rice was harvested, the Tet Offensive commenced and the valley was overrun by the National Liberation Front.[33] Across the Mekong Delta, the American presence in rural areas was so tenuous that the sustained attention necessary to raise a crop was not often possible. An American agricultural advisor

---

[31] Chandler 1992, 100–102.
[32] Chandler 1992, 108.
[33] LBJ Library 1967.

with the U.S. Agency for International Development described another failed experiment with IRRI rice where 47 varieties including IR8 were planted in a nursery near a relatively secure town in the Mekong Delta, Long Xuyen. The head of the experimental farm, however, was not from the area and did not fully appreciate the area's susceptibility to deep flooding. Floods arrived and the entire seed crop was lost.[34]

Instead of Americans, in 1967–68 Vietnamese entrepreneurs and other Asian advisors, especially Taiwanese, made the first sustained breakthroughs in raising high-yield rice. In some ways, this linking up of Vietnamese farmers and Chinese rice specialists reflected older linkages between Vietnamese farmers and Chinese rice brokers established several centuries earlier. Put simply, these individuals *knew rice*. The only portion of knowledge they lacked was the labscape essential for screening a variety such as IR8-288-3. However, with seed packs, access to motorized pumps and fields ideally situated in the well-drained *miet vuon*, this new network of Vietnamese and expat-Chinese farmers, technical experts, and businessmen provided a robust base for IR8's early distribution.

While the American-sponsored rice station near Long Xuyen failed to generate new seed, a private farmer just down the road became locally famous for harvesting his own crop of IR8 and quadrupling his rice yield. Interviews revealed that he had bought several kilograms of seed from an ethnic-Chinese seed dealer in the river port, My Tho. He planted the seed in a raised bed alongside a highway built on a natural alluvial bank. He applied fertilizers, supplied through American aid programs, and he irrigated the field with a small motor pump. By late 1968, this farmer had made a small fortune selling two successive harvests of seed to area farmers. A Vietnamese national television crew visited the farm as did several hundred farmers. So many came to see this "miracle rice" that he repeatedly complained of farmers stealing seed from his fields at night.[35] Thus, Taiwanese advisors played a more prominent role than Americans in 1967–68 in part because they could move more freely in delta towns. They worked closely with Vietnamese farmers for long spells in the field to develop simple, technological improvements. This work went largely unnoticed by Americans. Only in late 1967, did a Rhodes Scholar, Robert Sansom, note in a report to American officials at the U.S. Agency for International Development that farmers around Mỹ Tho had bought approximately 80,000 "shrimp-tail" boat motors and rigged them up as gas-powered water pumps.[36]

From 1968 to 1975, the success of IRRI varieties was repeatedly limited by war-related disruptions. Farmers interviewed in a former liberated zone described the difficulties involved in transporting such items as fertilizer from

[34] NARA-CP 1968.
[35] NARA-CP 1968.
[36] Sansom 1967.

government-controlled towns across free-fire zones into liberated zones. The high yield rice was for the most part limited to fields along key highways and in staunchly anti-communist areas.[37] The Mekong Delta's most famous rice researcher, Dr. Vo Tong Xuan, noted that in 1974, over 500,000 hectares or 25 percent of delta land was planted in IRRI rice; however, from the first major plantings in 1968, the Mekong Delta remained a net importer of rice. High yield varieties had failed to deliver because "development planners only think of a separate component of a new package of practices but never of local people's readiness to make full use of such innovations."[38] In other words, the actor-network essential to making IR8 successful required the full support of farmers, a viable transport system, and a functioning government. Popular herbicides such as 2,4-D were in short supply – likely due to high demand for the chemical as it was used by the U.S. military in Agent Orange. Fertilizer merchants also regularly engaged in price gouging during the peak season for planting; and others cut fertilizers with brick dust or sand thus reducing potency. Finally, Xuan suggested that the Saigon government may have overstated the area of land in cultivation; likely much of it was already abandoned as war refugees flooded into the cities.[39]

A closer study of Dr. Xuan's work with IRRI and high-yield rice in the Mekong Delta, especially in the 1970s and 1980s, shows that maintaining the *durability* of IRRI rice and maintaining higher yields was a struggle. In fact, IR8 never became the high-yield genome that launched Vietnam's Green Revolution. Its growing season was a few weeks too long, and it was very susceptible to one of the delta's fiercest rice predators, the brown plant hopper. When uncontrolled, this insect caused losses of roughly 60 percent in a crop. In 1971, the U.S. Agency for International Development signed a contract with IRRI to set up a plant breeding operation in the Mekong Delta near Mỹ Tho. IRRI scientists imported over a thousand rice lines from the headquarters. Dr. Xuan worked together with this new group of American and Vietnamese scientists that included IRRI's chief plant breeder, Dr. Dwight W. Kanter. In 1973 they released Tân Nông [TN, New Agriculture] number 73. Dr. Xuan, working from his offices at Can Tho University, then used a radio program broadcast across the Mekong Delta to educate farmers about techniques for controlling brown plant hopper through planting TN73 and two new IRRI strains, IR26 and IR30.[40]

The war ended in 1975, but still rice yields did not improve. The brown plant hopper evolved into a new biotype that soon plagued TN73, IR26 and IR30. In 1976–77, this new biotype ravaged over 700,000 hectares of high yield rice – once again threatening the survival of the variety. At the former

---

[37] Biggs 2002b.
[38] Vo 1975, 88.
[39] Vo 1975, 102–107.
[40] Vo 1995, 23.

IRRI fields near My Tho, just one Vietnamese researcher stayed behind to continue screening varieties in hopes of finding a new variety. Cut off from his American colleagues who returned to Los Banos after the war in 1975, Dr. Xuan wrote to his colleagues asking for help. They sent him an envelope containing four packets, each containing five grams of new high yield varieties. After multiplying one resistant variety, IR36, from five grams to two thousand kilograms a year and a half later, Dr. Xuan convinced the school rector to close the school for two months and send each student out with one kilogram of seed. Every student in the university received a crash course in preparing nurseries and transplanting. This variety's success won over most farmers and especially Vietnamese officials at all levels of government.[41]

Dr. Xuan's two encounters with the brown plant hopper and his success with IR36 reminds us that even with Green Revolution varieties, promiscuous transmission of genes and resistance occurred not only in rice but also in predators. Thus the notion here of a single, high-yield rice genome serving as the basis for widespread economic and ecological changes is misleading. The most important actors in this genome's survival were those people organized by Dr. Xuan and Can Tho University in 1978, later replaced by professional staff at rice research stations and agricultural extension programs across Vietnam. The IRRI research facility in Los Banos played a pivotal role, too, in supplying new genomes to combat an evolving brown plant hopper; but success in the Mekong Delta replied on the coordinated activities of approximately 2,000 students turning five grams of seed into several million tons covering 700,000 hectares! Several years later, with the market-oriented reforms, Vietnam emerged from being a net rice importer to one of the world's largest rice exporters. Vietnam's continuing role as a leader in rice exports depends on the continuation of this actor network built upon close coordination between farmers, politicians, and rice research institutions. Writes Dr. Xuan:

The effect of this work on a Vietnamese leader at the district, province, or national level has been very pronounced. When Vietnamese leaders – most of whom are politicians – talk about development, they talk about rice. When they talk about rice, they talk about new varieties from IRRI. This top-down approach by the Vietnamese government to agricultural development has accelerated the use of new varieties from IRRI throughout Vietnam. Even now, if we do not have new lines to release each year, scientists are criticized first by the farmers and then by national and provincial leaders. Consequently, every Vietnamese agricultural scientist is trying to develop new rice varieties adapted to each local situation. In addition, the Vietnamese farmer, especially the southern Vietnamese farmer, is very market oriented, always wanting something new. Most Vietnamese farmers want to replace the variety they

---

[41] Vo 1995, 25.

have been growing for two or three crop seasons to keep up with the evolution of the insects, pests, and diseases in the field.[42]

This quote from Dr. Xuan is insightful, for it suggests two things. First, the intensive organization of politicians, farmers, and rice scientists is a requirement to continue producing new strains of IRRI rice that can continue to adapt to changing ecological conditions. However, when one considers the intense pressures riding on these rice researchers to get it right or risk an economic disaster, is it possible that rice could be organizing us? In other words, rice genomes possess a remarkable ability to outcross and lose sought-after traits. As scientists move ever deeper into investigations of rice's encapsulated knowledge in its DNA, keeping up with the evolution of cultivars requires ever more discipline among the ranks of breeders, plant scientists, politicians, private firms, and farmers. Thus, a particular genetic variety such as IR36 can be viewed as an *assemblage* formed through repeated efforts to cross varieties, screen the offspring, and then isolate specific plants. Conversely, such an assemblage brings with it a very tightly defined set of procedures for maintaining it as a productive variety. With any serious disruptions in these networks, the variety fades into a genetic swamp of weedy relatives.

INTO THE PROMISCUOUS WILDERNESS

In the Mekong Delta today, one often gets the sense of living in a boom economy perched delicately on a razor's edge from disaster. Rice production continues to rise while old river towns grow into cities – some now with over a million residents. The delta's largest university, Can Tho University, is now sponsoring 1,000 students to pursue PhDs from internationally acclaimed schools in such fields as rice science, mechanical engineering, hydrology, and information sciences. Where a handful of PhDs such as Dr. Xuan were around to save the delta from the brown plant hopper in 1978, there are now hundreds of expertly trained rice scientists. While the future for many of the delta's twenty million people looks brighter and more peaceful than ever, there are nevertheless serious concerns, mostly environmental. The Mekong Delta is one of the world's flattest deltas – just a meter or so above sea level per one hundred kilometers; and sea levels are rising. Upstream on the Mekong various nations and private companies are moving ahead with plans to build hydroelectric dams on the Mekong mainstream. Nobody is exactly sure what effects this regulated river flow will have on the lower delta, but many are concerned about reduced silt, greater salinity, and subsidence. Finally, sustained alterations to paddy fields with chemical fertilizers and insecticides and widespread impoundment of water means that wild fish populations have

[42] Vo 1995, 27.

decreased severely. The once-ubiquitous catfish are harder to find in flooded fields. Fingerlings must either be imported from upstream in Cambodia or bred from eggs in high-tech hatcheries. Landraces of rice can still be found in some local markets; especially in years where rice futures are low, farmers like to grow landraces that require fewer expensive chemical inputs. However, the shift to mechanized agriculture and a high-yield harvesting regime has sent most young men into cities to find work. Knowledge about traditional breeding techniques, names for traditional tools and old landraces are dying with the older generation. Delta society has become more dependent, not less, on actor-networks built around IRRI, national rice research institutes, multinational food corporations, and global trade networks.

However, were farmers from past eras here to observe rice in the present, they might chide us by saying that growing rice has always been a struggle. True, much more land was wilderness before 1900; however, advancements in studying rice genomes have opened up a new world of wilderness at least at the genetic level. While landscapes may show increasing signs of human disturbance, rice and many other organisms such as the brown plant hopper show an incredible ability to evolve and proliferate. Just five grams of seed is sufficient to produce several thousand kilograms of seed in a year or two. In rice's promiscuity then there is at least a continuing potential for wildness. Concerns about loss of genetic biodiversity in rice in the Mekong Delta and elsewhere have prompted a new generation of IRRI and Vietnamese researchers to become bio-prospectors of sorts, gathering surviving strains of old landraces, wild rice (*O. rufipogons* and *O. officinalis*), and especially long-stem landraces. Rising sea levels, evolving pest ecologies and changing flood patterns challenge today's rice breeders as much as in the past. One might even say that where the seeds of cultivars encapsulate knowledge associated with actor-networks that maintain them, the seeds of wild and weedy species encapsulate the potential for wilderness. A grain-centered view of rice thus not only points to the extensive networks required to sustain it; it also reminds us that the history of rice is a living history. Within rice seeds, rice fields, and rice economies is a persistent, biological tension.

6

Red and White Rice in the Vicinity of Sierra Leone: Linked Histories of Slavery, Emancipation, and Seed Selection

Bruce L. Mouser, Edwin Nuijten, Florent Okry, and Paul Richards[1]

This chapter offers an account of the introduction of Carolina rice to communities surrounding the abolitionist settlement at Sierra Leone from the end of the eighteenth century. The abolitionists sought to encourage cultivation of rice with white pericarp, since this was thought to be more acceptable in export markets. Carolina rice was white. Most of this crop was grown in the region north of Freetown, on slave estates, where it displaced African red rice earlier produced for Atlantic slave ships. Carolina rice then appears to have become more widely disseminated, perhaps as a result of slave defections. Re-selected by free peasants for local use it became red, a colour preferred in the region around Sierra Leone.[2] Thus, our account describes two changes in rice seed type grown in the vicinity of Sierra Leone over a period of about 150 years under pressure for commodification. First we outline a shift from African to Asian rice in the late eighteenth and early nineteenth centuries, as the slave trade was ended and legitimate commerce took its place. Then we sketch a scenario for the modification of Carolina rice under farmer selection in the later nineteenth and early twentieth centuries. This second shift represents the reworking of rice as a commodity in international trade into an item more suited to local needs. Elsewhere such items have been termed anti-commodities.[3] Our chapter attempts to illustrate this process for rice.

Due to the interdisciplinary complexity of the argument the reader is offered some initial contextualization. First there is a need to explain the use of the terms "red" and "white" rice. West Africa has two distinct species

---

[1] All four contributors are to be regarded as joint first authors.
[2] This preference applies specifically to the region around Sierra Leone. Elsewhere in West Africa – e.g., Guinea-Bissau – white rice is preferred.
[3] Maat, Chapter 15, this volume.

of rice – *Oryza glaberrima* (African rice) and *O. sativa* (Asian rice).[4] African rice generally has a red (or more accurately a non-white) pericarp.[5] Asian rice has varieties with white or red pericarp types. Asian rice in international trade tends to be white, since this is a color favored by millers and merchants.[6] Many varieties of Asian rice consumed locally, however, are red. Thus red pericarp is found in indica and japonica variants of Asian rice, as well as in African rice. Pericarp color would have been an ideal indicator, as a white color is based on a single gene mutation.[7] As it is, it is not diagnostic of species or sub-species and we need to work with other less distinctive indicators. These other indicators (in Upper West Africa) include grain size (African rice tends to have smaller grains in the area covered by this chapter), farm location (Asian rice was planted – initially at least – in lowlands, and African rice on hills), and nutritional properties (African rice was considered superior, a view still espoused by peasant farmers today).

A second contextual point is to explain our interest in japonica rice. In the course of a larger study of rice varieties in the West African coastal belt we carried out assessments of the robustness and plasticity of farmer-selected types.[8] Specifically, the question whether West African farmer varieties are broadly adapted was posed. An argument in favor of modern varieties is that these have been selected for wide use. Farmer varieties are sometimes presumed to perform well only in local niches. We wanted to test this assumption. Representative farmer varieties were assembled from Senegal to Togo and assessed for genotype x environment (GxE) interaction. Many farmer varieties showed low GxE, implying they grow well over a range of environments. One set of varieties in one region stood out as an exception. This was the group of japonica rices from Sierra Leone. These rices showed high GxE responses, implying restriction to specific niches, perhaps because they are more recent introductions than other Asian rices in our sample. Thus, we wanted to know more about the history of this group of rices in the coastal region adjacent to the abolitionist settlement at Sierra Leone. The present chapter offers our findings on this topic.

---

[4] According to one authority African rice was domesticated in the Inland Delta of the Niger about 3000 years ago (Porteres 1962). This speculation has received some recent genetic support (Li et al. 2011). Consumption of wild rice (*O. barthii*) at an early date is reported for the Lake Chad basin (Klee et al. 2000). Selection pressure for domestication may have occurred over a wide area of West Africa (Harlan 1971).

[5] Gross et al. (2010) report a mutation for white pericarp in African rice (the rc-gl allele) and suggest that this may have occurred not long before the introduction of white pericarp Asian rices into West Africa, thus inhibiting the wider spread of the mutation.

[6] According to Grist (1975, 409) "modern taste in rice ... demands first and foremost appearance, so that flavor and health are sacrificed for the white appearance."

[7] Sweeney et al. 2007.

[8] Mokuwa et al. 2013.

One further point is in order. The introduction of Carolina rice to Sierra Leone is well-attested in late eighteenth and early nineteenth century sources. Our account of the later stages – adaptation to local use – is much more speculative. In part this stems from the limited documentary information available on maroon (slave runaway) communities and their transformation into self-sufficient peasantries from the second half of the nineteenth century. We have not attempted to hide the gaps in the later part of the story. What is offered here is a plausible scenario, tested by data drawn from history, anthropology, and crop science. In particular, the molecular information on current japonica rices in rural Sierra Leone gives us an end-line against which information on the historical and regional development of rice as a commodity can be further assessed.

RICE IN WEST AFRICA

Rice in West Africa is found in two major localities. It is associated with the great river valleys of the savanna, from Mauretania to Lake Chad, where it is now often a woman's crop.[9] It is also the main staple of the Upper West African coastal zone (from Côte d'Ivoire to Senegal), today grown mainly by peasant households.

Two major and dissimilar sorts of rice cultivation are practiced in the coastal zone, on coastal mangrove soils and on interior uplands. On the savanna section of the Upper West African coast rice is particularly associated with mangrove wetlands. The Jola people of Casamance were pioneers of this form of cultivation.[10] Other groups, such as the Baga of Guinea, may also have cultivated some rice in the mangrove zone at an early date.[11] Hawthorne shows that among the Balanta of Guinea-Bissau, however, large-scale mangrove rice cultivation developed only during the era of the Atlantic slave trade. Clearing mangroves and building dikes to exclude salt water made local farm labor more valuable, thus increasing incentives not to sell Balanta young men into captivity.[12]

The types of rice cultivated in the mangrove zone varied. Balanta rice cultivators were early users of imported Asian rice types "introduced to West Africa by Atlantic merchants in the sixteenth century," whereas Diola (Jola) grew only "an ordinary rice, very small," but with dark colour and "a good taste."[13] These latter characteristics indicate the African species.

---

[9] Carney 1993a, Nuijten 2010.
[10] Linares 1992, 2002.
[11] Fields-Black 2008.
[12] "This masculinized labor system [for diking rice polders] emerged during an agricultural revolution, the catalyst for which was the Atlantic slave trade" (Hawthorne 2003, 152).
[13] Hawthorne 2003, 159.

Mangrove rice cultivation along the Upper West African coast has occasioned an impressive body of scholarly literature.[14] The mangrove rice crop, however, was probably less important regionally than the output of African rice from the dryland zone.[15] The dryland system of rice cultivation involves planting specific varieties at different heights and dates on a soil catena stretching from hill crest to valley swamp.[16] This was a major source of rice for the slave ships in the heyday of the Atlantic trade.[17] Slave vessels trading higher on the coast sometimes sent cutters down to Sierra Leone or Cape Mount to purchase African red rice.

Despite the brutality of the trade, slave captains were conscious of a need to feed captives well, since this affected condition on arrival and thus profits. African red rice was acquired because it was a major staple food in parts of the Upper West African region, and readily available. Quite erroneously, it was thought less likely than white rice to induce "bloody flux" (dysentery), one of a slave voyage's greatest hazards.[18] African red rice was also considered (more plausibly) to be nutritionally superior to Asian rice, and sometimes was taken on board to feed the crew as well as slaves.[19] The abolitionist Thomas Clarkson wrote that "it is extraordinary that this rice should be finer in flavor, of greater substance, more wholesome, and capable of preservation, than the rice of any country whatsoever."[20]

WHITE RICE AND ABOLITION

A group of evangelical Christians centered around Granville Sharp and William Wilberforce spearheaded attempts to persuade the British parliament to abolish the Atlantic slave trade. A major step was to establish a settlement for freed slaves at Sierra Leone in 1787, at the heart of an important late-eighteenth century slave exporting region (Figure P.1b). Planned by Sharp, the first settlement at Sierra Leone (Granville Town) failed, and was replaced by a company venture intended to offer an economic basis for emancipation. The governor (at various periods from 1794 to 1799) of this second

---

[14] For example, Fields-Black 2008, Hawthorne 2003, Linares 1992, Littlefield 1981, Sarró 2009.

[15] Grist (1975, 179) notes that "Dryland rice is grown on nearly a quarter of the world's rice area [but] despite its importance ... has received far less attention than it deserves from both cultivators and investigators."

[16] Richards 1986, 28–44.

[17] Samuel Gamble, master of the slave vessel, the *Sandown*, recorded in his log for November, 12 1793 that he "receiv'd on board one ton and a half of red rice" (Mouser and Gamble 2002, 86).

[18] Rediker 2007, 271–2, 274, Richards 1996a, 217.

[19] The crew of a slave vessel from Sierra Leone (Bance Island) to Charleston in 1796 lived "upon red rice and salt beef ... the whole passage" (Mouser 1978, 260).

[20] Cited in Winterbottom 1803, 55. Thomas Jefferson imported African rice seed for trials at Monticello, and distribution to planters, to improve slave subsistence (Richards 1996a, 216–20).

settlement (Freetown) was a Scottish abolitionist, Zachary Macaulay. Trained in trade in Glasgow and apprenticed to plantation management in the West Indies, Macaulay applied his business and accounting skills to the problem of the economic survival of the infant colony. The Freetown settlement became a British Crown Colony in 1808, after the passing of a parliamentary bill outlawing the Atlantic slave trade. Macaulay maintained his connections to Sierra Leone as an adviser to his successor as governor (Thomas Ludlum) and through the activities of his London trading house, Messrs. Macaulay and Babington.[21]

A focus of Macaulay's advice was the need to develop export-oriented agriculture. Sierra Leone was not an agricultural colony. The topography was against it. Labor supply was also a problem, since slavery was banned. Macaulay proposed a system of indentured labor to replace slavery, but was criticized for reintroducing slavery by another name. In any case, those who acquired their freedom by being settled at Freetown preferred to trade. All-in-all, the infant colony had little potential for generating agricultural exports. It could, however, be a centre of agrarian commerce and stimulate agricultural exports from the surrounding region. Macaulay considered coffee, indigo, and cotton. Rice was also attractive, since Freetown constituted a considerable market for food shipments from surrounding districts, and some of this might be re-exported. Macaulay apparently hoped such exports would divert food supplies from the slave ships. He and Ludlum were clear, however, that the London commodity market would not accept red rice. If the plan was to succeed Freetown needed to broker the export of white rice.

> [...] it appears important to point out to [African chieftains] the advantage which they would derive from cultivating generally the *white* instead of the *red rice*, because in that case a vent might easily be obtained for their surplus produce of that article, either in Great Britain or in the West Indies; the former species being a marketable article, while the other, while equally useful as food, would not find a sale out of Africa.[22]

Macaulay offered "proof of concept," even as the abolition bill was before parliament, by importing a consignment of 100 tons of white rice from the region around Sierra Leone, for which he applied for a prize offered by

---

[21] Thomas Babington was Macaulay's brother-in-law, and his initial link with the Clapham Sect, a group of evangelical Christians committed to the abolitionist cause.

[22] Macaulay to the Right Honourable Viscount Castlereagh, May 8, 1807 (Macaulay 1815, Appendix p. 35, emphasis in original). Macaulay to Ludlum (governor of Sierra Leone) February 26, 1807: "It seems highly important that a ready market should be furnished to the Africans for the rice they may raise; and yet I fear the red rice will never find a sale out of Africa. Would it not be possible to induce the natives to cultivate exclusively the white rice, for which, if properly cleaned, it might be possible to obtain a market in the West Indies, or even in England?" (Macaulay 1815, Appendix, p. 19).

the African Institution.[23] The amount shipped was equivalent to between 10 and 15 percent of the total parliamentary estimate of annual commercial output of red rice for the slave ships.[24]

Where had the seed come from? As a merchant in London, Macaulay would have had contacts with white rice exporting regions, but we have found no evidence he introduced white rice to planters in West Africa. A more likely source would appear to be South Carolina. Several of the resident slave traders were Americans with direct contact with rice planters in South Carolina. The Rev. Leopold Butscher, a German missionary resident on the River Pongo from 1806 to 1812, reported that Carolina rice had been introduced to the area about 10 years before his arrival, adding that it was planted separately on burnt fields of Guinea grass and that "the natives do not think it so nourishing as their own kind."[25]

There were two main types of Carolina rice: Carolina White and Carolina Gold.[26] Gold was named for the color of its husk, not its pericarp. The Carolina rices are thought to have originated in Indonesia (and thus are probably tropical japonicas). Carolina Gold was hard to grow, since it was tall and lodged easily. Carolina White appears to have been the more widely cultivated variety. The slave trader Theophilus Conneau, resident on the Rio Pongo in the mid-1820s, was familiar with the local Carolina rice, reporting the grain to be whiter than African rice, though less solid and tasty.

The grain morphology of Carolina rice differed from the form generally thought to be typical for japonicas. One authority distinguished three main rice grain shapes: a "long, thin, cylindrical grain, known as Patna" (indica), a "short, stout grain, known as Spanish-Japan" (typical japonica), and a "relatively long and bold type" of grain (Carolina rice).[27] This longer grained morphotype remains especially common among japonica rices grown in Sierra Leone today, and is below interpreted as evidence of descent from eighteenth century Carolina rice.

A puzzle about these latter-day long-grain japonicas is that today they mainly have red pericarp. It is our argument that Carolina rice became red when it escaped from early nineteenth century slave plantations to be taken

---

[23] The African Institution (1807–1827) was an important group advocating for emancipation and the development of Africa, and linked royalty, parliamentarians, and leading abolitionists. The prize was a silver plate worth 50 guineas, awarded as the bill to abolish the slave trade was before parliament (in 1807).

[24] "The Quantity purchased annually for Consumption of the Ships and Factories may be from 700 to 1000 tons" (House of Commons Sessional Papers of the Eighteenth Century, Volume 69, George III: *The Report of the Lords of Trade on the Slave Trade 1789*, Part I, 66, 71 [ed. Sheila Lambert].

[25] Mouser 2000.

[26] Tibbetts 2006.

[27] Grist (1975 [1953], 95) cites C. E. Douglas, *Journal of the Royal Society of Arts*, July. 18, 1930.

up by peasants. Later in this chapter we will offer a scenario for such a trajectory, supported by molecular evidence. At this point it is sufficient only to note that in the 1790s white and red rices were planted in distinct localities. In distinguishing Guinea grass areas planted to Carolina rice and the "bushy places ... [used by local farmers] for the planting of their own sort [of rice]" Butscher provides us with evidence of an out-crossing barrier strong enough to have kept Carolina rice white, at least for a time. Guinea grass fields were unsuited to peasant cultivation methods. Soils occupied by rhizomatic Guinea grass are low in fertility and very hard to work. Today, in central and north-western Sierra Leone, their cultivation generally requires use of hired tractors.[28] Before the machine age only landlords with numerous slaves were likely to attempt the task. Encouraged by the abolitionists at Freetown, white rice was a commodity associated with newly emergent slave plantations.

RICE AS AN AFRICAN SLAVE PLANTATION CROP

The basic pattern of rice cultivation first observed in the vicinity of Sierra Leone by European visitors in the late eighteenth century was communal and subsistence-oriented. John Matthews, a trader on the Sierra Leone river, commented that "the natives ... at and about Sierra Leone ... cultivate little more rice than is necessary for their own consumption," adding that "the sides of the hills are generally preferred for their rice plantations."[29] Each village (according to Thomas Winterbottom, resident at Freetown in the 1790s) cultivated a large field and shared the harvest, pouring rice to height of the village chief as his portion. Winterbottom also noted, however, that slave-worked private farms were beginning to emerge in the region, especially among the Fula of Futa Jalon.[30]

Slave-based plantations also seem to have developed rapidly and extensively on the coastal plain north of Freetown. In the Mandingo state of Moria, founded about 1720, slaves were divided (as elsewhere) into two categories. Household slaves were often locally born into slave status, and were partially assimilated. Farm slaves came from outside Moria, and were war-captives or newly bought. They were assigned to outlying farming villages, where they were closely disciplined and watched. They had few rights, and were in danger of being sold into the Atlantic trade.

---

[28] Stobbs 1963.
[29] Matthews 1787, 23, 55.
[30] "Though each village and town has its plantation, individuals are allowed to cultivate others for their own private use, and this they frequently do, employing sometimes their own labor, but generally slaves for that purpose. This custom is very prevalent among the Foolas, where land, in consequence, begins to be considered ... private property ... subdivided into particular plantations ... " (Winterbottom 1803, 53).

Matthews estimated that about three-quarters of the population of this region was enslaved, remarking that "some of the principal men among the Mandingoes have from seven hundred to a thousand [slaves]."[31] But he also noted that "about the Riopongeos [River Pongo] they have three rice harvests in the year; one crop from the hills and two from the plains which [the rivers] overflow."[32] The (red) hill rice would have been directed toward the slave ships, but the annual "two [crops] from the plains" provided the vent for surplus through which Freetown was supplied white Carolina rice and which Macaulay hoped could be exported.

Cultivation of rice by slaves began as an *ad hoc* affair. Destined for the Atlantic trade, slaves were put to work temporarily to grow their own food. Matthews noted that "Every prisoner taken in battle was either put to death or kept as a slave ... those captured before the commencement of the rice season ... were reserved to cultivate the rice-ground; and sold after the harvest to ... tribes bordering the sea ... ."[33] From a peak in the 1760s (a decade in which more than 100,000 captives were exported from the region around Sierra Leone) exports dropped, in the decade of the 1780s, to less than half, in part because of imports being curtailed during the American Revolution.[34] Slave-raiding warlords were now forced to devise new forms of work for their unsold captives. By the 1790s the slave-holders were diversifying into white rice supply for the abolitionist settlement at Sierra Leone.

A more formalized system of slave plantations, as observed by Winterbottom in Futa Jalon, now began to emerge on the coastal plain. Increasingly, farm slaves on the coast claimed rights not to be sold overseas. Where these rights were breached, as in cases where trumped-up charges for witchcraft or other crimes were used as a pretext for selling a slave to the Atlantic dealers, the risk of desertion or outright rebellion increased.[35] In 1785 there was a major rising of Bullom, Baga, and Temne slaves from Moria.[36] The rebels received tacit support from the neighboring Susu state of Sumbuya. A maroon community took root at Yangekori, a camp at the base of the interior hills. Eventually the Susu and Mandingo slave holders of

---

[31] Matthews 1788, 149.
[32] Matthews 1788, 56. Butscher mentions the possibility of taking three crops of Carolina rice per year (Mouser 2000, 5 [no pagination]).
[33] Matthews 1788, 147.
[34] Rashid 2000, 663.
[35] See, for example, Richardson (2001), on slave revolts in Senegambia. Richardson argues that sale into the Atlantic trade of slaves with acquired rights was a trigger for revolt. On the process of social declassification see Lockwood (1990) and on its application to recent revolt in Sierra Leone see Richards (1996b).
[36] There is some variation in accounts of the Yangekori rebellion as to its social composition. Nowak (1986) and Rashid (2000) stress the role of farm slaves. Mouser (2007) stresses the involvement of domestic slaves as well. If the declassification argument is valid we should look for factors eroding the rights of both classes of slaves.

Sumbuya and Moria combined forces to destroy the camp in 1796.[37] This unexpected alliance among trade rivals is itself suggestive of the growing importance of slave-based agrarian production to the region as a whole.

The older pattern of trade in which caravans from the interior shipped down cattle, hides, rice, slaves, and gold, in return for salt, cotton cloth, and imported firearms and other European goods was far from changed overnight. The rulers of Moria and Sumbuya continued to sell slaves and red rice to European and American merchants on the coast. Theophilus Conneau found this trade still active in the 1820s.[38] But from 1808 a Royal Navy anti-slavery patrol was stationed at Freetown. Slave shipments from surrounding districts were progressively reduced, while at the same time the growth of Freetown demanded new sources of food supply. The extra two annual harvests that Matthews said the planters of Moria could get from farming their grassy plains must have seemed (as Macaulay hoped) a boon to legitimate trade.

Moria (with its capital at Forecariah) was the polity most directly in trading contact with the Freetown settlement. The landlord class elected a paramount ruler by selecting among candidates offered by leading families. In 1803 Moria accepted the rule of Almamy Amara, though not without some dispute as to his legitimacy and ability. For the next 20 years Amara became the strong man of Moria politics, and a determined opponent of British policy. After 1807 he remained stubbornly tied to American markets for slaves, as well as obsessed with what he considered to be British attempts to replace his control of Moria. In effect, Amara was caught between contradictory sets of market signals. Part of his wealth came from continued involvement in the slave trade. But an increasingly large part now came from taxing trade caravans headed across Moria territory for the emporium of Freetown. Many of these caravans carried the new Carolina white rice.

Shared trading interests brought Amara and the Freetown authorities into conflict over emancipation. In an incident in 1814 a large caravan from Moria arrived at Freetown with rice and cattle, whereupon a number of Moria carriers escaped their owners and requested [governor] Maxwell's protection. Amara's attempts to resolve the impasse included sending a fiery letter to Maxwell, in which he stoutly defended his interests in the slave trade.[39] His

---

[37] Mouser 1979, 80. Fendan Modu of Sumbuya told Richard Bright in 1802 "that commonly he makes 100 tons of salt and grows 100 tons of rice, exclusive of his own consumption." This must have taken a large labor force, and suggests that slave production was well entrenched by that date.

[38] Conneau 1976. Conneau worked for an Afro-European trader, Mongo John [John Ormond jun.]. On November 30, 1826 a Fula caravan arrived, carrying gold, 40 slaves, ivory, beeswax, 3,500 bullock hides, and 15 tons of rice. "The rice we purchased at a cent a pound" [comprising, at 22 dollars per ton about 4 percent of goods carried]. Hides and rice were agreed first "as these articles are generally exchanged for salt," needed by the Fula for their cattle.

[39] Mouser 1973.

own preference was to continue to supply the slave ships with red rice, but demand for white rice from the colony was of increasing interest to a number of the Moria landlords who had elected him as chief. Going against these interests risked mobilizing rivals for power.

By 1821 the British colony was receiving more than two-thirds of its white rice from the plantations of Moria and Sumbuya. Most came from the area loyal to Amara, but needed to cross lands in dispute before reaching Freetown. Trade tensions in these disputed areas erupted into open conflict when a rebellious Susu vassal town of Kukuna on the Kolenten (Great Scarcies) river continued to ship white rice down-river to Freetown. Amara was determined to bring the Kukuna rebels to heel, and allied himself with the Mandingo chief of Magbeti, a Temne-Bullom town below Kambia, to blockade the river. He also threatened Moriba of Port Loko, a key trading node for Freetown, with war if the sale of white rice was not halted.

Fearing a threat to its food supply, Freetown felt bound to act. Governor Grant sent Major Henry Ricketts and a Lieutenant Austin to Forecaria to ask Amara to re-open the road and allow the cultivation of white rice. Amara offered the excuse that trade in all commodities had stopped in the interior because the Moria people were afraid of ambushes by Dala Modu, a trade rival. But he also recognized that pressure for change was becoming increasingly hard to resist. The Atlantic slave trade was in terminal decline, and the pull of red rice weakening. Amara offered the British a white flag. Specifically, he claimed now to be actively recommending the planting of white rice.

FARM SLAVERY AND SELF-EMANCIPATION IN THE LATER NINETEENTH CENTURY

It was not only Amara who faced a dilemma in reconciling slavery and the new commodity trade. The commercial success of the abolitionist enclave also rested on a contradiction – strategic food supplies produced by interior slaves. Officials were not clear how to resolve the problem. Macaulay thought about offering the chiefs a bounty for emancipation, but realized that bounty-hunting might extend slave raiding and bankrupt the colony. Ludlum feared for trade if the slave-based plantation economy collapsed: "they will weave their own cloth, raise their own tobacco, smelt their own iron, and resume their bows and arrows."[40] In Ludlum's eyes a return to subsistence betokened barbarity.

No such reversion occurred, but neither did slavery disappear. The plantation system in Moria was better adapted to commerce in food than either Ludlum or Macaulay had anticipated. It remained the basis for a well-organized

---

[40] Ludlum to Macaulay, 1807, in Macaulay 1815, 50–1.

interior economy producing white rice for Freetown and red rice for Futa Jalon until the mid-nineteenth century.

The Rev. William Cooper Thomson, passing through Moria as an emissary from Freetown to Futa Jallon in 1842–3, noted that the "farms occupy much space ... cultivated by slaves" and that "export of rice to the colony" compensated for the decline in the slave trade. North of Kukuna rice was in short supply in Benna country, due to three years of locust attacks. But many people were said to be hoarding supplies "in the hope of purchasing slaves from their neighbors on the other side of the [Kolenten] river, who were much worse off than themselves."[41] Canny owners were maneuvering in anticipation that the plantation economy would rebound as soon as the locusts left.

It was about this time, however, that a new episode of slave revolt occurred, with long lasting consequences. Ishmael Rashid describes how Kukuna became embroiled in the long-lasting Bilali rebellion (1838–1872).[42] The son of Alimamy Namina Sheka Dumbuya, the Kukuna ruler, and a Koranko slave woman, and thus born a domestic slave, Bilali was denied the freedom he had been promised on his father's death. He fled from Kukuna and set up a refuge for runaway slaves in Tonko Limba country at Laminayah.[43] The Limba were a free peasant group with little use for slavery. With Limba support, Bilali was able to fend off many determined attacks over three decades.

The conflict drew in participants from as far away as Mende country, and so damaged the region's trade (not least its food exports) that the British in Freetown repeatedly tried to mediate a peace. Governor John Pope Hennessey, acting on advice from Edward Wilmot Blyden, finally brokered a compromise in 1872–3 that re-opened trade routes to Freetown. Bilali's enemies conceded his right to fight for his freedom, if not to run Laminayah as a refuge for run-away slaves (a "New Freetown"). But by the late 1870s "Moriah lapsed into another round of internal civil conflict."[44] With the Moria slave-owning elite weakened by in-fighting, the space for free peasants and self-emancipated slaves was enlarged. The pivot of the regional rice trade, in an ethnically mixed region of Susu plantations and Limba farms, Kukuna became the focus not only of a struggle for political freedom but also of local attempts to redefine seed technologies.

Free peasant and self-emancipated groups provided a conduit for movement of seeds out of the plantation corridor north of Freetown and into the grassy and at times inaccessible bolilands stretching away toward the southeast. The region is named after *boli*, which are seasonally flooded grassy depressions associated with an ancient lagoon system in the extensive coastal

[41] Thomson 1846, 113, 110, 123.
[42] Rashid 2000, 673–7.
[43] Laminaya was about 40 km ESE of Kukuna on the Little Scarcies (Kabba) river (Garrett 1892).
[44] Rashid 2000, 676.

plain behind Freetown. The boliland zone, however, contains more than *boli*. It is in fact a region with a huge range of both wetland and dryland niches for the determined cultivator to colonize.[45] Its more isolated recesses provided refuge for rebel groups in the Sierra Leone civil war in the 1990s.[46] A thinly populated mosaic of Guinea grass plains and forested islands, the area seems particularly suited to the Carolina rice that Butscher first associated with grassland sites along the River Pongo. The self-emancipated peasants of Laminayah and surrounding areas set about the task of adapting the seeds of the plantation economy to the requirements of the small-scale rice production systems found over much of lowland Sierra Leone today.

A NEW SOURCE OF SLAVE-BASED FOOD SUPPLY FOR FREETOWN

Before examining the evidence for these seed modifications "from below" we will trace the slave-based food-supply system down to the point of general emancipation of domestic and farm slaves. From 1882 the British and French delimited an international boundary through the plantation zone. Boundary demarcation was accompanied by French efforts to divert caravans from the interior away from Freetown and toward the new port of Conakry. Temne and Susu slave owners on the Sierra Leone side of the new border, sensing the threat of customs barriers and further interior slave revolts started to move their assets closer to the Freetown market for rice and the British protection it afforded. This followed discovery of a simple but ingenious technique to utilize hitherto neglected high-sulfur mangrove soils on the lower reaches of the Little and Great Scarcies rivers.[47] The technique involves keeping soils wet during the dry season through the daily pumping action of the tides, and delaying planting until rising fresh water in the rivers washes out excess salt during the first part of the rains. Tall varieties of rice (nursed in adjacent freshwater swamps and river terraces) are transplanted into the riverine mud to ripen on the falling flood.

Initial development of mangrove soils required more capital and labor than possessed by free peasant groups such as the Limba. Only landlords with large numbers of slaves, and the resources to feed these slaves until the land became productive, could undertake the task.[48] Mangroves took three

---

[45] Stobbs 1963.
[46] For example, rebel bases at Rosos (Sanda Tendaren chiefdom) and Yelima (Kamajei chiefdom).
[47] Brackish-water mangrove soils cannot be managed using the salt exclusion (diking) techniques found further up the coast. The soils contain sulfur oxidized by a bacterium (*Thiobacillus thio-oxidans*) as soon as soil moisture levels are reduced to about 50–60% (Grist 1975, 22). Polderization results in severe acidification of drying soil.
[48] An informant told Paul Richards that his father, a Susu chief on the Great Scarcies, had as many as 800 slaves growing mangrove rice, prior to emancipation.

years from initial clearing to the point where the rotting process was sufficiently advanced to allow planting to begin. Within two or three decades up to the start of World War I most of the area was reclaimed and turned into profitable rice plantations, linked to the Freetown market by riverine and coastal shipping routes. The British authorities opened up the chest of Empire white rices to the planters. A comparative trial of varieties from British Guiana, India, and Ceylon and local varieties was organized at Mambolo, on the Little Scarcies, in 1911–12.[49] The colonial authorities also assisted the planters by deflecting pressure for emancipation of slaves. The old compromise of an abolitionist settlement fed by slave labor became the basis for food supply for the capital of the newly formed Colony and Protectorate of Sierra Leone in the first three decades of the twentieth century.

The French abolished slavery in their West African colonies in 1905. The British delayed. The colonial government was threatened by an uprising of chiefs in 1898, and some officials thought the trouble was triggered by a threat to impose colony law (and its anti-slavery code) in the newly declared Protectorate. Buying and selling slaves was halted but those born as slaves were told that only the next generation would be born free. A concern was to head off claims for compensation were the slaves to be freed at a stroke. But mangrove rice supplies to Freetown were becoming increasingly vital, doubling in the first two years of World War I.[50] Freetown was an important station for Atlantic shipping, and wartime increased the city's food demands. Slave numbers were highest in the north-western part of the country, especially among groups such as the Susu and Mandingo involved in rice production in the Mangroves and along the rivers of the adjacent boliland zone. British authorities argued that slavery would die a natural death, but in effect they were protecting the capital's food supply.

The status quo was challenged soon after World War I ended. The newly formed League of Nations established an anti-slavery committee, and it began to take an interest in Sierra Leone. It became clear that farm slavery was more than an archaic institution fading away into a code of status and honor. Slave labor was the backbone of food production, especially that part of it organized on a sufficient scale to feed the growing urban centers. The League demanded progress toward emancipation, but still the government dragged its feet.

Matters came to a head with a revolt by Mandingo slaves in the Mabole valley, a location on the edge of the boliland zone, in 1926.[51] The rebellion made politicians and newspapers in Britain aware that slavery was still alive

---

[49] Moore-Sieray 1988, 66.
[50] Moore-Sieray 1988, 65.
[51] Arkley 1965.

in a country founded for freed slaves. The government's hand was forced. All slaves were declared free on January 1, 1928.[52]

Emancipation effectively ended half a century of expansion of mangrove rice cultivation, and nearly 150 years of symbiosis between abolition and slavery. An urban food security crisis loomed, and science attempted to take up the slack. The Rokupr Rice Research Station was founded in 1934, on the banks of the Great Scarcies, with a mandate to improve the productivity of mangrove rice farming systems through application of modern methods of plant improvement and irrigation management.

In an initial period very little was achieved. Ill-advised flood exclusion works at the end of World War II threatened to destroy the mangrove soil.[53] Modest improvements in the 1950s notwithstanding, urban food demands outstripped supply from the mangrove zone. Experiments with mechanization of rice cultivation in the bolilands also proved unsustainable. Freetown, ever more in need of rice, turned – postwar – to imported supplies. In the decade to independence in 1961 white rice increasingly came in bags from overseas.[54]

The search for secure urban food supply continued in the independence era. Hope was now focused on technology transfer (the importation with World Bank funding of an Asian wetland seeds and water management package for peasant farmers). This attempted Green Revolution foundered on unsolved problems of labor supply.[55] The Green Revolution package was labor intensive. Sierra Leonean rice farmers were constrained by labor shortages, and labor rates were high, with the result that local rice prices tended to be high. This threatened the food security of the urban poor. Faced with prospects of urban political agitation centered on food successive governments stepped in with imported, subsidized white rice, thereby undercutting the rise in rural wages necessary to effect the technical transition to which the Green Revolution aspired. Rural communities sought to tie young laborers to the land on low wages through the manipulation of customary law.[56] This drove many emancipated farm laborers out of agriculture altogether. Some went to the cities. Others opted to labor in the alluvial diamond pits, where sponsors of mining ventures fed their workers on imported rice.

Most attempts to modernize agriculture in Sierra Leone continue to be, in effect, disguised calls for a return to some kind of cheap labor system to replace bonded farm labor. The only real alternative was the post-1945

---

[52] Two slave owners had been prevented from reclaiming slaves who absconded during the 1926 revolt, but the decision was overturned by a higher court. This precipitated a public outcry in the United Kingdom (Arkley 1965, 132).
[53] Richards 1986, 12–14.
[54] From being an exporter of rice in 1935, Sierra Leone at the height of the alluvial diamond boom in 1956 imported a fifth of its national consumption in 1956.
[55] Richards 1986, 22–5.
[56] Mokuwa et al., 2011.

mechanization scheme.[57] Suitable machines proved hard to find, and maintenance problems and graft further undermined government-subsidized schemes. The option still has its proponents. Agri-business mechanization schemes might succeed, especially in the thinly populated grasslands, but international investors in Sierra Leone today show more interest in farming these areas for biofuels than for rice.

The problem of feeding the urban areas in Sierra Leone became endemic after emancipation in 1928. On the other hand, the agency of the ex-slaves was important in coping with hunger in the countryside.[58] We might wonder how this adaptation was achieved in a post-slavery age. A major contribution, it will be argued, came from seed selection activity by emancipated farmers. This reshaped many of the rices once associated with the plantation economy, resulting in a number of varieties effectively adapted to new socioeconomic conditions.

Later in the chapter we pay attention to two classes of rice planting material, in particular – niche-adapted (red-skinned) japonica rices, and farmer-selected interspecific hybrids. These local seeds differ from those provided by global technology for use with chemicals or machines. They respond well to limited amounts of labor and fertilization, and continue to be the basis for small-scale rice agriculture today, despite ill-advised attempts to replace them with "improved" types.

GENETIC CONSEQUENCES OF SELECTION OF RICE UNDER SLAVERY AND EMANCIPATION

The key to the success of local rice seeds is their robustness, in varied and challenging conditions. How was this adaptation for robustness achieved? The story can be inferred from evidence relating to seed selection dynamics, some of it deriving from molecular analysis.

The initial segregation of red and white rice will have required strong controls over seed selection. In the hinterland of Freetown in the late eighteenth century this was provided by a small number of estate landlords, responding to the strong color preferences of a distant market. Emancipation signaled a steep rise in selection intensity, as many thousands of peasants now began to make their own choices about which seeds to select.

A baseline and endline for this upward shift in selection intensity can be roughly fixed as follows. When Thomson passed through Moria in 1843 he encountered permanent estates worked by up to 150 enslaved persons. These were permanent farm slaves involved in food supply ventures, not temporary workers awaiting trans-Atlantic shipment. They worked on their own subsistence plots two or three days a week, so had some scope make their own

---

[57] Jedrej 1983.
[58] Richards 1986, 133–44.

seed choices. But there was little scope to move from village to village to pick up new types, as happens among experimentally minded peasant farmers today.[59] Nor will much in the way of seed reserves for planting have been accumulated. With only two days a week to work on their own plots many farm slaves surely will have consumed all they harvested, depending on the patronage of landlords for seeds in the following year, something that remains a marked feature of rice farming by the poorer classes in Sierra Leone today.[60] Thomson's report suggests that in Moria in the 1840s hardly more than a handful of persons – perhaps one in fifty – controlled the local seed choice decisions.

The end picture is very different. Today, an average sized Sierra Leonean rice-farming village of around 50–100 distinct farming households, will have between two and four adults per household involved in seed decisions.[61] Each household farm will be planted on average to between two and four distinct varieties. Every household will drop two or three varieties, and adopt (or re-adopt) the same number of new varieties, within a five-year period.[62] In all, a village of this size might have 30 to 50 distinct varieties in use at any one time, though the top five varieties will probably account for about three-quarters of the area planted each year.[63] Practically every person actively engaged in farming will have decision-making powers over at least one rice variety planted on the household farm or in associated personal plots. In short, modern varietal selection intensity is an order of magnitude higher than in the mid-nineteenth century.

The shift probably began during the late nineteenth century, as free peasant groups such as the Limba, farming niches in the backcountry, away from trade routes and plantations, became augmented by a rising maroon element in the local population, such as the settlement at Laminayah. Self-reliant and emancipated farmers had good reason to pay close attention to adaptive seed choices, since they were at times migrating into unfamiliar terrain with strictly limited resources for farming. The adaptive potential provided through *in situ* seed selection was a near-costless investment, since it depended only on ingenuity and observational awareness.

Catherine Longley has offered some interesting ethnographic evidence that observational acuity concerning seeds is today particularly marked in groups with a free peasant background.[64] She showed Susu and Limba informants from the Kukuna area (on the borders of the former Moria state) seed samples

---

[59] Richards 1989, Jusu 1999, Okry 2011.
[60] Richards 1986, 1990.
[61] Richards 1986, 1995.
[62] Richards 1997.
[63] Richards 1986.
[64] Longley 2000, 168–9. Her research design involved study in Kukuna itself, and in an adjacent Limba settlement.

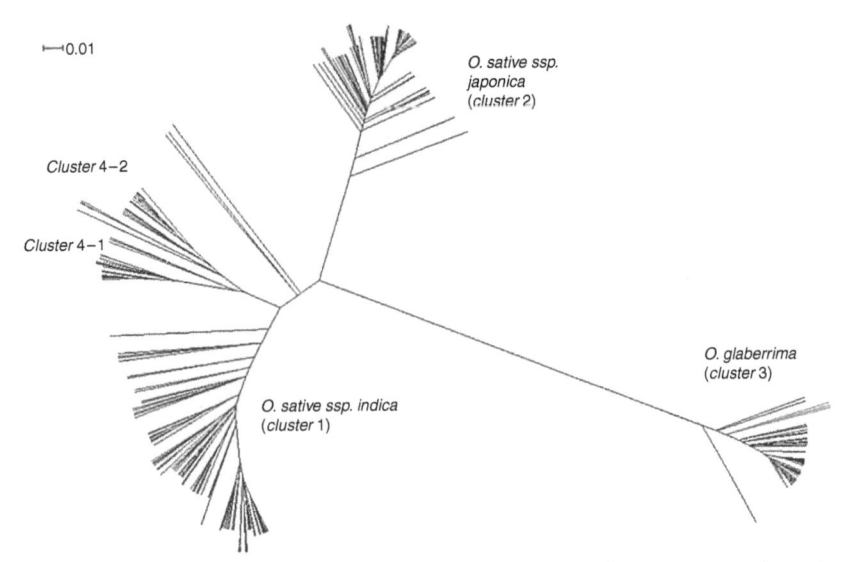

FIGURE 6.1 Phylogenetic relationships among 315 West African rice samples using UPGMA cluster analysis based on AFLP markers. Clusters 4–1 and 4–2 are farmer-selected hybrids.

collected from their own farms. "Without even examining the samples [...] Susu farmers usually declared them to be pure." Most Limba farmers, by contrast, "knew that samples from their own farms contained off-types and explained how the mixing had occurred as they picked them out."

Further evidence for an "indigenous" seed revolution comes from molecular and morphological examination of the rices themselves. First there is the finding that japonica rice (including Carolina rice) has been adapted to a range of niches in the coastal plain and boliland region of Sierra Leone, beyond the southern margins of the former Moria state. Second, there is evidence that farmer selection pressure has given rise to a group of inter-specific rice hybrids formed from out-crossing between African and Asian rice. These inter-specific hybrid rices are especially associated with the more hilly interior regions, where the niche-adapted japonica rices are perhaps less suitable.

A sample of 315 farmer varieties was collected in the West African coastal zone in 2008 and classified morphologically.[65] These rices were subsequently analyzed using AFLP markers.[66] The material separated into four clusters – African rice, japonica, indica, and a fourth cluster of farmer selected hybrid rices (Figure 6.1).

---

[65] Nuijten et al. 2009.
[66] Amplified Fragment Length Polymorphism, a molecular technique for genetic mapping and genotyping.

A close-up of the japonica cluster (Figure 6.2) shows the following patterns. Many of the Sierra Leone japonicas, including *nduliwa*, *jetɛ*, and *jɛbɛ-komei*, are found in the lower part of the cluster, where they sit on the stem rather than in a sub-cluster, and are thus genetically unrelated, suggesting that Sierra Leone has received japonicas from many parts of the tropical world. Two Sierra Leonean japonicas – *nduliwa* and *jetɛ* – that are genetically closely related are reported by farmers from Mogbuama in 1983 as belonging to an older stratum of Mende rice varieties than japonica types such as *gbɛngbɛn*.[67]

Gbɛngbɛn sits in a small somewhat more related group of mainly Sierra Leonean materials, and is a candidate for being one of the progeny of Carolina rice introduced to Guinea grass lowlands in the coastal plain adjacent to Freetown in the late eighteenth century. It is a japonica with red pericarp and a relatively long grain type, and is today particularly popular with farmers on the south-eastern edge of the boliland grassland zone.

Further up the stem there is a fan of material largely from Ghana and Guinea Bissau, with some degree of internal clustering. The separation between the Sierra Leonean materials lower down the stem and the Ghana-Guinea Bissau material sitting mainly above it could be explained by different processes of introduction, with the related Guinea Bissau and Ghana material a product of Portuguese influence radiating from long-established trade settlements at Cacheu (Guinea-Bissau) and Elmina (on the Gold Coast). Conceivably, this mixed sub-cluster contains progeny of japonica rices introduced by Portuguese and Cape Verdean traders up and down the coast during the earliest period of Atlantic trade, perhaps including the white rice reported by Donelha (a trader from Cape Verde) in the Orogu Valley of the Sierra Leone peninsula in about 1575, described as being as white as rice grown at Valencia.[68] Some of the Guinea Bissau and Ghana japonica material is morphologically strikingly similar – for example, Aqua Blue (Ghana) and Sefa Fingo (Guinea-Bissau). These two varieties share distinctive husk colors during flowering and ripening.

The separation of the two groups can be further explained by different selection processes. In Sierra Leone farmers grow the japonicas up and down a slope, in that way adapting them to both lowland and upland conditions.[69] But in Guinea-Bissau and Ghana farmers tend to grow japonicas only under upland conditions and use indicas for lowland cultivation, and in that way select for different types of japonicas.

As already noted, we know from experimental work on plasticity[70] that the Sierra Leone japonicas are strongly niche-adapted. In other words, they

---

[67] Richards 1986, 134.
[68] Donelha 1625.
[69] cf. Richards, 1986.
[70] Mokuwa et al., 2013.

FIGURE 6.2 Close-up of the phylogenetic relationships of the Japonica cluster and its subclusters. Based on UPGMA cluster analysis of 315 West African rice samples using AFLP markers, for methods see Nuijten et al. (2009).

flourish in local ecologies, but do much less well if moved outside their niche. This is in contrast to the more broadly adapted African rices, a group of Guinea-Bissau and Ghana japonicas and a group of indicas from Guinea. The niche-adaptation of Sierra Leonean japonicas seems consistent with our historical scenario, in which self-emancipated farmers pioneered a multiplicity of new farming sites in the interior grasslands abutting the historical zone of slave-based white rice cultivation.

Further evidence to link these present-day japonicas with earlier introductions can be found in data on the grain morphology of rices today grown on the eastern margins of the boliland zone. Thirteen rice types collected in 2008 from a Sierra Leonean village, Mogbuama, at the junction of the boli grasslands and interior uplands, were assigned to the japonica group according to both grain morphology and molecular markers (Table 6.1, Figure 6.1 and Figure 6.2). The average grain size in the group was 8.5 × 3.3 mm. This is longer than many Asian japonicas, but consistent with information that Carolina rice grains were bold and relatively long.[71] All the Mogbuama collection in 2008 had red pericarp with the exception of *nerigayei*, a recently introduced rice.

A comprehensive collection of rices grown in Mogbuama in 1983 included 41 Asian rices.[72] Using the average grain dimensions of the 2008 sample of japonica rices, 12 rices in this earlier collection can be assigned, retrospectively, to the japonica group (Table 6.1). This includes *gbɛngbɛn*, the most widely grown variety in 1983 (by 48 out of 98 farm households), and identified in the older sample as japonica solely on the basis of grain size, but confirmed to be a japonica in the 2008 sample on the basis of molecular evidence (Figure 6.2). Two japonica varieties in the 1983 older group had white pericarp (*banyalojɔ pɔ ihun* and *fɛlɛgbakoi*).

A second genetic effect plausibly linked to the scenario of diversification under emancipation is the emergence of inter-specific hybrid-derived rices in the repertoire of farmer selections.[73] West Africa is the only region where the two cultivated rice species co-exist in farmers' fields, thus providing opportunities for natural outcrossing and further selection of progeny by farmers.

The molecular data (Figure 6.1) show that West African farmers have selected and stabilized a number of rices of interspecific background (Clusters 4.1 and 4.2). Farmer hybrids are particularly common in Sierra Leone and Guinea Bissau and have their origin in these two countries. All farmer hybrids collected in Sierra Leone have a red pericarp, whereas all farmer hybrids from Guinea Bissau, except for the farmer hybrid *disi* (and related types) with a presumed origin in Sierra Leone, have a white to light brown pericarp. These farmer hybrids are distinct from recently released

---

[71] Grist 1975, 95.
[72] Richards 1986, 131–3.
[73] Barry et al. 2007, Nuijten and Van Treuren 2007, Nuijten et al. 2009.

TABLE 6.1 *Japonica rices at Mogbuama (Sierra Leone) in 1983 and 2007.*

Name of Rice, 1983 sample	Tones (Innes 1969)	Accession Number	Pericarp Color	Grain Length (mm)	Grain Width (mm)
banyalojo pɔ ihun		1983/1	white	8.2	3.3
felegbakoi		1983/13	white	8.4	3.4
gbεngben	LL	1983/15	non-white	7.6	3.7
gbεngben gole		1983/16	non-white	7.4	3.5
gbεngben tee		1983/17	non-white	8.3	3.7
gbolokondo		1983/18	non-white	7.6	3.9
gbondobai	LLHL	1983/12	non-white	8.2	3.5
gεtε * 1	HH	1983/20	non-white	7.6	4.4
helekpo	HHH	1983/21	non-white	7.6	3.6
jumukui		1983/22	non-white	7.6	4.1
puusawe		1983/30	non-white	8.4	3.4
kavunji	LHH	1983/36	non-white	8	4.1

Name of Rice, 2007 sample	Tones (Innes 1969)	Accession Number	Pericarp Color	Grain Length (mm)	Grain Width (mm)
bologuti		2007/174	non-white	8.6	2.9
gbεngben (1)		2007/175	non-white	8	3.4
gbεngben (2)		2007/176	non-white	7.8	3.4
jεbekomi		2007/177	non-white	6.8	3.8
jewule	HHH	2007/178	non-white	9.4	3.1
kondela		2007/179	non-white	8.7	3.6
konowanjei		2007/180	non-white	8.7	3.8
kotu gbɔngɔe	LH LH	2007/181	non-white	7.8	3.4
mabaji		2007/182	non-white	8.5	3.1
musugomei		2007/183	non-white	6.9	3.6
nerigeye		2007/184	white	10.8	2.9
giligoti		2007/185	non-white	8.7	3.2
yabasi		2007/186	non-white	9.8	3
yɔni		2007/187	non-white	8.5	2.9

* "A variety of short-grained rice" (Innes 1969)

(science-based) Nerica series interspecific hybrids, made by plant breeders by crossing African rice with japonica. The farmer hybrids are the result of crosses between African rice and indica rice. They also apparently predate the first Nerica releases. One rice from cluster 4.1 – *pa disi* – is attested from Guinea Bissau in the 1940s and north-western Sierra Leone in the 1920s.[74]

The suggested process for emergence of farmer interspecific rice hybrids involves in-field out-crossing and then spontaneous back-crossing, from which farmers interested in robust new planting materials are able to select fertile candidates for further testing.[75] In the area around Kukuna, noted for struggles between slave-holding rice producers and a self-emancipated peasantry in the mid-nineteenth century, some farmers today deliberately mix African and Asian rice in the same plot, actively looking to induce change in their seed stock.[76]

At the other extremity of the grassland zone running across central and northern Sierra Leone, chance crossing between Asian rice and weedy African rice, known to Mende farmers as *sanganyaa*, is a second possible source of rice hybrids. For farmers in Mogbuama, the presence of *sanganyaa* in a seed batch indicates that the rice was not rogued at harvest, and that it was thus probably intended for loaning by patrons to poorer farmers facing seed shortages at planting time.[77] Some of the recipients of these loans weed out the *sanganyaa*, but others protect it in the field, seeing it as a gift from God, and are unwilling to lose even one stand. In-field gene flow is then likely between the weedy and planted rice. Like Kukuna farmers, Mogbuama farmers have the motivation to nurse and test unusual off-types. In both locations it is the underclass that appears to provide much of the selection energy behind the emergence of farmer-selected hybrid rices, consistent with our emancipation hypothesis above.[78]

---

[74] Migeod (1926, 26) encountered "a rice called Pa deecee" named (as he supposed) in honor of the District Commissioner. "Pa" is in fact the Temne noun classifier for rice. The "disi" rice in our sample is a red-skinned farmer hybrid with African rice ancestry, clearly shown in its panicle form.

[75] The F1 cross will flower, and thus can cross back to a parent. Selection from a back-cross is more likely to be fertile. A presumed infertility barrier was a reason breeders hesitated to explore African x Asian rice hybrids until as recently as the 1990s.

[76] Longley and Richards 1993, Jusu 1999.

[77] Richards 1986, 139–40.

[78] The small rice farms of widows might be a good place to research in-field mechanisms of hybridity. These plots are often very mixed in terms of varieties, and the owners like it so, having the interest to select and experiment with off-types. Widows have weak land rights, and poor access to scarce male labor for clearing, so frequently "beg" to rework an old rice farm, where weedy off-types thrive.

SEED SYSTEMS IN THE "NORTHERN RIVERS" TODAY[79]

In the second half of the twentieth century, West African rice-producing countries, hardly noticing the ways in which local rice genetic resources had been shaped and re-shaped by an emancipated peasantry, reverted to top-down systems of seed selection, but this time shaped not by merchant-visionaries such as Macaulay, but the by the science visionaries of the Green Revolution. Food security was supposed to come from seeds designed by scientists and validated by peer review, not by tests of effectiveness in farmer conditions. In Guinea and Sierra Leone high-yielding exotic rice seeds were promoted first by public seed supply, and later by public-private partnerships, but none of these ventures proved sustainable. Meanwhile, the peasantry continued to invent. Local seed markets emerged as farmer needs diversified.

In the zone once occupied by the polity of Moria and its satellites, two rather distinct systems of local (farmer-driven) seed supply today share the terrain. A line of division follows the old watershed between rice supplied toward the coast, and the rice supplied into the hills of Futa Jalon. The Benna system, facing toward the interior, is run by established male farmers, who set aside some of their land each year to produce quality seed for sale. A range of contracts is offered, including patrimonial loans-in-kind. These dealers know local demand well. They choose to produce only a small number of varieties. These are the ones intensively selected by farmers to best match local conditions. Recent research has determined that these are robust seed types with an ability to produce reliably under a range of adverse conditions.[80] African rice is included; exotic novelties are not.

Then we turn to the local seed system on the coastal plain. Here agriculture is peri-urban, in the shadow of two large coastal cities, Freetown and Conakry. It is also a zone with a large number of wetland micro-niches to be exploited. Many of the farmers are women, driven out of the city by increasingly adverse economic conditions. The seed merchants are also mainly women. In addition to seed they produce themselves, they also travel up and down, seeking seed types they think their customers will buy. Some of the seeds caught in the nets of these well-traveled dealers are exotics. Whereas the seed merchants at the foot of the Benna Hills hardly needed to offer a word of advice about how to plant the old country seeds, the women seed merchants of the coastal plain are full of advice about their new seeds. Advice is part of what they offer, since many of their items come from far and are unknown to their clients, some of whom are opening up new wetland farming niches, or farming these wetland niches for the first time.

These two sets of local seed agents, between them, provide both red and white rice to those who need it, not based on dogma but on demand. A

---

[79] This section is based on Okry, 2011.
[80] Mokuwa et al., 2013.

gendered local pragmatism has helped to dissolve some of the divisions associated with the older, paradoxical abolitionist food security system built on the forced labor of slaves. It is these informal seed dealers (of both genders) who are perhaps the best channel through which a proposed New Green Revolution for Africa should apply its novel wares, since they are equipped to promote all types of seed, including the robust local products of a century or more of self-emancipation. In a period of rapid environmental change no source of adaptive capacity should be ignored.

CONCLUSION

Carolina rice, an export commodity produced by slavery in the United States, was introduced into West Africa in the late eighteenth century, where it was grown by slave labor as a mainstay of the abolitionist settlement at Freetown. White rice at Sierra Leone seemingly inverts the heartening story of Black Rice as an emancipatory element in New World rice cultivation.[81] It appears to support instead the idea that transfer of American seeds promoted the emergence of the harshest forms of chattel slavery in West Africa. But this would be to make the technological determinist's mistake of assuming that technology governs agency. The conclusion we wish to stress is somewhat different. By tracing the history of rice seeds in the region we have drawn attention to a process through which increasing levels of selection activity consequent upon emancipation pulled apart white rice as a commodity and rebuilt it as something more useful for local purposes. Locally adapted japonica rices, some of which may be derived from Carolina rice, are today important in peasant production in many parts of Sierra Leone, especially in higher rainfall districts adjacent to the grassland (boliland) zone of the coastal plain, where they contribute importantly to the food supply of provincial cities such as Bo, Makeni, and Kenema. No longer white-skinned, these japonica rices are successful in markets where local consumers often welcome redness in rice as a quality guarantee. This is not, therefore, a reversion to subsistence in the absence of slavery, as Governor Ludlum once feared. It is the story of the emergence of an anticommodity, shaped by the peasant selection energy released by emancipation.[82] This same selection energy "from below" also produced highly robust interspecific hybrid rices, apparently well suited to the needs of small-holders with poor soils and limited labor, and again welcomed by local consumers. Emancipated peasants were able to exploit the genetic potential of African red rice and two sub-species of Asian rice in a controlled way at a time when external science saw only insurmountable infertility barriers or promiscuous mixing. Furthermore, it was around the

---

[81] Littlefield 1981, Carney 2001.
[82] Maat, Chapter 15, this volume

products of this peasant selection activity that local cultures of seed commerce have emerged where external solutions failed. Those who suppose African food security requires outside intervention need to ponder the lessons of an emancipated peasant enterprise culture for seeds in the vicinity of Sierra Leone.

PART II

ENVIRONMENTAL MATTERS

Edda L. Fields-Black

INTRODUCTION

Throughout the long history of the crop, rice has been grown in a diversity of rainfed and irrigated ecological niches ranging from dry uplands, to terraced hillsides, lowlands, coastal wetlands, deep water environments, and brackish mangrove swamps. Controlling and channeling fresh water to nourish rice plants at critical stages of the cultivation cycle are simultaneously the keys to rice farmers' abilities to adapt the crop to diverse ecological niches as well as the impetuses of social, demographic, even epidemiologic, transformations within rice-growing societies. The continuous fluctuations in the environment, including the availability of fresh water therein, rice cultivators' interaction with their environment, as well as the impact of both lead to rich social history indeed. In short, the environment matters. Though rice farmers do not hold a monopoly on its manipulation, the environment is an important prism through which historians can examine key questions in social history, such as human interaction with the environment, the effects of the environment on human actors and their societies, and vice versa.

Examining rice-growing societies in West Africa, the Upper Guinea Coast and Senegal, the Atlantic and Indian Ocean zones, the U.S. South, and the Bengali and Punjab regions of South Asia reveals that the environment matters, not just locally, but globally. The environment matters wherever rice is grown. A global approach also reveals significant similarity in the ways that rice-growing societies have adapted the crop to their environment and adapted their environment to the crop. Both rainfed rice grown on coastal plains and irrigated rice require dramatically increased labor inputs to build the infrastructure for controlling and channeling fresh water. Many rice-growing societies globally have used coercion to recruit and maintain the necessary labor. In the nature of the coercive mechanisms – the state, slaveholders, or property-holding male elders – lies important differences between how rice-growing societies have adapted rice and rice cultivation to their environment.

The environment also matters in the investigation of the effects of rice-farming systems, particularly lowland production, on rice-growing societies. The transition to paddy rice production in different localities and at different moments in time exemplifies the tension between the local and the global. In South Carolina in the mid-eighteenth century, the expansion of both inland and tidal rice fields accompanied the dramatic increase in the number of African captives imported directly into the colony and the emergence of the commercial rice industry. Rice planters located their homesteads in close proximity to inland rice fields and slaves' quarters close to tidal rice fields. Enslaved laborers performed the back-breaking labor to clear the landscape and establish the fields. Low-lying rice fields created standing water where mosquitoes bred, carrying disease and death for both planters and slaves alike. In the mid-nineteenth century in Punjab and Bengal, the British colonial government constructed an enormous network of canals, promoting the establishment of "canal colonies" in the arid uplands of western Punjab, and expanding into millions of acres of uncultivated area. Rice, sugarcane, cotton, and wheat were "heating" crops, whose irrigation caused large-scale seasonal flooding and spreading of Anopheles mosquitoes from lowland riverine tracts to arid upland regions. As a result, malaria became the leading cause of debility and death for adults in Punjab by the late nineteenth and early twentieth century. Cash crop cultivators in Bengal and Punjab also utilized human and animal waste as green manure. Stored near human settlements, the waste products contaminated drinking water and caused widespread gastrointestinal infections and cross-infections between livestock and humans. In both of these societies, colonial South Carolina and South Asia, when rice became an important commercial crop, sickness and death prevailed.

There is a pregnant silence in the West African literature on rice and rice farmers in reference to whether or not disease rates increased as a result of intensive agriculture – mangrove rice cultivation. On the one hand, the silence in the literature could exist because many West Africans had biological immunity to Plasmodium falciparum malaria; many West and West Central Africans possessed the sickle cell allele which offered unique protection against falciparum and the two negative forms of the Duffy alleles, which provided complete protection against Plasmodium vivax malaria. In the Upper Guinea Coast, rice farmers may also have had acquired immunity to Plasmodium falciparum malaria. Populations of West African rice cultivators may have acquired higher levels of immunity – as did their counterparts in Bengal, but not Punjab where mosquito breeding and infection were much more seasonal – from living in environments where Anopheles mosquitoes breed.

On the other hand, the silence in the literature could also be a reflection of the larger vacuum of historical sources describing traditional rice cultivation techniques. Travelers' accounts recorded in Western Africa prior to the late eighteenth century have a "dry season bias." Due to the deadly nature of the coastal region, very few European observers travelled to coastal villages during the rainy season when coastal farmers prepared paddy rice fields and planted paddy rice. This critical stage in the agricultural calendar coincided to the season when Anopheles mosquitoes bred in the same swamps and infected coastal villagers. Rates of malarial infection among Upper Guinea Coast farmers were already high. The Upper Guinea Coast was the "Black Man's Hospital" long before the era of trans-Atlantic trade when it gained the reputation as the "White Man's Grave," because of high European death rates from malaria and yellow fever. That, unlike commercial rice farmers in colonial South Carolina, Upper Guinea Coast farmers did not locate paddy rice fields near their villages may contribute to the lack of evidence of higher death rates from malaria as a result of intensive agriculture in the region. It appears that Upper Guinea Coast farmers did the opposite – located their villages on higher ground and their rice fields on the low-lying peripheries – of their peers in South Carolina. The inhabitants of riverine inundated areas of Bengal, which experienced high levels of flooding, built their villages on higher ground and carved rice fields out of the surrounding inundated lowlands. Though rice-growing areas in Punjab did not experience high levels of flooding, villages located in or near floodplains were also built on higher ground. During the colonial and postcolonial periods, the time nursing mothers spent away from their infants, commuting back and forth and working in rice fields, contributed to negative nutritional impacts on infants during the rainy season. Upper Guinea Coast farmers continued to grow rice for subsistence as well as cash crops into the late twentieth century. Hence, a commercial rice industry did not develop in West Africa in the precolonial, colonial, or postcolonial period and did not drive the transition to intensive agricultural production in the region. In West Africa, trans-Atlantic trade, not in intensive agricultural production, transformed the region into a capitalist economy. Thus, the role of rice as a valuable cash crop in South Carolina's commercial rice industry, may have impacted the physical proximity of rice fields to human settlements and hence the health of rice-farming communities. Divergent effects of intensive agriculture in different local environments and at different moments in time exemplify the ways that the local both illuminates and challenges the global.

Taking the environment seriously necessitates careful historical interpretation. The nature of the questions asked by historians about the environment and societies' interactions with the environment confronts the limitations of historical sources on the subject. The field of environmental history is dominated by the theme of "encounter," European imperialists, colonizers, and/or slaveholders' interaction with indigenous peoples and indigenous land use systems. In the case of the New World, European and American planters were interacting with enslaved laborers who possessed West and West Central African land-use systems. Typically government – often colonial – officers, missionaries, and traders who recorded the majority of sources on which social historians rely had limited knowledge about – or patience for – indigenous land-use systems, complex and contested power relations with indigenous and enslaved peoples, and very different goals and objectives than social historians. The instances in which indigenous or enslaved peoples recorded their own experiences and left a proverbial "paper trail" for historians to interpret are few and far between. To take the environment seriously, social historians must use the available historical sources as evidence "in spite of themselves," reading "against the grain" to identify indigenous land-use systems, the complex power relations between indigenous and enslaved peoples and European/American colonizers and slaveholders, and the ways in which both of the aforementioned changed over time.

Taking seriously the role of indigenous societies and enslaved communities' interaction with the environment and the effects of the environment on these populations requires social historians to diversify the evidentiary base. The literature on rice and rice cultivators in Africa, Asia, and the U.S. South has been on the forefront of utilizing interdisciplinary sources, such as biological and botanical studies of land-use change and oral traditions, and methodologies, archaeology, the comparative method of historical linguistics, and plant genetics. The broader environmental history literature offers additional tools, such as botany, GIS/GPS mapping, paleohydrology, and palynology, whose employment could further deepen inquiry. Scientific disciplines are particularly attractive to social historians given the nature of the questions posed about the environment.

For social historians, however, interdisciplinary methods and sources are not a panacea. Like historical sources written by traders, missionaries, and state officers, interdisciplinary sources and methods present limitations and challenges. For example, because the studies were produced for other purposes, such as how shell middens, mangroves, languages, and crop varieties changed over time, social historians must make an additional layer of inference about how a particular society's engagement with shell middens, mangroves, languages, and crop varieties contributed to the ways in which it changed over time. In particular, comparative linguists analyze linguistic evidence to investigate how languages change over time. Social historians employing the comparative method of historical linguistics add another layer of investigation and inference employing linguistic and other interdisciplinary data to understand how the societies that spoke the languages changed over time. Unlike written documents, interdisciplinary sources or methods do not use calendar dates, positing that change registers much more slowly and measuring change very differently. Within several disciplines, such as the comparative method of historical linguistics, there are also active and healthy debates about the benefits and liabilities of dating.

The chapters in this Part exemplify how taking the environment seriously gives social historians an opportunity to look holistically at how colonial/planter, indigenous, and enslaved societies interacted with and impacted the environment. They confront the challenge of asking new questions of historical sources while simultaneously employing interdisciplinary sources and methods. In the end, they further the field by understanding more not only about the relationship between diverse societies and nature, but also about their relationship with one another.

7

Rice and Rice Farmers in the Upper Guinea Coast and Environmental History

Edda L. Fields-Black

"The Negroes from this part of the coast of Africa are well acquainted with the cultivation of rice and are naturally industrious."[1]

In 1789 Captain William Lyttleton testified before British Parliament's Committee of the Whole House to consider further the Circumstances of the Slave Trade about his two slaving voyages in the Gambia River region. By his own account, Lyttleton had traded from the mouth to 300 leagues up the Gambia River since serving as mate in 1762. He subsequently worked in the region as a merchant for more than 11 years and captained two slaving vessels, *Ulysses* and *Mentor*. The *Mentor* originated in London in 1784, purchased its complement of slaves on the River Gambia, and disembarked in Charleston, South Carolina in 1785. Lyttleton characterized the 1784–5 voyage as having a "very great and uncommon mortality," because, according to his recollection, 13 out of 140 captives died in the Middle Passage.[2]

Lyttleton testified to the Committee that the "natural productions" of the Gambia River region, "Country Corn, [...] Indian Corn, and Rice," were produced for subsistence and not for export. Captives imprisoned in coastal baracoons waiting to embark on slaving vessels were fed millet, rarely rice. Lyttleton proclaimed, "they never taste any Rice, unless they get it by stealth."[3] Prone to drought and crop failure, the region's provisions were often in too short supply to satisfy inhabitants' subsistence needs.

The African captives aboard the *Mentor* were victims of a famine that struck south-west of the mouth of the Gambia River in 1784.[4] During years of

---

[1] Donnan 1935, 477, n. 5.
[2] Though Lyttleton testifies that this voyage took place in 1786, it appears in a 1785 listing of the *South Carolina Gazette*, Ibid.
[3] Lambert 1975, 291, 285, 289, 292.
[4] Between ca. 1620 and ca.1860, drought, infestations of locusts, tropical diseases, and successive bad harvests led to long periods of famine in the Senegambia. Curtin 1975, app.1:4; Becker 1985, 14, 169.

inadequate rainfall, failed harvests, and swarms of locusts, the region that Lyttleton observed produced increased numbers of captives for sale to Mandinga, then European traders. When these three unfortunate natural phenomena intersected in 1784, a desperate situation ensued: inhabitants of the region "subsisted for some months on esculent roots, and whatever the country produced which had nourishment in it." When lineage groups ran out of nourishment and exhausted all other options, they were "driven to the dreadful necessity of selling each other to procure subsistence" in order to increase the likelihood that some members of the lineage would survive.[5] Mandinga traders purchased the captives from the Jola or "Floups" for "Country Corn," that is, locally produced millet, and European goods.

Once the slaves passed through quarantine in Sullivan's Island, they were auctioned off to the highest bidder in Charleston, South Carolina. In a May 30, 1785 advertisement of the *Mentor*'s arrival in the *South Carolina Gazette*, the ship's owners marketed the enslaved "cargo" to buyers in the region by associating the Gambia River region with rice production, stating: "The Negroes from this part of the coast of Africa are well acquainted with the cultivation of rice and are naturally industrious." The description by factors in Charleston of the captives as "well acquainted with the cultivation of rice" seems to stand in stark contrast to Lyttleton's description of the Gambia River region and its inhabitants as victims of famine and cultivators of millet before they were captured and sold to European traders. Were the inhabitants of the Gambia River region "well acquainted" with rice by 1785? Was the drought-prone Senegambia subregion or the remainder of the Upper Guinea Coast (Figure P.1b), specifically subregions further south of the Gambia River, "uniformly committed" to rice production by the late eighteenth century?

In a 2007 *American Historical Review* article, David Eltis, Philip Morgan, and David Richardson have suggested that West Africa's Upper Guinea Coast was "never uniformly committed to rice production."[6] Composed of a multitude of microenvironments, each with its own relationship to cereals and its own body of interdisciplinary source materials, the Upper Guinea Coast, first and foremost, is hardly "uniform." The slave ship *Mentor* is a prism into the complex and uneven nature and history of rice production in the Upper Guinea Coast and the limits of the sources available to historians for understanding the region's early and precolonial history. This chapter will attempt to understand the complex relationship that captives who originated in different subregions of the Upper Guinea Coast may have had to rice and rice production. By employing interdisciplinary sources, historical linguistics, archaeology, and European travelers' accounts, it will investigate the role that rice played in a complex farming system that was designed in its earliest

---

[5] Lambert 2002, 285.
[6] Eltis et al. 2007, 1345.

forms to decrease the effects of drought and transformed centuries later to simultaneously take advantage of new commercial opportunities and mitigate the inherent violence both generated by the trans-Atlantic slave trade.

THE UPPER GUINEA COAST AND ITS INHABITANTS

In his canonical *History of the Upper Guinea Coast 1545 to 1800*, Walter Rodney defines the Upper Guinea Coast as an irregularly triangular area that is connected by more than two dozen rivers flowing in a southwesterly direction. The region stretches toward the coast along the Gambia River (in present-day Senegal) in the north to Cape Mount (in present-day Liberia) in the south and is bounded in the east by the plateaus of the Futa Jallon Mountains, which lie at the head of the Gambia River. Rodney's location of the Upper Guinea Coast reflects his examination of the region as geographically, politically, socially, and economically distinct from areas to the west or south and his focus on regional inhabitants' interaction and commercial relations with Europeans, primarily the Portuguese.[7]

The Upper Guinea Coast is home to two unrelated language groups, Atlantic and Mande, whose speech communities have lived alongside each other for thousands of years. Dense populations of Mande language speakers overwhelmingly dominate the interior and cover the western Sahara from the present-day Mauritania border in the north, to the Atlantic coast in the west, and Nigeria in the east. The Mande language group consists of as many as 72 relatively well-documented languages, which have been described as "predatory," because widely spoken languages such as Mandinka threaten smaller Atlantic languages when two speech communities are in contact. Smaller sometimes isolated bands of Atlantic language speakers are sprinkled along the Atlantic coast from Senegal to Liberia. The Atlantic language group consists of approximately 50 languages with many Atlantic languages having less than 5,000 speakers. A few Atlantic languages, such as Koba/ Kalum, Banta/Banda, Mo-peng, and Mani, have already "died"; several others, such as Mbulungish and Mboteni, are in imminent danger of language death in a generation or two. Smaller Atlantic languages are threatened with language death by more widely spoken Atlantic languages, such as Wolof, Fulbe, and Temne, in addition to Mande languages.[8]

Using an interdisciplinary approach, the latest classification of Mande languages[9] analyzes independent evidence from lexicostatistical data and "Improved glottochronology,"[10] as well as evidence from paleoclimatology

---

[7] Rodney 1970, 2.
[8] Childs 2008, 1, 14.
[9] Dwyer 1989, 46–65; Grégoire and de Halleux 1994, 142, 53–71; Kastenholz 1991, 12–13, 107–58.
[10] Starostin 2000.

and archaeology. It situates the proto-Mande homeland in the southern Sahara Desert, in the southwestern portion of present-day Mali near the Mauritania border locating it there in the second half of the fourth millennium BCE. At the time, the Sahara was densely populated with hunters, cattle-keepers, and farmers. For the next 2,500 years, Mande speech communities inhabited the edge of the Sahara desert where periods of aridity punctuated periods of relatively high, stable rainfall and Mande languages began to diverge. Prior to approximately 1000 BCE, large-scale and long-distance migration was not a significant factor in the divergence of Mande languages. An arid crisis in ca. 1000 BCE followed by several hundred years of sharp rainfall fluctuations resulted in large-scale population shifts southward out of the Sahara. This pattern coincides with the further divergence of proto-Mande daughter languages. Lastly, another period of increased aridity ca. 500 CE coincided with the divergence of Mande language groups into individual language families.[11] Today, three of the four branches of the Mande language group, Eastern-Southern, Northwest, and Central-Southern are located within the Upper Guinea Coast regions.[12]

To date, Atlantic languages remain relatively less documented and researched than their Mande neighbors. Like Mande languages, the Atlantic language group is a member of the Niger-Congo language family. Unlike Mande, Atlantic languages have presented a conundrum to linguists who have debated for decades whether or not these languages are genetically related and constitute a unified language group. Linguists seem to agree that there are two branches, North Atlantic and South Atlantic, and one isolate language, Bijogo, in the Atlantic "group" and that languages within the sub-groups are genetically related. Linguists cannot agree, however, on whether or not the North Atlantic and South Atlantic branches and Bijogo are genetically related to one another and share genetic unity. These languages do share grammatical features, noun classes and systems of consonant alternation, which linguists have used to confirm earlier classifications based on lexicostatistics.[13] The latest research suggests that North Atlantic and South Atlantic diverged from proto-Niger-Congo independently at relatively the same time and shortly before the Mande language group diverged from proto-Niger-Congo. Bijogo diverged from proto-Niger-Congo much later.[14] If in fact proto-North Atlantic, proto-South Atlantic, and proto-Mande have been in contact for several thousand years since the languages diverged from proto-Niger-Congo, future research is necessary to determine what cultural vocabulary these ancestral

---

[11] Vydrin 2009, 107–16.
[12] Vydrin et al. 2010. Maps on the site by Matthew Benjamin are also very helpful.
[13] Doneux 1975, 41–129; Pozdniakov 1993; Sapir 1971, 45–112.
[14] Blench 2006, 118; Childs 2001; Childs 2003; Segrer 2000, 183–191.

languages share and what the shared cultural vocabulary tells historians about how the speech communities adapted to the changing environment on the edge of the Sahara Desert.

In West Africa's interior, speakers of Mande languages formed politically centralized societies, sometimes rising to the level of large hierarchical empires from the mid-thirteenth century. The Mali Empire's conquest of the Senegambia effectively integrated the region into its trans-Sahara trading networks, which reached east across the Niger River and south through the salt- and rice-producing mangrove regions along the coastal forests. It gained control of the Buré and Bambuk gold fields and denied Muslim traders direct access to the sources of gold. Trade in West-African gold stretched across the Sahara and into the Mediterranean World. The Mali Empire's contact with Berber traders in the Sahel resulted in its rulers and traders converting to Islam in the late tenth to eleventh centuries, though the masses of its people continued to practice indigenous religions for hundreds of years. Thus, the Mali Empire also represented the earliest point of connection between West African Muslims and the Islamic World.

In contrast to the politically centralized and Islamicized Mande, the overwhelming majority of speakers of Atlantic languages, such as the Jola, Beafada, Papel, Balante, Bainuk, Nalu, Mbulungish, Mboteni, Sitem, Mandori, and Landuma, remained politically de-centralized, stateless in the coastal reaches of the region. For the most part, these kin-based societies settled into the heavily forested coastal floodplains and mangrove swamps, spanning the lower Casamance River in present-day Senegal to the Pongo River in present-day Guinea. Here they produced salt and invented agricultural technology for producing rice in mangrove swamps and coastal floodplains. There were certainly exceptions to this rule, for example the Jolof Confederation was a former tributary of the Mali Empire, which asserted its independence in the sixteenth century and filled the political vacuum along the coast between the Senegal and Gambia Rivers. With the decline of the Mali Empire in the sixteenth century, which also coincided with environmental change, Mande-speakers, such as the Susu, expanded westward and southward settling alongside stateless societies imposing some "Mande" political and social institutions, and founding the Kaabu Kingdom and several other smaller states.

Though the Upper Guinea Coast is vastly different in terms of its language groups and their political formations, rice production in the lowlands and the uplands united the economy of Atlantic- and Mande-speakers, politically decentralized and centralized societies alike during the precolonial period. The question is, however, were inhabitants of the Upper Guinea Coast "uniformly" committed to rice production and if so, by when? Probing this historical conundrum will require interdisciplinary sources and methods. To these historical tools this analysis now turns.

INTERDISCIPLINARY SOURCES AND METHODS: THE COMPARATIVE METHOD OF HISTORICAL LINGUISTICS

The earliest evidence of rice in the interior of the Upper Guinea Coast/ Senegambia region comes from archaeological excavations of Jenne-jeno located along the Inland Niger Delta in present-day Mali, a region inhabited by Mande speech communities. The oldest sample of domesticated *Oryza glaberrima*, rice species indigenous to West Africa, dates to 300 BC to 200 BC. It was found in the earliest occupation phase of Jenne-jeno, which dates back to 250 BCE to 50 CE. The earliest inhabitants of this urban center made iron implements and sand-tempered pottery, subsisted on fish and bovids, which included domesticated cattle. By 500 to 400 CE, they added domesticated African rice to their diets. By 1000 CE, Jenne-jeno participated in a thriving trans-Saharan trade, exchanging agricultural products including rice for copper and salt.[15] Currently, the availability of archaeological sources is uneven at best; there is no additional archaeological evidence of *O. glaberrima* in the Upper Guinea Coast.

In the center of diversity on the upper Niger Delta, the inhabitants grew *O. glaberrima* in the floodwaters using floating rice cultivars. Non-floating cultivars subsequently spread to brackish waters in the coastal region of the Upper Guinea Coast between present-day Gambia and Guinea-Bissau and to rain-fed uplands in the forest region between present-day Sierra Leone and Ivory Coast.[16] Jack Harlan, on the other hand hypothesized that ancient hunter-gatherers selected *O. glaberrima* species from wild *O. barthii* species in multiples centers within the forest and savanna region.[17] All of these regions would have been inhabited by Mande- and Atlantic-speech communities.

Given the unevenness of the archaeological and botanical sources, linguistic sources and the historical linguistics methodology make important contributions to the history of rice in the Upper Guinea Coast. The comparative method of historical linguistics provides the earliest evidence for subregions within the Upper Guinea Coast and their inhabitants. Understanding how genetically related languages change over time and reconstructing the history of languages are the goals of the comparative method. It reconstructs the history of a language group by determining the relationship among its genetically related member languages and the changes that these languages have undergone over time. Then, it reconstructs ancestral or "proto-" forms of the languages in question.

A small number of Africanist historians, many but by no means all of whom work on the Bantu language group of Eastern, Central, and Southern parts of Western Africa,[18] have employed the comparative method of

---

[15] McIntosh 1995; McIntosh and McIntosh 1981, 15–6, 20.
[16] Portères 1970, 43–58.
[17] Harlan 1971, 468–74.
[18] Ehret 1967, 1–17; Ehret 1968, 213–21; Ehret 1979, 161–77; Klieman 2003; Nurse 1997, 359–91; Schoenbrun 1998; Schoenbrun 1993; Vansina 1995, 173–95; Vansina 1990.

historical linguistics for ends and in ways that linguists never intended. First, these "linguist historians" of Africa draw on the field of historical linguistics to reconstruct languages that are poorly documented. The comparative method was initially developed to examine Indo-European languages, which possess long histories of written documentation. Versions of languages, such as Old English, date back more than one millennium. However, the earliest recordings of the languages spoken in West Africa's Upper Guinea Coast, for example, only date back a few centuries, particularly some of the aforementioned little-documented, sparsely researched, and dying Atlantic languages. Where they are available, dictionaries and wordlists were written by explorers, missionaries, and colonial officers who were not native speakers of the African languages. There are often few or no dictionaries or wordlists available for many languages or for different dialects within the same language and hence little basis for historical comparison. Linguist historians have combated the paucity of language data by conducting fieldwork and collecting their own word-lists from present-day speakers. Thus, though the comparative method of historical linguistics was not designed for poorly documented languages, linguist historians of Africa have modified the method to suit the particular challenges of African languages.

Second, though the goal of the comparative method of historical linguistics is to reconstruct the history of genetically related languages, linguist historians reconstruct language history as an initial step and subsequently apply this data to reconstructing the human history of the groups who spoke the languages in question in the distant past.[19] In the case of Africa, linguist historians have employed linguistic tools, usually one quiver in an arsenal of interdisciplinary sources that includes archaeological, ethnographic, botanical, and ecological evidence, to reconstruct the early precolonial history of portions the continent. In many cases, including in the Upper Guinea Coast and other regions where oral traditions cover a relatively recent period in history, archaeological studies are few and far between and Arab, or more likely Portuguese, traders did not travel to, or stay long enough in, the region to record much of historical value, language evidence is the earliest data available. Without language sources and linguistic methods, historians would know a lot less about the early precolonial history of large swaths of the African continent.

---

[19] Klieman (Oliver et al. 2001, 48) argues that linguist historians have not been effective at articulating to historical linguists that the two groups do not have the same goals. She suggests that linguist historians also need to demonstrate better to fellow historians the additional modes of inquiry that they use to reconstruct human history using language sources and linguistic methods. Koen Bosteon critiques linguist historians, stating that their analysis of linguistic data does not follow best practices, often covers more linguistic data than can be thoroughly analyzed, and does not yield sufficient detail upon which to write sweeping histories. See also Bosteon 2007 and 2006, 223–4.

For linguist historians employing the "Words-and Things" method of historical linguistics, words are historical sources for every facet of society for which speech communities have designated a name. A speech community is a group of people who communicate with each other or are connected by chains of speakers who communicate with each other.[20] The speech communities that spoke the words in the past and present are the central actors of any history based on linguistic sources. Once analyzed, their words contain a fascinating and inherently social history. Clusters of vocabulary words provide historians with a variety of clues about the speech communities that spoke the vocabulary words, such as: who was an ancestral speech community?; where did they originate?; what tools did they use?; what did they value?; how did they adapt to their changing environment?; and, with whom did they interact? By employing the comparative method to analyze the words spoken by present-day speech communities and published in dictionaries/word lists, ethnographies, and travelers' accounts, historians can reconstruct the history of the speech communities who spoke the words in the distant past, a past which in the Upper Guinea Coast is currently otherwise unrecoverable using traditional historical sources.

All languages are comprised of sounds. The human vocal apparatus is equipped to produce a fixed number of vowel and consonant sounds. Linguists studying languages around the world have found that all human languages are comprised of sounds from the same limited set. At some point in their existence, members of a speech community subconsciously chose to communicate among themselves with a set of vowel and consonant sounds from this fixed set of sounds and a unique system of rules for combining them. These are the basic building blocks for every language. No two languages possess an identical set of sounds or rules for combination.

Languages change over time as a result of an ongoing series of subconscious choices by language speakers, which, though usually small, can have profound implications for their dialects, eventually resulting in the creation of new languages. Most of the subconscious changes result from speakers of the same dialect or language having less contact and less opportunity for communication with each other and/or more contact and more opportunity for communication with speakers of another dialect or language. This state of affairs may arise as a result of a variety of internal and external factors, for example: individual members of speech communities move or migrate; they come into contact with people speaking other languages; sometimes, individuals attempt to improve their social status by altering their use of language. Language shift is by no means always the result of physical movement. Dialects will begin to diverge as the language speakers make subconscious changes in the pronunciation of their language's sounds, the combination of

---

[20] Durie and Ross 1996, 16.

their sounds, or the words and meanings that they use rendering communication within the speech community more difficult and/or facilitating communication with speakers of neighboring dialects/languages. As long as the two groups, now speakers of different dialects, can still understand each other, they are still speaking one language and remain members of the same speech community. However, if the two dialects continue to evolve separately over a period of time to the point where they are no longer mutually intelligible, two separate daughter languages are born. A historical linguists' work can begin.

The comparative method is applied to genetically related languages, languages that descended from a common linguistic ancestor. Genetically related languages have their basic building blocks in common; they share a system of sounds and rules for combining them. This makes languages a particularly powerful tool of historical reconstruction. A preponderance of evidence from languages worldwide reveals the existence of regularities in sound change among genetically related languages. When pronouncing the fixed set of sounds, the human vocal apparatus tends to subconsciously become more efficient at sound production. Over time, language speakers subconsciously change sounds that require greater effort to produce to sounds that require less. As individual dialects diverge from a common linguistic ancestor, the regular correspondence will exist among the sound changes they undergo. Regular sound correspondences provide a genealogy of how daughter languages have changed, which historical linguists analyze to reconstruct the common linguistic ancestor. These are the basic assumptions underlying the comparative method. Rather than describe all of the technical operations of the method, the remainder of this section will be focused on the aspects of the method which this linguist historian of Africa has employed in reconstructing the history of the Rio Nunez region, one corner of the Upper Guinea Coast, its inhabitants, and the development of their rice-growing technology.

Linguist historians usually begin by analyzing a small sample – usually 100 or 200 – core vocabulary words. Common grammatical words, numerals, basic kinship terminology, parts of the body, elements in nature, and common verbs comprise core vocabulary. Linguists have found that core vocabulary words are some of the most stable words in any given language worldwide. When speech communities come into contact with each other, they are unlikely to exchange these basic vocabulary words, such as "'one,' 'two,' 'three,' 'father,' 'mother,' 'rock,' 'tree,' 'to eat,' and 'to sleep,'" because every language possesses its own terminology to describe these basic aspects of the human experience. A preponderance of cross-cultural data shows that typically, speech communities must be in contact with another speech community for a long period of time before sound change begins to affect their core vocabulary words. Core vocabulary words are less likely than other kinds of vocabulary words to undergo sound change. Linguist historians analyze core vocabulary to identify "cognates," pairs of words that share similar meanings and regular sound correspondences. Identifying cognates provides the linguist historian with a list of prospective regular sound correspondences, the sound system, rules for combining sounds, and the ways that the language groups' sounds have changed over time. These prospective sound changes must be found and confirmed in an analysis of non-core vocabulary words in the languages in question. Once cognates and regular sound correspondences have been identified using core vocabulary words, linguists calculate the percentage of cognate vocabulary shared by all of the member languages in the group and create a hierarchy of languages based on cognate percentages and degrees of relatedness.

The next step, determining linguistic subgroups requires using the tools of the comparative method of historical linguistics to identify shared lexical, phonological, and morphological innovations among genetically related languages that share a relatively high percentage of cognate vocabulary. Linguistic subgroups possess remnants of the common linguistic ancestor in their cognate vocabulary, regular sound correspondences, and other common grammatical features, such as noun-classes among many Atlantic languages spoken in the Upper Guinea Coast. For linguist historians, linguistic subgroups have intrinsic historical reality and profound historical importance. At a particular moment in time, the speech communities within a linguistic subgroup possessed a common language as well as common practices, technology, values, and institutions, which linguist historians can begin to reconstruct by using linguistic tools.

In addition to "core" vocabulary words, a second category of vocabulary, "cultural" vocabulary, is an important source in reconstructing the social history of a speech community in a linguistic subgroup that spoke an ancestral language. Words for social, political, cultural, and ritual institutions comprise cultural vocabulary. In languages worldwide, linguists have determined that when speech communities are in contact with one another, they are more likely to exchange cultural vocabulary than core vocabulary words; cultural vocabulary is much more vulnerable to change when speech communities no longer find the information that they describe to be relevant. For example, if one speech community migrates to a different ecological niche, its language speakers are more likely to borrow words for the farming techniques and tools that they will need to learn to survive in their new locale from the speech communities that they encounter in their new locale than they are to borrow kinship terminology or other core vocabulary words that they already possess in their own language.

Within a linguistic subgroup, there are three categories of cultural vocabulary, inherited, innovated, and borrowed words, which can be distinguished by whether or not they possess regular sound correspondences. Linguists have found from analyzing languages spoken worldwide that inherited vocabulary words are more likely to possess regular sound correspondences. Speech communities inherit cultural vocabulary words when they continue to pass down these cultural vocabulary words, because the information that the words describe remains relevant. However, some loan words were borrowed so long ago that they also exhibit regular sound correspondences. To guard against these unusual cases, comparative linguists must include in their analysis branches of the language family that are more distantly related and language data from speech communities that are located in the vicinity of the linguistic subgroup in question, but whose languages are not genetically related.

In addition to inheriting words, speech communities also create and acquire new words. Since innovated vocabulary possesses regular sound correspondences, linguist historians must investigate whether or not the words exist in the neighboring languages. If they are in fact unique to a particular linguistic subgroup and they possess the phonological characteristics of the linguistic subgroup, then they can be categorized as innovated vocabulary. Speech communities in a linguistic subgroup coin vocabulary words when they need new words to describe technology, social and political institutions, for example. To linguist historians, innovated vocabulary words are evidence of change, innovation, and sometimes a rupture with the inherited patterns of the past.

Speech communities also borrow loanwords from neighbors. If the word can be traced to a language that is not genetically related to the linguistic subgroup in question, then the word is classified as a loanword. To the linguist historians, loanwords are historical evidence of contact between two speech communities. Groups of loanwords give historians important clues about the nature of contact and possibly even the power dynamics between the two groups. Each category of cultural vocabulary is an invaluable historical source, because it provides evidence of how a speech community's practices, values, institutions, technology, and relationships with neighboring groups have changed over time.

Linguist historians use "glottochronology," a subset of the comparative method, to give absolute dates to linguistic subgroups within a language's genealogy. Glottochronology uses a mathematical constant to measure the cumulative effect resulting from individual random changes occurring on the vocabulary of a proto-language. From this figure, linguist historians infer an approximate length of time since the divergence of linguistic subgroups. Glottochronology measures "the patterned accumulation of individually random change among quanta of like properties."[21] Like the comparative method itself, glottochronology was developed on the basis of Indo-European languages, for which comparative linguists have written samples dating back approximately one millennium.

Among linguists and historians, glottochronology has its critics. Some comparative linguists have criticized the universality of its claims: Can the

---

[21] Ehret 2000, 373.

rate of word replacement be the same in all of the world's languages and throughout their entire histories? Can word loss and grammatical change really be measured? Others have suggested that the time depth of language divergence can be overestimated if regular sound correspondences and cognates are undercounted and underestimated if chance similarities and borrowed words are counted as cognates. At the core of critics' reasoning is also a critique of broader aspects of historical linguistics, particularly lexicostatistics, cognate percentages, and family trees.[22]

Some Africanist historians who have utilized the comparative method of historical linguistics to reconstruct the early precolonial history, primarily of Bantu speech communities in East and Central Africa, have echoed and added their voices to the aforementioned critiques. Objecting to the premise that words in all languages are replaced at a steady rate, Jan Vansina advocates using the relative chronology generated by the genealogy of a language group, which the application of historical linguistics methodology yields. Language groupings with lower cognate percentages are more distantly related and diverged from their common linguistic ancestor at an earlier period in the past; conversely, language groupings with higher cognate percentages are more closely related and diverged from their common linguistic ancestor more recently in the past. Vansina also advocates estimating that one half of a millennium elapsed between one level of a language's genealogy and another, but these estimates would remain unconfirmed.[23]

However, a second group of Africanist historian linguists, including Christopher Ehret and David Schoenbrun, continues to use and to refine glottochronology. Ehret demonstrated correlative chronologies from linguistic evidence and pottery traditions in languages throughout Africa, reviewing empirical data from linguistics and archaeology in four languages and in four different regions of Africa to test for correlation between dates generated by glottochronology and by archaeology. Over a 10,000-year period, Ehret concluded that the two methodologies independently generated roughly similar dates. Over a 1,000-year period of individual random changes, the language families in Africa shared 74 percent of their retentions. However, critics of glottochronology continue to question the underlying assumptions of Ehret's findings, because Ehret does not test his findings against a third independently generated chronology.[24]

In the Rio Nunez, a subregion of the Upper Guinea Coast, historical linguistics including glottochronology – in the absence of archaeological and botanical studies – provides the earliest historical evidence for the area, which predates the recording of European travelers' accounts. Two genetically, though distantly, related linguistic subgroups in the Atlantic language

---

[22] Embleton 2000.
[23] Vansina 2004, 4–5, 8.
[24] Ehret 2000.

family, which I have called Coastal and Highlands, inhabit the Rio Nunez region. Proto-Coastal-speakers were the earliest inhabitants to occupy the coast and have inhabited the coast of present-day Guinea-Conakry since antiquity. Whereas migration from the north along the coast may have played a role in the divergence of Nalu, divergence of the other Proto-Coastal daughter languages, Mbulungish, and Mboteni, diverged on the coast, practically in situ. Several months of "tornadoes,"[25] and torrential rains during the rainy seasons, severing canoe transportation and communication between villages for a significant portion of the year were more important factors in the divergence of these Coastal languages than was migration from the interior to the coast. Today, Nalu, Mbulungish, and Mboteni speech communities occupy small, sparsely inhabited villages in the region's coastal floodplains and mangrove swamps.

Proto-Coastal-speakers have inhabited the coastal fringe of present-day Guinea-Conakry and Guinea-Bissau since ca. 3000 to 2000 BCE. There they inherited knowledge of salt *-mer from their linguistic ancestors whose languages were spoken north of the Rio Nunez region in Senegal and Guinea-Bissau, which like Coastal languages, form part of the Northern branch of the Atlantic language family. In addition, the ancient Proto-Coastal-speakers had knowledge of white mangrove, *Avicenna Africana* *-yop, which biological and botanical studies of the mangroves find occupy zones close to dry land. The roots of *A. Africana*, "pneumatophores," are not adapted to grow in waterlogged soils with high levels of salinity. After the proto-Coastal language diverged ca.1000 CE, its daughter speech communities, Nalu, Mbulungish, and Mboteni, gained knowledge of red mangroves (*Rhizophora racemosa*) -*mak* and for the shellfish, which make their home in the roots of the red mangrove trees, -*nep* (crab, generic) and –*laŋ* (type of crab). Red mangroves have long, tangled aerial, stilt, or prop roots, which grow above ground and provide the main physical support for the tree. These roots are specially equipped to gain oxygen from submerged and waterlogged soils. Unlike words for "salt" and "white mangrove," words for "red mangroves" and "crabs" cannot be traced back to the proto-Coastal language. According to the linguistic evidence, Coastal speech communities first established a coastal land-use system that included salt and white mangroves, located closest to their settlements. They subsequently ventured out into zones of red mangroves located closer to the ocean and incorporated shellfish. They became specialists at exploiting the coastal environment before they integrated rice cultivation into their subsistence strategies. Among the earliest inhabitants of the Rio Nunez region, the development of a coastal land-use system is much more ancient than rice cultivation.

Unlike Coastal speech communities, proto-Highlands speech communities are relative newcomers to the Rio Nunez Region. Highlands languages are

---

[25] Conneau 1976, 272; Mouser 2000, 5 n.19.

part of the Southern branch of the Atlantic group, whose languages are distantly related to Coastal languages and other languages in the Northern branch. The Proto-Highlands homeland is located in the forest-savanna, just beyond the coastal region in the south of present-day Guinea, near the Konkoure River. Also unlike Coastal speech communities, East-West migration likely played an important role in the divergence of proto-Highlands into its daughter languages whose present-day speech communities inhabit a large territory along the coast and into the interior of present-day Guinea-Conakry, Sierra Leone, and Liberia. Reconstructed vocabulary for the proto-Highlands language is evidence that proto-Highlands-speakers were well-adapted to the forest-savanna region by ca.500 to 1000 CE: from their linguistic ancestors, they inherited knowledge of *-sɛm (animal, quadruped, wild animal, meat venison, or beef), *-cir (blood), *-na (cow), *-ir (goat), *-bamp (bird), *-wul (loop, noose trap for catching venison and birds), *-kom (oil palm), *-lop (fish), and *-buk (snake). Proto-Highlands-speakers also coined unique terminology related to iron production: *-fac (iron, iron cooking pot), *-unt (coal), and *-ima (smoke). Lastly, proto-Highlands-speakers borrowed loanwords related to cattle and herding from Fulbe, a distantly related Atlantic language from the Northern branch: -col (livestock breeding, to rear as cattle, tend, mind, attend to, take care as of cattle or men, shepherd, one tending cattle). After the divergence of Highlands languages ca.1000 CE, one inherited word, *-cap, "to wound, chop, fell," underwent semantic shift to include a new meaning, "to cut trees at the bottom before turning earth with wooden fulcrum shovel used by rice farmers in the Rio Nunez region." This semantic shift may be evidence of speech community migration from the forest-savanna to the coast. Highlands speech communities may have added new meanings to an old word to make it reflect their new circumstances. Coastal speech communities were agents of continuity in the Rio Nunez region, establishing the coastal land-use system; Highlands-speakers were agents of change within the region, bringing a diverse set of strategies, which included iron, land clearing, and animal trapping from the forest-savanna to the coastal region. Both Coastal and Highlands speech communities played essential, yet quite different roles in the development of coastal rice-growing technology.

An analysis of cultural vocabulary reveals that much of the material culture and farming techniques used by Coastal and Highlands speech communities in the Rio Nunez region to create dikes and bunds to trap fresh water along the coast and to channel this fresh water for desalinating tidal floodplains and mangrove swamps is indigenous to Atlantic speech communities. It cannot be reconstructed to either the Coastal or Highlands speech communities or to their linguistic ancestors. Instead, it was coined after the migration of Highlands speech communities to the coastal Rio Nunez region and the divergence of proto-Highlands ca. 1000 CE; it spread areally and locally among the Nalu, Mbulungish, Mboteni, and Sitem speech communities in the Rio Nunez region. For example, in the Rio Nunez region, Nalu, Mbulungish, Mboteni, and Sitem innovated vocabulary for water control technology – mounds and ridges, "-nɛk" – and transplanting technology. Most significantly, "ma-kumbal," the wooden fulcrum shovel, which farmers in the Upper Guinea Coast use to carve the dikes and bunds out of coastal soils is also indigenous. The areal vocabulary suggests that the earliest fulcrum shovels were probably fabricated completely out of wood, without the metal blade. In the Rio Nunez region, the birth of the coastal rice-growing technology was the result of collaboration between Coastal and Highlands speech communities. It produced a sophisticated farming system uniquely adapted to the floodplains and white mangrove swamps of this corner of the Upper Guinea Coast approximately 500 years before the arrival of the Portuguese, the first Europeans, in the region.

Finally, a linguistic analysis of words from the Susu language reveals language contact between Atlantic speech communities who spoke Coastal and Highlands languages and Susu speech communities between ca. 1500 to 1800 CE. Susu is part of the Mande language family, which is not genetically related to either the Coastal or Highlands languages in the Atlantic language family. The Susu language was the source of important innovations in the coastal Rio Nunez region. Susu-speakers inherited words for agriculture in the savanna-woodlands such as rice, fonio, sorghum, mound (for cultivation), and hoe from their linguistic ancestors who spoke proto-Susu-Jallonke. Nalu, Mboteni, Mbulungish, Sitem, Kalum, and Landuma subsequently borrowed these words and meanings from Susu. Susu-speakers coined a second set of words which cannot be reconstructed to proto-Susu-Jallonke, including vocabulary for iron working, the iron foot affixed to the end of the fulcrum shovel, and a general term for the wooden fulcrum shovel. Semantic shift in Mbulungish and Mboteni resulted in the shift in the meaning of the Susu word for iron, -fɛnc, into words for the metal blade at the bottom of the fulcrum shovel. Atlantic speech communities in the Rio Nunez borrowed Susu technology, using it to extend coastal rice-growing technology into zones of red mangroves. Atlantic language speakers in the Rio Nunez region also borrowed Susu terminology and added it to their specialized terminology for their coastal rice land-use system.

The Rio Nunez is the only subregion to date where historical linguistics has been used and employed to investigate the development of rice-growing technology. Thus, there is insufficient evidence in the rest of the Upper Guinea Coast subregions to determine that these findings would also apply to other areas. Additional interdisciplinary research is warranted. Simultaneously however, the sheer cultural, linguistic, social, political, and environmental diversity of the Upper Guinea Coast works against gathering and interpreting interdisciplinary data. This chapter will make one last attempt at answering this important question using European travelers' accounts.

HISTORICAL SOURCES: TRAVELERS' ACCOUNTS

The earliest historical sources for the Upper Guinea Coast were recorded by Portuguese and Luso-African traders who traveled up and down the rivers between present-day Senegal and Sierra Leone, spending short periods of time in different ports during the dry season. Because of the deadly disease environment created by mosquitoes, malaria, and yellow fever, rarely did European and Eur-African traders travel upriver or spend the deadly rainy seasons in port. Neither did they have commercial relationships with and hence firsthand knowledge of every group inhabiting the coast. The earliest written sources for the Upper Guinea Coast describe production, trade, and consumption of rice, primarily during the trade season, by regional inhabitants with whom Portuguese and Luso-African traders had commercial relations.

André Alvares de Álmada whose travels and trade between Gambia and Sierra Leone spanned the 1560s to 1580s described an agricultural cycle in Cape St. Mary south of the Gambia River in which the "winter" or rainy season began at the end of April or the beginning of May when the "blacks work in their rice-fields." According to Álmada, the subregion's inhabitants planted rice seeds first in rice nurseries, which became inundated with flood waters: "the rice-fields remain under water for more than three months, since the rising of the river floods all the lalas between June and November." They then transplanted rice seedlings from nurseries to fields once the seedlings had germinated: "from the flooded lalas the blacks recover their rice-plants, and transplant them into drier lalas, where they soon give their crop."[26] From a variety of locations between present-day Gambia to Sierra Leone, such as the kingdoms of Jolof, Gambia, and Buramos, the Biafadas and Banhuns territory, the shoals of St. Anne, south of Cape St. Mary, and Turtle Islands, Álmada witnessed a small, but growing, trade in grains, particularly rice, millet or "millet maçaroca," sorghum or "white millet," and fonio, as well as other foodstuffs.[27] Only among the Baga Sitem located on Cape Verga, does Álmada observe clean or husked rice and rice in the husk as available foodstuffs.[28] For the Upper Guinea Coast, Álmada's mid- to late-sixteenth-century account provides the earliest description of wet rice farming in coastal areas for subsistence and commercial production.

Almost one century after the publication of Álmada's account, Francisco de Lemos Coelho traveled and traded in the Upper Guinea Coast, centering his commercial operations in present-day Guinea-Bissau, further south than

---

[26] Álmada (1984, 57) may have been slightly confused in his description of planting rice seeds in submerged nurseries then transplanting them into drier rice fields. Typically, at least today in mangrove rice production in the Rio Nunez region, farmers transplant in the inverse direction, from drier nurseries with a lower percentage of salinity in the soil to wetter rice fields with higher levels of salinity.

[27] Álmada 1984, 18, 43, 61, 78, 82–83, 116, 139–140.

[28] Álmada 1984, 139.

Álmada's Gambia River nexus. By the late seventeenth century, commercial relations between European and Eur-African traders and Upper Guinea Coast inhabitants had increased. Portuguese and Luso-African traders were active in rivers that were unknown or unavailable to the Portuguese a century prior. They were also connecting coastal ports to overland caravan routes that brought trade goods to the coast from the interior. Lastly, Portuguese and Luso-African traders' monopoly over commercial activity was less secure. Lemos Coelho encountered European traders from multiple nations, British, Dutch, and French, who competed for goods and relationships with coastal rulers.

Like Álmada, Coelho described abundant rice production among the Jola in the Kingdom of Jame. Among the Baga Sitem in the Rio Nuñez region of present-day Guinea, Coelho witnessed an active trade in salt, which was taken to the port on the Nuñez River "where there is none," and rice, which was taken south to the port on the Pongo River "this being the same commodity taken to this port, where they load ships with it."[29] By the end of the seventeenth century, the Eur-African provision trade had opened up in the southern portion of the Upper Guinea Coast. Groups, such as the Baga Sitem who had a long history of producing rice, but had previously had limited commercial relationships with Eur-Africans, were drawn into the trade. In present-day Sierra Leone, Coelho described rice farming in inland valleys, possibly located in the bolilands, and irrigated by freshwater. According to Coelho, wet rice farming systems in these microenvironments were far less labor-intensive than mangrove rice farming, lacked components such as transplanting, and typically produced two rice harvests annually: "in return for the few labours its inhabitants perform for it, it pays them the tribute of two crops of rice a year."[30] Lastly, Coelho described the Balanta of present-day Guinea-Bissau trading in foodstuffs, but not in rice. They brought a "plant they cultivate called 'yams', which grows underground like turnips" to the coast for trade.[31] This observation represented an exception to what was increasingly becoming the rule – Luso-African traders describe rice cultivation in three separate microenvironments using different irrigation systems – along the Upper Guinea Coast at the end of the 1600s.

The end of the seventeenth century also brought change in the character of the provision trade and in the commodities traded. Cleaned or husked rice emerged as an important commodity in many ports supplanting the sale of unhusked rice for several coastal Eur-African markets, provisioning growing numbers of captives, and feeding growing Eur-African trade communities. For example, Mandinga traders on the southern side of the port of Jagra, and the inhabitants of the Kingdom of Manjagar sold husked rice and captives.

---

[29] Coelho and Hair 1985, 127.
[30] Coelho and Hair 1985, 138.
[31] Coelho and Hair 1985, 81; Hawthorne 2003.

In the port of Manjagar, the Mandinga traders also sold wax and ivory. Inhabitants in port of Cação offered many foodstuffs for sale, including hens, husked rice, milk, and fat.[32] In the port of Baracunda to which caravans of local merchants travel, there was so much husked rice that "ships could be loaded with it."[33] Surrounded by uninhabited islands where villagers grew rice, the Island of Oracao off the coast of present-day Guinea-Bissau produced abundant foodstuffs, especially husked rice.[34] Lastly, "a large quantity of husked rice" was available in Havana Island for ships coming from Sierra Leone.[35] Though rice production for local consumption and trans-Atlantic trade was escalating by the end of the seventeenth century, it was still not yet "uniform" throughout the Upper Guinea Coast.

By the end of the seventeenth century, Eur-African traders accessed portions of the Upper Guinea Coast where previously they did not have commercial relations, including areas such as the port of Jagra and the port of Benar where shoals of mud and sand-banks lined the waterways. Coelho's access gives historians a glimpse into the agricultural techniques and production, as well as the commercial activities of more Atlantic groups. In the northern reaches, rice had supplanted millet and fonio as the primary foodstuff in Coelho's description of the provision trade.[36] His account revealed that although production of and trade in rice, particularly husked rice had become more common, it was not yet "uniform" throughout the Upper Guinea Coast. However, the majority of the Upper Guinea Coast was producing rice for consumption and increasingly for sale by the end of the seventeenth century.

Was the Upper Guinea Coast "uniformly committed to rice production?" The answer is this: available evidence suggests that the overwhelming majority of Atlantic and possibly Mande groups in the Upper Guinea Coast were producing rice for subsistence and increasingly for trade in the mid-seventeenth century, the birth of the plantation complex in the U.S. South. The inhabitants of the Upper Guinea Coast were not "uniformly" committed. The inhabitants of the Senegambia still grew millet, particularly in years of too little rain. Further south, the inhabitants of present-day Guinea and Sierra Leone grew fonio. Both grains were part of complex farming systems whose delicate balance was designed to mitigate the effects of rainfall fluctuations and increase food security. Unfortunately, in the Senegambia, the balance periodically went awry, leading to tens of thousands of people captured and sold into slavery on slaving vessels, such as the *Mentor*, in the late eighteenth century.[37]

---

[32] Coelho and Hair 1985, 27, 31.
[33] Coelho and Hair 1985, 45.
[34] Coelho and Hair 1985, 101.
[35] Coelho and Hair 1985, 136.
[36] For a full analysis of the provision trade from 1700 to 1860, see Searing 1993.
[37] Carney 2001, 44.

Though the available interdisciplinary evidence is still quite uneven, it highlights the diversity of the Upper Guinea Coast and its inhabitants and the limits of the interdisciplinary sources available to reconstruct their precolonial history. Historical sources give historians the best grasp of the period of Eur-African trade when rice was already established in most Upper Guinea Coast communities. More interdisciplinary evidence is still necessary to enable historians to understand how and when rice became established as a primary economic activity in the diverse societies inhabiting the Upper Guinea Coast.

CONCLUSION: THE HISTORY OF WEST AFRICAN RICE FARMERS AND ENVIRONMENTAL HISTORY

The question of whether or not rice farmers in precolonial Upper Guinea Coast were "uniformly committed to rice" is a symptom of a larger phenomenon: there has been too little dialogue among the following literatures: the history of West African rice farmers, environmental history, and the histories of indigenous people's interactions with the environment, which for a variety of reasons have not identified as part of the environmental history cannon. At first sight, the literature on the global history of rice and rice farmers, including but not limited to that of Africanists, and the growing field of environmental history appear analogous to two parallel lines, which extend in the same direction without intersecting. There are several reasons for the perception that, excluding a few notable exceptions,[38] the global history of rice, particularly in Africa, is running parallel to and not intersecting with the environmental history literature.

The roots of the environmental history cannon primarily explore European imperialists taming nature and indigenous peoples, particularly Indians in the Americas.[39] On the one hand, the focus of the smaller, but growing historiography on Africa's environmental history, has mainly chronicled African initiative in the face of European colonization and capitalist exploitation. Chronologically, the literature is heavily weighted toward the colonial/imperial period. Thematically, it stresses encounters between Europeans, particularly European missionaries and settlers in East and Southern Africa, and African farmers and pastoralists, and clashes between subsistence/sustainable and commercial/capitalist systems of production.

On the other hand, the literature on African rice and rice farmers has overwhelmingly been focused on the West African region where *Oryza glaberrima*, the rice species that is indigenous to Africa, was domesticated and where large populations have continued to grow rice for subsistence as their staple crop into the postcolonial period.[40] Despite the growing use of

---

[38] Stewart 2002a and 2002b.
[39] Crosby 1986; Cronon and Demos 2003.
[40] Richards 1985; Linares 1992; Carney 2001; Hawthorne 2003; Fields-Black 2008.

quinine to prevent malarial infection in the late nineteenth century, West Africa did not attract a European settler population because of its disease environment and high European death rate relative to North, East, and Southern Africa. Hence, it was least affected by colonial land alienation policies. Not only did the land remain in the hands of West African peasants, but West African entrepreneurs, not European settlers, developed the commercial agricultural industries around cash crops such as palm oil, peanuts, and cocoa and rice to a lesser extent in the earlier period of trans-Atlantic trade. As a result, farmers in West Africa, including, but not limited to rice farmers, were able to develop innovative forms of indigenous agriculture, some of which were intensive.[41] If encounter and clash between European and indigenous knowledge systems are the rule in the environmental history literature, West African rice farmers are the exception.[42]

Despite these differences, there are many interesting points of connection between the literature on the global history of rice and environmental history. Both of these bodies of work have been on the cutting edge of employing interdisciplinary sources and methods, though the environmental history literature's tilt toward to the colonial and postcolonial period has generally translated to the dominance of archival sources. The Africanist environmental history literature has drawn effectively on oral traditions and histories, a methodology that the broader field of African history has employed since its inception to reconstruct the precolonial history of many groups in Africa, particularly those inhabiting regions that were not described by Arab traders or European missionaries or traders.[43] In the use of historical linguistics to understand indigenous people's development of complex and diverse land-use strategies to ensure food security, Africanists in both the environmental history and the rice and rice-farmer literature have led the way.[44] This chapter has laid out the potentials and limitations of the comparative method of historical linguistics for reconstructing early and precolonial history, including environmental history and the global history of rice.

The use of science, including palynology, paleohydrology, fossil pollen, biomedical analysis of lake sediment, tracings of river volumes, in historical analysis has been integral to both literatures.[45] Unlike this flowering of interdisciplinary source materials, Erik Gilbert was faced with silence in the West African literature on the introduction of O. sativa and travelers' accounts that hinted that O. sativa was introduced into East Africa in the

---

[41] Richards 1985.
[42] Carney 2001 and Hawthorne 2010a are notable exceptions, because they deal with captives from the Upper Guinea Coast of West Africa who were enslaved in South Carolina and Brazil and forced to labor on rice plantations in these regions.
[43] Shetler 2007; Giles-Vernick 2000, 2.
[44] Schoenbrun 1998; Fields-Black 2008.
[45] Schoenbrun 1998.

nineteenth century. Gilbert (Chapter 9, this volume) uses plant genetics to distinguish between O. *sativa* varieties that were introduced to West Africa and the Americas on one hand and Southeast Asia and East Africa on the other. Historians of global rice and the environment have in large part integrated scientific sources into their analyses, because of the nature of the questions posed about the interaction between humans, animals, and their environment and the incompleteness of traditional historical sources on such questions. In Africa, as always, the paucity of traditional historical sources, particularly for the precolonial period, is ever-present.

Environmental historians, in particular those reconstructing precolonial land-use patterns, have drawn effectively on archaeological studies of the role of agriculture in human settlement and evolution of complex societies, even reaching back several thousand years into the ancient past.[46] Archaeological evidence is much more limited for the environmental history of large swaths of the globe's populations that inhabit wet, forested, tropical regions where farmers plant seedless crops. Within the global rice literature, a glaring discrepancy exists in the archaeological record for Africa and Asia, because there are few visible ancient fields in Africa where fields rarely fossilize, unlike Asia.[47] Archaeologists working along the Yangtze River, east of the Taihu Lake, have found evidence of ancient paddy rice fields, small fields between one and fifteen square meters in size connected by canals and reservoirs whose layout reflects local topography.[48] To date, these kinds of studies have not been conducted in Africa, West or East, where archaeologists have been primarily focused on questions such as human settlement, state formation, and trade. In the literature on African rice and rice farmers, questions about agricultural technology and field systems have been secondary, if not tertiary.

Richly textured recent work using archaeology, historical linguistics, and oral traditions in the Africanist environmental literature is a call to arms. It challenges global specialists of rice and environmental historians specializing in other regions of the world who have yet to exploit these important interdisciplinary sources and methodologies to their fullest potential. As the Africanist literature on environmental history, rice, and rice farmers exemplifies, interdisciplinary sources and methods may be particularly illuminating for regions of the world and for time periods when indigenous peoples did not leave copious documentation written in their own hands.

Can parallel lines be re-routed to a point of intersection? Putting the history of West African rice farmers in dialogue with the environmental history literature elucidates whether or not the inhabitants of the Upper Guinea Coast were "uniformly committed to rice production" in the precolonial period. In the Upper Guinea Coast and in diverse far away locales, such

---

[46] Mitchell 2002; Giles-Vernick 2000; Shetler 2007.
[47] Sutton 1984, 25–6, 28.
[48] Fuller and Ling Qin 2009, 1, 94–8.

as the woodlands of North-central Namibia, semi-arid and arid areas of southern Kenya and northern Tanzania, Kalahari desert of Namibia and South Africa, indigenous communities do not base their subsistence on a single crop or land-use strategy.[49] Diversification would have decreased vulnerability to rainfall fluctuations and increased food security. For the drought-prone Senegambia, however, even diversification was not sufficient to stave off the effects of decades of poor rainfall and locust plagues between the seventeenth and nineteenth centuries. Beginning in the 1600's, these interlocked waves of disaster contributed to the sale of approximately 350,000 captives[50] from the sparsely populated Senegambia into the trans-Atlantic slave aboard slave ships such as the *Mentor*.

---

[49] Kreike 2004; Spear et al.1993; Wilmsen 1989; Gordon 1992.
[50] See David Eltis and Martin Halbert, www.slavevoyages.org [accessed July 24, 2014].

8

Reserving Water: Environmental and Technological Relationships with Colonial South Carolina Inland Rice Plantations

Hayden R. Smith

Reservoir-irrigated rice cultivation was the first successful type of plantation agriculture developed in South Carolina, and it served as the foundation for the South Carolina colonial economy. But despite its significance, Lowcountry inland rice cultivation has had an elusive history. Unlike the visible tidal rice embankments still standing along South Carolina tidal rivers, remnant inland fields are harder to find and many presently lie in overgrown wooded watersheds. The lack of cultivation has transformed the once carefully managed fields into second or third growth forests and wetlands, some of which are protected as conservation lands today in ways that have obscured these past histories of human land use. The sparseness of primary records also has deterred historians from fully examining the impact that this early plantation complex had on Lowcountry history, as few plantation journals and ledger books survive from the colonial period that speak of inland rice culture. When tidal rice irrigation took hold in the mid-eighteenth century, most planters began focusing their slave labor and documentation on this new technology because of the efficiency in irrigation and higher yields. Yet, inland cultivation continued in the antebellum period, as evidence from nineteenth-century plans and journals make clear. Far from being a primitive early approach to rice growing, inland cultivation has a history that parallels and interweaves with that of tidal cultivation.[1]

---

[1] Earlier histories note that inland cultivation was the first economically successful rice plantation. These interpretations also describe a single method of inland rice cultivation. See: Gray 1933, 1: 280–4; Heyward 1937, 11–6; Clowse and South Carolina Tricentennial Commission 1971, 122–33; Clifton 1978, ix–xi; Hilliard 1978, 98–100; Coclanis 1989, 44–5, 61–3, 96–8. On inland rice plantations continuation in the antebellum period, see: Smith 2012. Small scale inland rice cultivation continued beyond the traditional Lowcountry rice zone during the post-bellum period, documented in Vernon 1993, and Coclanis and Marlow 1998.

This chapter fills the gap in historiography by explaining how planters both adapted to and altered their environment by planting rice in South Carolina's inland swamps during the colonial period. It shows how attention to the environment leads to a historical analysis of the close relationship between Lowcountry cultivators and the land. Inland cultivation began as a simple process for growing rice by taking advantage of suitable sites. As demand for the crop and land values increased, planters needed larger harvests and so spent more energy expanding old inland fields and crafting new inland rice environments. The need to adapt to the diverse landscapes of the South Carolina Coastal Plain prompted planters to make each tract unique in order to maximize available land for rice cultivation. The cultivators themselves worked within the limitations of this environment to manage water flow and lessen the impact of storms, flooding, and drought, but as time went by they also transformed these environments in increasingly sophisticated ways.[2]

Inland rice cultivation also provides a significant story about slave labor systems in the Americas. When experimenting initially with rice cultivation, colonists used African slaves to plant seeds in a variety of microenvironments. Reacting to the opportunities of the global economy, inland planters used enslaved labor continually to clear more land and expand the crop's output, just as tobacco planters in the Chesapeake set slaves there to clear new land. This practice encouraged the ever-expanding slave trade in South Carolina and the diaspora of Africans through the New World. Ways of mobilizing labor by task instead of by gang also took shape on inland rice plantations. The task system that developed in the Lowcountry is found nowhere else in American history. The ecological foundations of inland rice plantations are the keys to understanding the emergence of a highly intricate labor and environmental management system in the dense South Carolina woodland watersheds.[3]

Rice sprouted in the Lowcountry approximately a decade after the first British inhabitants founded Charles Town (Charleston) in 1670 (Figure 8.1). Originally, European colonists experimented with rice, one of many subsistence crops, by cultivating the plant on high dry ground with periodic

---

[2] Water control and soil management are two themes found through environmental history literature. In discussing people's attempt to control both land and labor in the Georgia lowcountry, Stewart (1996) explains how tidal rice fields represented a hybrid landscape that integrated power, nature, and people. Also see: Porcher 1987. Literature contributing to understanding water control is found in Fiege 1999 and White 1995. Further explorations by Steinberg (1991) and Kirby (1995) reveal tensions over water, even when set in damp regions. Works discussing the importance of microenvironmental influence upon agricultural practices are found in Donahue 2004. For works documenting Southern soil use, see: Stoll 2002; Nelson 2007; Steinberg 1991, 99–165; and Sutter 2010.

[3] Morgan 1982; Coclanis 2000.

watering. As a result of poor husbandry, the upland method of cultivation was not very productive. Not until the creolization of African and European knowledge maintaining consistent irrigation methods, using low-lying wetlands as fields, did the crop produce a surplus above subsistence by the early eighteenth century. These plantations originally existed in the cypress groves and woodland streams roughly 5 to 30 miles inland from Charles Town. As prospective planters started migrating – and enslaved Africans shipped – to colonial South Carolina, partially motivated by a brief rice boom in the 1720s, did inland plantations soon stretch from the Savannah River up to Winyah Bay.

Demand for the grain exploded in both Europe and America by 1730, which initiated more capital investment in rice plantations. One key pull factor led to this demand for South Carolina rice. The British Parliament relaxed the Navigation Acts for rice in 1731. This change in policy allowed for the direct export of rice on British ships headed to Southern Europe, which consumed 20 percent of colonial rice exports by the 1730s. In 1699, Charles Town merchants exported 291 barrels of rice; by 1715, the total rose to 5,262 barrels. Fifteen years later, however, South Carolina merchants exported 44,385 barrels and by 1745 the total had grown to 63,433 barrels. Despite rising rice exports, prices fluctuated dramatically during a 21-year period beginning in 1739. A series of economic depressions in England and Charles Town – stemming from King George's War (1739–48), the Stono Rebellion (1739), and yellow fever (1739, 1745, 1748, 1758) and smallpox (1738, 1758, 1760) epidemics – led to deflated rice prices. Nonetheless, shipping increased between Europe and North America after the end of King George's War in 1748, and lower transportation costs, the consequence of faster shipping and higher volume, increased profits. English merchants could purchase less expensive rice from India or Africa at the end of the seventeenth century, yet they obtained a higher quality grain at a lower price from South Carolina by the mid-eighteenth century.[4]

The South Carolina rice market began another upward economic and manufacturing cycle in 1760. International events advanced rice prices in the second half of the eighteenth century, spurring an increase in Lowcountry rice production. European demand for rice grew dramatically after a series of poor English and European grain harvests during the late 1760s and early 1770s. This motivated the British Parliament to remove tariffs and import more of the South Carolina cash crop. Climate fluctuations between 1767 and 1771 created abnormally high rainfall in the summer and autumn, while cold and long winters prolonged snow cover. The cumulative moist seasons created damaging effects on European grain production, with wet autumns diminishing wheat production in the European lowlands and long winters depleting hay crops in

---

[4] Dethloff 1982, 236; Hardy 2001, 116; McCusker 2006, 5–763, 5–764.

the uplands. These environmental hardships suffered by European grain producers, and the relaxation of English trade restrictions, led to a 50 percent increase in imports of Carolina rice between ca. 1760 and ca. 1775.[5]

This dramatic growth of the cash crop rippled through South Carolina society, resulting in the rise of wealthy planters and creolization from slave importation. Creolization is an anthropological concept that denotes the development of a new culture formed from two or more diverse societies. The "response and interaction" between various people in a specific environment, such as a rice plantation, involves the exchange of ideas, beliefs, and objects.[6] Through interweaving on plantations, both whites and blacks took a portion of the others' cultural practices, whether ideological or physical, and adopted them for their own benefit. Although one culture may have dominated another through labor control, the transfer of culture flowed freely between captors and slaves. As Peter Wood explains in *Black Majority*, more than 40 percent of enslaved Africans who reached British mainland colonies between 1700 and 1775 arrived in South Carolina to grow rice. This migration brought a remarkable interaction between European and African settlers.[7] Depending on the direct interaction between Africans and Europeans on American soil, each culture adapted the other's language, foodways, material culture, and work patterns to function in a new land. The rice plantation is a unique model for creolization because the isolated settings provided a direct transfer of ideas between planter and slaves. At the same time, the transfer of ideas reflected how people altered the environment they worked upon.[8]

By the first decade of the eighteenth century, rice had become South Carolina's most successfully cultivated product. Freshwater wetlands ideal for this cultivation were nestled in tributaries and swamps several miles away from the South Carolina coast. Geographer Judith Carney describes these wetlands as "an array of microenvironments which include valley bottoms, low-lying depressions, and areas of moisture holding clay." The inland terrain challenged planters to recognize what features would successfully sustain rice. Once they identified these features, planters used enslaved Africans to re-vamp these available natural features for cash crop production. From hardwood depressions down to the cypress riverbanks, various ecosystems within the Lowcountry were modified for inland swamp plantations. The critical requirement for widespread cultivation was active water flow through these landforms.[9]

---

[5] Coclanis 1982, 539–43; Nash 1992, 679, 684, 686–9, 692; Hardy 2001, 116. For eighteenth-century climate fluctuations and European agriculture, see: Pfister 1978, 233–4, 239–40.
[6] Joyner 1984, xxi; Brathwaite 1971, 296.
[7] Wood 1974, xiv; Joyner 1984; Ferguson 1992, xli–xlv.
[8] Joyner 1984, xviii; quote, xx.
[9] Carney 2001, 58; Hilliard 1978, 97; Edelson 2007, 390–3.

Inland rice cultivation depended upon the simple principle that water flows from high ground to low ground. Water dispersed from rainstorms and springs flowed down hill, of course, while watersheds pulled this resource into creeks and streams. Inland planters found land in the Lowcountry that was level enough for rice cultivation, yet with sufficient angle of 2 to 3 percent grade to allow drainage. Inland rice fields soon took shape throughout the Inner and Outer South Carolina Coastal Plain, mostly in areas that were naturally suited to them. The physiographical coastal plain is generally downward sloping from the edge of the North American tectonic plate, the "fall line," to the Atlantic Ocean shoreline. The Lowcountry topography provided ideal situations for inland rice cultivation. As the Atlantic Ocean's shoreline alternately encroached and retreated during the Pleistocene Epoch (~2 million to ~ten thousand years ago), barrier island chains and corresponding tidal flats formed over the millennia to create terraces and scarps. Similar to modern barrier island systems, prehistoric terraces consisted of sand and shells, while the backside of these ridgelines consisted of clay loam from former tidal marshes and lagoons. Scarps serve as physical lines of demarcation between the terraces, forming either from erosion of the receding coastline or during the depositional stage of former barrier islands.[10] Water's movement through these sedimentary deposits shaped the land, forming knolls, ridges, and troughs between 4 to 40 feet in elevation, which became critical features to rice plantations and the people who lived on them. Islands of "high pine land" lying within and around plantation swamps provided sites for buildings and grazing fields, while creeks flowing around these landforms provided the water sources and floodplains needed for cultivating rice. The early agricultural practices were of necessity diverse, as planters adapted their economic activities to the various microenvironments located on their property. Rather than altering their environments extensively, early inland rice planters used the environments that they found (Figures 8.1 and 8.2).[11]

Once European colonists recognized the importance of impounding water to the irrigation of the rice crop and the simultaneous eradication of competing grass, a dramatic shift in landscape perceptions and in agricultural activity occurred. Rice farming moved from the upland and savannah ecosystems down to the cypress-hardwood stream systems. Colonists looked beyond the "wasteland" to see unlimited potential in transforming the low-lying small-stream floodplains, located "at the head of creeks and rivers," into orderly agricultural zones. The flow of water through wetlands fed the dense vegetation that created the apparently "inexhaustible fertility" of the South Carolina Lowcountry.[12] As the vegetation died and

---

[10] Colquhoun and South Carolina State Development Board Division of Geology 1969, 23, 6; Soller and Mills 1991, 290–1.
[11] Kovacik and Winberry 1987, 20–1.
[12] Reclamation of Southern Swamps 1854, 525; Catesby quoted in Merrins 1977, 93.

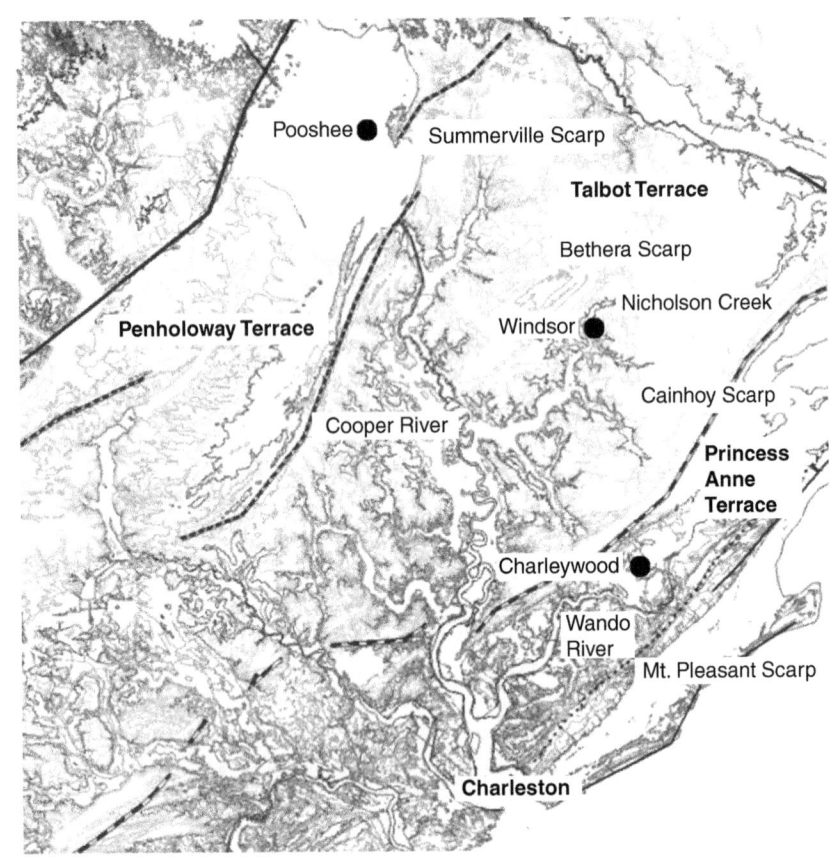

FIGURE 8.1. Scarps and terraces of the Lower Coastal Plain, central South Carolina. Image adapted from Donald J. Colquhoun, "Cyclic Surfical Stratigraphic Units of the Middle and Lower Coastal Plains, Central South Carolina," in Robert Q. Oaks and Jules R. DuBar, eds., *Post-Miocene Stratigraphy Central and Southern Atlantic Coastal Plain*, (Logan, UT: Utah State University Press, 1974), 181.

decomposed, nutrients accumulated and added to the soil's fertility that inland rice plantations exploited. Colonial naturalist Mark Catesby noted that inland swamps were "impregnated by the washings from the higher lands, in a series of years are become vastly rich, and deep of soyl [sic] consisting of a sandy loam of a dark brown colour."[13] One rice planter

---

[13] Catesby quoted in Merrins 1977, 92; Noting the tremendous amount of physical labor needed to transform this environment into agricultural fields, Catesby commented that "this soil is composed of a blackish sandy loam, and provides good rice land, but the trouble of grubbing up and clearing it of the trees and underwood has been hitherto a discouragement to the culture of it," in Merrins 1977, 93; Wood 1974, 59–62; Carney 1996, 14–16.

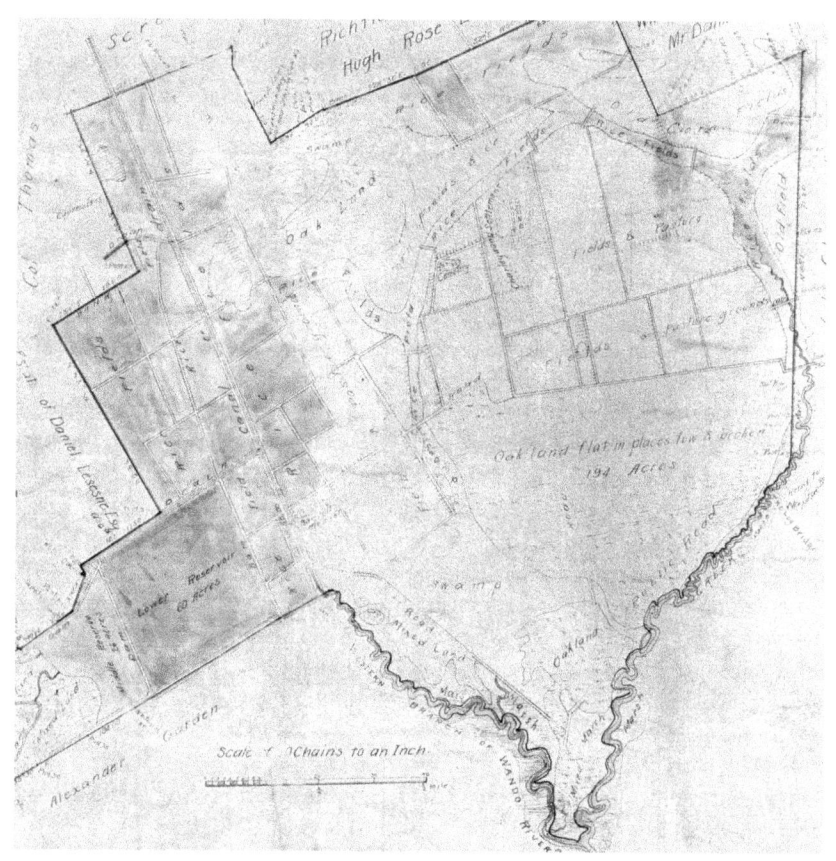

FIGURE 8.2. Charleywood Plantation with new rice fields on the left and old rice fields on the right. Image from "A Plan of Charleywood Plantation," McCrady Plat Collection, 954, Charleston County Register of Mesne Conveyance, Charleston, SC.

described inland swamps as having a "better foundation and soil than any other lands" and "by nature more durable" for cultivation because of the "fine supplies of decayed vegetable, which are deposited while the waters are passing over said lands."[14]

Planters' success or failure began with selecting a site with the right soil content. Impounded rice fields best retained water in less permeable loam and clay in low-lying wetlands. Planters' and slaves' knowledge of soil content became crucial for the construction of reservoirs and fields. Although inland fields were localized in distinct watersheds, the microenvironments used for

[14] Observations on the Winter Flowing of Rice Lands 1828, 531.

inland rice cultivation contained the same soil features. Meggett loam, as it was later known, was the soil type often associated with impounded inland rice zones. This soil had a mixture, or a loam, of sand, clay, silt, and organic matter. These watersheds – or second-order stream-floodplains – fed into the Cooper-Ashley-Wando (CAW) Basin, the Ashepoo-Combahee-Edisto (ACE) Basin, and the Savannah River, among others, meandering throughout the South Carolina coastal plain.[15]

Slow water permeability and high water-holding capacity were two characteristics found in the inland fields. Slow water permeability means that the soil content prevents water from efficiently draining through the ground. This feature allowed rice cultivators to retain water in the reservoirs and the fields. Because of their low water permeability, soil from these zones was also used to construct the embankments. By reinforcing the retaining walls with clay, slaves created a basin to hold water within the natural terrain. South Carolina Governor James Glenn wrote that "the best land for rice is a wet, deep, miry soil; such as is generally to be found in Cypress Swamps; or a black greasy Mould with a Clay Foundation; but the very best lands may be meliorated by laying them under water at proper Seasons." However, the compacted soil that created desirable conditions for retaining water also created hardship for enslaved laborers shaping the landscape. One Wando River plantation overseer complained that his hoes were "too broad and soft to dig up the clay land." The hoes were useless "for digging up light clay land," as "they duble [sic] up like a sheet of lead and manney [sic] become useless before they are halfe [sic] wore [sic]." Inland plantations' clay loam posed difficulties in excavation, yet the soil provided an accessible medium for Africans and African-Americans to express their cultural identity making colonoware – an earthenware pottery – and architectural features revealed in clay walled houses and outdoor chimneys.[16]

---

[15] Information about soil content derives from modern soil surveys, primary sources, and archaeology excavations. The Soil Conservation Service in the United States Department of Agriculture classifies, defines, and maps specific soils to current physical formations. Surprisingly, the physical remnants of inland and tidal rice fields still exist. Aerial photographs that contribute to the soil maps, or boundaries, for each unit reveal the inland fields and reservoirs. The soil content is a representation of what impact occurred on this land. As a result, the soil scientists acknowledge which soils were conducive for rice cultivation. For example, a 1916 soil survey explained that this soil type was "not used for agriculture, but abandoned canals, ditches, and dikes indicate that a considerable acreage was at one time used for the production of rice." The soil scientists observed that agricultural activity had not occurred for some time and that the land had become reclaimed "with a growth of cypress and gum, with longleaf and black pine, beech, and myrtle in the areas of slight elevation." United States Department of Agriculture 1980a; United States Department of Agriculture 1971; United States Department of Agriculture 1980b; quote: Latimer 1916, 515.

[16] Glen (1761) in Milling 1951, 14; Rash 1773; Singleton 2010, 157–70; Ferguson 1992, 18–22, 68–92.

Planters' ability to draw a steady amount of water to the fields was the second characteristic needed to successfully cultivate inland rice. Consistent access to water in these cultivation zones enabled planters and slaves to grow rice in these inland settings. Unlike tidal rice cultivation where planters and slaves harnessed the "estuary hydraulics" of the river's ebb and flow, inland planters relied on water simply flowing from higher elevations down to their fields. These cultivators had to contain the natural resource from reliable surface and ground water sources – represented in drainage basins, swamps, bays, and springs. Watersheds composed of Meggett loam were relatively level, so water flowed through these zones as a slow moving current.[17]

The size and shape of inland rice fields were adaptations to topography. The basic inland rice field consisted of two earthen dams enclosing a low-lying area bordered by ridges. Enslaved people built up the "strong banks" with available fill from adjoining drainage trenches. The dam on higher elevation contained stream or spring fed water to form a reservoir, or a "reserve," that would provide a water supply to the lower rice fields. Once cultivators released water from the reservoir, a second dam retained this resource to nourish rice fields. Between these two earthen structures was a series of smaller embankments and ditches to hold and drain water effectively during the cultivation process.[18]

Water control for inland rice cultivation required not only precise construction of earthen embankments, but also an understanding of the surrounding topography. Inland cultivators had to choose where to put reservoirs and fields in relation to watercourses and terrain. To retain water in the reservoir and rice fields, the soil required a substantial clay foundation to prevent impounded water from seeping out. The subtle elevation change, in some cases just three or four feet from sandy highlands to alluvial swamps, allowed different types of vegetation to take root. This variation of flora provided cultivators insight into soil composition. For example, longleaf pine and oak communities grew in well drained sandy soil while cypress and tupelo gum communities grew in less permeable soil. To aspiring rice cultivators who did not have access to the insights of soil science until the middle of the nineteenth century, the distribution of trees and other plants directed them toward appropriate inland sites. Colonial historian Alexander Hewatt observed that "nature points out to [the planter] where to begin his labours; for the soil, however various, is every where easily distinguished, by the different kinds of trees which grow upon it."[19] In

---

[17] Hilliard 1975, 97.
[18] Hilliard 1978, 97; Hewatt et al. 1779, 303; Stewart 1996, 168.
[19] Hewatt 1779, 305; South Carolina Governor James Glenn wrote in 1761 that "the best land for rice is a wet, deep, miry soil; such as is generally to be found in Cypress Swamps; or a black greasy Mould with a Clay Foundation; but the very best lands may be meliorated by laying them under water at proper Seasons." in Milling 1951, 14; Joyce Chaplin notes that although

discussing how to locate "good soil," Jean-Francois Gegnilliat explained, "one recognizes [the soil] by the difference in trees, which are big oaks and nut trees of three or four types." Planters needed a "careful observance of topography and water flow" in selecting sites for rice cultivation. With substantial start-up costs to grow rice, planters had to understand hydrology and topography to avoid commercial failure before beginning the expensive endeavor.[20]

Topography determined the natural boundaries for reservoirs and fields, as highland enclosed plots and retained water. Elevation change from knolls to bottomlands helped enclose the reservoir and fields, eliminating the need for additional embankments. Because planters relied on geographical features to contain flooded fields, the boundaries of these agricultural systems initially resembled tributaries' fluid contours. Traveling through coastal South Carolina, Catesby observed how these inland landscapes took shape: "the further parts of these marshes from the sea, are confined by higher lands, covered with woods, through which by intervals, the marsh extends in narrow tracts higher up the country, and contracts gradually as the ground rises." Elevation differences between highlands and the rice fields ranged from four feet at Charleywood Plantation on the Wando River to 40 feet at Newington Plantation located on the upper Ashley River. Compared to tidal rice fields, inland fields were smaller and contained within the topography of the wetlands. Tidal fields, on the other hand, sprawled across the riverbanks. The floodplains allowed planters to devote more land to tidal cultivation if the fields were built within the ebb and flow of the river.[21]

"Swamps had to be diked to separate land from water," observes historian Theodore Rosengarten, and this work was done by enslaved people who, "cleared and chiseled [the floodplain] with hoes until it was as level as a billiard table." Dense hardwoods, such as bald cypress, tupelo, and sweet gum, were removed with axes and saws. John Norris observed in 1712 that stumps and roots took 12 to 15 years to rot out of the fields, leaving slaves to plant rice around the remnant vegetation. Clearing the dense forests took an unimaginable amount of labor. Slashing and burning the fields expedited the decomposition process, as fire "softened" the landscape. Environmental historian Stephen Pyne notes, "with fire it was possible to reshape the pieces of the landscape mosaic and rearrange them into new pictures." Enslaved cultivators burned the underbrush and then hoed out the weed roots to prevent recurring

---

soil sciences did not evolve until the mid-1800s, people developed a basic understanding of which soils were fertile and which soil did not allow proper drainage (Chaplin and Institute of Early American History and Culture (Williamsburg) 1993, 144–5); Porcher and Rayner 2001, 89–96; Edelson 2007, 386–90.

[20] Cohen and Yardeni 1988, 8.
[21] Catesby quoted in Merrens 1977, 92; Elevation determined from current data referenced from the United States Gological Survey 2012.

growth of competing vegetation. Field hands spent January and February, "down" months in the agricultural cycle, burning leftover stubble on existing rice fields or clearing new acreage. Once vegetation was removed in South Carolina inland tracts, slaves leveled potential fields to accommodate rice planting and water drainage. After fields were developed to drain standing water, enslaved people dug precise quarter ditches to remove floodwaters more effectively. Such geometrically shaped fields by the 1730s had replaced the fluid landscape, redefining the non-human landforms of streams, banks, and knolls.[22]

The mechanical devices used to allow water on and off of the fields became a critical technical component for inland rice agriculture. Rice cultivators used gates, or "trunks," to control water flow from reservoirs onto the rice fields. Originally made from hollowed out trees, trunks were traditional African devices used to regulate water flow through a conduit by plugging the end of *Brassus* palms. Enslaved Africans in the Lowcountry substituted domestic *Sabal* palms and cypress for this device. European colonists contributed to the process of water control by introducing the use of "valves" when constructing inland rice fields. Valves were rectangular boxes open on one end with a perpendicular sliding gate on the other to control water flow. These valves were used in draining fens and could serve a similar role on South Carolina tidal plantations; both trunks and valves were used to manage the downward flow of water while simultaneously preventing incoming tides from flowing onto the fields.[23]

Field engineers placed trunks in sloughs, or stream channels, so water efficiently ran out of the holding pond from the embankment's lowest point. Sloughs were an important natural feature for draining the wetlands, for they served as a "gutter," or a depression in the subtle elevation change.[24] After these floodwaters nourished the soil and rice crop, and killed competing weeds, the fields were drained through trunks located at the second embankment. The water released from these fields flowed downhill toward nearby tidal rivers.[25]

---

[22] Rosengarten 1998, 40; Carney 2001, 86; Merrens 1977, 93; Littlefield 1981, 89; Clifton 1978, x. Period historian Alexander Hewatt speculated rice cultivation as "so laborious is the task of raising, beating, and clearing this article, that though it had been possible for attacking to the thick forest and clearing the grounds for the purpose, thousands and tens of thousands must have perished in the arduous attempt," (Hewatt et al. 1779, 120); Gibbs, 2 January 1845, 28–31 January 1845, 1–10 February 1845; Norris in Merrens 1977, 45; Pyne 1997, 466, 468. Cateby believed that stumps would rot out in fields between six to eight years, Merrens 1977, 93.

[23] Littlefield 1981, 97; Carney 2001, 95–6; Doar 1936, 12; Groening 1998, 158–9. English farmers also used "hatches" to control water when floating meadows. Although hatches are associated with English technological transfer to Carolina rice fields, these devices did not resemble rice trunks in design. See: Kerridge 1967, chapter 6; Martins and Williamson 1994, 21–30. For an image of a English hatch, see: Boswell 1779, plan # 5.

[24] Merrens 1977, 92.

[25] Hilliard 1978, 97; Carney 1996, 25.

Inland rice planters were limited in terms of flood control by the single downward direction of water flow. Ironically by impounding water in reservoirs, planters actually created a precarious situation if freshets or droughts occurred. Freshets occurred when storms or hurricanes provided more rain than the soil could absorb and streams could channel, causing "rapid torrents" that were "sudden and violent" as they flowed down hill.[26] This rush of water would flood the reservoir, causing an overflow that would breach the dam.[27] Droughts presented another problem for inland rice planters, as reservoirs that did not receive enough water would eventually dry up. Without plentiful "reserve water" to flood the fields, competing weeds overtook the orderly agricultural landscape.[28]

By focusing on specific examples located in the Cooper River and Wando River watersheds, this chapter will discuss how topography helped define irrigation patterns, field design, and settlement patterns. This spatial setting consists of the Eastern and Western branches of the Cooper River, converging with the Wando River to form the eastern half of the Charleston Harbor. Both rivers originate in the Lower Coastal Plain and flow relatively short distance compared to the neighboring Santee River, where headwaters begin approximately 440 miles away from the coast. Including land covered by a twentieth century hydro-electric dam project, the Cooper River flows approximately 60 miles and traverses four of the five Lower Coastal Plain terraces. The Wando River flows approximately 20 miles through just one terrace. Establishing inland rice cultivation systems in the Penholoway, Talbot, Pamlico, and Princess Anne Terraces, planters and their enslaved laborers worked within the boundaries of these landscapes to create agricultural modes of production. At the same time, these topographical boundaries influenced settlement patterns and provided a pallet for inhabitants to construct a unique cultural identity.[29]

Early forms of inland rice systems took simplistic shape following available stream communities in each of the four terrace complexes. Early eighteenth-century planters relied on small tributaries' definable floodplains to experiment with modes of irrigation control such as dams, embankments, ditches, and drains. In the French Huguenot enclave encompassing Biggin Swamp, at the headwaters of the Cooper River, neighboring planters tapped into the basin streams. Pooshee Plantation was one of 30 properties relying on Biggin Swamp tributaries for rice irrigation. The Lord Proprietors granted Peter St. Julian, a Vitré Brittany Huguenot, 1,000 acres in May 1704,

---

[26] Catesby quotes in Merrens 1977, 96.
[27] Hilliard 1978, 79; Hilliard 1975, 58; Matthew 1992, 64.
[28] Stewart 1996, 93; Chaplin and Institute of Early American History and Culture (Williamsburg) 1993, 229–230; Clowse and South Carolina Tricentennial Commission 1971, 127.
[29] Colquhoun 1974, 181; Cantrell and Turner 2002, 2.

becoming Pooshee. St. Julian sold the plantation to his brother-in-law, Henry LeNoble, in 1711, who three years later gifted Pooshee to his daughter Susanne and her new husband René Lewis Ravenel.[30]

Ravenel used a limestone spring, formed from a "downdip" in the Floridian aquifer system, to irrigate his Pooshee Plantation rice fields. Occurring more frequently in the Penholoway Terrace, these artesian springs, or "fountains" as the local residents called them, provided consistent water flow for rice plantations throughout the Biggin Swamp community. Pooshee Springs was one of six notable fountains bordering the basin that established this area as one of the central rice zones in colonial South Carolina. Enslaved labors at Pooshee, as S. Max Edelson notes, "made comparatively simple alterations to the land that took advantage of the existing contours of its topography." Slaves dug into Pooshee's "gray, sticky sandy clay" loam and "threw a dam" between the higher fine sandy loam to form a reservoir. Ravenel's enslaved laborers then constructed a second dam to impound spring fed water and maintained the modest 12-acre field.[31]

Toward the coast, the Princess Anne Terrace's brackish tidal rivers presented new challenges for early rice cultivators. Because of the terrace complex's close proximity to the ocean, Princess Anne began at sea level with a "gently inclined slope" up to 20 feet. The ocean's incoming tide pushed a "salt wedge" of brackish water against the downward flowing rivers. While freshwater hydrology became a critical component for tidal irrigation on the Cooper River, the Wando River's limited watershed did not generate enough flow to initiate this "hydraulic machine." Over millennia the Wando's ebb and flow through the maritime floodplains created an interwoven chain of creeks and tributaries. These tributaries "arise from low, springy or marshy lands, and, as they branch out far and wide, innumerable navigable creeks are every way formed throughout the country." To utilize this environment, planters had to construct earthen barriers to prevent the brackish tidewater from flowing into these low-lying watercourses.[32]

Richard Beresford's use of tidal creeks reflected how planters utilized other environments besides small-stream floodplains to cultivate inland rice. Emigrating from Barbados to Charles Town in 1683, Beresford began his career as a merchant owning 1/4 share of the *Mary of Carolina*. He became active in politics, serving on the Grand Council, he represented Berkeley and Craven counties in five General Assemblies, and he was a member of the First Royal Assembly. Beresford's political ambitions correlated with his land

---

[30] History of Transfer of Pooshee to 1756 (n.d.); Van Ruymbeke 2006, 59, 86.
[31] Aucott and Speiran 1985, 738; Siple 1960, 2; Cooke 1936, 75; Aucott 1988, 9; Ravenel 1860, 28–31; Holms 1849, 187; Map of Pooshee 1920; quotes: Edelson 2006, 104, and United States Department of Agriculture 1980b, 516, 506; Miscellaneous Inventories and Wills 1750, 77B: 578.
[32] Willis 2006, 5–12; McCartan et al. 1984; Willoughby and Doar 2006.

acquisitions. Between 1690 and 1714, he received nine proprietary grants totaling 5,040 acres. Charleywood, a plantation named after a Hertfordshire manor, derived from a series of seven 1711 grants of 4,350 acres.[33]

Building capital from the mercantile trade, cattle ranching, and naval stores, Beresford amassed a sizable labor force for rice cultivation. As one Santee Huguenot *émigré* explained, growing rice "can only be done at great expense and only rich people could undertake it." By 1715, Beresford had acquired 50 enslaved people. Seven years later, Beresford had doubled his enslaved population and was well within the 29 percent of Carolina slaveholders with 30 people or more by the 1720s. Beresford shuttled this substantial labor force between his seven plantations, where they herded cattle, extracted tar and pitch, and grew mulberry trees, corn, and rice. Beresford's labor force was not large enough to alter more than the 75 acres of Charleywood rice fields. More labor could build larger field systems. Compared to period rice plantations, more laborers were needed to build earthen barriers separating saline from fresh water zones, and to properly maintain the human-made environments against the natural tidal surges.[34]

Charleywood rice fields contained the same basic structure as at Pooshee, yet the subtle elevation change on the Wando River floodplains created a different aesthetic. Whereas Pooshee Swamp consisted of a relatively straight watercourse from the spring, Charleywood's tidal creeks came from multiple directions, wrapping around subtle highland knolls, and converging in Guerin Creek. Pooshee's rice field consisted of a single system of two dams bordering the rice. Charleywood, however, relied on dams to partition 75 acres into seven field divisions that, when compared to flooding a single unit, allowed improved irrigation control. Because early inland fields were limited to narrow watercourses, their acreage did not compare to later tidal systems sprawling across broad floodplains. Beresford had to work around the low profile of the floodplains, where "highland" that enclosed the rice fields was only four feet above the rice fields.

To retain water within the subtle elevation change, enslaved laborers had to construct embankments flanking each side of the field. Part of the challenge of establishing rice within this area was the limited elevation change separating the fields from the settlement. Compared to Pooshee's 10-foot difference between the fields and the settlements, Charleywood's four-foot difference did not allow much depth to the rice fields. Beresford had to build retaining embankments around the fields to hold more floodwater as the plants grew in size. Early inland cultivators had to pay attention to subtleties of the land, realizing when an

---

[33] Baldwin 1985, 22; Bailey and Edgar 1977, 77–8; Society for the Propagation of the Gospel in Foreign Parts 39: 102–3, 311, 315.
[34] McClain and Ellefson 2007, 392; Society for the Propagation of the Gospel, 16: 120; Coclanis 1989, 98.

impounded field was too big to draw water effectively on and off the fields. By subdividing the fields, even in situations where water directly flowed from one field to the next, cultivators could manage the amount of water on individual plots and flood the entire crop more consistently in shorter distances with a low elevation run compared to one elongated field with a greater elevation change. Charleywood fields averaged five acres for five of the divisions, yet expanded to an average of 25 acres for the remaining two divisions. Even with planters modifying their fields, problems resulted from having to flood each division in order from the lowest elevation to the highest elevation.[35]

By 1740, planters and their enslaved laborers began settling into new inland environments and expanding previously unaltered terrain. The developing irrigation methods emphasized that rice cultivators take "command of water" to secure systematic flooding and draining of fields. Inland planters also sought solutions to relieve pressure from freshets breaching reservoir dams. Flanking canals, which were dredged waterways that abutted exterior field embankments, provided a solution to this problem. Planters referred to flanking canals as "wasteway" or "washway" drains. The canals stretched the length of the field system. As naturalist William Bartram noted, these reservoirs were sometimes connected to "sluices to let ye redundant waters out." A similar concept of channeling water and relieving pressure from milldams also existed. Millowners installed canals that redirected water downstream from the reservoirs to prevent freshets from breaching their dams. Although millowners did not use the water released into their wasteway drains, Lowcountry inland rice planters channeled their wasteway water from the dam to the fields. Rice cultivators accomplished this water redirection by inserting trunks between the flanking canal and the upper and lower portion of each field division. Water would enter the field through the upper trunk and drain out of the field through the lower trunk. This adaptation allowed trunk-minders to irrigate fields without having to flow each division simultaneously. The flanking canal also served as a gutter to capture any downward flowing water from higher ground perpendicular to the fields.[36]

Flexibility to control water was essential when rice fields were on different cultivation schedules. Trunk minders could add or remove water as they saw fit without having to disrupt flood stages on adjoining fields. The staggering of flood schedules avoided possible depletion of impounded water, as springs

---

[35] Plan of Charleywood Plantation 1788; Judith Carney explains that inland rice fields similar to Charleywood are reminiscent West African mangrove systems (Carney 2001, 86–8). Edda L. Fields-Black provides a more detailed discussion of Rio Nunez cultivators' specialization of mangrove rice environments (Fields-Black 2008, 36–46, 57–106); for plantation elevations, see: United States Geological Survey 2012.
[36] Edelson 2006, 103–9; Heyward 1937, 13; Moore 1994, 292–6; Bartram quote: Groening 1998, 79; Commissioners of Fortified Estates 1786.

and creeks could recharge the reservoirs before the next flood cycle. "Every planter has his reservoirs or ponds of water which are attended by drains and ditches that he can at any time set his plantation afloat," cited eighteenth-century attorney Timothy Ford, who observed "[the planter] must know more from his own judgment and observation than anything else, when, how often, and how long his fields must be under water."[37]

During freshets, trunk minders could release excess water through the flanking canals, bypassing the rice fields and relieving pressure on the back dam. Flanking canals provided partial relief to the inland planter who had too much water in the winter and early spring. Mathurin Gibbs, an inland rice planter in St. Stephen's Parish revealed this frustration in his nineteenth-century agricultural journal. On trying to keep water out of the fields as he was attempting to contain the natural resource in his reservoir, he wrote, "The season has been backwards and the floods of the rain have drowned the greater portion of rice sown in two fields and preventing my sowing the other fields till now." Ten days later, Gibbs explained, "The labor of man is vain for no sooner does his industry and perseverance remove the water from one field than it is filled by the rain and the labors [...] applied to be again disappointed." The ability to control water, harnessing this natural resource when needed, became the primary concern of the inland planter. Inconsistent water flow would ultimately deter inland cultivation, yet the eighteenth-century use of flanking canals provided a new flexibility for rice cultivators attempting to control natural conditions.[38]

Planters who grew rice within narrow floodplains had to make different decisions compared to inland planters cultivating along the broad tidal floodplains. These separate microenvironments led to planters using new methods of drawing water onto and off of the rice fields. Windsor Plantation on the headwaters of the East Branch of the Cooper River, for instance, demonstrated how flanking canals took shape. Windsor's fields fit within the tight boundary of the Nicholson Creek floodplain. The elevation difference between pineland communities and the cypress hardwood forest varied between 30 and 40 feet (Figure 8.3). The watershed was dramatic in elevation change compared to the five to ten foot decline in elevation located five miles away on the Cooper River tidal floodplains. Through the eighteenth century, the Roche family optimistically surveyed four divisions within the confines of the scarp to the northwest and the Talbot plain highlands to the southeast. The Roches relied on the predominant knoll forming Nicholson Creek's southern boundary to contain the inland rice fields. Forming a crescent shape around a 40-foot bluff, Nicholson Creek connects with Turkey Creek to form Huger Creek and serves as the

---

[37] Barnwell 1912, 183.
[38] Gibbs, 1 June 1846, 11 June 1846.

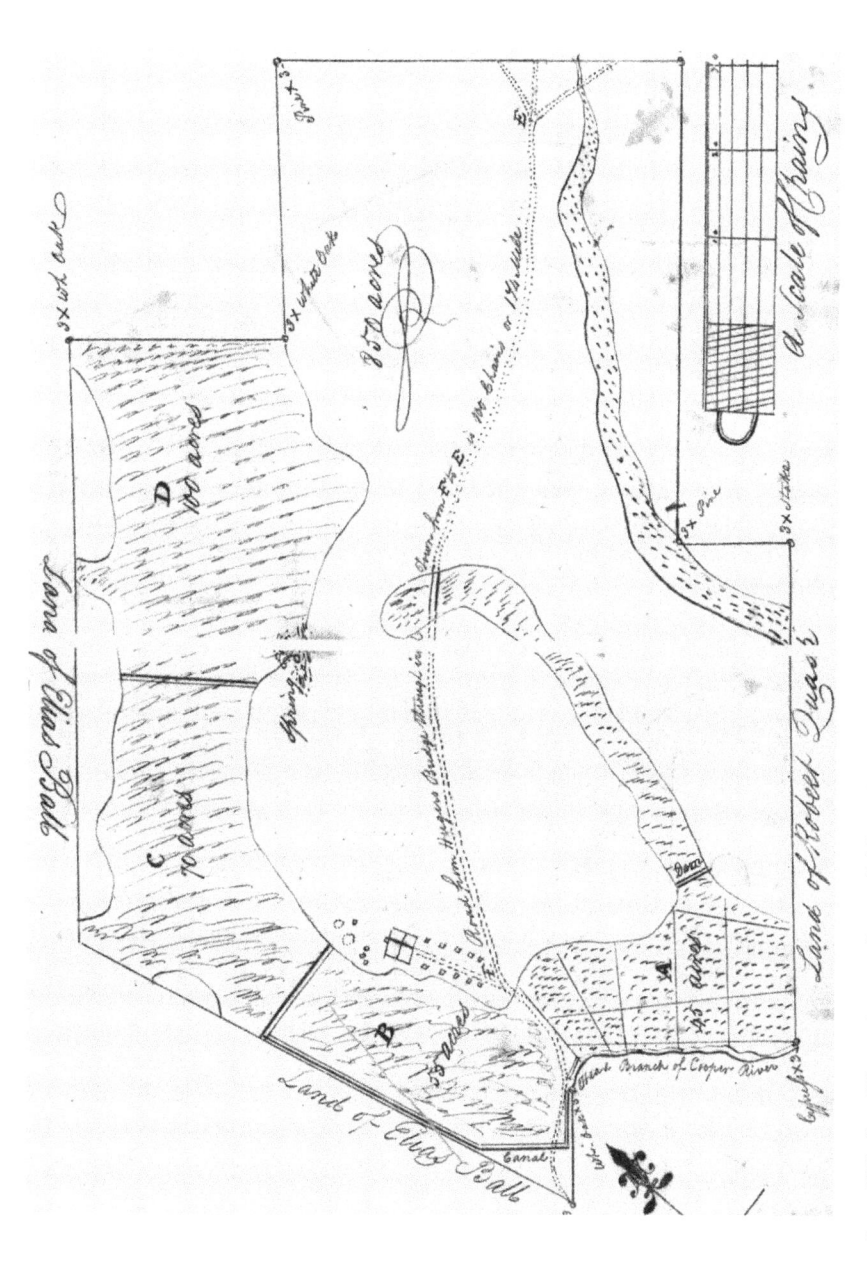

FIGURE 8.3. Windsor Plantation, with rice fields in division "A" and flanking canal wrapping around division "B." Image from "Plan of Windsor Plantation, March 1790," Book D7: 199, Charleston County Register of Mesne Conveyance, Charleston, SC.

headwaters of the Eastern Branch of the Cooper River. This bluff served as an optimal site for the Windsor house, slave settlement, and outbuildings.[39]

Planters placed their rice fields in relation to the low-lying topography, which dictated the slaves' positioning of the flanking canal. At Windsor, Patrick Roche ordered 12 enslaved labors to sculpt fields out of the Nicholson Creek cypress bottomlands by 1725. Fishbrook Field, named after the neighboring plantation, was the result of cutting trees, removing cypress stumps, and shaping 45 acres of land. Nicholson Creek's meandering channel passed the western boundary of Fishbrook Field, separated by an earthen embankment; Roche's slaves altered the natural watercourse by embanking a 55-acre division and channeling the water toward a flanking canal. An upstream field division impeded the natural watercourse with an earthen dam and then redirected the creek around the western perimeter. A variation on this system consisted of two canals, flanking the fields on each side. Dual canals increased the efficiency of moving water around fields during freshets and also provided additional flexibility in flooding and draining individual divisions. Flanking canals varied in length and width, relative to the size of the plantation watershed and rice fields. John Coming Ball's Back River Plantation, for example, utilized a 50-foot wide northern flanking canal as its reservoir while the southern flanking canal drained impounded water off the fields.[40]

As the mid-century Lowcountry plantation enterprise became firmly entrenched within Atlantic markets, inland planters began to initiate more aggressive cultivation practices. Expansion of inland landscapes stemmed from increased enslaved labor, acquired agricultural knowledge, improved canal networks, and lands suitable for cultivation. The developing inland field systems took on a new aesthetic, moving away from small acreage within natural boundaries and toward larger field divisions with geometrically rigid embankments.

On the Wando River, Richard Beresford, Jr. forced upward of 253 enslaved laborers to expand his father's inland rice fields. The younger Beresford inherited Charleywood and other sizable holdings upon his father's death from a falling tree limb in 1722. Richard, however, was only two years old at the time. Lieutenant Governor Thomas Broughton, executor of the Beresford estate, managed the plantation affairs for 10 percent of the annual profits until the younger Beresford reached 21 years of age. Educated in England and working as a London merchant until 27 years old, Richard returned to Charles Town in 1747 to manage his plantation enterprise. Like

---

[39] Irving 1840–1888; Weems et al. 1989; Colquhoun and Atlantic Coastal Plain Geological Association 1965, 29–31, quote: 29; Miscellaneous Inventories and Wills 1784, A: 378; *City Gazette* 1784.

[40] Deed Book D7: 199; United States Geological Survey 2012; Hateley 1792.

his father, Beresford maintained an active life, representing the Parish of St. Thomas and St. Dennis in three Royal Assemblies.[41]

Charleywood's rice fields encompassed nearly 600 acres of the Wando River floodplain. Whereas the banks resembled the broad and expansive floodplains of sought-after tidal rice landscapes, the Wando's brackish water made this floodplain useless to tidal planters. Inland planters channeled upland fresh water down to the brackish floodplains to grow rice. In comparison to the narrow Nicholson Creek watercourse, Charleywood's topography provided a vast foundation for Beresford's massive enslaved labor force to carve an intricate grid-like formation of canals, ditches, embankments, and dikes. The new, expanded field system was built on Pleistocene deposits of clay and shell, which provided more effective water retention and higher nutrient yields, compared to the elder Beresford's earlier field system, which was a sandy-loam. To irrigate Charleywood's larger rice fields, enslaved cultivators relied on two reservoirs located on the Cainhoy Scarp. The reservoirs impounded more than 40 acres of water flowing from the meandering creeks and bays common to the Lower Coastal Plain scarps, while canals channeled the water in a linear downward motion.[42]

Charleywood's settlement patterns shifted in relation to the plantation's rice cultivation. Early Charleywood inhabitants lived on slightly elevated land located approximately one-tenth of a mile west of the original rice fields. However, the settlement was abandoned by 1772 in favor of living quarters located in the upland pinelands. Geographer H. Roy Merrins and historian George D. Terry describe how the close proximity of inland rice plantation settlements to the rice fields represents early colonial perceptions of land use. "According to one [eighteenth-century] resident," cited the authors, "planters built their homes on the 'Edge of Swamps, in a damp moist Situation' because they wanted "to view from their Rooms, their Negroes at Work in the Rice Fields." By gazing over developed agricultural spaces, planters viewed progress, order, and labor management that reflected the Enlightenment. They perceived this as a non-human world transformed from "savagery" to "civilization." However, early eighteenth-century colonists did not understand the connections between malaria-carrying *Anopheles* mosquitoes and low-lying habitats. In terms of this disease, the settlement pattern proved ill conceived and resulted in significant higher mortality rates.

Approximately 37 percent of white males and 45 percent of white females born between 1721 and 1760 and surviving into adulthood in St. John's

---

[41] Society for the Propagation of the Gospel 16:115; Bailey and Edgar 1977, 78–79.
[42] Miscellaneous Inventories and Wills 1773, 94B: 423; Porcher and Rayner 2001, 40–41; Plan of Charleywood Plantation 1788; McCartan et al. 1984; Mart Stewart discusses the interconnection between social and environmental formations on tidal rice plantations (Stewart 1996, chapter 3).

Parish died before their fiftieth birthday. Charleywood's Christ Church Parish offered more dire statistics, where 85 percent of all white males born between 1721 and 1760 and surviving into adulthood died before their fiftieth birthday.[43] Malaria did not contribute to all of these cases, yet Merrins and Terry argue that 43 percent of recorded Christ Church deaths occurred within a four-month period between August and November suggesting an infectious cause.[44]

By the 1770s, Beresford ordered two new settlements positioned in strategic locations. The upper Charleywood settlement, built in the Awendaw Scarp's sandy pine flatwoods community, was more than likely relocated for healthier living conditions. Because Beresford was an absentee planter, the upper Charleywood settlement housed the plantation overseer and some select slaves. The other percentage of Charleywood's enslaved population, however, had to endure exposed and sickly conditions at the second settlement located in the middle of the new rice fields. The centrally located Bay Hill settlement consisted of four houses, a corn house, a "mite pen," and a sick house. Bay Hill residents lived on an isolated stretch of highland approximately 100 feet wide and 460 feet long between the Fairlawn Canal and surrounding rice fields.[45] Bay Hill reflects the "separate residential zones," defined by anthropologist John Michael Vlach, which were conceived to divide the planter's family from their ever-increasing enslaved rice laborers. These zones, according to Vlach, "frequently [were] set miles away from the planter's residence; the quarters were sizable villages where slaves developed social routines of their own." Bay Hill was separated from the Charleywood settlement by the middle reserve and rice fields. This put slave dwellings closer to the work place and farther away from the upland residence. Moving slave settlements away from the big house, and closer to the work site, allowed enslaved laborers to travel from residence to work in less time.[46]

The efforts of inland planters to control water moved beyond their plantation borders and expanded into larger projects involving neighboring plantations or plantation communities. A movement of public and private canal initiatives took place throughout the eighteenth century to assure water for the effective transport of commodities and, simultaneously, for use to drain wetlands and flood their fields. With a majority of inland rice environments located on non-navigable waterways, landowners petitioned the proprietary and royal government for public canals for commerce. Inland planters also

---

[43] *South Carolina Gazette* 1772; Rash 1773; Merrens and Terry 1984, 543–5, quote: 547. For understanding the intellectual framework of Enlightenment perceptions of the non-human landscape, see: Cronon 1995 and Merchant 1995.
[44] *South Carolina Gazette* 1772; Rash 1773; Merrens and Terry 1984, 543–5, quote: 547.
[45] Rash 1773; Plan of Charleywood Plantation 1788.
[46] Plan of Charleywood Plantation 1788; Vlach 1993, 155, 187; Chaplin and Institute of Early American History and Culture (Williamsburg) 1993, 262–71.

recognized the importance of these water highways to drain water from the broad low-lying wetlands. With the transformation of inland swamps into agricultural landscapes, those planter communities fanning out of Charles Town began to construct canals on the Wando River and Biggin Swamp. Some requested the legislative assistance to fund internal improvement projects between 1719 and 1768 in Cooper River headwaters, Back River, the Ashley River headwaters, Caw Caw Swamp, and the northern branch of the Stono River.[47]

Daniel Ravenel's canal represented the extent and scope of private projects. Ravenel of Somerton Plantation constructed a mile and a quarter long canal in Biggin swamp. The canal was fifty feet wide between his Somerton and Wantoot Plantations, powering his mill and providing manageable water flow to the inland rice fields. Also, the canal connected the four swamps into a single conduit and flowed into the Biggin Swamp Canal, a confluence of three canals stretching over 13 miles through the surrounding wetlands. Ravenel's slaves constructed an artery between property holdings that was "traversed and intersected by dikes and tributary canals," and carved through "the dense growth" of Biggin's cypress swamp. Through the engineering of the canal, clearing of trees, movement of earth, and interaction with rice trunks and fields, Black Oak Agricultural Society's president Samuel Dubose considered Ravenel's canal "to have been the greatest work undertaken by a private citizen of this State up to the period of its construction."[48] Reflecting on the previous generation's innovation, Dubose wrote of Ravenel's plantations, "[it is] a source of surprise and wonder to examine the amount of labor and skill some in the [inland rice] fields in this neighborhood exhibit." Noting the broader complexity of the consolidation of water management by Biggin Basin inland rice planters, Dubose believed "to unite and concentrate these [canals] into one, and bear off the water when in excess, as well as distribute it into the fields of different plantations, called for judgment, perseverance and an amount of labor not easily understood."[49]

The private canal projects involved specific inland rice plantations and a small population that directly benefited from the improvements. Unlike the public improvements in navigation on creeks and rivers occurring throughout the eighteenth century, these new private canals did not benefit the greater population. Isolated to the few plantations bounding the watercourse, private canals improved navigation and irrigation for neighboring plantations of the planters involved. Also, the amount of slave labor needed was coordinated between the parties involved. Inland canals were wide enough for rice-flats

---

[47] Terry 1981, 176–80; Petitions to the General Assembly 1782–1866; Journal of the Commons House of Assembly of South Carolina, 1695–1775; Cooper and McCord 1836–1841, Acts: 417, 442, 506, 508, 509, 519, 526, 533, 537, 540.
[48] Ravenel 1898, 44–5.
[49] DuBose and Black Oak Agricultural Society Charleston SC. 1858, 9–10.

transporting barrels of rice to Charles Town, while in addition, the canals flooded or drained individual field divisions. Unlike tidal cultivators, who could flood and drain fields with the same canal utilizing the ebb and flow of the river, inland planters were limited to the downward flow of water. Planters could use these canals only to flood fields located below the canal or drain fields above the canal. For example, a mile and a quarter long drainage canal bisected Charleywood Plantation, creating a division between the upper and lower settlements and fields. The Fairlawn Canal stemmed from the neighboring Fairlawn Plantation and was wide enough for barges to transport rice and goods to Guerin Creek. In addition, the canal's central location provided irrigation to Charleywood's lower fields while draining water off Fairlawn's inland rice fields.[50]

CONCLUSION

Combining increasing water control projects and ever-expanding enslaved labor populations with an established Lowcountry rice market economy and emerging tidal irrigation technology, inland rice field practices changed dramatically by the eve of the Revolutionary War. Where planters in these environments were limited by water control on and off their fields, the increasing network of canals and drains made expanding field divisions more economically accessible. Yet enslaved African-Americans were forced to dam more streams for reserve water, dig up soil for earthen embankments, and cultivate more acres of rice. Studying places like Pooshee and Charleywood reveals the ecological complexity of these plantation systems. This form of rice cultivation not only required that cultivators maintain a critical understanding of how to grow rice, but also how to utilize the surrounding landscape to the best of their ability. Planters had to control water through floodplains, yet not fall victim to natural disasters, such as freshets or droughts. Seeing how these planters dealt with water control provides a clearer understanding of specific cultivation methods. This story moves beyond how people planted the crop, but also how they shaped the land within geographical limitations to provide effective irrigation for rice. Also, the specific microenvironments played a crucial role in supporting the cash crop. Nutrient rich soil, formed by decaying organic material and soil composition, congregated in these inland watersheds. Planters identified these sites through forest aesthetics and topographical formations. The importance of how land and water came together in these microenvironments presents an interpretation of how the environment supports a sustainable agricultural center.

[50] Plan of Charleywood Plantation 1788; Plan of Fairlawn Plantation 1794.

Built on top of environmental understanding is the role that geography plays in determining settlement patterns. This investigation of inland rice presents a microhistory of how people identified suitable land to live and work, by explaining that high permeable soil presented ideal space for dwellings and low less-permeable soil suited rice cultivation. Further investigation must follow the inhabitants outside of these microenvironments. How did enslaved people view the environment on and outside these plantations? Did portals of access to other plantations, like trails and navigable rivers, exist for slaves? Through what environments did transportation networks exist for free and enslaved plantation residents to interact with a larger society outside of their isolated inland plantations? By connecting the larger environment with these specific agricultural centers, one may understand how the Lowcountry topography played a role in shaping culture and society as a whole.

9

Asian Rice in Africa: Plant Genetics and Crop History

Erik Gilbert

The African continent is home to two species of domesticated rice. One of these, *Oryza glaberrima* was almost certainly domesticated in West Africa and is cultivated nowhere else in the world. The other is *Oryza sativa*, which was originally domesticated in Asia and has spread through Eurasia, Africa, and the Americas. *Sativa*, or Asian, rice is the second most important cereal crop globally, second only to maize in annual production, but unlike maize, rice is mostly consumed by humans whereas much of the world's maize production is fed to livestock or more recently used for biofuels. Asian rice has become an important food crop on the African continent. In areas where African *glaberrima* rice was once predominant, Asian rice is now the preferred crop. In many other parts of the continent where native rice was never domesticated and riziculture is relatively new, Asian rice is the only rice cultivated. Using a new body of genetic data, this chapter examines the processes by which Asian rice came to the African continent. I contend that there were three, possibly four, separate introductions of Asian rice to the African continent. These waves of crop diffusion resulted in the existence of three distinct populations of *sativa* rice on the continent with a possible, but less obviously distinct, fourth population. None of the three main populations of *sativa* rice in Africa are limited to the continent, rather they are intercontinental and embrace the Americas, southern Europe, and Southeast Asia, leaving a botanical trace of human contacts between continents. While it is not possible to date the arrival of any these rice populations with certainty, I will propose possible historical explanations for the introduction of the ancestor of these modern rice groups.

O. GLABERRIMA: THE AFRICAN RICE

Much of the scholarship on rice in Africa concerns *O. glaberrima* and the complex and labor-intensive agricultural systems associated with it.[1] *Glabberima* rice was probably domesticated in the first millennium BCE in the inland delta of the Niger River. It is related to the wild species *O. barthii*, from which it was most likely domesticated. The main center of genetic diversity for *glabberima* rice is in the inland delta of the Niger, but there is a secondary center of diversity in the Upper Guinea region where *glaberrima*s are grown both as upland crops and in complex tidal systems that have garnered most of the scholarly interest in African rice production.[2] These tidal cultivation systems involve clearing mangrove swamps and then carefully and laboriously managing tidal water flows to keep salt water out of the fields and fresh water in.[3] Farmers who grow mangrove rice have selected for salt tolerance in their crops, with the result that some *glaberrima*s are much more tolerant of salt than *satvia*s. *Glaberrima*s are also resistant to other types of stress: drought and pests, for example.[4] At present, although some *glaberrima* rice is still cultivated in West Africa and it is sometimes sown in mixture with *sativa* rice, it has largely been supplanted by *sativa* rice because the latter has better yields and is much easier to process without breaking the grains.

Unlike other cereals that were domesticated in West Africa, *glaberrima* rice remained confined to its West African homeland. This is surprising in that in the recent expansion of rice into the eastern reaches of West Africa and Central Africa there were not environmental obstacles to the expansion of the *glaberrima*s' range. By contrast pearl millet and bicolor sorghum, which were also domesticated in the sahel region of West Africa, spread widely within the continent. These two grains also spread out of the continent; in fact, the oldest archaeological evidence for them comes from India and dates to the second millennium BCE.[5] Thus, there is no obvious reason why *glaberrima* cultivation should not have spread more widely within the continent or even out of the continent like other African domesticates.

Recently, the idea that *glaberrima* rice is a local domesticate or even a distinct species has been challenged by Nayar, who contends that *glaberrima*s are simply *sativa*s that have been subject to intense local selection in West Africa.[6] He posits that *sativa* rice arrived early in West African history probably across the Sahara from North Africa or across the continent from East Africa. From this introduced rice, African farmers bred the varieties that are now considered *glaberrima*s. He notes that it is very difficult to

---

[1] Carney 2001; Fields-Black 2008; Linares 2002; Portères 1962.
[2] Sweeney and McCouch 2007.
[3] Carney 2001, 55–68.
[4] Fields-Black 2008, 29.
[5] Fuller and Boivin 2009, 16.
[6] Nayar 2011.

distinguish visually *glaberrima*s from *sativa*s.[7] Further, the *glaberrima*s were not identified as a separate species until the late nineteeth century and occasionally rice with *glaberrima*-like physical traits turns up in India, suggesting that many of the *glaberrima* features may be latent in the *sativa* genome. However, the strong sterility barriers between *sativa*s and *glaberrima*s and recent molecular studies of *glaberrima*s, suggest that they are a distinct species.[8] My work suggests that an early introduction of *sativa*s to West Africa either via the Sahara or by way of East Africa is unlikely. So, for now the status of *glaberrima* as an Africa domesticate seems safe, though the question of why it did not spread to what seem like suitable environments it still present.

O. SATIVA: A BOTANICAL PRIMER

Sativa rice was domesticated earlier than *glaberrima*. The consensus position is that the *sativa*s were first domesticated in south China from O. *rufipogon* (a wild rice species) by the middle of the fifth millennium BCE. The domestication process in south China led to the creation of one of the two main sub-populations of O. *sativa*, the japonicas. A second major sub-population the indicas, derive from a different wild ancestor called O. *nivara*. As the name suggests, the indicas were first cultivated and gathered in north India and subsequently domesticated through crossing with japonicas. The indicas are still disproportionately found in the Indian Subcontinent. The japonicas are associated with East Asia and are further subdivided between the tropical japonicas and temperate japonicas. The tropical japonicas are connected geographically to Southeast Asia. So strong is this connection that they were formerly known as javanicas, after the island of Java. The temperate japonicas are historically associated with China and Japan. The other two groups are the aus rices and the aromatics. Aus rices are especially adapted to the monsoon regime of South Asia and are heavily concentrated there. Aus rices are genetically linked to the indicas. Aromatics, which include the basmatis, are more closely related to the japonicas, which is interesting given that they are most often grown in South Asia and have the long grains that are frequently, though not uniformly, associated with the indicas.[9]

These populations are quite genetically distinct. They are sufficiently distant from each other that indicas and japonicas do not always produce fertile offspring when crossed. So if a population of temperate japonicas is introduced into a new area, that population may be subject to great selective

---

[7] This is certainly the case. By way of example in the process of doing the genetic testing on which this chapter is based, we tested four rice varieties that the USDA germplasm database described as *glaberrima*. Three of the four turned out to be *sativa*.
[8] Nayar 2011; Semon et al. 2005.
[9] Sweeney and McCouch 2007.

pressure as famers choose seed from plants that have qualities they desire. This will have the effect of producing new varieties of temperate japonicas. It will not produce tropical japonicas, aus, or indicas.

ASIAN RICE COMES TO AFRICA

There has been surprisingly little interest in the historical processes that brought Asian rice to the African continent. In West Africa interest in the locally domesticated *glaberrima*s has overshadowed questions about the origins of Asian rice in the region. Because there is no archaeobotanical evidence that permits the dating of Asian rice for West Africa, it is not at all clear when it arrived. There is archaebotanical evidence of *glaberrima*s as early as 300 BCE in the inland delta of the Niger River, but it is not clear whether these were fully domesticated.[10] Because it is difficult for the lay person to determine whether a rice plant or seed is a *sativa* or a *glaberrima*, early reports by Arab travelers of rice in West Africa could refer to either local *glaberrima* or introduced *sativa*. The only reliable way to determine when the first Asian rice arrived would be to recover *sativa*s (preferable identified genetically) in a dateable archaeological context and this has yet to happen.

Several pathways for the introduction of Asian rice to West Africa have been proposed. Several authors have suggested that it may have been introduced to West Africa via the trans-Saharan trade.[11] Rice has been present in North Africa and the Mediterranean since the seventh or eighth centuries. It seems to be part of the larger movement of South Asian crops and agricultural technology into the Mediterranean associated with the rise of Islam.[12] It seems entirely possible that rice might have been intentionally introduced to West Africa sometime after the ninth-century opening of trade routes across the Sahara. Rice might also have served as provisions for caravans, though it seems unlikely that caravans would bring unhulled rice (the only kind that would be viable seed) or sufficient water to cook rice en route.

Some scholars have suggested that rice might have moved overland through the wetter parts of central Africa from East Africa to West Africa. On some levels this also seems plausible. Other Asian crops, like the banana and taro made this transcontinental journey. West Africa is the global center of genetic diversity for domestic plantains (a triploid member of the banana family) which suggests that although they are an introduced crop, they have been present for a long time. Phytolith evidence puts bananas in Cameroun by 600 BCE, though some archaeologists challenge the validity of this claim, but not necessarily the possibility of an early presence of bananas in West

---

[10] Sweeney and McCouch 2007.
[11] Fields-Black 2008, 31; Nayar 2011.
[12] Watson 1974.

Africa.[13] The travels of bananas and taro, both of which are of Southeast Asian origin are evidence that it is at least possible that rice could have transited the continent from east to west after its introduction to East Africa. In fact, Fuller and Boivin have proposed that there was a corridor linking the Horn of Africa by way of southern Ethiopia to West Africa through which African crops might have been carried to Asia.[14] Two early West African domesticates pearl millet and bicolor sorghum, arrived in South Asia before the first millennium BCE and are now widely dispersed in Asia. Fuller and Boivin suggest that they may have passed through this northern corridor on the way to West Africa. Though the routes may not be absolutely clear, West African cereal crops (millet and sorghum) have crossed the continent to Asia and Asian vegetative crops (banana, taro and water yam) have travelled overland in the opposite direction. Thus, it is not inconceivable that an Asian cereal – rice – might have followed a similar path across the continent, linking the rice cultures of East Africa to those of West Africa. Of course it is also conceivable that *glaberrima* rice might have crossed the continent and reached Asia through this northern corridor just like millet and sorghum, though for some reason this did not happen.

It is also possible, and, as I will argue below, probable, that Asian rice was unknown in West Africa until the European expansion and that it was introduced by the Portuguese or some other group of Europeans after they had opened the sea route around the southern tip of the continent.

For East Africa we are fortunate to at least have some reliable dates to work with. Sarah Walshaw's pioneering archaebotanical work on the East African island of Pemba found that rice was present on the East African coast by the 800 CE and was a the preferred staple by 1000 CE (at least at the sites she excavated on the island of Pemba).[15] Archaeologists have also found rice in the Comoro Islands by 800 CE and a bit earlier in Red Sea ports, though this is presumed to be imported cargo rather than locally produced rice.[16] The traditional explanation for the spread of rice cultivation to East Africa is that it is associated with the settlement of the island of Madagascar by a people from Southeast Asia whom we now call the Malagasy.[17] Archaeological and linguistic evidence puts the Malagasy in Madagascar by 750 CE, which matches nicely with the dates for the arrival of rice on the Swahili coast and in the Comoros Islands. The Malagasy were also presumed to be the agents in the spread of bananas, taro, and water yam as well various musical instruments, but the new earlier dates for bananas and their relatives in West Africa have clouded the picture a bit, and some scholars have begun to suggest that

---

[13] Fuller and Boivin 2009; De Langhe and De Maret 1999; Blench 1996.
[14] Fuller and Boivin 2009.
[15] Walshaw 2005, 247, 250.
[16] Walshaw 2005, 72.
[17] Nayar 2011.

there may have been earlier, pre-Malagasy, contact between Africa and Southeast Asia, though all concerned are at a loss to describe how that might have happened.[18] An additional complication in the Malagasy as crop diffusers scenario is that it is not at all clear that they had significant interaction with the East African mainland. This is especially true early in their history, when the Malagasy seem to have been present in very small numbers.[19] While there is little evidence of Malagasy influence on the Swahili, there is ample evidence of South Asian and Arabian influence on the Swahili coast, so it seems just as likely that visiting Indian merchants might have introduced rice to mainland East Africa.

To sum up the current state of knowledge, Asian rice can be confidently dated to the eighth century CE in the Mediterranean. The Islamic expansion is almost certainly responsible for introducing rice to the Mediterranean.[20] In East Africa, rice was present by 800 CE, but it remains unclear whether it reached East Africa across the northern arc of the Indian Ocean via South Asia or across a more southerly route from Southeast Asia. In West Africa, African rice was used by 300 BCE, though whether this was domesticated rice or not is ambiguous. Certainly African rice was domesticated by the middle of the first millennium CE and cultivated in the inland delta of the Niger and on the Upper Guinea coast a bit later. It is still unclear when and how Asian rice came to West Africa. At present West Africa produces significantly more Asian rice than East Africa, even though it seems almost certain that Asian rice was present there before it was available in West Africa.

Genetic Evidence

Until now, efforts to determine the origins of Asian rice in Africa have relied upon linguistic evidence, a few archeological finds, and historically informed speculation. Genetic evidence offers the potential to see links between rice populations within the continent and to link those populations to other regions of the world. Because genetic evidence is not routinely used by historians, I will explain at some length my use of genetic evidence and describe what I see as the virtues and potential problems of this type of evidence for historians.

My foray into rice genetics began as an effort to see whether rice was introduced to mainland East African as part of the same process that brought rice to Madagascar, or whether rice came to the two places through independent historical processes. Reasoning that genetic links between food crops might be used in much the same way that archaeologists use pot sherds and other bits of material culture to track cultural continuities or discontinuities

---

[18] Blench 1996.
[19] Randrianja and Ellis 2009, 23–4.
[20] Watson 1974; Nayar 2011.

and trade connections, I enlisted the help of the USDA-ARS Dale Bumpers National Rice Research Center in Stuttgart, Arkansas. In collaboration with Anna McClung, who is research director at the Center, I initially arranged to have 100 varieties of rice from around the Indian Ocean rim genotyped to test my hypothesis that mainland East African rices derived from South Asia while Madagascar rices came Southeast Asia. Because I was also curious about possible links between East and West African/Atlantic rices I included a few varieties from Congo, Ghana, and Brazil. We obtained our samples from the USDA's small grains collection, which is part of a much larger germplasm collection of crop species. USDA maintains an online data base of their holdings and provides seed samples for free. When looking for samples we chose varieties that were labeled as landraces and when possible chose material that was collected as long ago as possible. "Landrace" is a somewhat ambiguous term that refers to crop varieties that are grown by traditional farmers who keep seed and replant it rather than purchasing commercial seed. My assumption was that modern landrace rice descends from much more ancient varieties that were introduced long ago and thus offers a sort of genetic window to the past and the processes by which rice was introduced to Africa. Above all, I tried to avoid the recently introduced improved varieties that are the result of the Green Revolution. Because the Green Revolution plant breeders used lines from all over the rice growing world, these newer cultivars would have obscured the earlier connections I was looking for.

Having made the sample selection I ordered the seed from the USDA and I turned it over to Dr. McClung. She and her co-workers used approximately ten dehulled seeds from each accession, performed a chemical extraction of the DNA, then amplified the DNA in the sample (using a technique called a polymerase chain reaction or PCR) and tested 60 microsatellite markers. Thousands of these markers occur across the 12 rice chromosomes. These markers are known DNA sequences that can vary among different varieties due to base pair changes, insertions, or deletions within the DNA sequence resulting in different allele sizes. One can determine how closely or distantly related varieties are by the number of marker alleles that they share in common. The next step is to subject the data on the distances between the markers to statistical analysis. This is a particularly obscure part of the process that is done by bioinformatics specialists. There are established protocols for how this is done (for this project we used principal coordinate analysis in the JMP Genomics and GenAIEx softwares, structure analysis in the STRUCTURE software, and Nei's genetic diversity index analyzed with the PowerMarker softwares and visualized MEGA4), but I was struck by how specialized a task this is.[21] For historians, who usually lack training in

---

[21] Nei's 1973 article in the *PNAS* has been cited 6,367 times according to Google Scholar, which gives a sense of the extent to which the protocol he devised has become the standard in the field. Amazingly, the article is a mere 2.5 pages long.

statistics, this is all rather opaque. I was utterly dependent on the expertise of others during this part of the process.

The results of this initial effort were ambiguous at best. We could not discern any obvious relationships between East African or Madagascar rices and other regions of the Indian Ocean. We attributed this to a low sample size. While there were an abundance of landrace rice lines from Asia in the USDA's collection, there were very few from East Africa. In fact, for Tanzania, which is East Africa's biggest rice producer after Madagascar, there were only two landraces lines available. By contrast there were hundreds of landraces available from Asia. However, we did notice two interesting things in the pilot study. The first of these was that there appeared to be a clear separation between West African and East African rices. Rice from Kenya and Tanzania was unrelated to West Africa rice. Rice in the Congo River basin fell in the West African group and there appeared to be a genetic frontier between the Congo and the Lakes region of East Central Africa. This suggested that there was a rice population structure that parallels the geographical watershed that separates the parts of the continent that drain into the Atlantic from those that drain into the Indian Ocean. The second intriguing finding of the pilot study was that most of the West African rices we looked at, including those from Congo, were closely related to the varieties found in Brazil. The type of close relationships I had expected to see linking rice from East Africa to populations across the Indian Ocean were much more apparent in the Atlantic than in the Indian Ocean.

Following up on the pilot study we decided to try to get a clearer picture of the Indian Ocean situation and to examine the possibility of a trans-Atlantic rice population. For the Indian Ocean this meant expanding our sample size. It is difficult to move viable seed across international borders. This reflects concerns about the spread of plant pathogens and concerns about the use and patenting of genetic material. Thus, rather than immediately try to tap into the much larger rice seed bank held by the International Rice Research Institute in the Philippines or to collect more landraces in the Africa, I decided to use varieties that the USDA describes as "cultivated material." I reached this decision after an email correspondence with the director of the USDA small grains collection. He suggested that if I were careful to select material that was relatively old, that it would likely be close to landrace status. The term "landrace" is fairly arbitrary and USDA holds a fair amount of material that it received from other seedbanks that use different descriptors than USDA's. Thus, there are frequent judgment calls about terminology when material from other system is catalogued in the USDA system. Taking this broader view of what constituted acceptable seed stock let me expand my East African samples from nine to fourteen. Only one of the new lines was collected before the 1970s, so it is possible that some of these might be improved varieties. To pursue the Atlantic population I expanded the sample of Atlantic rice accessions from 11 to 41. This group included varieties from

Brazil, Suriname, Guyana, Central America, North America, the Caribbean, the Upper Guinea Coast, the Lower Guinea Coast, West Central Africa, and from landlocked Burkina Faso and Mali. Within this West African group were four varieties that were labeled as *glaberrima*s in the USDA, though, as a result of this analysis, I now think they were mislabeled. (It is worth noting that these labels reflect the collector's or the donor's idea about what they have donated to the USDA and not the USDA's determination of what they are receiving.) We were also curious about the possibility that rice from the Mediterranean might be related to the rices of the Atlantic or West African rices so we added 17 varieties from the Mediterranean. These included both southern European rices and North African and Turkish rices.

The results produced with the larger sample size of 167 accessions did little to clear up the confusion with respect to East Africa but yielded intriguing results for the Atlantic and the Mediterranean. The second and larger study yielded six population clusters. There were the usual indica, aus, aromatic, and temperate japonicas. What was surprising was that in our sample the tropical japonicas divided into two subgroups, which we dubbed tropical japonica 1 (TRJ1) and tropical japonica 2 (TRJ2). These are shown in Figure P.1a, Figure P.1b, and Figure P.1c. Figure P.1a, Figure P.1b, and Figure P.1c show the six populations plus a number of admixtures that do not fit any of the groups. Also interesting was that three of the four lines that were supposed to be *glaberrima*s grouped neatly with TRJ1. My collaborators are confident that is a case of mislabeling of these accessions in the collection. The fourth appears to be an aromatic and is probably a true *glaberrima*.

I then plotted each of the lines on a map (Figure 9.1a) indicating the subpopulations with the same scheme that appears in Figure P.1a, Figure P.1b, and Figure P.1c. Representatives of all of the subpopulations of Asian rice are found on the African continent. However, some groups have only token representation – there are only three Aus and they all came from the cultivated material rather than landrace part of the study so may be the result of recent efforts to improve African rice. There are six indicas in West Africa and four in East Africa.

The preponderance of the Asian rices in Africa are japonicas of one sort or another. There are a few temperate japonicas in North Africa and one and four respectively in West and East Africa. But the biggest single group is made up of tropical japonicas. The tropical japonicas within the continent fall into two subpopulations, the TRJ1 and TRJ2. TRJ1 is found almost entirely in West and West Central Africa. TRJ2 is found almost entirely in East Africa.

As I mentioned in the introduction, none of the major japonica populations on the continent is unique to Africa. Rather the main populations of japonicas are part of larger transcontinental populations that include the Americas, the Mediterranean, and the Indian Ocean. TRJ1 is found in West and West Central Africa as well as the Americas. TRJ2 reaches from the Congo-Tanzania border to the tropical japonica heartland in Java.

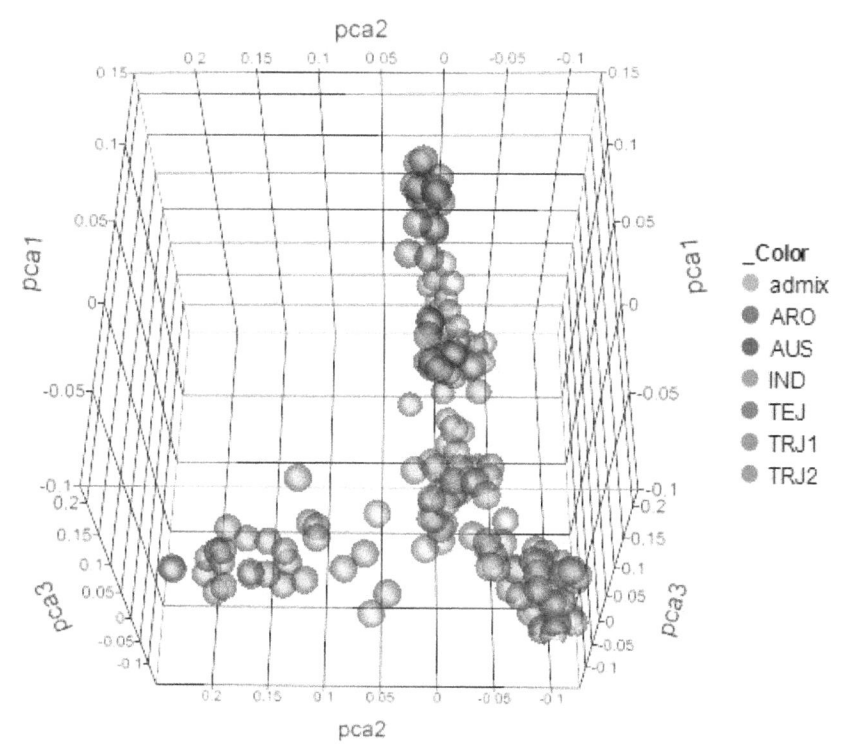

FIGURE 9.1a Population clusters identified by PCA in JMP Genomics software. The *glaberrima* (classified as an aromatic in structure) is not included in this figure. Aaron Jackson of the USDA-ARS made this chart and the tree charts in Figures 9.1b, 9.1c and 9.1d using PowerMarker software with the trees created with MEGA4.

The temperate japonicas of North Africa are clearly part of a larger population of temperate japonicas that are found all over the Mediterranean. Not surprisingly the population structure of Asian rices in Africa reflects major zones of human interaction between the continent and other regions of the world.

In addition to sorting the rice into genetic populations and then charting the geographical relationships between those populations we also sorted the lines by region and then looked for the degree of difference between the different regional populations. We did these regional comparisons both for all the genetic populations and as comparisons within genetic populations. These confirmed some of the findings that resulted from mapping the populations. Rice in Atlantic Africa is indeed related to rice in the Americas and rice in East Africa is related to Southeast Asian rice (see Figure 9.1b, Figure 9.1c, and Figure 9.1d).

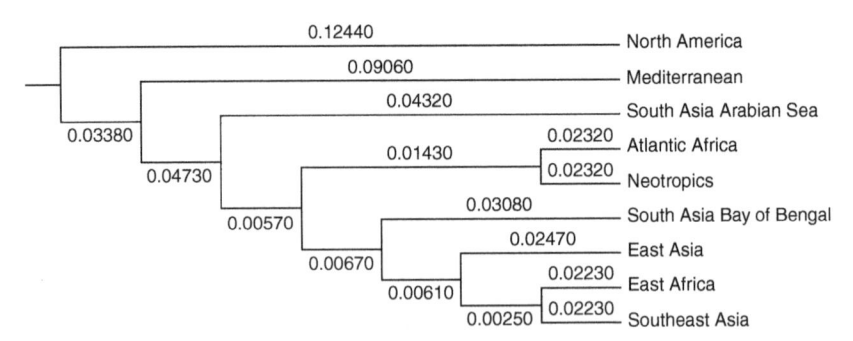

FIGURE 9.1b Cluster analysis of all populations ($n = 168$) by region (Nei 73).

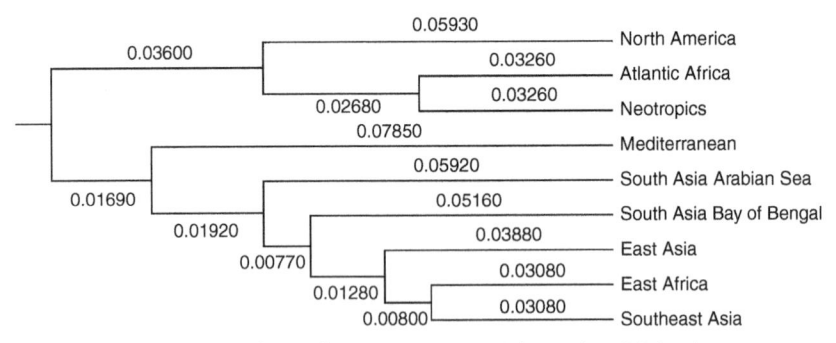

FIGURE 9.1c Cluster analysis of Japonicas ($n = 78$) by region (Nei 73).

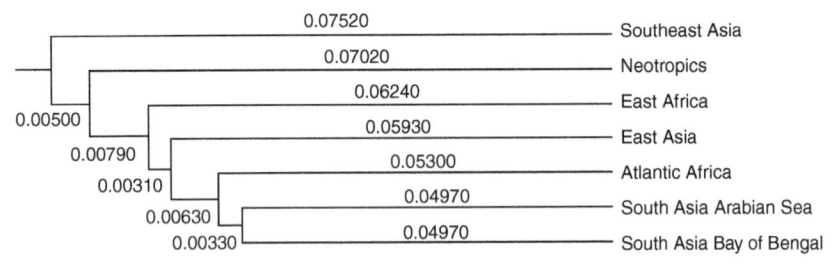

FIGURE 9.1d Cluster analysis of Indica and Aus ($n = 54$) by region (Nei 73).

POTENTIAL PROBLEMS WITH GENETIC DATA

Although I am convinced that genetic evidence in general is potentially useful to historians and that the genetic data in this study offer useful insights into the history of rice in Africa, genetic data have some serious shortcomings.

Foremost among these is the subjectivity of sampling.[22] Because genetic analysis yields quantitative results that look quite concrete, it is easy overlook the degree to which the subjectivity of the choice of samples affects outcomes. In this study, for example, I have been looking for rice varieties that I think reflect the genetic heritage of the past. My assumption has been that the best way to do achieve this is to use landraces. But landrace is a slippery concept that cannot be defined scientifically. It is a bit like the idea of "tradition" in folklore wherein there is thought to be a past characterized by limited change and surviving pockets of tradition, isolated Appalachian fiddlers for example, are thought to offer a window on that past. The African farmers who cultivate landraces exist in history and no doubt traded rice and rice seed long before the Green Revolution. There is evidence that rice varieties from India were introduced early in the twentieth century to East Africa and that they were quite popular.[23] Because we have to depend upon the descriptor information in the USDA germplasm database, we do not know whether the people who collected this rice and classified it as a landrace were able to distinguish the recent introductions from true landraces. Moreover, the USDA collection is a working collection of viable seed that was established over the last century whose purpose is to preserve as much germplasm diversity as possible. It is intended for plant breeders and more broadly concerned with long-term food security. Thus, it is not designed with historical research in mind and I am trying to use it to accomplish something it was not intended for.

The concerns above apply to any genetic study, whether it involves plants or animals, but there are also some issues particular to this study. Because I have been dependent on genetic material from existing sources in the United States, my analysis is limited to USDA's accessions which have been acquired through years of donations, collection trips, and international exchange agreements. Oddly, the USDA's holdings include no accessions classified as landraces from the two nations that are the continent's leading rice producers, Nigeria and Egypt. Africa in general is little represented in the USDA's rice holdings by way of comparison with Asia, where most of the world's rice is cultivated. So there is always the possibility that the rather small sample I have has skewed the results and that some of the patterns I think I have detected would be less apparent in a larger sample of accessions if they were available.

INTERPRETING THE RESULTS: WEST AFRICA AND THE ATLANTIC

The genetic data I have collected allow us to weed through the existing ideas about the spread of Asian rice in Africa. First, the genetic evidence argues against a straightforward diffusion of rice from the East African coast to West

---

[22] Pakendorf et al. 2011.
[23] Monson 1991, 64.

Africa. The TRJ1 population that is found in West, West Central Africa, and the Americas is quite distinct from the TRJ2 population found in East Africa. It is possible that a member of the East African TRJ2 population slipped across the continent into West Africa and then diversified, in what is called a founder effect, into the many closely related TRJ1s. However, there are good reasons to doubt this possibility. The general consensus is that rice did not move away from the East African coast into the interior until the nineteenth century. Christopher Ehret maintains that linguistic evidence suggests that rice is quite new in the interior and travelers' accounts from the nineteenth century I have been working with suggest that rice was in the process of being introduced on the caravan routes by coastal merchants in the middle of the nineteenth century.[24] So, if such an introduction took place, it failed to leave any trace of its passage. Our hypothetical rice-carrying migrants would have passed over thousands of miles of land capable of growing rice before deciding to stop and cultivate their rice. In the case of crops that are known to have spread across the continent like millet, sorghum, and bananas, there are populations of these crops in suitable environments marking their passage across the continent. That most of the TRJ1 group is found in coastal areas or in places with riverine links to the Atlantic also suggests something other than an overland transmission route. It seems much more likely that *sativa* rice arrived on the East African coast and then made no further progress into the interior until the nineteenth century. It is also clear that Asian rice was not introduced to West Africa from the Mediterranean. The Mediterranean rices in our study were uniformly temperate japonicas and we found only one temperate japonica in West Africa and that was on the southern desert edge in Mali. So, if Asian rice was not introduced to West Africa overland from East Africa or the Mediterranean, then the only remaining explanation is that it was introduced by sea. This would explain the apparent leapfrogging of the interior of the continent.

Unfortunately, our work does not allow us to date the split between the TRJ1 and TRJ2 groups. However, the mostly likely scenario is that the ancestor of the TRJ1 group was introduced by a European ship returning from Asia sometime after the Portuguese opened the sea route around the African continent, that is, sometime after 1500. By the middle of the sixteenth century the Portuguese were present both in South Asia and in Southeast Asia. The Portuguese were involved in the rice trade in the Indian Ocean and rice almost certainly was on board ships making the return voyage from India. There were formal Portuguese settlements in Angola, at El Mina, on São Tomé, and in the Cape Verde Islands and small informal communities of Portuguese settlers, called *lançados*, all along the West African coast. These Portuguese outposts may have grown rice for their own use, possibly with

---

[24] Ehret 2011, 229.

seed that they obtained from India. Carney has suggested that the Cape Verde Islands may have been a stepping stone for African food crops into the Atlantic. Some Portuguese ships retuning from Asia called at Cape Verde and wet rice production in Cape Verde provided provisions for ships bound for the Americas.[25] One might argue that they would be more likely to plant seed obtained from Portugal, but seed from South or Southeast Asia would almost certainly be better adapted to the tropical environment of West Africa than would seed from Portugal or other parts of the Mediterranean. African farmers who were already familiar with the cultivation of African *glaberrima* rice might have experimented with Asian rice obtained from these Portuguese settlements. In regions with no prior experience of rice growing, people may have begun to adopt Asian rice from the Portuguese in much the same way that they did maize. Interestingly, in regions where African rice was previously cultivated, Asian rices are called by names that are rooted in the words for *glaberrima* rice. In contrast, in areas where rice was a novelty the words for rice tend to derive from European languages, frequently form the Portuguese "arroz."[26] This I think reinforces the argument that Asian rice was recently introduced by Europeans.

The TRJ1 population is not exclusively African. TRJ1 rices are found all over the Atlantic world. In fact, TRJ1s seem to be connected on some fundamental level with the slave trade. There are TRJ1s in Brazil, Suriname, Guyana, Mexico, Congo, Ghana, and Puerto Rico. Carolina Gold, the rice variety most associated with the South Carolina rice complex is a TRJ1. Texas Star and Mortgage Lifter (an Arkansas variety) are TRJ1s. Clearly, West African rice is also Atlantic rice.

Judith Carney's *Black Rice* (2001) and *In the Shadow of Slavery* (2009), which she co-wrote with Richard Rosomoff, have argued that rice in the Americas and the agricultural knowledge associated with its cultivation crossed the Atlantic with enslaved Africans. According to Carney, Africans from the rice growing regions of West Africa, Upper Guinea in particular, were the primary historical actors in this crop transfer. Carney's critics have argued that her work fails to deal with the specific regional origins of the Africans present in the rice growing regions of the Americas.[27] Often they were not from rice growing regions of Africa. For example, when rice growing was introduced to South Carolina, most of the slaves there were from Angola, which is not a rice growing region. Later, enslaved Africans from the Upper Guinea region came to dominate and almost certainly played a role in the development of the tidal rice system there.[28]

---

[25] Carney 1998, 553.
[26] Blench 2006, 218; Carney 2001, 36. "Arroz" itself derives from the Arabic word for rice, so it is just possible that some of these terms derive directly from Arabic rather indirectly through Portuguese.
[27] Eltis et al. 2007; Hawthorne 2010b, 139–40.
[28] Hawthorne 2011.

The genetic evidence lends partial support to Carney's thesis. It certainly suggests a strong association between Asian rice in the Atlantic and the slave trade. It is clear that rice moved in the same web of connections that brought Africans to the Americas, and that the worlds of African slaves and rice are closely intertwined. What is less clear is the directionality of those movements and the agency behind them. It seems entirely plausible that the TRJ1 population was introduced first to the Americas and subsequently to West Africa, or perhaps to the Atlantic islands first and subsequently to the African mainland and the Americas. Furthermore, TRJ1 is not well represented in the Upper Guinea region of West Africa. While this may be skewed by the small sample size of the study, indicas and aus seem to be more common in the Upper Guinea rice country than TRJ1. While this does not rule out Upper Guineans as central to the development of the rice industry in the Americas, it does suggest that it if that is the case, they ended up applying their knowledge of rice cultivation to varieties that were not their own. If Asian rice was introduced into the Atlantic world after 1500, then presumably those African rice-growing systems that adopted it were themselves undergoing changes at the same time that rice cultivation was being introduced into the Americas. It seems probable that rice farming on both sides of the Atlantic was dynamic and changing in the centuries after 1500. What is clear is that something more complicated than a simple and direct transfer of rice seed and agricultural knowledge from Upper Guinea to the Americas occurred. Rather this looks like a transoceanic process, with multiple agents and innovators adapting their knowledge in new environments with new varieties of rice.

INTERPRETING THE EVIDENCE: EAST AFRICA

No one population dominates rice in East Africa the way TRJ1 dominates the Atlantic or the temperate japonicas dominate the Mediterranean. Rather the two main groups are the TRJ2 population of tropical japonicas and indicas. The diversity of rice seems much higher in East Africa than West Africa, possibly because of the antiquity of the rice trade in the Indian Ocean and multiple waves of migration and trade that have no doubt clouded the picture.[29] However, there are a few things we can discern from the data. First, the presence of a significant number of TRJ2s on both Madagascar and the mainland lends credence to the idea that the Malagasy are responsible for at least one introduction of rice into East Africa. The tree charts in Figure 9.1b, Figure 9.1c, and Figure 9.1d show a strong relationship between East African japonicas and Southeast Asian japonicas, so there is probably some validity to the received wisdom that the Malagasy introduced rice to

---

[29] Alpers 2009.

East Africa. But there are also indica, aus, and temperate japonica rices in East Africa. Our relatively large sample for Southeast Asia turned up just a couple of indicas and only one in insular Southeast Asia, which is thought to be the Malagasy homeland. By contrast indicas and aus are the norm in South Asia. I suspect that this means that there is a second layer of rice introduced from South Asia. This may have occurred later than the Malagasy introduction of TRJ2, and indeed may reflect the fairly recent – that is, in the last couple of centuries – movement of people from South Asia to East Africa.

Here linguistic evidence offers some interesting perspective. The Swahili have several words for rice, but the word for cooked rice is *wali*. This is similar to and probably cognate with, the Malagasy word for rice, which is *vary*. However, *vary* is not an Austronesian (the family to which Malagasy and most Southeast Asian languages belong) rooted word, rather it derives from the proto-Dravidian *vari* which itself is the source of the Sanskrit *vrihi*.[30] So, there are two possibilities here. Either the word *vary* is present in Malagasy because the Malagasy left their Southeast Asian homeland for Madagascar after the spread of a veneer of Indian culture into Southeast Asia or Indians played a sufficiently important role in the spread of rice into East Africa that both the Swahili and the Malagasy adopted Dravidian terms for rice. The introduction of rice to East Africa is, if anything, more complex and multi-layered than the situation in the Atlantic and the ambiguity of the genetic evidence reflects the multiple streams in this introduction.

CONCLUSION

The introduction of Asian rice to Africa was not a straightforward, point source event. Rather there were multiple introductions yielding a number of discrete regional populations. There appear to have been two introductions of rice to East Africa, first the TRJ2 from Southeast Asia and the almost certainly separate introduction of the indica-aus rices. In the Mediterranean (a temperate environment) there is a population of temperate japonicas, but there is no evidence that they spread into sub-Saharan Africa (a tropical environment) or into the larger Atlantic world. In West Africa the presence of the TRJ1 group and the cluster of indicas in the Senegambia suggest at least two introductions of rice there. The presence of TRJ1 on the slave routes in the Americas shows us how closely connected Atlantic Africa was with the Americas. What is interesting is the contrast between the dense web of oceanic connection that is visible in the rice genetics and the limited overland spread of rice within the continent. TRJ1 looks like it exploded across Atlantic, but shows fewer connections to inland rice growing areas. Rice seems to have struggled to travel overland. *Glaberrima*s did not escape West Africa. Asian

---

[30] Pierre Sagart, personal communication.

rice in East Africa was present on the coast for nearly a millennium before it began its journey into the interior. Even then, the East Africa TRJ2s sort of peter out once they reach the eastern Congo.

Rice, it seems, requires special conditions to spread. These include climate, topography, and available technology, but also social and economic conditions. That the temperate japonicas that are characteristic of the Mediterranean did follow the trade routes across the Sahara to tropical West Africa is probably attributable to environmental factors. However, environmental factors do little to explain the slow spread of Asian sativas in East Africa or the failure of *glaberrima*s to spread into Central or East Africa. Asian rice is now widely cultivated in central and eastern Tanzania, but something other than environment prevented its expansion into the interior until the nineteenth century. Similarly, Morgan has noted that although Tamilnad and eastern Tanzania have similar environments rice cultivation and irrigation practices are quite different.[31] Rice requires a certain amount of moisture and warmth, but the limits to its expansion in Africa do not seem to have been primarily environmental.

A recent paper by Fuller and Qin argues that the early spread of rice in Asia took place only in societies that were moving toward hierarchies.[32] While their work concerns a much earlier period than mine, I think this idea may be applicable to the spread of rice in Africa. If one considers the spread of Asian rice in Africa, it appears to follow trade routes. This may simply have served as the vector that moved the plants' seeds, but I suspect that the social changes that are a by-product of trade also tend to make societies more interested in rice production. That rice seems to follow oceanic trade routes may not be just because they provide transportation, instead it may reflect the hierarchies that emerge alongside long-distance trade.[33]

---

[31] Morgan 1988.
[32] Fuller and Qin 2009.
[33] A number of people made critical contributions to this chapter. Anna McClung organized the genetic analysis of the rice and provided essential guidance on plant genetics and how to obtain and choose rice samples. Other contributors at the USDA-ARS were Aaron Jackson, Georgia Eizenga, Eric Christiansen, Hesham Agrama, and Bob Fjellstrom. The research for this project was funded by a grant from the Arkansas Biosciences Institute at Arkansas State University. Sarah Walshaw was kind enough to let me pick her brain about rice in East Africa and to share a copy of her dissertation with me. Of course, any failure of interpretation, fact, or method this chapter may contain is mine.

10

When Jola Granaries Were Full

Olga F. Linares

The factors responsible for the uneven trajectories followed by crop productions among smallholder farmers around the world constitute an important dimension to all "histories of rice." In different regions of the world, but also within neighboring subareas, the quantity of yearly rice produced by rural farmers may fluctuate markedly. This rise and fall in production, whether short- or long-term, obeys a multitude of causes, and has serious consequences for the food security of millions who depend on rice for their livelihood. This chapter explores the reasons why some, though not all Jola sub-groups living in the Lower Casamance region of southern Senegal (Figure P.1b), who were once surplus producers of grains have now become net purchasers of rice and other foodstuffs. It is instructive to examine the forces that have led them to reduce subsistence production, to engage in ecologically destructive forms of commercial agriculture, and to migrate to urban areas in large numbers. Here is the story of how the effects of adverse climatic conditions, principally drought, have affected production. Structuring changes around a single event, felt in different ways and variable intensities within different Jola regions and communities, allows us to explore how ill-conceived economic policies, inadequate infrastructures, unfavorable terms of trade, and the ever-present urban bias have affected agricultural outputs.

DROUGHT AND FOOD SHORTAGES

Until the mid-1960s – that is up to 50 years ago – Lower Casamance was subject to a five-month rainy season with annual precipitations averaging well over 1,500 mm in the Ziguinchor area, the area's capital city. The rains were abundant and reliable, raising expectations that Lower Casamance would be the future grain basket of Senegal. Unfortunately, these conditions have changed dramatically.

Beginning in 1968, the very year after bumper crops were harvested, Senegal, and indeed all West African countries and beyond, entered a desperate, drought-ridden period lasting 17 years or more. Drought has been variously defined and differentiated. Glanz distinguishes between various kinds of drought.[1] A meteorological drought refers to the degree and duration of dryness (stated as the percentage reduction from a long-term mean), whereas a hydrological drought results when stream flow falls below a predetermined level, and an agricultural drought results when there is not enough moisture available at the right time for the growth and maturation of crops. Here, we will begin with a discussion of a meteorological drought as reflected by the total amount of yearly precipitation measured in four separate localities within the Lower Casamance Region. Three of the stations are near the communities that we have been discussing. The fourth is in Ziguinchor which, because it is midway between the other localities, and also has the longest available record, shall be used as a reference point and control.

Rainfall variability, in Lower Casamance and elsewhere, can be expressed either in terms of yearly fluctuations, of cyclical oscillations covering several years, or of long-term trends. With respect to yearly fluctuations, the second half of the 1960s ushered in a marked deterioration in climatic conditions unprecedented in length or magnitude. The decade began auspiciously enough, with rainfall averages well above 1,200 mm. Then, in 1968, rainfall plunged, decreasing by 1,124 mm from the year before, to attain a low of 883 mm. This marked the beginning of a prolonged meteorological drought. In Ziguinchor, the capital of Casamance, the years 1972, 1976, 1980, 1982–83, 1986, and 1992, had accumulated rainfall totals of less than 1,000 mm. These figures were several hundred millimeters below the 1,489 mm mark representing a 40-year average (1920–80). In two other stations of the same region, where rainfall records go back to the 1960s, the same general pattern could be discerned. After one or two decades of fairly "normal" oscillations, rainfall plummeted. In the town of Oussouye, located near the Sambujat community, it went from 1,844 mm the year before to 898 mm in 1968, and in Bignona, near the Jipalom and Fatiya communities, it went from 1,795mm to 826 mm in 1968, or a drop of very close to one meter in both areas. From then on, years of insufficient precipitation followed each other, though not necessarily directly.

The use of running averages, based on a statistical mean for several years, smoothes out yearly rainfall variations, exposing more clearly long-term trends. Figure 10.1 represents a graph of 5-year running rainfall averages for our four stations. These reveal an unquestionable sustained, overall decline in rainfall in the long term everywhere. Whereas both Ziguinchor and Oussouye had received more than 1,400 mm of rain during the decades from 1930 to 1960, with many years above the 1,600 mm line, there was a

---

[1] Glantz 1987.

When Jola Granaries Were Full

Lower casamance, senegal 5-year running average

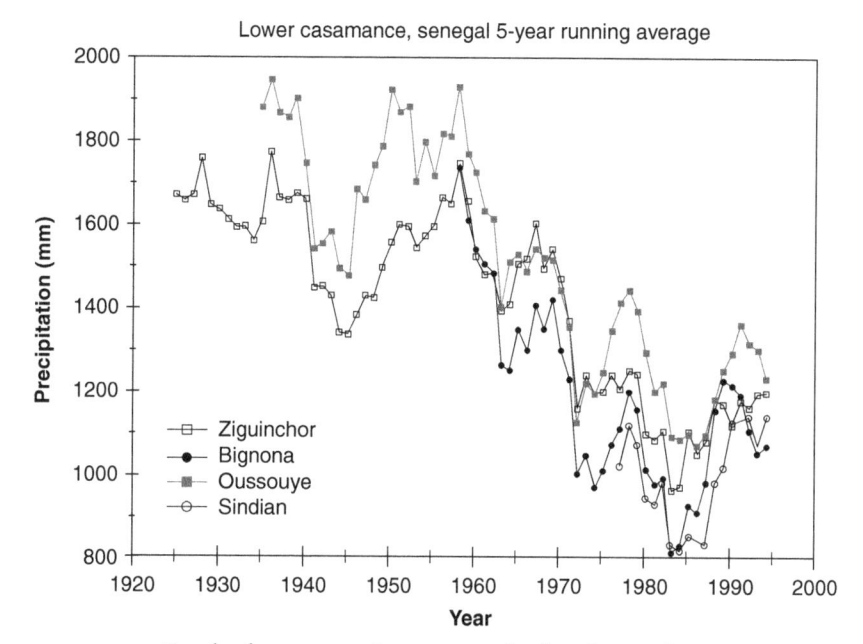

FIGURE 10.1 Graph of 5-year running averages for four Lower Casamance stations located near our study communities, to wit Sindian near Jipalom, Bignona near Fatiya, and Oussouye near Esudadu. The Ziguinchor station is used as a control.

steady decline beginning in 1960, first to the 1,400 mm line, then to the 1,200 mm line, until it finally reached the 1980s, with rainfall lows hovering around or below the 1,000 mm mark in Bignona and Sindian, near the Jipalom community.

Posner et al. suggest a rainfall minimum for each of the sub-regions, a benchmark below which the cultivation system is in imminent danger of failure, to wit 1,000 mm for Ziguinchor, 1,100 mm for Oussouye, and 900 mm for Bignona.[2] With these benchmarks in mind, Ziguinchor and Oussouye have experienced insufficient rain in five out of the last fifteen years, while Bignona has experienced four deficit years in the same period, with three additional years only slightly above the 900 mm minimum.

The decline in precipitation brought food shortages, but not famine, to Jola communities in the Casamance. However, such shortages must be evaluated in the context of cultural preferences. For the Jola, rice is synonymous with food, so a decline in the availability of this grain is seen as a threat to the general welfare of the population. Although millet and manioc were available at these precarious times, most Jola, with the exception of those in the Fatiya

---

[2] Posner et al 1985, 4, figure 1.

and surrounding villages, where millet is a staple food, refused to eat them on a daily basis. Hence, for most Jola, a shortage of food meant a shortage of rice, pure and simple.

A BRIEF ACCOUNT OF RICE PRODUCTION IN THREE JOLA VILLAGES

In Lower Casamance, agricultural conditions have been shaped by the local interplay between particular environmental conditions, specific social techniques, and the history of colonial and, later-on, state control of resources and commerce. To understand the remarkable feat that the Jola peoples have accomplished requires a cultural approach to agrarian and ecological change. In the process of producing rice to insure their own future social reproduction the Jola have profoundly altered the marshy landscape they inhabit. They have created a thoroughly modified, anthropogenic environment.

The communities discussed below are found within a radius of less than 100 kilometers as the crow flies, and a few hundred kilometers by road (Figure 10.2), yet they differ markedly in their rice-growing technologies, and in the social organization of production. These factors account in large measure for the successes and failures experienced by rice yields throughout the years. Each of the geo-cultural regions where they occur – namely the Kajamutay, Kalunay, and Esudadu – share similar ecological and sociocultural features.[3]

When it comes to agricultural production, the gender division of labor is a cultural construct of primary importance in shaping the ways field activities are performed. How a particular division of labor has come about, however, is not an easy task to determine. In two of the communities discussed later, namely Jipalom and Fatiya, it is quite probable that the nearly complete separation of cropping tasks has been influenced by the presence of the neighboring Malinke or Manding people who are well-known for the strict separation of the sexes in most aspects of life, from domestic arrangements to work out in the fields. Not surprisingly, among the Malinke, as well as the inhabitants of Jipalom and Fatiya, groundnuts, the principal cash crop, are grown by men who reap the benefits. But ecological conditions also play a part. Women, even when pregnant, or with infants on their backs, are able to perform such tasks as transplanting and harvesting the rice crop in Jipalom and Sambujat, whereas in Fatiya they also hoe the lighter soils in flooded fields. The heavier tasks of soil preparation and water control fall on the shoulders of the male population.

An ecological argument for the existence of a particular gender separation of agricultural tasks is not very compelling, however. What is more important is

[3] Linares 1992.

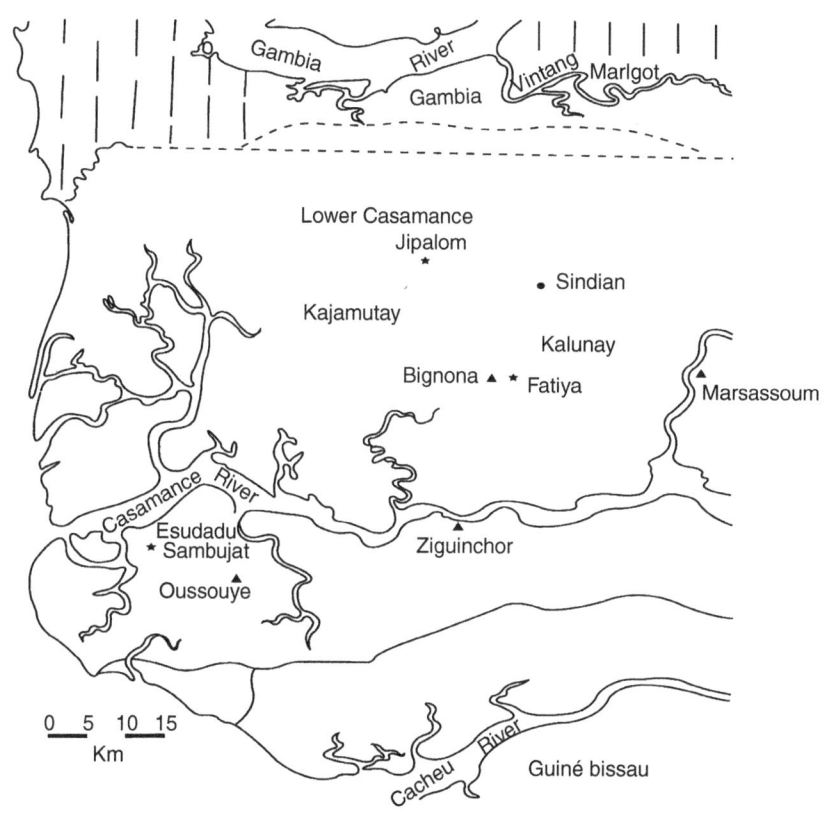

FIGURE 10.2 Location of our Jola study communities and the regions where they are found.

that in communities where women hold considerable ritual power by commanding important spirit-shrines, as in Sambujat, they are empowered. They control rice production on an equal footing with men, and they can command the labor of others. In areas where Islam devolves power and agency mostly on males, women are less independent and more reliant upon their husbands. Hence, a certain gender division of labor is legitimated and made operative by a specific system of cultural sanctions based on the different religious ideologies and practices that exist among various Jola communities.

The introduction of groundnuts as a cash crop into Senegal dates from French colonial rule which "turned Senegal into a monocrop exporter by harnessing a large share of land and labor, predominantly in the central basin, to the production of groundnuts."[4] The principal actors in opening land to

---

[4] Boone 1992, 106

groundnut production in this basin were members of the Mouride brotherhood, a powerful Islamic sect of marabouts or religious clerics belonging to the Wolof ethnic group, the dominant group in Senegal, who to this day control most of the groundnut trade by harnessing the labor of peasants or disciples (the talibés). Hence, from its beginnings, groundnut cultivation was associated with Islam and its practicioners. Although Mouridism has no following among Jola peoples, it was indirectly responsible for the introduction of groundnuts into the north-shore communities. In the minds of the Jola Islam and groundnuts are intimately related, so much so that most non-Muslims do not grow this crop. The north-shore Foñi Jola began to plant groundnuts after 1910, when the trade in wild rubber collapsed.[5] Instrumental in the introduction of this cash crop were the neighboring Manding or Malinke peoples who, encouraged by the French authorities, were cultivating groundnuts in the Middle Casamance by the 1850s. Despite a slow start, by 1935 the Jola north of the river were completely dependent on cash revenues from the groundnut trade. Hence, Islamization, cash cropping, and colonialism were interrelated processes ending centuries of relative economic independence by north-shore Jola.

Jipalom in the Kajamutay

The Jipalom village is one of about 30 communities located in the sub-region the Jola call the Kajamutay, within the basin of the Baila marigot. Before the end of the 1960s, the rice-growing system was vigorous and expanding, and Jipalom's granaries were full year after year. Here, the inhabitants combined rice growing in the alluvial lowlands extending from the compounds down to the tidal channels or marigots, with the cultivation of dry crops such as millet and sorghum for subsistence, and groundnuts as a commercial crop, in the uplands surrounding village lands. The main emphasis here is on the cultivation of rice in the alluvial lands.

The low lands that extend behind the Kajamutay communities, including Jipalom, are covered with hundreds of paddy fields varying in size, function, and location in the toposequence. Cultivated parcels range from the sandy nurseries behind the dwellings, to the diverse rainfed fields in the middle ranges, and on to the deep and salty fields recovered from the mangrove. Dozens of small, bunded parcels belonging in each of these categories have different soil properties and water retention qualities. They are also prepared (i.e., hand-plowed) by building up ridges and furrows, and are transplanted upon the ridges with varieties of rice seed requiring different moistures and having staggered maturing rates. In order to spread the risk, it is very important for each household head in the community to own fields belonging to the various categories.

[5] Linares 1992, 98–102

In general, men ridge and furrow the parcels using a unique long-handled tool, the kajandu, or fulcrum-shovel, and women broadcast the seed on the nurseries, transplanting the seedlings onto the ridges. They also harvest the crop and carry it to their household granaries. Figures for yields obtained from the various categories of fields in the 1965 season average 1,500 kg of paddy (unmilled rice) per hectare. Such yields are not spectacular, but they were quite sufficient to feed household members and even produce a surplus.

Fatiya in the Kalunay

The Kalunay sub-region is located north of the Casamance River, to the east of the town of Bignona. The communities located here, including Fatiya, differ from those in the Kajamutay by practicing a complete separation of cropping tasks along gender lines. Briefly, rice is grown solely by women, away from the tidal river channels or marigots, in the alluvial valleys and depressions dividing communities and wards, where freshwater accumulates and soils are not saline, whereas upland crops are grown solely by men on the plateaus.

Rice parcels themselves are large and flat; they are bunded around their peripheries by a low dike to retain rainwater. The fields are not functionally differentiated, as is the case in Jipalom, and there is no complex classification of fields into different categories. Even though it is the wives who work the rice land, it is their husbands who are lent paddy fields by the founding members of the village who hold inalienable rights to land.

In the 1960s, when the rains were abundant, the women of Fatiya did a great deal of work in the rice fields. By the end of June, the women tilled the rice fields flat, without ridging, using the long-handled hoe (the ebarai). Each section was weeded, then hoed, and either directly seeded in the shallower parts, or transplanted in the flooded sections. The harvest began by mid-October and usually concluded by the end of December. After a woman's field has been harvested her husband would arrive with the donkey cart and transport the crop home to store in the granary. This is one of the few occasions when men came down to the rice fields. The rice stored in the common granary belonged to both, a man and his wife (or wives), but each must ask the other for permission to dispose of rice not consumed by the family.

Even when the rains were favorable, several households belonging to immigrant men needed to purchase two or more 100 kg bags of rice a year. This is a small quantity, however. On the other hand, the wives of men belonging to the households of village founders consistently harvested enough rice to feed their families, and in rainy years even produced substantial surpluses.

Sambujat in the Esudadu area

The Esudadu Jola live south of the Casamance River, not far from the border with Guinea Bissau. At present, they occupy a string of five, small to large communities, at a distance of 4 to 5 km from the sea, and less than 20 km directly west from the Casamance River estuary. Facing the villages one finds a wide zone of low-lying lands or swampy depressions, separated from the brackish river channel by a broad mantle of mangrove vegetation. Here, in these lowlands, the Esudadu Jola cultivate aquatic rice intensively. They grow seedlings in nurseries on higher ground, and transplant them into mid-elevation fields or deep paddy fields that were recovered from the mangrove vegetation.

In contrast to the Kajamutay Jola of Jipalom, or the Fatiya Jola of the Kalunay, in the Esudadu both men and women grow rice as a monocrop using labor-intensive techniques. Men build sturdy and lengthy dikes to keep out brackish waters from the marigot, and distribute rainwater to the various paddies by means of sluices and canals. Women manure the nurseries where rice seedlings grow, and transplant them onto the various kinds of paddy fields. None of Sambujat residents grow plateau crops.

Transforming swampy lowlands, regularly swept by marine tidal waters and covered with mangrove vegetation, into deep and productive paddy fields is very labor-intensive. It is critically important to control and contain the brackish waters that are constantly being pushed inland along creeks or marigots by the daily tides. To this end, the Jola have created an ingenious and effective system of tidal control. They have carved out their mangrove paddy fields, a process that may take years, by constructing retaining dikes, then desalinating the soil and poldering it. In the end, all rice production depends upon the rainfall that accumulates during the rainy season within the sacred forest, which constitutes a protected watershed and water is then is distributed to the other paddies by way of a main canal backed by a dike. A duct, made from the trunk of the Borassus palm, pierces the dike and enters the canal. It is plugged or unplugged as needed for freshwater to flow, first to the mid-position fields, then all the way to the mangrove paddies.

Mangrove fields may be the most productive in good years, but they are also the riskiest. In years with insufficient rain, as has been the case during the last two decades, they accumulate toxic acids and salts. In years with abundant precipitation, however, as was the case up to the late 1960s, mangrove fields may yield 3,000 kg or more per hectare. The other rainfed fields regularly produced 1,500 kg/ha or more rice on average. Substantial surpluses underscored a vigorous trade in rice with members of villages located in less endowed areas.

THE IMPACT OF DROUGHT YEARS ON THE THREE COMMUNITIES

Before the drought began, domestic rice production met household needs almost everywhere in Lower Casamance. It has been calculated that in 1962–63 the per capita surplus of rice being produced in the Kajamutay and Kalunay regions was at least 100 kg, while in the Esudadu region it was 181 kg or more.[6] The effect of rainfall deficits was felt in different ways and intensities in the three Jola communities discussed.

Jipalom: The fact that adequate precipitation occurred in some – albeit only a few years – added to the general incertitude. The individuals who fared better chose their seed carefully, prepared their fields early, did not ridge but tilled the land flat, and mostly direct seeded rather than transplanted. At the same time, many of the rice varieties planted, differing in important characteristics, were abandoned.

With reduced precipitation levels, a high proportion of rice fields in the Jipalom community had to be abandoned due to salt intrusion in the lowest paddies, and drought stress on the upper fields. Not surprisingly, rice production declined markedly. Posner calculated that the surface cultivated in rice in declined to 53 percent of what it had been in 1960–64.[7]

By 1981, domestic rice production in Jipalom covered only 55 percent of the family's needs.[8] The per capita rice deficit was 170 kg; household supplies of home-grown rice lasted only for six months after the harvest, and often for much less. Everyone was buying imported low-quality rice from Southeast Asia. Imports of rice into the Basse Casamance had gone up, from 2,000–3,000 tons in 1960–65, to 30,000 tons in 1982–83.[9] In the Kajamutay and Kalunay regions there was a marked extension of surfaces cultivated in millet, sorghum and, most importantly maize. These are not preferred cereals for the local inhabitants, but they prevented famine. Here, also, the income generated by the groundnut trade was used to buy rice during the height of the scarce period.

Because rice in the Esudadu area in general, and in the Sambujat community in particular, is grown as a monocrop it does not compete with plateau crops for time or labor. Not far into the drought, however, some rice fields began to fail. In 1980, at times of strong tides, sections of the big dike that protected the deep fields recovered from the mangrove broke in parts, and saltwater invaded a few of these large and very productive fields. In 1981, PIDAC, the government agency, distributed free of charge bags of fertilizer, mostly phosphates, to all the Sambujat households. But very few people used it. One elder explained that using strong chemicals in badly watered fields simply "burned" the rice. The government also distributed sacks weighing 100 lb (45.56 kg) of milled rice which the American government had contributed as food aid. The free distribution of milled rice to self-sufficient residents only served as a disincentive to production.

In the Esudadu area the rice defecit of the less-endowed residents during drought years was about 121 kg. Most of the inhabitants, however, had

---

[6] Posner 1988, 8
[7] Posner 1988, Table 2, 9.
[8] Jolly and Michigan State University, Dept. of Agricultural Economics 1988: 1
[9] Posner 1988, 8.

extensive paddies producing enough rice to feed their families. Customarily, the inhabitants of Sambujat, especially the wives of elder men, sold rice locally. This was part of the ongoing, somewhat secretive informal trade. Even at the height of the drought, quite a bit of rice was being sold locally, not always in small quantities. In fact, in 1985 I witnessed a considerable amount of paddy rice being exchanged for palm wine and fish.

Besides experiencing occasional crop failures, or having to buy small quantities of rice, or needing to travel further south to tap palm wine, the drought did not bring any major change to Sambujat's rice economy. People did not take up direct seeding, nor did they abandon their old rice varieties.

Certainly, the drought did not affect the Sambujat social division of labor in any significant manner either. Work-groups, be they made up of men or of women, went on being used as before. What did affect production were labor shortages caused by the youth's flight to the cities. Although a good number of them came back during the rainy season to help their parents, many did not.[10] The resident elders feared that there would be nobody to repair the big dike that kept the brackish waters of the marigot from invading the most productive mangrove fields. In 2000 the dike broke, and salty water ruined these highly productive fields.

In many important ways, the agricultural system of Fatiya is fundamentally different from the other two regions. For one, the rice fields of Fatiya are located inland, in valleys and depressions away from the marigot, and for that reason do not have salinization problems. For another, precipitation is slightly less, and the rainy season is shorter, so the women are used to growing rice during a foreshortened season. Moreover, rice is only one of the subsistence crops grown in Fatiya; millet, sorghum, and recently introduced maize, are regular items of the diet.

In the Kalunay, the the 1970s and 1980s witnessed years of drought interspersed with years of satisfactory, though not abundant rains. 1980 was one of the driest years in the entire century; in Fatiya, it rained a scant 619 mm, hardly enough even for the less demanding crops such as sorghum and millet. Because the rice crop failed miserably in the following year women direct-seeded fast ripening Chinese varieties in rows, to facilitate weeding, and the young men sprayed insecticide on the rice plants. They were fortunate in that the rains were sufficient (1,033 mm that year), and the rice harvested was satisfactory. Even then, household heads needed to purchase two or more 100 kg sacks of milled rice because the millet, sorghum, and maize crops, which had not been sprayed, had been devoured by insects. In the following year, the Senegalese authorities distributed two 50 kg bags of milled U.S. rice to each of the household heads.

---

[10] Linares 2003.

In 1985, the rains were satisfactory, however, (1,114 mm) so the rice crop did well, as did maize and sorghum, with some households harvesting up to 600 kg of sorghum and 440 kg of maize, some of which they sold. Beginning this same year, both men and women were benefiting from the services of PIDAC, the government extension service. Agents would come to the villages, ask the men what kind of equipment they needed, and make available a plough, a cart, a seeder and so on for an annual payment.

The women also received help from the PIDAC extension agents. In fact, beginning in 1983, agents helped to establish garden projects in five surrounding villages by digging wells to irrigate the vegetables during the off season. To this day, women successfully cultivate a large vegetable garden every dry season and sell the product in the nearby Bignona market. With the profits averaging 8,000 CFA francs ($32.00) each, a considerable sum by local standards, women rented the ox-plough for a day, to prepare their gardens, and also bought fertilizer and improved seed. In 1994, the millet crop failed in part; there simply was too much water around for upland crops, though not for the rice crop, which prospered. Thus, when one crop succeeds, another one fails.

The big change that occurred in 1994 was that men began to help women cultivate by tilling the rice fields using the classic Jola tool, the kajandu. To witness men working in their wives' rice fields for the first time was quite astonishing. However, the devaluation of the CFA franc had brought much higher prices for purchased rice; an increase from 6,500 CFA francs ($24) for the 50 kg bag the year before, to 9,500 CFA francs ($35) this year. Household heads could no longer cover the cost of buying imported rice with what they earned from the sale of groundnuts. So they had little choice but to go down to the fields and help their wives hoe and polder their rice fields. This situation was not permanent, however. As the precipitation increased, and normal times ensued, men went back to growing plateau crops, leaving to the women all tasks having to do with rice cultivation. This phenomenom confirms the fact that a particular sexual division of labor is part and parcel of an overreaching and complex system of gender attributes and practices crosscutting all aspects of society. As such, it has legitimacy and continuity, making it particularly resistant to change.

CONCLUSIONS: FACTORS THAT AFFECT PRODUCTION

It should be emphasized here that drought, or more accurately decreased precipitation, was only one – perhaps the proximal but not the ultimate – cause of the agrarian transformations that have been discussed above. Even though the Sub-Saharan drought of the mid-1970s may have increased the plight of African farmers, Bates believes that "the problems lie deeper than the vagaries of the weather." He argues quite persuasively that governments manipulate the major markets affecting African farmers. They do so by paying farmers well below world-market price for their cash crops, and investing state earnings in urban industrial and manufacturing enterprises, and in increasing salaries for the bureaucratic elite.[11] Governments often compete directly with rural producers by engaging in food production, or by subsidizing farm inputs for a few, privileged farmers, thus providing low-priced food to urban consumers.

Explanations for the pronounced decline in agricultural productivity in Lower Casamance must be sought in the complex interactions that exist between climate, political economy, and other sociocultural and technological parameters. The forces that shape agrarian outputs operate at several levels, beginning with the general political and economic decisions made by state administrators, and ending with particular local community processes and procedures. Here, I will first consider how the reactions of the Senegalese state before and after the onset of drought conditions affected rural populations and their agricultural outputs. The important question to ask is not whether rainfall shortages have affected agricultural performance. Obviously, they have, and still do. What is worth examining is how, or indeed if, the government policies that were in place at the time disaster struck were helpful to farmers.

During the 1950s and 1960s, the dominant ideology of economic development emphasized the central role played by the Senegalese State in ensuring the proper functioning of agricultural markets. In the decades that followed, skepticism over flourishing bureaucracies and mistaken policies led to a re-evaluation of the role of government in facilitating commercial transactions. A history of continued instability in state-promoted projects and controlled markets impeded making any significant progress in agriculture. Uncertainty surrounding outlets and prices has done a great deal to discourage increased production by farmers and the rural poor. Moreover, the reliance on a few export crops, whose prices fluctuate widely in the international market, did not offer a viable alternative to growing food for self-provisioning. Under conditions of political and economic precariousness, and when facing unpredictable climatic twists and turns, household members have for decades shifted crop repertories in and out of marketable channels.

Rice production in the Casamance cannot be divorced from groundnut production, for they may compliment, but also often compete for time and labor. Jola farmers have to cultivate crops, principally rice, for subsistence purposes alongside commercial crops, mainly groundnuts, for the export market for two principal reasons. First, because the income generated by commercial agriculture is insufficient to cover subsistence needs – that is, to meet all food expenses – and also pay for other essential charges, to wit taxes,

---

[11] Bates 1981, 1

schooling, clothing, medicines and, most important, additional agricultural inputs. Second, and more obviously, they must cultivate food and commercial crops because the production "climate" – whether we are talking about precipitation or politics – is highly unstable. Under these circumstances, growing food crops alongside commercial crops is a wise strategy. It provides farmers with the kind of secure, independent base and political leverage needed to manipulate, or at least to "circumvent regulations and organizations which work against their interests."[12] A secure subsistence base makes it possible for farmers to weave their way around the morass of often confusing and contradictory rules setting price and production parameters while securing their own best interest, or that of their families.

Unfortunately, however, the postindependence Senegalese administration has continued to apply the same interventionist agricultural policies that characterized the colonial era. Governmental institutions, including agricultural extension services, state-organized cooperatives, and parastatal or parapublic agencies (i.e., filières) have controlled local cereal production as well as foreign cereal imports for many decades. They also regulated the exports of groundnuts (i.e., peanuts), until recently one of the main "engines" behind the Senegalese economy. After 1966, the role of establishing cooperatives, of buying, stocking and selling groundnuts, of purchasing and distributing imported rice, were all turned over to ONCAD (Office National de Coopération et d'Assistance au Développement). Jola farmers were left with little choice; they were obliged to use the official marketing outlets, the so-called cooperatives, if they wanted to sell their groundnuts. From 1966 to 1980, when ONCAD was in operation, its purpose – that of encouraging cooperatives and the development process – was progressively abandoned in favor of a purely marketing role. Whatever profits ONCAD may have made were transferred directly into the government coffers. Or they were used to compliment urban salaries by underwriting subsidies extended to imported rice. Technical services were poor, and corruption within the ONCAD ranks was rampant, leading to its dissolution 1980.

With reference to rice cultivation, the 1984–85 season can unqualifiably be classified as a drought year (949.4 mm precipitation in the Kajamutay). The two previous years had been even worse: 613 mm in 1983, and 924 mm in 1982. Household heads in Jipalom were now entirely dependent upon the profits they made from the sale of groundnuts to buy imported, broken rice from Southeast Asia to feed their families. In January 1985, just before the traite (i.e., the marketing) of the groundnut crop, a government decree increased the price of imported rice by 23 percent. Outside Dakar, it retailed for 162 francs CFA (about $1.00) per kilogram.[13] It is estimated that, on average, a household head was forced to buy 360 kg of imported milled rice a

---

[12] Barker 1989, 23.
[13] Newman et al., 1987, Table 4, 9.

year to feed his family during years of drought.[14] If this figure is correct, then eight out of eleven Jipalom households (or 73 percent) did not make enough money in 1985 (i.e., 58,320 francs CFA or $212) from the groundnut trade to buy the rice they needed.

The years from 1980 to 1985 were crucial for determining the future of government parastatals concerned with the grain trade. After ONCAD was abolished, a number of organizations were put in charge of buying and distributing local and imported crops.[15] The CPSP (Caisse de Péréquation et de Stabilisation des Prix) was reorganized to handle all imports of rice and millet/sorghum), PIDAC (Projet Intégré pour le Développement Agricole de la Casamance) was charged with buying local rice and millet. The CSA (Commissariat a l'Aide Alimentaire), coordinated, at least in principal, food aid and played a role in the assembly of local millet, sorghum, and maize, and finally, SONACOS (Société Nationale de Commercialisation des Oléagineux du Sénégal) bought the groundnut crops from village cooperatives and processed it for export. The rules governing the function of all these entities were confusing; "regulatory uncertainty," as it is called, also entered the domain of official prices. In macro-economic terms, Senegal's rice imports grew, from 31 percent of total grain available in 1974–77, to 38 percent in 1981–84, causing major foreign exchange losses. At the same time, the groundnut subsector ceased to be able to cover food imports; it registered an annual deficit of 13.5 billion francs CFA during the 1980–83 period.[16] Production was stagnant, per capita profits from commercial agriculture had declined, the land was degrading rapidly, and the filières were still creating huge deficits.[17] Because of this situation, in April 1984 the government put in place the Nouvelle Politique Agricole (NPA) with the aim of diversifying and augmenting local food production while reducing dependence on groundnut production and on rice imports.[18] Ten years later there had been some successes, but few of the principal aims had been achieved. Personnel in government agencies were resisting dismissal, farmers were paid less for their crops, agricultural production continued to grow at a snail's pace, and larger quantities of wheat and rice were being imported. Infrastructural projects were, as usual, neglected; roads and bridges fell into disuse, and river or sea transport continued to be limited.

Turning now to the local scene, it is important to emphasize the general characteristics that the rice economies of the Jola communities discussed above share with rice-growing communities everywhere. These is a dependence on adequate sources of water, a reliance on an ample supply of intensive labor, and a secure access to numerous rice varieties with different properties. As we

---

[14] Jolly and Michigan State University, Dept. of Agricultural Economics 1988, 23.
[15] Jolly et al. 1985
[16] Newman et al. 1987, 1–4.
[17] Duruflé 1994, 111.
[18] Martin and Crawford 1991.

have seen, however, the amount of precipitation varied considerably after the end of the 1960s, and in many years was insufficient to produce a satisfactory crop. One of the principal problems was that the decline in rainfall was not consistent. Here and there a year with adequate precipitation occurred, keeping farmers' hopes alive. To this day, good and bad years are interspersed. Thus, in 2007, Casamance granaries were empty[19] whereas in 2009, with more than 1,300 mm of rainfall in the areas near Esudadu, production was three times the previous figure, or 2.5 tons/hectare versus 1.5 tons/hectare.[20]

With regards to labor, the flight of the youth to the cities has caused severe shortages in the countryside. However, Jola communities differ profoundly among themselves in the time-depth of their engagement with migration, in the kinds of individuals who migrate, and in the rate at which migrants return to their home villages during the rainy season to participate in agricultural activities. In all cases, turn-around migration mitigates the negative effects of urban migration by returning some of the labor force to the countryside during crucial stages in the agricultural cycle. In Jipalom there is a veritable tradition of what Lambert has called "the culture of migration."[21] In my 1965 records, for example, 33 unmarried girls, and 34 unmarried boys, or roughly one-third of the labor force was listed as absent from Jipalom during the dry season.[22] Years later, in my 1990 sample of 106 youngsters 90, or 85 percent had left the village to work in nearby or distant cities, and even larger numbers were unemployed. In that same year, only 26 of the 90 youngsters, or 29 percent had returned to Jipalom during the rainy season to help their parents with agricultural work. Doubtless, in all the Kajamutay urban migration has had a significant negative impact on food production. This is clearly seen in the number of rice fields that were left idle for lack of labor.

The migration pattern of the Fatiya inhabitants differs somewhat from that of Jipalom. In 1990 neither of the two men in the elder's generation moved away. In the next generation, out of 28 adult men only 5 (or 18 percent) migrated permanently, 2 of them to rural areas to farm. This contrasts strongly with the situation in Jipalom, where 58 perecnt of this generation had gone away. When we come to the unmarried generation, conditions were similar to those of Jipalom. Of the 54 Fatiya boys and girls in this category, 43 (or 83 percent) had left for near or faraway cities. As elsewhere, the girls who moved to the city were employed as domestics. Of the 12 girls who were so-employed, 7 (or 58 percent) returned to Fatiya in 1990 to help their mothers with work in the rice fields. Among the boys, a much smaller percentage returned: of the 31 who had gone away, only 5 (or 16 percent) returned to help their fathers on that same year.

---

[19] IRIN News 2007.
[20] Sadio 2009.
[21] Lambert 2002.
[22] Linares 2003.

Again, the Sambujat pattern of migration differs from that of the other two aforementioned communities. In my 1990 census, not one of the elder's generation had left the village. In the next or mature men's generation, of the 32 men in the census only 6 (or 19 percent) had left. Interestingly, three (or half) of the migrants in this generation eventually returned to their natal village. With the unmarried or youth of both sexes migration began in earnest. All of the 102 youth in the census migrated during the dry season. In 1990, 52 percent of the boys, and 63 percent of the girls had returned during the rainy season to help their parents with agricultural work. Even though enough youngsters had returned to Sambujat to keep most rice fields nominally under cultivation, repairs to the big dike had been neglected. Under the constant pounding of unusually high tides the main dike, which protects the most productive rice fields, broke down in several places and salty water inundated an immense area just after it had been transplanted upon. Not only was that year's rice crop completely ruined but it will also take many years for the weng fields to be made cultivable again. Several rainy seasons are necessary to desalinate the affected parcels by flushing out the salts with fresh water. Thus, the absence of rural labor finally took its toll, and what was once a very productive rice system may never recover.

It is also interesting to note how the gender division of labor also affected productivity among these communities. I have argued elsewhere that, where men and women are out working in the fields from the first rains, cooperating in the preparation and seeding of the rice crop, as in Sambujat, or, conversely, where men and women work separately in their plateau and rice fields from the beginning, as in Fatiya, returns to labor are quite sufficient even during a foreshortened season.[23] Conversely, where women must wait until the men ridge and furrow their fields before they direct seed or transplant, as in Jipalom, returns to labor are roughly half.

To conclude, I have tried to show how a multitude of factors determine the disparate ways in which local Jola communities have coped with natural disasters such as drought. In doing so, I have emphasized the impact of exogenous forces as well as the workings out of social and cultural institutions. Theirs is the story of how the effects of adverse climatic conditions and ill-directed economic policies came to be felt in different ways and variable intensities within different regions and various communities. But it is also a chronicle of courage, ingenuity, and the ability to turn adversity around by adopting new crops such as maize and manioc, by trying out alternative forms of technology such as ox-plows, and by practicing new forms of temporary labor relations.

[23] Linares 1997.

11

Of Health and Harvests: Seasonal Mortality and Commercial Rice Cultivation in the Punjab and Bengal Regions of South Asia

Lauren Minsky

This chapter turns on a central paradox of the modern world: hunger, malnutrition, and disease severely haunt the people who produce the staple food grains that nourish and sustain the world's population. Related to this paradox is a second: that the health experiences of food grain producers are afforded considerably less attention than those of the consumers they feed. Histories of rice, as wheat and maize, tend to skirt the disease challenges faced by those producing them. And, when studies do turn to questions of cultivators' health, they typically posit deterministic formulations between particular ecologies, crops, and diseases – associating, for instance, the humid tropics with rice, and rice, in turn, with diseases like malaria and cholera simply by virtue of its being a "wet" crop.

This volume, then, provides a valuable opportunity to work toward developing a more complete and nuanced understanding of historical patterns of morbidity and mortality in agrarian regions that are central to global rice production and supply. In this exploratory spirit, I pursue a comparative and interdisciplinary analysis of the lived health experiences of rice cultivators in Punjab and Bengal – regions at opposite ends and ecological extremes of South Asia's Indo-Gangetic plain – during the nineteenth and early twentieth century. I find that in both regions a series of environmental changes were connected to an expansion and intensification in the production of high-input varieties of rice (among other crops) that were desired by urban and foreign consumers. Although regionally and even sub-regionally specific, these environmental changes ultimately led Punjabi and Bengali rice cultivators alike to experience a marked rise in disease morbidity during the principal commercial harvest seasons. Additionally, in both regions the dramatic increase in commodity production for global markets was accompanied by a concurrent increase in social inequality, as manifested in a growing disparity in entitlements to land and food and in the distribution of harvest labor and caloric demands. In this context, preharvest seasonal hunger, malnutrition, and immunological vulnerability became significant features of agrarian life, and rates of harvest mortality, and not simply morbidity, rose to record levels.

The analysis offered here ultimately contributes to a growing body of historical, social science, and biological scholarship[1] that questions both ecologically deterministic models for explaining the global distribution of hunger and disease in the modern world,[2] and mainstream approaches to agrarian development that promote commercial production for global markets as the best means for "growing out" of high rates of morbidity and mortality.[3] It also draws into question the practice of framing public health studies and interventions in terms of single, bio-medically defined diseases and exceptional epidemic and famine episodes. As this comparative study illustrates, Punjabi and Bengali rice producers "grew into," not "out of," routine struggles with sickness and hunger that were highly seasonal in nature, social in origin, and predictable in occurrence.

CULTIVATING A COMMERCIAL LANDSCAPE

Watered by rivers that originate in the Himalayas and flow eastward into the Bay of Bengal and westward into the Arabian Sea, the Indo-Gangetic plain is one of the largest alluvial expanses in the world. The plain is also notable because it stretches across a major climatic and ecological frontier that is widely seen as separating "the people of wheat" in semiarid and arid northwestern Asia and the Middle East from "the people of rice" in the wet tropics of southeast and eastern Asia. At its westernmost end lies Punjab, a semiarid region whose inhabitants rely upon a fickle two month monsoon during July and August coupled with the flooding of the Indus river and its major tributaries – the Jhelum, Chenab, Ravi, Satlej, and Beas – for successful cultivation (Figure P.1b). To the eastern extreme is Bengal, a humid region watered by both inundations from the Ganga-Brahmaputra-Meghna river system and a long and heavy rainy season lasting for four to six months.[4]

These ecological differences shaped the longue durée process of agricultural expansion in each region. In ancient Bengal, cultivators first settled higher parts of the seasonally inundated lowlands, where rice thrived as a crop, and later moved into both drier uplands and swampy lowlands along the coast where silt deposition continually formed new shoreline and island constellations. Adapting to such wetter environments required peasants to experiment with new strains of rice and systems of cultivation, while in drier ones peasants

---

[1] Komlos 1995; Komlos 1998; Feierman and Janzen 1992; Klein 2001; Guha 2001; McCann 2007; Packard, 2007; Bassino and Coclanis 2008; Cook et al. 2009; Samanta 2002; Iqbal 2010.
[2] Diamond 1999.
[3] Sachs 2005.
[4] Ludden 1999, 49–52.

incorporated wheat, millets, and pulses into their cropping regime. In Punjab, on the other hand, cultivation during ancient and medieval times moved steadily from seasonally inundated riverine tracts into arid uplands, and from the north and east where rainfall and flooding were heaviest to the increasingly sandy southwest. For much of the plains, harnessing sufficient water for cultivation posed a significant challenge, and peasants selected varieties of wheat, barley, millet, and rice that could withstand a fickle and often scarce supply. In both regions, agricultural frontiers were also shifting, as rivers changed their course on account of a complex combination of upstream deforestation, erosion, and siltation. Perhaps the most striking example is Bengal's river Ganga, which migrated eastward over the course of centuries until it eventually joined the Brahmaputra river during the eighteenth century.[5]

Yet as powerful as ecological factors were in shaping the early spread of agriculture, the inhabitants of both regions labored hard over the course of centuries to overcome these constraints. In thirteenth-century Punjab, for instance, nomadic pastoralists first adopted Persian wheel and *charas* (rope and leather bucket) technologies so that they could run deep wells for watering their herds and cultivating crops in the arid uplands.[6] Punjab's late medieval Tughluq and early modern Mughal and Sikh rulers also built enormous irrigation canals to extend cultivation into arid areas. Those with sufficient means, or those pooling resources, constructed seasonal inundation canals, as well as ponds and tanks to capture monsoon rainfall and extend cultivation.[7] Meanwhile, in medieval and early modern Bengal, rulers supported the construction of a variety of embankments, inundation and drainage channels, and tanks. These works were designed to control flooding and to maximize and regularize the reach of seasonal inundations and monsoon rainfall. They also ensured the fresh and sweet quality of water along the coast by preventing an influx of saline water from the sea.[8]

Such water-control works contributed not only to a steady expansion of agriculture, but to its growing diversification, intensification, and commercialization as well. In Punjab, peasant and tenant cultivators increasingly practiced *do-fasla* (double-cropping) by planting in succession crops that would ripen during the monsoon-fed *kharif* (autumn) harvest and the *rabi* (spring) harvest.[9] By the seventeenth century, irrigated rice – a crop dating to ca. 2000 to 1500 BCE in the region – had become second to wheat in commercial importance, and cotton, indigo, opium, and sugarcane were also prominent cash crops.[10] In Bengal, water-control technologies likewise

---

[5] Ludden 1999, 49–52.
[6] Singh 1985, 73–88.
[7] Grewal 2004, 6; Siddiqui 1986, 53–72.
[8] Kamal 2006, 194–9; Iqbal 2010, 40.
[9] Habib 2000, 27, 39–62.
[10] Grewal 2004, 4–6; Singh 1991, 107–9, 213–17.

enabled cultivators to intensify production such that rice became a major commercial export. As the Dutchman John Huyghen van Linschoten reported in 1506, Bengal "is most plentiful of necessary victuals, specially rice, for that there is more of it [in that country] than in all the East, for they do yearly lade divers shippes [therewith], which come thether from all places, and there is never any want thereof...."[11]

This trend toward agricultural commercialization expanded and accelerated at an unprecedented rate, and to an unprecedented degree, during the transition to capitalist empire under British colonial rule.[12] The East India Company (EIC), followed by the British Crown, sought to expand, intensify, and control commercial production across South Asia to serve British interests, beginning in coastal regions and later extending into the interior.[13] Toward this end, in 1793 the British instituted a permanent settlement in Bengal that at least theoretically concentrated power in the hands of large landlord revenue collectors, whom they hoped would enhance commercial production. They also invested in the construction of large embankments, canals, and an extensive network of raised railways to transport produce to the central markets of Calcutta. Additionally, the British promoted the ongoing clearing of forest and extension of the agricultural frontier and commercial production into eastern Bengal, where the river delta was most active.[14] The initial focus was the cultivation of indigo, but following a crash in indigo stocks on the London exchange jute was instead favored and ultimately became the region's leading commercial export during the late nineteenth and early twentieth century. Opium production also soared, while cotton, silk, and sugarcane cultivation, primarily destined for British or Chinese consumpion, rose as well.[15] It was in this wider context that Bengali rice, too, saw a substantial increase in production for global markets.[16] By the 1820s, rice exports from Bengal occupied a major share of northern European rice markets.[17] By 1912–13, exports of husked rice from Bengal reached a remarkable 10,099,692 cwts, with much of it headed to Ceylon (Sri Lanka), Britain, France, Germany, Mauritius, East Africa, South America, the West Indies, and Arabia.[18]

Although Punjab came under British rule several decades later than Bengal, the region experienced an even more dramatic expansion and intensification in commercial production for global markets during the colonial period. Here the British were especially determined to bring the region's vast and rich

---

[11] Watt 1891, 524.
[12] Richards et al. 1985.
[13] Bose 1993; Chaudhuri 1996; Ludden 1999; Subrahmanyam and Bayly 1988.
[14] Iqbal 2010, 18–26.
[15] B. Chaudhuri 1983, 315–25.
[16] Datta 1996, 109.
[17] Coclanis 1993b, 1057, 1067.
[18] Latham and Neal 1983, 263.

Of Health and Harvests

alluvial, but extremely arid, soils under cultivation – eliminating what they saw as "waste-land" in the west and southeast. Shortly after assuming formal control in 1858, they proceeded to settle cultivators' rights in land and invested in re-aligning and expanding the Mughal-era western Jumna canal in the arid southeastern plains.[19] During the 1870s, the British additionally began constructing an enormous network of perennial canals and promoting the settlement of new canal colonies in the arid uplands of western Punjab where nomadic pastoralism still predominated. New settlers, lured by the promise of land and tax incentives, were recruited from the densely populated and intensively cultivated areas in the northeast and central parts of the region.[20] By 1927, over 10 million acres had been added to the total cultivable area of Punjab.[21] Fed by massive canals and transported along an extensive network of newly constructed railways to urban market centers like Lahore, Karachi, and Delhi, commercial varieties of wheat became the principal spring crop in the region; similarly, autumn crops of rice, maize, sugarcane, cotton, and tobacco all assumed a growing percentage of the autumn harvest. The export of agricultural produce from the region, especially wheat and cotton, soared, with most of it destined for British and western European consumers.[22]

By the early twentieth century, export-oriented commercial agriculture was a central feature of agrarian production at both ends of the Indo-Gangetic plain. This trajectory was not a linear one, however. The sharp upward trend from 1880 until 1915 in prices for agricultural produce from India was primarily driven by demand from consumers in Europe. It was also shaped by the declining value of the rupee, which had the effect of raising prices for produce within British India as well.[23] World War I and the 1920s, on the other hand, was a time of significant instability in global prices and European consumers' demand, while the worldwide Great Depression of the 1930s was a time of marked declines in consumption and in prices paid for agricultural produce. As prices fell, the production of non-food crops like cotton and jute was especially affected, but prices of wheat and rice, among other food grain crops, also fell.[24] The protection of internal markets emerged as a central concern among Indian nationalists.[25]

Following World War II and independence from colonial rule in 1947, another boom in commercial food grain production occurred. Massive dams and canals were built to increase commercial production across the

---

[19] Government of India, 1908, 202–14.
[20] Ali 1988.
[21] Fox 1985, 53.
[22] Charlesworth and Economic History Society 1982, 26.
[23] K. N. Chaudhuri 1983, 851–4.
[24] McAlpin 1983, 880–91.
[25] Ludden 1999, 167.

Indo-Gangetic plains for purposes of both national food security and foreign export. During the Green Revolution of the 1960s and 1970s, high-yield varieties of rice that could be double-cropped with wheat were also introduced. This was especially the case in the canal-irrigated parts of Punjab, partitioned between India and Pakistan, which went from being a net rice importer to become a world leading rice, as well as wheat, producing region. Bengal, partitioned between India and East Pakistan/Bangladesh, also saw not only its rice yields increase but also its wheat production.[26] The subsequent adoption of neoliberal reforms during the 1990s provided yet another major push toward production for global markets – one that continues to the present day, albeit with growing resistance partly grounded in the environmental and health consequences of high-input irrigation and chemical fertilizer and pesticide use. While ecology indeed matters, to read a strict and timeless "wheat-rice" dichotomy onto the Indo-Gangetic plain's geography is to ignore a long history of efforts to reshape its landscape for commercial purposes.

CULTIVATING HARVEST SICKNESS

The story of how Bengal and Punjab's health environments were shaped by commercial production is also a long one that well pre-dates the Green Revolution. Well before the advent of high-yield varieties of crops and chemical additives, the cultivation of lucrative produce – including the particular "delicate" varieties of rice preferred by affluent urbanites and foreigners – required significantly greater water, fertilizer, and labor inputs to grow than did subsistence varieties. In turn, environmental changes connected to the practice of intensive, high-input commercial agriculture led to rising rates of disease morbidity during the principal spring and autumn commercial harvest seasons in both regions. This commercial cultivation of seasonal sickness became especially evident during the late nineteenth and early twentieth century boom in export-oriented commercial agriculture.

In Punjab, this rapid expansion and intensification of commercial production during the 1870s to the 1920s caused environmental changes that profoundly affected cultivators' health. Most of the rice that was grown in Punjab during these years was for commercial sale and consisted of copiously manured, -irrigated, and -weeded, "first-class" autumn varieties of *Oryza sativa*, including basmati, which were harvested in October and November and destined for export. A much smaller percentage consisted of "second-class" coarse and early-ripening *bhadoi* (late summer) varieties of *Oryza glutinosa* that were produced with few inputs and harvested in late August-September for local and regional consumption by cultivators and laborers.

---

[26] Govind 1986, 56–71.

Other prominent cash crops grown in the region, including wheat, cotton, and sugarcane, similarly required substantial time spent manuring, weeding, and irrigating relative to regional food staples like barley, sorghum, and gram.[27]

On account of the inputs required, Punjabis referred to rice, sugarcane, cotton, and wheat as "heating" crops – and, in point of fact, the cultivation of these crops did "heat" the region's landscape and its inhabitants over time.[28] The use of heavy irrigation created large ponds of stagnant water throughout much of the late summer/early autumn growing season. In addition, heavy and sustained irrigation contributed to a significant rise in the sub-soil water table level. The high embankments that flanked large irrigation canals and elevated railways also blocked the natural northeastern to southwestern drainage flow across much of the landscape. Consequently, when the summer monsoon arrived, the rainfall was neither absorbed into the soil nor naturally drained. Instead, enormous *jhils*, tracts of flooded and water-logged lands, formed in the most commercialized tracts of Punjab each year during late-summer and autumn.[29]

Such widespread surface flooding, in turn, created new ecological niches for species of anopheles mosquitoes to breed in Punjab's uplands, where malaria previously had but a tenuous presence. The relatively arid nature of the region's uplands, coupled with the migratory practices of small groups of nomadic pastoralists who inhabited such lands and the protection provided by zooprophylaxis, had long prevented the spread of malaria out from inundated and more densely populated riverine tracts, where the disease had ancient origins.[30] However, with the widespread cultivation of intensively irrigated crops like rice, this changed, and particularly lethal species of anopheles mosquitoes colonized Punjab's upland tracts. Among these were *An. culicifacies*, which came to be the most important rural vector of malaria in Punjab. It was an efficient transmitter of both P. *vivax* and P. *falciparum* plasmodium and it bred in a variety of clean and polluted bodies of still or lightly moving water in areas of slight rainfall, including river beds, irrigation ditches, rice fields, swamp pools, wells, borrow pits, and the edges of canals. *An. Stephensi* was another efficient vector of malaria in Punjab. It predominated in urban settlements, and was also a flexible breeder, laying eggs in still river beds, wells, cisterns, empty containers, roof gutters, hoof prints of animals, and rice fields. Both of these species of anopheles, along with others like *An. rossi* and *An. Fuliginosus*, experienced a tremendous expansion in habitat as cash crop irrigation and seasonal flooding expanded across the Punjabi landscape.[31]

---

[27] Watt 1891, 619–621.
[28] Kurin 1983a, 285; Kurin 1983b, 65–75.
[29] Klein 2001, 170–3; Agnihotri 1996, 37–59.
[30] Webb 2009, 45–6, 52–3.
[31] Learmonth 1957, 38–41; Klein 2001, 170–3.

The highly seasonal nature of flooding and mosquito breeding in Punjab's uplands also contributed to the severity with which cultivators experienced malaria. Flooding occurred during and immediately following the monsoon, such that the transmission of malaria was discontinuous throughout the year.[32] Spleen counts conducted by colonial epidemiologists revealed that malaria morbidity first appeared each year during August and September. Malaria mortality subsequently peaked during the labor-intensive autumn cotton and rice harvesting months of October and November and continued through the months of December and January when sugarcane was cut, after which it tapered off.[33] As a result, even adults who were annually exposed to P. *vivax* and P. *falciparum* by mosquito bites lost some of their acquired immunity during the following spring and summer months and became susceptible again by the following autumn. The growing population densities in the most irrigated and commercialized Punjabi uplands also likely enabled deadly P. *falciparum* to establish reservoirs of infection relative to the disabling (but seldom lethal) P. *vivax* that had long predominated in the region.[34]

As commercial production of rice, along with wheat, cotton, and sugarcane among other high-input commercial crops, soared during the late nineteenth and early twentieth century, malaria became the leading cause of debility and death in Punjab.[35] The overall annual fever death rate (comprised largely but not exclusively of malaria) even exceeded that of every other region of British India, including Bengal. Mortality rates ranged from approximately 10 to 20 per thousand in average years to between 20 to 30 per thousand during years deemed epidemic, which included 1876, 1878, 1879, 1884, 1890, 1892, 1900, and, above all, 1908, a year in which the most severe epidemic in the region's history claimed the lives of approximately 300,000 over the course of a few short months.[36] Malaria also came to be characterized by an epidemic area that neatly mapped onto the most intensively cultivated and commercialized subregions of Punjab's plains: the heavily rain-fed submontane region; the northern riverine tracts where substantial inundations and flooding occurred; and the uplands of the central, western, and southeastern plains where enormous perennial canals enabled intensive irrigated commercial production (Figure 11.1).[37]

In response, producers living in this epidemic zone petitioned the colonial government to prohibit the cultivation of heavily irrigated commercial crops on the grounds that they caused waterlogging and were injurious to their

---

[32] Packard 2007, 96.
[33] Christophers 1911, 6–1; Gill 1928, 64–5.
[34] Christophers and Bentley 1911; Christophers 1924.
[35] Das 1943, 170–2.
[36] Gill 1928, 58–61; Klein 2001, 170–2.
[37] Christophers 1911, 24–6; Gill 1928, 192–8, 525, and appendix III.

Of Health and Harvests 253

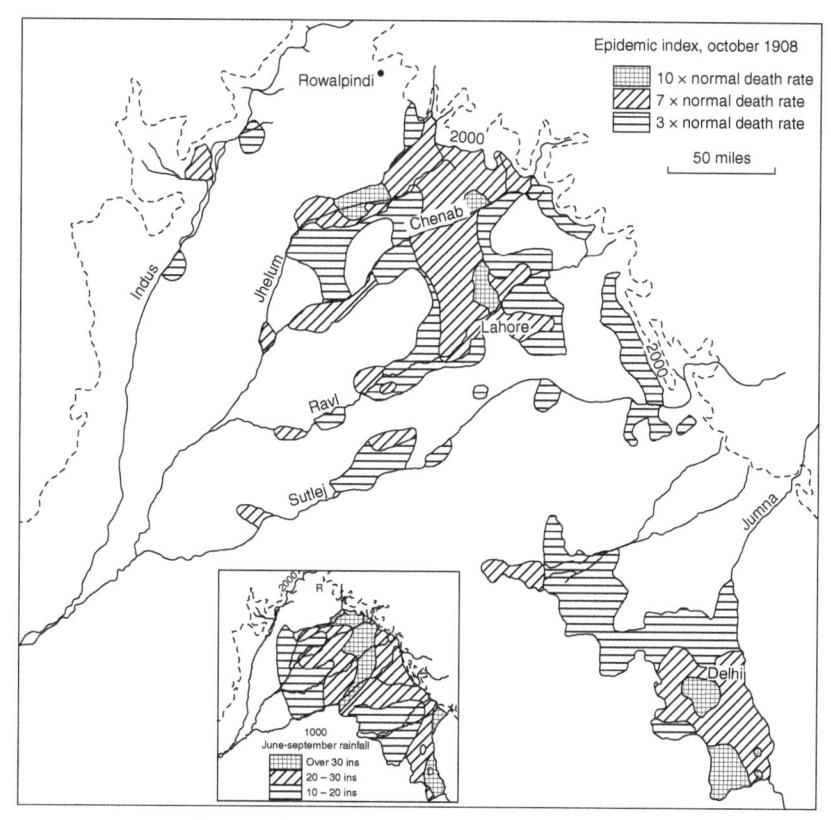

FIGURE 11.1. Death rates during the 1908 Malaria epidemic in Punjab, after S. R. Christopher's (1911) Maps I and IV, in A. T. A. Learmonth, "Some Contrasts in the Regional Geography of Malaria in India and Pakistan," in *Transactions and Papers (Institute of British Geographers)*, No. 23, (1957).

health. At times, they were successful in winning the support of local officials who had come to share their understanding. For instance, upon receiving petitions from villagers along the Hansi branch of the Western Jumna canal in the southeastern plains, A. Anderson, the Deputy Commissioner of Hissar wrote in 1890 that:

> I now beg to make definite the proposal that from the commencement of the agricultural year 1891–2 the irrigation of rice be prohibited in this district [...] It is admitted on all hands that the rice irrigation carried to excess is the cause of the water-logged state of the villages [...] The people themselves have admitted that rice irrigation is the cause, and whole villages have recently presented petitions to me to get it stopped [...].[38]

---

[38] Government of Punjab, Home Department Proceedings, Medical and Sanitary Branch, December 1890, no. 6, 95.

Similarly, Colonial L. J. H. Grey, Commissioner and Superintendent of Delhi Division, strongly endorsed petitions he received from cultivators along the main Western Jumna Canal, arguing that "If Government could be induced to refuse irrigation to rice and sugarcane in the villages you mention, men, cattle, and land would soon recover [from waterlogging and fever]."[39]

The expansion of irrigated commercial cultivation, including that of rice, also profoundly shaped the distribution and severity of malaria in Bengal. As in Punjab, not all of Bengal's rice varieties were of equal appeal to urban and foreign consumers and not all required the same amount of inputs. *Aush* (summer) varieties of rice required little in the way of inputs and were primarily grown to secure landowning cultivators' own subsistence and for sale to landless laborers. The seeds were sown broadcast following the initial spring showers in April to May on high sandy lands that were watered only by the summer monsoon. Quick-ripening in a period of 100 to 120 days, the mature grains were ultimately harvested in July or September.[40] The coarse and hard *boro* (spring) varieties of Bengali rice were similarly considered "self-sustaining." Unlike the summer varieties, however, these were grown on low-lying, naturally marshy, and deeply flooded lands, such as those found in the eastern coastal mangroves where strong river currents prevented saline water from entering inland. The spring varieties, which could withstand as much as 10 feet of water and intense heat, were typically transplanted from seed beds or sown broadcast between December and February and subsequently harvested in April-May.[41] Together, these "coarse" spring and summer varieties constituted the principal foods of the region's cultivators and laborers.[42]

Only the most commercially lucrative, late autumn/winter *aman* varieties of rice required significant water control for its successful cultivation. Winter rice – which, in contrast to the spring and summer varieties, consisted of several long, fragrant, and easily digestible forms that were in considerable demand on global markets – was preferentially grown on lands in the eastward-shifting active Delta that received seasonal river inundations and fertilizing silt depositions.[43] Here cultivators constructed paddies surrounded by bunds and inundation/drainage channels that could either confine or release water to protect their crops against flooding. While some autumn crops were sown broadcast, especially those grown in fields mixed with quick-ripening summer rice, most were seeded in nurseries and subsequently transplanted to paddies as each band around the fields was softened by the

---

[39] Government of Punjab, Home Department Proceedings, Medical and Sanitary Branch, December 1890, no. 6, 93.
[40] Watt 1891, 530; Iqbal 2010, 42.
[41] Iqbal 2010, 40.
[42] Mukherjee 1938, 51-4.
[43] Watt 1891, 556; Mukherjee and University of Calcutta 1938, 51-3.

Of Health and Harvests

rainfall and controlled river inundations. Gradually, over the course of the monsoon, the paddies steadily swelled until water covered all of the active Delta's landscape, excepting narrow elevated belts along the river-banks themselves where villages were situated.[44] Bengal's other major commercial crops, including jute, indigo, and sugarcane, were also "thirsty" crops that were grown in this same season and prone to damage from either too little or too much water. Jute, additionally, required soaking in stagnant pools of water for about two weeks before the fiber could be extracted.[45]

Fortuitously for commercial producers' health, however, when fields in the expansive delta were flooded by river inundations, the breeding of malaria vectors was largely suppressed. In Bengal, the most prevalent and efficient carrier of malaria parasites was *An. phillipinensis*, a species that preferred cattle to human blood and that bred well in the grassy edge of water collections and in temperatures below 80°F, such as that typically found in shaded tanks, pools, borrow-pits, and ditches with clear water. It most decidedly did not breed well in warm autumn fields containing silty river water.[46] Other efficient malaria vectors in Bengal, such as *An. varuna* and *An. fuliginosus*, also preferred clean, non-silty, and still collections of water for their breeding.[47] Consequently, where paddy fields were inundated by rivers, the available water edge was too small and the water too deep, silty, and warm for the region's predominant anopheles varieties to breed.[48] River inundations also flushed out mosquito larvae that had been laid beforehand and introduced predatory fish like carp. Lastly, unlike Punjab, in Bengal parasite transmission occurred throughout a much longer period of the year given the wetter environs. Due to their constant exposure, by the age of five Bengalis residing in endemic zones had typically acquired a significant and relatively permanent level of resistance to the disease.[49]

However, as Bengali cultivators increasingly sought to produce valuable winter rice, along with jute and other cash crops, the region's landscape changed in ways that greatly affected the prevalence of malaria. For one, the practice of non-inundated autumn rice cultivation outside of the active delta necessarily depended upon monsoon rainfall, which provided exactly the kinds of fresh, yet unsilty, and still tanks and paddy fields in which *An. phillipinensis* liked to breed.[50] Within the active delta, cultivators constructed bunds to contain water for paddies on higher ground and to prevent

---

[44] Watt 1891, 531–56.
[45] Samanta 2002, 29.
[46] Learmonth 1957, 41.
[47] Government of Bengal 1929, 3–5; Learmonth 1957, 38.
[48] Government of Bengal 1929, 13.
[49] Christophers 1924, 273–94.
[50] Government of Bengal 1929, 13; Klein 2001, 168.

floods from damaging those on lower grounds. Additionally, investors built a network of railway tracks – designed to move winter rice, jute, and other cash crops to Calcutta's markets – on high embankments to secure them from flood damage. All of these man-made efforts at water control to boost commercial productivity effectively blocked the natural seasonal flooding and recession of water and, with it, the annual "flushing out" of mosquito larvae that kept malaria in check after each monsoon. Long-standing inundation/drainage channels also began to silt up and to collect pools of water.[51]

By the nineteenth century, large tracts of land became so waterlogged during the annual monsoon inundation of rainfall and riverine flooding that they were transformed into stagnant swamps. These changes were especially pronounced in the intensively cultivated and densely populated western and central subregions of Bengal. Here, due to the gradual shifting of the Ganga river to the east, the delta was no longer active, and cultivators necessarily relied more heavily on irrigation works to produce cash crops. Moreover, in eastern Bengal the expanding agricultural frontier meant that the cultivation of winter rice and jute before 1920 was more extensive than intensive in nature. It was also in the southwestern plains that the densest network of embanked canals, including the Calcutta and Eastern canals, and railways was initially constructed. Bengal's railway network was later extended from its central hub in Calcutta into the eastern and northern plains during the late nineteenth and early twentieth century, thereby delaying the development of drainage problems and severe malaria epidemics in the east by several decades.[52]

During the 1820s through the 1880s, devastating epidemics of malaria struck portions of western and central Bengal that had previously been considered largely free of the disease.[53] Areas where commercial rice cultivation was most intensive, reliant upon irrigation works, and served by embanked railways were among the worst affected.[54] During the 1870s, malaria was estimated to affect 75 percent of the inhabitants of villages in western Bengal and to kill approximately 25 percent of its population, with most deaths occurring during the postmonsoon harvest months of August through December when waterlogging was severe and winter rice and jute were reaped.[55] As of 1911, spleen count data indicated that out of a provincial population of roughly 45 million, about 30 million people were afflicted

---

[51] Bentley and Public Health Department of Bengal 1925, 65–7; Iqbal 2010, 117–39.
[52] Roy 1876, 26–35; Bentley and Public Health Department of Bengal 1925, 28–9, 30–4, 48–55; Iyengar 1928, 12–14; Mukherjee 1938, 47–8, 68–72, 80–1; Klein 2001, 167–9; Iqbal 2010, 117–39.
[53] Klein 2001, 161–3; Samanta 2002, 74–113; Packard 2007, 4.
[54] Klein 2001, 164–5; Iqbal 2010, 43.
[55] Klein 2001, 162; Samanta 2002, 76.

with malaria, and of these, about 10 million severely so.[56] In western Bengal, there were an estimated 8 million cases out of a population of just under 8.5 million; in central Bengal, 8.4 million cases from just under 9.5 million; and in eastern Bengal, 5 million cases out of more than 17 million.[57] Between 1916 and 1934, the western and central subregions became even more "intensely malarious" and also expanded in size.[58] While eastern Bengal was increasingly affected, a 1938 study of malaria still found that the east largely consisted of "healthy plains" (with spleen rates less than 10 percent), while the disease was in a state of moderate to high endemicity of a more or less static character in the west, and a large portion in the central plains was so severely affected as to be declared hyper-endemic (Figure 11.2).[59]

As significant as post-monsoon, autumn episodes of malaria became in both Bengal and Punjab, commercial rice cultivators' lived health experiences were never reducible to this disease. Cash crops also demanded intensive fertilizing, and the provision of this input profoundly affected Bengalis' and Punjabis' health, as well. Historically, the most lucrative crops in both regions were sown in tracts that received seasonal inundations containing not only river water, but also highly fertilizing silt, fish to consume weeds and insect larvae, and sufficient water to inhibit weed growth. However, whenever cultivators practiced irrigated agriculture in uplands outside the reach of river inundations or saw the deposition of silt on their fields impeded due to embankments of some kind, they faced a predicament. As the Judicial Assistant Commissioner of Gurdaspur, Muhammad Hayat Khan explained during the late 1870s:

[i]t is an undisputed fact that a good crop depends upon the natural heat and moisture of the soil, and that if any of these two properties is exhausted, the land loses its productive power; hence the land which is properly manured and watered produces a good crop, while the land which is constantly watered but not manured, does not do so. The reason for this is that the moisture is increased by constant watering, but in the absence of the natural heat is soon absorbed.[60]

The unequivocal advice to all upland cultivators was: "[w]heat, sugarcane, maize and every other crop come to nothing without manure, don't forget this."[61]

Cultivators responded to the need for fertilizer by adopting a range of practices. They burned leftover straw and ploughed the ashes into the soil after each harvest. Nitrogen-fixing and fertility-restoring pulses and oil-seeds were deliberately included in crop rotations. With respect to rice, Punjabis

---

[56] Klein 2001, 168.
[57] Bentley and Public Health Department of Bengal 1925, 100–3.
[58] Mukherjee 1938, 212.
[59] Learmonth 1957, 38.
[60] Government of Punjab 1878–9, 311.
[61] Ram 1920, 23.

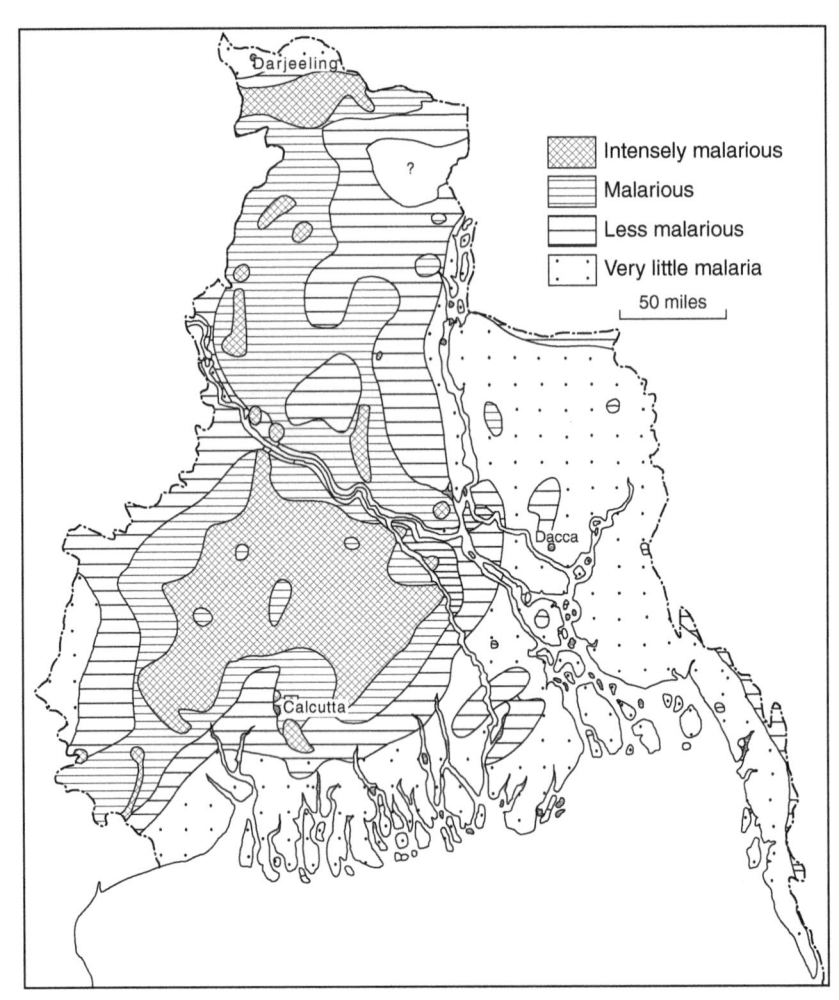

FIGURE 11.2. Malaria distribution in Bengal, after C. A. Bentley (1916) in A. T. A. Learmonth, "Some Contrasts in the Regional Geography of Malaria in India and Pakistan," in *Transactions and Papers (Institute of British Geographers)*, No. 23, (1957).

scattered the leaves and twigs of *basuti* (Adhatoda vasica) – an evergreen bush that was widely used to treat skin, eye, reproductive tract, and respiratory infections in humans – over recently flooded fields both as a form of green manure and as a medicine to kill off injurious aquatic weeds. The leaves and branches of *toon* (Cedrula toona), *neem* (Melia azadirachta), and *ak* (Calotropis gigantea) were similarly employed in Punjab as green manure. Bengalis, meanwhile, left the roots of a previous harvest to rot in the ground or burned the stubble to ashes as fertilizer for their *aman* rice. They also used the green grasses that sprouted in paddies as both a form of manure and a prophylaxis against the rice disease *kadamara;* in some places they also fertilized the soil by ploughing oil-cakes into their fields just before transplanting seedlings. Where land served year-round as paddy – typically to produce both an early summer and a late autumn/winter crop – Bengali cultivators additionally benefited from the presence of algae and aquatic plants which fixed nitrogen to the soil.[62]

However, it was cultivators' growing reliance upon livestock and human refuse as fertilizer that had significant health consequences. As irrigated commercial agriculture developed outside of riverine tracts, cultivators entered into contractual arrangements with nomadic pastoralists, who were invited to graze their livestock on leftover straw in exchange for the fertilizing dung they deposited and worked into the soil. Cultivators also grazed their own livestock on fields and defecated themselves on lands dedicated to their most valuable commercial crops. During the dramatic expansion and intensification of commercial production during the British colonial period, however, the demand for and use of dung as fertilizer increased dramatically. In colonial Punjab, "first-class" rice nurseries, along with sugarcane and cotton fields, were "highly" manured with dung, while the fields into which rice was transplanted were "manured to a limited extent also."[63] Fields dedicated to the cultivation of commercial wheat received substantial quantities of dung as well. Meanwhile in Bengal, the use of manure also grew. While rice crops depend primarily on adequate water supplies for most of its nutrients, the deposition of silt and rotting vegetation left by the seasonal inundations was critical.[64] Cultivators working lands outside of the active Delta, who were increasingly deprived of silt, began to regularly manure both the nursery plots where they grew winter rice seedlings and their jute fields with dung.[65] By the early 1900s, Bengalis in the interfluvial Hooghly-Damudar tract of central Bengal also reportedly applied dung at the rate of 20 baskets per *bigah* (roughly 1/3 acre) to their winter rice fields.[66]

As the demand for dung grew over the course of the nineteenth and early twentieth century, cultivators struggled to procure a sufficient supply. In Punjab, the especially rapid expansion of agriculture into the arid western and southeastern plains during the 1870s–1920s meant that nomadic pastoralism declined markedly, and that there were far fewer herds of sheep, goats, and camels available to graze over straw and directly fertilize fields. In Bengal, where there had never been the same degree of extensive nomadic pastoralism, the livestock population per capita was far lower to start. Consequently, although "[t]he raiyat [peasant] everywhere admits that the

---

[62] References of this paragraph are from Watt 1891, 543, 548, 555–8, 615–18.
[63] Watt 1891, 615.
[64] Datta 1996, 101–2.
[65] Watt 1891, 554–64.
[66] Watt 1891, 557.

application of cattle manure to the paddy fields is beneficial and peasants somewhat better off do use it and get better crops than their neighbours [...] the raiyat's stock is too limited to spare manure for transplanted rice, though he manures the nurseries heavily. Where the population is dense there is, of course, a larger supply of manure, but in no part of India is the natural supply sufficient [...]"[67] Due to fodder famines and devastating rinderpest epidemics, both regions' existing cattle and water buffalo populations also suffered serious declines during the late nineteenth century.[68] The deforestation that accompanied the expansion of agriculture also meant that Punjabis and Bengalis were increasingly reliant upon cow-dung as their primary source of cooking and heating fuel.[69]

In response, producers in both regions labored to cultivate their manure stores. Daily they collected excrement, including not only cattle and buffalo dung but also human nightsoil, and deposited it in heaps next to their huts or within their residential courtyards where it could be guarded.[70] According to Pandit Devi Chand, a Municipal Committee Vice-Chairman writing from Jullundur district in central Punjab in 1917,

[...] people are so fond of manure and similar articles that they would not only accumulate their own manure in their houses, where they live with their families, but would also engage private sweepers to deposit night soil and other kinds of manure in their houses [...] There is not a single village in which one does not meet with heaps and heaps of manure and night-soil, not only in the lanes and streets, but inside the houses of the people.[71]

To both meet and profit from the enormous demand, colonial-era urban conservancy and sewerage systems were also specifically designed and implemented not only out of concerns for "public health" but for the collection, storage, and sale of profitable livestock and human waste to nearby cultivators.[72] In this context, the populous and dense village and town settlements that characterized the most commercialized portions of the plains became extremely important during the colonial period not only as market and manufacturing centers, but also as sites for the production, storage, and distribution of manure.[73]

---

[67] Kenny 1910, 29.
[68] Government of India 1871, iii–xxviii.
[69] Watt 1891, 535; Kenny 1910, 28.
[70] Kenny 1910, 25; Government of Punjab, Home Department Proceedings, General Branch, 13 March 1869, no. 210A, 12; Government of Punjab, Home Department Proceedings, May 1879, 189–90 and 197.
[71] Government of Punjab, Home Department Proceedings, Medical and Sanitary Branch, July 1917, no. 48–50, 93–5.
[72] Government of Punjab 1882; 1884; 1885; 1894; 1895.
[73] Government of Punjab, Home Department Proceedings, Medical and Sanitary Branch, July 1917, no. 48–50, 93–5.

The accumulation and storage of large amounts of refuse in and around human settlements was also coupled with its concentrated application on fields in close proximity to where people lived. Cash crops were preferentially grown where they could be most easily watered, manured, and guarded. This practice was far from benign, however. Disease-causing bacteria, parasites, and viruses were shed in livestock and human waste, especially in the excrement of calves and children. Subsequent microbial survival within manure heaps was dependent upon many factors influencing core temperature and aerobic fermentation including pH, dry matter content, age, chemical composition, and microbial characteristics. Microbial survival was especially likely when the heaps were insufficiently turned, had insufficient dry matter content, were insufficiently aged, and/or did not receive sufficient exposure to sunlight; today scientists estimate that even an acre of cropland manured according to best practices still contains around one ton of bacteria.[74] Certainly, the practice of collecting manure in heaps and applying large quantities to fields around settlements at the same time in the cultivating cycle increased the risk of microbial transmission relative to smaller-scale fertilizing practices. For instance, when cultivating families instead defecated on their fields daily, they both distributed relatively small quantities of organic waste spatially over a large area around their households and ensured that direct exposure to sunlight would inhibit microbial survival and the risk of disease transmission.

Perhaps the gravest consequence of intensive fertilizing practices concerned the spike in gastrointestinal infections that occurred whenever sources of drinking water became contaminated with manure. Such occurrences were especially common during the monsoon season, when cloudy weather limited sunlight and heavy rains washed fresh refuse from the outside layer of manure heaps into inhabitants' water sources, including rivers, canals, tanks, and wells. As one sanitary official described from the central plains: "[there are] large accumulations of stable manure about many houses [...] the deposits are liquefied in the rains, carried by gravitation to distant parts, and thus distributed widely over the surface."[75] Manure applied to fields that had elevated sub-soil water-table levels caused by intensive irrigation also frequently contaminated drinking sources like unlined wells through a process of sub-soil seepage. For instance, in the autumn of 1896 the city of Amritsar's population experienced severe problems with gastrointestinal infections and its wells were found to be contaminated with refuse. Upon investigating the cause, a sanitary official explained

[...]. that the entire line of wells, which are sunk in the bed of an old branch of the Ravi are, on the north side, within 75 feet of land which is under cultivation, highly

---

[74] Kirk 2013, 1–7.
[75] Government of Punjab, Home Department Proceedings, General Branch, 13 March 1869, no. 210A, 12.

manured, and irrigated from wells worked by bullock power; in fact these lands lie on the watershed side of the wells, in the direction of the flow of the sub-soil water, and consequently are liable to pollution by soakage [...] especially as manure is freely employed here with irrigation.[76]

Among the most common contaminants of drinking water pollution were microbes that cross-infected between livestock and humans. These likely included *E. coli, Listeria, Salmonella, Mycobacterium bovis, Mycobacterium paratuberculosis, Cryptosporidiosis, L. monocytogenes, Giardia, Bacilla anthracis*, and *rotaviruses*.[77] Given human nightsoil was increasingly stored and used for manuring purposes by the nineteenth century, however, microbes that only infected humans also grew as a threat.

In this context, cholera, in particular, emerged as a leading cause of gastrointestinal infections in both regions. Historically cholera had only been mildly endemic (or at least discernibly so) in the densely populated flood plains of deltaic Bengal where people periodically consumed infected seafood. However, in 1817 – by which time intensive commercial production of rice, indigo, and other produce for pan-Asian and European markets had exploded – cholera abruptly emerged as a series of severe, multi-year, widespread epidemics in Bengal.[78] It is significant that cholera not only appeared in a serious epidemic form in Bengal at exactly the same time as did malaria, but also in the same subregions – namely the densely populated portions of the central and western plains. Cholera, like malaria, tended to become endemic in places where small tributaries and old inundation/drainage channels had silted up and become stagnant, and where cultivators relied each year upon irrigation works coupled with manure inputs to grow their cash crops. Whereas the cholera bacillus typically survived for an average of 18 hours in the Hooghly (and presumably other large rivers), it lasted four times as long – for an average of 72 hours – in stagnant irrigation tanks that were much smaller in volume and without a moving current.[79] This difference in microbial survival would have held true for a wide array of other microorganisms known to infect the gut of humans, as well.

Cholera morbidity, as with unspecified forms of diarrhea and dysentery, also followed a seasonal pattern that corresponded with the timing of Bengali commercial manuring and harvesting practices. Annually, the first large peak of cholera occurred during March-June when the *kalbaisakhi* (early summer rains) fell and nurseries and fields close to settlements were newly ploughed, manured, and sown in preparation for the autumn harvest crops of *aman* rice and jute.[80] These rains were also light – enough to wash refuse into sources of

---

[76] Government of Punjab 1897, 52.
[77] Kirk 2013, 1–7.
[78] Arnold 1993, 161–3.
[79] Klein 1994, 499, 510–13.
[80] Watt 1891, 533–4.

Of Health and Harvests

drinking water like tanks, wells, and channels, but not enough to dilute or flush them clean. Cases of and deaths from cholera, coupled with other gastrointestinal infections, continued at a significantly lower rate during the intensely rainy summer months, followed by a second marked seasonal peak in mortality during the autumn commercial harvest months in October through December.[81] Ultimately, cholera became such a significant part of Bengal's seasonal health environment that it killed over 3.75 million people during the last quarter of the nineteenth century, when epidemics of the disease peaked in frequency and intensity. An estimated 346,000 died in 1900 alone.[82] During the first two decades of the twentieth century, the disease was reported to routinely kill between 45 and 131 people per thousand annually.[83] Coupled with other kinds of diarrhea and dysentery, gastrointestinal infections were a leading cause of mortality in Bengal.

Over the course of the nineteenth century cholera also spread from Bengal across the intensively cultivated Indo-Gangetic plains, as well as from producers in these regions to the Asian, Middle Eastern, European, and North American consumers of their produce.[84] In Punjab, cholera first appeared as a well-documented epidemic in 1820 when it likely spread via British troops and commercial traders from Bengal as part of a pan-Indian and, ultimately, pan-Asian pandemic during 1817–1821.[85] The disease quickly localized and became endemic in Punjab itself over the course of the nineteenth century.[86] As in Bengal, the most highly commercialized and malarious plains – where heavy irrigation and manure inputs were used – were also the most frequently and severely affected by cholera and constituted the primary endemic loci of this disease. With the opening of the canal colonies and expansion of intensive commercial agricultural production into the western plains, this formerly arid zone of nomadic pastoralism came to be frequently affected by cholera as well.[87] The seasonal incidence of cholera in Punjab also reflected the region's cycle of commercial manuring practices. Specifically, cholera morbidity was tied to the annual "opening up" of manure heaps, and the manuring, ploughing, and sowing of the autumn harvest that occurred in May and June.[88] Rates of cholera mortality subsequently peaked during July, August, and September after monsoon rains washed microbes from fields and manure heaps into drinking water supplies and the summer rice crop was harvested.[89]

---

[81] Jameson and India Medical Department 1820, 1–2; Bryden 1874, 34–8, 59; Bouma and Pascual 2001, 147–56; Bannerjee and Hazra 1974, 27–33.
[82] Klein 1994, 498, 510.
[83] Samanta 2002, 109.
[84] For a critique of this narrative, see Hamlin 2010, 19–51.
[85] Arnold 1993, 161–4.
[86] Klein 1994, 497–99, 505–6.
[87] Government of Punjab 1882, 1–5 and 17–60; 1890a, 5–8; 1890b, 4–5.
[88] Government of Punjab 1889, 8.
[89] Das 1943, 15, 60–1.

Additionally, Bengali and Punjabi cultivators increasingly faced serious infections of the skin, eyes, and reproductive tract during the autumn harvest. Flies routinely bred in manure heaps and transmitted bacteria to people's eyes, causing ophthalmia. Exposure to infectious bacteria also occurred through direct physical contact with manure when ploughing, manuring, sowing, and harvesting work was undertaken. The ensuing skin infections and ulcers often caused significant temporary and even permanent disability of arms and legs. If such superficial infections spread to the bloodstream, as not infrequently happened, severe fever, sepsis, and even death resulted. The available statistical data for treatments administered at hospitals and dispensaries reveals that these infections ranked among the very top reasons why cultivators attended government facilities each autumn.[90] Because most births in Punjab and Bengal also occurred during the autumn, the autumn was also a season when infectious complications of childbirth such as postpartum puerperal fever occurred.[91] Lastly, monsoon flooding – flooding that worsened in conjunction with heavy irrigation – drove snakes out of their underground holes and into fields and homes where they bit people and were a not insignificant cause of disability and death around the time of the autumn harvest.[92]

The spring harvest months in Bengal and Punjab were also characterized by a peak in morbidity and mortality. In both regions, the spring harvest was primarily the season of highly contagious "eruptive" fevers like smallpox, measles, chickenpox, and bubonic plague, which were readily spread among densely settled populations via commercial trading activities. Among these, smallpox was historically the leading cause of mortality. Highly commercialized areas with the densest populations in both regions were especially affected.[93] However, in Punjab, where the spring harvest of wheat was the dominant commercial harvest in the region, cultivators experienced significantly higher rates of eruptive fever each spring as compared to Bengal. This difference was especially striking with respect to rates of morbidity and mortality from the global pandemic of bubonic plague that struck the subcontinent from the end of the nineteenth century through the early 1920s. Whereas Punjab led British India in plague related deaths – with a total of 2,992,166 reported deaths, or 29.2 of the subcontinent's total during the 20-year period from 1898 to 1918 – Bengal ranked last, with only 68,938 reported deaths or 0.7 of the subcontinent's total.[94]

Cultivators in Bengal and Punjab, thus, literally embodied the commercialization of agriculture in the form of sickness and death during the spring

---

[90] Government of Punjab 1882; 1894; 1922; Klein 1990, 46.
[91] Lam and Miron 1991, 73–88; Chatterjee and Acharya, 2000, 443–58.
[92] Wall 1883, 21, 161.
[93] Das 1943, 21; Arnold 1993, 116–20; Arnold 2000, 73.
[94] White 1918, 2; Yu and Christakos 2006, figure 2.

and autumn harvest seasons. This harvest mortality was not simply a by-product of ecology, climate, and weather, although these factors all played a crucial role. Most significant were environmental changes associated with the expansion and intensification of commercial agriculture. The growing application of irrigation and manure for the intensive farming of rice varieties that were in demand among urban and foreign consumers contributed, in particular, to the making of an autumn harvest season that was characterized by a range of autumnal fevers including malaria, cholera, and a range of opportunistic infections of the gastrointestinal tract, skin, eye, and uterus. Seasonal co-morbidity was, naturally, also critical. Infection with malaria significantly increased the risk of mortality from simultaneous infections, as well as spontaneous abortion and still-birth in pregnant women. Despite striking ecological differences between the two regions, then, Punjabi and Bengali rice cultivators came to share an autumnal struggle for survival as one of the defining features of their modern agrarian lives.

CULTIVATING INEQUALITY

Yet Punjabis and Bengalis did not experience their regions' deadly harvest seasons in the same way; nor were their chances of dying the same or constant over time. A sharp rise in social inequality occurred during the commercial agricultural boom of the nineteenth and early twentieth century, as reflected in declining entitlements to land and food; growing pre-harvest seasonal hunger and immunological vulnerability; and rising harvest labor and caloric demands among those who were directly engaged in cultivation. As a consequence, rates of harvest mortality, and not simply morbidity, rose to record levels during this period.

To begin, it is critical to recognize that some differences in relative immunity or susceptibility to disease among social groups were biological in their basis. In response to intensive exposure to particular microbes, humans are known to develop inheritable forms of immunity that greatly increase resilience to infection. For instance, people residing in areas of intensive plasmodium transmission acquired a range of important genetic mutations that decrease susceptibility to malaria. The best-known of these mutations come from West Africa: duffy negative red blood cells provide near complete protection against *P. vivax* malaria, while hemoglobin S (sickle cell anemia) mitigates the severity of *P. falciparum* infections.[95] Evidencing the long history of exposure to malaria in inundated tracts of Punjab and Bengal, populations in these regions also carry genetic mutations that protect against the disease. The HbD hemoglobin mutation, which offers significant resistance to malaria, exists in the highest percentage worldwide among Punjabis,

---

[95] Packard 2007, 29–30.

while a range of beta thalassaemias (inherited forms of anemia) are widely prevalent among Punjabis and Bengalis alike, with distinctive forms prevalent at different rates in each region.[96]

Acquired forms of biological immunity were also important.[97] With each successive harvest season that Punjabis and Bengalis sickened and survived, they gained immunity to the region's major disease threats – effectively becoming "seasoned." In the case of most spring eruptive fevers (smallpox, measles, bubonic plague, etc.), a single infection bestowed complete and lifelong acquired immunity. With respect to the characteristic autumn fevers, on the other hand, repeated infection afforded partial but critical protection. Gradually Punjabis' and Bengalis' immune systems were primed with a wide spectrum of antibodies as they were exposed to specific parasites, amoebas, bacteria, and viruses. These antibodies, in turn, decreased the likelihood that a subsequent infection would produce significant illness or prove lethal. Those who resided in hyper-endemic areas of any given disease usually acquired the fullest and most complete forms of acquired resistance. Consequently, people who lived in places in which plasmodium transmission was highly seasonal (as in much of Punjab) were more likely to fall seriously sick and die from malaria as adults than those who faced some level of year-round exposure, as in much of Bengal.[98] The phenomenon of acquired immunity also meant that, as a general rule, immunologically naïve infants and young children (especially those under the age of five) were always the most vulnerable to dying, followed by adult migrants who lacked prior exposure from their places of origin.

Statistics from the colonial period provide considerable evidence of the significance of acquired immunity in shaping Punjab and Bengal's epidemiological histories. The rise in mortality in Bengal and Punjab from the 1870s to 1920 corresponds to the relatively sudden appearance, spread, and intensification of diseases like malaria, cholera, and bubonic plague among populations that previously lacked such sustained, intensive exposure and, hence, high levels of acquired immunity.[99] Major epidemics of these and other diseases also tended to follow a cyclical pattern, striking hardest at intervals of several years when "herd immunity" had worn off and a critical number of unexposed children and vulnerable adults were again present in the population.[100] Additionally, when rates of mortality began to fall during the interwar period, the decline was most prominent among older children, adolescents, and adults who would have acquired immunity as young

---

[96] Garewal and Das 2003, 217–19; Garewal et al. 2005, 252–6; Sur and Mukhopadhyay 2006, 11–15.
[97] Klein 1989 and 1990.
[98] Gill 1928, 157; Packard 2007, 96.
[99] Klein 1989 and 1990.
[100] Gill 1928, 155.

children growing up during the previous decades. Mortality rates among immunologically vulnerable infants also declined somewhat, understandably given that they, too, acquired immunity when breastfeeding from immune mothers.[101]

As important as these forms of inherited and acquired biological immunity were, socially acquired immunity was also extremely important in determining which Punjabis and Bengalis were able to fight off infection and survive. Such immunity had several dimensions to it. One concerned disparities in exposure to major pathogens by virtue of differences in caste, occupation, gender, and age. Even among those who owned land and engaged in cultivation, risk of infection varied considerably between those who primarily performed field labor themselves and those who depended heavily on hired laborers. A second major type of socially acquired immunity took the form of differences in immune response as shaped by relative food entitlements. Malnutrition is well known to adversely affect a person's ability to successfully recover from infection, regenerate damaged tissue, and avoid secondary and subsequent infections. For instance, it is widely recognized to increase the lethality of *P. falciparum* infections.[102] Even the widely prevalent *P. vivax*, which ordinarily causes significant debility but very low rates of mortality, kills people who are malnourished.[103] The synergistic relationship between malnutrition and mortality from cholera (as well as other forms of gastrointestinal infections) is also well documented. Similarly, opportunistic infections of the eye, skin, and reproductive tract are more likely to become serious and lead to death when sufferers' immune systems are weakened by malnourishment. Thus, while differential exposure to pathogens plays a key role in shaping patterns of morbidity, relative food entitlements and levels of nutrition in relation to caloric demands can play a decisive role in determining who lives and who dies.[104]

Given this, it is necessary to apprehend how intensive agricultural production for global markets – and consumers located at a considerable spatial and social distance – shaped social inequality as reflected in differential food entitlements. Crucially, the commercial boom that occurred during the late nineteenth and early twentieth century was accompanied by a growing disparity in land ownership in both Punjab and Bengal. Colonial land surveys, revenue settlements, and colonization schemes invested the state with supreme rights of land ownership while granting individuals private property rights in exchange for their payment of a fixed land tax in cash to the state.[105] In setting the tax rates, revenue officials ignored important ecological

---

[101] Das, 1943, 12, 13–14; Guha 2001, 80.
[102] Zurbrigg 1992; Packard 2007.
[103] Webb 2009, 5–6.
[104] Guha 2001, 84–91.
[105] Ludden 1999, 170, 178.

differences and produced regressive schedules that assessed poor peasants with rights to dry or swampy lands at a proportionately higher tax rate than rich peasants and landlords with rights to prime inundated or irrigated lands. Moreover, because revenue demands were set as fixed payments in cash, even cultivators with small holdings had to grow cash crops in order to obtain money. Yet, growing cash crops came with higher input (as well as disease) costs, and the cost of these inputs, including irrigation and manure, had to be paid for as an investment in a future harvest and its returns.[106] Tax payments, meanwhile, fell due right at harvest time, effectively compelling cultivators to sell their produce when the market was glutted and prices were at their seasonal lows.[107] The colonial state also expected full payment of land taxes in cash, and would not revert to collecting revenue in kind regardless of how any given harvest turned out or of variation in market prices.[108] Failure to pay tax in full and on time, moreover, entitled the state to auction the land to others who could make the payments demanded.

In this context, professional merchant-moneylenders gained considerable power over the production process by issuing credit to cultivators so that they could meet a given harvest season's revenue demands and the input costs for sowing the next season's crop.[109] As debt accumulated, merchant-moneylenders steadily assumed additional control over cropping decisions, typically by binding cultivators in contracts that advanced credit in exchange for the production of lucrative and exportable cash crops and varieties of food grains.[110] Ultimately, a prolonged series of unlucky events – such as the repeated droughts and harvest failures that occurred in both regions at the end of the nineteenth century – drove many small landowners into such unrecoverable debt that they lost their land to creditors and joined the ranks of the growing population of tenants and landless laborers.[111] For instance, by 1870 in Bengal 500 *zamindars* (landlords) held vast estates exceeding 20,000 acres; 16,000 held estates between 500 and 20,000 acres; 138,000 landlords held properties less than 500 acres; and the remainder of the peasantry struggled to hold on to a few acres.[112] As of 1880, it was estimated that 39 percent of the region's population was significantly dependent upon labor alone for its subsistence.[113] Although the situation in the active delta of the east was considerably more favorable than this until the 1930s, in the Hugli and Burdwan districts, where rates of mortality were

[106] Ludden 1999, 172–3.
[107] Fox 1985, 16.
[108] Datta 1996, 115.
[109] Ludden 1999, 170, 172.
[110] Patnaik 1996, 295; Datta 1996, 109.
[111] Fox 1985, 39–40; Iqbal 2010, 168–74.
[112] Samanta 2002, 133; Arnold and Stein 2010, 233; Iqbal 2010, 18–38, 174.
[113] Ludden 1999, 209.

among the highest in all of Bengal, poor cultivators and field laborers comprised roughly 75 percent of the population.[114]

In Punjab, which came under colonial rule later than Bengal and where land settlement and revenue policies initially privileged peasants to a greater extent, approximately two-thirds of the land was cultivated by peasant landholders in 1860. As peasants' debt grew and they increasingly mortgaged their lands, however, this changed. By 1900 over 40 percent of the land was cultivated by tenants-at-will, with few or no occupancy rights, who worked for large landlords and were typically compelled by their landlords to grow lucrative cash crops and forced to pay heavy rents.[115] The percentage of land worked by owners and land worked by tenants-at-will was lowest and highest respectively in the arid southwestern areas of Punjab in particular.[116] The size of holdings also fell. As of the 1920s, 56 percent of Punjabi peasants cultivated less than five acres of land and, of these, half cultivated less than an acre – an amount which was, by any measure, insufficient to meet the basic subsistence needs of a family.[117] From 1911 to 1931 the number of male agricultural laborers in Punjab also increased by an estimated 40 percent.[118]

Alienation from land went hand in hand with alienation from secure entitlements to sufficient and nutritious food.[119] By the 1860s, several key factors had begun to converge: the land on which food was grown was privately owned; high-input commercial crops were cultivated in place of regionally consumed staple food grains; the quantity of food grain exports (especially wheat and rice) increased; regional food grain prices were determined by global demand; and compensation for labor took the form of cash rather than in-kind payments.[120] Throughout the early 1870s through the early 1920s, both regions experienced a significant rise in food grain prices.[121] In Bengal, the rising price of exportable winter rice varieties kept these grains beyond the reach of small-scale peasants and landless Bengalis, and even the price of the coarse spring and summer varieties were often beyond the reach of tenants and landless laborers.[122] In Punjab, between the 1880s and World War I wheat and rice often sold at "near famine-level" prices – well beyond the means of all but affluent landlords, merchants, and professionals, even in times of abundant harvests.[123] The prices of other food staples like early summer rice, barley, millet, sorghum, and gram also came to

[114] Iqbal 2010, 53.
[115] Fox 1985, 55; Zurbrigg 1992, PE-6.
[116] Fox 1985, 28.
[117] Zurbrigg 1992, PE-6.
[118] Bhattacharya 1985, 130-1.
[119] Sen 1981.
[120] Zurbrigg 1992, PE 5-6; Mukherjee 2005, 57-60.
[121] Narain 1926.
[122] Watt 1891, 523-29; Samanta 2002, 29, 73.
[123] Zurbrigg 1992, PE 5-6.

track that of wheat and to move as though they were one commodity.[124] Additionally, because landless laborers were increasingly compensated in cash, they were simultaneously deprived of the benefits that accrued to producers when food grain prices rose and rendered as dependent as any other consumer on the market for their food entitlements. As one report from Punjab explained: "[t]hose who have seen our villages and how agricultural labourers and *kamins* [servants] live, also know very well that these classes, have not benefited by the rise of prices. They live hand to mouth, and in their case the rise of prices, so far from being a source of gain, is frequently a cause of indebtedness."[125]

Thus, despite absolute rises in commercial agricultural productivity into the 1920s, growing numbers of Punjabis and Bengalis experienced a significant decline in the total quantity and quality of food they could afford to eat.[126] Conventional wisdom, to the contrary, claims that "per-capita" and "all-India" income and food availability increased during this period.[127] However, mean and national statistics ignore pronounced regional disparities in entitlements to income and food. During the period from 1880 to 1947, the availability of food grains per capita declined by 38 percent in Bengal and 18 percent in Punjab. It is also inaccurate to assume that, unlike inedible cash crops, food grains were produced for domestic consumption and were equally available "per capita," irrespective of class and social power relations. In fact, the heavily irrigated and manured export crops like wheat and winter rice were sold on domestic markets at prices that reflected global demand and purchasers' power, rendering them inaccessible to most Punjabis and Bengalis.[128] Reflective of this, a colonial official observed during the early twentieth century that "[i]n the Panjab [...] the poorer classes live on the millets grown in the rains, and on barley and gram; the richer classes eat principally wheat and rice. In Bengal proper [...] rice is the principal food, the coarse, early rice being mainly taken by the poor, the finer, late rice by the rich."[129]

Those who were landless were especially vulnerable to preharvest hunger, as well. The risk of being unable to satisfy one's daily caloric needs rose to a seasonal climax just before the harvests when food stores were exhausted, employment opportunities fell, and regional food prices soared.[130] Further exacerbating the situation in Punjab, exports and regional prices of wheat (and the other food grains that typically tracked it) peaked between June and

---

[124] Latham and Neal 1983, 270; Zurbrigg 1992, PE 5-6.
[125] Narain 1926, 49, quoted in Zurbrigg 1992.
[126] Zurbrigg 1992, PE 5-6; Samanta 2002, 73.
[127] Klein 1990, 34-5.
[128] Patnaik 1996, 301-2.
[129] Watt 1891, 531.
[130] Chambers et al. 1981; Zurbrigg 1992, PE2-26.

July – the leanest season of the year – to fill the gap between American and Australian exports on global markets.[131] As a result, during the weeks preceding the major harvests, those without sufficient food stores or purchasing power – typically indebted peasants, tenants, and landless laborers – endured extended periods without a meal or with only a single small meal a day.[132] Such preharvest hunger was especially significant because it occurred just before and as producers were called upon to perform the strenuous physical labor needed to reap and process cash crops during the ensuing harvest months. Adequate nutrition was also necessary to fight the many infections that peaked in incidence during the harvests. Ultimately, then, cultivators of rice and other food grains faced their greatest caloric demands at precisely the time of year when they were most hungry and least likely to be adequately nourished.

Such seasonal hunger is hard for historians to document precisely, much less to quantify. For this reason it largely escapes the attention of scholars who focus attention instead on overt starvation and dramatic famine episodes, with a few important exceptions.[133] It is, however, etched into Punjab and Bengal's available mortality data in striking ways. Throughout the period, mortality rates predictably rose during the harvest months when seasonally hungry and malnourished cultivators met with peak labor demands, metabolic requirements, and disease exposure (see Figure 11.3 for Punjab). As the colonial epidemiologist S. R. Christophers demonstrated in his work on Punjab, a high spleen rate (an indication of malaria parasite burden) only manifested in elevated rates of mortality from malaria during periods of, or immediately following, high food prices such as routinely occurred during the pre-autumn harvest season.[134] Mortality from cholera also predictably peaked in the hungry months before and during the autumn harvest. Preharvest seasonal hunger also helps to explain why periods of significant mortality from cholera, diarrhea, and dysentery often occurred during times and in places that were not experiencing outright famine – an observation that is sometimes advanced by scholars to dismiss or minimize the significance of nutrition in shaping the mortality patterns of gastrointestinal disease.[135]

Second, the prevalence of widespread seasonal hunger and malnutrition helps to account for the frequency, severity, and demographic features of epidemics in agrarian Punjab and Bengal during the late nineteenth and early twentieth century. If a harvest failed due to flooding or drought, large numbers of people who were already malnourished and immunologically vulnerable were at an increased risk of progressing rapidly to a point of starvation

[131] Fox 1985, 34.
[132] Narain and Brij 1932, 106.
[133] Chamberset al. 1981; Zurbrigg 1992; Ludden 1999, 17–36; Mandala 2005.
[134] Christophers 1911, 69–70, 107–9; Samanta 2002, 106.
[135] Klein 1994, 495.

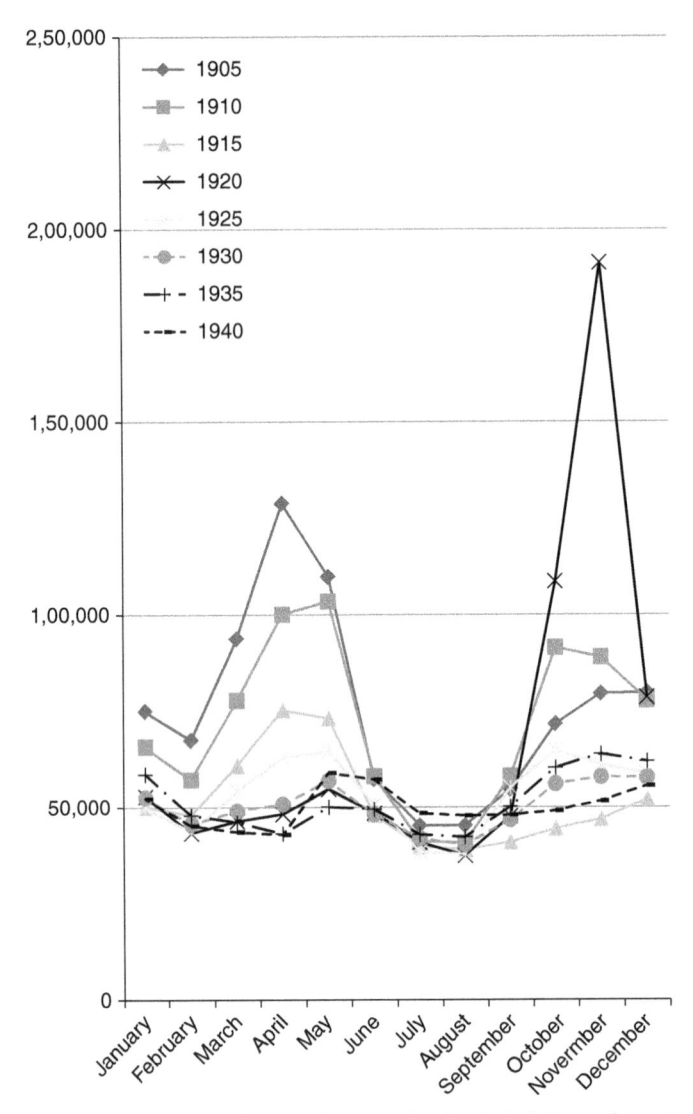

FIGURE 11.3 Seasonal mortality in the Punjab. Statistical Data from Das, *Vital Statistics of the Punjab*, 9–10.

and death from infection.[136] Indeed, epidemics in Punjab and Bengal were always comprised of a rise in the sum total of spring and/or autumn seasonal mortality, not of a single disease alone, even if one assumed dominance.[137] Typically, the main seasonal peak in mortality during times of famine, as in

[136] Singh 1996; Maharatna 1996, 63; Wakimura 1997.
[137] Das 1943; Dyson 1991, 6 , 22; Zurbrigg 1992, PE2–26; Maharatna 1996, 47–50.

non-famine years, occurred during the hungriest preharvest and early harvest months of August through November.[138] While infants and young children sustained the largest absolute increases in death rates, a majority of the "excess" or proportional increase in death rates that constituted epidemics occurred among older children, adolescents, and adults.[139] Without a state of widespread immunological compromise due to hunger and malnutrition, these older groups otherwise enjoyed the advantage of acquired immunity relative to the very young. The only exception to this pattern occurred with the introduction of novel disease strains to which the regions' adult populations lacked acquired biological immunity, such as bubonic plague and Spanish influenza. Reflecting well-known gendered differences in food entitlements both within families and in society at large across the northern subcontinent, a marked gendered pattern also characterized mortality during epidemic seasons, especially in the Punjab: the higher the mortality rate, the more that female deaths predominated over those of males across all age ranges.[140]

Strikingly, during the 1920s and 1930s mortality rates in Bengal and especially Punjab began to drop. It is significant that this decline took the form of a steady decrease in harvest mortality peaks (see Figure 11.3). It is also significant that it happened in the interwar context of a substantial fall in commodity and food grain prices, one that occurred faster than the corresponding fall in wages; a decline in the global demand for, and production of, input-demanding crops for export, including wheat and winter rice; a collapse in agrarian credit relations and the power of moneylenders over cultivators; and more stable food grain yields and an absence of major famines.[141] Together, these factors suggest that in this period *relative* social inequality declined and preharvest hunger and malnutrition was mitigated to the point that it no longer had a pronounced impact on the survival chances of the most vulnerable. This improvement in harvest mortality, however, does not imply that a majority of cultivators enjoyed a high standard of living, or even one that was not marked by malnutrition and extremely precarious. As the 1943–44 Bengal famine evidences, those who were landless remained highly vulnerable to major famines and epidemics during times of rising food grain prices. When the price of rice in Bengal rose in the midst of World War II, beginning in 1941 and ultimately quadrupling over an 18-month period, but wages failed to rise at anything close to that pace, between 2 and 3.5 million people died from starvation and epidemics.[142] Non-landowning

---

[138] Maharatna 1996, 24–5, 60–2.
[139] Das 1943; Drèze and Sen 1989, 80; Dyson 1991, 21; Maharatna 1996, 25–6, 173.
[140] Das 1943, 14; Dyson 1991, 21; Maharatna 1996, 77; Greenough 2009, 34.
[141] McAlpin 1983, 881–95; Fox 1985, 53, 55, 73; Bose and Jalal 1998, 146–8; Guha 2001, 84–6; Samanta 2002, 69; Iqbal 2010, 162–3.
[142] Sen 1981, 52–85; Patnaik 1996, 302–3; Maharatna 1996, 129.

groups including fishermen, those engaged in various agrarian petty trade and professions, and agricultural laborers ultimately suffered the greatest burden of this starvation and epidemic mortality.[143]

CONCLUSION

Widely held understandings that the global distribution of disease simply reflects the ecological characteristics of particular regions and crops, and that commercial agricultural production leads inexorably to better health and well-being, are in need of thoughtful reconsideration. As the findings here reveal, neither ecological nor rice determinism can fully account for the patterns of morbidity and mortality that were experienced by Bengali and Punjabi cultivators during the commercial boom of the late nineteenth and early twentieth century. Despite substantially different ecological settings, Punjabi and Bengali cultivators' lived health experiences were similarly shaped by environmental changes associated with the intensive production of water- and manure-demanding varieties of cash crops, including rice, for consumers located at considerable spatial and social distance from themselves. Additionally, commercial determinism cannot account for the sharp increase in rates of mortality that occurred during this commercial boom, much less for how this mortality was distributed spatially, socially, and seasonally. In both regions, a dramatic increase in commodity production for global markets was accompanied by a concurrent increase in social inequality, especially with respect to entitlements to land. In this context, preharvest seasonal hunger, malnutrition, and immunological vulnerability became significant features of life for those who were landless, and rates of harvest mortality, and not simply morbidity, rose to record levels. Ultimately, rice producers in both Punjab and Bengal grew into markedly seasonal struggles for survival, the basic contours of which came to characterize, for so many food grain producers across a wide range of ecological settings, the commercial harvests of modern times.

[143] Sen 1981, 70–5.

PART III

POWER AND CONTROL

Peter A. Coclanis

INTRODUCTION

Although the themes of power and control can be associated with any crop and any agricultural regime, such associations are particularly appropriate – and strong – in the case of rice. Whether we are speaking of cultivation practices, water management, labor protocols, market forces, or political imperatives, rice, especially under irrigation, has long been perceived as a crop predisposed to, if not demanding high levels of power and control, manipulation, and machination. One need not trot out theories of "irrigation societies," much less of "oriental despotism" or "hydraulic empires" to suggest that such perceptions correspond relatively closely with, and thus capture pretty well the realities of rice production – and the employment of nature, workers, capital, consumers, and rulers in the same – in many parts of the world over the millennia. In various ways the four chapters in this Part analyze rice in terms of power and control – or of resistance against such forces. In so doing, the chapters allow us to appreciate not only the complicated ways in which power and control have been inscribed upon (or contested in) landscapes of rice in Brazil, Japan, Indonesia, and the United States, but also some of the results and concomitants arising therefrom.

Rice can be grown – and, historically, has been grown – in innumerable ways. For most of its history in the parts of the world where it has proven most important, its cultivation has been considered heavy and exacting, often dangerous work, requiring considerable labor discipline, skill, and calibration. Not surprisingly, such factors meant that the exercise of power – whether familial/communal or legal/governmental – has often been instrumental, if not indispensable in recruiting and retaining workers with the requisite attributes needed for successful rice cultivation. Thus, in rice cultivation across space and time we find prominent roles for coerced labor of various kinds, whether corvée labor, slave labor, tightly circumscribed wage/sharecropping/tenant farmer arrangements, or more insidious kin- and community-based incentive/disincentive schemes.

In the case of rice, the exercise of power and need for control are also made manifest, as implied earlier, in the hydraulic realm. To be sure, it is important to remember that a significant proportion of the world rice crop has always been grown "dry," that is, without irrigation. Indeed, according to D. H. Grist, as much as one-quarter of the world's rice crop as late as the mid-1970s was still grown without irrigation. That said, rice, like other crops, grows best when supplied with adequate amounts of water at appropriate times, and sophisticated irrigation schemes have been associated with rice cultivation for millennia. Moreover, unlike other leading cereal grains, rice is often grown in standing water for at least part of the production cycle. As a result, hydraulic concerns are in a relative sense more integral to rice production than to the production of wheat or maize, rendering the exercise of power and maintenance of control over water into fixations in many rice cultivation regimes. When it comes to rice, then, words such as power, control, and domination come immediately to the fore, whether we are speaking about labor or water.

Furthermore, the association of power and control with rice extends to the realm of consumption. In many parts of the world rice has long dominated the diets of the resident populations, contributing a very high proportion of total caloric intake in many even in recent times. As recently as 2000, for example, rice accounted for almost 77 percent of daily caloric intake in Cambodia, nearly 76 percent in Bangladesh, 74 percent in Myanmar, 71 percent in Laos, 67 percent in Vietnam, and over half in Indonesia, the fourth largest country in the world in terms of population. There is no analogue in wheat – consuming areas to the powerful (and often deleterious) nutritional stranglehold of rice in these countries. And in those countries most dependent on the consumption of maize – Mexico and Guatemala – only among the poor does the proportion of total calories derived from that cereal approach 50 percent.

Once rice is consumed outside of the producing household and allocated via markets, which has been the case for millennia, other types of power come into play as well. To be sure, even before then, power was doubtless employed in allocative decisions, whether such decisions were infra or extra-household in nature. Who in the household gets to eat rice and in what quantities, for example, or how much rice goes into communal, religious, or state coffers – and on what terms? Such allocative decisions are still being made and still being affected by power considerations even today, of course, but the relative importance of market-mediated allocative decisions has become increasingly important over time. The allocation of rice via markets transforms, but hardly eliminates power and control from questions relating to consumption. The very existence of markets brings new personnel, institutions, ideas, and behaviors into play, and in cases wherein the market for rice is long-distance and/or organized along capitalist lines the degree of power and control informing the same is often amplified and intensified. Size and scope begin to matter more; logistics becomes a concern, specialists and middlemen emerge to handle matters relating to evaluating, certifying, financing, processing, shipping, and marketing output, as well as to manage inter-temporal and inter-spatial risks. So powerful are such middlemen in some cases (particularly when aided and abetted by the state) that they exercise considerable sway over the fates and fortunes of local rice producers and local consumers alike. If talk of "food security" and "iron rice bowls" often remains on the table, as it were – whether via state granaries, strategic reserves, production subsidies, or export curbs – the rise of capitalist markets has generally meant that such talk is increasingly cheap, often trumped by the allure of potential profits, wherever they can be taken. Fortunately for many, the international rice market is quite thin even today – only about 5–7 percent of total rice production is traded internationally, less than half the figure for small grains such as wheat – which means that the power of "the market" and the control of middlemen is still relatively constrained.

The particular characteristics of the rice market complicate matters further. Not only does rice constitute a large proportion of total food intake in many parts of the world, as we have seen, but numerous studies have also demonstrated that rice demand responds relatively sluggishly to changes in market prices and consumers' income. In technical terms, rice demand was in the past and is today highly price- and income inelastic in many parts of the world, particularly in Southeast, South, and East Asia, but in a number of other places as well (most notably, West Africa). In most parts of the West, of course, the place of rice is less prominent and its grip on consumers far less secure. Even in the West, though, there are places today – Guyana and Suriname, for example – where demand patterns look like those more characteristic of Asia. And in the past, too, there are places in the West, the coastal plain of South Carolina and Georgia in the southeastern United Sates comes immediately to mind in this regard, where the power of rice as a cereal grain approached levels in the East. Not for nothing did residents of the proud old city of Charleston, South Carolina – located in the epicenter of this once legendary rice-producing region – claim fictive kinship with the Chinese: people in both areas, it was said, lived on rice and worshipped their ancestors. For the record, many Chinese lived mainly on other grains, but one gets the point Charlestonians were trying to make. In any case, the upshot of the fact that in many parts of the world rice is so "sticky," so to speak, is that demand for the cereal responds only modestly to changes in income or price.

Power and control, our themes in this section, cannot easily exist in the absence of institutional supports, whether informal or formal, non-governmental or governmental in nature. Such supports could be legal – statutes legitimizing slavery, awarding riparian rights, or authorizing futures contracts, with attendant appropriations to enable/enforce/police the same – or non-legal, such as in the cases of some West African societies where workers who refuse to meet community obligations and perform honorably in rice work are shunned or stigmatized in other ways. In the latter cases, institutions are sanctioned informally, in the former, formally under governmental authority and auspices.

When governments are involved, such supports are generally more explicit, and in recent centuries more "objective" and rational. That said, in the case of rice, government power has often been wielded heavy handedly, leading to results far less impressive than overly confident officials assumed would be the case. Here, formulations associated with Foucault and Scott – "governmentality" and "high modernism" in particular – can prove helpful, as can be seen in two of the chapters included in this Part. That said, all four of the chapters in the Part shed light on questions relating to power and control, albeit in different ways.

In his provocative intervention into the "Black Rice" debate, Walter Hawthorne reframes the relevant issues in useful ways, in so doing, deepening our historical understanding of the power dynamics at work in rice fields in both West Africa and Brazil. For his part, Peter A. Coclanis offers an instructive case study regarding the manner in which a network of well-connected "outsiders" successfully established – even imposed – a new capital-intensive rice regime in the "Old Southwest" of the United States in the late nineteenth century, which regime marked a revolutionary disjuncture in the history of rice production. In their respective chapters Penelope Francks and Harro Maat provide insightful analyses of rice production in Japan and Sumatra, demonstrating the deployment and limits of power and coercion in the rice sector in each. Considered as a group, then, these four chapters at once punctuate and complicate the links between and among power, coercion, control, and one vital cereal grain.

12

The Cultural Meaning of Work: The "Black Rice Debate" Reconsidered

Walter Hawthorne

In the February 2010 issue of the *American Historical Review* (*AHR*), I offer a critique of what has come to be known as the "black rice debate."[1] The debate centers on the "black rice thesis," which Peter H. Wood, Daniel C. Littlefield, Judith A. Carney, Edda Fields Black, and Frederick C. Knight have contributed to over several decades. The thesis holds that skilled rice farmers from Africa's Upper Guinea coast introduced the technology important for the establishment and expansion of lowland South Carolina and Georgia's eighteenth century rice-based plantation system.[2] Carney applies the argument elsewhere, including Amazonia (Maranhão and Pará), Brazil.[3] David Eltis, Philip Morgan, and David Richardson challenge the thesis, and Max Edelson offers support for their argument.[4] At core, Eltis, Morgan, and Richardson argue that planter power, Atlantic winds and currents, and the demands of the Atlantic economy were the principal shapers of rice-based plantation systems. The African role in the making of American agricultural systems "should be highlighted," the trio states, "where it is attested," but Africans were not "the primary players in creating and maintaining rice regimes."[5]

In *AHR*, I argue that though Eltis, Morgan, and Richardson demonstrate that some of the black rice thesis' ancillary arguments should be rethought, we should not discard the thesis altogether. "Embracing the trio's approach," I write, "risks writing Africans and their descendants in the Americas once again out of history."[6] In this chapter, I situate, myself, again as someone who

---

[1] Hawthorne 2010b, 151–63.
[2] Wood 1974; Littlefield 1981; Carney 2001; Fields-Black 2008; Knight 2010. Also see Hall 2010. The definition of "Upper Guinea" that I use here is Senegal to Liberia and including the Senegambia, Windward Coast, and Sierra Leone slave-trading regions.
[3] Carney 2004.
[4] Eltis et al. 2007; Edelson 2006; Edelson 2010.
[5] Etis et al. 2007, 1335, 1357.
[6] Hawthorne 2010b, 152.

sees evidence for the application of African knowledge to some aspects of plantation agriculture and rice cuisines in Carolina and Amazonia. However, I reframe the debate by considering the cultural meaning that work had for Africans. In so doing, I argue that although many of the tasks Upper Guineans performed in rice fields on both sides of the ocean were the same, work over rice in the Americas was a "deculturing" experience. In their homelands, Upper Guineans never performed hard work for hard work's sake. They labored long hours over rice because society rewarded those who did so and punished those who did not. The American plantation system stripped away social rewards, making rice labor for white masters little more than drudgery.

THE CULTURAL MEANING OF WORK IN UPPER GUINEA

In an oft-quoted passage about black slavery in the Americas, Ira Berlin and Philip Morgan assert, "Slaves worked. When, where, and especially how they worked determined, in large measure, the course of their lives."[7] To be sure, the nature of slaves' labors was shaped by a great variety of things. Important were climate, geography, and the crops slaves engaged with. Important, also, were planters' decisions, which were shaped by slave resistance. Though slaves spent most of their time laboring over export crops, in many places plantation regimes permitted "peasant breaches" – times when slaves were allowed to work for themselves, often on provision grounds where they made culturally informed choices about what to plant, how to plant it, and how to harvest and process it.[8]

What is important about the black rice thesis is its insistence that slaves shaped agricultural practices beyond their provision grounds. The labor slaves undertook to produce a commodity crop on masters' fields was, backers of the thesis argue, the product of an African knowledge system. In Carney's words, Africans transferred "an entire agricultural complex of rice seeds, farming techniques, and milling" from one side of the ocean to the other.[9] As evidence, Carney cites similarities in the means of production on both sides of the Atlantic. But neither she nor we defenders of the black rice thesis pay much attention to profound differences in modes of production across time and space. We think it is significant that in South Carolina and Amazonia the instruments and subjects of labor were the same (or nearly so) as they were in Upper Guinea. But we don't dwell long enough on the obvious fact that on one side of the ocean African rice farmers labored under a lineage or domestic mode of production and on the other under a slave mode of production. On one side of the ocean, famers were one with what they

---

[7] Berlin and Morgan 1991, 3.
[8] On African agency and provision grounds, see Carney and Rosomoff 2010.
[9] Carney 2001, 167.

produced. On the other side, they were alienated from it. On one side, long days of carving rice paddies from the natural environment and of planting and harvesting rice transformed boys into men and girls into women. On the other, laboring over rice marked people as slaves.

These points are best made with examples from either side of the Atlantic. The group I know best in Upper Guinea is the Balanta, a rice growing society in the area of present day Guinea-Bissau. I have argued elsewhere that Atlantic merchants traded large quantities of iron to Upper Guinea coastal peoples for captives from the sixteenth through the eighteenth centuries. Coastal groups used iron to reinforce tools, and with them they dramatically expanded rice fields, particularly in the eighteenth century. It was in the eighteenth century that Balanta perfected mangrove rice farming, producing most years large surpluses of rice that fed growing populations.[10]

Like many groups in the area, Balanta relied on an age-grade system to group workers into bodies large enough to carry out the labor-intensive projects associated with mangrove rice agriculture. Among Balanta, age-grades divided village or *tabanca* males into two bodies: elders or *b'alante b'ndang* and youths or *blufos*. Females had a parallel system, but, since the gendered tasks they performed did not require it, they did not work in groups that were as large and coordinated as those of males. Each of the masculine bodies was subdivided into various grades, which were determined roughly by the age of those in them. Grades bound together males from the independent households that comprised *tabancas*, fostering an *esprit de corps*. Although people's identities were tied to households, they were also tied through the age-grade system to villages. Circumcision marked the passage of *blufos* into the ranks of *b'alante b'ndang*. Circumcised men sat on councils, *ko* or *beho*, and there made decision that had implications for the entire *tabanca*. On *beho*, men settled intra-*tabanca* disputes, carried out negotiations with neighboring *tabancas*, and organized groups for raids and war. They also organized *blufos* for large-scale and labor-intensive rice projects.

Mangrove rice farming was one of the most labor-intensive forms of agriculture carried out on the Atlantic rim in the eighteenth century. The first task that Balanta farmers undertook was the building of a large primary dike (*quididê*) through mangroves forests, which grew on the banks of brackish coastal rivers. Rice will not grow in salt water, so the *quididê* was built to hold back tidal surges. Males, organized by grade, built the *quididê*, first by cutting a path through mangroves, then by pounding wooden supports into the earth, and finally by mounding mud around the supports to form a long dike.

Once cordoned off, mangroves behind the *quididê* began to die. Elders then directed *blufos* grouped by grade to cut the mangroves with machetes

---

[10] Hawthorne 2003.

and axes. Next, the cleared area was desalinated with fresh water brought by rains, which was trapped within the *quididê*. The fresh water leached salt from the soil and was eventually discharged into the river during low tide. Age-grade based workers then created smaller secondary dikes that divided newly claimed land into paddies.

Throughout the rainy season, Balanta farmers labored to produce mangrove rice. Before the coming of the rainy season in June, they prepared nurseries on uplands near their compounds. With the first rains, rice was sown in these nurseries. When it reached a sufficient height, it was transplanted into paddies that had filled with fresh rainwater. There it matured, but not without near constant tending. Periodic weeding was necessary; dikes had to be reinforced; and birds, monkeys, and other animals had to be kept away. The latter task was reserved for the youngest boys, those in the first of the age grades.

Balanta harvested rice when it matured. *N'contu* (*O. glaberrima*), a rice native to West Africa, was ready for harvest as early as October. *O. sativa* varieties, which became popular later, and particularly in the twentieth century, were harvested in December. Farmers harvested rice by hand, cutting it midway down the culm with a curved knife (*cubom*) made by blacksmiths for the task. They bundled their harvest for transport to a cleared patch of land where women threshed it. Women then carried the rice to their households where they dried it in the sun and pounded it to remove the hulls. Once rice was harvested, fields had to be prepared for the coming rainy season, and dikes had to be reinforced, and nurseries prepared. All of this should make clear that paddy-rice agriculture required intense, organized, and year-long inputs of labor – difficult, exhausting, often painful labor.

Male age grades undertook most labor-intensive tasks – the building of dikes, clearing of mangroves, and, to a lesser extent, transplanting and harvesting rice. They did so because the work required was too great for a single household. Hence, for villagers, age grades were a means of placing young, strong workers from different households together into structured work groups. For the most arduous tasks, Balanta relied on males in their late teens who formed *nhaye* grades. One group of Guinea-Bissauan scholars has rightly labeled *nhaye* "the motor in Balanta society. It is the *nhaye* who do the most work [...]. A youth in this phase should be able to endure any type of physical labor, from the working of the *bolanha* to the harvesting of rice."[11]

Since *blufos* were central to rice production, *tabancas* did all they could to retain them and to convince them to work hard. Two strategies were important: punishments for the disobedient and rewards for the obedient. Punishments assumed two forms: ridicule and physical abuse. Name calling and ostracism were common, as they are today, when an individual or group

---

[11] Suba et al., n.d., 9.

was not doing what elders expected. And, indeed, there are few things worse in Balanta society than being dubbed lazy. But ridicule often escalated. As an informant told anthropologist Marina Temudo, rice farming in Upper Guinea is "enslavement" (*trabalhu catibu* in the Kriol language of the coast). "Trying to escape burdensome kinship obligations was," Temudo states, "rather risky." In days past, those who failed to follow through with obligations were beaten, banned, sold, or killed. Spirits seeking vengeance for the community could visit them. And often those who did not join in community agricultural projects could be labeled evil witches whose self-centered behavior undermined the whole. Sanctions against witchcraft were severe.[12]

The other way *b'alante b'ndang* insured the retention of young males was by fostering the age grade system described above. Over the long term, that system gave *blufos* incentives to remain in the *tabancas* of their birth. Though *b'alante b'ndang* held the prerogatives of power, all male youths regardless of household affiliation could attain the status of *b'alante b'ndang*. Hence, they had a reason to support the system, to submit to the authority of older men, to remain in the *tabancas* of their birth, and to work hard. In time, they too would be older men, *b'alante b'ndang*. Their hard work would be rewarded over the long term when they inherited their fathers' lands and prerogatives of power. Over the short term, *blufos* who worked well in fields were celebrated by everyone around them. Balanta society is today, like it was hundreds of years ago, stateless and decentralized. There are no inherited positions. All men recognized as successful are self-made. In adolescence, the hardest workers (and bravest warriors or, today, cattle thieves) attract the most attention from females, wear the largest number of bodily adornments, and are most recognized in rituals by spirits.[13] Hard workers are celebrated by those in this world and the spirit world.

All of this is to say that mangrove rice cultivation on the Upper Guinea coast is difficult and physically demanding. Balanta, like all mangrove rice societies, have constructed elaborate social structures and have clung to a system of social rewards and punishments to coerce and cajole young people to work. Up and down the coast, the incentives to work hard over rice have remained deeply engrained. Indeed, they are so much a part of Upper Guinean rice societies that people have resisted adopting alternative crops even as rice farming has become unviable in some places due to shifts in rainfall patterns. Noting this, anthropologist Joanna Davidson argues that Diola, a group occupying lands near Balanta, are committed to rice because they view alternative crops "as lazy work," a view that stems from an "adherence to a particular work regime" and to particular and particularly resilient religious and social structures. For most Upper Guineans, their sustenance system has never been "simply a means of survival, but [...] [has been] integrally tied to

---

[12] Temudo 2009, 49–50.
[13] Hawthorne 2003.

their conception of personhood, social relations, ritual obligations, and collective cultural identity."[14] This is certainly true of Balanta who define themselves as hard workers – people very different from "lazy" pastoralists and "lazy" farmers of crops other than rice. Many Balanta men go so far as to reject technological innovation such as draft animals and machines because these things are the tools of the lazy.

THE CULTURAL MEANING OF WORK IN THE AMERICAS

If, on the Upper Guinea coast hard work in rice fields made men and women, in the Americas it made slaves. To be sure, defenders of the black rice thesis have pointed to similarities in the means of production in Early Modern rice systems on both sides of the Atlantic. They have shown that aspects of an Upper Guinean knowledge system were transferred on slave ships to the Americas. And they have celebrated this as an indication of African slave agency. But would slaves, themselves, have taken solace in the fact that they performed some of the same tasks on one side of the ocean as they had on the other?

No slave voices survive today to give us a definitive answer to this question. But if we consider what Africans were not able to bring with them across the Atlantic, it seems doubtful that there was much to celebrate in American rice fields. In Upper Guinea, young men worked long hours because they received bountiful social rewards for doing so and because they might be ridiculed or killed if they did not. There is no indication that work in masters' fields in the Carolina lowlands offered African slaves social rewards that resembled those they had had across the ocean. In Carolina, slaves worked under a task system, being responsible for the completion of a set amount of work, after which they were "free" to do what they wished. Certainly, slaves who worked quickly and efficiently in fields eked out some time in the late afternoon when they might cultivate food crops of their choosing, produce their own handicrafts, or engage in other forms of cultural expression. But work over their masters' rice dominated slaves' lives.[15] With respect to this, Upper Guinea slaves would have been well aware that in Carolina gone were their age grade systems. Gone was praise from neighbors and ancestors. And in a place where black males far outnumbered black females, gone was the possibility of attracting female attention through success in rice cultivation. The same was true in Amazonia, where Upper Guineans comprised a majority of slaves in the second half of the eighteenth century and where they worked over rice on plantations owned by Portuguese settlers.[16] As a point of comparison to how I described Upper Guinean rice production in the paragraphs above,

---

[14] Davidson 2007.
[15] Coclanis 2000, 59–78.
[16] Hawthorne 2003.

I develop below a description of rice agriculture in Maranhão, one of Amazonia's two captaincies (Figure P.1c).

On slave plantations in Maranhão in the second half of the eighteenth century, the first stage of the annual rice cycle was field making. As in Upper Guinea, in Maranhão field making was men's work. However, from descriptions of field-making techniques in Maranhão, it is clear that for Upper Guinean males, the work of carving fields in Amazonian forest was deskilled and decultured. Field making took place in the context of the two types of rice agriculture – wetland and upland. Occasionally, slaves planted rice in freshwater wetlands. In 1771, Maranhão's governor, Joaquim de Melo e Póvoas, noted this, stating that on some plantations in the interior they "plant rice on fields that are marshy." There, he said, it "produces well and the grain is a perfect size, better than that grown on the upland fields."[17] Similarly, a 1787 report noted fields in "wetlands" along a number of the area's rivers.[18]

Nonetheless, not that many planters took up wetland rice agriculture. The Portuguese minister for the colonies complained in 1772 that despite the fact that Amazonia had "humid and swampy" lands, little rice was produced on them.[19] Discussing the more popular upland form of cultivation, the minister wrote elsewhere, "Here, the only way they farm the land is by cutting the jungle and when it is dry they set it on fire. If there have been no rains, it burns well, and the land is well prepared. However, if it burns badly ... it will never yield much."[20] Similarly, F. A. Brandão Júnior described field preparation in Maranhão in the early nineteenth century. In Maranhão, he said, there were two seasons: *tempo de chuva* or "time of the rain," which lasted from January to July, and *tempo sem chuva* or "time without rain," which stretched from August to December. "The first assignment of the [agricultural] cycle is the chopping down of the forests for the next year's planting, using a scythe to hack down smaller trees," he wrote. This work began mid-dry season and lasted about two months. In November or December, slaves cut large trees with iron axes. They then "set fire to the devastated jungle and cut and stack the branches and smaller tree trunks which have escaped the fire and which, occupying the surface of the earth, could hinder development of the crop." The stacks were lit ablaze, leaving a field "ravaged by fire and covered with ashes."[21]

The skills and knowledge required for clearing and farming of Maranhense upland forests were not nearly as difficult to acquire as those needed for the clearing and desalination of Upper Guinean lowland mangrove swamps. In

[17] APEM 12.
[18] ANTT mç. 601, cx. 704.
[19] AHU cx. 67, doc. 5793.
[20] APEM, 12.
[21] Brandão 1865, 31–8.

Maranhão, gangs of male slaves of multiple ages and ethnicities (most but not all of whom were Upper Guinean) were sent into forests to cut and burn large tracks of land. The work was dangerous and offered few rewards other than a bit of time in the evening if a defined task was completed before sunset. In Maranhão forests were consumed at a rapid rate because, unlike Upper Guinean farmers, white planters were interested in producing something other than food to sustain local populations. They produced rice for export, and the proceeds from rice sales enriched them. With capital from Lisbon and labor from Africa, white planters exploited their land and slaves. They pressed blacks to clear jungles as fast as they could and to reclear them as soon as possible. Forests were devastated and slaves' bodies broken. In Amazonia, Upper Guinean males did not win praise from their communities and from spirits for their hard work in fields. There the work preparing fields was void of any African-based cultural significance.

Processes of planting and harvesting also offered none of the social rewards common across Upper Guinea. To be sure, in Maranhão Upper Guinean slaves applied skills and knowledge to these stages of the agricultural cycle. Male and female slaves planted rice in January, at the start of the rainy season. Male slaves worked *roças novas*, or "new fields," with hoes that resembled fulcrum shovels known in coastal Upper Guinea.[22] When planting, male and female slaves pushed a stick into the earth to make a hole. Having dropped in some seed, they then covered the hole, moving dirt with the heel of a foot. The same technique was used across the ocean.[23] To be sure, prior experience with rice planting made Upper Guineans efficient workers in Amazonia. After the coming of rains, slaves were sent to weed – day in and day out – upland fields. Slaves uprooted weeds with iron hoes, tilling soils around sprouting rice and cotton plants so as not to disrupt roots. The work of weeding lasted for "as long as it takes for the plants [rice or cotton] to fully establish themselves."[24]

The next step in the agricultural cycle was harvesting. Male and female slaves harvested rice at the end of the *tempo de chuva*, when rice was knee to waist high. Slaves harvested it by moving in lines through fields, each worker holding "a small knife, cutting the stems one by one."[25] The knife was likely modeled on one used in Upper Guinea (the *cubom* among Balanta) for the same purpose. After harvested, they carried what they cut in large bundles to threshing stations. From contemporary descriptions, it is clear that that rice was threshed in much the same way as in Upper Guinea – "with a branch to loosen the grains" from grasses.[26] Slaves then gathered rice for milling. Slaves

---

[22] Carney 2004, 15; Hawthorne 2003, 162.
[23] Mello e Povoas's description in APEM, 12.
[24] Brandão 1865, 31–8.
[25] Brandão 1865, 96–9.
[26] Brandão 1865, 31–8.

from Upper Guinea who were skilled at using mortars and pestles often milled rice. When mechanical mills were available in an area, the work was done by machine.[27]

But no matter what knowledge Upper Guineans brought to agriculture in Maranhão, rice was a cruel crop. "At six o'clock in the morning," Brandão Júnior wrote, "the overseer forces the poor slave, still exhausted from the evenings labors, to rise from his rude bed and proceed to his work." An old man, who in the early twentieth century recalled his days as a slave in Maranhão, described a day beginning at four o'clock, "when a bell was struck and the overseers knocked at the houses of the slaves to be sure they awakened." Work, he said, continued until five in the evening.[28] In September and October, slaves' work consisted of 12 or more hours of slashing forest undergrowth. After the initial burn, they worked in shadeless fields, cutting and moving heavy trees to large piles. Of all the work in Maranhão, clearing fields was the most dangerous, often "fatal for a worker." Fires sometimes got out of control, resulting in some being burned alive and others being crushed by falling trees. "Rarely escapes some disgraced slave from becoming a victim," Brandão Junior wrote.[29]

Although less dangerous, weeding brought little relief. A constant chore throughout the early part of the rainy season, weeding was "painful labor for slaves, who, with nothing to work with but a weeding-hook, are forced to stand in a stooped position during the entire day, cutting the shoots of other native plants, and enduring a temperature in the sun of 40 Celsius [104 Fahrenheit]."[30] And harvesting brought no less discomfort. Slaves endured hot, shadeless 12-hour days, standing bent over to cut rice.

The physical toll that labor in fields took on slaves is obvious from plantation inventories, many of which justify lower-than-average values for slaves by listing injuries. Although there is no way of knowing how particular injuries occurred, we can assume that because plantation slaves spent 12 hours each day, six or seven days each week working for their masters, most injuries were directly related to their labor. Overworked and exhausted slaves could not avoid losing focus and accidentally cutting themselves or others with machetes, axes, scythes, planting sticks, and hoes. Sent into forests and fields without the protection of shoes or clothing beyond a loincloth or coarse cotton wrap, slaves suffered scrapes, cuts, and punctures to their extremities. Hazards were everywhere – from falling trees that could kill a man or break his bones, to sharply cut limbs and vines that could gouge an eye or slice a limb, to rice milling machinery that could catch a finger or whole

[27] AHU, Maranhão, cx. 45, doc. 4458.
[28] Eduardo 1948, 16.
[29] Brandão 1865, 31–8.
[30] Brandão 1865, 31–8.

arm in turning gears. Wounds that today would be considered minor often festered, becoming major health risks.

In inventories scribes made notes of slaves who were *aleijado* (crippled), *coxo* (lame), suffered *feridas* (wounds), or were *cego* (blind). On Antonio da Silva's plantation in 1824, seven slaves were blind in one or both eyes (and another had a seriously wounded eye), one had a "crippled" arm and one had a "crippled" foot, another had a "lame" leg, and another was listed as "sick in the legs."[31] On Felippe de Barros Vasconcellos's plantation in 1831, nine slaves were blind in one or both eyes (including several who were missing eyes), and 10 slaves had "crippled" limbs. In addition, eight were *ruim* ("defective" in a way that left them unable to work). Sometimes seriously wounded limbs were amputated and occasionally replaced with prosthetics.[32] Hence in 1813, Adão, a Bijago, was "crippled for not having a foot," and in 1810 an inventory taker noted that Julião had a "wooden leg."[33] Other possible work-related injuries recorded in inventories included broken ribs and shoulders and cuts on various parts of the body.[34]

One of the most common injuries from which slaves suffered was a *quebradura na verilha* – "rupture in the groin" or hernia of the inguinal or femoral variety.[35] Inguinal hernias are most often brought on by heavy lifting, which can result in the failure of an embryonic closure around the abdomen. When the embryonic closure herniates, the contents of the intestines descend into the hernia, causing a noticeable bulge. Hernias are not necessarily painful but can be uncomfortable. Moreover, if the intestines are pinched in the hernia, an obstruction can occur, resulting in strangulation followed by gangrene and death. Marçal, a 50-year-old Mandinka on Leonel Fernandes Vieira's plantation, may have suffered from a strangulated intestine as he was said to have a *quebradura na verilha* and obstruction. On the same plantation, 60-year-old Nastacio from Cape Verde also had a hernia.[36] And hernias are noted in many other inventories from the early nineteenth century. For example, in 1831 on Felippe de Barros Vasconcellos's plantation, five male slaves ranging in age from 20 to 60 had "bulges" or "ruptures" in their groins.[37] In 1807, on Antonio Henriques Leal's plantation, two male slaves had hernias, and in 1824 on Antonio da Silva's plantation, three male slaves had them.[38]

---

[31] Tribunal de Justiça do Estado do Maranhão (TJEM), São Luís, Maranhão, Brazil, Inventory of Antonio da Silva, 1821.
[32] TJEM, Felippe de Barros Vasconceallos, 1831.
[33] TJEM, Inventory of Antonio Joze Mesquita, 1813.
[34] TJEM, Inventory of Sargento Mór Manoel Joquim do Paço, 1823.
[35] See description of Miguel, in TJEM, Inventory of Jozefa Joaquina de Berredo, 1808.
[36] TJEM, Inventory of Leonel Fernandes Vieira, 1816.
[37] TJEM, Inventory of Felippe de Barros Vasconceallos, 1831.
[38] TJEM, Inventory of Antonio Henriques Leal, 1807.

The seriousness of some slaves' injuries is evidenced by the fact that after descriptions of wounds in inventories, notes were sometimes penned later in the margin stating *morto*, or "dead" and *falecido*, or "deceased." On Vasconcellos's plantation, 40-year-old Caetano, a Mandinka who was "crippled in an arm and leg," and 24-year-old Silvestre, a Bambara who was "crippled in the right leg," died shortly after notes were taken about them.[39] Similarly, in 1807 28-year-old Jacinto was listed in an inventory as "defective for having a wound on a leg." In the margin was later written "*falecido*."[40] In an 1813 inventory, 58-year-old Leonora was "sick with an illness of the foot." A short time later someone wrote beside her name, "This slave is dead."[41] In 1806, 50-year-old Alberto was said to have "an incurable illness in his right foot." Sometime later, *morto* was scrawled next to his name.[42]

Other records also reveal much about black slaves' treatment at the hands of their masters during Maranhão's plantation period. In the 1780s, a priest wrote of the treatment of slaves in Amazonia, "Those miserable slaves! There are *Senhores* who treat them like dogs. I have seen slaves crippled in the hands and feet, others with backs and lower parts covered with scars, the effects of punishment."[43] In a 1788 report from São Luís, Fernando de Foyoz emphasized "the horror" he felt when confronted with "the inhumanity with which slaves were treated" in Maranhão. Despite the fact that "slaves are very expensive," they were subjected to "great hunger, much work, greater punishments; everything consists of work without end or limit."[44] From observations made in 1819 and 1820, Friar Francisco de N. S. Dos Prazeres wrote that many slaves who arrived from Africa died each year from "mistreatment and sadness from knowing that they are separated forever from their country and relatives."[45] And D. J. G. de Magalhaens noted after his time in Maranhão in the 1830s that slaves "are treated with such barbarous rigor and when it is necessary to sustain them, they [the owners] don't: an ear of corn is lunch, rice and *farinha* [manioc flour] dinner; anything else they have is from stealing and hunting; they walk nude or covered with a small loincloth."[46] In the early nineteenth century, Antonio Pereira do Lago wrote that it was common for slaves to receive beatings from masters. The lives of slaves in Maranhão, he said, could be described in three words: "*misery, vice, and punishment.*" "There is not a population," he continued, "more disdained

---

[39] TJEM, Inventory of Felippe de Barros e Vasconceallos, 1831.
[40] TJEM, Inventory of Dona Anna Joquina Baldez, 1807.
[41] TJEM, Inventory of Jorge Gromuel, 1813.
[42] TJEM, Inventory of Anna Joaquina Gromuel, 1806.
[43] Quoted in Hoornaert 1992, 233.
[44] ANTT, Ministério do Reino, mç. 601, cx. 704.
[45] Dos Prazeres 1891, 140.
[46] Magalhaens 1865, 8.

and miserably treated and that suffers punishments more severe and capricious." "Punishment," he concluded, "is always and only corporal and painful."[47]

CONCLUSION

In this chapter, I have argued that although Upper Guineans brought knowledge of rice agriculture with them across the Atlantic, the system in which they applied that knowledge was oppressive to an extreme. The means of production were similar on either side of the ocean, but because the modes of production were different, Africans' hard work in rice fields brought few positive social rewards in the New World. By reframing the black rice thesis around questions about what Africans thought of the work they performed, the cruel brilliance of plantation rice systems becomes apparent. Those systems efficiently appropriated the skills of those they oppressed.

And this leaves us with the question of why? Why did Africans volunteer knowledge to a planter class that brutalized them? On provision grounds, it is likely that Africans chose the crops they raised, applying particular knowledge for the purpose of recreating culinary traditions. But in a master's field, what did an African gain from applying particular technologies? It may be that people do what they know how to do. Put rice farmers in rice fields, and they will work as they always have. It may also be that the incentives offered by the task system encouraged slaves to work efficiently. Whatever the case, a focus on the cultural meaning of work shows that plantation systems placed severe constraints on African's abilities to reproduce aspects of the cultures from which they came. Upper Guinean farmers brought with them knowledge of how to work efficiently over a difficult crop, but the ties between that work and African conceptions of personhood, ritual obligations, and collective cultural identity were broken.

---

[47] Pereira do Lago 1822, 25.

13

White Rice: The Midwestern Origins of the Modern Rice Industry in the United States

Peter A. Coclanis

The history of the U.S. rice industry isn't very well known even in the United States. There are many reasons for this lack of knowledge. Rice has never held a prominent place on the North American table, much less been considered the staff of life in the United States. In the entire history of rice cultivation in the United States, it has been cultivated in a major way in only a handful of places, and in relative terms, there have never been a lot of farmers involved in its production.[1] Today, of course, food studies are hot, but even with "commodity" histories all the rage, other cultigens and foods grab most of the attention, and to devotees of "food porn" rice is neither *outré* enough nor sufficiently controversial to capture market share from shark fins, high fructose corn syrup, baby calves, or foie gras.

Indeed, but for minor dust-ups regarding the burning of stubble in harvested rice fields in the Sacramento Valley of California and the introduction of GMO rice cultivars such as Bayer's LL62, the only rice story of note in the United States in recent years has been one concerning its purported "Black" origins. According to a number of prominent scholars, beginning with Peter Wood in 1974, and including among others Daniel Littlefield and, most notably and insistently, Judith Carney, the American rice narrative properly begins not with European and Euro-American populations in South Carolina in the late seventeenth century, but rather with enslaved West Africans, who transferred to South Carolina and other parts of the Americas their own "indigenous knowledge system" regarding risiculture. Once transferred, West African rice technology over time was appropriated by Euro-American slaveholders, who reaped the vast majority of the benefits of the same. Although proponents of the "Black rice" thesis differ in details, degree, and levels of adamancy, they generally contend that West African rice-growing practices and protocols regarding seed selection, cropping

---
[1] Coclanis 2010b, 411–31.

regimes, agricultural implements, irrigation systems, methods of milling, and the sexual division of labor – indeed, labor organization per se – were transferred to, or at least had analogues in the Americas, and that Africans and African Americans were the principal, if not the sole progenitors of the same. The white role in all of this – at least early on – is reduced essentially to one of expropriation of African and African American intellectual property.[2]

That the Black rice thesis has garnered considerable outside attention along with a good deal of scholarly acclaim is not surprising. A number of the scholars associated with the thesis are quite distinguished, and the thesis comports nicely with several broad scholarly trends of the past few decades, most notably "Atlantic" approaches to understanding developments in early American history and the seemingly urgent imperative among some to grant greater agency to any and all subaltern groups. Although I have been – along with David Eltis, Philip Morgan, and David Richardson – among the most vigorous critics of the "Black Rice" thesis, at least in its more categorical and perforce reductionist forms, I think that the evidence marshaled by proponents of the thesis is more than sufficient to demonstrate that an African "knowledge system" or, more likely, African knowledge systems, played a significant role in shaping the early history of rice cultivation in the Americas. I believe, however, that whites played a more significant role in shaping this history than proponents of the "Black rice" thesis allow. Indeed, without white capital, entrepreneurship, and organizational capacity – and, it should also be noted, without European and Euro-American indigenous knowledge systems pertaining to agriculture and trade – no rice industry *qua* industry would have emerged in the Americas in the so-called early modern period. In other words, without whites, rice would have been about as important in early America as Guinea corn (sorghum), another transplanted African crop. And, for the record, it should be pointed out that it was *O. sativa* – a species indigenous to Asia, though also grown in West Africa – rather than *O. glaberrima*, upon which the American rice industry was built.[3]

In any case, whether the American rice industry's origins were exclusively Black or otherwise, what we find is that, for hundreds of years after its original introduction, wherever rice was grown for markets in a systematic commodified way in the Americas – that is to say, mainly along the South Atlantic coast of North America and, to a lesser extent, in northeastern and later southern Brazil – production was characterized by arduous labor requirements and, thus, in a technical sense, by high labor inputs and great labor intensity. This was so even when rice was grown "dry," as it was at times in Brazil, in "humid swamp" ecosystems without benefit of irrigation. In North America, rice, from very early on, was cultivated in paddies irrigated

---

[2] Wood 1974, 55–62 esp.; Littlefield 1981, 74–114; Carney 1993b, Carney 1996; Carney 2001; Porcher 1993, 127–47; Porcher and Rayner 2001; Carney and Rosomoff 2009, 150–4 passim.
[3] Coclanis 2002, 247–8; Coclanis 2000; Eltis et al 2007; Eltis 2010.

in various ways, but principally via water impoundments and gravity-flow technology or, more commonly as time passed, via tidal rivers, whose diurnal water flows were manipulated onto and off of the fields through elaborate "rice works" comprised of bunds and embankments, sluices and gates, with canals of various size separating the paddy fields. The construction and upkeep of such rice works required heavy inputs of labor, and, because rice was cultivated as a row crop, weeding and hoeing requirements were also stringent. Although rice was not sown in nurseries in these areas and, thus, there was no need for transplanting, overall labor requirements in commercial paddy-rice production in the Americas were very heavy, particularly once harvesting and post-harvesting activities are figured in.[4]

Given these realities and the fact that the principal rice zones in the Americas were centered in malarial areas, the populations living in which were burdened by heavy disease loads and high mortality rates, it is not surprising that until the institution of slavery was abolished, African and African American slaves comprised the vast majority of the labor force in the American rice industry. Indeed, for decades after the demise of slavery in the Americas, African Americans, now free, continued to supply almost all of the labor power in the industry. And because of the economies of scale possible in commercial rice production in the Americas, most of the rice produced for markets was produced on plantations (or, later, so-called neo-plantations), employing large numbers of slaves/free Blacks doing specialized work on units subdivided into numerous small paddy fields, irrigated or otherwise. And, except in the case of milling – rice mills increasingly employed water and steam power in the nineteenth century – these laborers toiled without much in the way of mechanized equipment of any kind. These, then, were the facts on the ground for commercial rice production in the Western Hemisphere until the late nineteenth century.[5] Beginning in the mid-1880s, though, a small cohort of white Midwesterners – perceiving, then seizing opportunities opening up on the isolated prairies of southwestern Louisiana – succeeded through an act of what might be called agricultural transubstantiation in turning rice into wheat, as it were. In so doing, they ushered in a revolution, the results of which completely remade the U.S. rice industry (Figure 13.1a. and Figure 13.1b).

The spatial geographies of both the U.S. and the Brazilian rice industry changed dramatically in the nineteenth century. The rice industry in Brazil, which was far less important in commercial terms than that of the United States, shifted first, its center moving with the rest of the Brazilian economy from the northeast (Pará and especially Maranhão) to the south (Rio and São Paulo, and later further south to Rio Grande do Sul) beginning in the early

---

[4] Coclanis 2010b; Carney 2004; Pereira and Guimarães 2010, 445–6; Hawthorne 2010b.
[5] Hawthorne 2010b.

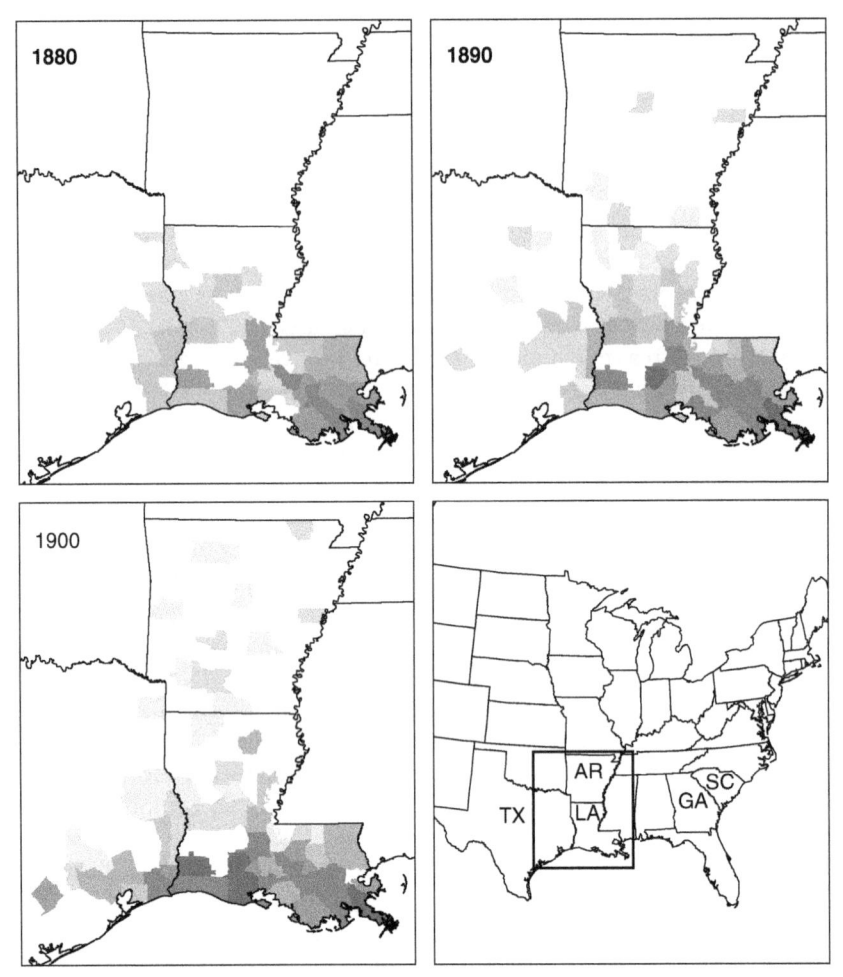

FIGURE 13.1A Geographic distribtion of pounds of rice produced in Southwestern states 1880–1900.
Data source: U.S. agricultural census. Maps by: GR Dobbs.

nineteenth century.[6] The shift in the United States came later and explaining its causes has proved far more controversial.

For the first 180 years of its existence the locus of the U.S. rice industry lay along the South Atlantic coast. Although the rice zone in this area stretched from the Cape Fear region of southeastern North Carolina to the St. Johns River region in northeast Florida, coastal areas in South Carolina and, later,

---

[6] Hawthorne 2010b; Mandell 1971; Alden 1984-1995.

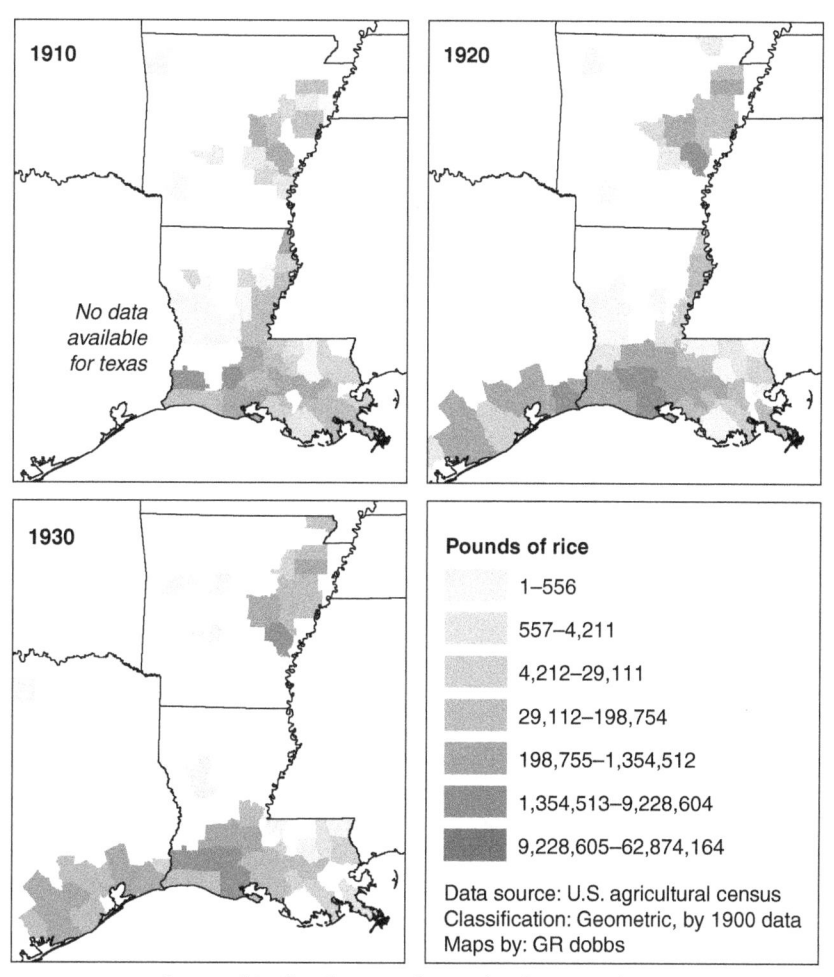

FIGURE 13.1B Geographic distribution of pounds of rice produced in Southwestern states 1910–30.
Data source: U.S. agricultural census. Maps by: GR Dobbs.

Georgia always dominated production in the region. This was so from the time the industry *qua* industry began in the early eighteenth century, through its supercession beginning in the mid-1880s by Louisiana and later other rice-producing states in the "Old Southwest" (Mississippi, Louisiana, Arkansas, and Texas), right down to 1920, by which time the South Atlantic rice industry had totally collapsed.[7]

---

[7] Coclanis 2010b, 1993. For detailed case studies of the epicenters of the South Atlantic rice industry, see Coclanis 1989; Stewart 1996.

The reasons for the difficulty in explaining the causes of this shift are many, and make for a wonderful textbook case regarding the complex nature of historical detective work. Because this chapter is principally about the rice revolution in the Old Southwest rather than the history of the rice industry in the South Atlantic region, I shall not tarry on the reasons for the collapse of the "first" rice industry in the United States. I have written at length on this question elsewhere, and interested readers can readily access my writings on this subject and assess the merits of the revisionist argument I make. The following brief discussion must suffice for our purposes here.[8]

To cut to the chase: With one notable exception – the Harvard economist Arthur H. Cole, writing in the 1920s – every scholar who wrote on the demise of the South Atlantic rice industry before me attributed its fate solely to domestic causes.[9] In so doing, they have attributed the industry's demise to a variety of factors ranging from entrepreneurial lethargy on the part of rice planters, factors, and merchants to an unfortunate series of weather shocks and disturbances in the late nineteenth century, an earthquake and several major hurricanes, most notably. Generally speaking, however, they have placed most of the blame in one way or another on the Civil War and its consequences. Whether it was wartime destruction to rice works, trade disruptions, emancipation, the difficulty of reorganizing the labor force in rice on the basis of something other than chattel slavery – or, more commonly, some combination of these factors – the Civil War was said to have brought a healthy industry to its knees (thence to be rendered completely prostrate, according to most writers, because of the indifferent entrepreneurial response by languorous planters and listless traders, as well as the aforementioned weather events of the late nineteenth century).

The problem with the Civil War/domestic demise explanatory line, so I discovered in the 1980s when I began studying the history of the international rice trade, was that it neglected almost entirely market considerations, particularly long-term changes in rice supply. As suggested at the outset of this chapter, the domestic market for U.S. rice has never been large – even today the United States generally produces less than 2 percent of the world's rice, but generally accounts for 10–12 percent of world exports – and in the eighteenth century and the nineteenth century up until 1860 most of the market rice produced in the South Atlantic region was exported.[10] During this period, the principal export markets for rice (and its byproducts) from this region were in northern Europe, where it proved a versatile and relatively cheap source of complex carbohydrates for humans and animals and a useful industrial crop. Between the middle of the eighteenth century and the 1830s, "Carolina" rice, which consisted of two principal varieties – both of which

---

[8] Coclanis 1989; Coclanis 1993b; Coclanis 1995; esp. Coclanis 2010a, xvii–xxxi.
[9] Cole 1927.
[10] Coclanis 2010b, 428–9; Coclanis 1993b, 1063 (Table 4), 1070 (Table 9).

were considered by northern Europeans to be of high quality and were thus relatively expensive – dominated the major markets in the United Kingdom, the Netherlands, and Germany. Beginning in the 1790s, however, cheap Asian rice began appearing in these markets, first, from Bengal, but also from Java in the late 1820s and 1830s, from Tenasserim and Arakan in the 1840s, and from Lower Burma, Siam, and Cochinchina in the 1850s.

One result, then, of increased market integration during the globalization wave of the long nineteenth century – a relatively minor result in the great scheme of things – was the supplanting of U.S. rice (and Western rice more generally) by cheaper Asian grain in the main markets where they competed with one another. In the first half of the nineteenth century, the main arena of competition was in the rapidly growing rice markets in urbanizing/industrializing northern Europe. Rice from the South Atlantic lost market share in northern Europe to Asian rice throughout the first six decades of the nineteenth century, and by 1860 had been rendered a relatively minor player in this market.

Although U.S. exporters tried to compensate by pushing expansion into markets closer to home – particularly into nearby Cuba and Puerto Rico, late-developing sugar plantation colonies in the West Indies – total U.S. rice exports in the 1850s (almost all of which originated in the South Atlantic states) were considerably lower than they had been in the 1830s, indeed, lower even than they had been in the 1790s. This, one should note, without compensating growth in the domestic market.

As the above summary suggests, the South Atlantic rice industry was in trouble, deep trouble, even before the advent of the Civil War, trouble signaled as well by the declining – even negative – profit picture in the industry in the 1850s. If all of this is true, why have scholars missed the (rice) boat? For a variety of reasons, I submit, including but not limited to the following facts: (1) it is fiendishly difficult to reconstruct Western rice markets during this period, not least because rice was a minor crop in these markets with many intermediate usages; (2) U.S. historians, until relatively recently, have been notoriously parochial and inward-looking, and therefore loath even to consider external, non-domestic explanatory variables; (3) the Civil War is the central event in the American historical imagination, and the key dividing point in American history (e.g., U.S. history survey courses are usually split into two "halves," U.S. History to 1865 and U.S. History after 1865); and (4) historians studying the rice industry have generally framed their enquiries too narrowly in a *temporal* as well as a spatial sense, leading them in a relative sense to neglect long-term market trends and, as a result, to succumb to the *post hoc ergo propter hoc fallacy* in explaining the rice industry's demise in the South Atlantic states.

The real decline narrative in my view goes something like this. As a global market for agricultural commodities, including rice, gradually emerged over the course of the long nineteenth century, the South Atlantic rice region, a high-cost producer in world terms, increasingly lost its competitive position in its most important markets (northern Europe) to Asian producers of cheaper rice. Principals in the South Atlantic rice industry became increasingly aware of what I have referred to elsewhere as the "distant thunder" emanating from Asia, and took various steps throughout the so-called antebellum period to adjust, attempting, for example, to modernize the industry, improve labor productivity, develop new export markets as well as the domestic market, and get tariff protection against foreign rice. They were successful to some extent in these endeavors – tariffs against foreign rice were first levied in the 1840s, for example – but not enough to turn the tide. One key problem related, ironically, to the rapid expansion of the cotton economy across the U.S. South. Bluntly put, the robust profit possibilities in cotton made it more difficult for rice interests to secure investments in rice. Indeed, many rice planters and merchants invested their own money in cotton rather than rice.

By the late 1850s, then, the rice industry was already in crisis: According to one careful econometric study, the average rate of return on South Carolina and Georgia rice farms and plantations in 1859 was a chilling –28.3 percent, and another close study puts the annual net rate of return in the Georgetown District of South Carolina – the epicenter of the industry in the South Atlantic states – at somewhere between –3.52 and –4.73 for the entire decade of the 1850s. And then the war came, with all its attendant disruptions, dislocations, and economic and social concatenations, the most important of which, obviously, was the end of chattel slavery.

To be sure, even with emancipation and with it the forced, uncompensated liquidation of a huge proportion of the rice region's wealth portfolio – over 50 percent of total wealth in the South Carolina low country in 1860 was held in the form of human beings – labor-intensive, non-mechanized rice production survived for a considerable period of time in the South Atlantic states after the war. As late as 1879, over 75 percent of total U.S. rice production (admittedly, a total less than 59 percent of that in 1859) came from the region (see Table 13.1). And, again, this rice was produced with free workers, employed in a complex variety of contractual arrangements, working much the same way as they had done prior to Civil War.

During the same period – the late 1860s and 1870s – rice production grew rapidly in another part of the United States: in low swampy grounds along the Mississippi River in the state of Louisiana. Small amounts of rice had been grown in southern Louisiana since the region was held by the French in the eighteenth century. During the late antebellum period, commercial production there for the first time became of some significance. In 1859, for example, about 3.4 percent of the total U.S. rice crop of 187.2 million pounds of clean rice came from Louisiana. In this part of Louisiana, rice was grown in much the same way as in the South Atlantic states, that is to say, on small paddy fields, with labor-intensive methods, and little mechanization. The principal difference between production in this region and production in the

TABLE 13.1. *Rice production in the United States, 1839–1919 (millions of pounds of clean rice)*

	1839	1849	1859	1869	1879	1889	1899	1909	1919
Total production	80.8	143.6	187.2	73.6	110.1	128.6	250.3	658.4	1,065.2
Primary production states (% of total crop)									
S. Carolina	75.0	74.3	63.6	43.9	47.3	23.6	18.9	2.5	0.4
Georgia	15.3	18.1	28.0	30.2	23.0	11.3	4.5	0.7	0.2
N. Carolina	3.5	2.5	4.1	2.8	5.1	4.6	3.2	0.0	0.0
Louisiana	4.5	2.0	3.4	21.5	21.1	58.8	69.0	49.6	45.3
Texas	0.0	0.0	0.0	0.1	0.1	0.1	2.9	41.2	15.0
Arkansas	0.0	0.0	0.0	0.1	0.0	0.0	0.0	5.9	19.2
California	0.0	0.0	0.0	0.0	0.0	0.0	0.0	0.0	19.6

Source: See Peter A. Coclanis. 1993. Distant thunder: the creation of a world market in rice and the transformations it wrought, *American Historical Review* 98 (October): 1050–1078, esp. p. 1070, Table 9.

South Atlantic states related to irrigation technology. In Louisiana methods of impounding/utilizing water for flooding the rice paddies were less costly and much less labor intensive than was the case in the South Atlantic tidal cultivation regimes, particularly by the 1850s when planters began to utilize steam engines connected to large, low-pressure pumps to draw water over the Mississippi River levees and onto and off of adjacent rice fields.[11]

The competitive advantage for growers along the Mississippi vis à vis growers in the South Atlantic states was such that the proportion of total U.S. rice production originating in southeastern Louisiana grew from 3.4 percent in 1859 to over 21 percent by 1879. Again, though, this only meant that growers in southeastern Louisiana – large planters mostly, many of whom had shifted production from sugar, which was even more labor-intensive than rice, after the Civil War – were claiming a bigger share of a smaller (rice) pie. Moreover, it should be noted that by 1879 the United States had been knocked out of export markets altogether by Asian exporters, and had itself become a major net importer of Asian rice. This, despite rising tariffs

---

[11] On the evolution of the U.S. rice industry during the period outlined above, see, Coclanis 1989, 133–42. On the price differentials between U.S. and Asian rice, see Coclanis 1989, 136, 281, note 57; Coclanis 1993b, 1066. For detailed information on the price differentials between "Carolina" rice and East Indian rice in the first half of the nineteenth century, see the collection of "Prices Current" from Liverpool and Rotterdam in the Enoch Silsby Collection, Southern Historical Collection, University of North Carolina, Chapel Hill, N.C. For an early assessment of rice cultivation in Louisiana, see Wilkinson 1848, 53–7; Knapp 1899, 17–21; Phillips 1951; Dethloff 1988, 60–5.

on rice imports. As the 1880s began, then, the U.S. rice industry as a whole was in crisis, despite the expansion of production along the Mississippi River in southeastern Louisiana. By the middle of that decade however, dramatic change was underway in the U.S. rice industry, as a result of an unusual, even uncanny convergence of actors, institutions, and processes in the southwestern part of that same state.

The upshot of this (harmonic?) convergence was the creation in relatively short order of an entirely new rice industry in the United States. This creation story, like most others, can be framed in a number of different ways. One can, for example, privilege economic discourse, emphasize relative factor prices, and tell a story of technological change via either induced innovation (*à la* Hayami-Ruttan) or more recent – and elaborate and sophisticated – endogenous growth models.[12] One can, however, take another path, as it were, and privilege historical discourse and tell a story of real people, discrete actions, and institutional imperatives and operations. Here, we shall take the latter path, but, in so doing, end up, as we shall see, more or less in the same place.

In recent decades an impressive literature has emerged in economic history and the history of technology on the role of technology networks in the innovation process. A good bit of work in this field has dealt with the role of networks in agricultural innovation, including innovation regarding the mechanization of production technology in small grains. None of the innovation networks involved in small-grains mechanization is more interesting – or implausible – than that treated here. Indeed, the social assemblage – to use Bruno Latour's terminology – that came together in southwestern Louisiana in the 1880s to spark the so-called rice revolution is difficult to imagine, much less to conjure up.[13]

What are the chances that a "network" of Midwestern developers, educators, and agronomists – all of them white and most with ties to Iowa – would successfully leverage their own intellectual, financial, and social/cultural capital with material resources from investors in the Northeast and Great Britain, the

---

[12] For the classic formulations of the Hayami-Ruttan approach, see Hayami et al. 1970, 1115–41; Hayami and Ruttan 1985. Simply put, the induced-innovation approach, articulated originally by Hicks (1932) views productivity gains as arising from output-augmenting and input-saving technologies involving the substitution of relatively cheap factors for relatively expensive ones. Note that Olmstead and Rhode (1993) usefully complicate the Hayami-Ruttan model with respect to U.S. agriculture and, more fully, in Olmstead and Rhode 2008, 1–16 and passim.

[13] On innovation networks and the mechanization of small-grains production in the late nineteenth century specifically, see, Evans 2007; Winder 2012. The networks treated by Evans and Winder – like those treated in this chapter – were transnational in nature. For an introduction to Bruno Latour's controversial approach, see Latour 2005. The term *social assemblage* is associated as well with other theorists such as Gilles Deleuze, Féliz Guattari, and Manuel de Landa.

state of Louisiana, and various and sundry railroads, banks, land development companies, and Louisiana capitalists in such a way as in a few short years to establish a dynamic new "high tech" rice industry on sparsely settled and scarcely developed land in "Cajun country" in southwestern Louisiana, that is, a part of the state inhabited at the time mostly by descendants of French Acadians from the Maritime Provinces of Canada, who had sought refuge in Louisiana after having been expelled from their homeland by the British after the Seven Years' War? What are the chances? Minuscule – yet this is what happened. Strange, but true. And if the expansion of the U.S. rice industry onto the prairies of the Old Southwest was less impressive and important in world historical terms than the more or less simultaneous expansion of production in Southeast Asian rice frontiers such as the Irrawaddy (Ayeyarwady) Delta of Lower Burma and the Mekong Delta in Indochina, it was hardly small potatoes either.[14]

Expansionism had been a constant theme in southern history since the seventeenth century, and the push into the "Old Southwest" (Mississippi, Louisiana, Arkansas, and Texas) proved particularly appealing both to planters and to capitalists of one sort or another – land developers, promoters, railroad men, merchants, and so on – beginning in the antebellum period. Regarding southwestern Louisiana *per se*: New Orleans interests, desirous of establishing rail links to Texas, began pushing west in the 1840s and had actually built a line westward into Cajun country before the Civil War. Dislocations associated with both the war and its aftermath slowed down further expansion, and it was not until the early 1880s that the line between New Orleans and Houston – via Orange, Texas on the Sabine River separating Louisiana from Texas – was completed. Once such links were established, development of some sort in the swamplands and the desolate prairies of southwest Louisiana became a realistic possibility for the first time – as actors of various kinds far and wide were quick to note.

Corporations – the Southern Pacific Railroad, the Southwest Immigration Company, and a British entity, the North American Land and Timber Company, Ltd., most notably – took the lead early on. They were aided and abetted in this project by officials of the state of Louisiana itself, who obviously was looking to promote development in a remote section of the state, along with a colorful cast of promoters, entrepreneurs, and agronomists, as well as assorted hustlers and flim-flam men. And, truth be told, the above efforts met with considerable success, as south central and

---

[14] For source material on the early days of the U.S. rice industry in the Old Southwest, see, for example, Southern Pacific Railroad Company 1899; Knapp 1899, esp 21–37; Southern Pacific [Railroad] Company 1901; Knapp 1910; Perrin 1910, 97; Small and St. Louis Southwestern Railway Company 1910, 3–8 and passim; *Arkansas* 1911, 9–10, 12; Surface 1911, 500–9; Chambliss 1920; Monroe and Fondren 1916; Jones et al. 1938; Spicer 1964. On the expansion of the Burmese rice industry into the Burma Delta and that of Indochina deeper and deeper into the Mekong Delta, see Adas 1974; Brocheux 1995; Biggs 2010.

southwestern Louisiana began to attract migrants from other parts of Louisiana – mostly whites, but some African Americans – and from other states, along with some foreign immigrants as well.[15]

The leading promoters of southwest Louisiana in the 1880s, particularly of its agricultural development, constituted a triumvirate of Midwesterners: Sylvester L. Cary, Jabez B. Watkins, and Seaman A. Knapp. They sometimes collaborated on settlement and development schemes, at other times pursued parallel projects, and at still other times found themselves competing with one another. What makes them interesting for our purposes was the degree to which they shared the same networks, networks that would prove ultimately prove central to the rice revolution.[16]

All three of these men had close connections to Iowa. Cary, a native Iowan, took up work as an immigration agent and land developer in southwest Louisiana in the early 1880s, supposedly "seeking a home where there was neither winter nor mortgages." If we take him at his word the fact that he teamed up at times with Watkins was in some ways ironic, for Watkins – something of a George F. Babbitt or even a Richard Roma *avant la lettre* – was a land speculator, farm-mortgage broker, and developer par excellence, whose business practices over the years were, shall we say, not without controversy. Working mainly out of Kansas in the early 1880s when his interest in Texas and Louisiana began to heat up, he, along with his affiliates at a branch office he had established in London, organized the North American Land and Timber Company in the United Kingdom, which company quickly raised sufficient capital to acquire huge amounts of undeveloped land in southwest Louisiana. When it came time to recruit settlers to the area and to develop the lands he had acquired, Watkins turned for help to his brother-in-law, Alexander Thompson, who was teaching agriculture at the Iowa Agricultural College [now Iowa State University] in Ames. His interest piqued, Thompson agreed to help promote agricultural development in the region, and, more importantly as it turned out, enticed Knapp, one of his colleagues at the Iowa Agricultural College – the president of the school, in fact – to join him in his promotional efforts in Louisiana.[17]

---

[15] Apart from the works mentioned already, see also Post 1940; Ginn 1940; Bailey 1945; Phillips 1951; Millet 1964; Babineaux 1967; Dethloff 1970; Daniel 1985; Dethloff 1988, 63–127; Coclanis 2010b, 422–9.

[16] For biographical data on these men, see anon. "Father Cary, Rice Missionary," *Rice Journal*, 1909, 137–8; "S.L. Cary Dies, Beloved by Many," *Times-Democrat* [Jennings, Louisiana], January 22, 1915, in Scrapbook; Bailey 1945, Speech [typescript], S. Arthur Knapp, February 26, 1953, McNeese State College, Lake Charles, Louisiana, Seaman A. Knapp Papers, Louisiana and Lower Mississippi Valley Collections, LSU; Bogue 1953, 26–59; Delavan 1963, 68–77; Cline 1970; Daniel 1985, 39–61; Dethloff 1988, 63–80.

[17] This discussion is drawn from materials found in the works cited in endnote 16. The quote from Cary can be found in Chapter 1 in Riser 1948. Thesis online at http://library.mcneese.edu/depts/archive/FTBooks/jennings.htm [accessed July 30, 2014].

In many ways Knapp was the key node in the complex, overlapping information, technology, and innovation networks that were in my view both necessary and sufficient to explain the rice revolution in southwest Louisiana. Not only was he an agronomist (and, later, breeder) of note, but also an agricultural journalist: he edited the *Western Stock Journal and Farmer*, out of Cedar Rapids, Iowa, progenitor of *Wallace's Farmer*, the celebrated agricultural journal. In addition, he played a leading role in the movement in the 1880s to create a system of government–funded agricultural experiment stations, which movement reached fruition with the passage of the Hatch Act of 1887.

Knapp's range of contacts inside and outside of Iowa was broad and deep. He was close friends, for example, with James ("Tama Jim") Wilson, a Scot, who, after migrating to Iowa as a young man, became a powerful political figure in the Hawkeye State, before serving as U.S. Secretary of Agriculture between 1897 and 1913. It should be noted that Wilson, while Secretary of Agriculture, appointed Knapp "Agricultural Explorer" for the Department, and sent him on two long – and ultimately, very successful – trips to Asia (1898, 1901) in search of better varieties of rice and other cultigens. It should be noted as well that Wilson, like Knapp and Thompson, was at various points a professor of agriculture at Iowa State. Wheels within wheels, in other words.

Knapp's contacts transcended the worlds of commerce, education, and government, pushing into the spiritual realm as well: he was a Methodist minister, and spent two years as pastor of a rural church in Vinton, Iowa, interacting closely with the types of Protestant farmers who came to constitute the Midwestern migrant pool to southwestern Louisiana. Indeed, Knapp, Cary, Watkins, and other promoters of southwest Louisiana (as well as of southeast Texas and, later, of east central Arkansas) worked faith communities in the rural Midwest assiduously and successfully when promoting migration south.[18]

They worked these communities – and others – by tapping old, and creating new information networks in very energetic and enterprising ways. Once the railroad opened up southwest Louisiana and individual and corporate promoters acquired vast chunks of marshland and prairie land in the region – dirt cheap, I might add – the trio began to settle and develop the same. Employing an impressive array of marketing strategies and tactics – circulars, pamphlets, planted newspaper articles, lectures and testimonials, free sightseeing tours, farm-inspection trips, and so on – agents

---

[18] Bailey 1945, 44–132; Daniel 1985, 40–46; Dethloff 1988, 69–80. Knapp's networks extended to the African American community as well. For example, his time at Iowa State Agricultural College – and, more specifically, his friendship there with James Wilson – connected him with the famous agronomist and distinguished Iowa State alumnus George W. Carver. Hersey 2011, 27–34, 128–30, 155–7.

representing railroads, land companies, syndicates, and, of course, themselves on the side enticed thousands of Midwestern farmers from Iowa, Illinois, Indiana, Ohio, Wisconsin, Nebraska, the Dakotas, Missouri, and Kansas to the Old Southwest.[19]

Between 1880 and 1900, the population of "southwest Louisiana" – broadly defined as the "Cajun" parts of southern Louisiana stretching westward to the Texas line from Baton Rouge – grew rapidly, with the southwestern prairie parishes alone almost doubling in size. To be sure, much of this population growth was due to newcomers from more settled parts of Louisiana, particularly in the east. But a critical part was comprised of expectant corn- and wheat-belt farmers, fleeing low commodity prices, snow, blizzards, and droughts, and hopeful of finding something better in the South. And the rapid populating of both the marshlands and the fertile but desolate prairie lands by white emigrés from the Midwest was due in large part to the success of "nodes" – to use the language of Social Network Analysis (SNA) – such as Knapp, Cary, and Watkins, whose networks in the heartland of America were widespread and distinct, even if they partially overlapped like Venn diagrams. In some ways, the fact that their networks were only loosely linked may even have been advantageous. In this regard, one thinks immediately of sociologist Mark Granovetter's famous "strength of weak ties" formulation, which seems apposite in attempting to explain the successful colonization of the predominantly Catholic Cajun country of southwest Louisiana by Protestant farmers from the Midwest, as the loosely aligned micro networks of the aforementioned promoters concatenated into a major macro development: the demographic and economic reconstitution of southwest Louisiana.[20]

---

[19] See the works cited in endnotes 15 and 16. For examples of such promotional materials, see "The Prairie Region: Southwestern Louisiana" [broadside], Jennings, Calcasieu Parish, 1885-86, Cary Scrapbook, pp. 290-1, Louisiana and Lower Mississippi Valley Collections, LSU; "Sioux City, (Iowa) Corn Palace 1889. Opens September 23d. Closes October 5th. Louisiana Exhibit!" [printed circular], Cary Scrapbook, pp. 459-60, Louisiana and Lower Mississippi Valley Collections, LSU. Rice is mentioned as being among the exhibited products. Also see Passenger Department, Southern Pacific Railway, comp., *Rice Cook Book* 1902. I used a copy included in the Seaman Knapp Papers, Louisiana and Lower Mississippi Valley Collections, LSU.

[20] Social Network Analysis (SNA), one of the leading tools in the social sciences, is concerned with relationships of various kinds between and among individuals, institutions, or organizations (between and among "nodes" and "ties" or "links"). Actor-Network Theory (ANT), which developed out of the field of STS (Science and Technology Studies), is related, though controversial among many because of its attribution of agency to nonhumans (networks, institutions, machines, and the like). Granovetter's famous thesis is laid out in Granovetter 1973. For a recent challenge to parts of Granovetter's argument, see Van der Leij and Goyal 2011. The literature on the relationship among social capital, networks, and knowledge/technology transfer is vast; Coleman 1988, 95-120; Adlerand Kwon 2002; Inkpen and Tsang 2005, 146-65; McFadyen and Cannella 2004; Huber 2009.

Although the demographic reconstitution of this region by Midwesterners was the result of well laid plans and considerable coordination, its economic reconstitution was anything but. That is to say, as the migration from the Midwest began to take off in the early 1880s, few of the early migrants coming down – however entrepreneurial and commercially minded they might be – explicitly did so in order to grow rice. Like the region itself, this cereal first had to be sold, and its sale owed much to many, none more so than Seaman Knapp.

After an initial fact-finding visit to the area, Knapp moved with his family to southwest Louisiana in November 1885. He did so, as suggested earlier, at the behest of Alexander Thompson, who had recruited him to work for his brother-in-law, Jabez Watkins, whose huge development syndicate, the North American Land and Timber Company, had recently acquired about 1.5 million acres of land in the region. Settling originally in the newly established town of Lake Charles in Calcasieu Parish [County], Knapp, as the well-paid "Assistant Manager" of the syndicate, was tasked with two related, but nonetheless distinct responsibilities: recruitment of hardworking, commercially minded Midwestern farmers to the area, and, with a nod to his expertise and experience in agronomy, finding a crop or crops with profit potential for those recruited to the region's marshes and vast prairies.

Until the 1880s – indeed, even afterward – the largely Cajun population in the marshes practiced subsistence agriculture, hunted and fished, and grazed livestock where they could. In limited ways, the prairies were also sites of subsistence agriculture and cattle-grazing, that is, when they were put into productive use at all. Given the area's remoteness and lack of access to centers of trade, it is clear that the latter activity – meat on the hoof, as it were – offered the small population living on the prairies, particularly on the western prairies, its best (and perhaps only) chance effectively to participate in market exchange of any kind. With the coming of the railroad – and a series of river-dredging projects and port improvements successfully advanced by Watkins and his allies – other economic options became possible, including, for the first time, commercial agriculture. In essence, then, what we are witnessing in the region is an attempt by Midwestern business interests and corporations to transform agriculture along large-scale capitalist lines.

So alluring was the portrait of southwest Louisiana painted by promoters, or, conversely, so poor did prospects at home seem to farmers from the corn belt and the wheat belt, that many rural Midwesterners quit the most fertile farmland in the United States – and, in so doing, left behind kith and kin – for the chance to break largely untilled prairie soil and attempt to start anew. At first most believed they would be able to cultivate the same crops as they had back at home, but when they did, they failed to do so profitably, which put promoters such as Knapp in a fix. The region had been touted in the overhyped advertising language of the time in Edenic terms as a land, if not of milk and honey, then of various and sundry field crops, livestock, fruit, and vegetables, any and all of which, it was said, would render farmers prosperous, if not rich.

Fairly quickly, though, it began to dawn on the newcomers from the North that neither of the principal Midwestern mainstays – wheat or corn – did very well in southwest Louisiana. As Knapp and the other promoters – along with the migrants themselves – began to acclimate to the region, however, they took note of the fact that a crop which they were unfamiliar, rice, was being grown in small quantities by many Cajun farmers on the prairies. The crop seemed to do well in the humid subtropical climate of southwest Louisiana, even though it was cultivated without benefit of modern irrigation, dependent solely on rainwater impounded in rudimentary reservoirs. Such dependence led the Cajuns to call what they were growing "Providence" rice.

The similarities between rice and wheat quickly registered with both Knapp and the Midwestern immigrants: one didn't have to teach agriculture at Iowa State to recognize that rice and wheat were both cereal grasses with some (but not all) of the same cultivation characteristics. Given the commercial bent of both the promoters and the migrants, the failed experiments with other field crops, and the paucity of alternatives, interest in rice cultivation soon took off. Not only did Knapp set up demonstration farms upon which rice (and other crops) were grown, but many of the migrants, particularly those with previous experience in wheat, also began experimenting with rice cultivation – employing Midwestern wheat-production methods and Midwestern wheat-production technology.[21]

But we are getting ahead of ourselves, for various matters relating to soil and water had to be addressed in conjunction with those relating to cultivation technology. If they weren't addressed successfully, attempts at technological transfer on the prairies of southwest Louisiana, however effective, wouldn't be worth a great deal. First, soil. Both Knapp and other newcomers experimenting with rice quickly found that although the heavy silt and sandy soils on the prairies were very different than what they were used to in the Midwest, they were well suited for rice cultivation. Why? Because they were fertile and because the virtual impenetrability of their subsoil hardpans allowed these soils to hold and retain water for long periods of time. If adequate water resources were found to be available and if appropriate water control/irrigation works could be put into place, these soils, clearly, promised much.

And so, agricultural trials were soon mounted with various sources of water for irrigation. Even prior to Knapp's entrance on the scene, several elaborate exercises in water control and capital-intensive cultivation were attempted by the Watkins syndicate in southwest Louisiana, not on the prairie per se but on marshlands in Cameron Parish near the coast. These schemes involved not only large-scale land reclamation, dredging, and canal construction, but also complicated – indeed overly complicated – technology,

---

[21] See the works cited in endnotes 14, 15, and 16.

to wit: Barges, mounted with engines, aligned with one another in parallel canals as much as half a mile apart, pulled by cables connected to heavy agricultural equipment, which (in theory) would allow highly efficient gang plowing, seeding, cultivating, harvesting, and so on, by boat. Such efforts, in retrospect, always had something of a Rube Goldberg air about them and never amounted to much. They do, however, presage the capital-intensive turn agriculture in the area would soon take.[22]

As Knapp himself later pointed out, the rice revolution *qua* revolution in southwest Louisiana started with simpler methods of water control, mainly consisting of modest, piecemeal improvements in the earlier reservoir/ impoundment systems associated with "Providence" rice and in simple irrigation schemes. According to Knapp, "Wherever prairies were found sufficiently level [generally with slopes of less than 1 degree], with an intersecting creek, which could be used to flood them, they were surrounded by a small levee [...] These levees were usually 12 to 24 inches high, and the interior ditch was 12 to 18 inches deep and 4 or 5 feet wide." That was basically it at first. Water from the adjacent creeks was drawn on to and off of the fields, but "[v]ery few interior ditches were made" and little attention was paid to drainage. Impoundment reservoirs continued in use, but in times of drought "creeks failed, and reservoirs were found to be expensive and unreliable."

Over time – not much time, in the 1890s – more sophisticated irrigation works (powered by windmills, steam engines, or gas turbines), were erected by growers, and enterprisers, with support and encouragement from the likes of Knapp, Watkins, and Cary, had begun to establish private canal and irrigation companies in the rice region, which developed elaborate water-control and pumping schemes and protocols specifically for the upland prairies. Custom "pumping outfits" could soon be rented out by growers, and such outfits helped to regularize and routinize irrigation and field drainage. Moreover, by 1895 or so, water engineers had discovered that the prairie was underlain by huge underground reservoirs of water – in strata anywhere from 125 to 600 feet beneath the surface – which made it possible almost immediately via pipe wells, engines, and pumping systems to grow irrigated rice far removed from rivers, bayous, and streams. Talk about Providence!

Sophisticated water-pumping schemes would later come to embody rice cultivation in the "Old Southwest" as much or more than anything else, with the possible exception of the region's almost impossibly high degree of mechanization and capital intensity. And, as was the case with water control, with respect to methods and cultivation technology, such tendencies were evident early on as Midwestern migrants in pursuit of the main chance

---

[22] Knapp 1899, 21–2; Knapp 1910, 8–12; Chambliss 1920, 3–5; Jones 1938, 3–7; Bailey 1945, 113–16.

worked to make of southwest Louisiana an improved version of the agricultural lands they left behind.[23]

Knapp, tellingly, likened the rice fields of southwest Louisiana in the 1880s and 1890s to "the bonanza wheat farms of Dakota," the huge, heavily mechanized wheat-producing domains that sprung up in the Upper Great Plains beginning in the 1870s. These domains – Midwestern latifundia – arose for much the same reasons as the rice farms further south: the presence of aggressive promoters and entrepreneurs; the ready availability of abundant, cheap, fertile land; new types of labor-saving farm equipment and implements; adequate stocks of harvest labor; the completion of railroad lines through the region; ready access to modern milling facilities and markets. Although the farms on the rice prairies weren't nearly so large as the Bonanza wheat farms – one such farm in North Dakota stretched to 100,000 acres (7 times the size of Manhattan Island), another was over 60,000, a number were over 15,000 acres, and the "average" size was about 7,000 acres – the migrant farmers in southwest Louisiana were just as eager to mechanize as their brethren further north. And they were going to employ, after adaptation, one part of their "indigenous knowledge system" – wheat-cultivating machinery – in so doing.[24]

Thus, we find that adjustments were quickly made to familiar equipment used in wheat cultivation – gang plows, disc harrows, drills, broadcast seeders, and the like – in order to render such equipment suitable for rice. One important implement proved somewhat more difficult to adapt to rice, however: the twine binder. Even so, by 1884 one of the entrepreneurial Midwestern farmers who had migrated to the area – an Iowan named Maurice Brien, who had settled in the new town of Jennings, of which town Sylvester Cary is considered the "father" – had succeeded in adapting a Deering binder for use with rice. Within a few years the Deering Company was flooding southwest Louisiana with rice binders from its factory in Illinois. By the early 1890s steam tractors (widely deployed in the Great Plains and Far West as early as the 1870s) and threshers were also in use in rice.[25]

And by then, just a few short years after the rice revolution in southwest Louisiana had begun and before irrigation systems were very far along in the

---

[23] Knapp 1899, 22–5; Knapp 1910, 10–12, 14–15, 27–9 (quotes in text are from pp. 27–8).

[24] Knapp 1899, 22; Knapp 1910, 27–8. On the era of bonanza farms in the Dakotas, see Shannon 1945, 154–61; Drache 1964, 3–33. The figures in the text on the size of bonanza farms are from Shannon 1945, 158. Note that in 1920, 5.1 percent of all farms in North Dakota were larger than 1,000 acres, while only 1.0 percent of farms in the United States as a whole passed that threshold (Drache 1964, 8).

[25] Knapp 1899, 22, 26–9; Daniel 1985, 42–45; Dethloff 1988, 72–5. On the steam tractor and other improvements in agricultural technology during this period, see Hurt 1994, 194–203; White 2008. For excellent photographs of some of the mechanized farm equipment used in the early rice industry in Calcasieu Parish, see Benoit and Archives and Special and Collections Department Frazar Memorial Library 2000, 25–7, 30.

region, Louisiana had already leap frogged South Carolina to become the predominant rice producer by far in the United States. Louisiana's rapid ascent in the 1880s can be seen in Table 13.1. Moreover, by the end of the 1880s, southwest Louisiana already accounted for a sizable share of the rice produced in the state, with Acadia Parish – whose seat, Crowley, was to become a major milling center – producing more rice than any other parish in Louisiana. The share of the state's rice emanating from southwest Louisiana would increase dramatically during the 1890s so that by the turn of the century the amount of rice produced in this region totally dwarfed production elsewhere in the state. Even using a "narrow" definition of southwest Louisiana – the area (comprised of eleven parishes today) between the Mississippi escarpment on the east and the Sabine River on the west, and from 31° N to the Gulf of Mexico – the increased relative importance of the region in the state's rice economy is striking, as can be seen in Table 13.2.

On the southern Louisiana prairies, which extend westward from St. Landry/St. Martin parishes to the Texas border, rice production began to take on something of a standard cast or form by the late 1890s: sizable landholdings (some of which were thousands of acres in size), operated by big companies or owner-operators, often divided into tenant farms, worked by relatively affluent tenants who owned a good deal of expensive equipment; large rice fields of 60 to 80 acres (or even more) rather than tiny paddies;

TABLE 13.2. *Southwest Louisiana's share of total rice production in Louisiana, 1879–1929.*

Year	Total Rice Production Louisiana (in millions of pounds, clean rice)	SW Louisiana's Share (%)
1879	23.2	4.5
1889	75.6	30.2
1899	172.7	72.7
1909	326.6	73.2
1919	482.5	85.7
1929	489.5	95.6

Sources: U.S. Bureau of the Census, *Tenth Census of the United States, 1880*, Vol. 3 (1883): 280–3; U.S. Bureau of the Census, *Eleventh Census of the United States, 1890*, Vol. 10 (1896): 421, 435; U.S. Bureau of the Census, *Twelfth Census of the United States, 1900*, Vol. 6, Part 2 (1902): 2: 94, 192; U.S. Bureau of the Census, *Thirteenth Census of the United States, 1910*, Vol. 5 (1914): 621, 623; Vol. 6 (1913): 690–5; U.S. Bureau of the Census, *Fourteenth Census of the United States, 1920*, Vol. 5 (1922:) 709, 771–2; Vol. 6, Part 2 (1922): 31, 608–13; U.S. Bureau of the Census, *Fifteenth Census of the United States, 1930*, Vol. 2, Part 2 (1932): 91. Note that the figures for rough rice for 1909, 1919, and 1929 were converted to clean rice by assuming that 48 pounds of rough rice were equal to 30 pounds of clean rice. "Southwest Louisiana" is defined here as the area comprised by the following present-day parishes: Acadia, Allen, Beauregard, Calcasieu, Cameron, Evangeline, Jefferson Davis, Lafayette, Saint Landry, Saint Martin, and Vermilion.

irrigation, via water pumped from streams and bayous by farm owners or canal companies, or via pump wells scattered through the fields; capital-intensive cultivation, mainly with heavily mechanized wheat technology adapted for use in rice; harvesting and threshing with self-binders and steam threshers; labor provided mainly by owner-operators and/or tenants, with some casual labor (mostly white, especially in Arkansas, with some African Americans) used seasonally, particularly during the harvest. This "cast" was not what we would call modern by today's standards, but it was a far cry from the labor-intensive methods used in rice cultivation in the South Atlantic states or on the Mississippi River in Louisiana, or, indeed, anyplace else in the world at the time. Rice was well on its way to becoming wheat, as it were.[26] Given the characteristics outlined above, it is not surprising that, once the irrigation works were in place, the labor inputs for cultivating prairie rice were minimal vis à vis rice-cultivation regimes elsewhere in the world. At the peak of the rice industry in the South Atlantic states, for example, planters calculated that one full slave "hand" was needed to produce five or six acres of rice, plus an acre of food crops. By the late nineteenth century, this acreage figure had increased slightly, and it was estimated that one rice worker, devoting his/her efforts solely to rice, could cultivate eight acres. Compare this to the situation on the "mechanized" prairies of southwest Louisiana, where ca. 1900 one worker, with a team of mules, could cultivate 80–100 acres of rice, except during the harvest, when an additional worker was needed. Weeding requirements were minimal on the prairies, where winter crops were often cultivated on the rice fields limiting weed growth, and mechanical reapers and binders meant that there was no need for laborious hand harvesting via rice hooks and sickles. In contrast, at roughly the same time, tens of thousands of weeders – mainly females working for wages – were employed each year in the Italian rice industry during the growing season, and the harvest proved hugely labor-intensive in every other rice-producing area in the world.[27]

Thus, turning rice into wheat, so to speak, drastically reduced labor inputs: by 1910 on the Grand Prairie in east central Arkansas, the amount of rice land that one worker could tend had grown to 200 acres (with a bit of additional

---

[26] See the works cited in endnotes 14 and 15. For the figure on the typical size of the rice fields in southwest Louisiana, see Knapp 1899, 22; Knapp 1910, 10, 20, 28; Bailey 1945, 121. On the racial composition of the harvest labor force in the Old Southwest, see Mitchell 1949, 115–32, 122–3; Daniel 1985, 44–9; West 1987, 39–42.

[27] See the works cited in endnotes 14 and 15. Knapp (1899, 20) gives rice acres per hand in the United States (both in the Carolinas and in the Old Southwest) compared to other parts of the world. Additional estimates for the South Atlantic rice region are in Gray 1933, 1: 284; 2: 731. McNair (1924, 7–9) describes respective labor requirements in rice and cotton in early-twentieth-century Arkansas. Large number of female weeders were employed in the Italian rice industry in the period between the opening of the Canal Cavour (1866) and the World War I (Zappi 1991, 1–33, esp. 9–10).

TABLE 13.3 *Mean yield of clean rice per acre, southwest Louisiana, 1879–1929*

Year	Mean Yield
1879	480.5
1889	681.4
1899	801.3
1909	936.9
1919	1034.4
1929	1222.5

Sources: Compiled from U.S. Bureau of the Census, *Tenth Census of the United States, 1880*, Vol. 3 (1883): 280–3; U.S. Bureau of the Census, *Eleventh Census of the United States, 1890*, Vol. 10 (1896): 421, 435; U.S. Bureau of the Census, *Twelfth Census of the United States, 1900*, Vol. 6, Part 2 (1902): 2: 94, 192; U.S. Bureau of the Census, *Thirteenth Census of the United States, 1910*, Vol. 5 (1914): 621, 623; Vol. 6 (1913): 690–5; U.S. Bureau of the Census, *Fourteenth Census of the United States, 1920*, Vol. 5 (1922:) 709, 771–2; Vol. 6, Part 2 (1922): 31, 608–13; U.S. Bureau of the Census, *Fifteenth Census of the United States, 1930*, Vol. 2, Part 2 (1932): 91. Figures for rough rice for 1909, 1919, and 1929 were converted to clean rice by assuming that 48 pounds of rough rice were equal to 30 pounds of clean rice. Wickizer 1941, 318–9 provides yields in other parts of the world in the early twentieth century. See also Grist 1959, 359; Cheng 1968, 28–29.

hired labor for "shocking and thrashing"), and rice people began to think in terms of man/hours rather than man/days per acre. This said, one thing the "rice revolution" did not lead to was spectacular increases in yields. Indeed, although yields on the prairies of southwest Louisiana (ca. 800–1,000 pounds of clean rice per acre) were considerably higher than yields in the collapsing rice economy of the South Carolina low country between 1899 and 1919, they were generally much lower than was the case in the small (in some cases, tiny), non-mechanized paddy fields in Italy, East Asia, and parts of Southeast Asia. During that period they were even lower than in Lower Burma – whose rapidly expanding, but still rather rudimentary frontier rice complex was marked by farms much larger than in other parts of Asia.[28]

These results regarding yields should not surprise anyone; indeed, they didn't surprise contemporaries in southwest Louisiana at the time. In most cultivation schemes, rice yields, *ceteris paribus*, will increase with greater labor intensity (at least up to a certain point) and labor inputs were minimized in the rice production function in southwest Louisiana. Indeed, the entire

---

[28] Perrin 1910, 97. On calculations of man/hours in rice production in the United States and man/days in in other parts of the world, see Grist (1959, 384–6). Figures for yields of clean rice per acre can be calculated from the U.S. Census. Figures for southwest Louisiana for 1879–1929 are given in Table 13.3.

rice-production system on the prairies was designed – per Hayami-Ruttan – to minimize (relatively) scarce, (relatively) expensive labor and to maximize the amount of (relatively) cheap land each laborer could tend. Initially, land was exceedingly cheap in the marshlands and on the prairies of the Old Southwest – sometimes even free, or as little as $0.20-$0.50 per acre in the 1880s, and U.S. Department of Agriculture data on wages for rice workers around the world, ca. 1900–1910 (compiled by none other than the ubiquitous Seaman Knapp) demonstrate that daily farm wages (with board) in southwestern Louisiana and Texas, at $1.50-$2.00 (U.S.), were far higher than anyplace else in the world at the time. But on the rice prairies, each laborer worked roughly 80 acres of rice, while, outside the United States, the largest average figure for acreage tended was five in Egypt and Spain, where daily wages with board were between 30 to 50 cents (U.S.).[29]

The relatively small size of labor inputs, coupled with the cheap price of land, rendered the rice industry in the Old Southwest quite profitable in the period from its beginnings until World War I, despite its capital intensity, its so-so yields, and the low rice prices in the United States in the 1890–1914 period. Abstracting a bit, one can in some ways view the seismic shift of the U.S. rice industry from the South Atlantic states to the Old Southwest as a market response to the creation of an integrated global market in rice, which process was nearing completion during this same period. As low-cost rice from Asia increasingly dominated markets the world over, labor-intensive rice production in the South Atlantic region of the United States (even with increasing tariff protection) was doomed. The revolutionary new regime established in the Old Southwest – beginning in southwest Louisiana in the 1880s, spilling over to southeast Texas in the 1890s, and spreading to east central Arkansas in the first decade of the twentieth century – at least gave the United States a chance. A fighting chance at that: after World War I, the revolutionized American rice industry – benefiting from impressive productivity gains, the rapid growth of commercial rice production in California, and tariffs on foreign rice – regained control of the domestic rice market and the United States became a net exporter once again. And, to reiterate, the revolutionaries were, first and foremost, promoters, entrepreneurs, and commercially minded farmers from the Midwest.[30]

---

[29] Southern Pacific Railroad Company 1889, 8-9; Bird 1886, 91. Once the prairies were drained and rice cultivation proved profitable, land prices rose accordingly. Bailey 1945, 121–2; Babineaux 1967, 28; Morris 1906, Section 2, 8. Knapp (1899, 20) gives daily farm wages around the world.

[30] See the works cited in endnotes 14 and 15. On the Texas rice industry, also see U.S. Department of the Interior 1898, 25–8; Scanlon 1954, 35–8, 41–2, 48–50. Brown (1906, 3) describes the early development of the Arkansas rice industry; Morris 1906, Section 2, 8; Vincenheller 1906, 119–29; "Rice Industry of Eastern Arkansas is Growing Rapidly From

To attribute the revolution primarily to Midwesterners is in no way to imply that locals were against modernizing agriculture, much less anti-revolutionary. After all, Louisiana's capital-intensive and intensively capitalistic sugar industry was being modernized in much the same way at roughly the same time, as John Heitmann and others demonstrated long ago.[31] Nor is attributing the rice revolution primarily to Midwesterners to deny that locals (and non-locals from places other than the Midwest) played roles as well, sometimes important roles. Locals, generally speaking, welcomed the newcomers and both appreciated and supported their developmental initiatives. Despite the usual business spats, native bankers, millers, and merchants (especially in New Orleans) provided investment capital and processed and marketed a good deal of the "revolutionary" rice. Moreover, some immigrants – most notably, Abrom Kaplan, who immigrated from Poland in 1890 and settled, improbably enough, in the prairie rice town of Crowley, founded in 1886 – were to prove integral to the revolution. In his case, Kaplan quickly got involved in rice growing and especially in rice-milling in southwestern Louisiana, and later (in 1902) founded a town in Vermilion Parish, which he called, eponymously, Kaplan. Others in his family later followed him to the area from Poland, and got involved in the rice industry as well.[32]

Immigrants, one should note, played important roles in the early development of the rice industry in Texas and Arkansas as well, albeit often after spending time in the United States. For example, the town of Stuttgart in Arkansas County, Arkansas – often considered the capital of the American rice industry – was founded in the early 1880s by Adam Buerkle, a native of Plattenhardt in the Esslingen District of Baden-Württemberg, who had migrated to the United States in 1852. Buerkle was a Lutheran

---

Year to Year," *Arkansas Gazette*, October 17, 1909, Part II, p. 12; Small and St. Louis Southwestern Railway Company 1910, 3–8; *Arkansas* 1911, 9–10, 12; Rosencrantz 1946, 123–37; Brown 1970, 76–9; Green 1986, 261–8. On the (successful) battle in the 1920s for tariff protection for rice, see Lee 1994. For materials on earlier efforts to support the southwestern rice industry through tariff protection, see, for example, Louisiana State Rice [Milling] Company, Board of Directors Minutes, 1911–1940, December 30, 1912, Vol. 2, p. 54, Rice Archives, Southwestern Archives and Manuscripts Collection (SAMC), University of Southwestern Louisiana [now University of Louisiana-Lafayette], Lafayette, Louisiana; Minutes, Meeting of the Rice Millers' Association Executive Committee, November 11, 1921, Box 1, Rice Millers' Association (RMA) Records, Rice Archives, SAMC, University of Southwestern Louisiana. Similar material is scattered throughout the Lazaro (Ladislas) Papers, Louisiana and Lower Mississippi Valley Collections, LSU. On the rise of the California rice industry, see "Great is California in Rice Growing," *California Cultivator* 49 (August 25, 1917), 181; Adams 1917, 441; Jones 1950; Bleyhl 1955; Wilson and Butte County Rice Growers Association 1979, 20–248.

[31] Heitmann 1987.
[32] Daniel 1985, 39–61; Dethloff 1988, 63–80, esp. 76. Also see the official websites for Kaplan (http://www.kaplanla.com) and Vermilion Parish (www.vermilion.org).

minister who, after pastoring in several northern states, bought 7,000 acres of land in the Grand Prairie region of Arkansas in 1878 and began promoting the migration into that region of German immigrant farmers from the Midwest. Once settled in the area, Buerkle established a post office near the site of present-day Stuttgart in 1880. The town of Stuttgart itself – named after the capital of Baden-Württenberg – was incorporated in 1884, and soon became a marketing center for farmers throughout the Grand Prairie region of east central Arkansas, where rice took off in a serious way in the early 1900s.[33]

But when all is said and done, it was not Poland or Germany but the Midwest that begat the revolution, and white Midwestern farmers (whether native or immigrant) – and their heavily commercialized values and culture – that made it. It was theirs. For every town of Kaplan or Stuttgart, there was an Iowa (in Calcasieu Parish) or a Vinton (also in Calcasieu, named by Knapp after the Iowa town wherein he had preached), or a Jennings, "a Northern village on Southern soil." To the names Knapp, Cary, and Watkins, we can add Midwesterners such as W. H. Fuller (Ohio and Nebraska), John Morris (Nebraska, albeit born in Wales), and W. E. Hope (Missouri), the founders of the rice industry in Arkansas, as well as that of the leading chronicler of the early rice industry in that state, J. M. Spicer, a native of Ohio, who made rice crops in the Stuttgart area for 51 consecutive years beginning in 1916. One contemporary put the number of Midwesterners in southwest Louisiana in 1900 at 7,000, and a survey of Arkansas rice farmers in 1930 found that 75 percent were born out of state – especially in the states of Iowa, Illinois, Indiana, Ohio, and Missouri.[34] The vision S. L. Cary had articulated in

---

[33] See "History of Stuttgart," *Grand Prairie Historical Bulletin* 6 (January 1963): 1–7; Hanley and Hanley 2008, 20–1; http://grandprairiemuseum.org/pages/history.htm, Website, Museum of the Arkansas Grand Prairie, Stuttgart, Arkansas [accessed July 30, 2014.

[34] Daniel 1985, 39–61, 44–5; Dethloff 1988, 63–94; Spicer 1964, esp. 1–31; Desmarias and Irving 1983, 12–24. For the 1930 survey of Arkansas rice farmers, see Dethloff 1988, 87. On Spicer's background, see Spicer 1964, 118–19. Note that another early historian of the Arkansas rice industry – the aforementioned Florence L. Rosencrantz – immigrated to Stuttgart, Arkansas from Carlinville, Illinois as a child in 1889. Her husband Joseph Rosencrantz became a large rice planter in the Stuttgart area, whose farm had grown to 2,600 acres by the mid-1940s. Rosencrantz 1946, 123. The Texas rice region – comprised of roughly 18 counties near Beaumont, with the epicenter in Jefferson – was basically an extension of the southwest Louisiana industry. Knapp was deeply involved in both states, obviously, but many other Louisianans such as Joseph Broussard and J. and L. Viterbo were pioneers in the Texas rice industry as well (Scanlon 1954, esp. 35–60); Dethloff 1988, 80–90; Dethloff, "Rice Culture," in *Handbook of Texas Online*, online at: https://www.tshaonline.org/handbook/online/articles/afro1 [accessed July 30, 2014]; Wooster, "Viterbo, TX," in *Handbook of Texas Online*, online at: http://www.tshaonline.org/handbook/online/articles/htv08 [accessed July 30, 2014].

an 1898 promotional piece entitled "A Paradise for the Immigrant," was in fact largely fulfilled:

> In all frankness we want the best farmers of the North. We have succeeded remarkably with such as we could get, such, often, who had made failures, who had experimented too long with a long winter. We shall not go to Europe or to Africa, and will find them at home as soon as they learn the facts as they exist.[35]

The Midwestern farmers who established the rice industry *qua* industry in the Old Southwest were cut from the same commercial mold as kith and kin they left behind: that is to say, the people who would bring us the Farm Bureau, established in Illinois in 1919, and the Hi-Bred Seed Company (later Pioneer), established in Iowa in 1926. They were of the same stock as the Iowa farmers who embraced the above-named seed company's great innovation – hybrid corn – so rapidly in the 1930s, the rapidity of which embrace was demonstrated and accounted for so powerfully in Zvi Griliches' classic 1957 paper in *Econometrica*.[36]

Although high-yielding rice hybrids were not developed until much later – in the 1960s and 1970s – the delay was due in large part to the fact that heterosis or hybrid vigor was more difficult to achieve in rice than in corn. Like their brethren further north, the Midwesterners who established the rice industry in the Old Southwest were from the start avid about improved seed varieties, which they sought by various means.

After many years of disinterest or neglect, the history of biological innovation in U.S. agriculture – including seed breeding – is getting more play, in large part because of the work of economic historians Alan L. Olmstead and Paul W. Rhode, whose award-winning 2008 book *Creating Abundance: Biological Innovation and American Agricultural Development* has already had a major impact. In their book Olmstead and Rhode argue convincingly that in explaining American agricultural development economic historians and historians of technology have paid too much attention to labor-saving mechanical technology and insufficient attention to biological innovation. According to Olmstead and Rhode, this problem is especially pronounced in explanations of American agricultural development in the two centuries prior to World War II. In making their case for the importance of biological innovation, they marshal a huge array of evidence regarding productivity gains emanating (germinating?) from increasingly systematic – and increasingly successful – innovations in plant- and animal breeding over the centuries, in so doing, putting the lie to the widely held notion that biological innovation in American agriculture began in the 1920s – in Iowa, one should note – with Henry Wallace and the Hi-Bred

---

[35] Cary 1901, 68–73. The quote is from p. 70. Note that this essay appeared originally in the New Orleans *Picayune*, September 1, 1898.

[36] Griliches 1957, 501–22.

Seed company, and didn't amount to much until the advent of hybrid corn in the 1930s.[37]

To be sure, Olmstead and Rhode may overstate slightly the degree to which other scholars have neglected biological innovation – the name Jack Ralph Kloppenburg, Jr., immediately comes to mind – but their overall point is well taken.[38] Although they don't treat rice in *Creating Abundance*, it is clear, moreover, that the historical evidence – at least that from the Old Southwest – fits their thesis very well. Virtually from the start, agronomists (whether working privately or at state agricultural experiment stations) and growers in the area were interested in improved varieties, and in the period between 1900 and 1929, 10 new rice cultivars were developed in Louisiana (nine) and Texas (one), including important ones such as the regional bellwether Blue Rose – a durable, medium grain rice – developed by the famous Crowley, Louisiana rice farmer Solomon Lusk ("Sol") Wright, who was sometimes called "the Luther Burbank of the rice industry." Wright, almost predictably, was a Midwesterner, born in Indiana, and a former wheat farmer, before moving just outside of Crowley in Acadia Parish in 1890 to try his hand at growing rice.[39]

Some of the other rice cultivars that became popular in the Old Southwest were "imports," most notably, Honduran, a long-grain variety introduced in 1890, and so-called Kiusha or "Jap" rices, short grains introduced to the region by Seaman Knapp in 1902 after the second of his bio-prospecting trips to Asia as "Agricultural Explorer" for the USDA. Clearly, then, the principals involved in the early rice industry in the Old Southwest were interested in biological as well as mechanical innovation, and some of the cultivars they developed, especially Wright's Blue Rose and some of his later varieties such as Early Prolific, brought both improved yields and reduced losses in the milling process.[40]

They were interested as well in creating the organizational, marketing, and educational infrastructure and "capabilities" appropriate for a "modern, scientific" industry. From modest beginnings – Knapp's demonstrations farms in the mid-1880s – the rice industry's infrastructural portfolio soon included agricultural experiment stations and private breeding farms, a specialized journal (the *Rice Journal and Gulf Farmer*, published out of

---

[37] Olmstead and Rhode 2008, 1–16, 386–402 and passim.
[38] Kloppenburg 1988; Coclanis 2001.
[39] Hong et al. 2005, 66–76, 68. Fontenot and Freeland (1997, v. 2, 14–36) delineate Solomon Lusk Wright and his role as a rice breeder; Dethloff 1988, 78, 91–92, 148; "Solomon Wright was 'Burbank' of Industry," Lafayette [Louisiana] *Daily Advertiser*, August 26, 1997; Crystal Rice Heritage Farm, "The Wright Stuff," online at: http://crystalrice.com/familyv2.htm [accessed October 14, 2011]; Website, The Wright Group (http://www.thewrightgroup.net/about/rice-history/) [accessed October 14, 2011]. The "Luther Burbank" quote in the text is from Dethloff 1988, 148.
[40] Dethloff 1988, 78–94; 148–9.

Crowley beginning in 1897), coops and trade associations of various kinds (the earliest of which, the Farmers' Cooperative Rice Milling Company and the Rice Association of America, were both the handiwork of Knapp in the 1890s).[41]

The modern, scientific (and ultra-capitalist) form of rice farming outlined above soon carried the day throughout the Old Southwest and shortly thereafter in the emerging California rice complex centered in the Sacramento Valley.[42] It has dominated the American rice industry ever since, nowhere more so than in the Grand Prairie region of east central Arkansas. It is a long way from here to there, but the roots of the hyper capital-intensive, exceptionally efficient, and extremely anomic and alienating agricultural "rice scape" on the Grand Prairie today – near places such as Stuttgart, for example – are to be found in southwest Louisiana in the late nineteenth century. People from the same Midwestern stock – and with much the same *mentalities* – that brought the steam tractor and modified mechanical reapers and binders to Crowley and Jennings in the 1890s are responsible for the rice-cultivation regime on the Grand Prairie in 2014, a regime characterized by laser-guided field leveling, seeding by air, self-propelled farm equipment (with GPS mounts connected to the satellites of the USDA's Soil Tilth Laboratory located in, yes, Ames, Iowa!), and massive water-pumping stations interspersed in the huge rice fields.[43]

If one by chance finds oneself in the Stuttgart area in the summer months, mosquitoes will be abundant, but humans scarce, for during the growing season one farmer can tend a thousand acres on the Arkansas rice prairies The system that exists today in Arkansas began to take shape 125 years ago, an early manifestation of the "indigenous knowledge system" brought south by white Protestant developers and farmers from the Midwest in search of economic salvation. Whether or not America's first risiculture regimes were African in inspiration remains an open question, but the origins of *modern* rice cultivation in the United States were without a doubt Midwestern and white.

---

[41] Bailey 1945, 109–32; Cline 1970, 335–40. Spicer 1964, 7–14, 32–3, 34–8; Dethloff, 1988, 110–27; Lee 1996; Lee 1994, 435–54. The Rice Association of America was the antecedent of another millers' group, the Rice Millers' Association (RMA), formed in 1896 or 1897. The records of the RMA are located at both the Rice Archives, SAMC, University of Louisiana-Lafayette, and the Special Collections Division, University of Arkansas Libraries, Fayetteville, Arkansas.

[42] Bleyhl 1955, 83–494; Willson and Butte County Rice Growers Association 1979, pp. 20–248.

[43] Hart 1991, 301–14; Coclanis 2010b, 429–30.

14

Rice and the Path of Economic Development in Japan

Penelope Francks

Rice and its cultivation have always been seen as central to any understanding of Japan's historical development. Some time in the mythical past, the originator of the imperial line received the first Japanese rice seeds from the sun goddess Amaterasu and his present-day successor still oversees a paddy field in the grounds of the Imperial Palace in Tokyo. In the popular imagination, it is the demands of irrigated rice that explain the "unique" Japanese propensity to work hard, operate in groups and value harmony; for the anthropologist Emiko Ohnuki-Tierney, "rice is self" in Japan.[1] The nation-wide panic that threats to its supply could still cause, even in the late twentieth century, seemed only to confirm its key role in the conception of Japanese identity.[2]

More prosaically, for economic historians, the real and symbolic significance that rice bears in Japan has made it the basis of "the role of agriculture" within the "Japanese development model." The vast majority of farm households have counted rice as their main crop throughout Japan's modern history, so that, by the time that national-level statistics were first compiled in the 1880s, rice occupied a little over 50 percent of the total value of agricultural output, a share that did not start to fall significantly until the 1960s.[3] Hence, in the standard account of Japan's economic development, it is the efforts of rice farmers, from the mid-nineteenth century onward, to raise yields and output that are held to have generated a major part of the resources on which modern industrialization depended. For long, this process was seen as predicated on state-led investment in the imported technology of modern industry that enabled a backward Japan to "catch up" with the West in the years following the Meiji Restoration of 1868. In this context, the capacity of

---

[1] Ohnuki-Tierney 1993.
[2] The poor harvest of 1993, which caused the government's Food Agency to resort to imports (of "inferior" non-Japanese rice), led to panic-buying on a large scale and considerable national soul-searching.
[3] Hayami et al. 1991, Table 1-6.

rice-cultivating farm households to supply both the government's tax income and the nation's food supply appeared to play a crucial role.[4]

More recently, however, the assumptions underlying this top-down narrative of Japan's development have increasingly been challenged by the quantitative and qualitative work of a new breed of economic historians. For them, long prior to the adoption of a state-led catch-up strategy, early-modern Japan, like its Western counterparts, was witnessing the output growth and spread of the market that are now seen as preconditions for industrialization. Their work has slotted into the emerging field of comparative and global history inspired by Kenneth Pomeranz's *The Great Divergence* and has been held to demonstrate that in Japan, as in other regions of East Asia, well before the impact of the modern West was felt, a rural economy centering on rice cultivation was already generating rising living standards based on commercial production of both agricultural and manufactured goods.[5] The "role of agriculture," hence of rice cultivation as the central element in the rural economy, thus appears to have a longer history than once thought and to involve much more than simply the release of resources to the modern sector in the late nineteenth century.

As the only non-Western country to achieve significant levels of industrialization before World War II, Japan is of course the exception that might prove the rule as regards the Great Divergence. The recognition that there too growth in the production and consumption of everyday goods such as food products and textiles was already taking place prior to modern industrialization has led to new research into those parts of the economy that in fact continued to produce expanding quantities of such goods well beyond the "opening to the West" and the emergence of new forms of industry based on imported technology. These constituted the "traditional sector" of small-scale agriculture and rural manufacturing, the persistence and indeed development of which has led to a reassessment of the significance, before and during the industrialization process, of areas of production and consumption that do not conform to the large-scale, mass-market, capital-intensive forms seen to characterize both the industrial and agricultural revolutions of northern Europe.

The observation of such historical developments, not only in Japan but also in other parts of East Asia, has led a number of scholars within the global history field to propose "alternative" models of industrialization that do not necessarily follow the same path as laid down in the standard description of the industrial revolution in the West. Japan is now argued to exemplify a different pattern – one that other parts of East Asia have subsequently

---

[4] See for example the classic paper by Gustav Ranis (1969) and other contributions to the same volume. For a more detailed discussion of the original "Japanese model," see Francks 1999, chapter 6.

[5] See Pomeranz 2000. Evidence of the growth of production and consumption, and of the spread of the market, in pre-industrial Japan is presented throughout chapters 2 and 3.

followed – according to which technological and economic developments within the "traditional sector" enabled labor resources to be utilized in effective ways that generated output growth along a "labor-intensive path" distinct from that followed in the more land- and capital-abundant nations of Europe and North America.[6] At the same time, the reassessment of development in the "traditional" economy, both as a precondition for modern economic growth and as an under-recognized element within it, has placed renewed emphasis on the production and consumption of everyday goods, such as food and clothing, that are the staples of that economy and central to rising living standards and the spread of the market.

In the light of this, the purpose of this chapter is to consider how rice might fit into such a new view of the path of development in a key example of non-Western industrialization. It was Francesca Bray who first set out the seminal idea that the pattern of economic growth in the "rice economies" might differ from that observed in the industrialized West.[7] Here I build on this approach to argue that the particular characteristics of rice, both as a consumer good and as the key determinant of rural economic and institutional structures, have to be taken into account in any analysis of Japan's long-term development path. The argument begins from a brief demonstration that, although rice continued to be grown in small-scale and labor-intensive ways, it cannot be regarded as straightforwardly a staple or subsistence crop in the context of the growing and developing Japanese economy. As other chapters in this volume demonstrate for various parts of East Asia, rice can represent a differentiated, high-status product that consumers substitute for "lesser" grains as they get richer, so that in Japan too, it has acted as a modern consumer good, the demand for which grew with rising incomes and the spread of the market. The remainder of the chapter then seeks to show how the continuing significance this demand-side process gave to rice conditioned the technological, economic, and institutional structures, not only of agriculture but also of an expanding manufacturing and services sector deeply entwined with it. In this way, rice can be seen as playing a crucial role in setting Japan on a distinctive development path involving the survival and growth of small-scale and labor-intensive forms of production. The ways in which rice has been produced and consumed cannot, therefore, be ignored in any interpretation of Japanese economic development, and are indeed central to understanding how Japan might have come to follow the particular path that it pioneered in East Asia.

---

[6] For a statement of the model, see Sugihara 2003. Other scholars, most notably Saitō Osamu (e.g., 2008), are pursuing similar lines of argument and research, and the concept of an alternative "East Asian path" in general underlies revisionist work on East Asia in the global economy, such as that of Andre Gunder Frank and Giovanni Arrighi. For more detailed analysis of "labor-intensive industrialization," see Austin and Sugihara (2013).

[7] Bray 1986. See also Bray 1983 and Palat 1995.

CONSUMING RICE

There is no doubt that rice has played a key part in Japanese life for a very long time. When it was introduced from the Asian mainland around 300–400 BCE, its cultivation was difficult and costly, in terms of infrastructure investment and labor time, and its consumption was reserved for those who could command the necessary resources to acquire it and appreciate its association with the superior civilization of China. Nonetheless, by the early-modern Tokugawa period (1600–1868), it had come to be grown widely, wherever conditions permitted, even though the bulk of output continued to be monopolized by the ruling class of feudal lords and samurai, in the form of the taxation in kind that they were able to levy on cultivators. The majority of this rice, together with any other "surplus" output, was marketed in the expanding cities of the period, and it was there that versions of what we now think of as Japanese cuisine – bowls of plain white rice with fish or vegetable side-dishes and pickles – came to be consumed, both by the samurai and mercantile better-off and by the many who came to work for them as permanent or temporary urban residents.[8]

Rice thereby acquired its status as central to a civilized, Japanese-style diet and indeed way of life. Consuming it in the correct way required access to suitable cooking equipment (stoves in kitchens rather than single cooking pots hung over a fire in the living room), to appropriate eating utensils (an assortment of ceramic bowls and dishes), and frequently to market facilities for the acquisition of the processed ingredients, such as soy sauce, required to give flavor to an otherwise bland menu. As knowledge of urban practice spread, the rural elite too began to adopt the more sophisticated ways of the cities, to the extent that they could, but for the majority in the countryside, a diet based on one-pot stews of non-rice grains and vegetables, with fish and commercial flavorings when they could be obtained, continued to fit better with their facilities and their cultivation and commercial practice.[9] The non-rice grains and vegetables that they ate, and also increasingly marketed, could be grown on unirrigated land or on paddies in the winter, while rice was cultivated to pay taxes, to market and perhaps to consume on special occasions. A diet in which non-rice grains played a major part, though nutritionally superior to one based on white rice alone, thus came to be associated with rural life and lack of sophistication.[10]

---

[8] On the origins of Japanese-style cuisine and meal patterns, see Watanabe M. 1964 or Ishige 2001. There is some debate as to how much of the rice crop remained to be consumed in the countryside during the Tokugawa period and wide regional variation in grain consumption patterns clearly existed. However, where rice was eaten by its cultivators, it was typically in unpolished brown form and mixed with other whole-grains. Polished white rice, served on its own as in the urban diet, was reserved for special occasions, if consumed at all. See Kitō 1998.

[9] Hanley 1997, 77–94; Watanabe 1964, chapter 11.

[10] For the argument that rice has typically acted as a luxury food in Asia in general, see Latham 1999. The chapters by Cheung and Lee in this volume demonstrate such a role for rice in the pattern of food consumption elsewhere in East Asia.

This pattern of tastes carried over to condition food consumption beyond the end of the Tokugawa regime, so that, once industrial urbanization took off around 1900, consumption of the white rice diet became synonymous with a modern urban identity for growing numbers of people moving into the cities and for those left behind in their rural backwaters. The resulting growth in demand for Japanese-style rice led to price rises and eventually, during the industrial boom of the late 1910s, to urban and rural rioting in protest.[11] As Michael Lewis shows, the so-called Rice Riots did not mean that there was nothing to eat – there were other grains and even cheap imported "foreign" rice – but reflected the fact that inability to afford Japanese-style rice threatened one's identity as a modern Japanese person. Having to eat rice mixed with other grains had become symbolic of poverty and backwardness.[12]

The consolidation of the role of rice as the symbol of an authentic Japanese life is, therefore, a product of the way in which modern consumer development took place over the course of the pre-World War II period. In the years since, the centrality of rice to the diet has undoubtedly continued to condition consumption patterns and responses to the globalization of food. Despite the postwar economic miracle that completed the process of turning Japan into a rich, industrialized society, it was not until the late 1960s that per capita consumption of rice began to decline and the universally observed correlation between rising incomes and a shift away from staple grain toward a diet involving more meat and dairy produce began to be observed there.[13] In what follows, I shall argue that the historically central role of rice, along with all its trappings and accompaniments, as the desired food in Japan is significant, not only as an element in Japanese culture, but also as a major influence on the technology, economic structure, and institutions of agriculture and, through that, on the manufacturing and modern industrial sectors that emerged within the process of growth and development. Because rice came to matter

---

[11] By the 1910s, domestic production was no longer adequate to meet the growth in demand for rice, resulting in the price rises that eventually triggered the riots. Imports available on the world market were of Indica varieties and considered inferior by Japanese consumers, who have consistently demonstrated a strong preference for domestically grown Japonica rice. The policy of promoting the cultivation of Japanese-style rice in Korea and Taiwan, once they became Japanese colonies, was intended to alleviate the problem, although price differentials between Japanese and all forms of imported rice persisted. For more detail, see Francks 2003.

[12] See Lewis 1990. For further evidence and examples, see Francks 2007, 155–61.

[13] Annual per capita consumption of polished white rice stood at around 100 kg in the first half of the 1950s, rising to 115–118 kg by the mid-1960s, before beginning a steady decline. Consistent data series that cross the World War II divide do not exist, so that it is difficult to make comparisons with prewar consumption levels. Estimates based on production data and measured in terms of unpolished brown rice show per capita consumption rising from around 100 kg in the second half of the 1870s to peaks of over 160 kg in the 1930s. Prewar data from Bank of Japan Statistics Department 1966, Table 129; postwar from Nōrinsuisanshō Tōkeijōhō-bu, various years.

in the way that it did as a food, it played a significant part in determining the characteristics of an economy and society that proved capable of producing much more than food alone.

RICE, LABOR INTENSITY AND THE MULTI-FUNCTIONAL RURAL HOUSEHOLD

The data and analysis presented in *The Rice Economies* showed how the particular technological, organizational, and institutional requirements of rice production might influence the long-term pattern of economic development in societies where irrigated rice cultivation is the dominant agricultural activity. The subsequent accumulation of research into Japan's economic history makes it possible to demonstrate the argument in greater detail, within the context of the boom in comparative modeling of paths of economic development and industrialization. The Japanese case, as summarized later, can thus be used to show how, in societies where rice is the preferred grain, the demand for which grows as incomes rise, the development of forms of production and consumption across the board can follow a different path from that observed in those societies with different agricultural structures that pioneered the industrial revolution, as it has come to be characterized. Central to this argument is the proposition that the scope for productive labor absorption is particularly high in rice-cultivating societies, not only in rice production itself, but also because of the scope to combine rice cultivation with other activities, on and off the farm.

As Bray showed, rice as a crop has the potential, if grown under suitably irrigated conditions, to generate significantly higher yields of food grain per hectare than the kinds of grain, such as wheat, typically grown in Europe and North America. However, this depends on a high level of labor input, with the result that rice can both demand and sustain a more densely packed population on the cultivable area than can, say, wheat. Japan was a key example in demonstrating that the labor-absorptive capacity of rice cultivation was not necessarily "involuntary."[14] The "Ishikawa curve," propounded by the Japanese economist and historian Ishikawa Shigeru, which describes a positive relationship, in the early stages of development at least, between growth in yields and increased labor input per hectare, became highly influential in development policy.[15] The detailed demographic work that led Hayami Akira to develop his concept of an "industrious revolution" in early-modern Japan demonstrated that, on the basis of an agricultural structure that revolved around Japanese-style rice cultivation, rising

---

[14] Possibly not even in Java, which had provided Clifford Geertz with the original case of "agricultural involution." See the chapter by Boomgaard and Kroonenberg in this volume.

[15] For the original data and argument, see Ishikawa 1981, chapter 1; for a more recent summary, see Sugihara 2003, 84–5.

population density on a limited cultivable area was consistent with improving standards of living, even if this involved more work and increased labor intensity in agriculture.[16]

The ability of rice cultivation to generate growth through productive labor absorption clearly has implications for the wider structure of the rural economy. The work required to achieve increases in yield involves care and skill, both in its execution and in its timing and management, and is difficult to organize and oversee on a large scale. There is substantial evidence that, as a result, where appropriate irrigation facilities are available, small-scale, typically family-based, cultivation units have advantages over larger enterprises and can achieve higher yields.[17] At the same time, as with all crops, the labor demands of rice cultivation are not evenly spread throughout the year so that, while at peak times such as transplanting and harvest all available labor time needs to be mobilized, at other points in the year considerable labor resources are available for other activities. These can be agricultural, and rice fits well into double-cropping and other rotations, but they do not have to be, and rice-farming households typically engage in a range of subsidiary income-earning activities, as and when these are available. In Japan at least, rice-based agriculture thus favored the small-scale, multi-functional rural household, seeking ways to utilize its available labor resources as effectively as possible.

Historical research on Japanese rice cultivation and the wider rural economy both provides more detailed evidence of the mechanisms that resulted in productive labor absorption and demonstrates a number of its implications for long-term patterns of growth and structural change. There is now widespread documentation of the development and diffusion, from at least the middle of the Tokugawa period onward, of a package of technological improvements that generated slow but steady increases in agricultural output at a national level.[18] These depended on investment in irrigation facilities that made possible improved control over the extent and timing of water flows, but otherwise involved incremental changes to seed varieties, increased use of commercial fertilizer, and improved tools and cultivation methods that enabled small-scale cultivators to get more from their land, in return for increased labor input over the course of the year. During the Tokugawa period and to a significant extent later, such improvements were largely diffused by means of private travel and communication among an emerging class of literate village leaders who cultivated and rented out land, although

---

[16] Hayami's industrious revolution is therefore a supply-side concept, rather different from the demand-driven model of the same name developed by Jan de Vries. See Hayami 2009, 64–72 and de Vries 2008, 78–82. Saitō Osamu and others have raised problems with the data and approach that Hayami used to support his concept in relation to Japan, but not with the basic assumption that increased labor intensity lay behind the growth in output in the Tokugawa period and beyond.

[17] See, e.g., Bray 1986, 150.

[18] For more detail on these changes, see Francks 1999, chapter 7.

the governments of feudal domains also promoted agricultural improvements that raised their tax revenue, and by the late nineteenth century national-level, state-funded research and extension services were pursuing technological development and diffusion along the same lines.[19]

This story is now well known and accepted, but what is also striking about the pattern of technical change in Japanese agriculture is the degree to which improvements both raised yields and facilitated diversification in the activities of farming households. Hence, irrigation investment and varietal improvement were intended not just to increase rice output but also to enable rice cultivation to be combined with multiple cropping of commercial crops, while improved tools and equipment contributed both to better cultivation (such as deep plowing) and to speeding up peak operations and easing bottlenecks in the agricultural cycle.[20] Hence, Tokugawa-period rural households were able to maintain their rice output, so keeping their tax-gathering feudal masters happy, while taking advantage, in whatever ways locally possible, of the opportunities opened up by the spread of the commercial economy and the growth in urban markets. This pattern of development was not undermined by the overthrow of the Tokugawa system and the beginnings of modern industrialization in the second half of the nineteenth century, and continued to determine the direction of technical change in agriculture through into the interwar period and beyond.

The diversification around rice that technical change facilitated could take more-or-less agricultural form – growing other commercial crops, keeping silk-worms – but it might also involve manufacturing or service activities, so long as these could be accommodated to the requirements of rice cultivation. It is now accepted that, by the mid-nineteenth century, the Japanese economy included a substantial manufacturing sector, the major part of which took the form of production in rural areas using the available labor time of workers based in farming households.[21] A wide range of

---

[19] The key role of cultivators themselves in developing and applying technological improvements in the cultivation of rice, as compared with other grain crops, is also implied by the Black Rice hypothesis. However, it is interesting to compare the Japanese path of technical change, and the economic and institutional structures that promoted it, with their counterparts in the case of the "Old Southwest" of the United States, as described by Coclanis in this volume. The Japanese case represents a bottom-up development of existing techniques, diffused by those with local knowledge and interests, as compared with the top-down, land- and capital-intensive package through which the mass-market American rice industry as we know it today was established in the late nineteenth century.

[20] The adoption of the whole technological package hinged on investments in irrigation systems that made it possible to drain paddy fields in the winter, thus enabling them to be double-cropped. The conversion of flooded to drainable paddies (*shitsuden* to *kanden*) can therefore be used as an indicator of the spread of higher-yielding agricultural technology through the nineteenth century and into the twentieth. See Arashi 1975, chapter 1.

[21] The first known survey of output at a national level, the Fuken Bussanhyō of 1874, suggests that manufacturing output constituted around 30 percent of the total (Yamaguchi 1963, 13–14).

household goods and textiles, as well as all kinds of processed food, was manufactured in the countryside by networks of producers, working at home or in local workshops and coordinated by rural-based merchants and entrepreneurs. As a result, it can now be demonstrated that by-employment generated a significant share of the total income of farming households in many parts of Tokugawa Japan and that non-agricultural income, from processing and manufacturing work in the home or from changing forms of wage work off the farm, continued thereafter to make a major contribution to rural households' budgets.[22]

This growing recognition of growth in the rural economy during the Tokugawa period and beyond, and of the role of household diversification within it, has generated a substantial reassessment of the long-term pattern of Japanese development in comparative context. It is now accepted that Japan too experienced proto-industrialization in the countryside and that, far from being static and "feudal," the Tokugawa economy was a growing commercializing one, accommodating a dynamic "traditional sector" that continued to play a major role in the growth of the economy even after the onset of imported modern industrialization. Attempts to estimate the total incomes of multifunctional households have allowed the conclusion that income per capita and living standards in early-modern Japan may not have been significantly below those in at least parts of Europe at comparable times, supporting Pomeranz's case for equality in levels of development across the Eurasian divide prior to the industrial revolution in the West.[23] However, what is striking is that, in at least some of the rice economies of the East, proto-industrialization and so-called Smithian growth, while based on the division of labor in production activities, did not result in agriculture/industry specialization at the level of the household, but rather in the persistence of the small-scale, multifunctional, "pluriactive" rural unit centering on rice cultivation.[24] The next section will consider the institutional basis that sustained this in Japan, before suggesting what it might mean for the possible paths of long-term development.

---

[22] The best data illustrating this come from the domain of Chōshū (in the south-west of Honshū) during the late Tokugawa period. Here, by the 1840s, income from non-agricultural sources ranged from 20 to 30 percent of total household income in the most agricultural areas to over 70 percent in the least (Smith 1988, 82). For evidence of the continued significance of multiple sources of income for farm households, see Francks 2005, 454–9.

[23] Saitō 2008, chapter 4. Others, using wage-rate data or other indicators developed for the comparative analysis of European economies (for example, Broadberry and Gupta 2006), come to a different conclusion, but Saitō shows how their methods fail to capture the full spectrum of income growth in a pre-industrial economy organized as Japan's was.

[24] Thus, Saitō sees the convergence of living standards across both ends of pre-industrial Eurasia as based on a structural divergence (Saitō 2008, especially chapter 8). For a detailed account of the history, theory, and practice of the multifunctional rural household in Asia in general, see Rigg 2001.

INSTITUTIONS, FACTOR MARKETS, AND THE DEVELOPING RICE ECONOMY

The historical trajectory of technical and economic change in Japanese-style rice-based agriculture could be summarized as involving increases in the input of labor time over the course of the year, growing use of divisible inputs, such as fertilizer, improved seed varieties, and locally made tools, and the management of a variety of diversified and sometimes skilled work operations. It does not appear to have been characterized by economies of scale or to have required investment in large-scale capital items, except as regards the irrigation infrastructure. This would suggest that the organizational and institutional arrangements that it suited and fostered might differ from those appropriate to developments in more capital- and land-intensive forms of agriculture. In the Japanese case we can observe the institutional mechanisms by means of which factor and output markets operated, as a rice-based rural economy commercialized and developed, generating the framework within which a distinctive pattern of labor-intensive industrialization was born.

The pioneering work of Thomas C. Smith demonstrated how the direction of technical and economic change in the pre-industrial Japanese countryside served to consolidate the position of those households that cultivated no more than one or two hectares on the basis of their resident work-forces, supplemented if necessary by short-term hired labor.[25] Through the early Tokugawa period, as labor costs rose and the demands of increasingly commercialized and diversified cultivation began to place a premium on careful work and time management, extended-family organizations cultivating larger areas of land were broken up.[26] From then on, households in control of more land than they could manage, given the constraints of their available labor forces and the possibilities of technical and commercial development, found it more advantageous to rent out parcels of their holding to tenants and branch households who would manage cultivation of it themselves. Although there was a market for agricultural labor, few rural households ever relied solely on wage income; although some households in most villages were able to accumulate ownership of larger-than-average areas of land, they never attempted to consolidate their holdings for the purpose of larger-scale cultivation. The small-scale, family-based household, managing its operations on the basis of its available labor resources, has remained the unit of management in Japanese agriculture ever since.[27]

---

[25] Smith 1959.

[26] For a more detailed examination of the establishment of the "small farm economy" and the "stem-family system" in the early Tokugawa period, see Saitō 1988, 201–10. Farris (2006, e.g., 154–5) presents evidence of the origins of the stem-family system significantly earlier than this.

[27] For data to support this, see Francks 2006, 136–8.

Such households were typically organized so as to be able to take advantage of any available opportunities for productive use of their resident labor forces, while maintaining and improving the cultivation of the land they managed. According to the principles of the *ie* household form that was adopted wherever feasible, management responsibility for the household's cultivation and other activities was vested in the household headship, which was ideally passed on from father to eldest son, although other arrangements, such as adoption, were possible if necessary to ensure the household's continuity. The head and his wife, together with their successors, constituted the central household labor force; any siblings of the future head worked on or off the farm to contribute to the household's income until they were able to marry and establish households of their own. Although in practice household fortunes could rise or fall, the village community was constituted as a grouping of continuing households of varying landholding scale but common commitment to cultivation of the village's paddy and other land.[28]

This institutional framework clearly did not prevent the growth and commercialization of a rural economy that continued to center on rice cultivation, despite the limitations it presented to the development of factor markets. Under the Tokugawa system, households did not technically own land and in theory no market in landownership was possible. Even after cultivating households were given title to their land under the Meiji Land Tax Reform of 1872, it was rarely sold outright and even today agricultural households are reluctant to sell ancestral land (unless it has non-agricultural development potential and a very high price). Nonetheless, the rental market offered an alternative mechanism whereby households could adjust the area they cultivated to their labor resources. Tenancy relationships are, therefore, increasingly interpreted, less as the means for class-based exploitation, and more as arrangements for the effective allocation of land and labor, under prevailing technological conditions, that also served to reduce the burden of risk to landlord and tenant and helped to diffuse improved techniques.[29]

Meanwhile, the labor market that emerged was conditioned by the fact that wage work had to be compatible with the demands of cultivation and with the requirements of different stages in the life-cycle of the rural household. Short-term wage work – day-labor on local farms; seasonal employment in agriculture or manufacturing, locally or on a migratory basis – certainly took place, both before and after 1868, providing a crucial supplement to the income of those with only small holdings, while enabling larger cultivators to cope with peaks in the agricultural cycle. Younger sons and daughters might undertake contract work off the farm, as and when they were not required on it, with a view to accumulating skills and finance that

---

[28] For presentation of Japanese research on this, see Sakane 2002 and Watanabe T. 2002.
[29] See Sakane 2002 for this institutional-economics approach to land tenure arrangements.

would enable them to set up on their own or marry, as well as contributing to the income of their natal households.

At the same time, the engagement of rural households with markets was supported, but also conditioned, by the institutions of the villages to which they belonged. Village communities, represented by increasingly literate and well-connected heads from the elite of larger-scale landowning households, operated with considerable autonomy during the Tokugawa period and remained the basic institution of rural life and local administration, despite subsequent Meiji-government attempts to achieve greater centralization. The strength of the village derived in part from the reliance of rice-cultivators on irrigation systems that had to be organized at a village or inter-village level. However, village bodies also kept records, tried to resolve disputes and in particular sought to regulate land transactions so as to ensure that village land remained in the hands of village cultivators.[30] As commercialization proceeded, villages developed facilities that were beyond the scope of individual household investment and eventually provided the basis for agricultural co-operatives offering marketing and credit services, as well as for the provision of extension advice and many other forms of interaction between cultivators and the state.

Hence, while the institutions and factor markets of Japan's rice economy may not have looked like, or produced the same results as, their equivalents in pre-industrial and industrializing Europe, they nonetheless operated in ways that permitted diversification and commercialization and promoted overall growth, without undermining the position of the small-scale, family-based, rice-cultivating household. Markets emerged but in particular forms that did not result in land consolidation on the basis of private property rights or the emergence of a wage-laboring class in the countryside. Rather, they provided the framework within which households were able to take advantage of opportunities to utilize their available labor resources both in higher-yielding rice cultivation and in a range of other agricultural and non-agricultural activities. Saitō's detailed comparative analysis of the available data concludes that, as a result, the distribution of income between the ruling class and the mass of cultivators was probably considerably more equal in pre-industrial Japan than in much of Europe at comparable times.[31] By the time that national-level data on cultivation scale and ownership status became available in the 1910s, no more than 10 percent of households farmed more than two hectares and two-thirds farmed less than one, while over 70

---

[30] In addition, Philip Brown has shown that the practice of joint ownership and periodic redistribution of agricultural land among village members was also not uncommon and did not disappear completely until after World War II (Brown 2011). In general, private land-ownership rights were everywhere circumscribed by community customs and social relations.

[31] Saitō 2008, chapter 5; for an earlier presentation of some of this material in English, see Saitō 2005.

percent continued to own at least some of the land they cultivated.[32] Developments during the interwar and wartime periods only served to strengthen the position of such small-to-medium, often owner/tenant households who held the key to the supply of the crucial food crop. The postwar Land Reform finally gave them full ownership of their land and locked them in place, ready to play their part in Japan's economic miracle.[33]

THE MULTIFUNCTIONAL RURAL HOUSEHOLD AND INDUSTRIAL DEVELOPMENT

In Japan's case, therefore, a pre-industrial structure of economic and technological development based on rice cultivation proved capable of generating a steadily growing and commercializing rural-based economy that involved relative income equality and a gradually improving standard of living for the majority. Proto-industrial manufacturing activity represented an expanding part of this economy, intertwined with the growth of agriculture through the operations of the multifunctional rural household and the institutions that supported it. However, what is remarkable about the Japanese case is the accumulating evidence that this form of economy continued to operate beyond the proto-industrial stage and was not undermined by the introduction of new forms of technology and production organization that took off after the opening of Japan to increased contact with the Western industrial powers in the mid-nineteenth century. What used to be regarded as the traditional or small-scale sector of manufacturing persisted and is increasingly being shown to have played a dynamic part in Japan's development as an industrial power.[34] This sector had its roots in the rural economy as it emerged during the Tokugawa period and its characteristics were clearly conditioned by its interlocking relationship with the rice-cultivating rural households who formed the basis of that economy.

During the Tokugawa period and beyond, as long as rural households were committed to the cultivation of rice and of other crops around it, non-agricultural producers who sought to make use of their labor had to adapt their methods and organization to the concurrent labor demands of agriculture. By the second half of the eighteenth century, those seeking to take advantage of the growing market for processed and manufactured goods in the great cities that emerged after the establishment of the Tokugawa regime were shifting their operations into the countryside in order to utilize the labor time of rural households. Here they established local networks of producers,

---

[32] Kayō 1958, Tables D-a-1 and E-a-1.
[33] See Tomobe 1996. In addition, the important work of Mori Takemaro describes the growth in the local political role of the small-to-medium, owner/tenant farm household in the interwar and World War II period (Mori 1999).
[34] For a reassessment in English, see the papers collected in Tanimoto 2006.

working within their homes or in small-scale workshops, whose finished products could be marketed in the cities and beyond. Local domain governments often helped to promote such industries, which provided both distinctive products that could be "exported" outside the domain and a source of income for tax-paying farm households.[35] In textiles but also ceramics, lacquer-ware, paper, metal-goods and many more areas of production, such local concentrations produced the wide range of regionally branded, differentiated goods that met an expanding consumer demand in the towns and cities, and also eventually in the countryside too. Meanwhile, throughout the country, local food-processing facilities, such as sake breweries and salt refineries, were being established to take advantage of seasonally available labor from nearby or further afield.[36]

Through the later Tokugawa period and into the second half of the nineteenth century, such rural industries continued to adapt and develop. In textile production, especially weaving, the putting-out system was increasingly widely adopted as the means to enable merchant-organizers to control the design and quality of cloth produced by home-based rural weavers. With the switch to factory-spun cotton, synthetic dyes and improved loom technology, small-scale producers with strong links to the agricultural economy were able to meet growing demand for Japanese-style fabrics in a competitive domestic market based on locally distinctive "brands." Tanimoto's detailed study of the accounts of a late nineteenth/early twentieth-century rural clothier shows how the piece rates paid to household-based weavers varied, not with demand for the product, but with the peaks and troughs of labor demand in the local agricultural cycle, as he adapted, in this and other ways, to the fact that the workers who made his business possible were also participating members of agricultural households.[37]

In less traditional industries too, producers continued to find ways to make use of labor based in the countryside. Manufacturers in an assortment of industries abandoned their attempts to set up urban factories and instead established coordinated networks of workshops and home-workers, operating at different stages in the production process, in rural areas.[38] Even modern industries such as cotton spinning and silk reeling, while adopting the factory system, still adapted their employment practices so as to be able to recruit the young female workers that rural households were willing and able to spare, for at least part of the year, from agricultural and other work at home.[39] The

---

[35] For examples, see Roberts 1998; Ravina 1999.
[36] For examples, see Pratt 1999.
[37] Tanimoto 1998, 304–7. For a summary of this research in English, see Tanimoto 2006.
[38] For examples, see Takeuchi 1991.
[39] Female textile-mill workers were typically allowed to go home at peak points in the agricultural cycle and were hired on fixed-term contracts on the assumption (actually not always justified) that they would return to their villages when they married (Hunter 2003, 287).

availability of the electric motor made small-scale production activities feasible in a range of industries, and rural industrial districts, where small-scale and home-based producers congregated to coordinate their activities and share commercial and technical knowledge, continued to develop to produce a range of differentiated or specialized products, both modern and traditional.

Nonetheless, from around the time of the World War I boom in the Japanese economy, growing numbers of rural people began to move to the towns and cities in response to better employment opportunities. However, while some did undoubtedly succeed in finding blue- or white-collar work in factories or offices, employment in the modern sector remained limited and the vast majority of urban workers were to be found employed in forms conditioned by rural practice and requirements. Girls left the countryside in large numbers to work in urban domestic service, with the aim of contributing income to their parental households and developing skills prior to marriage.[40] Meanwhile, their brothers, apart from the eldest, might use whatever connections they had to gain experience in urban commerce or industry, with a view to setting up on their own in due course. The majority of urban businesses thus continued to take the form of household enterprises or small-scale workshops operating within coordinated networks of similar organizations.[41] Although those who left for the cities to work for the most part eventually broke all but familial and social relations with their parental agricultural households, they took with them to their urban industrial employment the principles and practices that had generated the small-scale, labor-intensive but dynamic, rural economy from which they came.

As a result, even after the postwar economic miracle, Japan's by-then world-beating industrial economy continued to be characterized by an exceptionally large small-business sector and by high levels of family business and self-employment. Meanwhile, once the Land Reform had secured small-scale cultivators in the ownership of their land, rural households set about using all the means that the modern industrial economy offered them to continue to raise household income through the diversification of activities. Government food and agricultural policy ensured that the cultivation of rice (though not of many other crops) remained viable for small-scale cultivators, but the development of suitable small-scale machinery meant that it could be carried out with less-and-less labor time, freeing even household heads and successors for work off the farm, and David Friedman's study, *The Misunderstood Miracle*, describes village industries in which high-tech industrial equipment operated in the back-yards of what continued to be cultivating farms.[42] Part-time farming, whereby most rural men worked full-time in the rural or small-

---

[40] Odaka 1993.
[41] For a case-study, see Tanimoto 2013.
[42] Friedman 1988.

town facilities that grew to employ them, while their wives managed the farm, thus became the norm in the Japanese countryside and the key to achieving rural income levels comparable to those of urban industrial households. It also meant that the cultivation of rice, the key crop which, through years of technological and economic adaptation, small-scale farmers were best able to combine with other activities, had to be protected and supported, whatever the cost.[43]

CONCLUSION

By the late twentieth century, given the mounting cost of agricultural support and protection and the dwindling supply of young people willing to take on the work of the part-time farmer and his wife, the sustainability of Japan's form of rice cultivation had come into question, while the small-scale and rural industry with which it had so long been linked was being threatened by competitors from other parts of Asia. Nonetheless, the intractable difficulties that this situation now presents merely reinforce the significance of the role that rice cultivation and consumption have played, over the very long term, in conditioning the pattern of Japan's economic development and its social and economic structures and institutions.

There has long been discussion as to whether this pattern represents a "model" for other developing countries or whether it is simply "unique," but the recent resurgence in global and comparative history has begun to cast Japan's path in a new light. In the context of the Great Divergence debate, it has become possible to view the structures underlying the relatively high level of development in parts of early-modern East Asia as the foundations for a different and distinctive, "labor-intensive" path of industrialization, pioneered in Japan but later followed elsewhere in the region. The activities of the rice-cultivating rural household represent a key element in these structures, and it is in the nature of agricultural growth and its institutional framework that the origins of the divergence between the East Asian and European forms of industrialization are seen to lie.

By examining the role of rice in relation to Japan's path of development, it is possible to tease out the mechanisms by means of which technical and economic change in its cultivation, in response to the expansion of demand for it as a consumer good, might have conditioned the pattern of growth and eventual industrialization. Central to this was the capacity for productive labor absorption, both in rice cultivation itself and in the activities with which it could be combined. It was this capacity that the small-scale, multifunctional, household-based production unit was best placed to exploit,

---

[43] In fact, the policy of explicit protection and subsidy for the small-scale rice cultivator had its origins in the government's response to the Rice Riots crisis of the late 1910s. See Francks 2003.

so that the features of the agricultural revolution that are seen as facilitating the industrial revolution in the West – increased cultivation scale, greater land and capital intensity, the emergence of land-owning and wage-labor classes, and the specialization of agriculture and industry – did not emerge in Japan's rice economy. As a result, the small-scale cultivating household persisted, taking advantage of whatever opportunities emerged to enable it to utilize its available labor as effectively as possible. Not only did this mean steady improvements in rural livelihoods supported by both agricultural and non-agricultural income-earning activities, and a more equal distribution of the benefits of economic growth than was perhaps the case in Europe, but it also required industrial producers to adapt their technology and organization to the needs of the multifunctional, rice-cultivating, rural household. Hence, in due course, major sectors of the expanding industrial economy came to utilize the small-scale organization, institutional arrangements and technological adaptations that enabled them to employ the labor and skills of the majority of the workforce who remained based in households still practicing the cultivation of rice.

As a result, therefore, because of the way rice had to be grown in Japan, and the kinds of technological change necessary to expand output of it to meet growing demand, there emerged a path of industrial development that continued to involve small-scale, labor- and skill-intensive production of differentiated products, even when producing modern goods or adopting elements of imported technology. As far as agriculture is concerned, post–World War II policy-makers may have come to rue the survival of what was at that stage, by international standards, very small-scale and high-cost production of the crop that, both symbolically and statistically, dominated the modern Japanese diet. But the argument of this chapter, and of the Japanese research that it brings together, implies that the central role of such production in determining the path of Japan's economic development cannot be denied. Rice, and those who grow it, matter most significantly because they have helped to create the rich and productive, but distinctive, industrial economy that Japan had become by the second half of the twentieth century and that other Asian countries are now in the process of emulating.

15

Commodities and Anti-Commodities: Rice on Sumatra 1915–1925

Harro Maat

The start of World War I in 1914 was shocking news for the Dutch as it was to the rest of the world. The Netherlands, by maintaining a neutral status, avoided direct military involvement. The main concern, therefore, was the effect on the economy. In particular the capacity to import and export goods over sea was an issue as belligerent powers either sunk or confiscated steam vessels.[1] The disruption of overseas trade routes caused anxiety among the Dutch population in the Netherlands Indies as well. In particular plantation companies were dependent on international shipping routes for the export of their produce. Perhaps an even bigger worry for the planters than putting their goods to the international markets was the effect of the war on the imports of rice. A prime area that concerned both private planters and government officials was the coastal zone on the eastern part of Sumatra (Figure P.1a). Here, many thousands of migrant laborers, usually recruited on a three-year contract basis, formed the productive backbone of Sumatra's plantation belt.[2] The advent of war terrified the Sumatran planters. However, immediate panic-stricken orders for rice proved unnecessary as the rice markets in South East Asia continued to function during most of the war period.[3] Toward the end of the war the situation worsened, rice prices went up and many countries restricted rice exports. This time the situation seriously threatened the international rice trade and in 1918 the colonial government issued a long list of decrees to restrict exports of rice and other food crops from and across various places in the archipelago. Securing food provisions to the Sumatran plantation workers was a central target.

---

[1] The neutral position of the Netherlands hinged on the use of the Rotterdam harbour for imports to Germany. Obviously the British and allied forces put pressure on the Dutch to block this German trade route, a diplomatic battle escalating in 1918 (Frey 1997).
[2] Stoler 1985.
[3] According to Lulofs and van Vuuren (1918, 3), the pointless rush on rice by Sumatran planters in 1914 implied a loss equivalent to half a ton of gold.

The crisis of the late 1910s reveals what seems to be a paradox in the production and marketing of rice on Sumatra. Rice was grown all over Sumatra and although rice imports were common to most parts of the island, rice production was considered to be enough to feed the population. Rice exports, in particular from West Sumatra, were not uncommon. Why, then, were planters and the colonial government so worried about rice imports for several hundred thousand plantation workers on a relatively small strip of a rice-producing island that has a size bigger than Germany? The answer, this chapter argues, is that rice grown on Sumatra was an anti-commodity. The way farmers on Sumatra produced rice and other food crops did not fit with the common notion among planters and colonial administrators of agricultural produce as a commodity. This was not because Sumatran farmers were lazy and lacked an economic mentality, as most colonizers preferred to believe, but because the ecology and the social landscape of Sumatra made intensive cultivation, producing enough rice to turn it into a commodity, an unrealistic and unattractive option. This chapter addresses both the commodity and anti-commodity character of rice on Sumatra. In subsequent sections the notion of anti-commodity is elaborated before turning to the agricultural landscape of Sumatra. The chapter continues with a sketch of the rice and plantation sectors, the food situation and rice imports during the war period. The final sections describe the attempts of planters and the colonial government to intensify rice cultivation on Sumatra. This includes several attempts, spurred by the rice crisis, to introduce commodity rice production on Sumatra.

PRODUCING ANTI-COMMODITIES

The history of colonial agriculture has paid considerable attention to the transfer of European production methods, technologies, and scientific knowledge. These histories mainly focus on the activities of European colonizers, in particular plantation agriculture and colonial policies toward agricultural modernization. Other studies address local forms of production and the indigenous population more generally, as developed over many centuries.[4] In many cases European techniques and production methods blended with locally available practices. The notion of hybridity or creolization is often used to argue that European colonizers did not bring their methods, techniques, and knowledge to areas void of any of these matters but encountered farming systems, knowledge, and techniques that had proven to work and not rarely continued to work when European production came to a halt. A clear example is the cane sector on Mauritius as described by Bill Storey, showing

---

[4] For colonial Indonesia studies focus mostly on the plantation sector of Sumatra (Thee 1969, Pelzer 1978) or the sugar sector on Java (Bosma, Giusti-Cordero and Knight 2008). Moon (2007) addresses colonial policies for agricultural modernization.

that conflict and rebellion are often an incentive for the emergence of such hybrid technologies and production methods. Colonial scientists "paid more attention to small planters after the 1937 riots, when they promoted their own knowledge to help the colonial government control rural rebellion."[5] Similar processes are found in other colonial regions, in the cane industry as well as other sectors.[6]

The notion of anti-commodity takes the hybridization argument one step further and points at the production of different items, and producing items closely resembling commodities in very different ways, in response to introduced commodity production. Such items, crops or varieties of crops in the case of agriculture, receive their anti-commodity status due to the emergence of forms of production for global markets.[7] Anti-commodity thus focuses on production processes that are complementary to processes of commodification but are generally perceived to be of lesser or no significance because production is smaller or more dispersed in terms of acreage, has lower or undefined monetary value, and not rarely takes place in geographical and social spaces that are remote or at the fringes of the commodity production sites. Anti-commodity thus refers to production processes in the shadow of commodity production and for those reasons these processes rarely have a prominent place in official records and statistics.[8] A key feature of anti-commodity production, also apparent in the hybridization argument, is the complementarity and, not rarely, mutual dependence between commodity and anti-commodity. Just as anti-commodities emerge in response to processes of commodification, the latter only works because of the presence and with support of the first. Jonathan Curry-Machado, writing on agricultural development in Cuba during the nineteenth century, shows that the expansion of sugar plantations went hand in hand with a steep rise in the number of smallholdings and an increasing diversity of crops grown in these areas. A crop like banana initially was taken up as an anti-commodity but production gradually oriented on international export markets.[9] The production of food crops and an overall diversifying production were not mere side effects of plantation agriculture but a key ingredient of the overall

---

[5] Storey 1997, 189.
[6] Arnold (2005) reviews the issue for European colonies.
[7] The notion of anti-commodity emerged from a contribution from Paul Richards and the author to a workshop of the Commodities of Empire network in London, June 2007. Subsequently it was used to frame a research grant from the Netherlands Organization for Scientific Research Science, received in 2009.
[8] A number of exceptions were presented at a workshop titled "Local forms of production as resistance against global domination, anti-commodities" in Amsterdam, June 2010. These included cases outside the agricultural domain. A similar point about (technical) processes overlooked by historians is made by Edgerton (2007).
[9] Curry-Machado 2010.

dynamics of the agricultural sector. The notion of anti-commodities creates a counterpoint to the focus on the economically dominant form of production without excluding a commercial role anti-commodities may play. Rice, as presented in this chapter, can be commodity and anti-commodity at the same time. However, rice is not a singular object and what makes a rice an anti-commodity or commodity is connected to biological, material, and social characteristics, for example the varieties used or cultivation methods employed (see also Mouser, Nuijten, Okry, and Richards, this volume). Materiality matters and it is the way people employ the material environment in response to the pressures put forward by international trade networks and the commodification of products and resources that shapes the anti-commodity.

The affinitive relationship between commodity and anti-commodity resembles an argument elaborated by James Scott in his recent book about the upland cultures of Southeast Asia. Scott points at a symbiotic connection between hill societies and lowland states. By connecting the political and social histories to the geographical and agro-ecological characteristics of hills and valleys, he shows how mountain areas formed a refuge for people escaping the pressures from state rulers in lowland areas. The extraction of food and labor through administrative taxation or by military suppression formed the necessary element for states to ensure and expand their power. Hill societies, Scott argues, are formed out of people escaping state exploitation in the lowland regions by moving to hill regions. The symbioses points at this connection, also implying that hill peoples may not cut off all connections with valley states. Trade or temporary labor exchange between the hills and lowland areas are common. The distinct nature of hill societies typically expresses in agricultural activities. What Scott terms "escape agriculture" is characterized by a preference for shifting cultivation (or swiddening) and growing "escape crops" that are adapted to rugged terrains and the high mobility of the people cultivating them.[10] There is overlap between Scott's escape agriculture and anti-commodity insofar as that the latter implies forms of agricultural production by groups that escaped from plantations (maroon settlements) or resisted to become involved in the production of cash crops for global markets. However, anti-commodity more specifically refers to production in response to processes of commercialization that may be supported or even introduced by states but are not exclusively state-driven nor follow a clear geographical division between hills and valleys.[11]

---

[10] Scott 2009, 187–207.
[11] However, Scott clarifies that the economic reach of states went far beyond the lowland areas. "The higher the value and smaller the weight and volume of the commodity (think silk and precious gems as opposed to charcoal or grain), the greater the reach," Scott 2009, 35.

RICE AND ROBBERY

The landscape, agriculture, and forms of social organization on Sumatra are a close match to Scott's non-state hill societies.[12] A volcanic ridge, the Barisan mountains chain, running from north to south on the western side of the island, and the tropical rain forest that covers most of the island creates an ideal terrain for dispersed social formations that rely on shifting cultivation and forest products for the provision of food and shelter. Colonial interest in the island was low until the early nineteenth century when British colonial officers from Malaysia explored the island resulting in extensive ecological and ethnographic descriptions. During most of the nineteenth century the Dutch had an ambivalent strategy toward the island. Extraction of commercial products, most notably pepper, was considered more important than administrative control. Later efforts to exert colonial rule over the island appeared difficult as a result of restricted financial and military means, resistance from the local population and agreements with Britain. The situation started to change after 1860 when colonial rule was established more rigorously, even though the sultanate of Aceh in the north was only subordinated after several military campaigns that continued until the early 1900s.[13]

The troublesome imposition of colonial rule over the island resulted in an overall negative assessment of the island by government officials and military commanders. The cultivation methods of the local population and their way of life more generally was portrayed in terms of vagrancy and robbery. Swidden agriculture was targeted as a major problem because the wide dispersion of fields over a densely forested area made it very difficult for the Dutch military expeditions to seize rice or other foodstuff for their troops and carriers. Control over the food supply was one of the first problems the colonial government tried to solve.[14] Although shifting cultivation was the dominant form of growing rice and other food crops, permanent rice fields were found in various places. These fields were usually swamps or rain-fed fields and found across the island. In the bordering areas of colonial settlements, primarily coastal ports and strategic inland locations, permanent and

---

[12] Scott 2009, 39 quotes Sir Stamford Raffles, the British governor of colonial Indonesia in the period of the Napoleonic wars, in his assessment of Sumatra as an unruly collection of "innumerable petty tribes."

[13] British rule over the Indonesian archipelago formally lasted from 1811 to 1816 but settlements on Sumatra, most notably Bengkulu in the southwest, remained under British control until 1824. The Anglo-Dutch treaty of that year arranged free trade in the region and a neutral status for Aceh. The Dutch conquest of Aceh in the late nineteenth century violated the treaty, conceded by Britain (De Jong 1998).

[14] Schneider (1992, 36–7) gives various examples of chiefs and villagers refusing food to the Dutch soldiers. Scott (2009, 191) asserts that "[t]o choose swiddening (...) is to choose to remain outside state space."

more intensive forms of rice cultivation were stimulated to catch up with the quickly growing population in such areas. The permanent rice fields emerging around these populated areas did not produce enough rice and a lively trade in rice to Sumatra emerged by the turn of the century. The trade in rice was not an entirely new phenomenon. Reports of inland rice trade as well as small-scale overseas trade appear in accounts from the early nineteenth century.[15] The demand for agricultural products, timber, and other forest products from Sumatra for export to nearby or further overseas markets contributed to the growing rice shortage.

Despite the rather stable food situation, colonial depictions of local agricultural practices on Sumatra remained negative. Where the portrayal of vagrancy and robbery of the mid-nineteenth century was related to a staggering colonial conquest, the image did not change very much in the early twentieth century. A major factor was the emergence of plantation agriculture. The main region where these plantations emerged, from the 1860s onward, was the northeast where, within two decades after 1864, over a hundred tobacco estates emerged, later followed by rubber and oil palm estates. Although concentrated in the northeast, estates emerged all over the island and included other crops like coffee, tea, and fibers.[16] These estates got hold of the land through lease contracts that not only arranged land use but also things like compensation for felled fruit trees or displacement of kampongs. Moreover, the contracts allowed for shared use of lands, implying that after the tobacco harvest villagers could use the plots for rice and other crops (Figure 15.1). Although these arrangements tried to prevent too strong resistance from the local population against the emerging plantations, the arrangements favored the interest of plantation owners at the cost of the opportunities for the Sumatrans to use the land and surrounding forest. Moreover, there was little control on implementation of these regulations. Compensation to the local population and other rules were generally considered as inconvenient hassle and planters, for example, preferred to let their own workers, rather than the nearby villagers, grow food on the harvested tobacco fields.[17] In short, the European staff on the plantations tried to keep the local population at a distance and justified this by portraying the Sumatrans as lazy and their cultivation practices as inefficient and exhaustive. The Dutch word commonly used for shifting cultivation is *roofbouw*, that translates as robbery cultivation. Such negative depictions of swiddening were not typically Dutch and reflect, in past and present, the conflicting interests over forest areas between governments, planters, and local farmers.[18]

---

[15] Mansvelt et al. 1978, Schneider 1992.
[16] Pelzer 1978.
[17] Breman 1987, Pelzer 1978.
[18] Dove 1983.

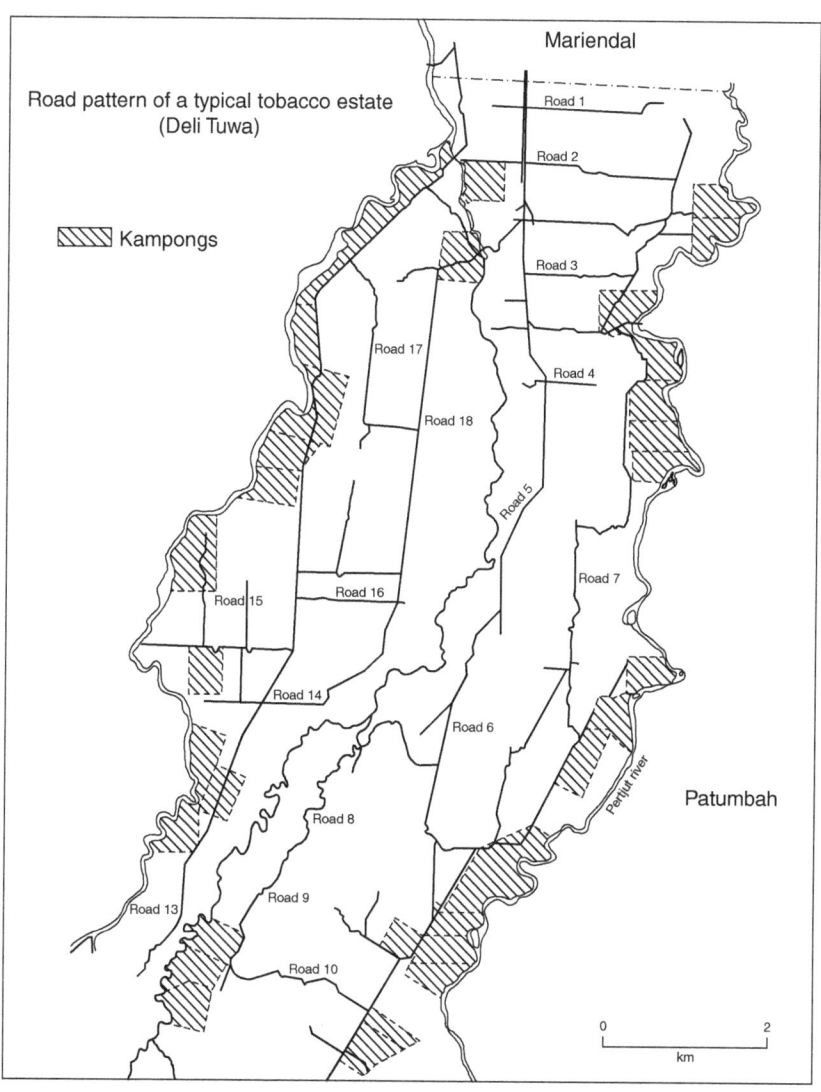

FIGURE 15.1. Map of a tobacco estate on Northeast Sumatra. The areas indicated as Kampongs are surrounding village fields.
Source: Pelzer 1978

RICE INTENSIFICATION

The Sumatran plantation economy attracted many laborers of diverse ethnic background. Between 1880 and 1900 the number of plantations had remained relatively stable but enterprises quickly expanded the cultivated area, resulting in an increasing labor demand. The European planters initially recruited mainly Chinese and Malayan workers but more and more relied on labor migrants from Java.[19] The overall population of the plantation belt in east Sumatra, an initial 150,000 in 1880 had more than tripled by 1900 and would continue to increase to 1.5 million in 1930.[20] A comparison of the years 1905 and 1917 by the statistical bureau shows an increase of 50 percent for the east coast and over 20 percent for the entire island.[21] Food supplies, in particular provisions of rice, played a crucial role in the organization of labor. Ann Stoler describes the enduring rebellious dynamics of the plantation system in which plantation owners tried to keep a balance between production costs, the threat of labor revolts, and a colonial administration that tried to keep both planters and laborers satisfied. The availability of rice for the workers at low cost, in particular in periods when rice prices were high, was important to maintain peace and quiet among the workforce.[22] Wages being partially paid with rice coupons that were exchanged in the plantation food stores was a common phenomenon.[23] Breman's account of work and living conditions in the early twentieth century reveal a harsh life, caused by the physical demands of the work and the repressive labor regime to prevent escape and rebellion. Plantation owners, usually large investment firms with offices in the colonies and the Netherlands, intensively lobbied national and colonial governments.[24] The arrival of war in 1914, creating a potential threat to the shipping of rice supplies to the plantation belt, was reason for alert and pressure on the government to guarantee food security.

By the mid-1910s the colonial government had gained some experience with food production and food distribution. Given that the Dutch had a rather effective statistics of imports and exports, it was able to create a rough picture of areas in the archipelago with food shortages and surplus production. The export figures provide little information on how food is actually produced, the potential for productivity increase and where such increases are to be expected. That was the sort of information to be produced by the Department of Agriculture that was added to the colonial administration in 1905. Where the first director, Melchior Treub, promoted on-station research to achieve higher productivity, his successor,

---

[19] Pelzer 1978, Thee 1969
[20] Breman 1987, Stoler 1985.
[21] The largest concentrations of Europeans were in the East Coast (2,667 in 1905; 6.270 in 1917) and West Coast (2,923 in 1905; 3,532 in 1917). In most other areas the number of Europeans was lower than five hundred. The total population on Sumatra for 1917 was about five million. The official census figures of the time include warnings that they are based on estimates rather than counting. Figures taken from Lulofs and van Vuuren (1918, 154–5).
[22] Because high rice prices were usually temporary and the colonial government subsidized rice, it was more attractive to provide rice directly than to increase wages. (Stoler 1985, 42).
[23] Breman 1987, 143.
[24] Taselaar 1998.

Herman Lovink, put more emphasis on the collection of regional and local information about food production and cultivation methods. From 1908, when he came to office, the number of agricultural advisors (or extension officers) quickly rose. Besides promoting implements or methods recommended by the research stations, these advisors collected detailed information about farm activities, cropping patterns, soils, weeds, and pests in the area they worked.[25] The cultivation methods of the Indonesian farmers thus received more attention, also on Sumatra.

In response to the war situation and the dependency on rice supplies from other countries in Asia, the Society for Study of Colonial Issues requested two colonial officials to report on the food supply and advise on appropriate measures.[26] The authors of the two studies had worked on Sumatra and paid considerable attention to the food situation on the island. The first report, written by the colonial civil servant C. Lulofs, argued that Sumatra was self-sufficient in rice would there not be the inflow of migrant workers to the plantations. He proposed to find solutions close to the cause: food production at or nearby estates and the migration of Javanese farmers, familiar with sawah rice cultivation, to Sumatra.[27] The author of the second report, the agricultural advisor M. B. Smits, came to a different conclusion. He started his report by putting the effect of the eastern plantation district on the overall food shortages in perspective. In his calculation this accounted for a rough 20 percent of the total imports. The rest was mainly an effect of an overall growing export production on Sumatra. The situation, he argued, was almost opposite to Java where farmers first produced rice and spent their remaining time as laborers on the plantations. On Sumatra, production of export crops was much more lucrative than rice and because fiber crops, rubber, coffee, and pepper were doing well in the Sumatran ecology, farmers opted to grow such crops themselves rather than sell their labor to the European plantations.[28] Consequently, improving the food situation by creating areas for intensive rice production run by migrant Javanese rice farmers envisions, according to Smits, an unrealistic transformation of the agricultural sector. The only option he saw for Sumatra was the intensification of upland or dry rice. This somewhat peculiar idea was based on a more profound understanding of the rice economy of Sumatra.

---

[25] Maat 2001.
[26] This society (in Dutch *Vereeniging voor Studie van Koloniaal-Maatschappelijke Vraagstukken*) issued the journal *Koloniale Studiën* (Colonial Studies) and consisted mainly of members from the colonial elite. The chair in the 1910s was J. Gerritzen, president of the Javasche Bank.
[27] Lulofs and van Vuuren 1918.
[28] Smits 1919a, 56.

Smits was appointed in 1915 and stationed on West Sumatra.[29] His explorations of his new work area resulted in a paper on the different forms of rice cultivation on the island. He was untypically positive about the shifting cultivation practices of Sumatran farmers. For most areas, he argued, the soil conditions in combination with the abundance of available forest area and low population density made swiddening an economically balanced system. His overall findings were confirmed some years later in a detailed study of a district at the south-west coastal area. "There is no way one can proof that swiddening applied in the way as described would have detrimental effects for the land."[30] He added that the commonly used term 'robbery culture' (*roofbouw*) makes no sense. Moreover, he argued that attempts to persuade farmers to change to more permanent forms of agriculture, either by pushing for a second crop on the swidden fields or the construction of irrigation systems, disrupted these swidden systems and would never sustain in most parts of Sumatra. Smits' reasoning was partly agronomic and partly economic. The structure and composition of the majority of the soils on Sumatra, the rugged terrain and the low availability of labor, made shifting cultivation a well-suited system. Instead of repeating the commonplace that Sumatran farmers were incapable and unwilling to grow rice, Smits made clear that no one can expect farmers to grow more rice in an environment that is unfriendly to more intensive forms of rice cultivation and operating in a plantation economy in which the price of rice is tied to the price of labor. His advice to intensify upland rice followed that logic. If rice on Sumatra had to be produced at a level below or equivalent to international trade prices, the government had basically two options. Subsidize rice farmers or grow rice on government farms. Clearly, the latter was the most attractive option from a political perspective.

INTENSIFIED INTENSIFICATION

Responses to the crisis situation around 1918 came from the planters and the colonial government. The planters, in particular the private research stations that were created from collective funds, had experimented with food crops from the very beginning. In particular the Deli research station for tobacco had a continuous program on food crops. One reason was the growth cycle of tobacco. Immediate after clearing the land was taken by local farmers to grow rice. As Pelzer describes the cycle: "A rice field invariably contained young bushes and trees, which took over the land once the rice had been harvested in

---

[29] His appointment is mentioned in the Annual report of the Department of Agriculture over 1915 (Jaarboek 1917). Biographical details are not found but it is likely he had started his career as agricultural advisor in the Netherlands.

[30] Smits 1919a, 16.

Commodities and Anti-Commodities

November or December. The land then lay fallow for a period of not less than seven years."[31] From the late 1900s the agronomist of the Deli research station experimented with numerous crops on the cleared fields, some fibre crops but most prominently food crops such as maize, soy bean, groundnut, cowpea, and rice.[32] Besides the production of food or additional commodities, the experiments were also set up to reduce slime disease, a bacterial infestation of tobacco plants of which the cause was only revealed during the 1910s. Several plants were suspected to act as intermediate host of the disease and were therefore forbidden. None of these experiments had spectacular results, meaning that normal yields were achieved but not at a level that made any of these crops attractive for commercial exploitation.

In the same period the colonial government had started an experiment with migration of Javanese farmers. Jürg Schneider's analysis of the transmigration to Sumatra makes clear that this was led by the assumption that the Javanese were better farmers and more interested in hard work than the Sumatrans. The "model farmers" transferred to the island were supposed to provide a clear example to follow by the Sumatrans. Colonial officials selected families from a region on Java where wet rice was combined with upland fields to accommodate adjustment to the conditions on Sumatra. Starting with a small number of families, about a hundred persons were transferred from Java to Sumatra each year during the 1910s.[33] The transmigration policy continued in following decades but clear effects appeared hard to assess. Although the share of intensive wetland (sawah) cultivation increased, upland dry fields, permanent or swiddens, remained by far the dominant form of cultivation. Rice surpluses of considerable volume were never achieved. The transmigration further filled the already densely populated areas where more intensive (wet) rice production by and large kept pace with the growing demand. In the late 1910s, when effects were pretty much unknown, transmigration was widely considered an adequate, albeit long-term, solution to reduce rice imports to Sumatra (see Table 15.1 for the origins of rice imports in the mid-1910s and Table 15.2 of rice imports of four major districts of Sumatra in the mid-1910s).

The plantation sector required quicker solutions for the shrinking availability of rice on the Asian markets. One option was to reduce the rations. In 1919 a degree from the government had set the ration on 15 kg rice per worker per month. Suggestions to further reduce this and supplement with other food, maize for example, were considered risky as there was disgruntlement among workers about the rice rations. Another option was to find rice on other markets. The society for rubber planters had even purchased rice

---

[31] Pelzer 1978, 49.
[32] Reports on the experiments are in the publication series of the station (*Mededeelingen van het Deli-Proefstation te Medan*).
[33] Schneider 1992, 67.

TABLE 15.1. *Origins of rice imports of the Netherlands Indies, in the mid-1910s (in million kg or 1,000 ton). Source: Smits (1919a)*

	Burma	Saigon (Cochinchina)	Siam	Other	Total
1912	328	30	77	17	452
1913	219	163	116	8	506
1914	173	185	107	6	471
1915	176	231	170	7	584
1916	329	114	245	5	693

TABLE 15.2. *Rice imports of four major districts of Sumatra, in the mid-1910s (in million kg or 1,000 ton). Negative figures imply exports. Source: Lulofs (1919)*

	East Coast	Aceh	West Coast	Palembang
1915	95	7	−0.5	20
1916	127	13	−0.8	19
1917	147	13	−4.0	19

from California (United States) but that appeared a very costly deal.[34] A third option was to take up food production themselves. The challenge was to grow large amounts of rice in an economic viable way. A crucial factor was labor. As the rice was supposed to feed the laborers on the plantations, recruiting additional laborers for rice production made no sense. The only other options was to mechanize the process. In 1920 the Deli Company (*Deli Maatschappij*) started experimenting with mechanized rice on one of the tobacco concessions. This tobacco company was large enough to afford investments in a crop that had never been cultivated in this form before.[35] Using tractors and disc plows it cleared and plowed over 200 ha of tobacco land for rice cultivation.[36] The works continued for several years but were stopped because economic benefits never exceeded the costs. The overall losses were about 400,000 guilders.[37] A similar initiative came from the research station for rubber. The director of the station considered a rice farm similar to that of the Deli Company a feasible option. However, the plan was never realized

---

[34] The society calculated price differences with rice from Saigon at 26 guilders per 100 kg. The price difference of the total lot purchased from California was over three million guilders. Figures and accounts over rations taken from Jaarverslag Algemeene Vereeniging van Rubberplanters ter Oostkust van Sumatra 1919–1920.

[35] The Deli Company had an estimated share capital of more than 18 million Dutch guilders in 1921. Beside tobacco it owned rubber and palm oil estates (Taselaar 1998, 70–2).

[36] *Mededeelingen van het Deli-Proefstation te Medan* 16 (1920).

[37] Volker 1928, 71.

because investment capital was lacking.[38] The two private-sector initiatives for mechanized rice farming were inspired by a much bigger and more ambitious plan that was run by the government.

In early 1919 the government had started with land preparation for a government rice farm, located in the lowlands of the Musi river at a place called *Selatdjaran*, near Palembang on the southern part of the island. The chosen area was a river bed in a delta region where the tidal effects produced intermittent inundation of the soil. To take control over the tidal flow, a ring dike with sluice gates was constructed. The first rice harvest was in 1921. However, the harvested amount was just a tiny fraction of the projected yield. Results did not improve in subsequent years and the farm was closed in 1923. The overall costs were calculated at 1.14 million guilders and the income from sold rice and equipment at 91 thousand.[39] The rice farm was generally considered an experiment and the outcome clearly negative. Besides an experiment in the agronomy and economics of rice cultivation, it was also an experiment in the politics of commodification.

STATE COMMODIFICATION OF RICE

The driving force behind the experiment was the director of the Department of Agriculture J. Sibinga Mulder. Mulder had a background in the sugar industry and was known as a champion of free enterprise, in particular European free enterprise. The person who left office, H. Lovink, had gained substantial respect from Indonesian opposition groups for his work on indigenous food production. The arrival of Mulder was therefore seen, as one newspaper put it "a serious attempt to wind back the film of agronomic people-development."[40] Mulder arrived at the right moment to show that the European entrepreneurial spirit could not just create booms in rubber or tobacco but also in rice. His proposal to start an experiment with mechanized rice farming on Sumatra was sent to the Governor-General in January 1919. He was inspired by the mechanized rice schemes he had seen in the

---

[38] The newspaper *Indische Mercuur* of January 21, 1921 summarizes the plans presented by A. A. L. Rutgers, director of the AVROS research station. AVROS stands for *Algemeene Vereniging voor Rubberplanters ter Oostkust van Sumatra* (General Society for Rubber planters on the East coast of Sumatra). The same newspaper mentions on May 21, 1921 that the plan is cancelled. According to Volker (1928, 71), the low rubber prices right after the war were the reason companies were unwilling to invest in the rice farm.
[39] The most detailed account on the rice scheme is an unpublished report by Van der Stok (1924). In a letter to the minister of colonies the governor asked if the report should be made public. The minister decides not to because "the interest in the experiment has quickly gone down."
[40] The quote, cited in the *Indische Gids* (40, 1493) comes from the newspaper *Locomotief*. On the role of the indigenous and Indo-European groups in the 1910s, see Moon (2007) and Bosma (2005).

United States. Mulder informed the governor that "the [American] companies are very profitable even with normal (prewar) prices."[41] When the experiment succeeded, the only thing the government would have to do would be "to urge the spirit of capitalist agricultural enterprises to take up the challenge, and to provide the necessary land and water concessions without the usual formalities." His letter to the government and various other statements about the plans reveal his enthusiasm. Suzanne Moon aptly described it as "a colonial Liberal's dream solution: Solve the food problem with private enterprise and boost investments in export agriculture simultaneously."[42]

Mulder's enthusiasm was not shared among all the experts. The team that was responsible for the rice scheme consisted of a soil scientist (E. C. J. Mohr), an irrigation engineer (J. H. Levert), a planter (T. Ottolander), and an agricultural advisor (M. B. Smits). Smits was sent to the United States to study the mechanized rice farms in the southern states. Between March and October 1919 he visited the rice industries in California, Texas, and Louisiana. His report, most detailed on the Californian situation, points out various of the critical factors the Sumatran rice farm would have to cope with in order to be viable. One critical factor was weed control. As Smits explained, in California rice was grown on almost bare soils, irrigated with water pumped up from the Sacramento river. A second crop or a fallow period reduced the weed problem. If needed the land was laid fallow and dry for a full year to choke the weeds. On Sumatra the climate was too humid to apply the same method. Another issue was the bearing capacity of the soil. Given the low rainfall in California, the water control system allowed for enough drainage whenever machines had to enter the fields. This was different on Sumatra. The higher rainfall at Selatdjaran made the soil muddy and thus required a dense network of drains and ditches to take the water out, resulting in smaller plots. Together, these factors made small, light tractors the best options.[43] Smits bought tractors toward the end of his trip that were shipped to Sumatra. In his report he points at various other critical factors, such as variety choice and soil fertility that require "utmost care" in *Selatdjaran*. Most of these points indeed appeared to be critical factors.

In 1924, when the *Selatdjaran* scheme was closed, the head of the indigenous crops division of the Department of Agriculture, J. E. van der Stok, wrote a detailed report on the experiment. The concerns expressed by Smits after his visit to the United States only scratched the surface of all the things that were beyond control in *Selatdjaran*. The dike construction embraced an area of 700 hectares. An immediate problem and major bottleneck for the advancement of the rice scheme, was clearing the land. The soil contained

---

[41] Creutzberg 1973, 248.
[42] Moon 2007, 84.
[43] Smits 1920, 50.

many more roots and stones than expected, causing delay and damage to the equipment. Moreover, the rainfall pattern over 1920, the year clearing started, was higher than average. Most of the time the soil was too muddy to allow any tractors to go in, adding to the delay. The drainage of the soil, working against the rainfall, caused contraction of the peat subsoil, creating low spots in the terrain that filled with water. Only 50 hectares were cleared before the first sowing period in November 1920. There was yet too much water on the fields to allow the tractors to go in and sowing was postponed to March the next year. The seeding worked out well this time but from the moment the rice came up, rats and bugs also entered the fields and ate most of the crop. An attempt to reduce rat damage by letting in more water failed because the water level in the river was too low. It was decided to plow the remains of the crop and start anew with land preparation. The months of June–August of 1921 were exceptionally wet. Tractors again got stuck in the mud. September was dryer so ultimately 120 hectares were sown. Besides rats and bugs, weeds also threatened the harvest. To test machine harvesting and threshing, laborers were recruited for manual weeding of 65 hectares, which saved part of the crop. The rice varieties that were used appeared not very suitable for mechanical harvesting and threshing. Over the year 1922–23 results were slightly better but there was no real control over any of the problems and the experiment was stopped. The land, machinery, and buildings were sold and even that appeared difficult.

The *Selatdjaran* experiment created considerable noise in the colonial press and Peoples Council (*Volksraad*), an advisory body to the government with representatives from various layers and groups in the colonial society. The atmosphere of crisis made people sensitive to large government expenditures on a project that appeared such a failure. Moreover, critics attacked the head of the Department of Agriculture, Mulder, for disrespecting the indigenous farming and overall food situation and favoring the European plantation sector. The rice scheme on Sumatra became a target for the emerging Indonesian indigenous movements and their opposition against the plantation sector, most prominently the sugar industry on Java.[44] My earlier account of the *Selatdjaran* scheme portrays the mechanization as a technical detour from the overall focus on plant breeding and other intensification techniques that characterized the research work on food crops at the Department of Agriculture.[45] These interpretations however overlook some of the crucial differences between rice on Java and rice on Sumatra. In fact, most colonial actors were unaware of the disparity of the two islands. On Java rice was much more a commodity crop than on Sumatra. The Indonesian and Dutch critics of colonial domination and European capital considered the

[44] Moon 2007.
[45] Maat 2001.

cultivation of sugar cane, commonly grown on fields that were also used for paddy production, a threat for the indigenous rice sector. As Boomgaard and Kroonenberg (this volume) show, the situation on Java was not that clear-cut but it was even more remote from the situation on Sumatra where rice was grown as an upland crop, part of more diversified cropping systems. Mulder ignored the differences between the islands and the lack of control over the technical complexity of the rice scheme combined with his background in the Java sugar industry made him an easy target for political opponents.[46] However, Mulder was advised by experts who were much better acquainted with rice on Sumatra, most notably the agricultural advisor Smits, who was put in charge of the rice scheme.

Why did Smits embark on the implementation of an irrigated-rice scheme when he had written an extensive report, just before he left for the United States, to argue that the only option to improve rice production on Sumatra was through improvement of upland rain-fed rice? Whether he considered the experiment worth a try or simply obeyed orders is unclear. The 1924 report by Van der Stok states that Smits was replaced by another agronomist in March 1921, before the first rice was sown. Members of the Peoples Council who questioned Mulder on the bad results of the experiment also asked about the "discharge" of Smits and his troubled relationship with Mulder.[47] They never got an answer but most likely Smits realized that given the setbacks they faced from the very beginning the whole enterprise was doomed to fail. His study of the rice schemes in the American Southwest had provided a clear picture of the huge difference between the two situations. What made the American schemes specific was not just the terrain, climate, soil structure, and water control but also the social and economic conditions (Coclanis this volume). Unlike in the United States, the ecological conditions of Sumatra and a colonial economy embedded in an active Southeast Asian rice market made it almost impossible to turn Sumatran rice into a commodity product of any significant scale. After the war rice markets recovered and shipping routes became safe. Rice prices went down and the imports of foreign rice to the plantation belt and cities on Sumatra continued the trend from before the war. The colonial government continued to invest in irrigation to encourage wet rice cultivation, mostly combined with the transmigration of Javanese families to these areas. This happened primarily in those areas where the Sumatrans already had developed rain-fed sawah and swamp rice cultivation.

---

[46] Mulder resigned from office after Van der Stok had written his report. Causality between the two is not confirmed in official documents but given that Mulder in the late 1920s tried to undermine Van der Stok's position when he was a professor in Wageningen suggests he had an axe to grind.

[47] Handelingen van de Volksraad July 1922.

SMALLHOLDERS AND COMMODIFICATION

Rice on Sumatra was a commodity product when focusing on the imported amounts from other Asian rice regions. The overall commodification of agriculture on Sumatra was a major cause for rice imports from the 1900s onward. Attempts from private companies and the colonial government to include rice produced on Sumatra into a commodity market had only marginal effects. The large rice schemes that were initiated in the late 1910s in order to give a boost to the commodification of Sumatran rice failed. The experiments revealed that commodification of an agricultural crop involved more than an entrepreneurial spirit, investment capital, and heavy machinery. Most colonial officials considered these ingredients the essence of the European approach, which made it superior to the Indonesians, in particular the Sumatran farmers. The mechanized upland rice farm of the Deli Company and the government wet rice scheme in *Selatdjaran* were hard and costly lessons that it was not quite that simple. Sumatran farmers must have observed these projects with some head-shaking amusement. The shifting cultivation practices they had developed over the centuries were not just a way of using an extensive forest area but a sophisticated farming system that balanced the available labor, soil fertility, and a portfolio of crops suitable to the environment. Moreover, from the early nineteenth century they had learned that crops like pepper, coffee and, somewhat later, rubber were crops that could be included in these farming system quite well and became attractive given the prices at which these products could be sold.

The inclusion into a global market economy during the colonial period did not imply that Sumatran farmers abandoned rice cultivation. Just like the uptake of commercial crops, other food crops were included but rice, cultivated in upland fields, remained a crucial crop. These upland fields were mostly swiddens although permanent upland fields were not uncommon. Even in areas, such as southwest Sumatra, where irrigated and rainfed lowland (wet) rice cultivation was stimulated did upland rice fields remain dominant, covering over 70 percent of the total rice area up to the 1960s.[48] Rice was not just one of the food crops but had a special status in most parts of the archipelago. The collective interest in the availability of rice was expressed in rituals and cautionary tales. A clear example is Michael Dove's explanation of an omen-dream among the Dayak in Borneo about rubber trees eating rice. This was a warning signal to ensure the cultivation of rice within a society that quickly adopted commercial rubber production during the early decades of the twentieth century. "The dream of the rice-eating rubber illuminates Bornean tribespeople's consciousness of the threat posed by overcommitment to global commodity markets."[49] The importance of rice for the Dayak on

---

[48] Schneider 1992, 97.
[49] Dove 1996, 35.

Borneo was not very different from the importance of rice among the Batak or other communities on Sumatra.[50] The similarities between the islands were also known by colonial officials. Soon after the Selatdjaran experiment started, Mulder had send a team to Borneo to mark out suitable terrain for similar wetland rice schemes that were never implemented.[51] Rice production on islands like Borneo and Sumatra thus resisted the "overcommitment to global commodity markets." Rice was an anti-commodity rather than a commodity.

In colonial histories of islands like Sumatra, the opposing interests between the local farming population and the European colonial companies and government create an effective explanatory framework for the agricultural and social dynamics during the early twentieth century. The opposition is not between commercial cash crop production as the main interest of the Europeans versus subsistence farming as the prime concern of smallholders. The Sumatran farmers, like their colleagues on Borneo and in other places incorporated cash crop production in their farm system, not rarely outcompeting the estates in quality, quantity, and capacity to adapt to fluctuating markets. As Dove aptly put it: "what was signified by the Dutch term for swidden agriculture, 'robber economy', was not that this system of agriculture robbed either the physical environment, its practitioners, or the country as a whole, but that it 'robbed' the colonial government which had little way of controlling and hence exploiting such dispersed, uncapitalized, peasant farmers."[52] This provides an appealing explanation to the negative descriptions of swiddening and indifference by colonial officials to examine these farming systems. However, the publications by Smits in the 1910s seem to contradict to such a conclusion.

The level of detail of Smits' observations and his calculations of time allocated by farmers to activities suggest that he spent considerable time in the field, most likely supported by local assistants with an agricultural training. Smits was part of an emerging research and extension system for indigenous agriculture. In 1915 the entire service consisted of 29 Europeans and 32 Indonesians, trained either in the Netherlands or at agricultural schools in the archipelago. In 1915 a total of six European and Indonesian advisors covered Sumatra, all the others were stationed on Java and Madura.[53] The nature of Smits work and his institutional position make clear that providing a more objective analysis of smallholder farming was not an easy task. In other words, the colonial government lacked the instruments to come to a better assessment of smallholder farming. Even for Java, where most studies of indigenous farming systems took place, the picture was scattered and

---

[50] Sherman and Sherman 1990.
[51] Nationaal Archief, Den Haag, Openbaar Verbaal, inventaris 2496.
[52] Dove 1983: 91.
[53] Jaarboek 1915.

effects limited.[54] The difference between what Smits proposed and what was implemented in *Selatdjaran* makes clear that even when better assessments of local agriculture became available, the arguments of one agricultural advisor could not change prevailing views in the colonial administration. Smits argued for better suited plans and methods to improve production of rice on Sumatra, methods that would fit the local farming systems. The failure of the mechanized rice experiments on tobacco fields and the polder in *Selatdjaran* demonstrated his point that agriculture is not a simple technique that can be pushed in any desired direction or shaped according to models from other places.[55] If rice production on Sumatra had to be intensified and produced to serve commercial markets, a necessity Smits did not deny, it had to be adapted from local forms of production.

CONCLUSION

The notion of anti-commodity sheds light on the organization of agricultural production and the way farming systems operate within a wider agrarian economy. Crop production directed at international commercial trade networks triggers production of other crops or other varieties of the commercial crop that separated or protected from commodification. Whether this implies production for subsistence, ornamental, and ritual purposes, or production for alternative markets is an empirical issue. The case presented here makes clear that Sumatran farmers had found a solution to incorporate rice as an anti-commodity in their farming systems because they were increasingly connected to international trade networks. The plantation companies and colonial government were largely unaware of this connection and considered every form of crop production amendable to commercial production once the necessary technical adjustment were made. It requires an understanding of agriculture and, most crucially, farming. Such understanding was not widely available in the colonial society of the Netherlands Indies, perhaps with the exception of colonial agricultural advisors who worked for the research and extension services for indigenous agriculture. In his 1919 report about the food situation in the colony, Smits underlines the importance of seeing farming as a business looking for a balance between various crops, appropriate levels of intensification for each of these crops and the allocation of labor. The plantation sector, Smits continues, is in that sense not a farm but more an industrial company.[56]

---

[54] Maat 2007.

[55] Smits repeated the point in 1934 when commenting on plans for mechanized rice farming in Surinam. "When the issue of mechanised rice farming is addressed, one fully has to let go of the American example and set up an entirely new system, based on well-established indigenous experience" (Smits 1934, 629).

[56] "These people [planters] are industrialists and their entire enterprise is in fact a single factory. (...) They may be good rubber planters or coffee farmers but about 'farm business' they usually know very little"(Smits 1919b, 100).

The emphasis on an industrial approach to agriculture and the neglect and derision of farming as the combined production of commodities and anti-commodities is a phenomenon of the twentieth century rather than a feature of colonial agriculture. The type of investments and scale of operation of the mechanized rice schemes on Sumatra were multiplied on an international level during the second half of the twentieth century. The planners of the Green Revolution in the 1950s considered, Nick Cullather shows, the industrial orientation of plantations the exemplar for the backward smallholder agriculture in Asia.[57] Although in the 1950s there was much more knowledge available about smallholder production than in the 1910s, "this picture of a dynamic, diversified globally linked agriculture was absent from discussion among American donors and scientists." Agriculture, Cullather proceeds, was "a category invented by city folk, a designation for a subordinate sphere within a presumptively urban-centered economy." Where the "miracles of modernization" in the 1910s were expected to appear from the introduction of tractors and disc plows, the trick was repeated in the 1960s and 1970s with dwarf varieties and chemical fertilizer. The underlying rationale is identical. Rice was considered a commodity, given the huge trade in rice perhaps even the primary commodity of Southeast Asia.[58] Surplus production of rice is typically related to intensified wetland (sawah) cultivation practices. In many areas, where different ecological, economic, and social factors are in play, rice is an anti-commodity. It is the type of rice production that remains invisible when commodification is used as the only lens through which rice cultivation is observed.

[57] Cullather 2010, 181.
[58] Latham 1998.

Bibliography

Adams, R. L. 1917. Rice – California's new profitable crop. *California Cultivator* 51:441.
Adas, Michael. 1974. *The Burma delta: economic development and social change on an Asian rice frontier, 1852–1941*. Madison WI: University of Wisconsin Press.
Adler, Paul S., and Seok-Woo Kwon. 2002. Social capital: prospects for a new concept. *Academy of Management Review* 27 (Jan):17–40.
Agnihotri, Indu. 1996. Ecology, land use and colonization in the canal colonies of Punjab. *Indian Economic and Social History Review* 33 (1):37–59.
AHU Arquivo Histórico Ultramarino, Pará. Para.
Alden, Dauril. 1984–1995. Late colonial Brazil, 1750–1808. In *The Cambridge history of Latin America, vol III*, edited by L. Bethell (pp. 601–60). Cambridge UK: Cambridge University Press.
Ali, Imran. 1988. *The Punjab under imperialism, 1885–1947*. Princeton NJ: Princeton University Press.
Álmada, Andre Alvares d, A. Teixeira da Mota, Paul E. H. Hair, and Jean Boulègue. 1984. *Brief treatise on the rivers of Guinea. Part I: translation by Paul E. H. Hair*. An interim and makeshift ed. 2 vols. Liverpool: Department of History, University of Liverpool.
Alpers, Edward A. 2009. The western Indian Ocean as a regional food network in the nineteenth century. In *East Africa and the Indian Ocean*, edited by E. A. Alpers (pp. 23–38). Princeton NJ: Markus Wiener Publishers.
An Pingsheng安平生. 1958. Yao shi fanshu cheng jibei de zengchan 要使番薯成幾倍的增產 (How to increase potate yields). In *Liangshi shengchan shudu keyi jiakuai* 糧食生產速度可以加快 (Food production can be accelerated), edited by Zhao Jinyang. Guangzhou: Guangdong renmin chubanshe.
Anon. 1998. Wonder wheat, *Science* 280 (24 April):527.
ANTT Arquivo Nacional da Torre do Tombo, edited by M. d. Reino. Lisbon, Portugal.
Anderson, Robert S., Edwin Levy, and Barrie M. Morrison. 1991. *Rice science and development politics: research strategies and IRRI's technologies confront Asian diversity (1950–1980)*. Oxford: Clarendon Press.

APEM Arquivo Publico do Estado do Maranhão, Livros de registro das ordens, livro 12. edited by l. Livros de registro das ordens.

Arashi Kaiichi 嵐嘉一. 1975. *Kinsei Inasaku gijitsu shi: sono ritchi seitaiteki kaiseki* 近世稲作技術史: その立地生態的解析 (History of rice cultivation techniques in the early modern period: analysis of local ecologies). Tōkyō: Nōsangyōson Bunka Kaigi.

Arkansas, Lonoke county and city. 1911. Lonoke AR: Lonoke County News.

Arkley, Alfred S. 1965. *Slavery in Sierra Leone.* Vol. s.n.: S.I.

Arnold, David. 1993. *Colonizing the body: state medicine and epidemic disease in nineteenth-century India.* Berkeley CA: University of California Press.

——. 2000. *Science, technology, and medicine in colonial India.* New York NY: Cambridge University Press.

——. 2005. Europe, technology and colonialism. *History and Technology* 21:85–106.

Arnold, David and Burton Stein. 2010. *History of India.* 2nd ed. Chichester: Blackwell Publishers Ltd.

Arrighi, Giovanni, Takeshi Hamashita, and Mark Selden, eds. 2003. *The resurgence of East Asia: 500, 150 and 50 year perspectives.* London UK, New York NY: Routledge.

Ashby, Jacqueline. 1990. Small farmers' participation in the design of technologies. In *Agroecology and small farm development*, edited by M. A. Altieri and S. B. Hecht. Boca Raton FL: CRC Press.

Aucott, Walter R. 1988. *The predevelopment ground-water flow system & hydraulic characteristics of the coastal plain aquifers of South Carolina*, edited by USGS. Washington DC: GPO.

Aucott, Walter R., and Gary K. Speiran. 1985. Ground-water flow in the coastal plain aquifers of South Carolina. *Ground Water* 23 (Nov/Dec):736–45.

Austin, Gareth, and Kaoru Sugihara. 2013. *Labour-intensive industrialization in global history.* Abingdon, Oxon; New York NY: Routledge.

Babineaux, Lawson Paul. 1967. A history of the rice industry of Southwestern Louisiana. MA Thesis, University of Southwestern Louisiana, 1967.

Bailey, Joseph Cannon. 1945. *Seaman A. Knapp, schoolmaster of American agriculture.* New York NY: Columbia University Press.

Bailey, N. Louise and Walter Edgar, eds. 1977. *Biographical Directory of the South Carolina House of Representatives, Volume II: The Commons House of Assembly, 1692–1775.* Columbia: University of South Carolina Press.

Baldwin, Agnes Leland. 1985. *First settlers of South Carolina, 1670–1700.* Easley SC: Southern Historical Press.

Ball family papers. South Caroliniana Library, University of South Carolina, Columbia SC.

Banerjee, Bireswar, and Jayati Hazra. 1974. *Geoecology of cholera in West Bengal: a study in medical geography.* Calcutta, Hazra: K.P. Bagchi Venus Printing Works.

Bank of Japan. 1966. *Hundred-year statistics of the Japanese economy.* Tōkyō: Statistics Department, Bank of Japan.

Barker, Jonathan. 1989. *Rural communities under stress: peasant farmers and the state in Africa, African society today.* Cambridge UK; New York NY: Cambridge University Press.

Barnwell, Joseph W. 1912. Diary of Timothy Ford, 1785–1786. *South Carolina Historical and Geological Magazine* 13 (Jul):132–47; 14 (Oct):181–204.

Barry, M., J. Pham, J. Noyer, C. Billot, B. Courtois, and N. Ahmadi 2007. Genetic diversity of the two cultivated rice species (O. sativa & O. glaberrima) in Maritime Guinea: evidence for interspecific recombination. *Euphytica* 154:127–37.

Barton, Gregory. 2011. Albert Howard and the decolonization of science: from the Raj to organic farming. In *Science and empire: knowledge and networks of science across the British Empire, 1800–1970*, edited by B. M. Bennett and J. Hodge (pp. 163–86). Basingstoke: Palgrave-Macmillan.

Bassino, Jean-Pascal, and Peter A. Coclanis. 2008. Economic transformation and biological welfare in colonial Burma: regional differentiation in the evolution of average height. *Economics and Human Biology* 6:212–27.

Bates, Robert H. 1981. *Markets and states in tropical Africa: the political basis of agricultural policies.* Berkeley CA: University of California Press.

Becker, Charles. 1985. Notes sur les Conditions Écologiques en Sénégambie aux 17e et 18e siecles. *African Economic History* 14:167–216.

Beinart, William, Karen Brown, and Daniel Gilfoyle. 2009. Experts and expertise in colonial Africa reconsidered: science and the interpenetration of knowledge. *African Affairs* 108 (432):413–33.

Benoit, Robert, and Archives and Special and Collections Department Frazar Memorial Library. 2000. *Imperial Calcasieu, images of America*. Charleston, SC: Arcadia Publications.

Bentley, Charles A., and Public Health Department of Bengal (India). 1925. *Malaria and agriculture in Bengal: how to reduce malaria in Bengal by irrigation*. Calcutta: Bengal Secretariat Book Depot.

Bergère, Marie-Claire, and Janet Lloyd. 1998. *Sun Yat-sen*. Stanford CA: Stanford University Press.

Berlin, Ira, and Philip Morgan, eds. 1991. *The slaves' economy: independent production by slaves in the Americas*. London UK: Frank Cass Publishers.

Bhattacharya, Neeladri. 1985. Agricultural labour and production in Punjab: Central and South-East Punjab, 1870–1940. In *Essays on the commercialization of Indian agriculture*, edited by K. N. Raj, N. Bhattacharya, S. Guha, and S. Padhi. Trivandrum Delhi: Centre for Development Studies, Oxford University Press.

Biggs, David A. 2002a. Personal correspondence with Mr. Dung. Hoa An Agricultural Research Station, Vietnam.

——. 2002b. Interview with Ong Rờ. edited by O. Rờ. Hoa My Commune, Phung Hiep District, Can Tho.

——. 2010. *Quagmire: nation-building and nature in the Mekong Delta*. Seattle WA: University of Washington Press.

Biggs, Stephen. 1980. The failure of farmers to adopt new technological "packages" entirely may be a sign of creativity rather than backwardness. *Ceres* 13 (4):23–6.

——. 1990. A multiple source of innovation model of agricultural research and technology promotion. *World Development* 18 (11):1481–99.

——. 2008. The lost 1990s? Personal reflections on a history of participatory technology development. *Development in Practice* 18 (4/5):489–505.

Bird, T. J. 1886. *Biennial report of the Louisiana commissioner of agriculture*.

Blench, Roger. 1996. The ethnographic evidence for long-distance contacts between Oceania and East Africa. In *The Indian Ocean in antiquity*, edited by J. Reade (pp. 0417–38). London UK, New York NY: Kegan Paul International & British Museum.

———. 2006. *Archaeology, language, and the African past*, The African archaeology series. Lanham MD: AltaMira Press.
Bleyhl, Norris Arthur. 1955. A history of the production and marketing of rice in California. PhD dissertation University of Minnesota, Microfilms 1957, Ann Arbor.
Bogue, Allan G. 1953. The administrative and policy problems of the J. B. Watkins land mortgage company, 1873–1894. *Bulletin of the Business Historical Society* 27 (March):26–59.
Böhmer, G. 1914. Die Entwicklung der Sortenfrage und ihre Lösung durch Sortenprüfung. *Kühn-Archiv* 5:191–206.
Bonneuil, Christophe. 2001. Development as experiment: science and state building in late colonial and postcolonial Africa, 1930–1970. *Osiris* 15:258–81.
Bonneuil, Christophe, and Frederic Thomas. 2009. *Genes, pouvoirs et profits: recherche publique et regimes de production des savoirs de Mendel aux OGM*. Versailles and Lausanne: Editions quae and fondation pour le progres de l'homme.
Boomgaard, Peter. 1989. *Children of the colonial state: population growth and economic development in Java, 1795–1880*, CASA monographs. Amsterdam, Netherlands: Free University Press: Centre for Asian Studies Amsterdam.
———. 1991. The non-agricultural side of an agricultural economy: Java, 1500–1900. In *In the shadow of agriculture: non-farm activities in the Javanese economy, past and present*, edited by P. Boomgaard, P. Alexander, and B. White (pp. 14–40). Amsterdam: Royal Tropical Institute.
———. 1999. Het Javaanse boerenbedrijf, 1900–1940. *NEHA-Jaarboek voor Economische, Bedrijfs- en Techniekgeschiedenis* 62:173–85.
———. 2007a. *Southeast Asia: an environmental history*. Nature and human societies series. Santa Barbara CA: ABC-CLIO.
———. 2007b. From riches to rags? Rice production and trade in Asia, particularly Indonesia,1500–1950. In *The wealth of nature: how natural resources have shaped Asian history, 1600–2000*, edited by G. Bankoff and P. Boomgaard (pp. 185–203). New York NY: Palgrave Macmillan.
Boomgaard, Peter, and Jan Luiten van Zanden. 1990. *Food crops and arable lands, Java 1815–1942*. Amsterdam, Netherlands: Royal Tropical Institute.
Boone, Catherine. 1992. *Merchant capital and the roots of state power in Senegal, 1930–1985*. Cambridge UK, New York NY: Cambridge University Press.
Booth, Anne. 1988. *Agricultural development in Indonesia*. Sydney, Boston MA: Allen and Unwin.
Bose, Sugata. 1990. Starvation amidst plenty: the making of famine in Bengal, Honan and Tonkin, 1942–45. *Modern Asian Studies* 24 (4):699–727.
———. 1993. *Peasant labour and colonial capital: rural Bengal since 1770*. Cambridge UK, New York NY: Cambridge University Press.
Bose, Sugata, and Ayesha Jalal. 1998. *Modern South Asia: history, culture, political economy*. New York NY: Routledge.
Bosma, Ulbe. 2005. The Indo: class, citizenship and politics in late colonial society. In *Recalling the Indies: colonial culture & postcolonial identities*, edited by J. Coté and L. Westerbeek (pp. 67–98). Amsterdam NJ: Aksant.

Bosma, Ulbe, Juan A. Giusti-Cordero, and G. Roger Knight, eds. 2008. *Sugarlandia revisited: sugar and colonialism in Asia and the Americas, 1800–1940*. New York NY and Oxford UK: Berghahn Books.

Bosteon, Koen. 2006. What comparative Bantu pottery vocabulary may tell us about early human settlement in the Inner Congo Basin. *Afrique & histoire* 5, 1:221–63.

—. 2007. Pots, words and the Bantu problem: on the lexical reconstruction and Early African history. *The Journal of African History* 48 (2):173–99.

Boswell, George. 1779. *A treatise on watering meadows*. London UK: J. Almon.

Bouma, Menno Jan, and Mercedes Pascual. 2001. Seasonal and interannual cycles of endemic cholera in Bengal 1891–1940 in relation to climate and geography. *Hydrobiologia* 160 (1–3):147–56.

Brandão Júnior, F. A. 1865. *A escravatura no Brasil precedida d'um artigo sobre agricultura e colonisação no Maranhão*. Brussels: H. Thiry-Vern Buggenhoudt.

Brathwaite, Kamau. 1971. *The development of Creole society in Jamaica, 1770–1820*. Oxford UK: Clarendon Press.

Bray, Francesca. 1979. Green revolution: a new perspective. *Modern Asian Studies* 13 (4):681–8.

—. 1983. Patterns of evolution in rice-growing societies. *Journal of Peasant Studies* 11:3–33.

—. 1986. *The rice economies: technology and development in Asian societies*. Oxford UK and New York NY: Blackwell.

—. 1997. *Technology and gender: fabrics of power in late imperial China*. Berkeley CA: University of California Press.

—. 2007a. Instructive and nourishing landscapes: natural resources, people and the state in late imperial China. In *A history of natural resources in Asia: the wealth of nature*, edited by G. Bankoff and P. Boomgaard (pp. 205–26). Basingstoke UK: Palgrave Macmillan.

—. 2007b. Agricultural illustrations: blueprint or icon? In *Graphics and text in the production of technical knowledge in China: the warp and the weft*, edited by F. Bray, V. Dorofeeva-Lichtmann, and G. Métailié (pp. 519–66). Leiden Netherlands: Brill.

—. 2008. Science, technique, technology: passages between matter and knowledge in imperial Chinese agriculture. *British Journal for the History of Science* 41 (3):319–44.

Breman, Jan, J. van den Brand, and J. L. T. Rhemrev. 1987. *Koelies, planters en koloniale politiek: het arbeidsregime op de grootlandbouwondernemingen aan Sumatra's oostkust in het begin van de twintigste eeuw*. Dordrecht, Netherlands and Providence RI: Foris.

Broadberry, Stephen, and Bishnupriya Gupta. 2006. The early modern great divergence: wages, prices and economic development in Europe and Asia, 1500 – 1800. *Economic History Review* LIX:2–31.

Brocheux, Pierre. 1995. *The Mekong Delta: ecology, economy, and revolution, 1860–1960*. Madison WI: Center for Southeast Asian Studies, University of Wisconsin-Madison.

Brook, Timothy. 1998. *The confusions of pleasure: commerce and culture in Ming China*. Berkeley CA: University of California Press.

Brooks, Sally. 2011. Living with materiality or confronting Asian diversity? The case of iron-biofortified rice research in the Philippines. *East Asian Science, Technology & Society* 5:173–88.

Brown, Philip C. 2011. *Cultivating commons: joint ownership of arable land in early modern Japan.* Honolulu HI: University of Hawaii Press.

Brown, Robert J. 1906. Rice fields of Arkansas revolutionize conditions in a large territory. *Arkansas Gazette (Little Rock)* (July):3.

Brown, Walter L. 1970. Notes on early rice culture in Arkansas. *Arkansas Historical Quarterly* 29 (Spring):76–9.

Bryden, James L. 1874. *Cholera epidemics of recent years viewed in relation to former epidemics: a record of cholera in the Bengal presidency from 1817 to 1872.* Calcutta: Office of the Superintendent of Government Printing.

Buck, John Lossing. 1956. *Land utilization in China: a study of 16,786 farms in 168 localities, and 38,256 farm families in twenty-two provinces in China, 1929–1933.* New York NY: Reproduced by the Council on Economic and Cultural Affairs.

Bundesverband Deutscher Pflanzenzüchter e.V (BDP), ed. 1987. *Landwirtschaftliche Pflanzenzüchtung in Deutschland. Geschichte, Gegenwart und Ausblick.* Gelsenkirchen: Thomas Mann.

Buoye, Thomas M. 2000. *Manslaughter, markets, and moral economy: violent disputes over property rights in eighteenth-century China.* 1. publ. ed. Cambridge UK: Cambridge University Press.

Cai Chenghao 蔡承豪, and Yang Yunping 楊韻平. 2004. *Taiwan fanshu wenhua zhi* 台灣番薯文化誌 (Traces of Taiwan's sweet potato culture). Taibei: Guoshi chuban.

Callison, C. Stuart. 1974. *The Land-to-the-Tiller Program and Rural Resource Mobilization in the Mekong Delta, South Vietnam.* Papers in International Studies Southeast Asia Series 34, Ohio University Center for International Studies, Southeast Asia Program.

Camprubi, Lino. 2010. One grain, one nation: rice genetics and the corporate state in early Francoist Spain (1939–1952). *Historical Studies in the Natural Sciences* 40 (4):499–531.

Cantrell, Wade M., and Larry E. Turner. 2002. *Total maximum daily load: Cooper river, Wando river, Charleston harbor system, South Carolina.* edited by Bureau of Water South Carolina Department of Health and Environmental Control. Columbia.

Capus, Guillaume. 1918. *Production et amélioration du riz d'Indo-Chine. Rapport introductif présenté au Congrès d'agriculture coloniale de 1918, par G. Capus.* Paris France: imprime de G. Cadet.

Cary, S. L. 1901. A paradise for the immigrant. In *Louisiana rice book*, edited by Southern Pacific Company. Houston TX: Passenger Department of the Southern Pacific *Sunset Route*.

Carney, Judith Ann. 1993a. Converting the wetlands, engendering the environment: the intersection of gender with agrarian change in the Gambia. *Economic Geography* 69 (4):329–48.

———. 1993b. From hands to tutors: African expertise in the South Carolina rice economy. *Agricultural History* 67 (July):1–30.

———. 1996. Landscapes of technology transfer: rice cultivation and African continuities. *Technology & Culture* 37 (Jan):5–35.

——. 1998. The role of African rice and slaves in the history of rice cultivation in the Americas. *Human Ecology* 26 (4):525–45.
——. 2001. *Black rice: the African origins of rice cultivation in the Americas*. Cambridge MA: Harvard University Press.
——. 2004. With grains in her hair: rice in colonial Brazil. *Slavery and Abolition* 25 (Apr):1–27.
Carney, Judith Ann, and Richard Porcher. 1993. Geographies of the past: rice, slaves, and technological transfer in South Carolina. *Southeastern Geographer* 33 (Nov):127–47.
Carney, Judith Ann, and Richard Nicholas Rosomoff. 2010. *In the shadow of slavery: Africa's botanical legacy in the Atlantic world*. Berkeley CA: University of California Press.
Catling, H. D., D. W. Puckridge, and D. HilleRislambers. 1988. The environment of Asian deepwater rice. In *International deepwater rice workshop, 26–30 Oct 1987*. Bangkok: Los Banos, Laguna (Philippines) International Rice Research Institute.
Ceccarelli, S. 1989. Wide adaptation: how wide? *Euphytica* 40:197–205.
Cernea, Michael M., and Amir H. Kassam, eds. 2006. *Researching the culture in agri-culture: social research for international development*. Wallingford: CABI Publishing.
Chambers, Robert. 1977. Challenges for rural research and development. In *Green revolution? Technology and change in rice-growing areas of Tamil Nadu and Sri Lanka*, edited by B. H. Farmer (pp. 398–412). London UK: Macmillan.
Chambers, Robert, Richard Longhurst, and Arnold Pacey. 1981. *Seasonal dimensions to rural poverty*. London UK, Totowa NJ: F. Pinter, Allanheld, Osmun.
Chambliss, Charles E. 1920. *Prairie rice culture in the United States*. Washington DC: US Department of Agriculture.
Chandler, Robert. 1992. *An adventure in applied science: a history of the International Rice Research Institute*. Los Banos: IRRI.
Chang, C. C. 1931. *China's Food Problem*. Shanghai: China Institute of Pacific Relations.
Chaplin, Joyce E., and Institute of Early American History and Culture (Williamsburg). 1993. *An anxious pursuit: agricultural innovation and modernity in the lower south, 1730–1815*. Chapel Hill NC: The University of North Carolina Press.
Charlesworth, Neil, and Economic History Society. 1982. *British rule and the Indian economy, 1800–1914*. London UK: Macmillan.
Chatterjee, U., and Acharya R. 2000. Seasonal variation of births in rural West Bengal: magnitude, direction and correlates. *Journal of Biosocial Science* 32 (4):443–58.
Chaudhuri, Binay Bhushan. 1983. Eastern India, Part II. In *The Cambridge economic history of India. vol.2, c.1757-c.1970*, edited by D. Kumar and M. Desai (pp. 87–177). Cambridge UK: Cambridge University Press.
——. 1996. The process of agricultural commercialisation in Eastern India during British Rule: a reconsideration of the notions of "forced commercialization" and "dependent peasantry". In *Meanings of agriculture: essays in South Asian history and economics*, edited by P. Robb (pp. 71–91). Delhi: Oxford University Press.

Chaudhuri, K. N. 1983. Foreign trade and balance of payments (1757–1947). In *The Cambridge economic history of India. vol.2, c.1757-c.1970*, edited by D. Kumar and M. Desai (pp. 804–77). Cambridge UK: Cambridge University Press.

Chen Bikuang 陳必貺. 1934. Wuhu miye zhi shikuang yu qi jiuji fangfa 蕪湖米業職實況與其救濟方法 (The situation of Wuhu rice business and methods for its revival). *Dongfang zazhi* 31 (2):21–9.

Chen Chunsheng 陳春聲. 1992. *Shichang jizhi yu shehui bianqian: shiba shiji Guangdong mijia fenxi* 市場機制與社會變遷－十八世紀廣東米價分析 (Market mechanisms and social reform: analysis of rice prices in Guangdong during the eighteenth century). Guangdong: Zhongshan daxue chubanshe.

Chen Gongbo 陳工博. 1936. *Sinian congzheng lu* 四年從政錄 (Report of four year's engagement into politics). Shanghai: Shangwu yinshuguan.

Chen Shiyuan 陳世元 (d. 1785). Qianlong edition. *Jinshu chuanxi lu* 金薯傳習錄 (Record on the transmission of sweet potato). Zhengzhou: Henan jiaoyu chubanshe.

Cheng, Siok-Hwa. 1968. *The rice industry of Burma, 1852–1940*. Kuala Lumpur: University of Malaya Press.

Cheung, Sui-wai. 2008. *The price of rice: market integration in eighteenth-century China*. Bellingham WA: Center for East Asian Studies, Western Washington University.

Childs, G. Tucker. 2001. What's so Atlantic about Atlantic? In *31st colloquium on African languages and linguistics*. Leiden, Netherlands: University of Leiden.

——. 2003. A splitter's holiday: more on the alleged unity of the Atlantic Group. In *33rd colloquium of African languages and linguistics*. Leiden, Netherlands: University of Leiden.

Childs, G. Tucker. 2008. Language death within the Atlantic language group. *West African Research Association (WARA) Newsletter*: 1–25.

Christophers, S. R. 1911. *Malaria in the Punjab, scientific memoirs by officers of the medical and sanitary departments of the government of India*. Calcutta: Superintendent Government Printing, India.

——. 1924. The mechanism of immunity against malaria in communities living under hyper-endemic conditions. *The Indian Journal of Medical Research* 12:273–94.

Christophers, S. R., and C. A. Bently. 1911. *Malaria in the Duars: being the second report to the advisory committee appointed by the government of India to conduct an enquiry regarding blackwater and other fevers prevalent in the Duars*. Simla: Government Monotype Press.

Chuan, Han-sheng, and Richard A. Kraus. 1975. *Mid-Ch'ing rice markets and trade: an essay in price history*. Cambridge MA, London UK: East Asian Research Center, Harvard University Press.

City Gazette 1784. (14 June) Charleston, SC.

Clifton, James M. 1978. *Life and labor on Argyle Island: letters and documents of a Savannah river rice plantation, 1833–1867*. Savannah GA: Beehive Press.

Cline, W. Rodney. 1970. Seaman Asahel Knapp, 1833–1911. *Louisiana History: The Journal of the Louisiana Historical Association* 11 (Sep):333–40.

Clowse, Converse D., and South Carolina Tricentennial Commission. 1971. *Economic beginnings in colonial South Carolina, 1670–1730*. Columbia SC: The University of South Carolina Press.

Coclanis, Peter A. 1982. Rice prices in the 1720s and the evolution of the South Carolina economy. *Journal of Southern History* 48 (Nov):531–44.
——. 1989. *The shadow of a dream: economic life and death in the South Carolina low country, 1670–1920*. New York NY: Oxford University Press.
——. 1993a. Southeast Asia's incorporation into the world rice market: a revisionist view. *Journal of Southeast Asian Studies* 24 (2):251–67.
——. 1993b. Distant thunder: the creation of a world market in rice and the transformations it wrought. *American Historical Review* 98:1050–78.
——. 1995. The poetics of American agriculture: the United States rice industry in international perspective. *Agricultural History* 69 (2):140–62.
——. 2000. How the Low Country was taken to task: slave-labor organization in Coastal South Carolina and Georgia. In *Slavery, secession, and southern history*, edited by R. L. Paquette and L. Ferleger (pp. 59–78). Charlottesville VA: University Press of Virginia.
——. 2001. Seeds of reform: David R. Coker. Premium cotton, and the campaign to modernize the rural south. *South Carolina Historical Magazine* 102 (July):82–98.
——. 2002. Review of Carney, Black Rice. *Journal of Economic History* 62 (March): 247–8.
——. 2006. Atlantic world or Atlantic/world? *William and Mary Quarterly 3rd Series* 63 (4):725–42.
——. 2010a. Introduction. In *Twilight on the rice fields: letters of the Heyward family, 1862–1871*, edited by A. H. Stokes and M. B. Hollis (pp. xviii–xxxi). Columbia SC: University of South Carolina Press.
——. 2010b. The rice industry of the United States. In *Rice: origin, antiquity and history*, edited by E. D. Sharma (pp. 411–31). Enfield NH, Oxford, IHB: Science Publishers.
Coclanis, Peter A., and J. C. Marlow. 1998. Inland rice production in the South Atlantic states: a picture in black and white. *Agricultural History* 72 (Spring): 197–213.
Coelho, Francisco de L., and Paul E. H. Hair. 1985. *Description of the coast of Guinea. Introduction and English translation of the Portuguese text*. Liverpool: Department of History, University of Liverpool.
Cohen, Robert, and Myriam Yardeni. 1988. Un suisse en Caroline du sud à la fin du XVIIe siècle, translated by Harriott Cheves Leland. *Bulletin de la Société de l'Histoire du Protestantisme Françias* 134 59–71.
Cole, Arthur H. 1927. The American rice-growing industry: a study of comparative advantage. *Quarterly Journal of Economics* 41 (Aug):595–643.
Coleman, James S. 1988. Social capital in the creation of human capital. *American Journal of Sociology* 94 (Supplement):95–120.
Colonial land grants, 1688–1799. edited by South Carolina Department of Agricultural History. Columbia SC.
Colquhoun, Donald J., 1974. Cyclic surficial stratigraphic units of the Middle and Lower Coastal Plains, Central South Carolina. In *Post-Miocene stratigraphy Central and Southern Atlantic Coastal Plain*, edited by Robert Q. Oaks and Jules R. DuBar, Logan: Utah State University Press, 179–90.
Colquhoun, Donald J., and Atlantic Coastal Plain Geological Association. 1965. *Terrace sediment complexes in central South Carolina*. Columbia SC: University of South Carolina.

Colquhoun, Donald J., and South Carolina State Development Board Division of Geology. 1969. *Geomorphology of the lower coastal plain of South Carolina*. Columbia SC: Division of Geology, State Development Board.

Comité agricole et industriel de la Cochinchine. 1872. Soixante-Quinzième Séance, 17 Octobre 1868, *Bulletin du Comité agricole et industriel de la Cochinchine*, Vol. 2, No. 7 (1872): 8–9.

Conneau, Theophilus (also known as Canot). 1976. *A slaver's log book, or 20 years of residence in Africa*. Englewood Cliff NJ: Prentice Hall. Original edition, 1856.

Cook, Harold John, Sanjoy Bhattacharya, Anne Hardy, and Wellcome Trust Centre for the History of Medicine at UCL. 2009. *History of the social determinants of health: global histories, contemporary debates*. Hyderabad: Orient BlackSwan.

Cooke, C. Wythe. 1936. *Geology of the coastal plain of South Carolina*. Washington DC: Government Printing Office, United States Department of the Interior, Geological Survey.

Cooke, Nola. 2004. Water world: Chinese and Vietnamese on the riverine water frontier, from Ca Mau to Tonle Sap (c. 1850–1884). In *Water frontier: commerce and the Chinese in the lower Mekong region, 1750–1880*, edited by N. Cooke and T. Li (pp. 139–57). Singapore, Lanham MD: Singapore University Press & Rowman & Littlefield.

Cooper, Frederick. 2010. Writing the history of development. *Journal of Modern European History* 8 (1):5–23.

Cooper, Thomas, and David J. McCord, eds. 1836–1841. *The statues at large of South Carolina*. Columbia: A.S. Johnston.

Cowan, Michael, and Robert Shenton. 1996. *Doctrines of development*. London, UK: Routledge.

Creutzberg, Peter, ed. 1973. *Het Economisch Beleid in Nederlandsch-Indië; Capita Selecta: een Bronnenpublikatie* 2. Groningen, Netherlands: CBNI.

Cronon, William. 1995. The trouble with wilderness: or, getting back to the wrong nature. In *Uncommon ground: rethinking the human place in nature*, edited by W. Cronon (pp. 69–90). New York NY: Norton.

Cronon, William, and John Demos. 2003. *Changes in the land: Indians, colonists, and the ecology of New England*. New York NY: Hill and Wang.

Crosby, Alfred W. 1986. *Ecological imperialism: the biological expansion of Europe, 900–1900*. Cambridge UK, New York NY: Cambridge University Press.

Crossley, Pamela Kyle. 1990. *Orphan warriors: three Manchu generations and the end of the Qing world*. Princeton NJ: Princeton University Press.

Cullather, Nick. 2004. Miracles of modernisation: the green revolution and the apotheosis of technology. *Diplomatic History* 28 (2):227–54.

———. 2010. *The hungry world: America's cold war battle against poverty in Asia*. Cambridge MA: Harvard University Press.

Curry-Machado, Jonathan. 2010. In cane's shadow: the impact of commodity plantations on local subsistence agriculture on Cuba's mid-nineteenth century sugar frontier. *Commodities of Empire Working Paper, Milton Keynes, Open University* 16:201.

Curtin, Philip D. 1975. *Economic change in pre-colonial Africa: Senegambia in the era of the slave trade*, Madison: University of Wisconsin Press.

Cwiertka, Katarzyna Joanna. 2006. *Modern Japanese cuisine: food, power and national identity*. London UK: Reaktion.

Dahlberg, Kenneth. 1979. *Beyond the green revolution: the ecology and politics of global agricultural development*. New York NY, London UK: Plenum.

Dai Nam Thuc Luc: Quoc Su Quan Trieu Nguyen. 1963. vol. 1. Ha Noi: Su Hoc.

Daniel, Pete. 1985. *Breaking the land: the transformation of cotton, tobacco, and rice cultures since 1880*. Urbana IL: University of Illinois Press.

Daniels, Christian, Nicholas K. Menzies, and Joseph Needham. 1996. *Science and civilisation in China. Volume 6, Biology and biological technology. Part 3, Agro-industries and forestry* Cambridge UK: Cambridge University Press.

Das, Dial. 1943. *Vital statistics of the Punjab, 1901 to 1940*. Lahore: Civil and Military Gazette.

Datta, Rajat. 1996. Peasant productivity and agrarian commercialism in a rice-growing economy: some notes on a comparative perspective and the case of Bengal in the eighteenth century. In *Meanings of agriculture: essays in South Asian history and economics*, edited by P. Robb (pp. 92–131). Delhi: Oxford University Press.

Davidson, Joanna 2007. Feet in the fire: social change and continuity among the Diola of Guinea-Bissau. PhD thesis, Emory University, Atlanta.

De Langhe, Edmond, and Pierre De Maret. 1999. Tracking the banana: its significance in early agriculture. In *The prehistory of food: appetites for change*, edited by C. Gosden and J. G. Hather (pp. 369–86). London UK, New York NY: Routledge.

De Vismes, Maurice-Paul, and Henry, Yves. 1928. *Documents de démographie et riziculture en Indochine*. Hanoï-Haiphong: Imprimé d'Extrême-Orient.

De Vries, Jan. 1994. The industrial revolution and the industrious revolution. *Journal of Economic History* **54** (2):249–70.

—. 2008. *The industrious revolution: consumer behavior and the household economy, 1650 to the present*. Cambridge UK, New York NY: Cambridge University Press.

De Vries, J., and Gary Toenniessen. 2001. *Securing the harvest: biotechnology, breeding and seed systems for African crops*. Wallingford UK: CABI Publishing.

Deed books. edited by Charleston County Register Mesne Conveyance. Charleston, SC.

Delevan, Wayne. 1963. *The North American Land and Timber Company, Limited. Some notes on its beginnings*. Edited by American Academy of Science. Vol. 17. Agricultural History Museum.

Departement van Landbouw Nijverheid en Handel. 1925. *Landbouwatlas van Java en Madoera*. Weltevreden Netherlands: Departement van Landbouw, Nijverheid en Handel.

Desmarias, Ralph, and Robert Irving. 1983. *The Arkansas Grand Prairie*. Stuttgart: The Arkansas County Agricultural History Museum.

Dethloff, Henry C. 1970. Rice revolution in the Southwest, 1880–1910. *Arkansas Historical Quarterly* **29** (Spring):66–75.

—. 1982. The colonial rice trade. *Agricultural History* **56** (Jan):231–43.

—. 1988. *A history of the American rice industry, 1685–1985*. College Station TX: Texas A&M University Press.

—. 2013. *Rice culture*. Texas State Historical Association 2010. Onlina at: http://tsha.utexas.edu/handbook/online/articles/RR/afrl1.html [accessed Feb. 23, 2013].

Diamond, Jared M. 1999. *Guns, germs, and steel: the fates of human societies*. New York, NY: W.W. Norton & Co.

Ding Ying 丁穎. 1957. Woguo daozuo quyu de huafen 我國稻作區域的劃分 (Corn regions and divisions of our country). In *Ding Ying daozuo lunwen xuanji* 丁穎稻作論文集 (Collected essays on grains by Ding Ying), edited by Ding Ying. Beijing: Nongye chubanshe.

——. 1983. *Ding Ying daozuo lunwen xuanji* 丁穎稻作論文集(Collected essays on grains by Ding Ying). Beijing: Nongye chubanshe.

Dix, Walter. 1911. Forderung des staatlichen Eingreifens zum Schutz des Saatguthandels und zur Förderung der Pflanzenzüchtung. *Illustrierte Landwirtschaftliche Zeitung* 31 (15 Feb):102–3.

Doar, David, A. S. Salley, and Theodore D. Ravenel. 1970. *Rice and rice planting in the South Carolina low country*. Charleston SC: Charleston Museum.

Donahue, Brian. 2004. *The great meadow: farmers and the land in colonial concord*. New Haven CT: Yale University Press.

Donald, C. M. 1968. The breeding of crop ideotypes. *Euphytica* 17 (3):385–403.

Donelha, Andre. 1625. *Descricao da Serra Leoa e dos Rios de Guine do Cabo Verde/ An account of Sierra Leone and the Rivers of Guinea of Cape Verde*, 1977 edition of Portuguese text by Avelino Teixeira da Mota, notes and English translation by Paul E. H. Hair. Lisbon: Junta de Investigacoes Cientificas do Ultramar.

Donnan, Elizabeth. 1935. *Documents illustrative of the history of the slave trade to America. 4 The border colonies and the southern colonies*. Washington DC: Carnegie Institute.

Doneux, J. L. 1975. Hypotheses pour la comparative des Langues atlantiques. *Africana linguistica* 6: 41–129.

Dos Prazeres, Francisco de N. S. 1891. Poranduba maranhense ou relação histórica da província do Maranhão. *Revista trimensal do Instituto do Histórico e Geographico Brazileiro* 54:140.

Douglas, Mary. 1966. *Purity and danger: an analysis of concepts of pollution and taboo*. New York NY: Praeger.

Dove, Michael R. 1983. Theories of swidden agriculture and the political economy of ignorance. *Agro Forestry Systems* 1:85–99.

——. 1996. Rice-eating rubber and people-eating governments: peasant versus state critiques of rubber development in colonial Borneo. *Ethnohistory* 43:33–63.

Drache, Hiram M. 1964. *The day of the bonanza: a history of bonanza farming in the red river valley of the North*. Fargo ND: North Dakota Institute for Regional Studies.

Drèze, Jean, and Amartya Sen. 1989. *Hunger and public action*. Oxford UK, New York NY: Oxford University Press and Clarendon Press.

Dubose, Samuel, and Black Oak Agricultural Society Charleston SC. 1858. *Address delivered at the seventeenth anniversary of the Black Oak agricultural society, April 27th, 1858*. Charleston SC: A. E. Miller.

Dumont, René, and J. Nanta. 1935. *La culture du riz dans le delta du Tonkin: étude et propositions d'amélioration des techniques traditionnelles de riziculture tropicale*. Paris France: Société d'éditions géographiques, maritimes et coloniales.

Duras, Marguerite, translated by Barbara Bray. 2008. *The lover*. London UK: Harper Perennial.

Durie, Mark, and Malcolm Ross. 1996. *The comparative method reviewed: regularity and irregularity in language change*. New York NY, Oxford UK: Oxford University Press.

Duruflé, Gilles. 1994. *Le Sénégal peut-il sortir de la crise? Douze ans d'ajustement structurel au Sénégal, Les Afriques*. Paris France: Editions Karthala.

Duvick, Donald N. 1990. The romance of plant breeding and other myths. In *Gene manipulation in plant improvement II*, edited by J. P. Gustafson (pp. 39–54). New York NY: Plenum Press.

———. 2002. Theory, empiricism and intuition in professional plant breeding. In *Farmers, scientists and plant breeding: integrating knowledge and practice*, edited by D. A. Cleveland and D. Soleri (pp. 189–212). Wallingford UK: CAB International.

Dwyer, David. 1989. Mande. In *The Niger-Congo languages: a classification and description of Africa's largest language family*, edited by J. Bendor-Samuel and R. L. Hartell (pp. 47–65). Lanham, MD: University Press of America.

Dyson, Tim. 1989. *India's historical demography: studies in famine, disease and society*. London UK: Curzon.

———. 1991. On the demography of South Asian famines: Part I. *Population Studies* 45 (1):5–25.

Edelson, S. Max. 2006. *Plantation enterprise in colonial South Carolina*. Cambridge MA: Harvard University Press.

———. 2007. Clearing swamps, harvesting forests: trees and the making of a plantation landscape in the Colonial South Carolina lowcountry. *Agricultural History* 81 (Summer):381–406.

———. 2010. Beyond "Black Rice": reconstructing material and cultural contexts for early plantation agriculture. AHR exchange: the question of "Black Rice". *American Historical Review* 115:125–35.

Edgar, Walter B., N. Louise Bailey, Alexander Moore, and General Assembly House of Representatives Research Committee South Carolina. 1974. *Biographical directory of the South Carolina House of Representatives*. Columbia SC: University of South Carolina Press.

Edgerton, David. 2007. Creole technologies and global histories: rethinking how things travel in space and time. *History of Science and Technology* 1:75–112.

Eduardo, Octavio da Costa 1948. *The negro in Northern Brazil* New York NY: J. J. Augustin Publishers.

Ehret, Christopher. 1967. Cattle-keeping and milking in eastern and southern African history: the linguistic evidence. *The Journal of African History* 8, (1): 1–17.

———. 1968. Sheep and central Sudanic peoples in southern Africa. *The Journal of African History* 9, (2): 213–21.

———. 1979. On the antiquity of agriculture in Ethiopia. *The Journal of African History* 20, (2): 161–77.

———. 2000. Testing the expectations of glottochronology against the correlations of language and archaeology in Africa. In *Time depth in historical linguistics*, edited by C. Renfrew, A. McMahon, R. L. Trask, and McDonald Institute for Archaeological Research (pp. 373–99). Cambridge UK: McDonald Institute for Archaeological Research.

———. 2011. *History and the testimony of language*. Berkeley CA: University of California Press.

Eltis, David, Philip D. Morgan, and David Richardson. 2007. Agency and diaspora in Atlantic history: reassessing the African contribution to rice cultivation in the Americas. *American Historical Review* 112 (Dec):1329–58.

——. 2010. Black, brown, or white? Color-coding American commercial rice cultivation with slave labor. AHR exchange: the question of "Black Rice". *American Historical Review* 115:164–71.

Elvin, Mark. 1973. *The pattern of the Chinese past: a social and economic interpretation*. Stanford CA: Stanford University Press.

——. 2004. *The retreat of the elephants: an environmental history of China*. New Haven CT: Yale University Press.

Elvin, Mark, and Ts'ui-jung Liu, eds. 1998. *Sediments of time: environment and society in Chinese history*. Cambridge UK, New York NY: Cambridge University Press.

Embleton, Sheila. 2000. Lexicostatistics/Glottochronology: from Swadesh to Sankoff to Starostin to future horizons. In *Time depth in historical linguistics*, edited by C. Renfrew (pp. 143–66). Cambridge UK: McDonald Institute for Archaeological Research.

Engledow, F. L. 1925. The economic possibilities of plant breeding. In *Imperial botanical conference: report of proceedings*, edited by F. T. Brooks (pp. 31–40). Cambridge UK: Cambridge University Press.

Evans, Sterling. 2007. *Bound in twine: the history and ecology of the henequen-wheat complex for Mexico and the American and Canadian plains, 1880–1950*. College Station: Texas A & M University Press.

FAO, United Nations Food and Agriculture Organisation. 2004. *The state of food and agriculture, 2003–04: agricultural biotechnology – meeting the needs of the poor?* Rome Italy: FAO.

Farmer, B. H. 1979. The "green revolution" in South Asian ricefields: environment and production. *Journal of Development Studies* 15 (4):304–19.

——. 1986. Perspectives on the green revolution in South Asia. *Modern Asian Studies* 20 (1):175–99.

Farris, William Wayne. 2006. *Japan's medieval population: famine, fertility, and warfare in a transformative age*. Honolulu: University of Hawai'i Press.

Faure, David. 1989. *The rural economy of pre-liberation China: trade expansion and peasant livelihood in Jiangsu and Guangdong, 1870 to 1937*. Hong Kong, New York NY: Oxford University Press.

——. 1990. The rice trade in Hong Kong before the second world war. In *Between east and west: aspects of social and political development in Hong Kong*, edited by E. Sinn (pp. 216–25). Hong Kong: Centre of Asian Studies, University of Hong Kong.

Feierman, Steven. 1992. *The social basis of health and healing in Africa*. Berkeley CA: University of California Press.

Feierman, Steven and John M. Janzen, eds. 1992. *The social basis of health and healing in Africa*. Berkeley: University of California Press.

Feng Liutang 灃柳堂. 1934. *Zhongguo li dai minshi zhengce shi* 中國歷代民食政策史 (A history of provisional policies in Chinese dynasties), Zhongguo jingji xue she congshu. Shanghai: Shangwu yinshuguan.

Ferguson, Leland G. 1992. *Uncommon ground: archaeology and early African America, 1650–1800*. Washington DC: Smithsonian Institution Press.

Fiege, Mark. 1999. *Irrigated Eden: the making of an agricultural landscape in the American West*. Seattle WA: University of Washington Press.

Bibliography

Fields-Black, Edda L. 2008. *Deep roots: rice farmers in West Africa and the African diaspora.* Bloomington IN: Indiana University Press.

Finlay, Robert. 2010. *The pilgrim art: cultures of porcelain in world history.* Berkeley CA: University of California Press.

Flynn, Dennis Owen, Lionel Frost, and A. J. H. Latham, eds. 1999. *Pacific centuries: Pacific and Pacific Rim history since the sixteenth century.* London UK, New York NY: Routledge.

Fontenot, Mary Alice, and Paul B. Freeland. 1997. *Acadia Parish, Louisiana.* 2 vols. Baton Rouge LA: Claitor's Pub. Division. Original edition, 1976.

Fox, J., and J. Ledgerwood. 1999. Dry-season flood-recession rice in the Mekong Delta: two thousand years of sustainable agriculture? *Asian Perspectives* 38:37–50.

Fox, Richard Gabriel. 1985. *Lions of the Punjab: culture in the making.* Berkeley CA: University of California Press.

Francks, Penelope. 1984. *Technology and agricultural development in pre-war Japan.* New Haven CT: Yale University Press.

——. 1999. *Japanese economic development: theory and practice.* London UK, New York NY: Routledge.

——. 2003. Rice for the masses: food policy and the adoption of imperial self-sufficiency in early twentieth-century Japan. *Japan Forum* 15:125–46.

——. 2005. Multiple choices: rural household diversification and Japan's path to industrialization. *Journal of Agrarian Change* 5:451–75.

——. 2006. *Rural economic development in Japan: from the nineteenth century to the Pacific war.* London UK, New York NY: Routledge.

——. 2007. Consuming rice: food, traditional products and the history of consumption in Japan. *Japan Forum* 19:147–68.

——. 2009. *The Japanese consumer: an alternative economic history of modern Japan.* Cambridge UK, New York NY: Cambridge University Press.

Frank, Andre Gunder. 1998. *ReOrient: global economy in the Asian age.* Berkeley CA: University of California Press.

Frey, Marc. 1997. Trade, ships, and the neutrality of the Netherlands in the First World War. *International History Review* 19:541–62.

Friedman, David. 1988. *The misunderstood miracle: industrial development and political change in Japan.* Ithaca NY: Cornell University Press.

Fruwirth, Carl. 1907. *Sorten, Saatfruchtbau und Pflanzenzüchtung in Württemberg.* Plieningen Germany: Friedrich Find.

——. ed. 1909. *Die Züchtung der landwirtschaftlichen Kulturpflanzen.* Vol. 1. Berlin Germany: Parey.

Fuller, Dorian, and Nicole Boivin. 2009. Crops, cattle and commensals across the Indian Ocean: current and potential archaeobotanical evidence. *Etudes Océan Indien* 42:13–46.

Fuller, Dorian Q., and Ling Qin. 2009. Water management and labour in the origins and dispersal of Asian rice. *World Archaeology* 41:1, 88–111.

Garewal, Gurjeewan. 2005. Nucleotide -88 (C-T) promoter mutation is a common Thalassemia mutation in the Jat Sikhs of Punjab, India. *Americal Journal of Hematology* 79:252–6.

Garewal, Gurjeewan, and Reena Das. 2003. Spectrum of B-Thalessemia mutations in Punjabis. *International Journal of Human Genetics* 3 (4):217–19.

Garrett, G. H. 1892. Sierra Leone and the interior: to the upper waters of the Niger. *Proceedings of the Royal Geographical Society and Monthly Record of Geography* 14 (7):433–55.

Geertz, Clifford. 1963. *Agricultural involution: the process of ecological change in Indonesia.* Berkeley CA: The University of California Press.

Gibbs, Mathurin Guerin. 1824–1874. *Plantation registers.* Charleston SC: South Carolina Historical Society.

Giles-Vernick, Tamara. 2000. Doli: translating an African history of loss in the Sangha river basin of equatorial Africa. *Journal of African History* 41:373–94.

——. 2002. *Cutting the vines of the past: environmental histories of the Central African rain forest.* Charlottesville VA: University of Virginia Press.

Gill, C. A. 1928. *The genesis of epidemics and the natural history of disease: an introduction to the science of epidemiology based upon the study of epidemics of malaria, influenza & plague.* London UK: Baillière, Tindall and Cox.

Ginn, Mildred Kelly. 1940. A history of rice production in Louisiana to 1896. *Louisiana Historical Quarterly* 23 (Apr):544–88.

Glantz, Michael H. 1987. Drought in Africa. *Scientific American* 256 (6):34–40.

Glen, James, George Milligen-Johnston, and Chapman J. Milling. 1951. *Colonial South Carolina: two contemporary descriptions, South Caroliniana.* Columbia SC: University of South Carolina Press.

Gordon, Robert J. 1992. *The Bushman myth: the making of a Namibian underclass.* Boulder CO: Westview Press.

Government of Bengal, Public Health Department. 1929. *Malaria Problem in Bengal.* Calcutta: Bengal Government Press.

Government of India, Cattle Plague Commission. 1871. *Report of the Commissioners appointed to inquire into the origin, nature, etc. of Indian cattle plagues: with appendices, 1871.* Calcutta: Office of the Superintendent of Government Printing.

——. 1908/1991. *Imperial gazetteer of India.* Vol. 1. New Delhi India: Atlantic Publishers and Distributors.

Government of Punjab. 1869. *Home Department Proceedings*, General Branch, 13 March 1869, no. 210A, 12.

——. 1878–79. Punjab report in reply to the inquires issued by the famine commission. Lahore Pakistan: Central Jail Press.

——. 1879. *Home Department proceedings*, May 1879, 189–90 and 197.

——. 1882, 1885, 1890. Report on the sanitary administration of the Punjab for the year 1880, 1884, 1880. Lahore Pakistan: Central Jail Press.

——. 1885. *Report on the Sanitary Administration of the Punjab for the year 1884.* Lahore: Civil and Military Gazette Press.

——. 1882, 1894, 1922. *Annual report on dispensaries in the Punjab for the year 1881, 1893, 1921.* Lahore Pakistan: Central Jail Press.

——. 1890, 1895. *Report on the sanitary administration of the Punjab for the year 1889, 1894.* Lahore Pakistan: Civil and Military Gazette Press.

——. 1890a *Home Department proceedings*, Medical and Sanitary Branch, December 1890, no. 6. Chandigarh: Punjab State Archives.

——. 1890b. *Report on the Sanitary Administration of the Punjab for the year 1889.* Lahore: Civil and Military Gazette Press.

———. 1897 *Home Department proceedings*, Medical and Sanitary Branch, February 1897, no. 10. Chandigarh: Punjab State Archives.

———. 1917. *Home Department proceedings*, Medical and Sanitary Branch, July 1917, no. 48–50, 93–5. Chandigarh: Punjab State Archives.

Govind, Nalini. 1986. *Regional perspectives in agricultural development: a case study in wheat and rice in selected regions of India*. New Delhi: Concept Publishing Company.

Granovetter, Mark S. 1973. The strength of weak ties. *American Journal of Sociology* 78:1360–80.

Gray, Lewis Cecil. 1933. *History of agriculture in the Southern United States to 1860*. 2 vols. Gloucester MA: P. Smith.

Great Britain Parliament, House of Commons, and Sheila Lambert. 1975. *House of Commons sessional papers of the eighteenth century*. 147 vols. Vol. 68. Wilmington: Scholarly Resources.

Green, D. Brooks. 1986. Irrigation expansion in Arkansas: a preliminary investigation. *Arkansas Historical Quarterly* 45 (Autumn):261–8.

Greene, Jack P., Rosemary Brana-Shute, and Randy J. Sparks. 2001. *Money, trade, and power: the evolution of colonial South Carolina's plantation society*. Columbia SC: University of South Carolina Press.

Greenough, Paul. 2009. Asian intra-household survival logics: the "Shen Te" and "Shui Ta" options. In *History of the social determinants of health: global histories, contemporary debates*, edited by H. J. Cook, S. Bhattacharya, and A. Hardy (pp. 27–41). Hyderabad India: Orient BlackSwan.

Grégoire, Claire, and Bernard de Halleux. 1994. Etude lexicostatistique de quarante-trois langues et dialectes mandé. *Africana Linguistica XI, Annales du Musée Royal de l'Afrique Centrale, Sciences Humaines* 142:53–71.

Grewal, J. S. 2004. Historical geography of the Punjab. *Journal of Punjab Studies* 11 (1):1–18.

Griffin, Keith. 1974. *The political economy of agrarian change: an essay on the green revolution*. London UK: Macmillan.

Griliches, Zvi. 1957. An exploration in the economics of technological change. *Econometrica* 25 (Oct):501–22.

Grist, D. H. 1975 [1953]. *Rice*. 5th edition London UK: Longmans.

Groening, Richard I. 1998. The rice landscape in South Carolina: valuation, technology, and historical periodization. MA thesis, University of South Carolina, Columbia.

Gross, B. L., F. T. Steffen, and K. M. Olsen. 2010. The molecular basis of white pericarp in African domesticated rice: novel mutations at the rice gene. *Journal of Evolutionary Biology* 23:2747–53.

Guangdong sheng yinhang jingji yanjiushe. 1938. *Guangzhou zhi miye* 廣州之米業 (Rice business in Guangzhou). Guangzhou: Guangdong shenyinhang jingji yanjiushi.

Guangdong sheng zhongshan tushuguan. 1992. *Guangdong jinxiandai renwu cidian* 廣東近現代人物詞典 (Dictionary of prominent persons from Guangdong in modern history). Guangzhou: Guangdong keji chubanshe.

Guha, Sumit. 2001. *Health and population in South Asia: from earliest times to the present*. London UK: Hurst & Co.

Guoji maoyi daobao 國際貿易導報 (Journal of foreign trade) 1930–1937. Nanjing: Guomin zhengfu shiyebu.

Guoli gugong bowuyuan 國立故宮博物院. 1977–79. *Gongzhong dang Yongzheng chaozouzhe* 宮中檔雍正朝奏摺 (Memorials of the palace archive of the Yongzheng era). Taibei: Guoli gugong bowuguan.

——. 1982–89. 1982. *Gong zhong dang Qianlong chao zou zhe* 宮中檔乾隆朝奏摺 (Throne memorials of the palace archive of the Qianlong era). Taibei: Gai yuan.

Habib, Irfan. 2000. *The agrarian system of Mughal India, 1526–1707*. Delhi India, Toronto Canada: Oxford University Press.

Hall, Gwendolyn Midlo. 2010. Africa and Africans in the African diaspora: the uses of relational databases. *American Historical Review* 115 (1):136–50.

Hamblin, J. 1993. The ideotype concept: useful or outdated? In *International Crop Science*, edited by D. R. Buxton (pp. 589–97). Madison WI: Crop Science Society of America.

Hamilton, Gary G, and Wei-An Chang. 2003. The importance of commerce in the organization of China's late imperial economy. In *The resurgence of East Asia: 500, 150 and 50 year perspectives*, edited by G. Arrighi, T. Hamashita, and M. Selden (pp. 173–213). London UK, New York NY: Routledge.

Hamilton, Roy W. 2004. *The art of rice: spirit and sustenance in Asia*. Seattle, WA, Chesham: University of Washington Press.

Hamlin, Christopher. 2010. *Cholera: the biography*. Oxford: Oxford University Press.

Hammond, Winifred. 1961. *Rice. Food for a hungry world*. New York NY: Fawcett Publications Inc.

Handelingen van de Volksraad, 1918. Batavia: Landsdrukkerij.

Hanley, Steven G., and Ray Hanley. 2008. *Arkansas county*. Charleston SC: Arcadia Publication.

Hanley, Susan B. 1997. *Everyday things in premodern Japan: The hidden legacy of material culture*. Berkeley CA: University of California Press.

Hardy, Stephen G. 2001. Colonial South Carolina's rice industry and the Atlantic economy: patterns of trade, shipping, and growth, 1715–1775. In *Money, trade, and power: the evolution of colonial South Carolina's plantation society. The Carolina lowcountry and the Atlantic world*, edited by J. P. Greene, R. Brana-Shute, and R. J. Sparks (pp. 108–40). Columbia SC: University of South Carolina Press.

Harlan, Jack. 1971. Agricultural origins: centers and noncenters. *Science* 29 (4008):468–74.

Harrell, Stevan. 2007. Recent Chinese history in ecosystem perspective. In *Conference on New Paradigms in Chinese Studies*. UC San Diego, April 2007: online at: http://faculty.washington.edu/stevehar/Chinese%20History%20as%20an%20Ecosystem.pdf [accessed August 5, 2014].

Harriss, Barbara. 1990. The intrafamily distribution of hunger in South Asia. In *The political economy of hunger. Vol. 1, Entitlement and well-being*, edited by J. Drèze and A. Sen (pp. 351–424). Oxford UK: Clarendon.

Hart, John Fraser. 1991. *The land that feeds us*. New York NY: W.W. Norton.

Harwood, Jonathan. 2005. *Technology's dilemma: agricultural colleges between science and practice in Germany, 1860–1934*. Frankfurt, Bern, New York NY: Peter Lang.

——. 2012. *Europe's green revolution and others since: the rise and fall of peasant-friendly plant-breeding*. London UK: Routledge.

Hateley, Charles. 1792. Hateley to John Coming Ball. 6 August 1792. Ball Family Papers. South Caroliniana Library, University of South Carolina, Columbia, SC.

Hawthorne, Walter. 2003. *Planting rice and harvesting slaves: transformations along the Guinea-Bissau coast, 1400–1900*. Portsmouth NH: Heinemann.

———. 2010a. *From Africa to Brazil: culture, identity, and an Atlantic slave trade, 1600–1830*. Cambridge UK, New York NY: Cambridge University Press.

———. 2010b. From "black rice" to "brown": rethinking the history of risiculture in the seventeenth and eighteenth century Atlantic. *American Historical Review* 115 (1):151–63.

———. 2011. African foods and the making of the Americas. *Common-place* (3), online at: http://www.common-place.org/vol-11/no-03/reviews/hawthorne.shtml [accessed August 5, 2014].

Hayami Akira 速水融. 1967. Keizai shakai no seiritsu to sono tokushitsu 經濟社會の成立とその特質 (The emergence of economic society and its characteristics). In *Atarashii Edo Jidaizo o Motomete* edited by Shakai Keizaishi Gakkai 社会経済史学会編. Tōkyō Japan: Tōyō Keizai Shinposha.

———. 1989. Preface. In *Economic and demographic development in rice producing societies: some aspects of East Asian economic history, 1500–1900*, edited by Akira Hayami and Yoshihiro Tsubouchi. Tōkyō: Keio University, 1–5.

———. 1992. The industrious revolution. *Look Japan* 38 (436):8–10.

———. 2009. Industrial revolution versus industrious revolution. In *Population, family and society in pre-modern Japan: collected papers of Akira Hayami*, edited by A. Hayami and O. Saitō, Folkestone UK: Global Oriental.

Hayami Akira, and Saitō Osamu. 2009. *Population, family and society in pre-modern Japan collected papers of Akira Hayami*. Folkestone UK: Global Oriental.

Hayami Akira, and Tsubouchi Yoshihiro. 1990. *Economic and demographic development in rice producing societies: some aspects of East Asian economic history, 1500–1900*. Edited by Leuven. *Proceedings: 10th International Economic History Congress*, August 1990. Leuven: Leuven University Press.

Hayami Yujiro, and Vernon W. Ruttan. 1970. Factor prices and technical change in agricultural development: the United States and Japan, 1880–1960. *Journal of Political Economy* 78:1115–41.

———. 1985. *Agricultural development: an international perspective*. Baltimore MD: Johns Hopkins University Press.

Hayami Yujiro, Saburo Yamada, and Masakatsu Akino. 1991. *The agricultural development of Japan: a century's perspective*. Tōkyō Japan: University of Tōkyō Press.

Heitmann, John Alfred. 1987. *The modernization of the Louisiana sugar industry, 1830–1910*. Baton Rouge LA: Louisiana State University Press.

Henley, David. 2006. From low to high fertility in Sulawesi (Indonesia) during the colonial period: explaining the "first fertility transition." *Population Studies* 60 (3):309–27.

Henry, Yves. 1906. *Le Coton dans l'Afrique Occidentale française*. Paris France: A. Challamel.

Henry, Yves, and Inspection générale de l'agriculture de l'élevage et des forêts French Indochina. 1932. *Économie agricole de l'Indochine*. Hanoi Vietnam: Imprimerie d'Extrême-orient.

Hersey, Mark D. 2011. *My work is that of conservation: an environmental biography of George Washington Carver*. Athens GA: University of Georgia Press.

Hewatt, Alexander, John Locke, and South Carolina Constitution. 1779. *A historical account of the rise and progress of the colonies of South Carolina and Georgia*. 2 vols. London UK: Alexander Donaldson.

Heyward, Duncan Clinch, Institute for Southern Studies University of South Carolina, and South Caroliniana Society. 1993. *Seed from Madagascar*. Columbia SC: University of South Carolina Press.

Hicks, John. 1932. *The theory of wages*. London UK: Macmillan.

Hilliard, Sam B. 1975. The tidewater rice plantation: an ingenious adaptation to nature. In *Geoscience and man*, edited by H. J. Walker. Baton Rouge LA: Louisiana State Press.

———. 1978. Antebellum tidewater rice culture in South Carolina and Georgia. In *European settlement and development in North America: essays on geographical change in honour and memory of Andrew Hill Clark*, edited by J. R. Gibson and A. H. Clark. Folkstone UK: Dawson.

"History of transfer of Pooshee to 1756." Ravenel Land Papers. 1695–1880. South Carolina Historical Society, Charleston, SC.

Ho, Ping-ti. 1974. *Studies on population of China, 1368–1953*. Cambridge MA: Harvard University Press.

Holms, F. S. 1849. Notes on the geology of Charleston SC. *American Journal of Science and Arts* 7 (March):655–71.

Hong Lu, Marc A. Redus, Jason R. J. Coburn, Neil Rutger, Susan R. McCouch, and Thomas H. Tai. 2005. Population structure and breeding patterns of 145 rice cultivars based on SSR marker analysis. *Crop Science* 45 (Jan-Feb):66–76.

Hong, Xingjin 洪興錦 ed. 1936. *Gongshang ribao* 工商日報 (Hong Kong industry and commerce daily). Xianggang/ Hongkong.

Hoornaert, Eduardo. 1992. *História da igreja na Amazônia*. Pretrós: Vozes.

Huang, Philip C. C. 1990. *The peasant family and rural development in the Yangzi Delta, 1350–1988*. Stanford CA: Stanford University Press.

Huang, Yinhui 黃陰晦. 1998. Lijin kanke shi baoguoqing weile: ji Chen Zupei xiansheng de aiguo shiji 歷盡坎坷事報國情未了: 記 陳祖佈先生的愛國事記 (Having gone through rough affairs, a patriotic mind is not enough: reminiscences of Mr. Chen Zupei's patriotic life). *Guangdong wenshi ziliao* 79 (1):65.

Huber, Franz. 2009. Social capital of economic clusters: towards a network-based conception of social resources. *Tijdschrift voor economische en sociale gographie* 1000 (Apr):160–70.

Hugenholtz, W. R. 2008. *Landrentebelasting op Java, 1812–1920*. Proefschrift, Universiteit Leiden.

Hunter, Janet. 2003. *Women and the labour market in Japan's industrializing economy: The textile industry before the Pacific war*. London UK: Routledge-Curzon.

Hurt, R. Douglas. 1994. *American agriculture: a brief history*. Ames IA: Iowa State University Press.

India, Government of. Census of 1931. Online at: http://censusindia.gov.in/Census_And_You/old_report/Census_1931_tebles.aspx.

Ingram, James C. 1955. *Economic change in Thailand since 1850*. Stanford CA: Stanford University Press.
Inkpen, Andrew C., and Eric W. K. Tsang. 2005. Social capital, networks, and knowledge transfer. *Academy of Management Review* 30 (Jan):146–65.
Innes, Gordon. 1969. *A Mende-English dictionary*. Cambridge UK: Cambridge University Press.
International Rice Research Institute. *World rice statistics* 2012. Available from http://ricestat.irri.org.
Iqbal, Iftekhar. 2010. *The Bengal delta: ecology, state and social change, 1840–1943*. Basingstoke UK: Palgrave Macmillan.
IRIN News. 2007. *Empty granaries in Casamance*. United Nations Office.
Irving, John B. 1840–88. *Record of Windsor and Kensington Plantations, 1840–1888*. Charleston Library Society, Charleston, SC.
Ishige, Naomichi. 2001. *The history and culture of Japanese food*. London UK, New York NY: Kegan Paul.
Ishii, Yoneo. 1978. History and rice-growing. In *Thailand, a rice-growing society*, edited by Y. Ishii. Honolulu: University Press of Hawai'i.
Ishikawa, Shigeru. 1981. *Essays on technology, employment and institutions in economic development: comparative Asian experience*. Tōkyō Japan: Kinokuniya.
Ishikawa, Shigeru, and K. Ohkawa. 1972. Significance of Japan's experience – technological changes in agricultural production and changes in agrarian structure. In *Agriculture and economic development – structural readjustment in Asian perspective*, edited by Japan Economic Research Centre. Tōkyō Japan: Japan Economic Research Centre.
Iyengar, Mandayam Osuri Tirunarayana 1928. *Report on the malaria survey of the environs of Calcutta*. Calcutta: Public Health Department, Bengal.
Jameson, James, and India Medical Department. 1820. *Report on the epidemick cholera morbus, as it visited the territories subject to the Presidency of Bengal, in the years 1817, 1818 and 1819*. Calcutta India: Balfour.
Jedrej, Charles. 1983. The growth and decline of a mechanical agriculture scheme in West Africa. *African Affairs* 83 (329):541–58.
Jennings, Peter R. 1964. Plant type as a rice breeding objective. *Crop Science* 4:13–15.
Jolly, Curtis M., and Michigan State University. Dept. of Agricultural Economics. 1988. *Farm level cereal situation in lower Casamance: results of a field study*. East Lansing MI: Department of Agricultural Economics, Michigan State University.
Jolly, C. M., O. Diop, and Institut sénégalais de recherches agricoles. 1985. *La filière de commercialisation céréalière en Basse et Moyenne Casamance*. Dakar: Bureau d'analyses macro-économiques.
Jones, Jenkin W. and J. Mitchell Jenkins 1938. *Rice culture in the southern states*. Washington DC: US Department of Agriculture.
Jones, Jenkin W., Loren L. Davis, and Arthur H. Williams. 1950. *Rice culture in California*. Washington DC: US Department of Agriculture.
Jong, J. J. P. de. 1998. *De waaier van het fortuin: van handelscompagnie tot koloniaal imperium. De Nederlanders in Azië en de Indonesische archipel, 1595–1950*. Den Haag Netherlands: Sdu.
Journal of the Commons House of Assembly of South Carolina, 1695–1775. edited by the Department of Archives & History. South Carolina, Columbia, SC.

Joyner, Charles W. 1984. *Down by the riverside: a South Carolina slave community*. Urbana, IL: University of Illinois Press.

Juma, Calestous. 1989. *The gene hunters: biotechnology and the scramble for seeds*. London UK, Princeton NJ: Zed Books, Princeton University Press.

Jusu, Malcolm. 1999. Management of genetic variability in rice (Oryza sativa L. and O. glaberrima Steud.) by breeders and farmers in Sierra Leone. PhD thesis, Wageningen University.

Kamal, A. 2006. Living with water: Bangladesh since ancient times. In *A history of water: water control and river biographies*, edited by T. Tvedt and E. Jakobsson (pp. 194–216). London UK: I. B. Taurus.

Kastenholz, Raimund. 1991. Comparative mandé studies: state of art. *Sprache und Geschichte in Afrika* 12/13:107–58.

Kawakatsu Mamoru 川勝守. 1992. *Min Shin Kōnan nōgyō keizaishi kenkyû* 明清江南農業經濟史研究 (Economic and agricultural history of Jiangnan during the Ming and Qing era). Tōkyō Japan: Tōkyō daigaku shuppankai.

Kayō, Nobufumi 加用信文. 1958. *Nihon nōgyō kiso tōkei* 日本農業基礎統計 (Basic statistics of Japanese agriculture). Tōkyō Japan: Nōrin Suisangyō Seisan Kōjō Kaigi.

Kenny, John. 1910. *The coconut and rice*. Madras India: Higginbotham & Co.

Kerridge, Eric. 1967. *The agricultural revolution*. London UK: Allen & Unwin.

Kiessling, Ludwig. 1906. Die Organisation einer Landessaatgutzüchtung in Bayern. *Fühlings Landwirtschaftliche Zeitung* 55:329–38.

———. 1924. Zur Problemstellung, Begriffsbestimmung und Methodik der Pflanzenzucht. *Beitrage zur Pflanzenzucht* 7:11–21.

Kirby, Jack Temple. 1995. *Poquosin: a study of rural landscape & society*. Chapel Hill NC: University of North Carolina Press.

Kirby, William C. 2000. Engineering China: birth of the developmental state, 1928–1937. In *Becoming Chinese: passages to modernity and beyond*, edited by W.-H. Yeh (pp. 137–60). Berkeley CA: University of California Press.

Kirk, John H. 2013 Pathogens in manure. School of Veterinary Medicine, University of California Davis, online at: http://www.vetmed.ucdavis.edu/vetext/INF-DA/pathog-manure.pdf.

Kitō, Hiroshi. 1998. Edo jidai no beishoku (The Edo-period rice diet). In *Kome, Mugi, Zakkoku, Mame* (Rice, Other Grains and Beans). *Zenshū Nihon no Shoku Bunka* (Series: Japanese Food Culture) 3, edited by Noboru Haga and Hiroko Ishikawa. Tōkyō: Yūzankaku, 47–58.

Klee, M., B. Zach, and K. Neumann. 2000. Four thousand years of plant exploitation in the Chad basin of north-east Nigeria 1: the archaeobotany of Kursakata. *Vegetation History and Archaeology* 9:223–37.

Klein, Ira. 1990. Population growth and mortality in British India. Part I: the climacteric of death. *Indian Economic and Social History Review* 27:33–63.

———. 1994. Population growth and mortality in British India. Part II: the demographic revolution. *Indian Economic and Social History Review* 31:491–518.

———. 2001. Development and death: reinterpreting malaria, economics and ecology in British India. *Indian Economic and Social History Review* 38 (2):147–79.

Klieman, Kairn A. 2003. *The Pygmies were our compass: Bantu and Batwa in the history of west central Africa, early times to c 1900 CE*. Portsmouth NH: Heinemann.

Kloppenburg, Jack Ralph. 1988. *First the seed: the political economy of plant biotechnology, 1492-2000*. Cambridge UK, New York NY: Cambridge University Press.

Knapp, Seaman Asahel. 1899. *The present status of rice culture in the United States*. Washington DC: United States Department of Agriculture, Division of Botany.

——. 1910. *Rice culture*. Washington DC: United States Department of Agriculture, Division of Botany.

Knight, Frederick C. 2010. *Working the diaspora: the impact of African labor on the Anglo-American world, 1650-1850*. New York NY: New York University Press.

Koloniaal Verslag. 1855-1930. Den Haag Netherlands: Staatsdrukkerij.

Komlos, John. 1995. *The biological standard of living on three continents: further explorations in anthropometric history*. Boulder CO: Westview Press.

——. 1998. Shrinking in a growing economy? The mystery of physical stature during the industrial revolution. *Journal of Economic History* 58:779-802.

Kovacik, Charles G., and John J. Winberry. 1989. *South Carolina: the making of a landscape*. Columbia SC: University of South Carolina Press.

Kreike, Emmanuel. 2004. *Re-creating Eden: land use, environment, and society in southern Angola and northern Namibia*. Portsmouth NH: Heinemann.

Kryzymowski, Richard. 1913. Beziehungen zwischen der Betriebsintensitat und der Sortenfrage. *Jahrbuch der Deutschen Landwirtschafts-Gesellschaft* 28:456-67.

Kühle, Ludwig. 1926. Der Stand und die Lage der deutschen Pflanzenzucht. *Mitteilungen der Deutschen Landwirtschafts-Gesellschaft* 41:856-65.

Kulisch, Paul. 1913. Die staatliche Forderung der Saatzucht und des Saatgutbaues in Elsass-Lothringen. *Jahrbuch der Deutschen Landwirtschafts-Gesellschaft* 28:467-87.

Kurin, Richard. 1983a. Indigenous agronomics and agricultural development in the Indus basin. *Human Organization* 42 (4):283-94.

——. 1983b. Modernization and traditionalization: hot and cold agriculture in Punjab, Pakistan. *South Asian Anthropologist* 4 (2):65-75.

Lam, D.A, and J.A. Miron. 1991. Temperature and the seasonality of births. *Advances in Experimental Medicine and Biology* 186:73-88.

Lambert, Michael C. 2002. *Longing for exile: migration and the making of a translocal community in Senegal, West Africa*. Portmouth NH: Heinemann.

Lambert, Sheila, ed. 1975. *House of Commons sessional papers of the eighteenth century: minutes of evidence on the slave trade: 1788 and 1789: George III. Vol. 68*. Wilmington: Scholarly Resources.

Lang, Hans. 1909. Einiges über Saatgutzüchtung. *Badisches Landwirtschaftliches Wochenblatt* (29):613-14.

Lansing, J. Stephen. 2006. *Perfect order: recognizing complexity in Bali*. Princeton NJ: Princeton University Press.

Latham, A.J.H. 1998. *Rice: the primary commodity*. London UK, New York NY: Routledge.

——. 1999. Rice is a luxury, not a necessity. In *Pacific centuries: Pacific and Pacific Rim history since the sixteenth century*, edited by D.O. Flynn, L. Frost, and A.J.H. Latham (pp. 110-24). London UK, New York NY: Routledge.

Latham, A.J.H., and Larry Neal. 1983. The international market in rice and wheat, 1868-1914. *The Economic History Review, New Series* 36 (2):260-80.

Latimer, W. J., ed. 1916. *Soil survey of Berkeley county, South Carolina. Field operations of the Bureau of Soils*. Washington DC: Bureau of Soils.

Latour, Bruno. 2005. *Reassembling the social: an introduction to actor-network-theory, Clarendon lectures in management studies*. Oxford UK, New York NY: Oxford University Press.

Law, John. 2009. Actor network theory and material semiotics. In *The new Blackwell companion to social theory*, edited by B. S. Turner (pp. 141–58). Chichester UK, Malden MA: Wiley-Blackwell.

Learmonth, A. T. A. 1957. Some contrasts in the regional geography of malaria in India and Pakistan. *Transactions and Papers (Institute of British Geographers)* 23:37–59.

Lee, Brian, and International Rice Research Institute. 1994. *IRRI 1993–1994: filling the world's rice bowl*. Manila: International Rice Research Institute.

Lee, Christopher M. 1994. Organization for survival: the rice industry and protective tariffs, 1921–1929. *Louisiana History: The Journal of the Louisiana Historical Association* 35 (Autumn):433–54.

——. 1996. The American rice industry's organization for a domestic market: the associated rice millers of America. *Louisiana History: The Journal of the Louisiana Historical Association* 37 (Spring):187–99.

Lee, Seung-joon. 2011. *Gourmets in the land of famine: the culture and politics of rice in modern Canton*. Stanford CA: Stanford University Press.

Lewis, Michael. 1990. *Rioters and citizens: mass protest in Imperial Japan*. Berkeley CA: University of California Press.

Li, Bozhong. 1998. *Agricultural development in Jiangnan, 1620–1850, Studies on the Chinese economy*. New York NY: St. Martin's Press.

Li, Cho-ying. 2010. Contending strategies, collaboration among local specialists and officials, and reform in the late-fifteenth-century Lower Yangzi delta. *East Asian Science, Technology and Society: An International Journal* 4 (2):229–53.

Li, Zhi-Ming, Xiao-Ming Zheng, and Song Ge. 2011. Genetic diversity and domestication history of African rice (Oryza glaberrima) as inferred from multiple gene sequences. *Theoretical and Applied Genetics* 123:21–31.

Li, Zidian 李自典. 2006. Zhongyang nongye shiyansuo shulun 中央農業實驗所述論 (On the central agricultural experiment center) *Lishi dang'an* 104 (Nov):113–20.

Lin, Man-Houng. 2001. Overseas Chinese merchants and multiple nationality: A means for reducing commercial risk (1895–1935). *Modern Asian Studies* 35 (July):985–1009.

Linares, Olga F. 1981. From tidal swamp to inland valley: on the social organization of wet rice cultivation among the Diola of Senegal. *Africa: Journal of the International African Institute* 51 (2):557–95.

——. 1992. *Power, prayer, and production: the Jola of Casamance, Senegal*. Cambridge UK, New York NY: Cambridge University Press.

——. 1997. Diminished rains and divided tasks: rice growing in three Jola communities of Casamance, Senegal. In *The ecology of practice. Food crop production in Sub-Saharan West Africa*, edited by E. Nyerges (pp. 39–76). New York NY: Gordon & Breach.

——. 2002. African rice (Oryza glaberrima): history and future potential. *Proceedings of the National Academy of Sciences (PNAS)* 99 (25):16360–5.

——. 2003 Going to the city .... and coming back? Turn-around migration among the Jola of Senegal. *Africa* 73 (1):113–32.

Lipton, Michael. 1978. Inter-farm, inter-regional and farm-nonfarm income distribution: The impact of the new cereal varieties. *World Development* 6 (3):319–37.

Littlefield, Daniel C. 1920. *Map of Pooshee*. edited by Berkeley County Register of Mesne Conveyance. Monks Corner SC.

———. 1981. *Rice and slaves: ethnicity and the slave trade in colonial South Carolina*. Baton Rouge LA: Louisiana State University Press.

Lockwood, David. 1990. *Solidarity and schism*. Oxford UK: Oxford University Pres.

Longley, Catherine, and Paul Richards. 1993. Farmer innovation and local knowledge in Sierra Leone. In *Cultivating knowledge*, edited by Walter de Boef, Kojo Amanor, Kate Wellard, and Anthony Bebbington. London UK: Intermediate Technology Press.

Longley, Catherine Ann. 2000. A social life of seeds: local management of crop variability in north-western Sierra Leone. PhD thesis, University College London UK, s.n.

Ludden, David E. 1999. *An agrarian history of South Asia*. Cambridge UK, New York NY: Cambridge University Press.

Lufu zouzhe 奏摺錄副 (Recorded notes and memorials). Beijing: Zhongguo diyi lishi dang'anguan.

Lulofs, C., and Louis van Vuuren. 1919. *De Voedselvoorziening van Nederlandsch-Indië. Door C. Lulofs, met medewerking van L. van Vuuren*. Weltevreden Netherlands: n.d.

Lynam, John. 2011. Plant breeding in sub-Saharan Africa in an era of donor dependence. *IDS Bulletin* 42 (4):36–47.

Lyndon Baines Johnson Presidential Library. 1967. *Memorandum for the Honorable Orville L. Freeman secretary of agriculture: silver lining to disaster or how IR-8 rice came to Vietnam in a big way*.

Maat, Harro. 2001. *Science cultivating practice: a history of agricultural science in the Netherlands and its colonies, 1863–1986*. Dordrecht Netherlands, Boston MA: Kluwer Academic Publishers.

———. 2007. Is participation rooted in colonialism? Agricultural innovation systems and participation in the Netherlands Indies. *IDS Bulletin* 38 (5):50–60.

Macaulay, Zachary. 1815. *A letter to his royal highness the Duke of Gloucester, President of the African institution*. London UK: Ellerton and Henderson, for John Hatchard.

Maddison, Angus. 2005. *Growth and the interaction in the world economy: the roots of modernity*. Washington DC: AEI Press.

Magalhaens, D. J. G. de. 1865. *Memoria historica da revolução da provincia do Maranhão (1838–1840)*. Rio de Janeiro Brazil: Livraria de B. L. Garnier.

Maguin, François-Henri, and Comité Agricole de l'Arrondissement de Metz. 1868. *Bulletin du Comice Agricole de l'Arrondissement de Metz*. Metz France: F. Blanc.

Maharatna, Arup. 1996. *The demography of famines: an Indian historical perspective*. Delhi India: Oxford University Press.

Malleret, Louis. 1959. *L'archéologie du Delta du Mékong, Tome premier. L'exploration archéologique et les fouilles d'Oc-Èo*. Paris France: Ecole française d'Extrême-Orient.

———. 1962. *L'archéologie du Delta du Mékong. Tome troisième, la culture du Fou-Nan*. Paris France: École française d'Extrême-Orient.

Mandala, Elias Coutinho. 2005. *The end of Chidyerano: a history of food and everyday life in Malawi, 1860–2004*. Portsmouth NH: Heinemann.
Mandell, Paul I. 1971. The rise of the modern Brazilian rice industry: demand expansion in a dynamic economy. *Food Research Institute Studies in Agricultural Economics, Trade, and Development* 10 (2):161–219.
Mansvelt, W. M. F., P. Creutzberg, and Petrus Johannes van Dooren. 1978. *Changing economy in Indonesia: a selection of statistical source material from the early nineteenth century up to 1940 / Vol. 4, Rice prices*. The Hague Netherlands: Nijhoff.
"Map of Pooshee," 1920. Berkeley County Register of Mesne Conveyance, Monks Corner, SC
Marglin, Stephen A. 1996. Farmers, seedsmen and scientists: systems of agriculture and systems of knowledge. In *Decolonizing knowledge: from development to dialogue*, edited by F. Apffel-Marglin and S. A. Marglin (pp. 185–248). Oxford UK: Clarendon Press.
Marks, Robert. 1998. *Tigers, rice, silk, and silt: environment and economy in late imperial south China, Studies in environment and history*. Cambridge UK, New York NY: Cambridge University Press.
Marmé, Michael. 2005. *Suzhou: where the goods of all the provinces converge*. Stanford CA: Stanford University Press.
Marshall, D. R. 1991. Alternative approaches and perspectives in breeding for higher yields. *Field Crops Research* 26:171–90.
Martin, Frédéric, and E. Crawford. 1991. The new agricultural policy: its feasibility and implications for the future. In *The Political Economy of Senegal Under Structural Adjustment*, edited by C. L. Delgado and S. Jammeh (pp. 85–96). New York NY: Praeger.
Martins, Susanna Wade, and Tom Williamson. 1994. Floated water-meadows in Norfolk: a misplaced innovation. *Agricultural History Review* 42:30–7.
Mathew, William M., ed. 1992. *Agriculture, geology, and society in Antebellum South Carolina: The private diary of Edmund Ruffin, 1843*. Athens: University of Georgia Press.
Matthews, John. 1788. *A Voyage to the River Sierra Leone, on the Coast of Africa...* London: B. White and Sons
Mazumdar, Sucheta. 1998. *Sugar and society in China: peasants, technology, and the world market*. Cambridge MA: Harvard University Asia Center.
McAlpin, Michelle. 1983. Price movements and fluctuations in economic activity (1860–1947). In *The Cambridge economic history of India*, vol. 2 *c.1757–c.1970*, edited by D. Kumar and M. Desai (pp. 878–904). Cambridge UK: Cambridge University Press.
McCann, James. 2007. *Maize and grace: Africa's encounter with a new world crop, 1500–2000*. Cambridge MA, London UK: Harvard University Press.
McCartan, Lucy, Earl M. Lemon, R. E. Weems, Geological Survey (US), and U.S. Nuclear Regulatory Commission. 1984. *Geologic map of the area between Charleston and Orangeburg, South Carolina*. Reston VA: US Geological Survey.
McCay, David. 1910. *Investigations on Bengal jail dietaries, with some observations on the influence of dietary on the physical development and well-being of the people of Bengal*. Calcutta India: Superintendent Government Printing, India.

McClain, Molly and Alessa Ellefson. 2007. A letter from Carolina, 1688: French Huguenotsin the New World. *William and Mary Quarterly*, 3rd series **64** (April): 377–94.
McCrady Plat collection edited by Charleston County Register of Mesne Conveyance. Charleston, SC.
McCusker, John J. 2006. Colonial Statistics. In *Historical Statistics of the United States*, vol. V, edited by S. B. Carter (pp. 681–84). Cambridge UK, New York NY: Cambridge University Press.
McFadyen, M. Ann, and Albert A. Cannella Jr. 2004. Social capital and knowledge creation: diminishing returns of the number and strength of exchange. *Academy of Management Journal* **47** (Oct):735–46.
McIntosh, Susan Keech. 1995. *Excavations at Jenné-Jeno, Hambarketolo, and Kaniana (Inland Niger Delta, Mali), the 1981 season*. Berkeley CA: University of California Press.
McNair, A. D. 1924. *Labor requirements of Arkansas crops*. Edited by United States Department of Agriculture. Vol. **1181**. Washington DC: United States Government Printing Office.
Mededeelingen van het Deli-Proefstation te Medan 1920. Medan: Deli Proefstation.
Meillassoux, Claude. 1981. *Maidens, meal, and money: capitalism and the domestic community*. Cambridge UK, New York NY: Cambridge University Press.
Merchant, Carolyn. 1995. Reinventing Eden: western culture as a recovery narrative. In *Uncommon ground: rethinking the human place in nature*, edited by W. Cronon. New York NY: W.W. Norton & Co.
Merrens, H. Roy. 1977. *The colonial South Carolina scene: contemporary views, 1697–1774*. Columbia SC: University of South Carolina Press.
Merrens, H. Roy, and George D. Terry. 1984. Dying in paradise: malaria, mortality, and the perceptual environment in colonial South Carolina. *Journal of Southern History* **50** (Nov):533–50.
Migeod, Frederick William Hugh. 1926. *A view of Sierra Leone*. London UK: K. Paul, Trench, Trubner.
Migu tongji 米穀統計 (Rice statistics). 1934. Nanjing: Quanguo jingji weiyuanhui nongyechu.
Millet, Donald J., Sr. 1964. The economic development of Southwest Louisiana, 1865–1900. PhD thesis, Louisiana State University.
Milling, Chapman J., ed., 1951. *Colonial South Carolina: Two contemporary descriptions*. Columbia: University of South Carolina Press.
Mintz, Sidney W. 1985. *Sweetness and Power: the Place of Sugar in Modern History*. New York: Viking.
Miscellaneous inventories and wills, Charleston County, 1687–1785. edited by South Carolina Department of Archives & History. Columbia SC.
Mitchell, John B. 1949. An analysis of Arkansas' population by race and nativity, and residence. *Arkansas Historical Quarterly* **8** (Summer):115–32.
Mitchell, Laura J. 2002. Traces in the landscape: hunters, herders and farmers on the Cedarberg frontier, South Africa, 1725–95. *Journal of African History* **43**:431–50.
Mokuwa, Alfred et al. 2013. Robustness and strategies of adaptation among farmer varieties of African rice (Oryza glaberrima) and Asian rice (Oryza sativa) across West Africa [Short title: "How robust are rice varieties in West Africa?]. *PloS ONE*, 8(2).

Mokuwa, Esther, Maarten Voors, Erwin Bulte, and Paul Richards. 2011. Peasant grievance and insurgency in Sierra Leone: judicial serfdom as a driver of conflict. *African Affairs* 110 (440):339–66.

Monroe, J. T., and H. C. Fondren. 1916. *Southwest Louisiana: It's [sic] agricultural and industrial developments and its potential wealth along Southern Pacific lines.* No publisher, no place of publication.

Monson, Jamie. 1991. Agricultural transformation of the inner Kilombero. PhD thesis, UCLA, UCLA, Los Angeles.

Montesano, Michael J. 2009. Revisiting the rice deltas and reconsidering modern Southeast Asia's economic history. *Journal of Southeast Asian Studies* 40 (2):417–29.

Moon, Suzanne. 2007. *Technology and ethical idealism: a history of development in the Netherlands East Indies.* Leiden Netherlands: CNWS Publications.

Moore, Alexander. 1994. Daniel Axtell's account book and the economy of Early South Carolina. *South Carolina Historical Magazine* 95 (Oct):280–301.

Moore-Sieray, David. 1988. The evolution of colonial agricultural policy in Sierra Leone, with special reference to swamp rice cultivation, 1908–1939. PhD thesis, School of Oriental and African Studies, University of London, 1988.

Morgan, Philip D. 1982. Work and culture: the task system and the world of Lowcountry Blacks, 1700 to 1880. *William and Mary Quarterly* 39 (Oct):563–99.

Morgan, W. T. W. 1988. Tamilnad and Eastern Tanzania: comparative regional geography and the historical process. *Geographical Journal* 154 (1):69–85.

Mori, Takemaro 森武麿. 1999. *Senji Nihon nōson shakai no kenkyū* 戦時日本農村社会の研究 (A study of rural society in war time). Tōkyō: Tōkyō Daigaku Shuppan Kai.

Morris, Grover C. 1906. Rice has transformed the barren prairies into fertile lands. *Arkansas Gazette (Little Rock)* 30 (Sep):8.

Morris, Morris D. 1983. The growth of large-scale industry to 1947. In *The Cambridge economic history of India, c.1757–c.1970*, edited by D. Kumar, and M. Desai (pp. 551–676). Cambridge UK: Cambridge University Press.

Mouser, Bruce, ed. 2000. *Account of the Mandingoes, Susoos, & Other Nations c. 1815, by the Reverend Leopold Butscher, University of Leizig Papers on Africa, History and Culture Series 6* SFAX: Ifriqiya Books.

Mouser, Bruce L. 1973. Moria politics in 1814: Amara to Maxwell, March 2. *Bulletin de Institut Fondamental d'Afrique Noire* 35, B (4):805–12.

———. 1978. The voyage of the good sloop Dolphin to Africa, 1795–1796. *The American Neptune* 38 (4):249–61.

———. 1979. Richard Bright Journal 1802. In *Guinea journals: journeys into Guinea-Conakry during the Sierra Leone phase, 1800–1821*, edited by Bruce L. Mouser (31–113). Washington DC: University Press of America.

———. 2007. Rebellion, marronage and 'jih'ad': strategies of resistance to slavery on the Sierra Leone coast, c. 1783–1796. *Journal of African History* 48:27–44.

Mouser, Bruce L., and Samuel Gamble. 2002. *A slaving voyage to Africa and Jamaica: the log of the Sandown, 1793–1794.* Bloomington: Indiana University Press.

Mukherjee, Mridula. 2005. *Colonizing agriculture: the myth of Punjab exceptionalism.* New Delhi: Sage.

Mukherjee, Radhakamal, and University of Calcutta. 1938. *The changing face of Bengal – A study in riverine economy, Calcutta University Readership Lectures.* Calcutta: The University of Calcutta.

Myren, Delbert T. 1970. The Rockefeller foundation program in corn and wheat in Mexico. In *Subsistence agriculture and economic development*, edited by C. R. Wharton (438–52). London UK: Cass.
Nalini, Govind. 1986. *Regional perspectives in agricultural development: a case study of wheat and rice in selected regions of India*. New Delhi India: Concept Publication Co.
Narain, Brij. 1926. *Eighty years of Punjab food prices, 1841–1920, Rural Section publication*. Lahore Pakistan: Civil and Military Gazette Press.
Narain, Raj, and Narain Brij. 1932. *An economic survey of Gijhi, a village in the Rohtak district of the Punjab*. Lahore Pakistan: Civil and Military Gazette Press.
Nash, R. C. 1992. South Carolina and the Atlantic economy in the late seventeenth and eighteenth centuries. *The Economic History Review, New Series* 45 (Nov):677–702.
National Archives and Records Administration – College Park, NARA-CP. 1968. Rice 1967.
——. 1970. Small rice mills in the Mekong delta. Pacification Studies Group, Box 22, CORDS Historical Working Group, 1967–73, Record Group 472.
Nayar, N. M. 2011. Evolution of the African rice: a historical and biological perspective. *Crop Science* 51:505–16.
Needham, Joseph. 1969. *The grand titration: science and society in East and West*. London UK: Allen & Unwin.
Nei, Masatoshi. 1973. Analysis of gene diversity in subdivided populations. *Proceedings of the National Academy of Science (NAS)* 70 (12):3321–3.
Nelson, Lynn A. 2007. *Pharsalia: an environmental biography of a southern plantation, 1780–1880*. Athens: University of Georgia Press.
Netting, Robert McC. 1993. *Smallholders, householders: farm families and the ecology of intensive, sustainable agriculture*. Stanford CA: Stanford University Press.
Newman, Mark D., Alassane Sow, Ousseynou Ndoye, and Institut sénégalais de recherches agricoles. 1987. *Tradeoffs between domestic and imported cereals in Senegal: a marketing systems perspective*. East Lansing MI: Department of Agricultural Economics, Institut Sénégalais de recherches agricoles, Bureau d'analyses macro-économiques.
Nguyen Duc Tu. Rice Production and a Vision for Vietnam's Wetlands. In *Successful cases on sustainable rice paddy farming practices and wetland conservation in Asia*, edited by George Lukacs. Tōkyō: Ministry of Environment, Japan, 2011: 46–9.
Nguyen, Huu Chiem. 1994. Studies on agro-ecological environment and land use in the Mekong delta, Vietnam. PhD thesis, Kyōto University, Kyōto.
Nguyên ng'oc, Hiên. 1997. *Lê-thành-hâu-nguyên-h'uu-Canh-1650–1700: (vói-cōng-cuōc-khai-sáng-miên-Nam-nuóc-Viêt-cuōi-thê-ky-17)*. Tái-ban-lân-thú-hai. ed. Thành-phō-Hō-chí-Minh Vietnam: Nhà-xuât-ban-Van-hoc.
Nilsson-Ehle, H. 1913. Über die Winterweizenarbeiten in Svalöf. *Beiträge zur Pflanzenzucht* 3:62–88.
Norimatsu, Akifumi 則松彰文. 1985. Yōzeiki ni okeru beikiku ryūtsū to beika hendō: Sōshū to Fukken no kanren o chūshin to shite 雍正期における米谷流通と米價變動―蘇州と福建の連關を中心として―(Rice price changes and customs during the Yongzheng era – Relations between Suzhou and Fujian). *Kyûshû daigaku tōyōshironshû* 14:157–88.

Nōrinsuisanshō Tōkeijōhōbu (農林水産省統計方情報部). Various years. *Poketto Nōrinsuisan Tōkei* (ポケット農林水産統計) (Statistics of Agriculture, Forestry and Fishing, Pocket Edition). Tōkyō: Nōrin Tōkei Kyōkai.

Nowak, Bruce 1986. The slave rebellion in Sierra Leone in 1785–1796. *Hemispheres (Warsaw)* 3:151–69.

Nuijten, Edwin. 2005. Farmer management of gene flow: the impact of gender and breeding system on genetic diversity and crop improvement in The Gambia. PhD thesis, Wageningen Universiteit, Wageningen.

———. 2010. Gender and the management of crop diversity in The Gambia. *Journal of Political Ecology* 7:42–58.

Nuijten, Edwin, and Paul Richards. 2013. Gene flow in African rice farmers' fields. In *Realizing Africa's rice promise*, edited by M Wopereis, D. Johnson, N. Ahmadi, E. Tollens, and A. Jalloh. Wallingford UK: CABI Publishing.

Nuijten, Edwin, and Robert van Treuren 2007. Spatial and temporal dynamics of genetic diversity in upland rice and late millet (Pennisetum glaucum (L.) R.Br.) in The Gambia. *Genetic Resources & Crop Evolution* 54 (5):989–1005.

Nuijten, Edwin, et al. 2009. Evidence for the emergence of new rice types of interspecific hybrid origin in West African farmers' fields. *PloS ONE*, 4(10), e7335.

Nurse, Derek. 1997. The contribution of linguistics to the study of history in Africa. *Journal of African History* 38: 59–91.

Oaks, Robert Q., and Jules R. DuBar. 1974. Post-miocene stratigraphy central and Southern Atlantic coastal plain. In *Post-Miocene stratigraphy, central and southern Atlantic coastal plain*, edited by R. Q. Oaks and J. R. DuBar. Logan: Utah State University Press.

Observations on the winter flowing of rice lands, in reply to Mr. Munnerlyn's answers to queries, & c. by a rice planter. 1828. *Southern Agriculturalist and Register of Rural Affairs* 1 Dec 1.

Odaka, Kōnosuke. 1993. Redundancy utilized: the economics of female domestic servants in pre-war Japan. In *Japanese women working*, edited by J. Hunter (16–36). London UK, New York NY: Routledge.

Ohnuki-Tierney, Emiko. 1993. *Rice as self: Japanese identities through time*. Princeton NJ: Princeton University Press.

Okry, Florent. 2011. Strengthening rice seed systems and agro-biodiversity conservation in West Africa: a socio-technical focus on farmers' practices of rice seed development and diversity conservation in Susu cross border lands in Guinea and Sierra Leone. PhD, Wageningen University.

Oliver, Roland, Thomas Spear, Kairn Klieman, Jan Vansina, Scott MacEachern, David Schoenbrun, James Denbow, et al. (2001) Comments on Christopher Ehret, "Bantu history: re-envisioning the evidence of language." *International Journal of African Historical Studies* 34, (1):43–81.

Olmstead, Alan L. 1998. Induced innovation in American agriculture: an econometric analysis. *Research in Economic History* 18:103–19.

Olmstead, Alan L. and Paul Webb Rhode 1993. Induced innovation in American agriculture: a reconsideration. *Journal of Political Economy* 101 (Feb): 100–18.

———. 2008. *Creating abundance: biological innovation and American agricultural development*. New York NY: Cambridge University Press.

Packard, Randall M. 2007. *The making of a tropical disease: a short history of malaria*. Baltimore MD: Johns Hopkins University Press.

Pakendorf, Bridgitte, Koen Bostoen, and Cesare de Fillippo. 2011. Molecular perspectives on the Bantu expansion: a synthesis. *Language Dynamics and Change* 1:50–8.

Palat, Ravi Arvind. 1995. Historical transformations in agrarian systems based on wet-rice cultivation: towards an alternative model of social change. In *Food and agrarian orders in the world economy*, edited by P. McMichael. Westport CT: Greenwood Press.

Panyu xian xuzhi 番禺縣續集 (Gazetteer of Panyu county). 1911. Panyu: n.d.

Paris, Pierre. 1931. Anciens Canaux Reconnus Sur Photographs Aeriénnes dans les Provinces de Tak Ev et de Chau Doc. *Bulletin de l'École française de l'Extrême-Orient* 31:221–3.

Patnaik, Utsa. 1996. Peasant subsistence and food security in the context of the international commoditisation of production: the present and history. In *Meanings of agriculture: essays in South Asian history and economics*, edited by P. Robb. Delhi India: Oxford University Press.

Pavie, Auguste, and Walter E.J. Tips. 1999. *Travel reports of the Pavie missio: Vietnam, Laos, Yunnan, and Siam*. Bangkok Thailand: White Lotus Press.

Pelzer, Karl J. 1978. *Planter and peasant: colonial policy and the agrarian struggle in East Sumatra 1863–1947*. The Hague Netherlands: Martinus Nijhoff.

Petitions to the General Assembly, 1782–1866. edited by South Carolina Department of Archive & History. Columbia SC.

Pereira do Lago, Antonio Bernardino 1822. *Estatistica historica-geografica da provincia do Maranhão*. Lisbon Portugal: Academia Real das Sciencias.

Pereira, J.A., and E.P. Guimarães. 2010. History of rice in Latin America. In *Rice: origin, antiquity and history*, edited by S.D. Sharma (432–51). New Delhi India: Oxford University Press and IBH.

Perkins, John. 1997. *Geopolitics and the green revolution: wheat, genes and the cold war*. New York NY: Oxford University Press.

Perrin, Frank L. 1910. Arkansas rice. *Farm Journal* 34 (Feb):97.

Pfister, Christian. 1978. Climate and economy in Eighteenth-Century Switzerland. *Journal of Interdisciplinary History* 9 (autumn):223–43.

Phillips, Edward Hake. 1951. The Gulf coast rice industry. *Agricultural History* 25 (Apr):91–6.

Pineiro, M., and Eduardo Trigo, eds. 1983. *Technical change and social conflict in agriculture: Latin American perspectives*. Boulder CO: Westview Press.

Pinstrup-Andersen, Per, and Peter Hazell. 1985. The impact of the green revolution and prospects for the future. *Food Reviews International* 1 (1):1–25.

Plan of Fairlawn Plantation. 1794. St. Thomas Parish, Charleston District (May.) John McCrady Plat Collection. no. 4339. Charleston County Register of Mesne Conveyance, Charleston, SC.

Ploeg, Jan Douwe Van der 1992. The reconstitution of locality: technology and labour in modern agriculture. In *Labour and locality*, edited by T. Marsden, P. Lowe and S. Whatmore (19–43). London UK: David Fulton.

Pomeranz, Kenneth. 2000. *The great divergence: China, Europe, and the making of the modern world economy*. Princeton NJ: Princeton University Press.

———. 2003. Women's work, family, and economic development in Europe and East Asia: long-term trajectories and contemporary comparisons. In *The resurgence of East Asia: 500, 150, and 50 year perspectives*, edited by G. Arrighi and M. Selden (124–72). London UK: Routledge.

Porcher, Richard D. 1987. Rice culture in South Carolina: a brief history, the role of the Huguenots, and the preservation of its legacy. *Transactions of the Huguenot Society of South Carolina* 92:1–22.

Porcher, Richard D., and Douglas A. Rayner. 2001. *A guide to the wildflowers of South Carolina*. Columbia SC: University of South Carolina Press.

Portères, Roland. 1962. Berceaux agricoles primaires sur le continent Africain. *Journal of African History* 3 (2):195–210.

———. 1970. Primary cradles of agriculture in the African continent. In *Papers in African prehistory*, edited by J.D. Fage and R.A. Oliver (43–58). Cambridge UK: Cambridge University Press.

Posner, Joshua Lowe. 1988. *A contribution to agronomic knowledge of the lower Casamance: bibliographical synthesis*. East Lansing MI: Department of Agricultural Economics, Michigan State University.

Posner, Joshua Lowe, Mulumba Kamuanga, and Mamadou Gueye Lo. 1991. *Lowland cropping systems in the Lower Casamance of Senegal: results of four years of agronomic research (1982–1985)*. East Lansing MI: Department of Agricultural Economics, Michigan State University.

Posner, Joshua Lowe, Mulumba Kamuanga, and Samba Sall. 1985. Les systèmes de production en Basse Casamance et les stratégies paysannes face au déficit pluviométrique. edited by I. Institut Senegalais de Recherches Agricoles, Travaux et Documents. Dakar: Département Systéme et. Transfert, Centre de Djibelor, Institut Sénégalais de Recherches Agricoles.

Post, Lauren. 1940. The rice country of Southwest Louisiana. *Geographical Review* 30 (October):574–90.

Pozdniakov, Konstantin. 1993. *Сравнительная грамматика атлантических языков (Grammaire comparée historique des langues Atlantiques)*. Moscow Russia: Nauka.

Pratt, Edward E. 1999. *Japan's protoindustrial elite: the economic foundations of the gōnō*. Cambridge MA: Harvard University Asia Center, Harvard University Press.

Public Health Department of Bengal (India). 1929. *Malaria problem in Bengal*. Calcutta India: Public Health Department of Bengal, India.

Pyne, Stephen J. 1997. *Vestal fire: an environmental history, told through fire, of Europe and Europe's encounter with the world*. Seattle WA: University of Washington Press.

Qu, Dajun 屈大均. 1985. *Guangdong xinyu* 廣東新語 (New words from Guangdong). Beijing: Zhonghua shuju.

Ram, Rai Bahadur Ganga. 1920. *Punjab agricultural proverbs and their scientific significance: being a lecture delivered by Rai Bahadur Ganga Ram, on 27th September, 1920 before a public meeting in Simla under the presidency of Sir Edward Maclagan*. Lahore Pakistan: Ram.

Randrianja, Solofo, ed. 2009. *Madagascar, le coup d'etat de mars 2009, Hommes et sociétés*. Paris France: Karthala.

Randrianja, Solofo and Stephen Ellis. 2009. *Madagascar: A short history*. Chicago: University of Chicago Press.
Ranis, Gustav. 1969. The financing of Japanese economic development. In *Agriculture and economic growth: Japan's experience* edited by K. Ohkawa, B. Johnston, and H. Kaneda (440–54). Tōkyō, Japan: Tōkyō University Press.
Rash, Matthias, 1773. Rash to Peter Taylor. 18 March 1773. Taylor Family Papers. 1709–1829. South Caroliniana Library, University of South Carolina, Columbia, SC.
Rashid, Ishmael 2000. Escape, revolt and marronage in eighteenth and nineteenth century Sierra Leone hinterland. *Canadian Journal of African Studies* 34:656–83.
Ravenel, Henry Edmund. 1860. The limestone springs of St. John's Berkeley. Paper read at Proceedings of the Elliott Society of Science and Art, 1 Feb 1859, at Charleston, South Carolina.
———. 1898. *Ravenel records. A history and genealogy of the Huguenot family of Ravenel, of South Carolina; with some incidental account of the parish of St. Johns Berkeley, which was their principal location*. Atlanta GA: Franklin Printing and Publishing Co.
Ravenel land papers, 1695–1880. edited by South Carolina History Society. Charleston SC.
Ravina, Mark. 1999. *Land and lordship in early modern Japan*. Stanford CA: Stanford University Press.
Rawski, Evelyn Sakakida. 1972. *Agricultural change and the peasant economy of South China*. Cambridge MA: Harvard University Press.
Reclamation of Southern swamps. 1854. *DeBow's Review and Industrial Resources* 17 (Nov):525.
Rediker, Marcus. 2007. *The slave ship: a human history*. New York NY: Viking.
Remy, Theodor. 1908. Nochmals einige Worte über die Gefahren und Nachteile des modernen Pflanzenzuchtbetriebes. *Deutsche Landwirtschaftliche Presse* 35 (36):385–7.
Rénaud, J. 1880. Étude d'un Projet de Canal Entre le Vaico et le Cua-Tieu. *Excursions et Reconnaissances* 3:315–30.
Richards, John F., Edward S. Haynes, and James R. Hagen. 1985. Changes in the land and human productivity in Northern India, 1870–1970. *Agricultural History* 59 (4):523–48.
Richards, Paul. 1985. *Indigenous agricultural revolution: ecology and food production in West Africa*. London UK: Hutchinson.
———. 1986. *Coping with hunger: hazard and experiment in an African rice-farming system*. London UK, Boston MA: Allen & Unwin.
———. 1989. Farmers also experiment: a neglected intellectual resource in African science. *Discovery & Innovation* 1 (1):19–25.
———. 1990. Local strategies for coping with hunger: northern Nigeria and central Sierra Leone compared. *African Affairs* 89:265–75.
———. 1995. The versatility of the poor: indigenous wetland management systems in Sierra Leone. *GeoJournal* 35 (2):197–203.

———. 1996a. Culture and community values in the selection and maintenance of African rice. In *Valuing local knowledge: indigenous people and intellectual property rights*, edited by S. Brush and D. Stabinsky (209–29). Washington DC: Island Press.

———. 1996b. *Fighting for the rain forest: war, youth & resources in Sierra Leone*. Portsmouth NH: Heinemann.

———. 1997. Toward an African green revolution? An anthropology of rice research in Sierra Leone. In *The ecology of practice: studies of food crop production in sub-Saharan West Africa*, edited by E. Nyerges (201–52). Newark NJ: Gordon & Breach.

Richardson, David 2001. Shipboard revolts, African authority, and the African slave trade. *William and Mary Quarterly 3rd Series* 58:69–92.

Riello, Giorgio, and Prasannan Parthasarathi. 2011. *The spinning world: a global history of cotton textiles, 1200–1850*. Oxford UK: Oxford University Press.

Rigg, Jonathan. 2001. *More than the soil: rural change in Southeast Asia*. Harlow UK: Prentice Hall.

Riley, Ralph. 1983. Plant breeding – an integrating technology. In *Plant breeding for low input conditions* edited by K. ter Horst and E. R. Watts. Lusaka: Ministry of Agriculture & Water Development.

Riser, Henry LeRoy. 1948. *The history of Jennings, Louisiana*. MA thesis, Louisiana State University.

Rist, Gilbert. 2008. *The history of development: from Western origins to global faith*. London UK: Zed Books.

Robb, Peter. 1996. *Meanings of agriculture: essays in South Asian history and economics*. Delhi India: Oxford University Press.

Roberts, Luke Shepherd. 1998. *Mercantilism in a Japanese domain: the merchant origins of economic nationalism in eighteenth-century Tosa*. Cambridge UK, New York NY: Cambridge University Press.

Robertson, C. J. 1936. The rice export from Burma, Siam, and French Indo-China. *Pacific Affairs* 9 (2):243–53.

Rodney, Walter. 1970. *A history of the Upper Guinea coast, 1545–1800*, Oxford studies in African affairs. Oxford UK: Clarendon Press.

Rosencrantz, Florence L. 1946. The rice industry in Arkansas. *Arkansas Historical Quarterly* 5 (Summer):123–37.

Rosengarten, Theodore. 1998. In the master's garden. In *Art and landscape in Charleston and the Lowcountry*, edited by J. Beardslay. Washington DC: Spacemaker Press.

Roy, Gopaul Chunder. 1876. *The causes, symptoms, and treatment of Burdwan fever, or the epidemic fever of lower Bengal*. London UK: Churchill.

Rudra, A. 1987. Technology choice in agriculture in India over the past three decades. In *Macropolicies for appropriate technology in developing countries*, edited by F. Stewart (22–73). Boulder CO: Westview.

Ruffin, Edmund, and William M. Mathew, eds. 1992. *Agriculture, geology, and society in antebellum South Carolina: the private diary of Edmund Ruffin, 1843*. Athens GA: University of Georgia Press.

Ruttan, Vernon. 1977. The green revolution: seven generalizations. *International Development Review* 4:16–23.

Sachs, Jeffrey. 2005. *The end of poverty: economic possibilities for our time*. New York NY: Penguin Press.

Sadio, Moussa. 2009 Production triplé`a Ziguinchor. *Le Soleil* Mardi 24 Fevrie.
Saitō Osamu 齋藤修. 1988. Daikaikon, jinkō, shōnō keizai 大開墾、人口、小農經業 (Land reclamation, population and the small-farm economy) In *Nihon keizaishi. 1, Keizai shakai no seiritsu* 日本経済史. 1, 経済社会の成立 *(Economic history of Japan. 1. The establishment of economic society)*, edited by Umemura Mataji 梅村又次, Hayami Akira 速水融 and Miyamoto Matao 宮本又郎. Tōkyō Japan: Iwanami Shoten.
———. 2005. Pre-modern economic growth revisited: Japan and the West. *LSE/GEHN Working Paper Series.*
———. 2008. *Hikaku keizai hatten ron* 比較経済発展論 (Comparative economic development). Tōkyō Japan: Iwanami Shoten.
Sakane Yoshihiro 坂根嘉弘. 2002. Kindaiteki tochi shoyū no gaiken to tokushitsu" (The outline and characteristics of modern landownership) In *Tochi shoyū shi* 土地所有史 (The history of landownership), edited by Watanabe Takashi 渡辺尚志 and Gomi Fumihiko 五味文. Tōkyō Japan: Yamakawa Shuppansha.
Samanta, Arabinda. 2002. *Malarial fever in colonial Bengal, 1820–1939: social history of an epidemic.* Kolkata: Firma KLM.
Sansom, Robert. 1967, Oct. 18. *The use and impact of the four horsepower gasoline engine in rural Vietnam.* Lyndon Baines Johnson Presidential Library, Reel 1.
———. 2010. L'agriculture traditionnelle chinoise est-elle verte et jusqu'où? In *L'empreinte de la Technique. Ethnologie Prospective (Cerisy 2–9 Juillet 2009)*, edited by É. Faroult and T. Gaudin (pp. 117–40). Paris: L'Harmattan.
———. 2011. Rethinking the green revolution in South China: technological materialities and human-environment relations. *East Asian Science, Technology and Society* 5 (4):479–504.
Sapir, J. David. 1971. West Atlantic: an inventory of the languages, their noun class systems and consonant alternation. *Current Trends in Linguistics* 7, (1):5–112.
Sarasin, Viraphol. 1977. *Tribute and profit: Sino-Siamese trade, 1652–1853.* Cambridge MA: Council on East Asian Studies, Harvard University Press.
Sarró, Ramon. 2009. *The politics of religious change on the Upper Guinea coast: iconoclasm done and undone.* Edinburgh UK: Edinburgh University Press.
Scanlon, Sister Francis Assisi. 1954. The rice industry of Texas. MA thesis, University of Texas, Austin.
Scharnagel, Theodor. 1936. Stand und Aufgaben der Pflanbzenzüchtung im süddeutschen Raum. *Der Forschungsdienst* Sonderheft Nr. 3:34–40.
———. 1953. Die Bedeutung der Lokalsortenzüchtung für Bayern. *Landwirtschaftliches Jahrbuch für Bayern* 30 (June):174–81.
Schindler, Franz. 1907. Inwieweit hat die Getreidezüchtung auf die Landrassen Rücksicht zu nehmen und welche Massnahmen sind geeignet, die Saatgutzüchtung in wirksamster Weise zu fördern? In *VIII. Internationaler landwirtschaftlicher Kongress Wien*, edited by anon. Vienna Austria: F.A. Wachtl.
———. 1928. Über die Notwendigkeit der Erforschung und Erhaltung der Getreidelandrassen im Hinblick auf ihre züchterische und wirtschaftliche Bedeutung. In *Festschrift anlässlich des 70. Geburtstages Professor Dr. Julius Stoklasa*, edited by E. G. Doerell. Berlin Germany: Parey.
Schneider, Jürg. 1992. *From upland to irrigated rice: the development of wet-rice agriculture in Rejang-Musi, Southwest Sumatra.* Bern: Reimer.

Schoenbrun, David Lee. 1993. We are what we eat: ancient agriculture between the Great Lakes. *The Journal of African History* 34, (1):1–31.

——. 1998. *A green place, a good place: agrarian change, gender, and social identity in the Great Lakes region to the 15th century.* Portsmouth NH: Heinemann.

Schultz, Theodore. 1964. *Transforming traditional agriculture.* Chicago IL, London UK: University of Chicago Press.

Science. 1998. Wonder wheat. *Science* 280 (24 Apr):527.

Scott, James C. 1998. *Seeing like a state: how certain schemes to improve the human condition have failed.* New Haven CT, London UK: Yale University Press.

——. 2009. *The art of not being governed: an anarchist history of upland Southeast Asia.* New Haven CT: Yale University Press.

Searing, James F. 1993. *West African slavery and Atlantic commerce (Texto impreso): the Senegal River valley, 1700–1860. African studies series.* Cambridge UK: Cambridge University Press.

Segerer, Guillaume. 2000. L'origine des Bijogo: hypothèses de linguiste. In *Migrations anciennes et peuplement actuel des Côtes guinéennes: actes du colloque international de l'Université de Lille 1, les 1er, 2 et 3 décembre 1997,* edited by G. Gaillard and Université de science et technique de Lille (183–92). Paris France: Harmattan.

——. 2002. *La Langue Bijogo De Bubaque (Guinee Bissau).* Louvain, Belgium: Peters.

Semon, Mande, Rasmus Neilsen, Monty P. Jones, and Susan R. McCouch. 2005. Population structure of African cultivated rice Oryza glaberrima (Steud.): evidence for elevated levels of linkage. Disequilibrium caused by admixture with O. sativa and ecological adaptation. *Genetics* 169:1639–47.

Sen, Amartya. 1981. *Poverty and famines: an essay on entitlement and deprivation.* Oxford UK, New York NY: Clarendon Press, Oxford University Press.

Shannon, Fred A. 1945. *The farmer's last frontier, agriculture, 1860–1897, The economic history of the United States.* New York NY, Toronto Canada: Farrar & Rinehart.

Sharma, Shatanjiw Das. 2010. *Rice: origin, antiquity and history.* Enfield NH, Boca Raton FL: Science Publishers, distributed by CRC Press.

Shen Chiran 沈赤然. 1986. preface dated 1808. Hanye congtan 寒夜叢談 (Random notes of a chilly night) In *Youmanlou congshu* 又滿樓叢書 (Book collection of Youmanlou). Reprint 1986 of 1924 edition. Jiangsu: Guangling guji keyinshe.

Shen, Xiaobai. 2010. Understanding the evolution of rice technology in China – from traditional agriculture to GM rice today. *Journal of Development Studies* 46 (6):1026–46.

Shen Zonghan, 1980. Xiansheng jinian ji沈宗翰先生紀念集 (Collection of articles to commemorate Shen Zonghan). Taipei: Shen Zonghan xiansheng jinian ji bianyin weiyuan hui.

Shen Zonghan 沈宗翰. 1984. *Shen Zonghan zishu* 沈宗翰自述 (Memoirs of Shen Zonghan). Taibei: Zhuanji wenxue chubanshe.

Sherman, D. George, and Hedy Bruyns Sherman. 1990. *Rice, rupees, and ritual: economy and society among the Samosir Batak of Sumatra.* Stanford CA: Stanford University Press.

Shetler, Jan Bender. 2007. *Imagining Serengeti: a history of landscape memory in Tanzania from earliest times to the present, New African histories series.* Athens OH: Ohio University Press.

Shiba Yoshinobu 斯波義信. 1968. *Sōdai keizaishi no kenkyû* 宋代商業史研究 (Study of Song Dynastic economic history). Tōkyō Japan: Kazama Shobo.

Shina no kome ni kansuru chōsa 支那ノ米ニ關スル調査 (China and rice: analysis of their relation). 1917. Tōkyō Japan: Nōshōmushō nōmukyoku.

Siddiqui, Iqtidar Hussein. 1986. Water works and irrigation systems in India during Pre-Mughal times. *Journal of Economic and Social History of the Orient* 29 (1):53–72.

Simmonds, N.W. 1991. Selection for local adaptation in a plant breeding programme. *Theoretical and Applied Genetics* 82:363–7.

Singh, Chetan. 1985. Well-irrigation methods in medieval Panjab: the Persian wheel reconsidered. *Indian Economic and Social History Review* 22 (1):73–88.

Singh, Chetan. 1991. *Region and empire: Panjab in the seventeenth century*. Delhi: Oxford University Press.

Singh, Navtej. 1996. *Starvation and colonialism: a study of famines in the nineteenth century British Punjab, 1858–1901*. New Delhi India: National Book Organisation.

Singleton, Theresa A. 2010. Reclaiming the Gullah-Geechee past: archaeology of slavery in coastal Georgia. In *African American life in the Georgia Lowcountry: the Atlantic world and the Gullah Geechee*, edited by P. Morgan (151–87). Athens GA: University of Georgia Press.

Sinn, Elizabeth. 1990. *Between east and west: aspects of social and political development in Hong Kong*. Hong Kong: Centre of Asian Studies, University of Hong Kong.

Siple, George E. 1960. Some geologic and hydrologic factors affecting limestone terraces of tertiary age in South Carolina. *Southeastern Geology* 2 (Aug):1–11.

Small, John C., and St. Louis Southwestern Railway Company. 1910. *Rice, the white cereal of Arkansas*. St. Louis, MO: E.W. LaBeaume.

Smith, Hayden R. 2012. Rich swamps and rice grounds: the specialization of inland rice culture in the South Carolina Lowcountry, 1670–1861. PhD thesis, History, University of Georgia.

Smith, Thomas C. 1959. *The agrarian origins of modern Japan*. Stanford CA: Stanford University Press.

—. 1988. Farm family by-employments in pre-industrial Japan. In *Native sources of Japanese industrialization, 1750–1920*, edited by T. C. Smith (71–102). Berkeley CA: University of California Press.

Smits, M. B. 1919a. *De voedselvoorziening van Nederlandsch-Indië*, Batavia: Vereeniging voor Studie van Koloniaal Maatschappelijke Vraagstukken.

—. 1919b. Onderzoek naar de landbouwtoestanden in de Onderafdeling Aier Bangis (S.W.K.). *Mededeelingen van den Landbouwvoorlichtingsdienst* 2:1–16.

—. 1920. *De rijstcultuur in Noord-Amerika met behulp van mechanischen arbeid*. Weltevreden Netherlands: Landsdrukkerij.

—. 1934. Mechanische Rijstcultuur en haar betekenis voor de Nederlandsche Koloniën. *Landbouwkundig Tijdschrift* 46:617–29.

Society for the propagation of the gospel in foreign parts. South Carolina. Microfilm.

Soller, D. R., and H. H. Mills. 1991. Surficial geology and geomorphology. In *Geology of the Carolinas: Carolina Geological Society fiftieth anniversary volume*, edited by J. W. Horton, V. A. Zullo, and Carolina Geological Society (290–308). Knoxville TN: University of Tennessee Press.

South Carolina Gazette, Various years. Charleston SC.

Southern Pacific [Railroad] Company. 1899. *Southwest Louisiana up-to-date*. Omaha, Edition: n.p.
——. 1901. *Louisiana rice book*. Houston TX: Passenger Department of the Southern Pacific "Sunset Route".
——. 1902. *Rice cook book*. Houston: n.p. Passenger Department.
Southworth, F. C. 2011. Proto-Dravidian agriculture. In *Rice and language across Asia: crops movement and social change symposium*. Cornell University's East Asia Program.
Spear, Thomas T., Richard Waller, and African Studies Association Meeting. 1993. *Being Maasai: ethnicity & identity in East Africa*. London UK: J. Currey.
Spicer, J. M. 1964. *Beginnings of the rice industry in Arkansas*. Arkansas: Arkansas Rice Promotion Association and Rice Council.
Stadelmann. 1924. Saatzüchterische Tagesfragen. *Wochenblatt des landwirtschaftlichen Vereins in Bayern* 114:233–4.
Starostin, Sergei. 2000. Comparative-historical linguistics and lexicostatistics. *Time Depth in Historical Linguistics* 1:223–59.
Steglich, Bruno. 1893. *Über Verbesserung und Veredelung landwirtschaftlicher Kulturgesächse durch Züchtung (lecture, 2 Dec 1892 at Ökonomische Gesellschaft im Kgr. Sachsen)*. Leipzig Germany: Reichenbach.
Stein, Burton, and David Arnold. 2010. *A history of India*. Oxford UK, Malden MA: Wiley-Blackwell.
Steinberg, Theodore. 1991. *Nature incorporated: industrialization and the waters of New England, Studies in environment and history*. Cambridge UK, New York NY: Cambridge University Press.
Stewart, Mart A. 2002a. Southern environmental history. In *A companion to the American South*, edited by John B. Bowles. Malden, MA: Blackwell.
——. 2002b. *What nature suffers to groe: life, labor, and landscape on the Georgia Coast, 1680–1920, Wormsloe foundation publications*. Athens GA, London UK: University of Georgia Press.
Stewart, Mart A., and Peter A. Coclanis. 2011. *Environmental change and agricultural sustainability in the Mekong Delta*. Dordrecht Netherlands: Springer.
Stiven, A. E. 1908. Rice. In *Twentieth century impressions of Siam: its history, people, commerce, industries, and resources, with which is incorporated an abridged edition of twentieth century impressions of British Malaya*, edited by A. Wright and O. T. Breakspear (144–69). London UK: Lloyds Greater Britain Publishing Company, Ltd.
Stobbs, A. R. 1963. *The soils and geography of the Boliland Region of Sierra Leone*. Freetown Sierra Leone: Government of Sierra Leone.
Stoler, Ann Laura. 1985. *Capitalism and confrontation in Sumatra's plantation belt, 1870–1979*. New Haven CT: Yale University Press.
Stoll, Steven. 2002. *Larding the lean earth: soil and society in nineteenth-century America*. New York NY: Hill and Wang.
Storey, William Kelleher. 1997. *Science and power in colonial Mauritius*. Rochester NY: University of Rochester Press.
Stross, Randall E. 1986. *The stubborn earth: American agriculturalists on Chinese soil, 1898–1937*. Berkeley CA: University of California Press.
Suba, Agostinho Clode. As estruturas sociais Balantas. *Bombolom* 1:n.d.

Subrahmanyam, Sanjay, and C. A. Bayly. 1988. Portfolio capitalists and the political economy of early modern India. *The Indian Economic and Social History Review* 25 (4):401–24.

Suehiro Akira. 1989. *Capital accumulation in Thailand, 1855–1985*. Tōkyō Japan: Centre for East Asian Cultural Studies.

Sugihara Kaoru. 2003. The East Asian path of development: a long-term perspective. In *The resurgence of East Asia: 500, 150 and 50 year perspectives*, edited by G. Arrighi, T. Hamashita and M. Selden (178–23). London UK, New York NY: Routledge.

Sun Wen. 1957. *Guofu quanji*國父全集 (Completed works of Sun Yat-sen) Taipei: Zhongyang wenwu gongying she.

Sun Yixian 孫逸仙 et al. 1957. *Guofu quanji* 國父全集 (Completed works of Sun Yat-sen). 6 vols. Taibei: Zhongyang wenwu.

Sur, D., and S. P. Mukhopadhyay. 2006. Prevalence of Thalassaemia trait in the state of West Bengal. *Journal of the Indian Medical Association* 104 (1):11–5.

Surface, G. T. 1911. Rice in the United States. *Bulletin of the American Geographical Society* 43:500–9.

Sutter, Paul, S. 2010. What gullies mean: Georgia's "little Grand Canyon" and Southern environmental history. *The Journal of Southern History* 76 (Aug): 579–616.

Sutton, J. E. G. 1984. Irrigation and soil-conservation in African agricultural history. *Journal of Agricultural History* 25:25–41.

Sweeney, M. T. et al. 2007. Global dissemination of a single mutation conferring white pericarp in rice. *PloS Genetics* 3 (8):1418–24.

Sweeny, Megan, and Susan R. McCouch. 2007. The complex history of the domestication of rice. *Annals of Botany* 100 (5):951–7.

Taiwan Sōtoku kanbō chōsaka. 1925. *Saigon mai no chosa* 西貢米の 調査 (The survey of Saigon rice). Taipei: Taiwan Sōtoku kanbō chōsaka.

Takeuchi, J. Ozen. 1991. *The role of labour-intensive sectors in Japanese industrialization*. Tōkyō Japan: United Nations University Press.

Tamaki Akira 玉城哲. 1977. *Mizu no shisō* 水の思想 (The philosophy of water). Tokyo: Ronsōsha.

Tan Qian 談遷. 1960. *Beiyou lu* 北游錄 *(Record of Northern travels)* Beijing: Zhonghua shuju.

Tanimoto Masayuki 谷本雅之. 1998. *Nihon ni okeru zairaiteki keizai hatten to orimonogyō: shijō keisei to kazoku keizai* 日本における在来的経済発展と織物業 : 市場形成と家族経済 (Indigenous economic development and the textile industry in Japan: market formation and the household economy). Nagoya, Japan: Nagoya Daigaku Shuppankai.

——. 2006. The role of tradition in Japan's industrialization. In *The role of tradition in Japan's industrialization: another path to industrialization*, edited by M. Tanimoto (3–44). Oxford UK, New York NY: Oxford University Press.

——. 2013. From peasant economy to urban agglomeration: the transformation of labor-intensive industrialization in modern Japan. In *Labour-intensive industrialization in historical perspective*, edited by G. Austin and K. Sugihara (144–75). Abingdon UK: Routledge.

Taselaar, Arjen. 1998. *De Nederlandse koloniale lobby: ondernemers en de Indische politiek, 1914–1940*. Leiden Netherlands: Research School CNWS, School of Asian, African, and Amerindian Studies.

Tawney, R. H. 1932, reprint 1966. *Land and labor in China*. Boston MA: Beacon Press.
Taylor family papers. 1709–1829. edited by University of South Carolina, South Caroliniana Library. Columbia SC.
Temudo, Marina Padrão. 2009. From the margins of the state to the presidential palace: the Balanta case in Guinea-Bissau. *African Studies Review* 52 (2):49–50.
terHorst, K., and E. R. Watts, eds. 1983. *Plant breeding for low input conditions (Proceedings of a workshop on plant breeding for "lousy" conditions, held at Mt. Makulu Central Research Station, Chilanga, Zambia, 5 March 1982)*. Lusaka Zambia: Ministry of Agriculture & Water Development.
Terry, George D. 1981. "Champaign Country": a social history of an eighteenth century Lowcountry Parish in South Carolina, St. Johns Berkley County. PhD, University of South Carolina.
Thee, Kian Wie. 1969. Plantation agriculture and export growth an economic history of East Sumatra, 1863–1942. PhD thesis, National Institute of Economic and Social Research University of Wisconsin.
Thomson, William Cooper. 1846. Narrative of Mr. William Cooper Thomson's journey from Sierra Leone to Timbo, capital of Futah Kallo, in Western Africa. *Journal of the Royal Geographical Society of London* 16:106–38.
Tibbetts, John. 2006. African roots, Carolina gold, Coastal Heritage. *Coastal Heritage* 21 (1):3–10.
Tilley, Helen. 2011. *Africa as a living laboratory: empire, development, and the problem of scientific knowledge, 1870–1950*. Chicago: University of Chicago Press.
Tomobe Kenichi友部謙一. 1996. Tochiseido 土地制度 (The land system). In *Nihon Keizai no 200-nen* 日本経濟の 200年 (200 years of the Japanese economy), edited by Nishikawa Shunsuke 西川俊作, Odaka Kōnosuke 尾高煌 and Saitō Osamu 斎藤修. Tōkyō Japan: Nihon Hyōronsha.
Tripp, Robert, and et al. 2006. *Self-sufficient agriculture: labour and knowledge in small-scale farming*. London UK: Earthscan.
Tsao, Ellen. 1932. Chinese rice merchants and millers in French Indo-China. *Chinese Economic Journal* 11 (6 Dec):450–63.
Tsou, S. C. S., and R. L. Villareal. 1982. Resistance to eating sweet potatoes. In *Sweet potato*, edited by R. L. Villareal and T. D. Griggs (37–42). Shanhua: Asian Vegetable Research and Development Center.
Tu, Nguyen Duc. 2011. Rice production and a vision for Vietnam's wetlands. In *Successful cases on sustainable rice paddy farming practices and wetland conservation in Asia*, edited by G. Lukacs. Tōkyō Japan: Ministry of Environment.
United States Department of Agriculture. 1971. *Soil survey of Charleston County, South Carolina*. Washington DC: Government Printing Office.
——. 1980a. *Soil survey of Beaufort and Jasper counties*. Washington DC: Government Printing Office.
——. 1980b. *Soil survey of Berkeley county, South Carolina*. Washington DC: Government Printing Office.
United States Geological Survey. 2012. *The National Map*. Washington DC: online at: http://nationalmap.gov/ [accessed August 5, 2014).

U.S. Department of the Interior. 1898. *Water supply and irrigation papers of the United States Geological Survey.* Vol. 13, *Irrigation systems in Texas.* Washington DC: Government Printing Office.

Van der Leij, Marco, and Sanjeev Goyal. 2011. Strong ties in a small world. *Review of Network Economics* online at: http://www.bepress.com/rne/vol10/iss2/1 [accessed August 5, 2014].

Van der Stok, J. E. 1924. *Verslag over het rijstproefbedrijf Selatdjaran.* edited by I. K. National Archive. The Hague Netherlands.

Van Ruymbeke, Bertrand. 2006. *From New Babylon to Eden: the Huguenots and their migration to colonial South Carolina.* Columbia SC: University of South Carolina Press.

Vansina, Jan. 1990. *Paths in the rainforests: toward a history of political tradition in equatorial Africa.* Madison WI: University of Wisconsin Press.

——. 1995. New linguistic evidence and "the Bantu expansion." *The Journal of African History* 36 (2):173–95.

——. 2004. *How societies are born: governance in West Central Africa before 1600.* Charlottesville VA: University of Virginia Press.

Vaughan, D. A., Koh-ichi Kadowaki, Akito Kaga, and Norihiko Tomooka. 2005. On the phylogeny and biogeography of the genus Oryza. *Breeding Science* 55: 113–22.

Vernon, Amelia Wallace. 1993. *African Americans at Mars Bluff, South Carolina.* Baton Rouge LA: Louisiana State University Press.

Verschuer, Charlotte von. 2003. *Le riz dans la culture de Heian, mythe et réalité, Bibliothèque de l'Institut des hautes études japonaises.* Paris France: Collège de France, Institut des hautes études japonaises.

Vincenheller, W. G. 1906. *Rice growing in Arkansas.* Fayetteville AR: Arkansas Agricultural Experiment Station.

Vink, G. J. 1941. *De grondslagen van het Indonesische landbouwbedrijf.* Wageningen Netherlands: H. Veenman.

Virk, P. S., G. S. Khush, and S. Peng. 2004. Breeding to enhance yield potential of rice at IRRI: the ideotype approach. *International Rice Research Notes* 29 (1):5–9.

Vlach, John Michael. 1993. *Back of the big house: the architecture of plantation slavery, The Fred W. Morrison series in Southern studies.* Chapel Hill NC: University of North Carolina Press.

Volker, Tys. 1928. *Van oerbosch tot cultuurgebied: een schets van de beteekenis van de tabak, de andere cultures en de industrie ter oostkust van Sumatra.* Medan Indonesia: Deli Planters Vereeniging.

Vydrin, Valentin. 2009. On the problem of the proto-Mande homeland. *Вопросы языкового родства–Journal of Language Relationship* 1: 107–42.

Vydrin, Valentin, and T. G. Bergman. *Mandé language group of West Africa: location and genetic classification,* June 23, 2010 2010. Online at: http://www-01.sil.org/silesr/2000/2000-003/silesr2000-003.htm [accessed August 5, 2014].

Wakimura, Kohei. 1997. Famines, epidemics and mortality in Northern India, 1870–1921. In *Local agrarian societies in colonial India: Japanese perspectives,* edited by P. Robb, K. Sugihara and H. Yanagisawa (280–310). New Delhi India: Manohar.

Wall, A. J. 1883. *Indian snake poisons, their nature and effects.* London UK: Allen.

Walshaw, Sarah. 2005. Swahili urbanization, trade and food production: botanical perspectives from Pemba Island, Tanzania, AD 600–1500, PhD dissertation, Washington University.

Walton, J. R. 1999. Varietal innovation and the competitiveness of the British cereals sector, 1760–1930. *Agricultural History Review* 47:29–57.

Wang Xixian 黃希憲. preface 1640. *Fu Wu xilue* 撫吳檄畧 (Brief sketch of the administrator Fu).

Wang Yeh-chien 王业键. 1986. The food supply in eighteenth-century Fukien. *Late Imperial China* 7 (2):80–117.

———. 2003. *Qingdai jingji shilun wenji* 清代經濟史論文集 (Collected essays in the economic history of Qing China). Taibei Xian Banqiao: Daoxiang chubanshe.

Wang Zuoyue. 2002. Saving China through science: the science society of China, scientific nationalism, and civil society in Republican China. *Osiris* 17 291–322.

Warman, Arturo. 2003. *Corn & capitalism: how a botanical bastard grew to global dominance, Latin America in translation/en tradducción/em tradução*. Chapel Hill NC: University of North Carolina Press.

Watanabe Minoru 渡邊実. 1964. *Nihon shoku seikatsu shi* 日本食生活史 (A history of foodways in Japan). Tōkyō Japan: Yoshikawa Kobunkan.

Watanabe Takashi 渡辺尚志. 2002. Kinseiteki tochi shoyū no tokushitsu 近世的土地所有の特質 (The features of landownership in the early-modern period). In *Tochi Shoyū Shi* 土地所有史 (The history of landownership), edited by Watanabe Takashi and Gomi Fumihiko. Tōkyō Japan: Yamakawa Shuppansha.

Watson, Andrew. 1974. The Arab agricultural revolution and its diffusion, 700–1100. *Journal of Economic History* 34 (1):8–35.

Watt, George. 1891. *A dictionary of the economic products of India/ 5, Linum to oyster*. Calcutta India: Government Printing, India.

Webb, James L. A. 2009. *Humanity's burden: a global history of malaria, Studies in environment and history*. Cambridge UK, New York NY: Cambridge University Press.

Weems, R. E., Geological Survey (U.S.), Earl M. Lemon, and US Nuclear Regulatory Commission. 1989. *Geology of the Bethera, Cordesville, Huger, and Kittredge quadrangles, Berkeley County, South Carolina*. Reston CA, Denver CO: The Survey, Map Distribution.

West, Ellen Hillman. 1987. Itinerant farm worker – Charles Miller. *Grand Prairie Historical Society Bulletin* 30 (Apr):39–42.

White, Benjamin. 1983. "Agricultural involution" and its critics: twenty years after. *Bulletin of Concerned Asian Scholars* 15 (2):18–31.

White, Frederick Norman. 1918. *Twenty years of plague in India with special reference to the outbreak of 1917–18*. Calcutta India: Supt. Government Printing.

White, Richard. 1995. *The organic machine: the remaking of the Columbia river*. New York NY: Hill and Wang.

White, William. 2008. Economic history of tractors in the United States. In *Eh.Net Encyclopedia*: Robert Whaples online at: http://eh.net/encyclopedia/article/white.tractors.history.us [accessed October 13, 2011].

Wickizer, Vernon Dale, Merrill Kelley Bennett, and Institute of Pacific Relations. 1941. *The rice economy of monsoon Asia*. Stanford CA: Stanford University, Food Research Institute.

Wilkinson, R. A. 1848. Production of rice in Louisiana. *De Bow's Review* 6 (July):53–7.

Will, Pierre-Etienne and R. Bin Wong. 1991. *Nourish the people: the state civilian granary system in China, 1650–1850*. Ann Arbor MI: Center for Chinese Studies Publications.

Willis, Russell Austin. 2006. Genetic stratigraphy and geochronology of last interglacial shorelines on the central coast of South Carolina. MA thesis, Geology & Geophysics, Louisiana State University.

Willoughby, Ralph H., and Doar, W.R., III. 2006. *Solution to the two-Talbot problem of maritime Pleistocene terraces in South Carolina*. Columbia SC: South Carolina Department of Natural Resources, Geological Survey.

Willson, Jack H., and Butte County Rice Growers Association. 1979. *Rice in California*. Richvale CA: Butte County Rice Growers Association.

Wilmsen, Edwin N. 1989. *Land filled with flies: a political economy of the Kalahari*. Chicago IL: University of Chicago Press.

Winder, Gordon M. 2012. *The American reaper: harvesting networks and technology, 1830–1910*. Farham, UK: Ashgate.

Winterbottom, Thomas Masterman. 1803. *An account of the native Africans in the neighbourhood of Sierra Leone; to which is added, an account of the present state of medicine among them*. London UK: C. Whittingham, J. Hatchard.

Wittfogel, Karl August. 1957. *Oriental despotism; a comparative study of total power*. New Haven CT: Yale University Press.

Wong, R. Bin. 1997. *China transformed: historical change and the limits of European experience*. Ithaca NY: Cornell University Press.

Wood, Peter H. 1974. *Black majority. Negroes in colonial South Carolina from 1670 through the Stono Rebellion*. New York NY: Knopf, distributed by Random House.

Woolcock, Michael, Simon Szreter, and Vijayendra Rao. 2011. How and why does history matter for development policy? *Journal of Development Studies* 47 (1):70–96.

Wooster, Ralph. 2012. *Viterbo, TX*. Online at: http://www.tshaonline.org/handbook/online/articles/htv08 [accessed August 5, 2014].

World Bank. 2007. *World development report 2008: agriculture for development*. Washington DC: World Bank.

Wright, Arnold, and Oliver T. Breakspear. 1908. *Twentieth century impressions of Siam: its history, people, commerce, industries, and resources, with which is incorporated an abridged edition of Twentieth century impressions of British Malaya*. London UK: Lloyds Greater Britain Publishing Company, Ltd.

Wu Han 吳晗. 1960. Aiguo de lishijia Tan Qian 愛國的歷史學家談遷 (Tan Qian, A patriot-historian). In *Beiyou lu*, edited by T. Qian. Beijing: Zhonghua shu ju.

Xingzhengyuan nongcun fuxing weiyuan hui. 1934. *Zhongguo nongye zhi gaijin* 中國農業之改進 (The improvement of Chinese agriculture). Shanghai: Shangwu yinshuguan.

Xuan, Vo Tong. 1975. Rice cultivation in the Mekong delta: present situation and potentials for increased production. *South East Asian Studies* 13 (1):88–111.

——. 1994, 4–7 May *History of Vietnam-IRRI Rice Cooperation*. Paper read at Vietnam and IRRI: A partnership in rice research 1995, at Hanoi.

Yamaguchi Kazuo 山口和雄. 1963. *Meiji zenki keizai no bunseki* 明治前期經濟の分析 (Analysis of the Early Meiji economy), 2nd ed.. Tōkyō Japan: Tōkyō Daigaku Shuppansha.

Yeh Wen-Hsin. 2000. *Becoming Chinese: passages to modernity and beyond*, Studies on China. Berkeley CA: University of California Press.

You Xiuling 游修齡. 1986. Taihu diqu daozuo qiyuan ji qi chuanbo he fazhan wenti 太湖地區稻作起源及其傳播和發展問題 (The origin of grains, its development and spread in the Taihu era). *Zhongguo nongshi* 10:71–83.

Yu, Hwa-Lung, and George Christakos. 2006. Spatiotemporal modelling and mapping of the Bubonic Plague epidemic in India. *International Journal of Health Geography* (12), online at: http://www.ncbi.nlm.nih.gov/pmc/articles/PMC1448212 [accessed August 5, 2014].

Zader, Amy. 2011. Technologies of quality: the role of the Chinese state in guiding the market for rice. *East Asian Science, Technology and Society* 5 (4):461–77.

Zanden, J. L. van. 2000. The great convergence from a West-European perspective: some thought and hypotheses. *Itinerario* 24 (3/4):9–28.

Zappi, Elda Gentili. 1991. *If eight hours seem too few: mobilization of women workers in the Italian rice fields*. Albany NY: State University of New York Press.

Zhang, Xinyi. 1931. *China's food problem*. Shanghai: China Institute of Pacific Relations.

Zhao Fangtian 趙方田, and Yang Jun 楊軍. 2008. *Zhongguo nongxue huishi* 中國農學會史 (A history of China association of agricultural science societies). Shanghai: Shanghai jiaotong daxue chubanshe.

Zhao Lianfang 趙連芳. 1954. *Xiandai nongye* 現代農業 (Modern agriculture), Xiandai guomin jiben zhishi congshu. Taibei: Zhonghua wenhua chubanshi yewei yuanhui.

——. 趙連芳. 1970. *Zhao Lianfang boshi huiyilu* 趙連芳博士回憶錄 (Dr. Zhao Lianfang's memoir). Taibei: Zhaozhang xiaosong.

Zhupi zouzhe 硃批奏摺 (Throne memorials with imperial annotations) Edited by Z. d. d. a. guan. Beijing: Zhongguo diyi lishi dang'anguan, Microfilm.

Zuijin simian jian shiliang wenti wenxian mulu 最近四年來食糧問題文獻目錄 (Index of the works for food problem in recent four years). 1936. *Guoji maoyi daobao* 8 (6):267–78.

Zurbrigg, Sheila. 1992. Hunger and epidemic malaria in Punjab, 1968–1940. *Economic and Political Weekly* 25 (Jan): PE 2–26.

Zurndorfer, Harriet T. 2004. Imperialism, globalization, and public finance: the case of the late Qing. LSE, *Global Economic History Network (GEHN) Working Paper* 06/04.

Index

Academia Sinica 104
Acadia Parish, Louisiana 309
Adão, (Bijago, a slave, Amazonia) 288
Africa, African analyses 17
  African slaves in America and rice
    10–11, 226
  and Asian rice 224, 273
  and Black Rice debate 10
  comparative linguistics and historical
    reconstructionism 172
  creativity of societies 14, critiques 178
  differential modes of operation 280–281
  environmental history 185
  genetic distribution of rice 221, 222
  japonica rice 225
  study of rice farmers 185
  trade before the Green Revolution 223
  see also African rice, Black Rice debate,
    Green Revolution, individual countries
African Institution 143
African rice (*Oryza glaberrima*) 28, 139,
    172, 185, 212
  archaeobotanical evidence of use in
    Africa, 215
  centers of genetic diversity and
    origins of 213
  cultivation 225
  domestication 213
  geographical reach of 216, 227
  N'contu 282
  salt tolerance 213
  and US 292
  see also Asian rice
African role in the making of American
    agricultural systems 279–280
  and transfer of knowledge systems 284
African studies 17
  see also individual cultures; slavery; West
    Africa

Africanists 185, 186
Agent Orange 134
agrarian development, mainstream
    approaches to 246
Agricultural Advisory Corps of Republic of
    China at Vietnam (*Zhonghua minguo zhu
    Yuenan nongye jishu tuan*) 110
agricultural involution theory 3, 5, 10–11,
    40, 66
  creativity 14
  criticism of thesis 58
  inappropriateness of term 72
  modernization and progress 13
  and rice based dynamic 12
  rice industry and 12 *see also* Geetz
agricultural purification regimes 37–38
agricultural research, new directions in 51–52
agricultural revolutions 54
agriculture:
  as purification 37
  dynamics of agricultural sector
    337, 338
  history and historiography of rice and other
    crops compared 15
  and illness 264–265
  relationship with the economy
    95, 96
  and revolution through uniformity 41
  themes of power and control 275
agroecology 52
agronomists, economists, governments
    and efficient commodity
    production 20
Akifumi Norimatsu 92
Alberto (slave, Amazonia) 289
Alimamy Namina Sheka
    Dumbuya, 148
Álmada, André Alvares de 182
Almamy Amara 146, 147

aman rice 97
Amazonia (Maranhão and Pará), Brazil 279, 280
  absence of cultural significance of work 286
  methods of rice production 286
  planters and rice production 286
  planters and wetland rice agriculture 285
  planting and harvesting 286–287
  Amazonia 284, 285–289
  weeding 287
Anderson, A. (Deputy Commissioner of Hissar) 253
Angkor Borei 122, 124
Angkor Empire 97
Angola 224, 225
Anhui 90, 108
Annam geng rice 115
anopheles mosquitoes 164, 165, 251
anti-commodity, concept of 20, 21, 138
  acquisition of status 337
  complementarily and mutual dependence with commodities 337
  definition 337
  focus on production processes 337
  hybridization argument 337
  producing anti-commodities 336–338
  see also under Sumatra
Arkansas, US, rice industry in 314
aromatic rices 214
Ashepoo-Combahee-Edisto (ACE) Basin 196
Asia and rice 1, 31
  Asian oceanic trade 6
  importance of skills over economies of scale 19, -trade 7–8
  studies of rice systems 18
  see also under individual states
l'Archéologie du Delta du Mékong 122
Asian rice (Oryza sativa) 28, 126, 139, 186–187, 212, 214–215
  and African rice 225
  archaeobotanical evidence of use in Africa, absence of 215
  Balanta region 282
  domestication 214
  genetic evidence of migration 217–219
  in Mediterranean 217
  pathways for introduction into Africa 215
  spread of in Africa 227–228
  use in Africa 212–214
  and US 292

Asianists 19
Atlantic approaches to understanding American history 292
Atlantic economy, demands of the 279
Atlantic history and Atlantic world 1, 5, 31
Atlantic language group, Upper Guinea 169, 171, 176, 181
  classification and evolution 170–171
Atlantic region 3, 31, 163
Atlantic rice systems 14, 33
  Atlanticist rice history 15
Atlanticist debate 14, 15, 153
August Revolution, Vietnam 125
aus rice 97, 214, 222, 227
Austin, Lieutenant 147
Avicenna Africana *-yop 179
Ayutthaya (Siam) 123

b'alante b'ndang. grade Balanta 281
Back River Plantation 206
Baga Sitem 183
Balanta, Guinea-Bissau 281, 282
  age grade system 281, 282
  control of blufos grade 282–283
  councils (ko or beho) 281
  gender division 281
  mangrove rice agriculture 281
  preparation of rice 282
  resistance to technological innovation 284
  spirit world 283
  structure of Balanta society 283
  varieties of rice used 282
  witchcraft 283
Bali 18, 56
Ball, John Coming 206
banana 215–216, 224, 337
  phytolith evidence 215
Bangkok, Thailand, rice milling in 111
Bangladesh 132
  rice breeders in 47
Bangladeshi Rice Research Institute 46
Banten 75, 79
Bantu language group 172–173
Banyuwangi 81, 83
Barros Vasconcellos, Felippe de 288
Bartram, William 203
basmati rices 214
Batavia 75, 79
Bates, Robert 239–240
Bay Hill settlement, South Carolina 208
beans, China 90

Beijing, 88, 115, establishment of 87
Benar, port of 184
Bengal 7, 8, 9, 94, 127, 163, 164, 165, 246
   19th century malaria epidemics 256–257
   1943-44 Bengal famine 273–274
   acquired immunity to malaria 255
   agricultural practices 257, 258, 259
   anti-malaria mutations 265–266
   British rule 7, 248, 269
   cash crops and health 257
   changing inequality 265–273
   cholera 262
   commercial crops 255
   gastrointestinal infections 263
   health environment 250
   health of cultivators 245
   impact of agricultural change 255–256
   impact of waterlogging 256
   incidence of bubonic plague 264
   interwar decline in mortality rates 273
   livestock, human refuse and health 259
   malaria 252–253, 254, 262
   malnutrition and epidemics 271–273
   other infections 264–265
   patterns of morbidity 274
   peasants and rising prices 19th century 269
   rice agriculture development of 248–249
   rice production in 6, 25, 31
   rice varieties 254–255
   seasonal hunger 271
   situation in 1920s 270
   socially acquired immunity 267
   use of dung 259–260
   varieties grown 97
   water management 247–248
Benna system, Sierra Leone 160
Beresford, Jr., Richard 206–207, 208
   ecological complexity of plantations 210–211
   impact of slavery and canals 210
   planters and management of water control 210
Beresford, Richard 201–202
Bergère, Marrie-Claire 101
Berlin, Ira, 280
Biggin Swamp Canal 209
Biggin Swamp Huguenot enclave 200, 201
Biggs* 9, 39
Bignona, Senegal 230
Bilali rebellion 148
"biofortified" rice varieties 52
Black Athena 14

Black Oak Agricultural Society 209
Black Rice thesis, Chapter 12
   and Asia 2
   and Asianists 19
   and Carolinas 30, 291
   and cultural divisions 15
   debate on 1, 2, 3, 5, 30, 278
   debate and premises 30–31
   defined 10
   goals of 14
   Guinea-Bissau 23–24
   and knowledge system 15, 31
   re-zoning of rice history 31
   and rice history 31
   significance of 280
   United States 161
   West Africa 23, 31, 291–292
   white planter appropriation of 292
Black, Edda Fields 279
blast disease 132
Blue Rose rice 316
blufos grade, Balanta 281
Blyden, Edward Wilmot 148
Boeke, J.H. 67
bolilands, Sierra Leone 148–149, 154, 161
Bonanza wheat farms, United States 308
Borlaug, Norman 46, 49
Borneo transition between rice and rubber production 351, 352
boro rice 97
Boserup, Ester 71
Boserupian growth 71, 72
Brahmaputra river 247
Brandão Júnior, F. A. 285, 287
Bray, Francesca 310, 320, 323
Brazil, rice in 2, 3, 7, 15, 24, 30, 225, 275, 278, 292, 293–294
   Black Rice thesis and 10
   rice growing as deculturing experience 24
   slavery in 24
   spatial geography of rice industry impact on status 24
   and West African rice 219
breeding, agricultural 42, 44
   breeding strategies 53
Breman, Jan 342
Brien, Maurice 308
British East India Company 96, 248
Broughton, Lieutenant Governor Thomas 206
brown plant hopper 134, 136
   evolution of 134, 135
bubonic plague 264, 266

bubonic plague (cont.)
  and seasonal hunger 273
Buck, John Lossing 85, 86, 95, 96, 104
Buck, Pearl 104
buckwheat 85, 88, 89
Buerkle, Adam 313–314
buffaloes 65
Burma (Myanmar) and rice production 7, 8, 15, 31, 34
  export trade 32
Butscher, Rev. Leopold 143, 144, 149

Ca Mau Peninsula 123
Cação, port of 184
Caetano (Mandinka slave, Amazonia) 289
California Rice complex, Sacramento Valley 317, 348
California School 12, 13
Cambodia 121, 122, 137
  Vietnamese occupation of 124
Can Tho, Mekong Delta 124
Can Tho University 135, 136
Canton region, China 117
  Canton rice market 115, 117
  complexity of trade 32
  rice imports 103
Cape Fear region, North Carolina 294
Cape St. Mary 182
Cape Verde islands:
  and African food crops 225
  Portuguese and 224
  wet rice production 225
capitalism:
  American 14
  capitalist interpretations of efficiency and progress 9
  capitalist mode of production 9
  colonial-industrial 7, rise of 13–14, networks 4
  history of 5
capitalist enterprise, Jawa 62–63
Carney Judith 19, 23–24, 192, 225, 279, 280, 291
  Black Rice thesis 10
  critiques of 225
  genetic evidence in support of thesis 226
Carolina Gold Rice 225
Carolina rice (O. sativa) 126, 127, 130, 143, 149, 154, 296–297
  18th century-1830s exports 296
  and japonicas 143
  and Sierra Leone 138
  taste and durability 130
Cary, Sylvester L. 302, 304, 307, 308, 314
  promotional vision 314–315
Casamance River, Senegal 16, 171
  interrelationship between rice production and groundnut production 240
cassava 66, 71, 83
Catesby, Mark 194, 198
cattle 65
Center for Rice and Wheat Improvement 105
Central Agricultural Experimental Institute, (*Zhongyang nongye shiyansuo*) China 100, 104–105, 107, 108, 109, 110, 116, 117
  during Sino-Japanese War 108–109
Ceylon (Sri Lanka) 32
Champa rice, China 39, 85, 96
Charles Town (Charleston) 167, 190, 191, 277
  canal construction 209
  rice exports 191
Charleston Harbor 200
Charleywood Plantation, South Carolina 198
Charleywood rice fields 202, 204, 206–207, 210
  expansion of settlement 208
Chen Dashou, Jiangsu Governor 93
Chen Gongbo 104
Chen Hongmou, Fujian Governor 89
Chen Luquan 114
Chen Zupei 114
Chengdu 108
Chiang Kai-shek 102, 105
China, 2, 14, 17, 21
  18th century 40
  agricultural experts 100, 101
  agricultural revolution 10
  Asian rice trade 7, 110
  attitudes towards industriousness 23
  attitudes towards rice 116
  breeders 49
  Chinese elite 995 116
  commercialization and economic growth 25–26
  commoditization of rice and other grain trade 99
  demand for rice 97
  desire to eat well 88–90
  development of rice production 96
  economic policies 100
  economic policies of 100
  economy 7

Index 403

farming in 7
food and foreign trade 103
food crops 33
food problem 99, 116
food security 100
gender divisions and work 23
Green Revolution 11, 13, 34
historic production 19–20
historical growth in 3, 9
ideological status of rice farming 23
impact of consumers 26
impact of World War I 102, 103, 116
internal flow of rice 33
internal trade in rice 33
irrigation 11, 88
irrigation projects 11
knowledge market 34
land reforms 18
management of river systems 18–19
markets 86, 18th century 86
modernising tendencies 12
and Nanyang Zone 32
official knowledge system 34
officials and markets 34
organization of peasant labor 18
population and rice cultivation 85
proposed backwardness of 11, 12
quality of rice 110
reasons for decline 12
regional grain staples 84, 85
Republic 9, 26–27, 34–35, 95, 101–102, 103
rice and agriculture 99
rice as foundation of Chinese agriculture 98, 99
rice and national security 102–103
rice and taxation 21, 37, 38
rice imports 32, 99–100, 129
rice production 15, 33
rice shortages 111
rice trade imperial China 18, 86
river systems 18–19
role of the market 85
significance of rice in history 99
significance of rice 99
stagnation in 13, 68–69
staple foods 88, 277, 278
RH Tawney on 96
technological improvements in rice cultivation 99
trade with Europe 32
varieties of rice 86
see also Guomindang, Taiwan

China International Famine Relief Commission 106, 107
Chinese Civil War 109
Chinese Communist Party 18, 101, 109
  Nationalist government 105
Chinese dragon wheel 88
Chinese rice merchants 33, 49, 101, 112–113, 133
  Cantonese rice merchants 100, 113
  practical knowledge of 100
Cho Lon (Ho Chi Min City) 127, 128
cholera and Indo-Gangetic plain 262
  and malnutrition 267, 271
  morbidity 262–263
Cholon, Vietnam 111–112
Chongqing, Gomindang at 108
Christophers, S. R. 271
circumcision and African grade system 281
Civil War, US
  ending of chattel slavery 298
  impact on rice industry 298
  as US historical watershed 297
civilizations, non-Western 14
Clarkson, Thomas 141
"coarse food" (zaliang), 26, 49, 89, 90, 93
Coastal language speakers 179
  proto-Coastal speakers, geographical location 179
  language and location 139
Cochinchina 8, 31, 127
  Chinese monopoly in 112
  rice and European markets 127
Coclanis, Peter 8, 31, 126–127
Coelho, Francisco de Lemos 182–183, 184
Cold War 131
Cole, Arthur H. 296
College of Agriculture and Forestry, University of Nanking (Jinling daxue) 102, 106
College of Agriculture, National Central University in Nanjing (Guoli Zhongyang daxue), 106
College of Agriculture, University of the Philippines 109
colonialism
  colonial era and universals 9
  colonial policies towards agricultural modernization 336, 337
  colonial policy and attitudes 20
  colonial state and insurability of actor network 129
  colonialist attitudes 126
  and durability of tradition 129

colonialism (cont.)
  growth 1
  research 126
  rice and colonial development 15
Columbus, Christopher 6
commercial determinism 274
  change in inequality 274
commercial seed crops and non-standard
    growing environments 43
  cost of commercial varieties 44
Committee of Agriculture and Industry,
    Cochinchina 127
commodity production 20
  and global inequality 245–246
Comoro Islands 216
comparative modeling of paths of economic
    development and industrialization 323
Conakry 149, 160
Conneau, Theophilus 143, 146
consumer markets 2
consumers and economic growth 25
Cooper River 200, 201, 204
Cooper-Ashley-Wando (CAW) Basin 196
Cornell-Nanking Plant Improvement Project"/
    agricultural improvement program
    104, 106
Cornell-Nanking program 102
correlations, interpretation of 60–61
cosmopolitan breeding strategy 51, 52
  and local breeders 53
cotton 5, 6, 19
cotton farmers, Punjab 95
cotton, trade in 87
CPSP (*Caisse de Péréquation et de
    Stabilisation des Prix*) Senegal 242
creolization 192, 336–337
  and rice plantation 192
  see also anti-commodity
crop ideotype and "miracle varieties" 46
Cropping Systems Division, IRRI 47
CSA (*Commissariat a l'Aide Alimentaire*),
    Senegal 242
Cuba 337
Cullather, Nick 354
cultivars and biodiversity loss 126
  rise of 126–136
cultivation of commercial landscapes 246–250
Cultivation System, Java 10, 57, 68, 69
cultural diversity 48
cultural importance of food quality 49
Curry-Machado, Jonathan 337
Cwiertka, Katarzyna 22

Dailian 112, 114
Dala Modu 147
Davidson, Joanna 283
de Vries, Jan 13
dee-geo-woo-gen 132
  see also Taichung Native 1
Deering Company and Deering binder 308
Deheyong, rice firm 114
Deli Company (Deli Maatschappij) 346, 351
Deli research station for tobacco 344, 345
development, history of 54
Diola group, Upper Guinea 283
disease, nature of global distribution of 274
disi rice type 157, 159
do-fasla (double-cropping), Punjab 247
doi moi reforms Vietnam 121–122
dongchongmi 92
Douglas, Mary 37
Dove, Michael 351, 352
drought responses to 16
  West Africa 229–231
Dubose, Samuel 209
Dumont, Rene 130
dung, use of as fertilizer, India 259–262
Duras, Marguerite 128
Dutch East Indies 31, 32, 129
dwarfholdings, Java 65, 72
  defined 64
  and sugar 63

E'erda, Governor Guangdong 94
East Africa 213, 214, 215, 216, 219
  and Madagascar 217
  rice 217–219, 226–227
  trade with India 28, 217
East Asia 15
  and ideologies of Western supremacy 14
  involution debates 13–14
  see also individual states
East Asia-Atlantic comparison 15
East Asian debate 15
East Pakistan/Bangladesh 250
Edelson, S. Max 15, 16, 201
Ehret, Christopher 178, 224
Eltis, David 15, 24, 279, 292
Elvin, Mark 11, 12
environmental history 185, 186, 187
eruptive fevers, Bengal and Punjab 266
  impact on infants and children 266
escape agriculture 338
  and anti-commodities 338
Esudadu Jola 235–236

Esudadu, Senegal 232, 237
  rice deficit 237–238
Eurocentrism 14
Europe, and rice China trade creation of world market in rice 31–32
  research institutes 45
European imperialism 165, 185, 336
  European colonial expansion 7
Evelyn Rawski 96
Expansionism, southern 301–302
  rail network development 301
expert community 41–42

Fairlawn Plantation and Canal 210
famine 49
  famine relief programs and rice 30
FAO (Food and Agriculture Organization of the United Nations) 109
Farm Bureau, Illinois 315
Farmers' Cooperative Rice Milling Company 317
farming
  as combination of commodities and anti-commodities 354
  ecological and economic diversity 52
  farmers and rice breeding 51
  reasons for selection of varieties 8–9
  and rise of industrialization 38
farming systems research 50
Fatiya, Senegal 232, 235, 238, 244
  adjustment to drought 238
  gender cropping 235
  youth migration 243
Fengqiao, 93
Fengtairen, rice firm 114
fertilizers 68
  and agricultural development 42, 44, 71
  impact of 42
Fields-Black, Edda 1
Fishbrook Field 206
fonio 184
food and context 48
food grain production and hunger of food producers 245
  health experiences of 245
  links between environment and diseases 245
food security 277
food self-sufficiency 2
food studies 291, 321, food porn 291
Ford Foundation 46, 131
Ford, Timothy 204
Foshan 94

Forecariah 146
Foucault, Michel 278
Foyoz, Father Fernando de 289
Francisco de N. S. Dos Prazeres, Friar 289
Freetown, Sierra Leone 138, 142, 146, 147, 149
  civil war 149
  farming for 160
  and rice growing 142, 144
  Royal Navy patrol 146
  slave-based food supply 149
  white rice exports 142–143, 148
Friedman, David 332
Fujian 85, 87, 89, 91
  rice imports 97–98
  Fujian Guaongdong provinces 111
Fukien 123
fulcrum shovels, use of in Rio Nunez region 181
  use in Senegal 235
Fuller and Boivin, landbridge proposal of 216
Fuller and Qin 228
Fuller, W. H. 314
Futa Jalon 144, 145, 148, 160
  Mountains 169

Gambia River 167
  famine 1784
  and slavery 167
  slaves from 168
Ganga river 247, 256
Geertz, Clifford 10, 12, 13, 20, 40
  and agricultural income 67
  analysis of statistics 58–59
  analytical failures 72
  assumptions 20
  attitudes towards 20, 56
  influence of 11
  missing link between sugar and livestock 65
  non-correlation of statistics 58–59
  non-coverage of non-agricultural labour 62
  and population growth 69
  quantitative data 57–60
  and sugar agriculture 57
  statistics 58–59, 60
  sugar-rice link 69
  thesis 57, 60, 61, 66
  writing style 56
  see also agricultural involution
Gegnilliat, Jean-Francois 198
genotype x environment (GxE) interaction 139

Index

Georgia (USA) 3, 277
  antebellum economic decline of rice industry 298
  rice plantations in 279, 294
Germany, agricultural development in 42–43
  crops and regional ill-adaptation 43
Ghana, rice in 155, 157
Gibbs, Mathurin 204
Gilbert, Erik 186
Glanz 230
Glenn, Governor James 196
global distribution of hunger, models of 246
global history 3, 4
global South 41, 51, 53, 54
  Green Revolution in 45
global trade 5, 6
globalization, 19th century 297
glottochronology," 177–178
GMO rice *see* rice
Gold Blizzard" (*Jinfengxue*) rice 115
Golden Rice 9
Goldseed rice, Carolina 129
gotongroyong 18
Gourou, Pierre 130
governmentality, concept of 278
grain, trade in 86, 87
Grand Canal 88, 93
Grand Prairie region 314, 317
Granovetter, Mark 304
Grant, Governor 147
Granville Town 141
Great Depression 1930s 249
Great Divergence, Japan 319, 333
Great Leap Forward 90
Green Revolution 9, 26
  areas lying outside 8
  and Bengal and Punjab 250
  changing role 50
  China 11–12, 26–27
  controversy surrounding 47–48
  controversy over environmental impact 47–48
  criticism of 51
  critique 49–50, 51, 130, 131
  and development of rice variants 35, 46
  emphasizing quantity over quality 34, 46, 49
  establishment 132
  expense 48
  as an experiment 49
  flaws in policies 27
  frailties of Green Revolution 45–49
  and genetic analysis 218
  and global South 45, 54

  holistic approach 50, IR8-288-3 132
  irrigation schemes 39
  Java 56, 71
  limitations on knowledge 53
  Mekong Delta 16, 121, 125, 134
  nature of 38
  negative impact upon poverty 48
  1950s viewpoint 354
  reliance upon irrigation 48
  and rural poverty 48
  Sierra Leone 21, 151
  and smallholders 49–50, 51
  unsuitability of varieties 48
  Vietnam 134, 135
  West Africa 160
Grey, Colonial L. J. H., Commissioner and Superintendent of Delhi Division 254
Griliches, Zvi 315
Grist, D. H. 276
groundnut farming 17
  and government rice price change 241–242
  and Islam 234
  Senegal 232, 233–234, 237, 241
growth without development 3, 12
Guangdong 85, 88, 89, 91
  government 90
  rice trade 112
Guangdong Province 93
  poor quality of wheat 93–94
  types of rice 94, 97
  rice shortages 103
Guangdong Provincial Agriculture and Forestry Experiment Field 104
Guangxi 88, 94, 97, 105
  wild rice 106
Guangxi Provincial Agricultural Bureau 105
Guangzhou 86, 88, 97, 98, 114, 115, 123
Guerin Creek 202
Guinea Bissau 281, 282
  Balanta 140
  Black Rice thesis and 23–24
  rice in 155, 157
  rice production in 23, 24
  transferable riziculture skills 23
Guinea Coast 10, 27, 30
Guomindang regime, China 100, 101–102, 108, 109
  and Central Agricultural Experiment Institute 104

and China's food problem 116
and Guangdong's rice shortages 103
move from Nanjing 108

Hana barley 43
Hangzhou 86
Harlan, Jack 172
Hartlib, Samuel 16
Harwood, Jonathan, 38
Hatch Act, 1887 303
Havana Island 184
Hayami, Akira 13, 323
  see also industrious revolution
Hayami-Ruttan 300
Heitmann, John 313–314
Hennessey, Governor John Pope 148
Henry, Yves 130
Hewatt, Alexander 197
Hi-Bred Seed Company (later Pioneer), Iowa 315–316
high modernism, concept of 278
High Yielding Varieties 71
Highland language speakers 179, proto-Highlands 179
high-level equilibrium trap, concept of 12
hill societies, significance of 338
  relationship with lowland regions 338
Hispaniola 6
historical linguistics 172–181, 186, 187
  speech communities 174
  "Words-and Things" method of historical linguistics 174
  see also linguist historians
historiographies of rice, 2, 3
history of biological innovation in U.S. agriculture 315–316
  social historians 165–166
Ho Chi Minh 130
Ho Chi Min City 127
Ho, Ping-ti 85
Hong Kong 112
"Hong Kong residing buyers (zhougang maishou)." 113
Hong Kong rice masters 26
Hooghly-Damudar tract of central Bengal 259–260
Hope, W. E. 314
Huai River 86
Huang Huang Lee firm 111
Huang, Phiip 12
Hubei 85, 87, 93
Hue (Dai Viet) Court 123

Huizhou 88
Hunan 85, 87, 88, 93, 107, 108
Hushu Customs House 93
hybrid corn 315, 316
hydraulic empires and schemes 275, 276

immutable mobiles 9
Improvement of Chinese Agriculture (Zhongguo nongye zhi gaijin) 103
India 17
  Mughul 7
  British 3, 7, 32, 129, 164, 248
  1920s economy 270
  development of indica rice 214
  famine relief programs 30
  farmers and food 26
  and technological package-local variety debate 47
  varieties grown 46
Indian Ocean region 33, 163
  and rice 219, 224
  analysis of rice varieties 219–220
indica rice 132, 139, 214, 222, 227
Indochina 7
  French 9, 32, 34, 49, 111, 114, 125
  French absence of research stations 129
Indochina Wars 121
Indo-Gangetic plain 245, 246
  agricultural exports 249
  cholera 263
  development of 249–250
  ecology and agriculture 250
  gastrointestinal infections 262
  harvest and health 250–251
  socially acquired immunity 267
  see also Bengal, Punjab
Indonesia 15, 32, 275
  economic history 70
  indigenous movements 1920s 349
  living standards 70
Indus river 246
industrial capitalism, global networks of 1
  rise of 6
industrial rationality 9
industrial revolution, Western 334
industrialization and standardization 38
industrious revolution 3, 13, 64–65, 70
  and Japan 323–324
Inland Niger Delta 172
Inner and Outer South Carolina Coastal Plain 193

international development, visions or ideologies of 9
International Rice Research Institute (IRRI) 9, 35, 46, 48, 51, 52, 126
  actor-networks 137
  changing role 51
  development of IR8 132
  diversification 51, 136
  durability of rice 134
  founding 110
  rice breeders' doubts 47
  structural implementation issues of 134
  success of 133
  seed bank 219
  and Vietnam 131, 132, 134
  see also IR8
involution debate 10–11
Iowa 300, 302
IR-8 ("miracle rice" variety) 8, 37, 38, 39, 46, 47, 48, 49
  considered inferior 49
  development of 132
  Thailand 132
  Vietnam 126, 132, 133, 134
  vulnerability to pests 47
IR8–288–3 rice variety 132, 133
IR26 rice 134
IR30 rice 134
IR36 135, 136
Iraq 109
iron rice bowls 277
irrigation 276
  and inland rice cultivation 197
  and rice China 88
irrigation rights, Asia 18
irrigation strategies 2
Ishikawa curve 323
Ishikawa Shigeru 323
Ishmael Rashid 148
Islam and groundnuts 234
Islamic expansion and rice 217

Jagra, port of 184
Japan 2, 3, 7, 14, 17, 70, 96, 128, 132, 275, 278, Chapter 14
  association of rice and urban identity 322
  challenges to theses of Japan's development 319
  comparison with Europe 329
  cult of rice 18, 22
  development of part time farming 332–333
  diversification 325
  dynamic of extended-family organizations 327–328
  Emperor 22
  export of labor-intensive path of industrialization 333
  female employment 331, 332
  government food and agricultural policy 332
  growth of manufacturing sector 325–326
  growth of rural economy 328
  historical development of rice industry 321
  ideological status of farming 23
  importing Mekong Delta rice 129
  industrial development 319–320
  industrious revolution 3
  and industriousness 23
  industry and rural income 331
  institutional mechanisms in operation 327
  intensification of rice based farming 13
  Japanese models of rural societies 17–18
  Japanese models of society 17–18
  Japanese-style rice-based agriculture 327
  long term development 320
  Meiji government 8, 11, 13, 22, 54, 318, 329
  pattern of technical change 325
  political role of rice 22–23
  political role of rice 22
  post-WWII economic miracle 332, 334
  pre-industrial Japanese countryside and vectors for technical and economic change 327
  real and symbolic role 318
  research into Japanese economic history 323, 324–325
  as rice-centred civilization 22
  rice and development 310, 320
  rice and industrial development 334
  rice production 12–13, 15, 19, 21
  rice and taxation 22
  rice imports 33, 333
  rice labor intensity and rural households 323–326
  rice, development, and mechanisms of change 333–334
  role of rice 22–23
  rural economy 325–326
  rural households and industrial development 330–333
  rural households and markets 329
  rural-urban population movement 332
  significance of consuming rice 291, 321

significance of rice 318
as successful rice economy 19
symbolic status of rice 22, 23
taxation of rice 22
theory of Japaneseness 21–22
wage work 328
Japanese rice merchants 129
Japanese rice (Japonica rice) 91, 139, 143
in Africa 220, 222, 227
development of 214
Sierra Leone 139, 154, 155
Java 3, 12, 127, 349–350, 352
agricultural involution 20, 68
capital investment 67
Cultivation System 10, 58, 68
economic growth 71
farmers 344, 345
fertilizer use 68
Geertz and 10, 20, 56
Java Residencies 61
mechanization 67
population growth 69–71
regencies 17
rice and sugar production 20, 57, 59
rice imports 33
rice production, 59, 126
sugar production 59
javanica 214
Jenne-jeno 172
Jennings, Peter 132
Jiangnan 91, 92
Jiangsu 85, 87, 88
Province 90
Jiangxi 85, 87, 88, 90, 93, 108
jing (geng) rice 91–92, 93, 96, 97
supply of 92
Jipalom, Kajamutay, Senegal 232
agriculture 234–235
drought 237
youth migration 243
Jola villages, Casamance region, Chapter 10, 16–17, 140
change in socioeconomic activities 229
drought 17
factors affecting production 239–244
farming in 21
flight of youth to the cities 238, 243–244
gender and tasks 23, 235
gender division and productivity 244
gender separation of labour 232–233
general rice economy characteristics 242–243

pre-drought surplus 236
and rice 231–232
rice growing 183, 232–234
sugar estates 57
trade off between rice production and commercial crop production 240–241
transition from net production to net purchasers of rice 229
variable rainfall 243
women and ritual power 233
workforce distribution 62
Jolof Confederation 171
Jolof kingdoms 182
Julião (slave, Amazonia) 288
June Twenty-third Street of Guangzhou 115

Kajamutay, Senegal 232, 233, 234, 237, 241
kajandu (fulcrum-shovel) 235, 239
Kalunay, Senegal 232, 237
changing gender roles 239
drought in 237, 238–239
Kanter, Dr. Dwight W. 134
Kaplan (town) Vermilion Parish, Louisiana 313
Kaplan, Abrom 313, 314
Kedah 7
Khan, Muhammad Hayat (Judicial Assistant Commissioner of Gurdaspur) 257
King George's War 191
Kloppenburg, Jr., Jack Ralph 316
Knapp, Seaman A. 302, 303, 304, 305, 306
introduction of rice varieties 316
and rice growing 306, 307
statistics on wages 312
Knight, Frederick C 279
knowledge transfers 118
Korea 8
Kukuna (town) 147, 148, 159
Kuomintang (KMT) 26, 27

Lago, Antonio Pereira do 289–290
Lake Charles in Calcasieu Parish [County], 305
agricultural modernization 313
becomes predominant US rice producer 308–310
methods of production 310
rice yield 311
water control and agricultural innovation 306–307
Lake Tai 91
Lambert and 'culture of migration' 243

Laminayah 148, 149, 153
lançados (Portuguese settlers) 224
Land to the Tiller reform, Vietnam 125
Landbouwatlas van Java en Madoera
  (Agricultural Atlas of Java and Madura
  60, 81
landlordism 19
language, nature of 174
  core vocabulary 175
  "cultural" vocabulary, 176–177
  developments in 174
  dialects 174–175
  genetically related language 175
  linguistic subgroups 176
  loanwords 177
  transformation 175–176
  word creation 177
Lansing, Steven 18
Latham, A. J. H. 29
Latour, Bruno 9, 300
Latourian concept of assemblages 5, 39, 120
  see also under rice
Law, John 118
League of Nations 102, 150, 151
Leal, Antonio Henriques 288
Leizhou Peninsula 90
LeNoble, Henry 201
Leonora (slave, Amazonia) 289
Levert, J. H. 348
Lewis, Michael 322
Limba 149, 153
linguist historians 173, 174, 175, 176, 177
Littlefield, Daniel C. 279
livestock 65–66, 81–83
  correlation between livestock and rice
  production 65–66, 77
LL62 rice 291
local versus cosmopolitan crops 42–45
  ecological aspects 44
  local strategies 44–45
  value of local crops 44
local-global articulations 4
Long Xuyen, rice station near 133
long-handled hoe (ebarai) 235
Longley, Catherine 153–154
Los Banos 135
Louisiana 9
  Cajun country 301, 304
  Cajun farmers 305
  development of rice industry 298–300
  immigration 304
  irrigation technology 299

official promotion of enterprise 301
prairie agriculture 305
and railroads 301, 303–304, 305
rice in 295
suitability of soil for rice growing 306
Love, Harris H. (Harry Houser)
  104, 106
Lovink, Herman 342
Lower Casamance, Senegal 229
  decline in productivity in 240
  drought in 230
Lower Yangzi River 19, 20, 32, 85
Ludlum, Thomas 142, 161
Lulofs, C. (Sumatra civil servant) 343
Lyttleton, Captain William 167, 168

Maat * 20
  see also anti-commodity
Macau 96
Macaulay, Zachary 142, 143, 147, 160
Madagascar 216–217, 219, 227
  crop diffusion scenario 217
  and term for rice 227
Madura 79
Magalhaens, D. J. G. de 289
Magbeti, (town) 147
main food (*zhuliang*) 26, 89
maize 66, 71, 83, 276, Senegal 238
Malacca 96
malaria (*Plasmodium falciparum* and *P. vivax*)
  164, 165, 251, 271
  human genetic resistance 265
  impact of flooding 255
  India 207
  Indonesia 70
  inland planters and control of water
  208–209
  and malnutrition 267
  and monsoon 252
  private canals, impact of 209–210
  see also Bengal and Punjab
Malaya/Malaysia 18, 32, 339
Mali Empire 171
Malinke or Manding people, Senegal 234
Malleret, Louis 122
malnutrition impact of on illness 267
  and epidemics 271
Manchukuo 102
Manchuria, Japanese invasion of 102
Mande language group, Upper Guinea
  169, 171
  classification and evolution 169–170

Index

Mandingo slave rebellion, Sierra Leone
150–151
Mandingo traders 183–184
mangrove
  compared to wet rice farming 183
  farming by Balanta 281, 283
  mangrove rice farming 23, 124, 140–141,
    149–150, 151, 171
  red mangrove 179
  resistance to growing alternative crops 283
  Senegal 236
  tidal systems rice farming 213
  white mangrove 179
Manila 96
manioc 231
Manjagar, Kingdom of 183
Maranhão, Amazonia 285–289
  work as deskilled and decultured 285
Marçal, (Mandinka slave, Amazonia) 288
marigot 234, 235, 236, 238
maroons 140, 145, 153, 338
Marxist materialism 17
  Marxist literature 62
master-hand (gaoshou or nengshou)., Hong
  Kong 113
materiality, significance of 338
Matthews, John 144, 145, 146
Mauritius 336
Maxwell, Governor 146
  slave trade interests 146–147
McClung, Anna 218
Meggett loam 196, 197
Meiji Land Tax Reform of 1872 328, 330, 332
Meji government *see under* Japan
Mekong Delta 5, 16, 39, 97, 118, 119, 136
  Americans in 131, 132
  blurred boundaries between areas 125
  Chinese influx 123
  choice of rice varieties 123
  colonial era plantations 2, 125
  concern about loss of biodiversity 137
  flooding 121
  French attempts to improve rice 126
  hydro-ecological zones 119, 120
  impact of mechanization 137
  impact of elevation 122
  impact of geological depression
    123, 125
  impact of industrialization 122
  loss of biodiversity 137
  loss of knowledge 137
  material semiotics perspective 1212

as net importer of rice 134
plant breeding operation 134
rising sea levels 136
settlement patterns 122
Viet-Khmer relations 124
Vietnamese influx 123
seed repopulation of 131
terrain topography and hydrology 16
Mekong River and hydroelectric
  dams 136
  fish stocks 136–137
Melo e Póvoas, Governor Joaquim de 285
merchant cultures 2
Merrins, H. Roy 207, 208
Mexican Agricultural Program 46
Mid-Western model of rice farming 9
Midwest, US, faith communities and
  migration south 303
  indigenous knowledge system and
    agriculture 308
  migration to Southwest 304, 305–306
  and rice 306
  and rice revolution network 300–301
  transfer of wheat producing
    technology 306
miet vuon (garden strips), Vietnam 122, 123,
  125, 126, 133
millet 51, 85, 167, 184, 213, 224
  China 84, 88, 89, 90
  Country Corn 167–168
  pearl millet 213, 216
  Jola village 231
  Senegal 234, 237, 238, 239
  Upper Guinea 182
Ming government 84, 96
Ministry of Agricultural and Mining,
  China 104
miracles of modernization 354
Mississippi River 298, 299
  rice growers' competitive advantage over
    South Atlantic plantations 299
  see also Louisiana
modernity, emergence of 14
Mogbuama, Sierra Leone, analysis of rice
  varieties 157
Mohr, E. C. J. 348
molecular analysis of rice 21
money-merchants and moneylenders, Bengal
  and Punjab 268, 273
Mongol invasion of China 86
monsoon 247
  and malaria 252

morbidity and mortality rates, means of
    tackling 246
  patterns of morbidity 274
Morgan 228
Morgan, Philip 279, 280, 292
Moria, Sierra Leone 146, 148, 152, 153, 160
  British involvement 147
  formation 144
  slaves 144, 145
Moriba of Port Loko 147
Morris John 314
Mortgage Lifter 225
Mouride brotherhood, Sengal 234
Mulder. J. Sibinga 347–348, 349, 350, 352
multinationals, power of 53
My Tho 133, 134, 135

N'contu rice 282
Nagasaki 96
Nanjing 91
Nanyang 26, 32, 33
Nastacio (slave, Amazonia) 288
Nasutu, Governor-general 90
National Economic Committee (*Quanguo jingji weiyuanhui*) 102, 106
national identity and rice 2
National Liberation Front, Vietnam 124, 128, 132
Nationalist Government, China 101
Native Americans 16, 95
Navigation Acts (UK) and rice 191
Nayar, NM 213–214
near-universal" varieties 46–47, 52
Needham, Joseph 11
Nerica rice 159
Netherlands Indies 335
Netherlands, The 335
  and Sumatra 339
  see also Sumatra
New Green Revolution 38
new plant types, limitations on 52
New Treatise on Guangdong (*Guangdong xinyu*) 93
Newington Plantation, South Carolina 198
Nguyen Huu Canh 122–123
Nguyen Van Huyen 130
nhaye grades Blanta 282
Nicholson Creek 204–206, 207
Niger delta, and origins of African rice 213, 215
Norris, John 198
North American Land and Timber Company, Ltd., 301, 302, 305
Nouvelle Politique Agricole (NPA) 242

oats 88, 89
Oc Eo. canal nexus 122
  archaeological excavations 124
Ohnuki-Tierney, Emiko 22, 318
Old Southwest (Texas and Arkansas):
  labor inputs early 20th century 312
  Midwest farmers and rice industry 315
  post World War I entrepreneurship 312–313
  rice industry in 278, 295, 296, 301
Olmstead, Alan L. and Paul W Rhode. 315, 316
ONCAD, Senegal 241, 242
Oracao, Island of 184
Oriental despotism, concept of 11
Oryza species:
  O. barthii 172, 213
  O. glaberrimas see African rice
  O. officinalis, 137
  O. rufipogons 121, 124, 125, 137
  O. sativa see Asian rice
  distinction between *O. glaberrimas* and *O. satavia* 213–214
Ottolander, T. 348
Oussouye, Senegal 230, 231

Pan Siju, Fujian Governor 89
Panajachel, Guatemala 95
Pandit Devi Chand, Municipal Committee Vice-Chairman, Jullundur district, central Punjab in 260
Paris, Pierre 122
"participatory plant breeding" (PPB) 51, 52
Pasuruan 61, 73, 75
Pavie, Auguste 127
Pax Nederlandica 69
Pearl River Delta 19, 93, 94, 98
peasant agency and choices 20
  and commercially competitive production 2017
  peasant agriculture 20, 53
peasant labor, organization of 18
Pekalongan 78
Pemba 216
Penholoway, Talbot, Pamlico, and Princess Anne Terraces 200, 201
Peoples Council (Volksraad), Sumatra 349, 350
peta (rice type, Philippines) 132
Petkuser rye 43
phantom rice 125
Philippines 32, 131

and IR-8 rice 47, 126, 132
rice imports 32
Phnom Penh (Cambodia) 123
PIDAC (Projet Intégré pour le Développement Agricole de la Casamance) Senegal 237, 238–239, 242
  encouraging market gardening 239
"Plan for National Rice Self-Sufficiency (*quanguo daomi jigei jihua*)" 105, 108
"Plan for National Wheat Self-Sufficiency (*quanguo xiaomai jigei jihua*)" 105
plant breeders
  being out of touch with needs and diversity 48
  broadening scope of 51
  cosmopolitan strategy 42, 44, 48
  and the global South 53
  role of 41
  preference for local verities 44
  quasi-deductive approach 52–53
  see also universal varieties
plant breeding stations, development of 45, 53
plantain 215
plantation systems 7, 280
planters and slaves' resistance 280
plasticity 155
Pomeranz, Kenneth 318, 326
poor, fate of 25, and sweet potatoes 89
Pooshee Plantation 200, 201, 202
  slaves at 201
porcelain 5, 6, 96
Portuguese trade 96, 224
  and introduction of Asian rice 225
  rice and Cape Verde islands 224, 225
Posner, JL 231, 237
postindependence development programs 1
Post-War World Food and Agriculture Conference 109
power and control, basis of 277
Priangan 79
Principle of People's Livelihood, China 102
Probolinggo 61, 73, 75
proto-industrialization, Japan 326
Providence rice 306, 307
Provincial Rice Improvement Committee, Hunan province China 107
public health studies and interventions, framing of 246
Punjab 7, 25, 94, 163, 164, 165, 246, 247
  1908 Malaria Epidemic 253
  agricultural practice 257–258
  anti-malaria mutation 265–266

British rule 248, 269
canal system 250
cash crops and health 257
changing agricultural crops 247–248
cholera 263
crops grown 250–251, 252
development and impact on health 250
development of jhils, 251
flooding 251–252
growing inequality 265–273
health environment 250
health of cultivars 245
impact of high grain prices 269–270
incidence of bubonic plague 264
interwar decline in mortality rates 273
livestock, human refuse and health 259
malaria 252–253, 271
malnutrition and epidemics 271–273
other infections 264–265
patterns of morbidity 274
peasants, land settlements and alienation 269–270
prevention of malaria 251
relationship between malaria and intensity of cultivation 252
rulers of 247
seasonal hunger 270–271
situation in 1920s 270
socially-acquired immunity 267
technology 247
use of dung 259, 261
waterlogging as an issue 252–254
wheat cultivation 264–265
Pyne, Stephen 198

Qian Tianhao 104, 107
Qing dynasty 104, 123, 127
Qingdao 112, 114
Qu Dajun 93
Quanzhou 86
quididê dike, Balanta 281

racism, intellectual 14
Rajchman, Dr. Ludwig 102
Ravenel, Daniel 209
Ravenel, René Lewis 201
Ravenel, Susanne 201
rebel grasses, Vietnam 125
Rechengde, rice firm 114
Red River Delta, 130
refuse, use of, and disease 261
  and drinking water 261–262

regimes of subordination 14
Rembang 75, 79
reservoir-irrigated rice cultivation 189
Residencies, Java and sugar cane 61
  analysing data of 72
Revolutionary War 210–211
Rhizophora racemosa 179
Ricci, Matteo 85
rice 37, 275
  absence of archaeological evidence 187
  and actor-network theory 16
  adaptations to local environment, in Africa chapter 6
  and agricultural morbidity 25
  and Atlantic system 31
  as an African slave plantation crop 144–147
  as anti-commodity 353, 354
  as both commodity and anti-commodity 337, 338
  assemblages 5, 118, 119, 121, 131
  association with power and control 276
  botanical-social history of rice 40
  capacity to hybridize 119
  and capitalism 2, 3
  classification of rice 38
  commitment to rice 19, 21–28
  as a commodity 21, 29–30
  comparative history as component of diet 276
  comparative yields compared to other grains 323
  consumption of 29
  creation of global market 97, 98, 99, 277, 312
  cultivars 118, 119
  deepwater 123, 124
  demand for rice 31
  development of modern rice 9
  differences between West African and East African rice 219
  double-cropping 39, 85, 97
  ecological niches 8
  and economic development 2, 7
  and environment 2, 163
  European market 31
  and exercise of power 276
  factors behind spread 228
  floating 39, 123, 124, 125, 172
  and food self sufficiency 34
  French colonial era research 130
  gender and rice production 23
  genetic mapping of 21
  global rice 5–9
  global analysis of rice growing 163
  global and local attributes 5
  global rice trade 128
  GMO rice 291
  grain-centric view of rice 137
  hybrid rice systems 16
  high yield rice development 133, 315
  histories of rice 1, 3, 4, 5, 9, 118, 229, chapter 13
  holistic approach to grain cultivation 101
  ideology of rice breeding 2
  impact of labor input 323, impact of environment 164
  impact of rice and the industrial revolution on economic development 323
  and industrial revolution 13
  and innovation in science 119
  as influencing humans 136
  interbreeding of types 27–28
  interrelationship between literature on 166
  interrelationship between rice populations 118
  local production and international trade 353
  and involution 14
  landraces 37, 118, 119, 121, 123, 125, 126, 129, 131, 137, 218, 219
  longstem 123
  managing sustained production 120
  mapping of rice genome 121, 135, 136
  mass and niche markets 30
  means and mode of production 24
  means of production and mode of production 24
  mid-Western model of rice farming 9
  "miracle rices" *see* IR-8
  myth of rice 22
  new varieties 136
  New World rice systems 10
  19th century market transition from Western rice to Asian rice 297
  potential problems with genetic data 222–223
  presence in North Africa and Mediterranean 215
  purity of 39
  integrated world rice market 2, 33–34
  policy of the local versus policy of the universal 39
  reasons for eating rice 86
  reconceptualizing significance of 5

red rice 138, 141, 142, 143, 144, 146, 147, 148, 161
relationship between regional rices 219
rice-based societies and attitudes to emergence of modernity 13
rice breeders 29, 47, 52
rice cultivation and generating growth 324
rice cultivation as skill-orientated agricultural system 12–13, 19, 100
rice economies 19, rice ecosystems 119
rice farming East Asia 14
rice growing and personhood 23, 24
rice, markets and power 276
"rice is nice" perception 21
rice quality and consumers 116
rice, researchers and bio-prospecting 137
rice-sugar relationship 58–59
and robbery 339–340
and role of supply and demand 85–86
scientific seed breeding 9
Senegal rice production 234–239
significance in Chinese history 99
significance of as rice 28–30
and slavery 17
small scale farming, key aspects of 19
and society 15–21
status of 21
and sugar cane 62, 63
tensions between various interests 18
transfer over sea rather than land routes 227
transgenic rice 121
in 20th century 121
types of 27–28
universal varieties 40
using variability of 37
varieties as assemblages 136
varieties of 8, 16
varieties of rice 46, 58–59
West Africa 140–141
wet rice fields 22, 56, 183
wider context of rice 118
wild rice 105–106, 121
wonder seeds 129
as world cereal 119
and world economy 2
yields early 20th century China 84–85, see also agricultural involution, Black Rice, Green Revolution, individual countries
Rice Association of America 317
rice economies and the West 320
historical trajectory of rice based economies 10
rice farming systems, varieties of 163
Rice Journal and Gulf Farmer 316
rice plantations and response and interaction 192
and creolization 16, 192
rice revolution, US Midwest 300, 307, 314
innovation and research 316–317
irrigation systems 307–308
yields 311
Rice Riots 322
rice-based agriculture and technical and economic change 327–330
Richardson, David 279, 293
Ricketts, Major Henry 147
Rio Nunez region, 175, 178–179, 180
cultural vocabulary of inhabitants 180–181
Portuguese in 181
rice growing technology 181
Riopongeos area 145
Roche family, South Carolina 204
Roche, Patrick 206
Rockefeller Foundation 46, 131
Rodney, Walter 169
Rokupr Rice Research Station 151
roofbouw, (robbery cultivation) 340, 344, 352
Rosengarten, Theodore 198
Rosomoff, Richard 225
rubber 20
rural poverty 48
Ryuku Islands 33

Sacramento Valley of California, stubble burning in 291
Saigon 122, 123, 127, 128, 132, 134
salt production and trade 171
Sambujat, Senegal 230, 238
aquatic rice production 236
and drought 237
Esudadu Jola in 235–236
non-gendered agriculture 236
ritual power of women 233
social division of labor 238
system of tidal control 236
youth migration 244
sanganyaa rice 159
Sansom, Robert 133
Sao Tome 224
Savannah River 196

sawah, Java, 56, 58
  and dwarfholdings 63
  rice production 60
  and sugar cane production 61, 62
Schneider, Jürg 345
Schoenbrun, David 178
Schultz, Theodore 95
scientific analysis and global history 186
scientific and industrial revolutions 11
Scott, James C. 41, 278, 338, 339
secret abacus" (midi suanpan). China 113, 114
Selatdjaran scheme 348–349, 352, 353
Selatdjaran, near Palembang 347
Selatdjaran, Sumatra 348
Senegal 3, 9, 163, Chapter 10
  establishment of official organizations 242
  impact of drought in 236–239
  official ideology 240
  perceived administrative inefficiencies 240
  period of regulatory uncertainty and impact upon agricultural economy 242
  post independent state and interventionist agricultural policies 241
  rice growing in 139
  rice growing region 16
  state and drought 240
Senegambia subregion 168, 171, 188, 227
Shandong 114, 115
Shanghai market 98
Sharp, Granville 141
Shen Chiran 92
Shen Zonghan, Dr 105, 106–107, 109
  post war career 109–110
Shinriki rice, Japan 50
Siam (Thailand) 7, 8, 15, 31, 32, 111
  export trade 32, 33, 34, 98, 99
Sierra Leone 9, 21, 40
  abolitionist settlers in 138
  African red rice 138, 143, 144
  agri-business 152
  Anglo-French colonial boundary division 149
  farmer created rice varieties, analysis of 154–157
  formation of Colony and Protectorate of Sierra Leone 150
  Green Revolution 150–151
  introduction of Carolina rice 138, 140, 155
  japonica rices in 139, 140, 155–157
  League of Nations interest in 150
  modernizing agriculture 151–152
  post-slavery system 142
  seed merchants 160–161
  settlement for freed slaves 141
  slave based food systems 19th century 149–151
  slavery, emancipation and rice genetics 152
  trade patterns 146
  underclass farmers and innovation 159
  urban food requirements 151, 152
  use of rice varieties 153
  see also mangrove
Silk Sprout (Simiao) rice 115
silk, trade in 87, 88, 96
Silva, Antonio da (planter) 288
silver China 96, Japan 96, New World 96, 97
Silvestre (Bambara, slave) 289
Sino-Japanese War (1937–1945) 108, 116
slavery
slave trade 7
  Amazonia 284, 285–289
  Atlantic slave trade 30, 97, 138, 167, 169
  farm slavery 147
  French and abolition 150, 151
  impact on Africa 27
  indigenous African 144–146
  injuries to Amazonia slaves 287–289
  and rice 7, 10, 17
  and technology transfer 10
  United States 14, 24, 50, 280
  US Civil War and emancipation 298
smallholders 64–65, 72
  agricultural intensification 72
  and control of rice breeding 51
  and technology 49, 50
  changing analysis of 354
  Europe 45
  farming strategies 20
  innovative capacity of 50
  intensification and industrious revolution 63–64
  subsistence-orientated 62
  Sumatra 20, 351–353
  trajectories of crop production 229
  Vietnam 126
smallpox 70, 191, 264, 266
Smith, Adam 71
Smith, Thomas C. 327
Smithian growth 71, 72
Smits, M. B. (Sumatra civil servant) 343, 344, 348, 350, 352, 353
Société des Études Indochinoises 122

Society for Study of Colonial Issues, Netherlands 343
soil composition 197
SONACOS (*Société Nationale de Commercialisation des Oléagineux du Sénégal*) 242
Song Dynasty 11, 86, 96
sorghum 84, 213, 216, 224
  Senegal 234, 237, 238
  US guinea corn 292
South Atlantic coast rice rice industry 295, 296
  and cotton industry 298
  decline narrative 297
  and development of Asian rice industry 298
  exports 296
  impact of Civil War 296
  irrigation technology 299
  methods of rice technology 310
  postbellum rice production 298
  pre-Civil War problems 297
  reasons for demise 296–297
  requirements for production 310
  shift of rice industry to Old Southwest 312
  term market considerations 296
South Carolina 7, 15, 16, 164, 165, 277, 280, 294
  adaptation of rice cultivation 190
  antebellum economic decline of rice industry 298
  canals and wasteway drains 203
  colonial perceptions of land use 207
  creolization of African and European knowledge 191, 192
  development of rice agriculture 193
  droughts 200
  exports of rice 191–192
  flexibility in controlling water 203–204
  forest clearance 198
  impact of microenvironments 204
  inland cultivation 189, 190, 191
  inland cultivation and slave labor systems 190, 197
  inland rice cultivation 193, 195, 197
  introduction of rice 190
  and knowledge systems 10, 291
  Lowcountry cultivators 16, 190, 191
  Lowcountry plantation enterprise and Atlantic markets 206
  Lowcountry rice planters and wastewater removal 203
  Lowcountry slaves 199–200
  Lowcountry topography 192, 193
  mechanical water maintenance and control 199
  mid 18th century expansion 203
  mortality rates 207–208
  need for irrigation 197
  problems with inland cultivation 196
  reversion of the land 189
  rice as foundation of colonial economy 189
  rice plantations 279, 280
  rice yields, early 20th century 311
  rise of planters 16, 192, 194–196
  significance of topography 198
  slave trade 190, 191
  slavery and landscape restructuring 198–199
  slavery and wealth 298
  source of slaves 164, 225
  species grown 292
  swamp clearance and slavery 198
  tidal rice irrigation cultivation 189, 197
  topography and rice growing farming 200–210
  use of freshwater wetlands 192
South Carolina Coastal Plain 190
South China Sea rice trade 100, 110–112
  trade 123
South Vietnam 110, US and 132
Southeast Asia rice histories 17
  colonial authorities in 110–111
  rice trade 110, 112, 126–127
southern and northern trade (*Nanbei hang*), China 112, 113, 114
Southern Pacific Railroad 301
Southwest Immigration Company 301
Spain, trade from 96
Spicer, J. M. 314
Squarehead wheat 43
Sri Lanka civil war 149
St. Johns River region Florida 294
St. Julian, Peter 200–201
state commodification of rice 347
static expansion concept 67
Stoler, Ann 342
Stono Rebellion 191
Storey, Bill 336
Street of Nanbei hang. 112–113
strength of weak ties" formulation, 304
Stuttgart, Arkansas County, Arkansas 313, 314, 317
subak (Bali) 18
sugar 19, 57, 59, 61
  and population 71
  and rice production 58, 62–63, 80

sugar cane sector Mauritius 336–337
Sui-Wai Cheung 48
Sumatra, rice growing in 20, 278, Chapter 15
   1937 riots 337
   colonial government 20, 353–354
   colonial histories 352
   colonizers' view of commodity
     production 336
   Dutch statistical analysis of trade early 20th
     century 342
   East Asian markets 335
   establishment of colonial rule 339
   impact of WWI on international rice trade
     335, 342
   import of Javanese farmers 345
   local agricultural practices and
     accommodating change 351
   local crop emphasis 343
   negative portrayal of culture and agriculture
     339, 340
   plantation agriculture 314, 340, 342
   post WWI rice market 350
   recruitment of overseas workers 341–342
   rice as an anti-commodity 336, 352, 353
   rice as commodity 351–353
   rice cultivation 340
   rice production and marketing issues 336
   rice trade with 340
   Sumatran farmers' views of rice production
     336, 353
   upland or dry rice 276, 343, 345
   wetland rice 345
   WWI and rice imports 345–346
Sumbuya 145, 147
Sun Yat-sen 101, 102, 103, 105
sustainability and participation 51
sustainable cultivation practices 52
Susu language 181
Suzhou 86, 87
Swahili, linguistic influences on 217
   and rice 227
Swawah 58
sweet potatoes 88, 89–90, 91
   attitudes towards 89
swidden agriculture, Sumatra 338, 340,
   344, 352
   and shift to static cultivation 339

tabancas, villages, Balanta 281
Taichung Native 1 (*deegeo-woo-gen*)
   35, 132
Taichung Research Station 35

Taihexing, rice firm 114
Taiwan 8, 86, 108, 109, 128, 132
   Nationalist government 35
Tamilnad 228
Tân Nông [TN, New Agriculture] number 73
   rice 134
Tan Qian 84–85
Tan Tsu Huang 111
Tang Youheng 104
Tanggerang rice of Java 129, 130
Tanimoto, Masayuki 331
Tanzania 228
taro 215, 216
taste and rice 26, 27, 29, 47, 48, 49, 51, 115,
   120–121, 130, 322
   consumer 40, 97, 118
Tawney, Richard Henry 96
tea, trade in 19, 87, 96
technological determinism 116
"technological package" 47
   limitations of technology 55
technology networks, role of, in the innovation
   process 300
Temudo, Marina 283
Terry, George D. 207, 208
Tet Offensive 132
Texas Star 225
Thailand 132
Thompson, Alexander 302, 305
Thomson, Rev. William Cooper 148, 152–159
Three Principles of People, The 101
Tianjin 112, 114, 115
tobacco cultivation Sumatra 340, 341, 344,
   345, 346
Togo 139
Tokugawa period, Japan 321, 322, 324, 325
   agriculture and accommodating industrial
     labor 330
   autonomy of village communities 329
   and commercializing economy 326, 330
   impact of rising labor costs 327
   interaction with Western industrial powers
     19th century 330
   land ownership 328
   rural economy during period 326, 330–331
Tonkin, China 112
Tonko Limba country 148
traditional, non-capitalist social institutions 10
TRJ (Tropical japonica) 220, 224
   relationship between TRJ rice and
     slavery 225
   species involved 225

split between TRJ groups 224-225
spread across Atlantic world 224-, 225
spread of 226
and Upper Guinea 226

U.S. Agency for International Development 133, 134
UK Parliament and the Slave Trade 167
United Kingdom
  Bengal and rice 31
  and Carolina rice 31
  colonies and rice 31
  industrial revolution in 13
  and Sumatra 339
United States 3
  abolitionist movement 138, 141-143
  American South and rice 15, 163
  Bonanza farmers and agronomists 8
  California and rice 8
  Carolina rice 28, 30, 31, 97, 161
  Carolinas 15, 16, 24, 25, 30, 31-32
  Cultural meaning of work in the Americas 284-290
  cultivation system 292
  expansionism and southern history 301-302
  export programs 128
  gender inequality in rice plantations 284
  geographical distribution of rice 293, 295
  history of rice industry in US Chapter 13
  influence of Africa on 30
  Louisiana and rice 8, 293
  nature of plantation system 10, 293
  origins of rice growing in US 292
  relationship with Africa 14
  rice in 7, 8, 275
  and rice in Asia 32
  rice industry late 19th century 300
  rice system 24
  shift from net export to net import of rice 299-300
  slaves and rice plantations 14, 284
  slaves, sale of transported 168
  spatial geography of rice production 293
  use of slave labour 293
  white planter input 292
  see also Georgia, Old Southwest, slavery, South Atlantic, South Carolina
"universal varieties" (Universalsorten) 37, 39, 40, 43, 45-49, 53
  criticism of 44
  local strategy 53

and Black Rice thesis 291, 292
see also Black Rice
University of Nanking (Jinling daxue), 106
Upper Branch (Tien Giang) Mekong 123
Upper Great Plains, wheat production in 308
Upper Guinea 279
  Upper Guineans and American rice cultivation as deculturing 280
  and hard work 280
  cultural meaning of work in Upper Guinea 280
Upper Guinea Coast 163, 168-187
  changing rice exports 183
  extent of rice production 168
  geography 169-171
  issue of uniform commitment to rice 185
  language groups 169, 173
  level of commitment to rice production 184
  linguistic sources and regional history of rice 172
  location of rice fields 165
  need for diversification 187-188
  and origins of African rice 213
  rates of illness in 165
  rice as export commodity 97
  rice cultivation 172, 225
  rice varieties 226
  sustenance system 283-284
  trade in grains 182
  trade in iron and slaves 281
  travellers' accounts of 182-185
  and TRJ rice 226
Upper Guinean knowledge system 284, 290
USDA 219, 220
USDA database 218, 223
USDA's Soil Tilth Laboratory 317
USDA-ARS Dale Bumpers National Rice Research Center, Stuttgart, Arkansas 218

van der Stok, J. E. 348
van Linschoten, John Huyghen 6, 248
Vansina, Jan 178
Vasconcellos, Felippe de Barros 288, 289
Vieira, Leonel Fernandes 288
Vietnam 15, 32, 98, 122
  Chinese immigration 127
  Chinese merchants 127, 128
  colonial period 128
  colonial rule 128, 129
  disappearance of varieties of rice 126
  durability of tradition 129
  entrepreneurs 133

Vietnam (cont.)
  ethnic division in rice preparation industry 127, 128, 129–130
  failure of colonial state to improve rice 129, 130
  French importation of Javanese labor 129
  Green Revolution 134
  historical expansion 97
  hybridizing of rice varieties 129
  IRRI 131, 133
  markets 129
  Republic of 126, 128
  reunification 121
  rice cultivation in 97, 121
  as a rice exporter 135
  Socialist Republic of 126
  studies of rice 130, 131
  US and rice distribution 132
  US presence in 131
  French attitudes towards rice production 127
Vietnam War 110, 121, 125
  and agriculture 133
Vink, G.J. 67
Vlach, John-Michael 208
von Verschuer Charlotte 22

Wallace, Henry 315
Walshaw, Sarah 216
Wando River 200, 201, 207
"Wanglee" rice firm 111
war and agricultural science, China 108–110
Watkins, Jabez B. 302, 304, 305, 307, 314
Weihai 112, 114
West Africa 31, 163, 164, 277–278
  1960s drought and food shortages 229–232
  and anti-commodities 21
  anti-malaria mutations 265
  Asian rice in 217
  Carolina rice 161
  comparative method of historical linguistics 172–173
  dryland system 141
  Europeans, malaria and quinine 185–186
  French abolition of slavery 150, 151
  and Green Revolution 160
  impact of knowledge systems on American rice history 292
  japonica rice 161
  maritime trade and rice 97
  peasants and rice development 160, 161–162
  power and government 277–278

red and white rice 138–139, 141
red and white rice 138–139
rice cultivation 140
rice culture 100
rice farmers and environmental history 185–187
rice varieties 139, 140
slave trade 7, 10, 27, 50, 141
West Africa, rice and the Atlantic 223–226
West African entrepreneurship 186
West African gold trade 171
West African knowledge system 2, 10, 15, 30, 31, 186, 187, 225, 291
  see also Black Rice debate, mangrove
West Bonham Street, Hong Kong 112–113
West River, China, 86, 88, 93, 94
Western Jumna canal 253, 254
wheat 84, 85, 88, 89, 276, 277
  Guangdong Province 93–94
  China 103
wheat cultivating machinery, adaptation to rice 308, 310–311
Wilberforce, William 141
Wilson, James ("Tama Jim") 303
Windsor Plantation, South Carolina 204, 206
Winterbottom, Thomas 144, 145
Wittfogel, Karl 11
Wolof ethnic group, Senegal 234
women
  and creativity 14
  and the economy Indonesia 70
  Indonesia 70
  and West Africa rice cultivation 10
Wood, Peter H. 192, 279, 291
work brigades, China 18
World Bank 150, 151
Wright, Solomon Lusk ("Sol") 316
  Blue Rose variety 316
Wuzhou Prefecture 94

xian rice 91, 92, 93, 94, 97, 98, 99
  on West River, China 93–95
Xie Jiasheng 107
Xuan, Dr. Vo Tong 131, 134
  research 135
  on rice development 136–135

Yaerhashan, acting Governor Jiangsu 89
yams 51, 88, 89, 183, 216
Yan, rice merchant 115
Yangekori, 145–146

Yangzi Delta and rice production 19, 91, 93, 94
   archaeological evidence 186, 187
   rice imports 96, 98
   varieties of rice grown 97
Yangzi River 86, 87, 88, 94
   Yangzi Valley 18, 93, 97
Yenching University's rural reform project 107
Yogya 64, 74, 76, 83
Yogyakarta 63–64, 73–74, 75, 76, 83
You Xiuling 91
Yunlu 114

zaliang (coarse food) 89
zamindars, Bengal and Punjab 268
Zhangzhou 89
Zhao Lianfang, Dr 105, 106, 107, 108
   post war career 109
Zhaoqing 94
Zhejiang 85, 88
Zhong Shou 114
Zhong Xi 114
Zhongnong No. 4 rice 108
Zhongnong No. 34 rice 108
Zhu Zhixi 84
zhuliang 89
Ziguinchor area, Senegal 229, 230